Noble Frankland

THE LIFE OF BENJAMIN DISRAELI
EARL OF BEACONSFIELD

Emery Walker ph.sc.

Viscountess Beaconsfield
from the portrait at Hughenden
painted in 1873 by G.F. Middleton

THE LIFE OF
BENJAMIN DISRAELI
EARL OF BEACONSFIELD

BY GEORGE EARLE BUCKLE

IN SUCCESSION TO W. F. MONYPENNY

VOLUME V
1868—1876

WITH PORTRAITS AND ILLUSTRATIONS

Read no history, nothing but
biography, for that is life without
theory.—CONTARINI FLEMING.

LONDON
JOHN MURRAY, ALBEMARLE STREET, W.
1920

CONTENTS OF VOL. V.

LIST OF ILLUSTRATIONS TO VOL. V.

PREFACE

TO VOLUMES V. AND VI.

It was originally intended that the story of the last phase of Disraeli's life should be completed in one volume. This would only have been possible if his management of the Eastern Question, the most outstanding feature of his great Administration, were treated merely in general terms; a course which, however unsatisfactory in itself, appeared to be discreet and judicious, so long as Russia was our faithful ally in the war, and was governed by a friendly Sovereign, the grandson of that Emperor Alexander who was in antagonism in the later seventies to Queen Victoria and to her Minister. But the Revolution in Russia, the repudiation of the Alliance, and the murder of the Tsar have entirely changed the conditions. There can be now no reasons of international delicacy to prevent a full disclosure of Disraeli's Eastern policy; without which disclosure, indeed, the record of his life and accomplishment would be seriously imperfect. While the course of history has thus tended to promote an extension of plan, there has also been placed unexpectedly at my disposal a great mass of important new material for the final eight years, 1873 to 1881. It has, therefore, become inevitable to expand the single last volume originally contemplated into the two volumes now submitted to the public.

During more than half the period, 1868 to 1881, covered by these volumes, Disraeli was the First Minister of the Crown; and the principal documents not hitherto accessible to the world, bearing on his public policy, must necessarily be his correspondence with Queen

Victoria.   His Majesty the King has graciously permitted
me to make an extensive selection from these royal
papers, and thus to illustrate and elucidate in an ample
manner both the policy of the Minister and his relations
to his Sovereign.   I am deeply sensible of the magnitude
of the benefit that the book has received through His
Majesty's kindness, for which I desire to tender very
dutiful acknowledgments.

Only second to my obligations to the King are my
indebtedness and my gratitude to those who have
afforded me access to the new material mentioned above.
By the courtesy of the Bridgeman family, and, in particular, of the Dowager Lady Bradford, of Commander the
Hon. Richard Orlando Beaconsfield Bridgeman, D.S.O.,
R.N., Beaconsfield's godson and namesake, a gallant
officer who has since given his life for his country, and of
Lady Beatrice Pretyman, the present owner, I have been
enabled to make copious use of the voluminous correspondence which Disraeli in his last years carried on
with two sisters, Selina Lady Bradford and Anne Lady
Chesterfield.   The character of Disraeli's letters and
of the intimacy between him and these ladies is fully
explained in Volume V., chapter 7; and every subsequent chapter in both volumes bears witness to the
vital importance of the contribution thus made to
Disraelian biography.   Attention may perhaps be drawn
here to one feature of this familiar correspondence: the
highest in the land are often playfully alluded to in it
under fanciful names.   Thus Queen Victoria appears
frequently as the Faery or Fairy, Disraeli's imagination
conceiving of Her Majesty as a modern Queen Elizabeth,
a nineteenth-century Faery Queen, so that he could
write of and to her somewhat in the same romantic
fashion as Spenser or Raleigh employed in addressing
and describing their magnificent mistress.

I desire to thank the Proprietors of *The Times*,
to whose enterprise the inception and completion of
this biography are due, for the great consideration and

generosity with which they have treated Mr. Monypenny and me throughout. I have also to thank the
Beaconsfield trustees for the continuance of their confidence and encouragement; and to lament that death
has again been busy in their ranks. Mr. Leopold de
Rothschild, whose marriage reception in January, 1881,
was among the last social functions which Beaconsfield
attended, and Sir Philip Frederick Rose, of Rayners,
Penn, the son of Disraeli's confidential agent, have both
passed away since Volume IV. was published. There are
many others to whom I owe gratitude either for permission to use letters, or for more direct assistance in the
preparation of these final volumes. I would especially
mention Lord Derby, Lord Sanderson, Lord Salisbury,
Lord Iddesleigh, the Bishop of Worcester, Major
Coningsby Disraeli, Mr. Norton Longman, Mr. Murray,
and my wife.

It is with a sense of thankfulness and relief that I
bring to a conclusion a biography, the publication of
which has suffered so much through death and delay.
Lord Rowton, Beaconsfield's literary executor; Nathaniel
Lord Rothschild and Sir Philip Rose, the original trustees
of the Beaconsfield estate, and two of their successors;
Mr. Moberly Bell, who, at the request of the trustees,
undertook, on behalf of *The Times*, to arrange for
the publication and to supply a biographer; and
Mr. Monypenny, who projected the work and completed
the first two volumes—are all dead; and further delay
has been caused by illness and the war. The fact
that two writers have been successively engaged upon
the book has necessarily impaired its unity; though
I have not consciously departed from the lines upon
which Mr. Monypenny worked, save perhaps in making
an even more extensive use of the wealth of Disraeli's
letters at my command. Wherever possible, I have
preferred to let Disraeli tell his own story, rather than
to tell it for him. It is, I hope, a fair claim to make for

these six volumes that, whatever their imperfections, they largely enable the reader to realise Disraeli's life from the inside, through the evidence of his familiar letters to wife, sister, and friends, as well as of his political and personal letters to his Sovereign and his colleagues.

This method of biography, of course, precludes brevity. But a large canvas is required to display with anything like justice the character and achievement of one who did so much, and who was so much; who held the attention of the world, as man, author, Parliamentarian, and statesman, for between fifty and sixty years, from the publication of *Vivian Grey* till the last day of his life; whose career his rival Gladstone pronounced to be the most remarkable, with the possible exception of that of the younger Pitt, in our long Parliamentary history; who, apart from his political eminence, won a definite and distinguished place in literature; and who, to borrow the apt words of a reviewer of the fourth of these volumes, was also 'one of the most original, interesting, and interested human beings who ever walked through the pageant of life.'   Unlike as Disraeli was in most respects to the great Tory of a hundred years before him, Dr. Johnson, he resembled him in being a unique figure of extraordinary and, I would fain believe, perennial human interest; one of those men about whose personality and performance the curiosity of the world remains ever active.   It has been my aim, as it was Mr. Monypenny's, from the mass of papers bequeathed to Lord Rowton, and from an abundance of other original sources, to satisfy that legitimate curiosity.

G. E. B.

London,
   Christmas, 1919.

CHAPTER I.

THE IRISH CHURCH.

1868.

From February, 1868, till his death thirteen years later, Disraeli was the titular head, as he had long been the most vital force, of the Conservative party. But until after his victory at the polls in 1874 his authority was of an imperfect character, liable to question and dispute. Lord Derby lived for a year and a half after his resignation; and throughout that period many of his old followers still looked upon him as their leader, with Disraeli as acting deputy; a position which, indeed, Disraeli himself had gracefully volunteered to accept, though Derby's common sense and good feeling had repudiated the suggestion.[1] Derby's death, in 1869, converted Disraeli's regency over the party into actual sovereignty; but the ill-fortune which had attended the Conservatives at the General Election in November, 1868, continued to discredit the foresight and diminish the prestige of the new Chief until the by-elections from 1871 onwards showed that the tide had turned. With success came general and unstinted confidence; and during the Administration of 1874–1880, Disraeli exercised as undisputed a sway over his followers, and as complete a control over Parliament, as ever was attained in this country by Minister or party-leader. The confidence of his party was not seriously shaken by the crushing defeat of 1880; he retained it in almost undiminished measure to the last day of his life.

The nine months of his first Administration were, how-

[1] See Vol. IV., p. 590.

ever, a troubled and unsatisfactory time. Not that the unfavourable turn of events was due to the deficiencies of the Cabinet, which was constituted as follows:

First Lord of the Treasury	..	B. DISRAELI.
Lord Chancellor	.. ..	LORD CAIRNS.
Lord President	.. ..	DUKE OF MARLBOROUGH.
Lord Privy Seal	.. ..	EARL OF MALMESBURY.
Home Secretary	.. ..	GATHORNE HARDY.
Foreign Secretary	.. ..	LORD STANLEY.
Colonial Secretary	.. ..	DUKE OF BUCKINGHAM.
War Secretary ..	.. ..	SIR JOHN PAKINGTON.
Indian Secretary	.. ..	SIR STAFFORD NORTHCOTE.
Chancellor of the Exchequer	..	G. WARD HUNT.
First Lord of the Admiralty	..	HENRY J. L. CORRY.
President of the Board of Trade	..	DUKE OF RICHMOND.
First Commissioner of Works	..	LORD JOHN MANNERS.
Chief Secretary for Ireland	..	EARL OF MAYO.

Though not so powerful as Derby's original Cabinet in July, 1866, it was still a formidable combination, containing half a dozen members who were real statesmen, and several more who were experienced and competent administrators. If it had lost Cranborne, it had gained Cairns; and its principal loss, that of Derby himself, did not affect the Chamber in which the battle was immediately to be fought, though it undoubtedly affected the ultimate tribunal, the electorate, who had regarded him with respect, though not with enthusiasm, for nearly forty years. But the most efficient Cabinet is of no avail in the face of an adverse, and united, Parliamentary majority. In Parliament Whigs, Liberals, Radicals, and Irish, taken all together, had a majority of sixty or seventy over the Conservatives; and, with the settlement of the Reform question which had divided them, they would, however sore with one another, have a disposition to reunite in order to regain office.

One aspect of the Parliamentary situation demands especial notice. As Derby had been obliged by ill-health to give way to Disraeli, so Russell, owing to his increasing years, had retired this winter in favour of Gladstone. With the session of 1868 the protagonists of the two

parties in the House of Commons stood out as the party
leaders. Each admired and respected the great Parliamentary qualities of his rival; but Gladstone's respect
was combined with an alloy of deep moral disapprobation
—a frame of mind which was fostered by what Disraeli
had called the 'finical and fastidious crew' of high
Anglicans among whom Gladstone familiarly moved.
To them and to him Disraeli's elevation was an offence.
A brilliant journalist shrewdly diagnosed the Gladstonian
temper of the moment:

One of the most grievous and constant puzzles of King
David was the prosperity of the wicked and the scornful,
and the same tremendous moral enigma has come down to our
own days. . . . Like the Psalmist, the Liberal leader may
well protest that verily he has cleansed his heart in vain and
washed his hands in innocency; all day long he has been
plagued by Whig Lords and chastened every morning by
Radical manufacturers; as blamelessly as any curate he has
written about *Ecce Homo ;* and he has never made a speech,
even in the smallest country town, without calling out with
David, How foolish am I, and how ignorant ! For all this,
what does he see ? The scorner who shot out the lip and shook
the head at him across the table of the House of Commons last
session has now more than heart could wish; his eyes, speaking
in an Oriental manner, stand out with fatness, he speaketh
loftily, and pride compasseth him about as a chain. . . . That
the writer of frivolous stories about *Vivian Grey* and *Coningsby*
should grasp the sceptre before the writer of beautiful and
serious things about *Ecce Homo*—the man who is epigram-
matic, flashy, arrogant, before the man who never perpetrated
an epigram in his life, is always fervid, and would as soon die
as admit that he had a shade more brain than his footman—
the Radical corrupted into a Tory before the Tory purified
and elevated into a Radical—is not this enough to make an
honest man rend his mantle and shave his head and sit down
among the ashes inconsolable ? [1]

But inaction in face of such a moral paradox would
have been wholly out of keeping with Gladstone's vigorous
character. His 'teeth were set on edge,' as Gathorne
Hardy wrote, ' and he prepared to bite.' [2] It might be

[1] *Pall Mall Gazette,* March 3, 1868.
[2] Gathorne Hardy's *Life of Lord Cranbrook,* Vol. I., p. 264. Hardy's
diaries are most valuable evidence as regards the proceedings of Disraeli's

thought that the last session of an expiring Parliament—
a session which must be devoted mainly to the corollaries
of Reform and to necessary administrative work—would
afford him little opportunity. There was, however, a
weapon to his hand, but it was one which he had hitherto
hesitated to grasp, so completely would its employment
mark his severance from the most cherished of the ideas
with which he entered public life. On the other side,
nothing could recommend him so strongly to the party
which he had now finally adopted as to brandish the
sword of religious equality, even if only in Ireland. Gladstone's Church views had been the one great stumbling-
block to complete sympathy with his new party; and
hitherto he had declined to associate himself with that
attack on the Irish Establishment which had united
Whigs (when in opposition), Radicals, and the Irish
brigade ever since the days of Russell's motion in
1835 about the Appropriation Clause. He had, indeed,
he has told us, regarded the position of the Irish Church
as indefensible since 1863; but both in 1865 and in 1866 he
had, as Minister, resisted motions against it, and when he
was seeking re-election at Oxford in 1865 had informed a
clerical voter that he regarded the question as ' remote
and apparently out of all bearing on the practical politics
of the day.' At that time, so far as public declarations
went, it seemed even more unlikely that Gladstone would
effect Irish disestablishment than that Disraeli would
carry household suffrage.

But the Fenian conspiracy had forcibly directed public
attention to the defects of British government in Ireland,
and the leaders of both parties were preoccupied with
Irish policy. The object at which both aimed was the
reconciliation with England of the leaders of Roman
Catholic opinion in Ireland. With Roman Catholic
opinion in England Disraeli had established a *modus
vivendi* during Palmerston's Government, though, owing

two Governments; and the following pages will show how great are my
obligations to the admirable biography of the father by the son.

to an indiscretion of Derby's, its effect had been impaired
at the last General Election. In regard to Ireland he had
advocated conciliation, but conciliation through the
action of a powerful and vigorous executive, from his
early days in Parliament. In a famous speech[1] in 1844
he had said that it was the duty of an English Minister to
effect in Ireland by policy all those changes which a
revolution would effect by force; in 1847 he had urged the
liberal outlay of English gold to forward Irish economic
development; in the first Derby-Disraeli Government he
had endeavoured to pass into law a comprehensive reform
of Irish land tenure in favour of the tenant; and in the
second Derby-Disraeli Government he had contemplated
the grant of a charter to a Roman Catholic University in
Dublin, but had lacked the time to carry the policy into
act. It was this last scheme which he took up once more
in the years 1867 and 1868, being much encouraged by
Manning, who had recently become Roman Catholic
Archbishop of Westminster, and who was eager to assume
the lead in all movements for the benefit of his adopted
co-religionists. From May, 1867, to March, 1868, Disraeli
was in regular communication with the Archbishop, who
represented himself as fully acquainted with the views of
Cardinal Cullen and the other leaders of Irish Roman
Catholic opinion. After an informal conversation on an
early Sunday in May, Manning brought the Rector of
the existing Roman Catholic University in Dublin to
see Disraeli. In a letter arranging for the interview
Manning wrote, on May 21: 'I am able to say, of my
own knowledge, that any favourable proposal from
Government on the subject of the Catholic University
would not only encounter no opposition, but would be
assisted. I believe I may say that this includes the granting of a charter. What I write is not from second-hand.
I can add that the "Chief" I conferred with is in the
front, and he fully recognises the need of removing the
Catholic education of Ireland from the turbulent region

---

[1] See Vol. II., pp. 188-194.

of politics.' He urged Disraeli to disregard certain
expressions of Irish members of Parliament, hostile to
chartering a Catholic University. 'I am now able to
state,' he wrote on August 20, 'that they do not represent
the sense and desire of Cardinal Cullen or of the Irish
Bishops.' He warned Disraeli of the importance of
securing the co-operation of the Irish Bishops.

In the winter months the conversations were resumed.
On December 22 Manning wrote that he had just received
a letter from Cardinal Cullen 'on the subject of our last
conversation,' and requested a further appointment,
which apparently took effect on December 28. On
January 15, 1868, he suggested another talk, stating
in his letter that he had been reading 'with great
assent' Disraeli's speech on Irish affairs in 1844. Again,
on February 19, he accepted an appointment for the
following day. This was just after the reopening of
Parliament, when the grave news of Derby's relapse was
turning all eyes upon his Chancellor of the Exchequer.
'I fully understood your silence,' Manning wrote, 'knowing how much and anxiously you must be pressed. The
present moment is truly a crisis, but I trust that all may
issue in good.' Throughout these weeks Manning was
lending his assistance in maturing the Ministerial plan,
and he hailed Disraeli's elevation to the Premiership in
terms which showed not obscurely that he was looking
forward to co-operation with him in a policy of Roman
Catholic amelioration—a policy which involved, besides
University education, a reform of the Irish land laws, and
an ultimate vision of concurrent endowment in Ireland
for the Roman Church.

From Archbishop Manning.

8, York Place, *Feb.* 26, 1868.—The kindness and consideration I have received from you impels me to convey to you my
sympathy at this great crisis of your public life.

It is my privilege to stand neutral between political parties,
and I have been united, for nearly forty years, in close personal
friendship with Mr. Gladstone; nevertheless it is a happiness

to me to see you where your public services have justly placed
you as first Minister of the Crown, and to add an expression of
my best wishes.   I trust you may have health and life to carry
out the legislation which, as you one day told me, you thought
yourself too old to see realised.   That is not so; and the
season has set in sooner than you then looked for.

This letter needs no reply, but I could not let the moment
pass without assuring you of my sympathy.

There was undoubtedly a certain disposition to look to
Disraeli—a statesman who had always regarded Ireland
in a spirit alike of detachment and of sympathy—for a
settlement of the Irish question.   Early in the session of
1866 Bright had adjured both leaders, Gladstone and
Disraeli, to lay aside their Parliamentary rivalry and
combine with this object; and Bernal Osborne, shortly
after the formation of the 1866 Government, had recalled
the speech of 1844 and urged that now was the moment
for Disraeli to put in force the policy then proclaimed.
The successful settlement of the Reform difficulty by the
method of taking the House as a whole into council
suggested that the same man and the same method might
solve the still more intractable problem of Ireland.
A voice reached Disraeli in that sense from Australia.
Gavan Duffy wrote from Melbourne on November 26,
1867, congratulating him on his success in his Herculean
task of Reform, and urging that there was a ' crowning
work' for him still to do.   ' You could give Ireland peace,
and, after a little, prosperity.'   It was too late for half-
measures.

A statesman must offer the agricultural classes terms which
a reasonable man may regard as fairly competing with the
terms upon which he can obtain land if he emigrates to
America or Australia. . . .   If the State will buy up at a
reasonable valuation the waste lands now unproductive,
and let them at a rent yielding 3 per cent. on the purchase
money, and will further enable the more intelligent and
industrious Irish tenants on ordinary estates to purchase
the fee simple of their farms by a series of annual payments
representing the actual value, you will have tranquillised
Ireland for this generation.   The Church question and the
education question will remain to be dealt with, no doubt,

but these are the questions of the educated minority; the uneasy class *are* uneasy because of the perpetual uncertainty of tenure.

Subsequent history has shown that Gavan Duffy was right; that—putting the national question aside—the tenure of land was the crux of the Irish problem, and could only be solved by an extensive system of purchase. But the ' educated minority ' of Roman Catholics in Ireland were more vocal than the farmers and peasants; accordingly it was the Church question and the education question which were taken in hand at this time by leaders and parties in Parliament, the one by Gladstone and the other by Disraeli; though Disraeli had recognised in the past, and Gladstone, as his Irish researches proceeded, was to discover in the future, the supreme importance of a satisfactory settlement of the land question.

The idea of Disraeli and the Government was to establish in Dublin an institution which should stand in relation to Roman Catholics somewhat in the same position that Trinity College does to Protestants. The governing body should entirely consist of Roman Catholics, and the teaching be mainly conducted by them; but full security should be taken that no religious influence should be brought to bear on students who belonged to another faith. Five prelates, together with the President of Maynooth, were to be put on the governing body, the senate; but there was to be a strong lay element in its constitution, and the Government contemplated the appointment of a layman as the first Chancellor. The State would pay the establishment charges of the new University, but the general question of State endowment would be postponed. This scheme, in general terms, had Manning's approval; and, from his assurances, Disraeli had reason to hope that it would be accepted in substance by the Irish Bishops. Accordingly, after its promulgation on March 10 by Mayo in the House of Commons—where, though scoffed at by Bright as a pill good against the earthquake, it was received with benignity both by Chichester Fortescue on behalf of the official Liberals and by Monsell on behalf of the Roman Catholic laity—it was submitted to Archbishop Leahy and Bishop Derry, the appointed representatives of the hierarchy. Unfortunately, their attitude was widely different from what the Government had been led to expect. They demanded the submission of the new University to episcopal guidance. The Chancellor, they claimed, must always be a prelate, and Cardinal Cullen ought to be the first Chancellor. General control must not rest with the senate as a whole, a preponderatingly lay body, but with its episcopal members. These prelates must have an absolute veto on the books included in the University programme, and on the first nomination of the professors, lecturers, and other officers; and must also have the power of depriving such teachers of their offices, should they be judged by their Bishops to have done anything contrary to faith and morals.

Claims of this kind were so preposterous that the whole scheme had to be relinquished. Dr. Leahy and Dr. Derry were not men of affairs, and it has been suggested —and may well be true—that they asked for twice as much as they were prepared to take, and were astonished when the Government abandoned the negotiation as hopeless. But it is difficult not to connect the extremist attitude of the Irish negotiators with the development of Gladstone's policy of disestablishment. The preliminary reply of the Bishops was dated March 19, three days after Gladstone's announcement that the Irish Church, ' as a State Church, must cease to exist.' The final reply, expressing the episcopal views in detail, was dated March 31, after Gladstone had tabled his famous Resolutions, and while the debate on them in the House of Commons was in progress. Until Gladstone's announcement Manning was still active on behalf of the scheme; but his last letter to Disraeli was dated on the very day (March 16) when the announcement was made. From that moment he ceased all communication with the Prime Minister till the close of the Government in December, when he excused himself as follows:

From Archbishop Manning.

8, YORK PLACE, W., *Dec.* 2, 1868.—. . . I have felt that a ravine, I will not say a gulf, opened between us when the Resolutions on the Irish Church were laid upon the Table of the House. I regretted this, as I had hoped to see the scheme of the Catholic University happily matured; but with my inevitable conviction as to the Irish Church I felt that I ought not to trespass upon your kindness, which I can assure you I shall remember with much pleasure. . . .

It is not unnatural that Disraeli should have felt that he had been treated shabbily by the representatives of the Roman Catholics, and especially by Manning. He said on more than one occasion to Roman Catholic friends that he had been stabbed in the back. Manning's defence, when he heard the accusation, was that the University negotiations ' were entirely taken out of my hands by the Bishops who corresponded with you, and in a sense at variance with my judgment and advice.' Had he been left free to act, he maintained that he would have been successful; and he averred that he had never ceased to regret the failure of his efforts.[1]

Whatever the degree of Manning's responsibility, the facts and dates suggest that the Roman Catholic authorities were diverted from adhesion to Disraeli's programme by Gladstone's superior bid. It was impossible to resist the temptation of wreaking vengeance on the Anglican Church, though in the result they got nothing of the Church revenues, nor even, till after forty years, the Catholic University which was within their grasp; and the temporal power of the Pope, the importance of which to Roman Catholics Disraeli alone among British statesmen appreciated, perished a couple of years later, in 1870.

[1] Letter from Manning to Disraeli, dated Rome, May 7, 1870. Manning cited, as a witness to the accuracy of his account, Cashel Hoey, a well-known Irish journalist.

Gladstone allowed the new Government no close time, but, like a capable general, took the offensive at once. Derby's resignation and Disraeli's appointment as his successor were announced in both Houses on Tuesday, February 25; on Thursday, March 5, after nine days' adjournment, Disraeli and his colleagues presented themselves to Parliament and made their Ministerial profession of faith; only five days later, on Tuesday, March 10, came a debate on the Irish question initiated by an Irish member, and the Chief Secretary's exposition of policy; and on the last night of that debate, Monday, March 16, less than three weeks after Disraeli's acceptance of office, Gladstone launched the new policy of the Liberal party, the immediate disestablishment and disendowment of the Irish Church. It was Gladstone's most brilliant and successful stroke as a party leader. The settlement of the Reform question by Disraeli's statesmanship had deprived the Liberals of the popular cry which they had for long utilised at elections, if they forgot it in Parliament. If no new cry were raised, there was a fear lest the working man might be disposed to vote, not for those who had often promised but failed to perform, but for those who had actually given him the franchise. The Irish Church was in a very weak position, and could not long be left untouched; it was, at this very time, undergoing investigation by a Commission which the Government had appointed in the previous year. It claimed, indeed, to be, like the Church of England, the historical representative of the ancient Church of the country; and its maintenance, as an establishment united to its sister Church, was one of the provisions by which the assent of the then dominant Protestants in Ireland was secured for the Act of Union. But, though it was the Church of the ruling classes, it had failed to win the affections of the people. More than three-quarters of the total population were Roman Catholics, and of the remainder nearly a half were Presbyterians. The Church of Ireland ministered to only about one-eighth of the people of Ireland. Moreover, it was Evangelical in its tendencies, and had been very little affected by the Tractarian development. Here was an institution the attack upon which would rally to the Liberal banner Roman Catholics, Liberal Anglicans, Dissenters and Secularists, Whigs jealous of ecclesiastical power, and Radicals hostile to corporate property. Besides, a policy of disestablishment and disendowment gave a great opportunity for specious electioneering cries calculated to attract the new voter: ' religious equality,' ' justice to Ireland.'

How were the Government, how were the Conservative party, to meet it ? The Prime Minister, nearly a quarter of a century before, had declared that an ' alien Church ' was one of Ireland's legitimate grievances. He had refused to respond to Derby's urgent requests that he should speak on its behalf in Parliament, and had written to him shortly after the General Election: ' I do not think that any general resolution respecting the Irish Church could be successfully withstood in the present Parliament. It is a very unpopular cause, even with many of our best men.' [1] On the other hand, the party which Disraeli led was essentially the defender of the Church of England, and had been especially mobilised by himself in its defence. Moreover, any loosening of the bond between religion and the State was repugnant to all his theocratic ideas. One section of the Cabinet, headed by Hardy, and powerfully supported by Derby from without, desired that high ground should be taken and the proposal denounced as sacrilege; or, if unity could not be preserved on those lines, at least that a strong passive resistance should be offered to change. Another section, in which Stanley and Pakington were conspicuous, was ready to accept disestablishment as inevitable, and desired to concentrate on liberal treatment of the disestablished Church together with a utilisation of surplus revenues for the benefit of Roman Catholics.

[1] See Vol. IV., pp. 405, 406, 425, 426.

From Lord Derby.

Confidential. KNOWSLEY, *March* 3, 1868.—Anxious as I
am for the permanence of your Government, I cannot refrain
from expressing my apprehensions as to the forthcoming
discussions upon the Irish questions. . . .

Your real difficulty will arise when you come to deal with
the Established Church. You know that I have always
entertained a very strong opinion adversé to the right of
Parliament to alienate any part of the property of that or of
any other corporation, and this was the main ground of our
successful opposition to the Appropriation Clause, the object
of which was to convert to secular purposes any surplus, over
and above what might be deemed requisite for the maintenance of the establishment. It seems to be generally assumed
that this principle is no longer tenable; but the moment you
depart from it, you will find yourself involved in inextricable
difficulty. The obvious course would appear to be, at all
events, to wait for the report of the Commission which we
issued last year; but Stanley says, though I do not agree with
him, that Parliament will not, and Gladstone says that it shall
not, admit that ground for postponement of legislation. In
my opinion, however, the safest course for the Government will
be to abstain from making any proposition whatever. . . .
The difficulties of this question are such that I am convinced
your safety is to sit still, and, instead of showing your hand, to
compel your adversaries to exhibit theirs, with all their
discrepancies and contradictions. . . .

To Lord Derby.

10, DOWNING STREET, *March* 4, 1868.—. . . We have discussed our Irish policy for two days, and have arrived at
conclusions which are very much in unison with your suggestions—to bring in a Land Bill, which will deal with all those
points of the controversy on which there begins to be a concurrence of opinion; and with respect to the others, to propose
another Devon Commission.

The famine and State emigration have happened since the
labors of that inquiry, and we think that such a body of evidence will be collected as to the present improved state of the
country that a great effect may be produced on public opinion.

The Cabinet adopted unanimously the University scheme
which you had approved.

With regard to the great difficulty and the real danger, the
Church, although there was great difference of opinion in the
Cabinet on the merits of the question, there was unanimity

that it ought not to be treated except in a new Parliament; and also that no pledge should be given of maintaining absolutely unchanged the present state of ecclesiastical affairs. . . .

Disraeli was not likely to overlook one obvious method of contributing to the tranquillisation of Ireland—the presence of royalty in that country.   Like other Ministers, before and after his time, he was hampered by the unfortunate reluctance of Queen Victoria either to go to Ireland herself or to permit members of her family to go. No doubt the disturbed state of the country gave some reason for anxiety in case of a royal visit, but both the Lord-Lieutenant and the Chief Secretary, Abercorn and Mayo, each of them an Irishman with a wide knowledge of Irish feeling, urged the great advantage of a visit from the Prince of Wales; and the representations of Disraeli at length prevailed to secure Her Majesty's consent.

To Lord Derby.

Confidential. 10, DOWNING STREET, *March* 9, 1868.— . . . The Prince of Wales is to pay a visit to Ireland at Easter. This affair has given me much trouble. They invited the Prince without the previous consent of Her Majesty, and the occasion chosen for eliciting the loyal feeling of Ireland was a princely visit to some races at a place with the unfortunate title of Punchestown, or something like it. The Queen did not approve of the occasion, or a state visit agreed to without her authority; and the matter appeared to me, at one time, more serious than the Irish Church, but with much correspondence and the loyal assistance of General Grey, whose conduct is really admirable, I think we have got all right. Lords Abercorn and Mayo are pardoned, and, I hope, the Prince; and, if my humble suggestion be adopted, the inauguration of H.R.H. as a Knight of St. Patrick, in the renovated cathedral, will be an adequate occasion for the royal visit, and a more suitable and stately cause than a race, however national.

Stanley did more than well about *Alabama ;* strengthened the Government. He gives me daily good accounts of you, which are agreeable to your devoted D.

The Irish Government would have liked to follow up the Prince's visit by the establishment of a permanent royal residence in Ireland. But on this point the resistance of the Queen could not be overcome.

From Sir John Pakington.

Confidential. 52, GROSVENOR PLACE, S.W., *March* 14, 1868. —Is it not still possible that you may suggest in your speech a compromise on the Church question, which may at least diminish the effect of any move on the opposite side ? It is clear that a state of affairs which no one ventures to defend cannot be maintained.

I think we may consent to disestablishment, but we cannot consent to disendowment. Hardy hinted that any surplus may be dealt with. May not this hint be pushed further, and an outline be sketched for (1) disestablishing; (2) insuring a surplus by reducing the provision for the Church to the minimum of her real requirements; (3) devoting the surplus to providing glebes, parsonages, and good churches for the R.Cs.; (4) extending the powers of the Commission, if necessary, to arrange the details of such a plan ?

You will excuse the zeal which offers a suggestion to one who so little needs it.

The opinions expressed in the Irish debate, which lasted four days,[1] were very various, but the Liberals, Radicals, and Irish brigade all united in demanding the disestablishment of the Church as the first step. This policy united Lowe and Bright, Mill and Chichester Fortescue, Horsman and Monsell. The Government speakers ridiculed the idea that confiscation could be the proper way to start a healing policy. But the Chief Secretary disclaimed a merely negative attitude on the part of Irish Protestants, and hinted that levelling upwards and not downwards was the proper course. Gladstone dismissed the Government policy for Ireland as inadequate, though he agreed that the Roman Catholic grievance about University education ought to be remedied. But the Irish Church must first be dealt with, and must, as an establishment, cease to exist. He brushed aside the idea of waiting till the Commission then sitting had reported. If the Government would not move, the Opposition must

---

[1] March 10, 12, 13, and 16.

not be content with an empty declaration of opinion, but must proceed to act.

Disraeli began happily by contrasting the apathy and indifference on this question shown by Gladstone and his friends when in office, and their discovery of its instant importance when in opposition. 'I could not but feel,' he said, 'that I was the most unfortunate of Ministers, since at the moment when I arrived, by Her Majesty's gracious favour, at the position I now fill, a controversy which had lasted for 700 years had reached its culminating point, and I was immediately called upon with my colleagues to produce measures equal to such a supernatural exigency.' He defended the Irish policy of the Government as being one of dealing with all such points as were by general agreement sufficiently advanced for legislation, and referring to Commissions only those matters which were not ripe for decision. To suggest that the object was delay was 'the lees and refuse of factious insinuation.' He admitted that the Irish Church was not in the condition in which he could wish to see a national Church; but he dwelt earnestly on the importance of connecting the principle of religion with government, otherwise political authority would become a mere affair of police. If religion and government were to be associated, endowment was inevitable. The Irish, whether Presbyterian, Anglican, or Roman, were essentially a religious people, and therefore in favour of ecclesiastical endowments. This great principle was at stake, and Parliament had no moral competence to deal with it till after an appeal to the nation —an appeal which the Government were prepared to hasten. He pointed, as Mayo had, to some form of concurrent endowment. The moment had arrived, he said, when there must be a considerable change in the condition of the unendowed clergy of Ireland which would elevate their influence. But he did not mean what was vulgarly called 'paying the priests,' and so making them stipendiaries of the State, of which he strongly disapproved.

He did not shrink from meeting the challenge which had been thrown down to him to reconcile his present attitude with his famous dictum in 1844 about a starving population, an absentee aristocracy, and an alien Church.

With reference to that passage which has been quoted from a speech made by me, I may remark that it appeared to me at the time I made it that nobody listened to it. It seemed to me that I was pouring water upon sand, but it seems now that the water came from a golden goblet. With regard to the passage from that speech there are many remarks which, if I wanted to vindicate or defend myself, I might legitimately make. I might remind the House that that speech was made before the famine and the emigration from Ireland, and the whole of that passage about the starving people and the amount of population to the square mile no longer applies. I might remark that that speech was made before the change in locomotion and the sale of a large portion of the soil of Ireland, which has established a resident proprietary instead of an absentee aristocracy, though, so far as I can collect, the absentee aristocracy seems more popular than the resident proprietary. All this I might say, but I do not care to say it, and I do not wish to say it, because in my conscience the sentiment of that speech was right. It may have been expressed with the heedless rhetoric which, I suppose, is the appanage of all who sit below the gangway; but in my historical conscience the sentiment of that speech was right.

Disraeli's speech pleased his colleagues and impressed the House of Commons. Hardy was struck by its skill and humorousness as opposed to Gladstone's extravagant violence. Cairns wrote: ' I doubt if anything, at once so difficult and so perfect, was accomplished even by yourself. The issue on which you have placed our policy with Gladstone is excellent.' Lennox reported Lowe and Henry Cowper as being both decidedly of opinion that Disraeli had the best of it in his duel with Gladstone. But the speech, in view both of the divisions in the Cabinet and of Disraeli's strong feeling, in his ' historical conscience,' of the anomalous position of the Irish Church, was rather a debating answer to Gladstone than a definite statement of policy; and the Prime Minister felt the necessity of deciding promptly on some line of action on which he could hope to secure the united support of his colleagues. He accordingly outlined during the next few days to Cairns, who as an Irish Protestant was specially interested in the question, the policy which, with certain modifications, was eventually adopted by the Cabinet.

To Lord Cairns.

Secret. 10, DOWNING STREET, *March* 19, 1868.—I wish very much to confer with you, but as that is, I suppose, impossible, I must endeavor, without loss of time, to convey to you my present impressions as to the critical position at which not only the Cabinet, but the country, has now arrived.

I assume, from what reaches me, that Gladstone and his party will now propose the disestablishment of the Irish Church.

He seems to me to have raised a clear and distinct issue. I don't think we could wish it better put.

I think we ought to hold that the whole question of national establishments is now raised; that the Irish Church is but a small portion of the question; and that those who wish to demolish it must be held to desire the abolition of national establishments in the three kingdoms.

But we must detach the Irish Church as much as possible from the prominent portion of the subject, for, there is no doubt, it is not popular.

I think, if the principle that the State should adopt and uphold religion as an essential portion of the Constitution be broadly raised, a great number of members from the north of England and Scotland, called Liberals, would be obliged to leave the philosophic standard.

I am, therefore, at present inclined to an amendment which, while it admitted that the present condition of the Church in Ireland was susceptible of improvement, while it might be desirable to elevate the status of the unendowed clergy of that country, still declared it was the first duty of the State to acknowledge and maintain the religious principle in an established form, etc.

All this is very rough writing, and the amendment would require the utmost thought and precision. What I want at present to do is to call your immediate thought to the situation. It has come on us like a thief in the night. It is useless to launch such thoughts, as I suggest, in an unprepared Cabinet. You and I must settle all this together, and then speak to one or two leading spirits; but it is quite on the cards that we may have to take our course on Saturday in Cabinet.

There ought to be no faltering on my part in that case; therefore I beg your earnest and devoted attention to all this. We are on the eve of great events, and we ought to show ourselves equal to them.

To Sir Anthony de Rothschild.

10, DOWNING STREET, *March* 19, 1868.—You sent me some good stuff to keep up my spirits in the great battles at hand; so, if I beat my enemies, the ' great Liberal party ' will owe their discomfiture to your burgundy !

Would you like to be Lord Lieutenant of the county ? If so, you must return me at least six members. That's the quota for such a distinction. My love to your wife.

To Lord Derby.

10, DOWNING STREET, *March* 21, 1868.—I have been intending, and expecting, to write to you every day announcing the hostile motion, and requesting your advice on it; but it has been delayed so long that I am almost in hopes you may reach London before it is made public. We had anticipated considering it in Cabinet to-day, but, as you have observed, it was postponed last night, and the House was favored only with a notice that a notice would be given. Something new in Parliament ! We have, however, spent two hours and a half in the old room, from which I have just escaped to send you this line to let you know how we all were. We did a good deal of business, but nothing very striking except settling our Bill for the purchase of the telegraphs of the United Kingdom.

A person of authority, and a social friend of Gladstone's, told me yesterday that his present violent courses are entirely to be attributed to the paralytic stroke of the Bishop of Winchester.[1] Until that happened G. was quiet and temperate, and resisted all the anti-Church overtures of the advanced party. But when this calamity happened to the worthy prelate Gladstone became disturbed and restless, and finally adopted a more violent course even than his friends had originally suggested. Strange that a desire to make Bishops should lead a man to destroy Churches !

I hope Lady Derby is well, and that your followers will soon see you. Your very tired but devoted D.

Gladstone's Resolutions, though they were not ready so soon as Disraeli anticipated, were not delayed beyond

[1] Sumner.

a week, being laid on the table of the House on Monday, March 23. They were three in number. The first affirmed the necessity of immediate disestablishment; the second the desirability of preventing the creation of fresh interests in the Irish Church; the third proposed an address to the Queen asking her to place her interest in the temporalities of the Church at the disposal of Parliament. Disraeli immediately put forth his reply in the shape of a letter to Lord Dartmouth, who had forwarded to him a Conservative memorial expressing confidence in his leadership. In it he followed the line laid down in the letter to Cairns, insisting that there was a ' crisis in England ' rather than in Ireland; ' for the purpose is now avowed, and that by a powerful party, of destroying that sacred union between Church and State which has hitherto been the chief means of our civilisation and is the only security of our religious liberty.'

The Queen was greatly disturbed by Gladstone's proceedings, but with true statesmanship was very anxious to avoid raising a religious issue.

From Queen Victoria.

Windsor Castle, *March* 24, 1868.—The Queen has read Mr. Disraeli's account of Mr. Gladstone's proposed Resolutions with the deepest concern. She fears there is but too much truth in what Mr. Disraeli says of the spirit that may possibly be excited amongst the Protestants of the three kingdoms, and of the danger that exists of those old cries being revived which, in the name of religion, have worked evils which successive Governments have so long tried in vain to remedy. Mr. Gladstone must be aware that the chief difficulty in governing Ireland has always been to restrain the mutual violence of the old Orange party on the one side, and of the Roman Catholics on the other; and he might, the Queen thinks, to say the least, have paused before he made a declaration, of which the only effect will certainly be to revive and influence the old sectarian feuds and to render the administration of Ireland more difficult.

The Queen trusts, however, to her Government, and especially to Mr. Disraeli, *carefully to avoid* saying *anything*, however great the provocation may be to act otherwise, that can tend to encourage a spirit of retaliation amongst the Protestants or to revive old religious animosities. It seems to her essentially a state of things in which her Ministers will deserve and receive the support of all who look to what is really for the good of the country if they show moderation and forbearance in meeting this attack, and studiously avoid taking a course which, though it might give them a party advantage for the moment, would surely be injurious to the permanent interests of the Empire.

In view of their internal disagreement, the Cabinet determined to meet Gladstone's motion to go into Committee on his Resolutions by a temporising amendment to be moved by Stanley, which, while admitting that considerable modifications in Irish Church temporalities might be expedient, declared that the decision of the question should be left to a new Parliament. It was an eminently reasonable proposition, but naturally, as it avoided the issue of principle, was not combative enough to satisfy Derby, who wrote to Disraeli on March 25: ' It seems to me in the right sense, but it implies rather more of concession than pleases *me* ; for the expression " without prejudging the question of *considerable* modifications, etc.," appears practically to prejudge the question to an extent which will not satisfy your Protestant friends, and I shall be rather nervous as to Stanley's mode of handling the subject.' Derby's nervousness was justified; Stanley's mode of handling his subject dismayed and disorganised his party. Even Cairns found him ' colourless and chilling,' while Hardy in his diary pungently described his speech as ' the cry of a whipped hound.' Cranborne seized the opportunity to make an attack, in Hardy's words, ' sneering as regards us all; venomous and remorseless against Disraeli.' He went so far as to suggest that, having betrayed the party over household suffrage, Disraeli was preparing to betray them once more over the Irish Church, Stanley's ' Delphic ' amendment being the first step in a policy of disestablishment. Hardy made a spirited reply to this malicious outburst, quoted recent letters and speeches to show the suddenness of Glad-

stone's conversion, and defended the Irish Church and
the principle of establishment and endowment in eloquent terms.   All the leaders took part in the debate.[1]
Gladstone endeavoured to vindicate his consistency, and
asserted that the Church of England would be benefited
and not injured by being severed from a communion with
what was politically dangerous and socially unjust.
Lowe gave Liberals the catchword, ' Cut it down; why
cumbereth it the ground ?'

Disraeli had no difficulty, in his reply, in vindicating
the reasonableness of Stanley's amendment.   The
Government could not meet Gladstone's motion with a
direct negative, as they thought some modification
would be necessary.   They held, moreover, that, when
a fundamental law of the country was attacked, Parliament was not morally competent to decide the question,
unless some intimation had been given to the constituency which elected it.   Once again, as on the third reading of the Reform Bill, Disraeli dealt with the virulent
attacks made on him by Cranborne and Lowe.   The
former he let off comparatively lightly.   He recognised
the vigour and vindictiveness of his invective, but thought,
as a critic, that, in spite of all the study which Cranborne
had given to the subject, it lacked finish.[2]   He turned
to Lowe, Cranborne's ' echo ' from the Liberal side.

When the bark is heard on this side, the right hon. member
for Calne emerges, I will not say from his cave, but perhaps
from a more cynical habitation.   He joins immediately in
the chorus of reciprocal malignity, and ' hails with horrid
melody the moon.'   . . .   The right hon. member for Calne
is a very remarkable man.   He is a learned man, though he
despises history.   He can chop logic like Dean Aldrich;
but what is more remarkable than his learning and his logic
is that power of spontaneous aversion which particularises

[1] March 30 and 31, April 2 and 3.
[2] This was the last encounter between Cranborne and Disraeli in the
Commons.   During the Easter recess Disraeli's old colleague, Salisbury,
died, and Cranborne succeeded to the title.   Father and son had been
reconciled, and Salisbury had even espoused Cranborne's quarrel with
Disraeli, who, however, was able to write to Stanley on April 15: ' I am
glad that Lord Salisbury shook hands with me cordially before he died.'

him. There is nothing that he likes, and almost everything that he hates. He hates the working classes of England. He hates the Roman Catholics of Ireland. He hates the Protestants of Ireland. He hates His Majesty's Ministers. And until the right hon. gentleman the member for South Lancashire [Gladstone] placed his hand upon the ark, he almost seemed to hate the right hon. gentleman.

Disraeli maintained that there had been a great improvement in the state of Ireland since the Union, due to the steady policy of conciliation which had been for many years pursued by England, and especially by his own party. They had acted on the principle that in Ireland it was wise to create and not to destroy, and to strengthen Protestant institutions by being just to Roman Catholics, as in the University proposals then before Parliament. But Gladstone's policy would revive the acrimony of which they had hoped to get rid, place classes and creeds in antagonism, and indefinitely defer the restoration of political tranquillity. He strongly objected to disendowment. ' I view with great jealousy the plunder of a Church, because, so far as history can guide me, I have never found that Churches are plundered except to establish or enrich oligarchies.' There might be some palliation if there were a question of restitution to the Roman Catholics, but he could not in any circumstances agree that the endowments should be applied to what Liberals called secular purposes. ' A secular purpose is always a job.'

Towards the close of his speech Disraeli developed the argument on which he had touched in the previous debate, which he had pressed in his letter to Cairns, and which was especially congenial to one whose Jewish traditions gave a theocratic bent to his mind. He insisted on the vital importance of the union of Church and State; by which he meant ' that authority is to be not merely political, that government is to be not merely an affair of force, but is to recognise its responsibility to the Divine Power.' The divine right of Kings had properly been discarded, ' but an intelligent

age will never discard the divine right of Government.
If government is not divine, it is nothing. It is a mere
affair of the police office, of the tax-gatherer, of the
guardroom.'[1] If the Church in Ireland fell, he foresaw
attacks on the Church in Scotland and on the Church in
Wales; and the crisis in England, as he had said in his
letter to Lord Dartmouth, was fast arriving. 'High
Church Ritualists and the Irish followers of the Pope
have been long in secret combination, and are now in
open confederacy. . . . They have combined to destroy
that great blessing of conciliation which both parties in
the State for the last quarter of a century have laboured
to effect.'

Gladstone, in reply, deduced from Ministers' speeches
that their policy was some form of endowment for the
Roman Catholic Church, and condemned this alternative
as 'too late.' Gladstone's tone was the assured one of
a leader who knows that he has found a cause which
unites and inspires his party, and the division lobbies
justified him. Stanley's amendment was defeated by
sixty votes, and the motion to go into Committee was
carried by fifty-six.

From Lord Cairns.

Confidential. 5, CROMWELL HOUSES, W., *April* 4, 1868.—
. . . The division is larger than I expected, and yet I cannot
but hope that the numbers, together with the views which
Gladstone's supporters have expressed, will during the recess
make the country awake to the gravity of the position. The
issue, as you have placed it, is excellent, and I cannot express
my admiration of the whole of your magnificent speech.[2]

It was as an outwork of the Church of England that the
Church of Ireland especially appealed to Disraeli. The
same forces of Whiggery, Rationalism, and Dissent that

[1] In the General Preface to the novels, 1870, he reaffirmed this doctrine:
'The divine right of Kings may have been a plea for feeble tyrants, but
the divine right of Government is the keystone of human progress, and
without it government sinks into police, and a nation is degraded into a
mob.'

[2] On the other hand, to Hardy, the High Churchman, the speech appeared
obscure, flippant, and imprudent.'

had gathered to the attack on Church rates were once
more mobilised; and they were on this occasion reinforced
by the Roman Catholics and by some of the High
Churchmen and Ritualists, who were closely allied
with Gladstone and dreaded Erastianism more than
disestablishment. It was to this danger that Disraeli
called attention in the last words of his speech. His
statement was widely challenged, but he unhesitatingly defended it in a letter to a correspondent.

To the Rev. Arthur Baker.

HUGHENDEN MANOR, *Maundy Thursday*,[1] 1868.—. . . You
are under a misapprehension if you suppose that I intended
to cast any slur upon the High Church party. I have the
highest respect for the High Church party; I believe there is no
body of men in this country to which we have been more
indebted, from the days of Queen Anne to the days of Queen
Victoria, for the maintenance of the orthodox faith, the rights
of the Crown, and the liberties of the people. . . .
  When I spoke I referred to an extreme faction in the
Church, of very modern date, that does not conceal its ambition to destroy the connection between Church and State,
and which I have reason to believe has been for some time in
secret combination, and is now in open confederacy, with the
Irish Romanists for the purpose. The Liberation Society,
with its shallow and short-sighted fanaticism, is a mere instrument in the hands of this confederacy, and will probably be
the first victim of the spiritual despotism the Liberation
Society is now blindly working to establish. As I hold that
the dissolution of the union between Church and State will
cause permanently a greater revolution in this country than
foreign conquest, I shall use my utmost energies to defeat
these fatal machinations.

  It was, therefore, in Disraeli's view, essential that
the Church of England should collect her powers for
resistance. As a layman who had taken an active part
in diocesan affairs, he appealed to his Bishop, the
energetic Samuel Wilberforce, to give a lead to the clergy.
'What is the *mot d'ordre* to the diocese ?' he asked on

[1] The exaggerated ecclesiasticism of this method of dating his letter
exposed Disraeli to deserved criticism. Always an artist on the public
stage, he sometimes over-dressed his part.

April 15. It would be very unwise of the High Church clergy, he maintained, to let their imperfect sympathy with ' a Calvinistic branch of the establishment ' neutralise their action, as ' the fate of the Established Church will depend upon the opinion of the country as it is directed, formed, and organised during the next eight months.'[1] The Bishop had been much discomposed at his friend Gladstone's new move, which he attributed to ' the unconscious influence of his restlessness in being out of office '; and, in response to Disraeli's appeal, he set himself vigorously to work both in his diocese and in the Church at large, and took a prominent part in a great Church meeting of protest in St. James's Hall in May. In this Churchmen of all parties joined: Archbishop Longley with Dean Stanley, Bishop Tait with Bishop Wilberforce. Spofforth, the Conservative organiser, told Disraeli that the meeting was an unmeasured success, and would rouse the Protestant party throughout the country; but Shaftesbury, with more discernment, warned him that it was a failure. ' It was one mass of clergy with a sprinkling of peers. . . . The time is gone by when the country could be be-bishoped and be-duked on public matters. Unless you can get a mighty body of laity, bankers, lawyers, merchants, shipbuilders, etc.' The Liberal party, seldom behindhand in agitation, had taken the lead in organising great gatherings throughout the country in Gladstone's support, beginning with a meeting in London over which Russell presided; and it was manifest that the new policy had an increasing volume of public opinion behind it.

The large majority by which Gladstone had carried his motion against the resistance of the Government placed Ministers in a difficult situation. If that majority were maintained when the Resolutions were moved in detail, resignation or dissolution would in ordinary circumstances be inevitable. The circumstances, however, were not ordinary. Parliament had passed sentence of death upon

[1] *Life of Bishop Wilberforce*, Vol. III., p. 245.

itself by accepting a policy of Reform; but the policy was as yet incompletely carried out, as only the English Bill had become law, and the Irish and Scottish Bills were still under consideration.   Moreover, when they were passed, some months would be required to draw up the new registers and bring them into operation.   It was not reasonable to permit a moribund Parliament to decide without reference to the country a question of vital importance unexpectedly thrust upon its attention.   On the other hand, it was absurd to dissolve at once and appeal to the old constituencies; and it was doubtful whether the new constituencies could be properly created before 1869.   Strong influences were at work to prevent what apparently most of the Liberals expected and desired—namely, resignation.   Derby advised against it. The Queen would not hear of it, and expressed herself strongly in that sense in a private talk with Derby on the very morning of the initial vote.

From Lord Derby.

Most Confidential.   St. James's Square, *April* 3, 1868.— I would not have troubled you with a letter when I know how much your thoughts must be engaged, had I not thought that you would like to hear that the Queen, who has honoured me this morning with a visit of near an hour, spoke in most unreserved terms of condemnation of Gladstone's motion and conduct; and on my venturing to refer to the precedent of 1835, and the corresponding motion, and saying that its only result had been to turn out the Government, H.M. exclaimed with great emphasis, 'It shall not have that effect now!' I took on myself to say that I had strongly urged you, in the event of defeat, not to think of resigning, to which H.M. answered 'Quite right.' . . .

Disraeli, ever a fighter, agreed with Derby and the Queen; but several members of the Cabinet, of whom Hardy was the most prominent, were reluctant to sanction a course which would involve Ministers, in Hardy's words, ' in inextricable difficulties. The Opposition,' he wrote in his diary, ' has tasted blood, and will bully and endeavour to control us, so as to place us in minorities con-

stantly, and impede any legislation in our own sense.'
During the Easter recess the Queen entertained at Windsor
not only Disraeli, but also Hardy and Cairns, and impressed
her view very strongly upon them all.   Hardy wrote to
Disraeli, April 5: ' I have been much struck by the dread
which the Queen expresses of Gladstone and his scheme.
The Coronation Oath weighs upon her mind.   She thinks
she should be relieved of it legislatively with her own
consent, before being called upon to agree to the destruction of the Church of Ireland. . . .   The Queen is, as you
say, extraordinarily friendly, and anxious not to have a
change.'   Disraeli, after his visit, wrote to Cairns on April
8: ' The Queen is in a state of considerable excitement and
determination about the present state of affairs, which
she looks upon as very grave, tho' sanguine that the
country will rally to sound views.'

Before the recess concluded Disraeli had another
audience of Her Majesty on the question, and on the
resumption of Parliament, in anticipation of the forthcoming debate on the first Resolution, obtained the
general sanction of the Cabinet to a policy of dissolution
in preference to resignation.

To Lord Cairns.

Secret.   10, DOWNING STREET, April 22, 1868.—I shall open
the Cabinet to-day by giving the result of my audience last
Thursday at Windsor.

I shall indicate what I think is the duty of the Cabinet as
regards themselves and their party, and then, by Her Majesty's
especial desire and command, I shall refer to their duty, under
the circumstances, to the Queen personally.

When I have finished I shall request your opinion, and the
Queen hopes that you will confirm, from your personal
experience, the accuracy of my statement as to Her Majesty's
views.   She expects the same from Mr. Secy. Hardy, and for
the same reason; but I shall appeal to you first, not only
because you are my principal colleague, but because there is
only one black sheep in the Cabinet, the Duke of M[arl]borough],
and as he sits far from you, he will be governed by the
numerous opinions that will precede his own.

GATHORNE HARDY, FIRST EARL OF CRANBROOK.

From a portrait by W. E. Miller, at Hughenden.

From Queen Victoria.

OSBORNE, *April* 22, 1868.—The Queen received yesterday
Mr. Disraeli's letter, and thanks him very much for his full
explanation of the course which the Government propose to
recommend to her when Mr. Gladstone's first Resolution shall
be affirmed.

The Queen has always believed that that question, which has
been so unseasonably raised, cannot be settled without an
appeal to the country, and her Government may depend upon
her support in any measures which may appear to her calculated to effect that settlement in a satisfactory manner.

But as Mr. Disraeli postpones any specific recommendation
till the division on Mr. Gladstone's motion shall have taken
place, the Queen will only say now that any recommendation
she may then receive from her Government shall have her
careful and anxious consideration.   She would, however,
press upon Mr. Disraeli the importance of his *not* ' feeling,' as he
expresses it, ' for the opinion of the House,' as to the proper
time for appealing to the country, but that her Government
should consider this for themselves, and announce the decision
which they may think it right to submit to the Queen in a
manner that shall show no hesitation or doubt as to the policy
they mean to pursue.

Disraeli had some reason for thinking that, in spite of
the violent outcry of many Liberals and the Liberal press
for an immediate change of Government, Gladstone and
the more responsible leaders recognised the advisability
of waiting for the result of the appeal to the new constituencies.   He wrote to Hardy on the 23rd: ' Gladstone,
instead of wishing to upset us, has no Cabinet ready, and,
tho' sanguine as to his future, is, at present, greatly
embarrassed.   He wishes to build us a golden bridge, and
if we announce a *bona fide* attempt to wind up, he would
support Bills to extend the time of registration, which
would be necessitated by the passing of the Scotch and
Irish Bills.'   He added that ' the commercial Liberals . . .
look with the greatest alarm to Lord Russell's return to
the F.O., or even that of Ld. Clarendon.   They think the
peace of Europe depends upon Stanley's remaining.   I
am assured that there never was a moment in which a
want of confidence vote had a worse chance.'

The debate on Gladstone's first and main Resolution, that the Irish Church should cease to exist as an establishment, was carried over three nights,[1] but added little to the exhaustive arguments urged during the preliminary stage. Gladstone was able to show that the policy of joint endowment tentatively advanced by Disraeli was repudiated by other leading Conservatives, and that accordingly the only alternative to disestablishment was a course of procrastination. Disraeli's main point was that to carry the Resolution would, on the one hand, shake the principle of property throughout the kingdom, and, on the other, impair our security for religious liberty and civil rights by tampering with the royal supremacy.

The absence of a practicable alternative made a strong impression, and the majority increased to 65, 330 voting for the Resolution and only 265 against. Disraeli immediately moved the adjournment on the ground that the vote had altered the relation between the Government and the House; and proceeded on the next morning[2] to Osborne to tender to the Queen the advice which, in general terms, the Cabinet had agreed upon in the previous week. As the course to be followed had already been concerted with Her Majesty, there was no difficulty in obtaining her consent; but she very properly desired that her Minister's advice and her own answer should be formally recorded in writing.

To Queen Victoria.

[*May* 1, 1868.]—The division of this morning in the House of Commons, by which at half-past two o'clock a.m. Mr. Gladstone carried a Resolution for the disestablishment of the Irish Church by a majority of sixty-five, renders it necessary to call your Majesty's attention to the position of your Majesty's Government.

About two years ago Lord Derby undertook the management of your Majesty's affairs in a Parliament elected under the influence of his opponents, and in which there was a Liberal majority certainly exceeding seventy.

In the spirit of the Constitution he might have advised your

---

[1] April 27, 28, and 30.   [2] Friday, May 1.

Majesty to dissolve this Parliament, and, in the broken state of the Liberal party at that moment, perhaps not without success. But considering that the Parliament had been so recently elected he resolved to attempt to conduct affairs without that appeal. In the following year he had to encounter the Reform question under peculiar difficulties, and he succeeded in carrying a large measure on a subject which had for a long series of years baffled all statesmen and all parties.

Lord Derby would naturally have advised your Majesty to dissolve Parliament at the close of last year, had there not been some Bills supplementary to the Reform Bill, which time prevented carrying, but the principle of all which had been sanctioned by the House of Commons.

Was there anything in the general conduct of affairs by your Majesty's present Government which should have deterred them from this appeal to the opinion of the nation ?

The conduct of affairs has never been impugned during these two years in any department; on the contrary, in every department it has been commended by their opponents. On the grounds, therefore, that they assumed office in a large and avowed minority in a House of Commons elected by their opponents; that they succeeded in passing the Reform Act; that their policy has been never impugned, but has been entirely accepted, they would be acting only in the spirit of the Constitution, were they to advise your Majesty to dissolve Parliament.

In this state of affairs, while attempting to wind up the session and pass the supplementary Reform Bills, Mr. Gladstone at a few days' notice introduces a policy to disestablish the Church in Ireland.

The objections of your Majesty's Government to this measure are very grave.

1. It is a retrograde policy, and would destroy the effect of thirty years of conciliation.

2. It shakes property to the centre.

3. It dissolves for the first time the connection between Government and religion.

And fourthly and chiefly in their opinion it introduces a principle which must sooner or later, and perhaps much sooner than is anticipated, be applied to England, where the effects must be of a most serious consequence.

The Church will become either an *Imperium in Imperio* more powerful than the State, or it will break into sects and schisms and ultimately be absorbed by the tradition and discipline of the Church of Rome; and the consequence will be that the Queen's supremacy, the security for our religious liberty, and, in no slight degree, for our civil rights, will be

destroyed.   In fact, this will be a revolution, and an entire
subversion of the English Constitution.

Is the fact that this policy has been sanctioned, perhaps
heedlessly, by the House of Commons a reason for not appealing to the nation ?   Your Majesty's Ministers humbly think
not, and that no satisfactory settlement can be arrived at
without such an appeal.

Under these circumstances the advice they would humbly
offer your Majesty is to dissolve this Parliament as soon as the
public interests will permit, and that an earnest endeavor
should be made by the Government that such appeal should
be made to the new constituency.

In offering your Majesty this advice your Majesty's
Ministers would most dutifully state that if your Majesty
thought the question could be more satisfactorily settled, and
the public interest best consulted, by the immediate retirement of your Majesty's present Ministers from your Majesty's
service, they would at once place their resignations in your
Majesty's hands, with only one feeling of gratitude to your
Majesty for your Majesty's constant support to them in their
arduous duties, which has always encouraged and often
assisted them.

From Queen Victoria.

OSBORNE, *May* 2, 1868.—The Queen has given her most
serious consideration to Mr. Disraeli's letter, and cannot
hesitate, as she has already verbally informed him, to sanction
the dissolution of Parliament, under the circumstances
stated by him, in order that the opinion of the country may
be deliberately expressed on the important question which has
been brought into discussion.

The Queen admits the correctness of Mr. Disraeli's statement
of the circumstances under which Lord Derby undertook the
Government in the first instance, and Mr. Disraeli has since
continued to carry it on.

She has frequently had occasion to express her satisfaction
at the zeal and ability with which the several departments
of her Government have been administered; and while her
Ministers have done nothing to forfeit the confidence she has
hitherto reposed in them, she cannot think of having recourse
to the alternative which Mr. Disraeli has placed before her,
of accepting their resignations, till the sense of the country
shall have been taken on a question which, [it] is admitted on
all hands, cannot be settled in the present Parliament.

It will be seen that, while an alternative tender was
made of resignation, the advice given to the Queen was

to dissolve Parliament ' as soon as the public interests will permit,' coupled with a suggestion that, in the event of dissolution, Ministers should make ' an earnest endeavor ' to ensure that the appeal should be made to the new constituency; and that the Queen's reply was to refuse to accept resignation, but ' to sanction the dissolution of Parliament, under the circumstances stated,' without making any distinction between the old constituency and the new.

Disraeli had gone to the Queen without calling a Cabinet, relying on the general assent which his colleagues had given ten days before to a policy of dissolution rather than resignation. This somewhat high-handed departure from precedent was naturally resented. ' Disraeli has communicated with none of us, which is strange,' wrote Hardy mildly in his diary. Malmesbury, more roundly, noted: ' The Ministers are very angry with Disraeli for going to the Queen without calling a Cabinet, and the Duke of Marlborough wants to resign, but I have done all I could to dissuade him from this course.' The Duke, it will be remembered, was described by Disraeli, in writing to Cairns, as a ' black sheep ' on this question. It is evident from the entries in Hardy's diary, and especially one on May 6 ('A Cabinet before Osborne would have altered everything, but now ?'), that Disraeli avoided a preliminary Cabinet because he had good reason to fear that his colleagues would weaken in their resolution now that the moment for action had arrived, but might be trusted to accept a *fait accompli*. He returned from Osborne on the Saturday evening, May 2, saw on the Sunday two of the colleagues upon whom he principally relied, Cairns and Hardy, and perhaps others, and explained to them what had passed with the Queen. Hardy greatly doubted, and had a strong personal longing for resignation;[1] Cairns expressed agreement with his chief; and the Cabinet next day endorsed, though with

---

[1] In 1889, on reconsideration of the whole position, Hardy wrote: ' Looking back, I doubt if we could have done otherwise than we did ' (Gathorne Hardy, Vol. I., p. 273).

considerable hesitation, the bill which the Prime Minister had drawn upon its confidence.

A course which had only with difficulty been accepted by Disraeli's colleagues could hardly be expected to commend itself offhand to the Liberal majority in the House of Commons. Disraeli's recital of the successful conduct of affairs by Ministers since 1866, his justification by precedent of the constitutionality of government by a minority, his withdrawal of protracted opposition to the remaining Resolutions, and his promise to expedite public business so that the dissolution might take place in the autumn, did not prevent the Opposition from using, in Hardy's words, ' plenty of unpleasant language ' about the advice which Ministers had tendered to the Queen. Gladstone protested angrily against a penal dissolution, though, in view of Disraeli's readiness to facilitate debate on the remaining Resolutions, he did not persist in his announced motion to take the conduct of public business into his own hands. Lowe said that Parliament was asked to give a ten months' lease of office to Ministers whom it did not trust; Ayrton and Bouverie denounced Disraeli for bringing the Crown into conflict with the Commons; Bright said that it was merely for the sake of prolonging his own term of office that Disraeli was making this outrageous demand on the indulgence of Parliament. Disraeli, in reply, pointed out that, while he was ready to make all arrangements for an appeal to the new constituency in November, the Queen's permission to dissolve was unqualified, without any reference to old or new constituencies; and he challenged the Opposition to give Parliamentary effect to their taunts by moving a vote of want of confidence.

The challenge, as Disraeli expected, was not taken up. However ready the Liberal leaders might be to insult and to bluster, and their followers to annoy Ministers by putting them in a minority on this question and on that, the general sense of the House was that the Government which had passed Reform should remain in office to complete its work, and to pass the supplementary measures necessary to secure at the earliest possible date an appeal to the new constituency. The very reasonableness of this view only served to exasperate Gladstone and his friends; and for several days they kept recurring to Disraeli's statements about his audiences of the Queen and the advice he had given her, suggesting supposed discrepancies and denouncing supposed improprieties. One such occasion is described in the following letter:

To the Duke of Richmond.

CARLTON CLUB, *May* 5, 1868.—Mr. Gladstone,[1] to-night, without giving me any notice whatever, called on me to explain what he described as a discrepancy in our statements as to the Queen's declaration in my audience at Osborne.

Had he been courteous enough to give me the usual notice, I could have had the opportunity of conferring with your Grace, and learning from yourself what you had stated, instead of being referred to the mere extract of an alleged report in a newspaper.

All that I could do, therefore, was to repeat what Her Majesty had been pleased to declare, and to add, that if there were any discrepancy in our statements, as I was the Minister, who had waited on Her Majesty, it seemed to me, that the inquiry ought rather to be made in the House of Lords, than to myself.

I write this note, that your Grace should not suppose, that I hesitated to defend, or support, an absent colleague: but under the circumstances of the case, having had no notice from Mr. Gladstone, and having no evidence that the alleged quotation was authentic, I thought it best to take a course wh. suspended all judgment on the question.

Another occasion arose on the motion of a Liberal member condemning the policy of making any public grants whatever in Ireland to religious bodies, such as the *Regium Donum* to Presbyterians, or the Maynooth grant and the proposed University endowment for Roman Catholics. A warm discussion sprang up, chiefly among Liberal members themselves; and Ayrton, whose unconciliatory and overbearing demeanour in office was subse-

---

[1] 'In a white heat,' noted Hardy in his diary.

quently to bring discredit upon Gladstone's first Administration, commented severely upon the absence of the Leader of the House during the debate. Disraeli, who arrived during Ayrton's lecture, made the characteristic excuse that there had been, as he anticipated, a quarrel among gentlemen opposite over the plunder of the Irish Church, and that it was not his duty to give an opinion on the subject. This sneer seems to have caused Bright to lose all command over himself, and to use language which necessarily brought to an end the unconventional but undoubted private friendship which had existed between him and Disraeli for twenty years. Bright had been falling under the spell of Gladstone's influence, and apparently was ready now to regard Disraeli through his rival's eyes. This is what he permitted himself to say:

The right hon. gentleman the other night, with a mixture of pompousness and sometimes of servility, talked at large of the interviews which he had had with his Sovereign. I venture to say that a Minister who deceives his Sovereign is as guilty as the conspirator who would dethrone her. I do not charge the right hon. gentleman with deceiving his Sovereign. But if he has not changed the opinions which he held twenty-five years ago, and which in the main he said, only a few weeks ago, were right, then I fear he has not stated all that it was his duty to state in the interviews which he had with his Sovereign. Let me tell hon. gentlemen opposite, and the right hon. gentleman in particular, that any man in this country who puts the Sovereign in the front of a great struggle like this into which it may be we are about to enter—who points to the Irish people and says from the floor of this House, 'your Queen holds the flag under which we, the enemies of religious equality and justice to Ireland, are marshalled'—I say the Minister who does that is guilty of a very high crime and a great misdemeanour against his Sovereign and against his country; and there is no honour, there is no reputation, there is no glory, there is no future name that any Minister can gain by conduct like this, which will acquit him to posterity of one of the most grievous offences against his country which a Prime Minister can possibly commit.

It was an outrageous attack, and was suitably answered by Disraeli. Observers differed as to whether he was deeply moved or whether he merely spoke with quiet scorn. Lord Ronald Gower tells us that 'Dizzy quite lost his temper and shook his fist at Bright'; but Malmesbury's record is that the Prime Minister 'replied in the most gentlemanlike manner, and was cheered by both sides of the House.'

I shall not condescend to notice at length the observations of the hon. member for Birmingham. He says that, when it was my duty to make a communication to the House, of the greatest importance, and which I certainly wished to make—as I hope I did make it—in a manner not unbecoming the occasion, I was at once pompous and servile. Well, sir, if it suits the heat of party acrimony to impute such qualities to me, any gentleman may do so; but I am in the memory and in the feeling of gentlemen on both sides of the House— and fortunately there are gentlemen on both sides of this House; they will judge of the accuracy of this representation of my conduct. It is to their feeling and to their sentiment on both sides of the House that I must appeal; and no words of mine, if the charge be true, can vindicate me. The hon. gentleman says that he will make no charge against me; and then he makes insinuations which, if he believes them, he ought to bring forth boldly as charges. I defy the hon. member for Birmingham, notwithstanding his stale invective, to come down to the House and substantiate any charge of the kind which he has presumed only to insinuate. Let him prefer those charges; I will meet him; and I will appeal to the verdict only of gentlemen who sit on the same side of the House as himself.

This challenge, it need hardly be added, was not met, any more than the challenge to bring forward a vote of censure had been met. But the stream of calumny in the House, on the platform, and in the press, flowed on unabated. It was the cue of many Liberals to treat Disraeli as being capable of any trickery and of any breach of constitutional usage. When therefore Gladstone's second and third Resolutions had passed, the one suspending Irish ecclesiastical appointments, the other praying the Queen to place her interest in the temporalities at the disposal of Parliament, the absurd suggestion was made that Disraeli was likely to advise the Queen to set herself in antagonism to the House of Commons by returning an unfavourable answer to the third Resolution.

From General the Hon. Charles Grey.

OSBORNE, *May* 5, 1868.—. . . Her Majesty hears with much satisfaction what you say of the favourable prospects in the House of Commons; and trusts that your expectation of being able to surmount the difficulties still before you may be realised. She is very anxious to hear what you propose to advise her as to the answer to the Address, which is the object of the third Resolution. *The Times* assumes that the ' Suspensory Bill ' which the Address will ask the Queen to allow to be introduced, will certainly be thrown out in the House of Lords. This would place the H. of Lords in a position of antagonism to the House of Commons from which, in H.M.'s opinion, they ought, if possible, to be saved. Yet, after all that has passed, it seems difficult for the Govt. to advise the Queen to refuse the request of the Commons.

Could Her Majesty, without refusing it (on the contrary, expressing her anxiety to act with her *Parliament* in any measures calculated to give satisfaction to her Irish subjects), not require that, in a matter which cannot be settled without the concurrence of the House of Lords, the Address should be agreed to by both Houses ? . . .

Disraeli was too shrewd even to endorse this not unreasonable suggestion to withhold an answer to the Address till it had been adopted by both Houses; and the answer which, after special consultation with Cairns and Hardy, he settled in Cabinet stated that Her Majesty desired that her interest in the Irish temporalities should not stand in the way of the consideration by Parliament of legislation in the current session. Gladstone promptly introduced his Suspensory Bill, and the second reading was carried on May 22 by a majority of fifty-four, after a debate in which the Opposition leader insisted that the choice lay between a system of concurrent endowment such as had been hinted at by the Government and the general disendowment which he himself proposed to effect by repealing the Maynooth Act and discontinuing the *Regium Donum* to Presbyterians, as well as by disestablishing and disendowing the Church of Ireland. Disraeli was hampered, in his reply, by the disfavour with which the policy of concurrent endowment had been received by his own party and by the country. He accordingly minimised the extent to which the Government had committed themselves to it. He denied that their University proposals amounted to endowment, or that they contemplated paying the Roman Catholic clergy or increasing the *Regium Donum*. The logical position of Disraeli and his Government was necessarily much weakened by this public deprecation of the only alternative policy; a policy, moreover, which he favoured himself and which had the historical support of a succession of British statesmen from Pitt and Castlereagh down to Russell, who had only abandoned it that year. He had to fall back, as his main argument, on the resulting danger to the Church of England. ' I say this act is the first step to the disestablishment of the English Church.' The correctness of this view has recently received unexpected confirmation from Mr. Birrell, Chief Secretary for Ireland for many years and no friend of the Church of England, who has deplored in an important State paper that the Irish Church was disestablished rather from a desire to please the Dissenters in England than to do justice to Ireland. But a practical people like the English will never be deterred from dealing with a practical and admitted grievance by apprehension of possible but remote consequences.

The Suspensory Bill had been pushed forward rather to show that Gladstone and the Liberals were in earnest than with any expectation that it would pass into law. Disraeli having once registered his opposition to it, facilitated its speedy passage to the Lords, where it was promptly rejected by a majority of two to one, on the ground that the whole question should be left without prejudice to the judgment of the electorate.

From Lord Derby.

St. James's Square, *May* 29, 1868.—. . . I think . . . I may congratulate you on being master of the position for the remainder of the Session, which I presume you will close

as soon as you can. Will you allow me to suggest that, partly
to promote that object, it would be well to let it be understood that you do not mean further to oppose Gladstone's
Suspension Bill. . . . Our object should be to get it disposed
of in the Lords as soon, and as summarily, as possible. I
suggest this for your consideration as a matter of tactics,
of which however you are too great a master to stand in need
of any hint from me. . . .

To Lord Derby.

10, Downing Street, *May* 30, 1868.—I must thank you
for your kind letter, and for your invaluable counsel. I had
moved a little in the direction you advise, and will still
further prosecute that course. . . .

To Charles N. Newdegate.

Confidential. 10, Downing St., *May* 31, '68.—I think it
would be well to consider whether it may not be desirable to
place no further impediments to the passing of the Suspension
Bill in the House of Commons, so that the decision of the
House of Lords may be taken as speedily as possible.

It is probable that the Church Commission will report
towards the end of next month, and if they recommend any
modification of appointments it will be difficult for the Lords
to oppose the Suspension Bill and they will be driven to
define and limit its objects, instead of opposing the second
reading: and this the country will never understand.

No doubt Gladstone sees this chance and will not be in a
hurry to carry his Bill through our House, whereas, in my
opinion, our object should be to get it disposed of in the
Lords as soon, and as summarily, as possible.

I wish you would think over this and give me your opinion.

These letters were written during the Whitsuntide
recess, which roughly corresponded with the close of the
great party struggle of the session. If Disraeli was, as
Derby suggested, ' master of the position ' from that time
till the prorogation, it was largely because he had not
only evaded the snares of his foes, but had also brought
his somewhat distracted Cabinet into harmony and sub-
ordination.

To Mrs. Disraeli.

House of Commons, *May* 14, '68.—I think we have got
out of our danger, but it has been very ticklish.

May 19, '68.—The Cabinet was very satisfactory, and they signed a paper, projected and headed by the Duke of Richmond, to stand by me in any advice I should give the Queen on the great subject. This puts an end to one source of wearing disquietude, namely, the fear that the Cabinet might not stand firm and united.

The reunited Cabinet utilised the recess to come to an agreement as to the measure to expedite the new register so as to make possible a General Election in November and the summoning of the new Parliament in December. Disraeli was justifiably anxious that the acceleration should not be such as to arouse a suspicion in the new constituency ' that there is any design to neutralise the large franchises with which they have been wisely invested, by hurrying and hustling them in the establishment of their electoral privileges.' [1]   But Cairns and Hardy were particularly urgent in pressing for an early date, to maintain the honour of the Government and to save them from any possible charge of bad faith; and their scheme was accepted first by the Cabinet and then, amid general satisfaction, by Parliament.

This Registration of Voters Bill was one of five measures which Disraeli carried during this session to complete the work of Parliamentary Reform. The factiousness of the Opposition made the progress of the Irish and Scottish Reform Bills through the House of Commons a tedious and aggravating business, and Disraeli had need of all his tact and good temper to bring them safely into port.   On the Scottish Bill, particularly, he was subjected to some annoying defeats; but, in pursuance of his acknowledged principle of acting, in regard to Reform, in co-operation with the general sense of the House, he accepted the amendments of the majority with a good grace.   The Boundary Bill was the occasion of further worries.   The decisions of the Commission appointed by the Government in 1867 were not accepted in the House, and were submitted for revision to a Select Committee presided over by Walpole.   The Commission

[1] Letter to Cairns, dated May 29.

enlarged the Parliamentary boundaries of many big towns, but the Committee restored the old limits; and Government and Opposition, Lords and Commons, were set by the ears over the somewhat trivial questions as to which tribunal's decisions were to be followed, and whether a compromise accepted by the Prime Minister in the Commons was binding on the majority in the Lords. Disraeli repudiated the interpretation put by the Opposition on his words; but, after the Liberal Peers had adopted the childish expedient of leaving the House of Lords in a body, Malmesbury and the majority gave way.

To Lord Malmesbury.

10, DOWNING STREET, *July* 3, 1868.—I have learnt your proceedings in the House of Lords, last night, with astonishment. The interpretation placed on my words, when speaking of the progress of business in the House of Commons, is one painfully distorted. I was answering an enquiry as to the prospects of business in that House, and in estimating them, I mentioned, that certain measures, tho' they had not formally passed the House of Commons, might be considered virtually settled: that is to say, would lead, in the House of Commons, to no further debate or division.

A much more important reform was effected by the Corrupt Practices Bill; and it is to the lasting credit of Disraeli that he removed the trial of election petitions from the jurisdiction of a partisan Committee of the House of Commons and transferred it to an impartial tribunal consisting of His Majesty's Judges. In order to carry this simple and desirable reform he had to overcome many obstacles, in particular the united protest of the Judges themselves against the new duties it was proposed to put upon them. The Bill underwent several changes and, in order to pass, had to be made experimental in form and duration; but the principle was firmly established that irregularities committed in political elections, like other breaches of the law, should be investigated and punished by a legal tribunal and not by a committee of active politicians. A great purification

of public life has resulted from the firm determination of
Disraeli and his Government to associate the proper trial
and due punishment of corrupt practices at elections
with the extension of the Parliamentary suffrage.

If Disraeli's Parliamentary course was troubled, the
principal external venture of his Government was brilliantly conducted. At the beginning of the very week which
witnessed the decisive defeat of Ministers on Gladstone's
first Resolution, there came news of the complete success
of the Abyssinian expedition under the command of Sir
Robert Napier. It was on the morning of Sunday,
April 26, and about 11 o'clock, the present Lord Iddesleigh, on behalf of his father Northcote, the Secretary of
State for India, brought the intelligence to Disraeli. He
found him ' gorgeously arrayed in a dressing-gown and in
imposing headgear,' and, as might be expected, ' opulent
in compliment.'[1] The Queen told her Prime Minister that
she was ' truly delighted at the glorious and satisfactory
news from Abyssinia, which she thinks must have a
favourable effect on the general position of the Government.' There was, indeed, universal satisfaction; and
Gladstone joined in the compliments paid, not only to the
commander and his gallant force, but to the Government,
and especially the Indian Secretary, for their prudent
conduct of a difficult affair.

For it was a very difficult affair to rescue a British
envoy and a British consul, who with other captives were
imprisoned in an impregnable fortress, far inland in a
wild and inhospitable country, by a half-mad and only
half-civilised potentate. Ministers had only with great
reluctance accepted the necessity of sending an expedition,
Stanley characteristically writing to Disraeli in the autumn
of 1866, ' I sincerely hope the W[ar] O[ffice] will find the
country inaccessible. I think they will.' But, as Disraeli
explained when moving the credit of £2,000,000 in November, 1867, they felt that the honour of the Crown and the
duty of the country were involved; that magnanimity

[1] Lang's *Northcote*, p. 194.

and forbearance had been pushed to extreme limits; that
justice could only be had by recourse to arms. None
of the numerous little expeditions which England has
sent out was ever more completely successful. The
difficult country was safely penetrated, King Theodore's
army was defeated with insignificant casualties on our side,
his citadel Magdala was stormed, he himself committed
suicide, and the prisoners were duly brought away.
Disraeli may be forgiven the slight touch of pomposity
with which, in moving Parliament to thank the commander and his forces, he dilated on the difficulties overcome and the success attained. Napier, he said, had to
form a base on a desolate shore, to create a road through
a wall of mountains, and to guide his army across a
barren and lofty tableland, intersected with high ranges
and unfathomable ravines; leading ' the elephants of
Asia, bearing the artillery of Europe, over African passes
which might have startled the trapper and appalled
the hunter of the Alps.' Finally our troops ' had to scale
a mountain fortress, of which the intrinsic strength was
such that it may be fairly said it would have been impregnable to the whole world had it been defended by the
man by whom it was assailed.' Thus it was, said Disraeli,
linking modern achievement with Johnsonian romance,
that ' the standard of St. George was hoisted on the
mountains of Rasselas.'

It was not merely for its conduct that the expedition
was remarkable, but for its character. Disraeli pointed
out in November, 1867, that the country was going to
war, ' not to obtain territory, not to secure commercial
advantages, but for high moral causes and for high moral
causes alone.' Accordingly, when the prisoners had
been released and Theodore's capital destroyed, the
British force, having accomplished its object, completely
evacuated, by the orders of the Ministry, the country
which it had successfully invaded. Disraeli naturally
congratulated the House and the country on so unique
a spectacle.

When it was first announced that England was about to embark on a most costly and perilous expedition, merely to vindicate the honour of our Sovereign, and to rescue from an unjust but remote captivity a few of our fellow-subjects, the announcement was received in more than one country with something like mocking incredulity. But we have asserted the purity of our purpose. In an age accused, and perhaps not unjustly, of selfishness, and a too great regard for material interests, it is something, in so striking and significant a manner, for a great nation to have vindicated the higher principles of humanity. It is a privilege to belong to a country which has done such deeds.

Disraeli has been charged with lowering the standard of British foreign policy by basing it upon British interests rather than upon public right and justice. The Abyssinian expedition, which his detractors prefer to ignore, is incontestable evidence that he placed public right and justice high among British interests. The only criticism to which his policy on this occasion is fairly open is that he underrated the cost. Ward Hunt, in his Budget speech, estimated the total at £5,000,000, and raised the income tax from fourpence to sixpence in order to meet the expense; but it turned out that nearly as much again was required, and Gladstone's Chancellor of the Exchequer had in 1869 to provide for meeting the balance of an ascertained total of £9,000,000. The fault seems to have lain mainly with the Indian Government, who supplied the General and the troops; but the miscalculation must necessarily detract somewhat from the credit otherwise due to Disraeli and his Government. Disraeli himself, in retrospect, treated the cost as a trifling matter in comparison with the successful result.

To Lady Bradford.

2, WHITEHALL GARDENS, *Oct.* 2, 1875.— . . . I do not look back to the Abyssinian [war] with regret: quite the reverse. It was a noble feat of arms, and highly raised our prestige in the East. It certainly cost double what was contemplated, and that is likely to be the case in all wars for wh. I may be responsible. Money is not to be considered in such matters: success alone is to be thought of. Abyss.

cost 9 mills. or so, instead of 4 or 5 anticipated; but by that
expenditure we secured the business being accomplished in
one campaign. Had there been a second campaign, it wd.
probably have been 19 mill. and perhaps failed—from climate,
or an abler and more prepared military resistance. . . .

Though Parliament was prorogued at the comparatively early date of July 31, yet once more, in spite of the
time necessarily devoted to the corollaries of Reform,
and of the many days spent on the Irish problem and
Gladstone's new policy, there was a good harvest of other
legislation. The Queen's Speech enumerated as having
passed ' Bills for the better government of public schools,
the regulation of railways, the amendment of the law
relating to British sea fisheries, and for the acquisition
and maintenance of electric telegraphs by the Postmaster-
General, and several important measures having for their
object the improvement of the law and of the civil and
criminal procedure in Scotland.' A small measure, which
was not mentioned, was the Act which abolished, none too
soon, the degrading practice of public execution. The
purchase of the telegraphs was a question to which
Disraeli had paid special attention. To transfer the working of so essential a public service to the State was undoubtedly a great public benefit; but the price paid to the
telegraph companies was so high, and popular pressure
for cheap messages so persistent, that the transaction
has never yielded the profit to the State which those
who effected it contemplated. The educational bill upon
which the Cabinet had been closely engaged at the
beginning of the year[1] did not get beyond a second
reading in the House of Lords, where it was introduced by
the Lord President, the Duke of Marlborough. It had
the great merit of recognising the importance and dignity
of education by constituting a comprehensive education
department under a Cabinet Minister, a reform which
Disraeli had advocated in 1855[2] but which Parliament
did not accept till 1899, and it provided an effective con-

[1] See Vol. IV., ch. 16.   [2] See Vol. IV., ch. 2.

science clause; but Ministers hesitated to introduce the principle of a rate, without which a general system could hardly be established. It was a measure, in Disraeli's words, ' preliminary, but of magnitude '; but there was no time to consider it, and the whole question, as he anticipated, was left over to the next Parliament.

Through all the troubles and worries of this spring and summer Disraeli was greatly cheered and supported by the constant sympathy and encouragement of the Queen. Her Majesty considered that her Minister's conduct and the advice he had given her at the time of the crisis were perfectly correct and constitutional; and she was disgusted with what she held to be the factious and unworthy treatment which he received at the hands of the Opposition. The relations between Sovereign and Minister, which were eventually to become so intimate, were drawn very perceptibly closer during this May and June. The Queen began that practice of sending Disraeli spring flowers, which was a constant mark of their later relationship, and which has resulted in the permanent association of his name and memory with the primrose; and he, whose official letters to his Sovereign had always sounded a strongly individual and personal note, was encouraged to develop this tendency and entertain Her Majesty by such correspondence as he alone was able to write. Lady Augusta Stanley told Clarendon at this time that ' Dizzy writes daily letters to the Queen in his best novel style, telling her every scrap of political news dressed up to serve his own purpose, and every scrap of social gossip cooked to amuse her. She declares that she has never had such letters in her life, which is probably true, and that she never before knew *everything !*' [1]

Princess Christian to Mrs. Disraeli.

May 12.—Mama desires me to . . . send you the accompanying flowers in her name for Mr. Disraeli. She heard him say one day that he was so fond of may and of all those

[1] Letter from Clarendon to Lady Salisbury. Maxwell's *Clarendon*, Vol. II., p. 346.

lovely spring flowers that she has ventured to send him these, as they will make his rooms look so bright. The flowers come from Windsor.

Mrs. Disraeli to Princess Christian.

. . . I performed the most pleasing office which I ever had to fulfil in obeying Her Majesty's commands. Mr. Disraeli is passionately fond of flowers, and their lustre and perfume were enhanced by the condescending hand which had showered upon him all the treasures of spring.

From Queen Victoria.

May 14.—The Queen was glad to hear how very warmly Mr. Disraeli was received yesterday. It is very significant. The Queen trusts that the debate to-night[1] will be satisfactory, tho' Mr. Disraeli told her he had anticipated the worst.

WINDSOR CASTLE, *May* 16, 1868.—The Queen is most thankful to Mr. Disraeli for his very kind and feeling letter. She feels most deeply when others *do* sympathise as he does with her; Mr. Disraeli has at all times shown the greatest consideration for her feelings. . . .

The Queen sends by this evening's messenger a few more flowers for Mr. Disraeli.

BALMORAL, *May* 21.—The Queen was very sorry to hear from Mr. Disraeli what an unsatisfactory night they had on Monday.[2]

She feels very anxious to hear what course they intend to pursue, but trusts that this as well as other difficulties will be got over, and this annoying Session soon be brought to an end. . . .

May 23.—. . . Really there never was such conduct as that of the Opposition.

May 25.—The Queen thanks Mr. Disraeli for several kind letters. . . .

The Queen is really shocked at the way in which the House of Commons go on; they really bring discredit on Constitutional Government. The Queen hopes and trusts, however, that to-day's division will be satisfactory and then there will be quiet.

The sooner the Dissolution can take place the better. . . .

June 6.—The Queen thanks Mr. Disraeli very much for his kind, long letter. She hopes all will go smoothly. She regrets however the acrimonious discussion respecting the

---

[1] On the Boundary Bill.

[2] When the Government were defeated in important divisions on the Scotch Reform Bill.

letter[1] which she wishes could have been avoided. This personal bitterness in politics is a bad thing, and if possible should be prevented. But alas! it is often *impossible*.

The Queen trusts the Session will speedily be got to an end, for it is sure to be disagreeable as long as it lasts. . . .

June 21.—. . . Most grateful to Mr. Disraeli for the gift of his novels, which she values much.

It was particularly tactful and appropriate of Disraeli to present the Queen with his novels, as Her Majesty had herself entered the ranks of authorship in the beginning of the year by publishing *Leaves from the Journal of our Life in the Highlands*. There was thus a fresh link between the Minister and his royal mistress, which so accomplished a courtier could hardly fail to turn to good account. There is no reason to doubt the story which represents him as using more than once, in conversation with Her Majesty on literary subjects, the words: 'We authors, Ma'am.'

To Arthur Helps.

[*January*, 1868].—I am most obliged to you for sending me a copy, and an early one, of the royal volume.

I read it last night and with unaffected interest. Its vein is innocent and vivid; happy in picture and touched with what I ever think is the characteristic of our royal mistress—grace.

There is a freshness and fragrance about the book like the heather amid which it was written.

They say that truth and tact are not easily combined: I never believed so; and you have proved the contrary; for you have combined them in your preface, and that's why I like it.

The Queen was far from well in the spring of 1868. She informed Disraeli in May that the anxiety and worry of the last two or three years were beginning to tell on her health and nerves; that she often feared she would be unable physically to go on; and that she felt the necessity of rest in a pure and bracing air. A visit to Switzerland was accordingly arranged; and the Queen, travelling as Countess of Kent, left England at the beginning of

---

[1] Gladstone had written a letter imputing to the Government a policy of concurrent endowment.

August. She passed through Paris, where a slight *contretemps* occurred which gave Disraeli an opportunity of showing how tactfully he could offer somewhat unwelcome advice.

To Lord Cairns.

Private. HUGHENDEN, *August* 11, 1868.—. . . I heard from Lucerne to-day. Our Peeress is very happy and, as yet, quite delighted. Her house is on a high hill, above the town, with a splendid view over the lake; the air fine, the rooms large, lofty, cool. There has been rain and there is a grim world.

The gentlemen of the suite don't like the hill; *facilis descensus,* but the getting back will be awful. Stanley has not yet arrived, but he likes hills; a member of your Alpine Club.

There was a sort of Fenian outrage at Paris; one O'Brien, a teacher of languages, shook his stick at Princess Louise, and shouted ' A bas les Anglais,' and some other stuff. The Queen was not there.

I fear, between ourselves, the greater outrage was that our dear Peeress did not return the visit of the Empress. This is to be deplored, particularly as they had named a Boulevard after her, and she went to see it ! . . .

To Queen Victoria.

10, DOWNING STREET [*August*, 1868].—. . . There is no doubt that your Majesty acted quite rightly in declining to return the visit of the Empress at Paris. Such an act on your Majesty's part would have been quite inconsistent with the incognito assumed by your Majesty, for a return visit to a Sovereign is an act of high etiquette: which incognito is invented to guard against.

Nevertheless there is, Mr. Disraeli would ask permission to observe, perhaps no doubt that your Majesty was scarcely well advised in receiving the visit, as such a reception was equally inconsistent with incognito.

Certain persons, M. de Fleury notably among them, made a great grievance of the visit not being returned, but Mr. Disraeli hoped the matter would have blown over and been forgotten. The Empress, who is far from irrational, was not at first by any means disposed to take M. de Fleury's view, but everybody persists in impressing on her she has been treated with incivility; and there is no doubt that it has ended by the French Court being sore.

Mr. Disraeli thought it his duty to lay this matter before

your Majesty; as your Majesty perhaps on your return, with your Majesty's happy judgment, might by some slight act gracefully dissipate this malaise.

It was not found possible to arrange to make the return visit as the Countess of Kent passed through Paris on her way back to England; but Lady Ely wrote to Disraeli: 'The Queen desires me to tell you that H.M. has written to the Empress herself to express all her regrets, but to say H.M. has given up paying visits now and had declined going to her own relations, but hoped at some future time when she passed through Paris to call and see the Empress.'

Immediately upon her return to this country, Her Majesty commanded Disraeli's presence for ten days at Balmoral, where he had never before been Minister in attendance. Mrs. Disraeli did not accompany him, and he kept her fully informed of his doings and experiences.

To Mrs. Disraeli.

PERTH, *Sept.* 18, '68.

MY DARLING WIFE,—I telegraphed to you this morning, that all was well. Within an hour of this place, where we ought to have arrived a little after eleven o'clock, it was signalled that something had gone wrong with a goods train, and that the road was blocked up: and we had to sit in the dark for two hours and more ! However, this was better than being smashed. Everything, otherwise, has gone very well.

You provided for me so admirably and so judiciously, that I had two sumptuous meals: a partridge breakfast, and a chicken and tongue dinner: and plenty of good wine ! I did not slumber on the road, but had a very good night here, and have got up early, quite refreshed, to send you a telegram, and write a few letters, this particularly, which you will get to-morrow.

There was a great mob at Carlisle who cheered me very much, but I profited by our experience during our Edinbro' visit, and would not get out: so they assembled on the platform round the carriage. It was an ordeal of ten minutes: I bowed to them and went on reading; but was glad when the train moved.

I was greatly distressed at our separation, and when I

woke this morning, did not know where I was.   Nothing but
the gravity of public life sustains me under a great trial,
which no one can understand except those who live on the
terms of entire affection and companionship like ourselves:
and, I believe, they are very few.

Write to me every day, if it is only a line to tell me how
you are; but you, with your lively mind and life, will be able
to tell me a great deal more.   Montagu [Corry] will have discovered by this time the best mode of communication.   The
Queen's messenger goes every day by the same train I did—
10 o'clock Euston.   Adieu, with a thousand embraces, my
dearest, dearest wife.   D.

BALMORAL CASTLE, *Sept.* 19, '68.—Arrived here last night,
½ past nine; the household at dinner.   The Queen sent a
considerate message, that I need not dress, but I thought it
best, as I was tired and dusty, not to appear: particularly as
I found some important letters from Stanley on my table.
They served me a capital little dinner in my room, and I had
a very good night. . . .   I thought it right to appear at
breakfast to-day, as I had not presented myself last night.

Lady Churchill in attendance and Miss Lascelles, and
Lord Bridport, etc., etc.

Bridport told me that I need not wear frock coats, ' which,
as a country gentleman, I know in the country you must
abominate.'

Sept. 20.—I write to you whenever I can snatch an opportunity, and they are so frequent here, but so hurried, that I
hardly know when I wrote to you last, or what I said.   Yesterday, I dined with the Queen, a party of eight.   H.M., the
Prince and Princess Xtian, Princess Louise, the Duke of
Edinburgh, and myself, Lord Bridport and Lady Churchill.

We dined in the Library, a small, square room, with good
books—very cosy; like dining with a bachelor in very good
rooms in the Albany.

Conversation lively, though not memorable.   The Duke of
Edinburgh talked much of foreign fruits, and talked well.

Although my diet has been severe, and I have not tasted
anything but sherry since we parted, I have suffered much
from biliary derangement, which weakens and depresses
me. . . .   Yesterday morning I went out walking with Lord
Bridport, and made a tour of the place: so I quite understand
the situation, and general features: I much admire it.   Mountains not too high: of graceful outline and well wooded, and
sometimes a vast expanse of what they call forest, but which
is, in fact, only wild moor, where the red deer congregate.
The Duke of Edinbro' came from the Prince of Wales' place
with his keepers, and dogs, and guns. . . .   He wears the

tartan and dined in it: and so did Prince Xtian, but it was
for the first time; and the Duke told me he was an hour
getting it on, and only succeeded in getting it all right by the
aid of his wife and his affectionate brother-in-law. . . .

Sept. 21.—The Queen sent for me yesterday afternoon.
Her rooms are upstairs: not on the ground floor. Nothing
can be more exquisite, than the view from her window. An
expanse of green and shaven lawn more extensive than that
from the terrace of Clifden, and singularly striking in a land
of mountains: but H.M. told me, that it was all artificial,
and they had levelled a rugged and undulating soil. In short,
our garden at Hughenden on a great scale: except this was a
broad, green glade, the flower garden being at the other side
of the Castle. I dined with the household, and, between
ourselves, was struck, as I have been before, by the contrast
between the Queen's somewhat simple, but sufficient, dinner,
and the banquet of our humbler friends.

Sept. 22.—The weather here, instead of being cold as they
predicted, has been wet and warm: and my room every day
too hot; so I have written always with a fire, and the window
open. It is now, under these circumstances, 63: but my fire
nearly out.

Yesterday, after a hard morning's work—for the messenger
goes at 12 o'clock, and I rise exactly at seven; so I get four
hours' work—Lord Bridport drove me to see some famous
falls—of Garrawalt: and though the day was misty and the
mountains veiled, the cataract was heightened by the rain.
I never in my life saw anything more magnificent: much
grander falls often, as in Switzerland, but none with such
lovely accessories; such banks of birchen woods, and boulders
of colossal granite.

I dined with the Queen again yesterday. . . .

Sept. 23.—Yesterday we went one of those expeditions you
read of in the Queen's book. Two carriages posting and
changing horses. We went to the Castle of Braemar, where,
every year, the contiguous clans assemble, and have Highland
games. The castle was most picturesque, and is complete
and inhabited, and in old days must have been formidable,
as it commands all the passes of the valleys. I was very
glad that there were no games. The drive to it sublime, or
rather nobly beautiful. Then we went on to the Linn of
Dee—a fall of the Dee River; and on the bank we lunched.
One might take many hints for country luncheons from this
day, for our friends have great experience in these matters:
and nothing could be more compact and complete than the
whole arrangements. The party was very merry: all the
courtiers had a holiday. Lady Churchill said that, when she

asked the Queen, through the Princess Louise, whether she
was wanted this morning, the Queen replied 'No: all the
ladies are to go, to make it amusing to Mr. Disraeli.'

Returning we went to Mar Lodge, and took tea with Lady
Fife.   There we found Sylvia Doyle, looking more absurd
than any human being I can well remember.   The highlanders
call her 'The colored Lady.'   Her cheeks were like a
clown's in a pantomime, and she had a pile of golden hair
as high as some of the neighbouring hills.   However, she
smiled and cracked her jokes as usual, and gave me, as usual,
a long list of all the places she was going to.

Lord Bridport gave me the enclosed photographs for you.
I saw the Queen on my return home—on business.   We left
Balmoral at ½ past 12 and got home by 7: a very fine day:
no clouds on the mountains and the outlines all precise:
while we lunched, sunshine; and not a drop of rain the whole
day.

Sept. 24.—The Queen gives her Minister plenty to do: but
I will write every day, however briefly. . . .

Sept. 25.—Only a line to keep up the chain. . . .

The Queen has got a photographer and insists upon my
being *done*.   This gave me an opportunity to give your collection to Lord Bridport.   I said you had sent them for the
Queen, but I would not give them, etc., etc.: but he did; and
the Queen was delighted . . . 'and said many kind things
about Mrs. Disraeli.'   I shall try to find them out.

Sept. 26.—The bag has brought me no letter from you this
morning, which greatly distresses me: for although all goes on
well here, I am extremely nervous, my health being very
unsatisfactory. . . .   I have never tasted one of your dear
peaches, which I much wished to do for your sake, and have
drunk nothing but sherry.   However, the attack never
continues in the day, but then I am in a miserable state in
these morning hours, when I have to do the main work, and
the work is very heavy. . . .

I leave this on Monday, and get to Perth to sleep, and the
next morning to Knowsley, as I must see Lord Derby.   On
Thursday, I propose to be at Grosvenor Gate, after an absence of a fortnight ! . . .

This morning, the Queen has sent me two volumes of views
of Balmoral: a box full of family photographs, a very fine
whole-length portrait of the Prince, and 'a Scotch shawl for
Mrs. Disraeli, which H.M. hopes you will find warm in the
cold weather.'   To-day, I am resolved to keep in my room.

Adieu, my dearest love; though greatly suffering, I am
sustained by the speedy prospect of our being again together,
and talking over a 1,000 things.

Sept. 27.—The Queen sent for me yesterday after she came home from her ride: but said, when I left H.M., ' This is not your audience before leaving.'

Sept. 28.—A very rapid letter before departure. The joy at our soon meeting again is inexpressible.

Princess Christian said yesterday, that they were all very sorry I was going, but she knew who was glad, and that was Mrs. Disraeli. . . .

I had a long audience of the Queen at four o'clock, and shortly afterwards was invited to dine with H. Majesty again.

Disraeli's visit to Balmoral coincided with a great pressure of public work, and he realised the serious inconvenience caused to public interests by a ten days' sojourn of the Prime Minister in the remote Highlands. ' Carrying on the Government of a country six hundred miles from the metropolis doubles the labour,' he wrote to Bishop Wilberforce. He only repeated the experiment once, in 1874; for the rest of his second Administration he prevailed on Her Majesty to excuse him from taking his turn of Ministerial attendance at Balmoral.

CHAPTER II.

DEFEAT AND RESIGNATION.

1868.

The fate of the Irish Church and of the Conservative Ministry and party would be decided by the result of the General Election in November. To one competent observer it appeared a fairly matched fight. Clarendon wrote in June: 'Confidence in Gladstone seems on the increase thro'out the country, though it remains feeble and stationary in the H. of C. On the other hand a demoralised nation admires the audacity, the tricks, and the success of the Jew.' Disraeli realised the powerful effect that organisation might produce; and with his well-known disregard of money was ready to take a liberal lead in supplying the necessary funds. ' What we want,' he wrote to Stanley, ' is to raise one hundred thousand, which, it is believed, will secure the result. It can be done if the Cabinet sets a good example.'

To Lord Beauchamp.

10, DOWNING ST., *June 22,* '68.—The impending General Election is the most important since 1832, and will, probably, decide the political situation for a long period. The party that is best organised will be successful. No seat, where there is a fair prospect, should be unchallenged. To effect this, and to operate on a class of seats hitherto unassailed, it is necessary that a fund, to aid the legitimate expenses of candidates, should be raised, and that upon a scale not inferior to the range which democratic associations have, on more than one occasion, realised, in order to advance their views.

As it is natural that the success of such an effort must depend upon the example set by Her Majesty's Government, I have induced my colleagues in the Cabinet to subscribe a minimum sum of ten thousand pounds, tho', if they follow my example, it will reach a greater amount.

May I hope that you will support me in this enterprise ? Some more formal application may, possibly, be made to you; but, to so intimate a friend, I prefer to appeal myself.

One thing was clear to Disraeli, namely, that, in determining the result of the General Election, the Church of England, if united and resolved, must play a considerable, perhaps a preponderant, part. To secure her active support for a cause, in which, to his mind, her own ultimate fate was involved, he bent his energies; and it was with that temporal end largely in view that he distributed the ecclesiastical patronage of the Crown, which happened to be of a peculiarly momentous character in his nine months' premiership. Five sees had to be filled in that short period, including those of Canterbury and London; three or four deaneries, including that of St. Paul's; besides canonries, a divinity professorship, and important parochial cures. Both Low Churchmen and High Churchmen were restive. The former marked with alarm the rapid advance of Tractarianism and the resulting Ritualism, and many of them were disposed to quit for Dissent a Church which seemed to them to be heading straight for Rome; the latter were inclined to regard themselves as the only true inheritors of the Anglican tradition, to resent the want of recognition under which their leaders suffered, and to magnify the episcopal character of the Church at the expense of its national aspect. To Disraeli, who never forgot the popular outburst at the time of the Papal aggression, the political danger, at least, appeared to be greatest from the Low Church side; and, though he desired to make a fair distribution among all loyal schools, it was to placate the Evangelicals that he mainly set himself.

In this whole question of Church patronage he laboured

under two serious disadvantages: personal ignorance of
the leading clergy, and a multiplicity of divergent counsellors, eager to enlighten that ignorance.   Keenly interested as he was in the ultimate issues of religion, and
considerable as had been his study of the historical claims
and present needs of the Church of England, Disraeli had
never moved in ecclesiastical or even academical circles,
and knew only such clergy as he met in society; moreover,
though he regularly attended his parish church, he did
not go about to hear preachers of renown.   In Dean
Stanley's *Life*[1] there is a story of the Dean's meeting
Beaconsfield in the street, on the last Sunday in 1876, and
taking him to hear for the first time F. W. Farrar, whom
he had just made a Canon, preach in Westminster Abbey.
To Gladstone it would have been an ordinary experience;
to Beaconsfield it was a ' Haroun-al-Raschid expedition '
to be piloted into the north transept of the Abbey to
hear a popular preacher.   The Dean and the Premier
listened, unnoticed, for a few minutes, and then came
out.   ' I would not have missed the sight for anything,'
said Beaconsfield; ' the darkness, the lights, the marvellous windows, the vast crowd, the courtesy, the respect,
the devotion—and fifty years ago there would not have
been fifty persons there.'   It was the comment of an
artist and not of an informed churchgoer.   ' Send me
down to-morrow the clergy list.   I don't know the names
and descriptions of the persons I am recommending for
deaneries and mitres,' Disraeli wrote to Corry in August,
1868, from Hughenden; and again from Balmoral in
September, ' Ecclesiastical affairs rage here.   Send me
Crockford's directory; I must be armed.'   ' He showed
an ignorance about all Church matters, men, opinions, that
was astonishing,' said Wellesley, Dean of Windsor, in
November.   One leading Churchman Disraeli did know
well, his own Bishop, Samuel Wilberforce.   But much as
he admired his gifts both of oratory and of organisation,
he did not trust one who had been for years hand in

[1] Vol. II., p. 447.

glove with Gladstone; and he was convinced that the
great mass of his countrymen distrusted him still more.

The Bishop was one of those who were eager to direct
the disposal of the Crown patronage.   He and Hardy and
Beauchamp[1] plied Disraeli with recommendations on the
High Church side; while Cairns, on the Low Church side,
aspired to play the same part in Disraeli's ecclesiastical
appointments as Shaftesbury had in Palmerston's.
Derby's advice also was sought and given on every
important occasion.   Last, but by no means least, the
Queen had strong views of her own, founded partly on the
Broad Church traditions of the Prince Consort, but
largely on personal experience of distinguished divines.
Her Majesty, moreover, had naturally no political bias,
such as, consciously or unconsciously, swayed Disraeli
himself and most of his other counsellors; but was guided
solely by the good of the Church, as she saw it.

Disraeli's first important appointment was to the
Bishopric of Hereford.   There he disregarded both
his Low Church and his High Church advisers, and
nominated a hard-working parish clergyman of moderate
opinions, Atlay, the Vicar of Leeds.   This was in
May. It was in August that he made his great bid
for Protestant support by appointing to the Deanery of
Ripon Canon McNeile of Liverpool; 'a regular Lord
Lyndhurst in the Church,' as an Evangelical correspondent
wrote, who would make ' the Protestant party fight like
dragons for the Government.'   Cairns was naturally
' satisfied that nothing more politic could occur at the
present time.'   It would stop the feeling that was abroad
that the Bishop of Oxford was interfering and influencing
Church patronage—a feeling which was due, no doubt,
to the appointment of Wilberforce's chaplain, Woodford,
to succeed Atlay at Leeds. Derby was startled;

[1] Beauchamp had endeavoured to influence ecclesiastical appointments
while Derby was Prime Minister.   Disraeli wrote to him on Nov. 24, 1866:
' I will do my utmost, and immediately, to forward your wishes; but,
entre nous, I don't think my interference, in matters of that kind, is much
affected: at least, I fancy so.   I asked for a deanery the other day, for
Mansel, but he is not a Dean.'

McNeile's nomination seemed to him 'rather a hazardous bid for the extreme Low Church.' Disraeli did not disguise from his leading colleague his electioneering aim.

To Lord Stanley.

HUGHENDEN, *Aug.* 16, 1868.—. . . No human being can give anything like a precise estimate of the elections until the Registration is over. All that is certain at present is, that we have our men better planted than our opponents; more numerous candidates, and stronger ones. The enemy also have no electioneering fund. It is a fact that both the Duke of Devon[shir]e and D. of Bedford refused to subscribe. We, on the contrary, have a fund, tho' not $\frac{1}{2}$ large enough: but sufficient to stimulate and secure contests, where there is a good chance, and which, otherwise, would not have been engaged in.

What we want at this moment is a strong Protestant appointment in the Church. I have been expecting a Bishop to die every day, but there is hardly a 'good Protestant' strong enough to make a Bishop. I thought, however, of recommending Dean Goode, an Evangelical, but really an ecclesiastical scholar, and equal in Patristic lore to any Puseyite father.

Strange to say, instead of being made a Bishop, he has suddenly died: and I have recommended the Queen to make McNeile of Liverpool, Dean of Ripon, which is a Protestant diocese. I believe the effect of this will be very advantageous to us. . . .

Aug. 21.—. . . Things are rapidly maturing here: the country, I am convinced, is, almost to a man, against the High Ch. party. It is not the townspeople merely, but the farmers universally, the greater portion of the gentry, all the professional classes: nay ! I don't know who is for them, except some University dons, some youthful priests and some women; a great many, perhaps, of the latter. But *they* have not votes yet.

It's still a quarter of a year to the dissolution, and that's a long time for this rapid age: but I have little doubt it will end in a great Protestant struggle. The feeling in England is getting higher and higher every day: but it is Protestant, not Church, feeling at present. The problem to solve is, how this Protestant feeling should be enlisted on the side of existing institutions. I think it can be done: but it will require the greatest adroitness and courage.

Not a Cath. will be with us: not even Gerard. They can't. . . .

The Queen, like Derby, was startled at the nomination of McNeile, and only consented with reluctance. But Disraeli was so satisfied with what he had done that he was anxious, when the Bishopric of Peterborough presently fell vacant, to proceed with another strongly Evangelical appointment. Here he met with decided resistance from the Queen, to whom he explained at length his view of the ecclesiastical and political situation.

To Queen Victoria.

[*End of Aug.*, 1868].— . . . The appointment of the new Dean of Ripon has quite realised Mr. Disraeli's expectations: it has done great good, has rallied the Protestant party and has been received by the other sections with no disfavor or cavil.

Since Mr. Disraeli wrote last a long impending vacancy on the Episcopal Bench has occurred. There is no necessity to precipitate the appointment and the final decision can await your Majesty's return. Perhaps Mr. Disraeli may be permitted to wait on your Majesty at Windsor on your Majesty's return, before he attends your Majesty in Scotland, to which he looks forward with much interest.

On the nomination to the See of Peterboro' in the present temper of the country much depends. The new prelate should be one of unquestionably Protestant principles, but must combine with them learning, personal piety, administrative ability, and what is not much heeded by the world but which is vital to the Church, a general pastoral experience.

Mr. Disraeli after the most careful enquiries and the most anxious thought is strongly inclined to recommend to your Majesty Canon Champneys of St. Paul's and Vicar of Pancras. . . .

Affairs at this moment ripen so rapidly in England, that he must lay before your Majesty the result of his reflexions on a mass of data, that for amount and authenticity was probably never before possessed by a Minister. He receives every day regular reports and casual communications from every part of the United Kingdom. . . .

There is no sort of doubt that the great feature of national opinion at this moment is an utter repudiation by all classes of the High Church party. It is not only general: it is universal.

If the Irish Church fall it will be owing entirely to the High Church party—and the prejudice which they have raised against ecclesiastical establishment.

Mr. Disraeli speaks entirely without prejudice. The bias of his mind from education, being brought up in a fear of fanaticism, is certainly towards the High Church, but he has no sort of doubt as to the justness of his present conclusions and it is his highest duty to tell your Majesty this.

Nevertheless the Church as an institution is so rooted, and the doctrine of the royal supremacy so wonderfully popular, that if the feeling of the country be guided with wisdom Mr. Disraeli believes that the result of the impending struggle may be very advantageous and even triumphant to the existing constitution of the country. . . .

From Queen Victoria.

LUCERNE, *Sept.* 7, 1868.—The Queen thanks Mr. Disraeli for his two letters. She is glad that Mr. Disraeli has not pressed for an answer relative to the new Bishop, as the appointments are of such importance, not only for the present but for the future good of the Church in general, that it will *not* do merely to encourage the ultra-Evangelical party, than wh. there is none more narrow-minded, and thereby destructive to the well-being and permanence of the Church of England. Dr. McNeile's appointment was *not* liked by *moderate* men, but still, this having been done, it is not necessary or advisable to make more of a similar nature, and the Queen, with the greatest wish to support the Government and the Protestant feeling in the country, feels bound to ask for moderate, sensible, clever men, neither Evangelical or Ritualistic in their views, to be appointed to the high offices in the Church.

The Church of England has suffered from its great exclusiveness and narrow-mindedness, and, in these days of danger to her, *all* the liberal-minded men should be rallied round her and pressed into her service to support her and not to make her more and more a mere Party Church, which will alienate all the others from her. This is the more important as we are threatened with the loss of several more Bishops and of one most eminent man—the Dean of St. Paul's. . . .[1]

To Queen Victoria.

[*Sept.*, 1868].—. . . If, when the verdict is given, the Church of England is associated in the minds of the people with the extreme High Church school, the country will deal to that Church a serious, if not a deadly, blow.

Your Majesty justly observes that the appointment of Dr. McNeile did not satisfy moderate men. With becoming

[1] Milman, the ecclesiastical historian.

humility Mr. Disraeli would venture to observe it was not intended to do so.   But it satisfied some millions of your Majesty's subjects and acted as a safety valve to such an extent, that while, before that appointment, an extreme pressure on your Majesty's advisers existed to appoint to the vacant see some professor of very decided opinions, from the moment of the preferment of Dr. McNeile that pressure was greatly mitigated, and almost ceased.

With humility Mr. Disraeli would presume to observe, that he knows not, in his long political experience, any happier instance of seizing the *à propos*.

The country was on the eve of a series of public meetings on the Church, held by Churchmen, to protest against the imputed designs of the Crown and the Crown's Ministers in favour of Ritualism and Rationalism, when this preferment was decided on.   Twenty preferments of clergymen of the same type as McNeile but not of his strong individuality would not have produced the effect.

And what did he receive ?   A mock deanery which your Majesty could not have offered to some of the great scholars who sigh for such, etc.

The appointment of Dr. McNeile already allows your Majesty greater latitude in the selection of a Bishop.

Again, if a wise selection be made in this instance of Peterboro' your Majesty will find still more freedom in the impending vacancies which your Majesty is obliged to contemplate but which it is trusted may be at least postponed.

Your Majesty very properly wishes to appoint to the Bench 'moderate, sensible, and clever men' neither Ritualist nor Evangelical.   But Mr. Disraeli humbly asks, Where are they to be found ?   The time is not come, at least certainly not the hour, when Deans of St. Paul and Westminster, and men of that class of refined thought, however gifted, can be submitted to your Majesty's consideration.   It is not ripe for that; tho' with prudence it may be sooner than some suspect. The consequences of such a step at this particular moment would be disastrous.   And, as for men, qualified as your Majesty wishes, without the pale of that school, why your Majesty has already been obliged to go to New Zealand for a Prelate,[1] and even Dr. Atlay, whom Mr. Disraeli recommended to your Majesty as almost *ultimus Romanorum*, is denounced, tho' erroneously, as a creature of the Bishop of Oxford, a prelate, who, tho' Mr. Disraeli's diocesan, he is bound to see is absolutely in this country more odious than Laud.

As a matter of civil prudence, he would presume to say wisdom, Mr. Disraeli is of opinion, that the wisest course at

[1] Selwyn.

this conjuncture is to seek among the Evangelical school some man of learning, piety, administrative capacity, and of views, tho' inevitably decided, temperate and conciliatory in their application. He thinks that, with the more ardent satisfied by the tardy recognition of McNeile and the calmer portion, now alarmed and irritated, encouraged and soothed and solaced by such an appointment as that which he indicates, we might get over the General Election without any violent ebullition: and even if another vacancy were to occur in the interval, a man more conformable with your Majesty's views might be advanced, if Your Majesty could fix upon one.

The names which Mr. Disraeli, after the most anxious and painful investigation, places before your Majesty's consideration, are both of, as he believes, admirable men: and who by their standing, compass of mind, and tact in their intercourse with their fellow-clergy, are qualified for the office of a Bishop.

They are Canon Champneys of St. Paul's and Vicar of Pancras, Archdeacon Hone of Worcester.[1]

Doubtless neither of these appointments would please the sacerdotal school nor even satisfy the philosophic: that is not to be expected: but they would be received with respect alike by Ritualist or Rationalist; and with confidence and joy by the great body of your Majesty's subjects.

From Queen Victoria.

BALMORAL, *Sept.* 18, 1868.—Tho' the Queen will have an opportunity of seeing and conversing with Mr. Disraeli on this important and difficult subject, viz. the Church appointments, she thinks it as well to put down in writing the result of much reflection on her part.

First of all—it is to be remembered that any ultra-Protestant appointment, or at least any extreme Evangelical one, will only alienate the other party and not please the really moderate men—while it is bringing into the Church those who by their natural illiberality will render the Church itself more and more unpopular. . . .

The deanery of St. Paul's, which the Queen fears will soon be vacant, she thinks ought certainly to be given for eminence only—either as a *preacher or a writer*—irrespective of party, and she trusts that, should we lose the valuable, distinguished and excellent present Dean of St. Paul's, Mr. Disraeli will concur in this. Another very clever man, and the finest preacher the Queen has ever heard out of Scotland, and whom she would much wish to see promoted—is the Dean of Cork (Dr. Magee).

[1] 1805–1881: Rector of Halesowen, and Archdeacon of Worcester: a respected but hardly outstanding Evangelical.

To Lord Derby.

Private. PERTH, *Sept.* 18, '68.—. . . I wish I could consult you about the Bishop, but it would require a volume instead of a letter.   These questions, within the last few months, have become so critical and complicated.   They were always difficult enough.   I have begun to write to you several times on this subject, but have given it up in despair from the utter inability of conveying to you my view of the circumstances in a letter.

I think the deanery of Ripon has been a *coup*.   I was really surrounded by hungry lions and bulls of Bashan till that took place, but, since, there has been a lull, and an easier feeling in all quarters—strange to say—among all parties. Probably they were all astounded.

Oh ! for an hour of confidential talk in St. James' Square ! There are priests now, and men of abilities, who are as perverse as Laud, and some as wild as Hugh Peters ! . . . I am, as I always am, to you, most faithful, D.

The High Church party were deeply affronted by McNeile's appointment.   Even so moderate and representative a Churchman as Hook, Dean of Chichester, came out against the Conservative cause.   Disraeli complained to the Bishop of Oxford that ' in the great struggle in which I am embarked, it is a matter of great mortification to me that I am daily crossed, and generally opposed, by the High Church party.'   The Bishop replied on September 11: ' The vast body of sound Churchmen are entirely with you on the great question of the day. But I should not tell you all that I believe to be the truth if I did not add that there is at this moment a jealous and alarmed watchfulness of your administration of Church patronage.   Those who through the long period of Palmerston's Administration held their fidelity in an ostracised position are in danger of being alienated.' The Bishop assisted Disraeli by explaining to Hook that McNeile's appointment only meant that no allowed party in the Church would be excluded from promotion; but he repeatedly urged Disraeli to placate what he called ' the strong middle party of orthodox English Churchmen,' who alone could give him the support he wanted. Disraeli rejoined emphatically from Balmoral on September 28:

> There can be no doubt that every wise man on our side should attract the Protestant feeling, as much as practicable, to the Church of England. It has been diverted from the Church of England in Scotland. There the Protestant feeling is absolutely enlisted against us. If we let it escape from us in England, all is over. It appears to me that, if we act in the spirit of the Dean of Chichester, we may all live to see the great Church of England subside into an Episcopalian sect. I will struggle against this with my utmost energy.[1]

Disraeli, apparently, knew little or nothing of Magee, the great orator of the Irish Church, till his name was suggested by the Queen. But soon recommendations came from many quarters in his favour; and before the end of the month he attracted widespread attention as the preacher of a famous sermon of appeal from the Irish Church to her English sister, on the text: ' They beckoned unto their partners, which were in the other ship, that they should come and help them.' [2]

To Montagu Corry.

BALMORAL, *Sept.* 21, '68.—. . . The Queen, I found, very desirous to make Magee (Dean of Cork) the Bishop. I waived all this by saying he must be an Oxford man, and she suggested the Dean might be one: but I had no book to refer to, and I am not sure whether Crockford, shortsighted Crockford, biographises the Irish clergy. Generally speaking, I also discouraged the idea: but to my intense surprise I received yesterday a letter from John Manners, the highest Churchman in the Cabinet, proposing Magee himself for my consideration, as an appointment which would satisfy all parties. We should then, he said, by this, and the instance of Selwyn, prove our recognition of the *unity* of the Church: colonial and Irish, etc.

One objection to Magee is, that his appointment would give us nothing, and that is a great objection.

[1] *Life of Bishop Wilberforce*, Vol. III., pp. 266, 267.
[2] St. Luke v. 7.

The Queen prevailed, and Magee was appointed Bishop,[1] Champneys being preferred to the Deanery of Lichfield. For the Deanery of St. Paul's, Disraeli had a very suitable man of his own, Mansel, the distinguished Oxford metaphysician, who had been associated with him on the *Press*, and who shared and powerfully expressed the scepticism which Disraeli entertained of the value of the conclusions of German professors and theologians. The author of *Phrontisterion* was a congenial spirit with the orator of the Sheldonian theatre.

The appointments of Magee and Mansel gave very general satisfaction, approval being expressed by Derby, Hardy, and even Wilberforce. The latter's favourite candidate, Leighton, the Warden of All Souls, though disappointed of a Bishopric, was made a Canon of Westminster; and the High Churchmen were further placated by the appointment of the energetic Gregory to a Canonry at St. Paul's, and of the scholarly Bright to Mansel's chair at Oxford—the latter appointment pressed by Beauchamp, who warned Disraeli that the High Church party other than ' the old port-winers ' were holding aloof from the political contest. But a much more difficult and delicate selection was now laid upon Disraeli. In the end of October the Archbishop of Canterbury, Dr. Longley, died.

To Lord Derby.

Secret. 10, DOWNING STREET, *Nov.* 2, 1868.—Returning from Balmoral, I was disappointed in the opportunity of consulting you on two important matters: the Church appointments then pending, and my address, of which I would have brought you the draft. However, I got through those difficulties, and pretty well.

Now comes a greater one: the Archbishop.

[1] Magee, at the time Dean of Cork, had written to the Prime Minister, ' asking him, when filling up the deanery of St. Paul's, to give him one of the appointments that might be vacant in so doing.' Magee's biographer notes the touch of humour in Disraeli's reply, ' beginning with a refusal of the Dean's modest request on the first page, and then making the offer of the bishopric when he turned over the leaf.' MacDonnell's *Magee*, Vol. I., p. 197.

My Church policy was this: to induce, if possible, the two great and legitimate parties to cease their internecine strife, and to combine against the common enemies: Rits and Rats. This could only be done by a fair division of the patronage, and though at first beset by great difficulties, arising from party jealousy and suspicion, I think I have now succeeded in getting them well to work together. . . .

As I did not want a very High Churchman, or an Evangelist, for Archbishop, the materials from which I could select were very few. I was disposed in favour of the Bishop of Gloucester,[1] whom I don't personally know, but was pleased by his general career since your accession to office, and also by a correspondence which he held, subsequently, with me, arising out of the Ritual Commission. It seemed to me very desirable that the new Primate should not be mixed up with all the recent controversies, and clerical fracas, which have damaged all concerned in them. I sent my proposal, with well digested reasons: the boxes crossed, and one came to me saying that there could be no doubt what was to be done, as there was *only one* man fit for the position: the Bishop of London.[2] Then came another box, mine having been received, still more decided, if that could be. Now I think the Bishop of London an appointment which will please neither of the great parties—and only a few clerical freethinkers, who think, and perhaps justly, he may be their tool, and some Romanisers—for he supports sisterhoods as strongly as Oxford or Sarum.[3] I wrote in reply, acknowledging the two letters, and saying merely they should have my most serious attention, and I have been employed all this morning in drawing up a statement touching the whole case, which will be received, by the person to whom it is addressed, on her arrival on Thursday. That will be followed, probably, by an audience on Saturday, and before that time I should be deeply obliged if you would give me, through the ever faithful secretary,[4] some hints, and your general impressions. . . .

From Lord Derby.

Confidential. KNOWSLEY, *Nov.* 3, 1868.—. . . I am afraid that I can do but little towards relieving you from the difficulty in which you are now placed. . . . I agree in your general principle of dealing, in respect to patronage, with the rival parties in the Church; and you have been fortunate in having at your disposal a succession of appointments which has enabled you to distribute your favours with some appearance of impartiality. But the appropriation of the highest

[1] Ellicott.   [2] Tait.   [3] W. K. Hamilton.   [4] Lady Derby.

prize of all can hardly be hoped to give general satisfaction, and you must be satisfied if it does not produce general discontent. Your range of choice is limited, and your materials by no means first-rate. I cannot agree with H.M. that the Bishop of London would be either a popular or a judicious selection. I am perhaps prejudiced against the man, but I must confess that I have no confidence in his judgment. If you should be finally driven to promote him, which I hope will not be the case, the Bishop of Oxford, though ineligible for the Primacy, would make a very good and useful Bishop of London.

With the Bishop of Gloucester, whom you name, my acquaintance is only slight. He is undoubtedly a learned man, and I believe a sound Churchman, rather inclining to the High School. But I should doubt his having much strength of character, and he has a foolish voice and manner which make him appear weaker than I believe he really is. He is said, and I believe with reason, to be entirely under the influence of the Bishop of Oxford. Of the other Bishops, has the name ever occurred to you of my Bishop of Rochester, Claughton? If his opinions are not too High Church, he has many qualifications for the office—and I think that you might do worse. Harold Browne, the Bishop of Ely, is a man of very high reputation—but I do not know him personally, even by sight . . .

To Lord Derby.

Secret. 10, DOWNING STREET, *Nov.* 12, 1868.—Harold Browne is offered as a compromise. But what do I gain by Harold Browne? While H.M. will only be annoyed. I could win, if I had a man. I don't know personally the Bishop of Gloucester—and you can't fight for a person you don't know. I proposed him as one appointed by Palmerston, and yet not an Evangelical, and certainly, from his correspondence, not a follower of the Bishop of Oxford. The Bishop of Oxford is quite out of the running, so great is the distrust of him by the country. That is the great fact, that has come out of the canvass of England. I thought, last night, of taking the Bishop of London, and countervailing his neological tendencies, which I think form the great objection to him, and, of course, his great recommendation in the eyes of H.M., by raising Jackson[1] to London. He is orthodox and Protestant. . . .

Tait was a Liberal and a Broad Churchman, unacceptable to Disraeli on the score both of politics and of

---

[1] Bishop of Lincoln.

theology. Accordingly Disraeli fought with passion
against his appointment, coming out of the royal closet, it
was noticed, in great excitement, and telling Malmesbury
' Don't bring any more bothers before me; I have enough
already to drive a man mad.' But, having no really
satisfactory candidate of his own, he had to give way in
the end; and the Church thereby gained a statesman on
the throne of Canterbury, but one whose want of sympathy
with the Oxford school impaired his usefulness in the
troubled times which followed. Tait, in his diary, de-
cribed with a dry humour his interview with the Prime
Minister after the nomination.

He harangued me on the state of the Church; spoke of
rationalists, explained that those now so called did not follow
Paulus. He spoke at large of his desire to rally a Church
party, which, omitting the extremes of rationalism and
ritualism, should unite all other sections of the Church;
alluded to his Church appointments as aiming at this—
Champneys, Merivale,[1] Wordsworth, Gregory, Leighton,
myself, Jackson. He promised to support a Church Discipline Bill, but deprecated its being brought in by Lord
Shaftesbury. Remarked that, whether in office or out, he
had a large Church party. . . . I stated my views shortly,
and w: separated.[2]

For the see of London Dean Wellesley told Wilberforce that Disraeli proposed Christopher Wordsworth,
the nephew of the poet, the learned Canon of Westminster. ' The Queen objected strongly; no experience;
passing over Bishops, etc.; then she suggested Jackson,
and two others, not you, because of Disraeli's expressed
hostility; and Disraeli chose Jackson.' Though Jackson
made a good Bishop of London, Disraeli had better have
taken Derby's advice and proposed Wilberforce, whom
the Queen would have accepted. Wilberforce's energy
and organising power, his knowledge of the world and
of society, his high reputation and influence in the
Church, would have made him almost an ideal Bishop for

---

[1] The historian, appointed Dean of Ely.
[2] Tait's *Life*, Vol. I., p. 536.

London. Manners, writing to Disraeli two years later
about the lament in the General Preface to the novels
that no Churchman equal to the occasion had arisen
from the Oxford movement, says: ' I doubt whether a
Churchman was not produced by the Oxford movement—sufficiently a statesman, with all his faults,
to have helped you greatly; and I have never understood why, when, for reasons I can appreciate, you
sent Tait to Lambeth, you did not transfer Wilberforce to London.' The reason was that, as appears
in letter after letter, Disraeli was told, from the most
divergent quarters, that public opinion throughout the
country would resent the appointment, and visit its
displeasure at the polls on the Government responsible
for it. It must be borne in mind that, though the world
knows now how carefully and loyally the Bishop kept the
via media of Anglicanism, he was still in 1868 outside his
diocese widely suspected of Romeward tendencies, which
had operated with fatal effect in his own family. Since
he became Bishop all three of his brothers, and two
brothers-in-law, of whom Manning was one, had joined
the Roman Church; and in this very year the example
was followed by his daughter and her husband. Disraeli
can hardly be blamed for not facing the threatened storm;
but, had he shown his wonted courage here, he would
not have lost a useful ally or alienated a powerful party.

For the appointment of Wordsworth to the Bishopric
of Lincoln, of Bright to a professorship, and of Leighton
and Gregory to canonries, did not console the High
Church party for the slight to their principal champion;
and Wilberforce himself could not hide the bitterness of his
disappointment. He wrote in his diary, ' I am trying to
discipline myself, but feeling the affront,' and to a friend,
' In myself I really thank God; it very little disturbs me.
I in my reason apprehend that by the common rule in such
matters I had no right to be so treated; but I am really
thankful in feeling so cool about it.' He had resented
Gladstone's new policy and had been working cordially

with Disraeli to save the Irish Church. But now he resumed his former intimate association with Gladstone, who became Prime Minister next month; and he was unsparing in condemnation of his rival. He immediately began to contrast the two men greatly to Disraeli's disadvantage, ' Gladstone as ever: great, earnest, and honest; as unlike the tricky Disraeli as possible '; and to smooth the way for Gladstone's Irish policy, by writing to Archbishop Trench, of Dublin, urging him to arrange a compromise. Trench had suggested delay, till Gladstone had realised the difficulties before him. The Bishop replied that this would be a wise course if they were dealing with ' a master of selfish cunning and unprincipled trickery,' ' a mere mystery-man like Disraeli,' whose whole idea was ' to use the Church to keep himself in office '; but happily in Gladstone they had ' a man of the highest and noblest principle.'[1] And when *Lothair* was published, in which he himself was portrayed, the Bishop wrote: ' My wrath against D. has burnt before this so fiercely that it seems to have burnt up all the materials for burning and to be like an exhausted prairie-fire—full of black stumps, burnt grass, and all abominations.' Fortunately the Bishop was translated in 1869, on Gladstone's motion, from Oxford to Winchester, so that he no longer had among his flock the statesman with whom he had for a time so zealously co-operated, but of whom, since his disregard of his diocesan's claims to promotion, he had come to think so meanly.

In the general result, with the conspicuous exception of the neglect of Wilberforce, the appointments for which Disraeli was responsible were not unsatisfactory; and his policy of fair division and of a clear insistence on the national character of the Church was a right policy. But it cannot be denied that in its application he pursued a seesaw and zigzag course, and laid himself open to Dean Wellesley's criticism that ' he rode the Protestant horse

---

[1] *Wilberforce*, Vol. III., pp. 277-279.

one day; then got frightened it had gone too far and was injuring the county elections, so he went right round.' The result was that, so far as his object was a political one, he did not succeed in it; there was no such union at the General Election, as he hoped for, of all parties in the Church to resist Gladstone's Irish policy. ' Bishoprics, once so much prized, are really graceless patronage now,' he wrote ruefully during the year to Derby; ' they bring no power.' The Crown had intervened in Church patronage in a decisive way, largely owing to the Minister's ignorance; had carried the Archbishop of its choice directly in his teeth, and had proved the determining factor in other appointments, including the striking nomination of Magee. Both in the principles which Her Majesty laid down, and in the divines whom she recommended, the Queen's intervention must command respect, and it attained, as well as deserved, success.

Disraeli maintained intimate and confidential relations with his predecessor Derby throughout this Government, and had constant recourse in all difficulties to his counsel. He even submitted the Queen's Speech to be delivered on the prorogation of Parliament to his revision. Derby made considerable alterations in the form, though not in the substance, of the draft; but only advanced these as suggestions, and hoped Disraeli would not think he had taken too great liberties with his ' skeleton.' Sensible as he was of his obligations to Derby and the house of Stanley, Disraeli sought, as Prime Minister, for opportunities of showing his gratitude and friendship. Early in the spring he paid his old chief the graceful compliment of placing at his disposal the lord-lieutenancy of Middlesex; and at the close of the session he found an official vacancy for Frederick Stanley, Derby's younger son, afterwards War Secretary, Governor-General of Canada, and the sixteenth earl. Derby declined the lord-lieutenancy, as he had no local connection with the county, and no local interest; but he was gratified by the political opening afforded to his son.

To Lord Derby.

Private.   10, DOWNING STREET, *July* 31, 1868.—Parliament
being prorogued, I have had the pleasure of offering the Civil
Lordship of the Admiralty to Frederick, and shall be gratified
if he accept it.   At any rate, it is an introduction to official
life, and his tenure of office may last longer than some imagine.

We work at the elections with ceaseless energy.   I have
got the matter out of the hands of Spofforth, and placed in
those of a limited, but influential, Committee of gentlemen,
and it seems to work very well.

Lord Abercorn is to be an Irish Duke, and Mayo our Indian
Viceroy: so the Irish Government may be satisfied.   What
the Irish title is to be I can't tell you.   The Prince of Wales
wants it to be Ulster, of which he is Earl,[1] but as I would not
countenance this, H.R.H. is to go to the Queen to-morrow
anent.   I should think the regal brow would be clouded,
and that our friend must be content with being Duke of
Abercorn.   He is very happy, and six inches taller.

I had thought of offering the Irish Secretaryship to Elcho,
a friend of Lord Abercorn, but His Excellency seems to think
that the political connection might disturb the fervor of the
friendship.   If so, I think it must be John Manners, who is
sensible, conciliatory, and very painstaking, and certainly
will not 'override' Abercorn, or quarrel with anybody.
Then Elcho might have J.M.'s place.   But would he take it
without the Cabinet ?   And Henry Lennox will resign if he be
not promoted !   Nothing seems to satisfy him, and if he had
Henry Corry's place, he would soon want mine.[2]

The Cabinet to-day was very tranquil, a great contrast to
three or four months ago.   Cairns is a great success at the
Council Board.

Short as was Disraeli's term of office, he had not merely
to give an Archbishop to Canterbury, but a Governor-
General both to Canada and to India.   The first of these
two posts was offered in succession to Mayo and to
Manners, but was eventually filled by a seasoned administrator, Sir John Young, afterwards Lord Lisgar, who
had been High Commissioner for the Ionian Islands and
Governor of New South Wales.   Mayo, who had done

[1] Derby pointed out in reply that it was the Duke of Edinburgh, and
not the Prince of Wales, who was Earl of Ulster.
[2] Wilson Patten, created at the close of the Government Lord Winmar-
leigh, was ultimately appointed Irish Secretary.

yeoman service for his country and his party as thrice Chief Secretary for Ireland, was sent to India.

From Lord John Manners.

April 30, '68.—In spite of all your encouraging kindness, for which I shall never cease to be grateful, I have finally decided—mainly on private and family grounds—to decline the great post offered to me last week; and have written to the Duke of Buckingham to that effect.

Though private considerations have determined this decision, I own I derive satisfaction from thinking that it will enable me to remain by your side to the end of the most eventful chapter in our political life.

Let it terminate as it may, it will always be to me a source of unalloyed pleasure to have seen you at the summit of power, and to have had my humbler fortunes linked—unbrokenly—to yours.

To Sir Stafford Northcote.

10, DOWNING STREET, *June* 9, 1868.—I could have wished to have replied to your letter [1] instantly, but every moment, yesterday, was taken up. Although your loss to me would be not easily calculable, I don't think I could allow it to weigh against your personal interests, for which, I trust, I have always shown a due regard. But the Indian V. Royalty has always been destined for Lord Mayo, who did not wish to return to Ireland, and I spoke to Lord Derby, with that view, when his Government was formed, and when you did not occupy that great office of State, [2] which you have since administered with so much satisfaction to the country, and with so much credit to yourself. Certainly, Lord Mayo's administration of Ireland affords no reason for disturbing the prospect in which, for a considerable time, he has been permitted to indulge, and, being myself now at the head of affairs, it would hardly become me to shrink from the fulfilment of expectations, which I sanctioned and supported as a subordinate member of the Ministry.

I could not speak to you on this matter before, because, when the prospects of the Ministry were not as bright as they are at present, Lord Mayo had nearly made up his mind to go to Canada, when the next mail brought the news, that the

---

[1] Northcote's name had been canvassed, among others, as that of a possible Viceroy; and he wrote to say that, while he would very much like to go to India, he did not put himself forward as a candidate, and would most cheerfully accept Disraeli's decision. Only, for family reasons, he should like to know, as soon as might be convenient, what the decision was.

[2] Indian Secretary.

wise Parliament of the Dominion had reduced the salary of
the Governor-General from £10,000 to £6,000 per annum,
thereby depriving themselves of ever having the benefit of
the services of a first-class man.[1]

You did quite right in addressing me directly and frankly,
and I reply to you in the same spirit.   I should be more than
sorry to occasion you disappointment, because I highly esteem
and regard you, and am anxious, so far as it is in my power,
to advance, and secure, your fortunes.

How well Mayo justified Disraeli's choice is recorded in
English and Indian history.   But the Liberals, indignant
at the wealth of patronage that had fallen to a Ministry
which they maintained to have no constitutional claim to
remain in office, raised a loud outcry at the appointment
in their press, and intimated in no uncertain fashion
that, if they got a majority in the election, they would
cancel it.   This was no mere journalistic bravado, as
has sometimes been asserted since.   The correspondence
of the Liberal leaders shows that cancellation was
seriously contemplated.   'If you cancel Mayo's appointment,' Granville wrote to Gladstone on September 28,
'what do you think of Salisbury ?   It would be a teat
taken away from our pigs, but it would weaken the
Opposition.'   'I think the suggestion an excellent one,'
Gladstone replied.[2]   If Mayo was after all left undisturbed, and the Duke of Argyll, Gladstone's Indian
Secretary, was able to assert that no advice to remove
him was given to the Crown or contemplated by the
Gladstone Government, the reason may be found in the
following letters :

From Lord Stanley.

Private.   F.O.,   *Sept.* 17, 1868.—I hear from more than
one quarter, and in a manner that leaves no doubt on my
mind as to the truth of the report, that the Opposition have
decided, in the event of their coming in before the end of the
year, to remove Mayo, even if he should have sailed, from the
Gov.-Gen.ship. . . .

[1] The Queen was advised to withhold her assent to the bill reducing the
salary, which accordingly remains £10,000 per annum.
[2] Fitzmaurice's *Granville,* Vol. I., p. 541.

I think this worth naming, as you may be able to stop it *in limine* by getting the Queen to express her disapproval. The step is an extremely unusual one—the only precedent being the removal of Lord Heytesbury to make way for Lord Auckland, which caused the Afghan War. . . .

To Lord Stanley.

BALMORAL, *Sept.* 21, 1868.— . . .   Your hint about Mayo was *à propos,* for our Mistress herself touched upon the business. She thinks the contemplated recall of her representative will weaken her name and authority in India: as if she were a mere pageant !   This is the Constitutional view, and I confirmed it.   There is a material difference in recalling a Govr.-Genl. of the Company and the Vice-Roy of the Sovereign. Clearly.

H.M. recurs to her hope, that, whatever happens, we shall gain a material accession of strength.   I told her the truth— that all the stories about, respecting the result of the General Election, were alike untrustworthy: that the great body of the new constituency in towns were unpledged: that the new electors in the counties were reported as singularly conservative; and the victory, at the last moment, would be to the party, which was wealthiest, and best organised.

She does not conceal, from me at least, her personal wishes. . . .

Magnanimity to foes and gratitude to friends were among Disraeli's most notable qualities; and in both respects power revealed the man.   In all the early stages of his career he had been held up to ridicule by John Leech in *Punch* with a mercilessness which was far removed from the *bonhomie* with which the artist and the journal treated other public men.   But when his attention was called in 1868 to the fact that Leech's widow, who had been granted a pension by the Liberal Government, was dead, and that his two children were more than ever in want of assistance, he had no hesitation in continuing the pension to the family, remembering only the dead artist's genius and disregarding the persistent animosity of his pencil.   His enduring gratitude to a benefactor was manifested in a still more striking manner.

For many years after the caprice of the Duke of Portland, in calling in the money advanced by the Bentincks for the purchase of Hughenden, had thrown Disraeli back upon the moneylenders,[1] his private affairs were in an unsatisfactory condition and he was greatly hampered by the exorbitant interest on his apparently still accumulating debts.   In the winter of 1862–1863 fortune sent him a much-needed relief.   The Conservative cause in the North had a strong supporter in a Yorkshire squire, Andrew Montagu, of Melton, Yorks, and Papplewick, Notts; son of Fountayne Wilson, who had sat in Parliament for the undivided county of York; and representative, in the female line, of the famous Charles Montagu, Earl of Halifax, the Finance Minister of William III. Andrew Montagu was a bachelor of great wealth and of somewhat eccentric habits.   The story runs that he made inquiries in that winter of the Conservative headquarters as to how best he could use his wealth to promote the success of his party.   Among other suggestions he was told that a rich man could render no more acceptable service to the cause than by buying up the debts of the leader in the Commons, and charging him only a reasonable interest in the place of the exactions under which he was suffering.   He showed himself disposed to entertain the idea, and was put by Rose, through whom the negotiation was carried on, into communication with Disraeli's friend, Baron Lionel de Rothschild, who was himself ready to help Disraeli pecuniarily, but who, as Disraeli wrote, preferred to give, not lend, to his friends. Rothschild and Montagu met, with the result that, in return for a mortgage on Hughenden, accompanied, it may be, by some guarantee or assurance from Rothschild, Montagu assumed the whole responsibility for Disraeli's debts, charging him apparently merely the 3 per cent. which was then the interest on Consols instead of the 10 per cent. or more that he was previously paying.   The immensity of the service thus rendered to Disraeli may be gauged by the fact that he estimated the resulting increase in his annual income, in one letter at £4,200, and in

[1] See Vol. III., p. 152.

another at £5,000. His gross income in 1866 appears to have been nearly £9,000 a year; but by that time he had received £30,000 as Mrs. Brydges Willyams's residuary legatee.[1]

Disraeli was anxious to show his gratitude by recommending his benefactor for a peerage. It was perhaps rather a hazardous step; but Rose, who encouraged his chief, quoted as a precedent in its favour the Carrington peerage, conferred at Pitt's instance on Robert Smith, the banker, to whom the Minister was under great personal and pecuniary obligations. He advised Disraeli to disregard an anonymous letter of warning. He pointed out that this was no case of an obscure man of recently acquired wealth. Montagu's father had formerly refused a peerage, and he himself, though eccentric, was a man of great possessions, good family, and political influence in the county of York. Thus reassured, Disraeli made the offer.

To Andrew Montagu.

BALMORAL CASTLE, *Sept.* 20, 1868.—It is my intention, if agreeable to you, to recommend Her Majesty to confer on you the dignity of the Peerage.

Altho', unlike your father, who was the last representative of the undivided county of York, you have not chosen to avail yourself of a seat in the House of Commons, your vast possessions, noble lineage, and devotion to the Conservative party, fully authorise this act on the part of the Queen, as one in entire conformity with the social custom, and the Constitutional practice, of the Realm.

Montagu declined the honour, mainly on the ground that his usefulness to Disraeli and to the Conservative party in the forthcoming elections would be seriously impaired if he accepted a title. His friends in Yorkshire, where he was a leading worker for the Conservative cause, would think he wanted to save himself from a sinking ship. In other circumstances he might accept a favour from his ' best friend and benefactor,' but not in the autumn of 1868.

[1] See Vol. III., ch. 13.

The election was to be fought upon domestic issues, and it would avail Disraeli little with the new electors that he was able to boast, with good reason, that a great improvement had supervened in our foreign relations by the substitution of Stanley for Russell in the direction of our policy. He dwelt on this improvement on more than one occasion, but especially in a speech at Merchant Taylors' Hall in June.

When we acceded to office the name of England was a name of suspicion and distrust in every Court and Cabinet. There was no possibility of that cordial action with any of the Great Powers which is the only security for peace; and, in consequence of that want of cordiality, wars were frequently occurring. But since we entered upon office, and public affairs were administered by my noble friend [Stanley] . . . I say that all this has changed; that there never existed between England and foreign Powers a feeling of greater cordiality and confidence than now prevails; that while we have shrunk from bustling and arrogant intermeddling, we have never taken refuge in selfish isolation; and the result has been that there never was a Government in this country which has been more frequently appealed to for its friendly offices than the one which now exists.

The Liberals could only reply that a considerable improvement had been effected in Clarendon's few months of office after Palmerston's death, and reproach Disraeli, in Gladstone's words, with his language of 'inflated and exaggerated eulogy.' That Stanley's conduct of foreign affairs was eminently satisfactory was the general opinion of all parties.

It looked at one time as if Disraeli would have the good fortune of settling the acute questions which separated this country from America. His constant yet dignified friendliness to the United States throughout the troubled period of the Civil War merited such a success. The difficulty mainly arose from the negligence, in the observance of neutrality during that period, of the Palmerston Administration, and especially of Russell its Foreign Secretary, who had permitted the *Alabama* to escape from a British port to prey on American com merce. Russell had obstinately maintained the correctness of his action, or rather inaction, and refused to refer the questions at issue to arbitration in any form. Stanley, as Foreign Minister, had adopted a more reasonable course. He was prepared to accept arbitration; but he resisted, with practically universal approval here, an attempt by the American Secretary of State to include in the reference the question of the recognition by this country of the belligerent rights of the Confederate States—a recognition which the Federals had themselves made in proclaiming a blockade. But the speech in which Stanley announced his policy in March, 1868, was so conciliatory as well as firm that public opinion in America was favourably impressed; and, as a result, when a vacancy arose in the summer in the United States Ministry in London, a notable man, Senator Reverdy Johnson, was appointed Minister, with, as Stanley understood, 'very conciliatory instructions.' When Johnson arrived, Stanley was in Switzerland in attendance on the Queen; and so it fell to Disraeli to show the appreciation of the British Government. He immediately asked the newcomer down to Hughenden to meet a distinguished party, including the hero of the hour, Sir Robert Napier, just created Lord Napier of Magdala, and the historian Lord Stanhope.

To Lord Stanley.

HUGHENDEN, *Aug.* 16, 1868.—. . . Reverdy J. has not arrived. I will send a Secy. the moment he does, and ask him down here. The hero of Magdala is coming on the 24th. I should like to kill them with the same stone.

I have given orders for the new Adm[iralt]y Patent to be prepared, as I hear there is no danger, now, of any election being precipitated at Preston, so Fred. will be soon at work : Sir M. Hicks Beach to be U. Secy. Home, and Jem Lowther to have his place in the Poor Law Board, which he will represent in the Commons. Thus we get the young ones, who promise, into the firm, and they will sit on the front bench, wherever that may be.

To Montagu Corry.

HUGHENDEN, *Aug.* 21.—. . . Understand the Minister of the Un: States comes on Tuesday. . . . Remember, if you can, the venison: and oh ! don't forget some work of the illustrious and noble author,[1] bound, and let me have it in time to put book plate in: otherwise, enemy for life. . . .

Aug. 23.—. . . I count on your punctuality to-morrow: as I hear to-day, there is to be a triumphal arch at the entrance of the Park, and Mr. Coates and the tenantry on horseback to escort the hero ! I entirely rely on your being the Master of the Ceremonies. . . .

To Lord Stanley.

HUGHENDEN, *Aug.* 26, '68.—You sent me a most amusing letter. Do you know, I think you an excellent letter writer; terse and picturesque; seizing the chief points, and a sense of humor.

Reverdy Johnson is here, and gets on very well. The ladies like him. He has eleven children, and 33 grandchildren: so they call him Grandpapa. He has only one eye, and that a very ugly one; and, yet, at a distance, looks something like old Lord Lansdowne, after a somewhat serious illness. His manners, tho', at first, rather abrupt and harsh, are good; he is self-possessed, and turns out genial.

Stanhope, who is here, seems to delight in him, and thinks it a *coup de maître* to have asked him here, and that the *Alabama* and all other claims will be settled forthwith. His visit to Hughenden is to our joint credit.

They all like Napier of Magdala very much: he is interesting and graceful, and tells even a story—but not too long: Chinese or Abyssinian.

Stanley, in his speech in March, had expressed his readiness to consider a suggestion which Seward, the American Secretary of State, had thrown out, of a General Commission to which the claims of both countries might be referred. On these lines a convention was arranged in the autumn with Reverdy Johnson, with a special proviso for the reference of the *Alabama* claims to a neutral Sovereign, in case the Commission should not agree. Though the American Minister at the Lord Mayor's banquet in November spoke of the matter as settled,

---

[1] Lord Stanhope.

the good work was not actually completed when the Government went out of office; but Clarendon, the new Foreign Secretary, took it up and brought it to formal signature in January. Internal politics in the United States, however, caused the convention to miscarry. It had to pass the Senate, then in antagonism to President Johnson and his executive; and the electors in the autumn had chosen a new President, who would wish to have his hands free when he assumed office in March. More also might be hoped from England under a Liberal than under a Conservative Administration. All these considerations determined the Senate to reject the convention; and the difficulty was left to be settled in a costly and less satisfactory fashion by the Gladstone Government a few years later.

It is natural to search Disraeli's correspondence during this period of office, to see how far he realised the catastrophe which was impending over France and over Europe, owing to the rapid rise of Prussian power and the jealousy with which it was regarded to the west of the Rhine. In obedience to his own inclinations and the Queen's command,[1] he kept a watchful eye on the situation abroad; but it cannot be maintained that he saw much farther than his neighbours. In the August of 1867 the French Emperor and Empress had paid a visit to the Emperor of Austria at Salzburg, ostensibly to condole with him on the tragic fate in Mexico in the previous June of the Emperor Maximilian, Francis Joseph's kinsman. But the visit also signified a certain drawing together of two Powers, of which one had been defeated, and the other was threatened, by the growing might of Prussia. Disraeli's letters of that date show how he viewed the European kaleidoscope.

To Lord Stanley.

HUGHENDEN, *Sept.* 1, 1867.—. . . I have heard nothing from the R[othschild]s. I observe, they never write, and

[1] See Vol. IV., p. 473.

only speak, indeed, on these matters in a corner, and a whisper.

To form a judgment of the present state of affairs, one must be greatly guided by our knowledge of the personal character of the chief actors.

The Emperor will never act alone; Bismarck wants quiet; and Beust,[1] tho' vain, is shrewd and prudent.

Gortc[hako]ff[2] is the only man, who could, and would, act with the Emperor, in order to gain his own ends, on which he is much set, but if the Emperor combines with him, he will so alarm, and agonise, Austria, that she will throw herself into the arms of Prussia, in order that an united Germany may save her from the destruction of all her Danubian dreams.

I think affairs will trail on, at least for a time, and the longer the time, the stronger will be your position. In such a balanced state of circumstances, you will be master. . . .

GROSVENOR GATE, *Oct.* 14, 1867.—I thought it wise to reconnoitre, and called on our friend [3] yesterday.

He said the Emperor was no longer master of the position, and repeated this rather significantly.

In time, I extracted from him, that they had information from Paris, that there was a secret treaty between Prussia and Italy.

I rather expressed doubts about this, and hinted that it seemed inconsistent with what had reached us, that there was an understanding between France and Italy, that the Emperor should give notice of his course, etc.

He was up to all this, and showed, or rather read, me a telegram, I should think of yesterday, in precisely the same words as you expressed, so I inferred the same person had given the news to Fane and his correspondent. Probably Nigra[4] himself.

The information of the secret treaty had arrived subsequently, and he stuck to it, and evidently believed it. . . .

The Berlin Ministry have consulted another member of the family about ironclads. They are going to expend $1\frac{1}{2}$ mill. sterling immediately thereon, and told him they thought of having the order executed in America, as, in case of war with France, the ships would not be allowed to depart if they were constructed in England. . . .

In the spring of 1868 one of those pretended reductions of Prussian armament, which have occasionally been advertised since, was understood to be in progress at

---

[1] Austrian Foreign Minister.   [2] Russian Chancellor.
[3] Baron Lionel de Rothschild.   [4] Italian Minister in Paris.

Berlin; and Disraeli, who should have had enough experience to disbelieve, was caught by a story which was rightly treated by Stanley as not worth serious attention.

To Lord Stanley.

GROSVENOR GATE, *April* 23, '68.—This appears to me important: Charles [Rothschild] is virtually Bismarck.[1]

A few days ago, B. was all fury against France, and declared that France was resolved on war, etc.: but on Monday the Rs. wrote to Berlin, that they understood England was so satisfied with Prussia, so convinced, that she really wished peace, etc., that England would take no step, at the instance of France, which would imply doubt of Prussia, etc.

This is the answer. I can't help thinking, that you have another grand opportunity of securing the peace of Europe and establishing your fame. . . .

[ENCLOSURE.]

Charles Rothschild to Baron Rothschild.

(*Telegram.*) BERLIN, *April* 23, 9.45 a.m. — Tell your friend that from the 1st of May army reduction here has been decided upon, and will be continued on a larger scale if same system is adopted elsewhere. Details by post.

To Lord Stanley.

10, DOWNING STREET, *April* 24, '68.—Bernstorff never knows anything.[2] I am sure there is something on the tapis, and I want you to have the credit of it. Vide Reuter's Tels: in *Times* of to-day: 'Berlin, Ap: 23,' rumor on the Bourse, etc.

What I should do would be to telegraph to Loftus, and bring things to a point, and then act.

I feel sure it will be done without you, if you don't look sharp. You risk nothing, and may gain everything.

April 25, 4 o'c.—I feel persuaded it's all true. They have a letter this morning in detail, explaining the telegram, and enforcing it. The writer, fresh from Bismarck himself, does not speak as if doubt were possible: gives all the details of the military reductions to commence on 1st May, and the larger ones, which will be immediately set afoot, if France responds.

How can you explain all this ? What of Loftus ?

[1] 'They see one another daily,' was Stanley's note on the letter. To avoid misunderstanding, it should be added that there has not been, since 1901, any branch of the house of Rothschild in the German Empire.

[2] Stanley had replied that the Ambassador knew nothing of intended reductions.

From Lord Stanley.

Private. **Sat., 6** p.m. [*April* **25,** 1868].—The telegram confirms your friend's expectations. I spoke to La Tour [d'Auvergne][1] in anticipation of it, 'Supposing the news were true, what would you do ?' His answer was discouraging He says (and indeed the tel. confirms him in that respect) that Prussian reductions mean nothing. 'What security do they give, when it is admitted that the men can be brought back in a week's time, if not in 24 hours ?' I am compelled to own there is some force in the reply. Still, with the facts actually before us, we may press them a little.

Throughout the summer and early autumn Disraeli remained sanguine of success at the polls. Derby, however, told him in August that ' Stanley's language as to the result of the elections is absolute despondency— he hardly seems to think the battle worth fighting.'

To Lord Derby.

Private. HUGHENDEN, *August* 23, 1868.—. . . I heard from Stanley[2] to-day, who seems rather jolly, and wonderfully well. He makes excursions in the mountains, and takes very long walks. He confesses he is 'enjoying himself.' He has not seen much of his Royal Mistress, but he says that, on Sunday last, she was looking very well, and in high good humor—does not talk much politics, but highly disapproves of the Opposition, praises her Ministers, and is very anxious that the elections should go right. According to your last, she did not get hold of the right man to encourage her on that subject; but the fact is Stanley does not know anything about it; he reads newspapers and believes in them; and as they are all written by the same clique, or coteries almost identical in thought, feeling, life and manners, they harp on the same string. It is very difficult to say, in this rapid age, what may occur in a General Election, which will not now happen for nearly a quarter of a year, but I myself should not be surprised if the result might astonish, yet, the Bob Lowes, Higgins, Delanes, and all that class of Pall Mall journal intellect. . . .

The newspapers, and Stanley, who, like the newspapers, had a shrewd instinct for average opinion, saw more clearly

---

[1] Of the French Embassy in London.
[2] At Lucerne in attendance on the Queen.

than the Conservative leader and his advisers what was going to happen. The party Committee to whom was entrusted the duty of conducting the elections assured Disraeli that there was reason to expect that the Conservatives would make sufficient gains to give them more than half the House of Commons: 266 from England, 51 from Ireland, and 13 from Scotland; 330 in all out of a House of 658. With this report before him Disraeli, absorbed in the heavy and responsible work of Government, was apparently content to wait in comparative passivity for the country's verdict. He had given the vote to a hitherto unenfranchised million of his fellow-countrymen, belonging in the great majority to the working classes; but so absolutely incapable was he of demagogic arts that he neglected, almost to a culpable degree, to endeavour to utilise his great legislative achievement to secure their support for himself and his party. The Liberals went up and down the country explaining that, though the Conservatives had passed the Reform Bill, the thanks of the new voters for the boon were really due to Gladstone and Bright; and Gladstone and several of his colleagues undertook impassioned electoral campaigns in which the new Irish policy of their party was eloquently expounded. But Disraeli contented himself with issuing an address, undoubtedly of some length and elaboration, to the electors of Bucks; and, as there was no contest in his constituency, with one speech on the hustings on re-election—a speech which was not even delivered till after the verdict of the boroughs had been largely given against his Ministry.

The address was drafted early in September, and during the remainder of the month was submitted to his principal colleagues for criticism and emendation; particularly to Cairns, on whose judgment Disraeli had come very thoroughly to rely, and whom he begged ' to give his whole mind to the affair, and, if necessary, to rewrite it.' No serious alteration was suggested by Cairns or others, and at the beginning of October the document was

issued.   In the forefront Disraeli claimed the confidence
of the party and the country as Derby's political heir,
who had pursued his old chief's policy 'without deviation.'
The settlement of the Reform question on broad lines,
a foreign policy which established the just influence
of England, the successful expedition to Abyssinia, and
the strengthening of the naval and military forces, were
all put forward as grounds for support.   But, owing to
the tactics of the Liberal party, Ireland had necessarily
to be the main subject of the address.   He claimed that
Ministers had, by vigilance and firmness, baffled the
Fenian conspiracy, and had also pursued a wise policy
of sympathy and conciliation.   But Gladstone had
suddenly proposed 'a change of the fundamental laws
of the realm' and 'a dissolution of the union between
Church and State.'   To that policy Ministers had offered,
and would offer, 'an uncompromising resistance.   The
connection of religion with the exercise of political
authority is one of the main safeguards of the civilisation
of man.'   No doubt the new policy was only to be partially
applied in the first instance, but the religious integrity of
the community would be frittered away.   Confiscation,
too, was contagious.   Finally the religious security
which was the result of the royal supremacy would
be endangered, and Rome alone would profit.

Amid the discordant activity of many factions there moves
the supreme purpose of one Power.   The philosopher may
flatter himself he is advancing the cause of enlightened progress; the sectarian may be roused to exertion by anticipations
of the downfall of ecclesiastical systems.   These are transient
efforts; vain and passing aspirations.   The ultimate triumph,
were our Church to fall, would be to that Power which would
substitute for the authority of our Sovereign the supremacy
of a foreign Prince; to that Power with whose tradition,
learning, discipline, and organisation our Church alone has,
hitherto, been able to cope, and that, too, only when supported
by a determined and devoted people.

In this address Disraeli made his main appeal for
confidence to the Protestantism of the nation.   There

is no doubt that, misled by the violent outbreak at the
time of the Papal aggression, by the suspicions arising
out of the Roman missionary propaganda in society
during the sixties, and by the popular dislike of the de-
velopments of Ritualism, he overrated the electoral
strength of a feeling which undoubtedly was widely
spread.

As the election drew near, the signs of Liberal victory
became more evident, though Disraeli, still sanguine,
tried to explain them away.   Derby, surveying the field
now from an outside standpoint, anticipated unsatisfactory
results generally, save in his own county of Lancashire.
' I am afraid,' he wrote on October 29, ' that, where it has
any operation, the minority clause will operate unfavourably for us in almost every instance, and there
appears to be a lamentable apathy on the part of the
Conservatives in abandoning seats which might fairly be
contested, or even of availing ourselves of the rival
pretensions of Liberal candidates for a single seat.'

To Montagu Corry.

Private. 10, DOWNING STREET, *Nov.* 3, '68.—Might not
these two queries lead to a solution of the difficulty—perhaps
the fallacy—of yesterday's speculations on the General
Election ?

1 : Was there ever a General Election in which half the seats
were not uncontested ?

2 : Is it not a fact, that the winning side always, or generally, gains $\frac{2}{3}$rds of the contests ?

For illustration, examine Palmerston's two dissolutions:
China—and 1865.   And then Peel's in 1834 when he gained
100 seats : and dissolution of 1841 when he gained 80.

These are materials from which an expert might deduce
instructive results.

If I could have them before my audience I should be glad.

Nov. 10.—Send me a line of news.   Our men seem to be
running away. . . .

On the very eve of the dissolution came the celebration
of Lord Mayor's Day, and Disraeli at the Guildhall
banquet gaily affected to entertain a confident expecta-

tion that he would be the Lord Mayor's guest in the following November, and chaffed the Liberals over their boastful and braggart methods of conducting the campaign.

I think I have read somewhere that it is the custom of
undisciplined hosts on the eve of a battle to anticipate and
celebrate their triumph by horrid sounds and hideous yells,
the sounding of cymbals, the beating of terrible drums, the
shrieks and screams of barbaric horns.   But when the struggle
comes, and the fight takes place, it is sometimes found that the
victory is not to them, but to those who are calm and collected :
the victory is to those who have arms of precision, though
they may make no noise—to those who have the breech-
loaders, the rocket brigade, and the Armstrong artillery.

One of the most frequent and most telling weapons
which the Opposition used in their campaign was the
assertion that the Government were quite as ready to
disestablish the Irish Church as they were themselves.
' There is as much chance,' wrote Disraeli in the vain
hope of silencing this slander, ' of the Tory party proposing to disestablish the Protestant Church in Ireland
as there is of their proposing to abrogate the Monarchy.'
It was a great misfortune that Disraeli could not bring
his colleagues to agree to concurrent endowment; but,
that being so, Ministers, however ready for reform, could
hardly for the election take up any other position than
that of simple resistance to Gladstone's plan of destruction.   This was naturally distasteful to the reforming
section of the Cabinet, and especially to Stanley. He
pressed his views again on Disraeli in the autumn, and
Disraeli replied, on September 26, from Balmoral: ' I
highly appreciate your criticisms, as you well know;
but I think your views about the Irish Church are of
a school of thought that has passed.   Excuse my
presumption. I don't think compromise is now practicable.'   Both Derby and Disraeli feared that Stanley,
when he gave, according to promise, a full explanation
of his views to the electors of Lynn, might seriously
embarrass the future of the Conservative party; and
the father, now as on previous occasions, relied upon

Disraeli to keep the son straight. It was an immense relief to both chiefs to find from the next morning's paper that the Foreign Secretary had been cautious and discreet.

To Lord Stanley.

10, DOWNING STREET, *Nov.* 10, '68.—I should like to have seen you, for a moment, before you departed. I shall have sleepless nights, until I have read your Lynn words.

Pray don't stab me in the back after all the incredible exertions I am making for the good cause.

And don't believe newspapers, and newspaper writers, too much. The result of the General Election, rest assured, will surprise all the students of that literature.

Nov. 14.—Perfect !

I am told our own party are enthusiastic: but all praise it. It must do us great good.

Stanley's speech was at the opening of the polls. By the time that the county returns were beginning, and that Disraeli was elected unopposed for Bucks, it was clear that Ministers would be defeated;[1] and the Prime Minister, in marked contrast to Gladstone's bellicose utterances, felt himself justified in taking a detached and impartial view of the situation on the hustings at Aylesbury. To this happy contingency we owe a priceless appreciation of the Irish character.

The Irishman is an imaginative being. He lives on an island in a damp climate, and contiguous to the melancholy ocean. He has no variety of pursuit. There is no nation in the world that leads so monotonous a life as the Irish, because their only occupation is the cultivation of the soil before them. These men are discontented because they are not amused. The Irishman in other countries, when he has a fair field for his talents in various occupations, is equal, if not superior, to most races; and it is not the fault of the Government that there is not that variety of occupation in Ireland. I may say with frankness that I think it is the fault of the Irish. If they led that kind of life which would invite the introduction of capital into the country, all this ability might be utilised; and instead of those feelings which they acquire by brooding over the history of their country, a great

---

[1] 'Our shadows seem to grow very long,' Disraeli wrote on the day of the election to Northcote.

part of which is merely traditionary, you would find men acquiring fortunes, and arriving at conclusions on politics entirely different from those which they now offer.[1]

Derby, while singing the praises of his own county of Lancashire, gave Disraeli a gloomy exposition of the general upshot of the elections.

From Lord Derby.

Confidential. KNOWSLEY, *Nov.* 22, 1868.—On looking over the returns, which are now nearly completed, I am sorry to see that our numbers will not only greatly disappoint your sanguine hopes, but will fall considerably below even my more modest anticipations. Even talking the most favourable view of the elections which are yet to take place, I cannot make out that Gladstone's majority will be less, and probably more, than a hundred. I am happy to think however that my county at least has done its duty. I told you I hoped to secure 18 out of the 32 seats[2]—we have done that already, if, as I have every reason to believe, we have carried both seats in the North-East. There are four seats remaining, out of which I have every hope of carrying three, including this division, in which we shall defeat Gladstone by not less than a thousand. We have lost Wigan by sheer mismanagement, and Warrington temporarily by rascality; the Mayor's poll clerk, who has absconded, having omitted 50 or 60 of Greenall's supporters, whose votes appear on the books of both parties. . . .

In the midst of our disasters, let me congratulate you, which I do very sincerely, on your speech at your nomination. It was perfectly suited to the occasion, calm, temperate, and dignified, and a striking contrast to the balderdash and braggadocio in which Gladstone has been indulging on his stumping tour—and which, I am happy to say, has done him more harm than good. The fate of the Government however is, I apprehend, decided. . . .

Household suffrage, on its first experiment, produced results which were very unfavourable to its authors. The working men accepted the Liberal contention as to the real giver of their franchise; and were seduced by the captivating cries of religious equality and justice to Ireland. Accordingly, the boroughs, save in Lancashire,

---

[1] Aylesbury, Nov. 19, 1868.
[2] The final result for Lancashire showed 19 Conservatives to 13 Liberals.

declared with considerable unanimity against the Government; but the reduction of the occupation franchise in the counties operated favourably to the Conservatives, and enabled them to appear in Parliament as a considerable and coherent, if a reduced, minority. Unsatisfactory as was the general result, which, roughly speaking, doubled the majority of sixty which the Liberals had held in the last Parliament, there were several individual returns which were calculated, in some measure, to console the losers. Gladstone, in spite of a campaign of copious oratory, was rejected by the Lancastrian constituency which had come to his rescue after his defeat at Oxford; and he would sit in the new Parliament as the junior member for the metropolitan borough of Greenwich. Lancashire further gratified the Tory party and the house of Stanley by returning Frederick Stanley in the place of Lord Hartington; and in two important metropolitan constituencies victories were won for the party by two men who were to be among the ablest of Disraeli's younger colleagues in his last Administration—William Henry Smith ousted John Stuart Mill from Westminster, and Lord George Hamilton, then a young guardsman, came in at the top of the poll for Middlesex. If there was considerable slaughter among Tory lawyers, the failure of Roebuck, Milner-Gibson, H. Austin Bruce, Bernal Osborne, and Horsman—to name the more conspicuous of the Liberal notabilities who fell—must have brought some balm to Disraeli's spirit. By the operation of the minority clause a Conservative was returned also with three Liberals for the City of London, and Disraeli's Liberal friend, Baron Lionel de Rothschild, whom he had done so much to seat in the House, was rejected.

The country had registered a decisive verdict against Ministers. What ought they to do ? According to the old precedents, they ought to meet Parliament as if nothing had happened, and wait to be defeated either on the election of Speaker or on an amendment to the

Address.   This was the course pursued by Melbourne's
Government in 1841; but Disraeli had condemned it
then as a policy resting on constitutional fictions and not
on facts, and so causing harmful and unnecessary delay.[1]
Ministers, now as then, had been defeated in Parliament,
had thereupon appealed from Parliament to the country,
and had had at the polls their defeat confirmed and
emphasised.   It was advisable, he thought, to acknowledge the fact and resign at once.   As was his frequent
custom in this Government, he first talked the matter
over with Stanley, who had independently come to
the same conclusion.   Disraeli's two other most important colleagues, Hardy and Cairns, agreed; and the Queen
threw the weight of her influence into the scale.   Apart
from her invariable preference for realities and readiness
to accept political facts even if unpalatable to her, Her
Majesty was naturally anxious to have the political
changes completed, so far as possible, before the recurrence
of the sad anniversary of her loss on December 14.

While the concurrence of the Queen and of Disraeli's
principal colleagues made it probable that the assent of the
Cabinet would be secured for immediate resignation, it
was certain that the country would be surprised, and it
was possible that the party might be offended.   Accordingly, it was necessary, as Disraeli wrote to Derby, to
accompany resignation 'by some simultaneous act
which should reassure and satisfy the party'; 'some
proceeding,' as he wrote to Hardy, 'which leaves no doubt
in the minds of our friends, in Parliament and the country,
of our determination to stand by our policy of [? on] disestablishment.'   As Parliament was not sitting, this was
difficult.   At first Disraeli thought of effecting his purpose
by an open letter to Derby; but finally decided to send
a circular to all Conservative peers and members of
Parliament.   The Cabinet accepted the advice of the
Prime Minister, backed by his most influential colleagues,
in spite of a strong letter from Derby in the contrary sense,

[1] See Vol. II., p. 116.

written to Stanley, and read, at the writer's request, both to Disraeli and apparently also to the Cabinet. 'It does not alter my opinion,' Disraeli told Stanley. 'However, the Cabinet will consider and decide. If you think it expedient to read it, postpone its reading till we have ascertained the unbiassed sentiments of our colleagues.'

To Queen Victoria.

10, DOWNING STREET, *Nov.* 28, 1868.—Mr. Disraeli with his humble duty to your Majesty.

The Cabinet is over, and has arrived at the conclusion he wished, though after much criticism, and great apprehension, that the Conservative party, not only in Parliament, may be offended and alienated.

Assisted by Lord Stanley, and by the Lord Chancellor, Mr. Disraeli successfully combated these fears, and adopted several suggestions, which were made, sensible and ingenious, which are calculated to prevent their occurrence. . .

From General the Hon. Charles Grey.

WINDSOR CASTLE, *Nov.* 30, 1868.—The Queen commands me to return Lord Derby's letter. H.M. is still of opinion that you have taken the course which was most honourable and straightforward as regards the character of the Govt., and certainly best for the public interest. . . .

To Lord Derby.

10, DOWNING STREET, *Dec.* 2, 1868.—The Cabinet were unanimous on the subject of resignation, not so much from any sentimental feeling of personal honor, which would not bear discussion, but from a conviction that the course was more advantageous to the party.

I enclose you a copy of the circular, which I propose to forward to every member of the party in both Houses, and which will, of course, appear in all the newspapers.

I tendered my resignation yesterday.

In the circular Ministers explained that they had not modified their opinion that Gladstone's policy of Irish disestablishment and disendowment was 'wrong in principle, probably impracticable in application, and if practicable would be disastrous in its effects.' But they justified their immediate resignation in the following terms:

Although the General Election has elicited in the decision of numerous and vast constituencies an expression of feeling which in a remarkable degree has justified their anticipations and which in dealing with the question in controversy no wise statesman would disregard, it is now clear that the present Administration cannot expect to command the confidence of the newly elected House of Commons. Under these circumstances Her Majesty's Ministers have felt it due to their own honour and to the policy they support not to retain office unnecessarily for a single day. They hold it to be more consistent with the attitude they have assumed and with the convenience of public business at this season, as well as more conducive to the just influence of the Conservative party, at once to tender the resignation of their offices to Her Majesty rather than wait for the assembling of a Parliament in which in the present aspect of affairs they are sensible they must be in a minority.

The precedent thus wisely set has been followed on every subsequent occasion when the circumstances have been at all similar; by Gladstone after the General Elections of 1874 and 1886, and by Beaconsfield himself after that of 1880. In 1885 and in 1892 Salisbury took a different course on the reasonable ground that, though there was probably a majority against Ministers, it was not a homogeneous majority and might fairly be tested in Parliament; but on neither occasion did his Government survive the Address. For the moment in 1868 there was some doubt as to the constitutionality of the proceeding; but the press and the party were in general favourable.[1] Disraeli was able to report to Grey, for the Queen's information, on December 4: ' Montagu Corry tells me that he went into the Carlton Club yesterday, which was crammed and crowded, as it always is during a Ministerial crisis, and that there was only one, and even enthusiastic, opinion as to the propriety of the course which I had taken. This is a great relief to me; even the

---

[1] Even Derby changed his mind; and ' on further consideration of all the circumstances,' told Disraeli he was satisfied that the decision of the Government was right.

malignant *Times*, on second thoughts, finds it wise to approve.' Public opinion, on the whole, endorsed Grey's verdict in a letter to the Queen: ' Nothing more proper or manly than [Disraeli's] way of taking defeat.' Many Liberal journals paid a similar tribute. ' Mr. Disraeli's conduct,' said the *Spectator*, ' although astute, is still manly and straightforward. He is a gamester in politics, but having lost the rubber he pays the stakes without a squabble.' He knew how to lose like a gentleman.

When Disraeli quitted office he was just completing his sixty-fourth year and his wife had reached the advanced age of seventy-six. Considering the size and enthusiasm of the Liberal majority, it was most improbable that she at any rate would live to share office once more with her husband. Was it even worth *his* while to resume the toil of apparently hopeless Opposition ? He had reached the goal of his ambition, had become what he told Melbourne he meant to be, Prime Minister. Might he not reasonably now retire from the active fight, accept the honours to which his long service had given him a claim, and settle down to enjoy them with his wife in the few years during which he might yet keep her with him ? The vision attracted him; but, even if he could bring himself to forgo the joy of battle in the Commons, he must have felt the honourable obligation, so long as his health permitted, of remaining to rebuild the party from the ruin into which, according to his busy detractors in the ranks, it was his reckless Reform policy that had plunged them. If, however, he remained, he might still secure for his wife the honours which she would value the more highly as coming through him and on his account. In his audience of the Queen after the elections he broached the suggestion that Mrs. Disraeli might be created a peeress in her own right; and was encouraged to submit his exact proposal in writing to Her Majesty. It will be noticed that, in his memorandum, Disraeli treats the party which was about to go into opposition as in no mere conventional language but in a very real sense ' Her Majesty's Opposition,' to be directed not only with a view to the promotion of its own principles but with constant regard to the Queen's comfort, welfare, and advantage.

To Queen Victoria.

Nov. 23, 1868.—Mr. Disraeli with his humble duty to your Majesty. Pursuant to your Majesty's gracious intimation he will endeavour to succinctly state what passed in audience with reference to the condition of the Conservative party after the General Election and his personal relations to it.

It was to be considered, 1st, whether it was for your Majesty's comfort and advantage to keep the party together—and, 2ndly, whether if kept together it was expedient that Mr. Disraeli should continue to attempt the task or leave the effort to younger hands. It seemed desirable that the party should be kept together because, although not numerically stronger, its moral influence appeared to be increased from the remarkably popular elements of which the Conservative party was now formed under the influence of the new Reform Act. Viewing England only, the Conservative party in the House of Commons will represent the majority of the population of that country.

This is a strange and most unforeseen result. It did not appear after great deliberation that any person could guide this party for your Majesty's comfort and welfare with the same advantage as Mr. Disraeli, as no one could be so intimately acquainted with your Majesty's wishes and objects as himself.

It had been the original intention of Mr. Disraeli on the termination of this Ministry to have closed his political career and to have humbly solicited your Majesty to have bestowed upon him some mark of your Majesty's favor, not altogether unusual under the circumstances.

When the Leader or Speaker of the House of Commons has been elevated by the Sovereign to the peerage, the rank accorded to him hitherto has been that of Viscount. And on this ground, that otherwise his inferiors in political position, who had been elevated often by his advice while he held either of these great posts, would take precedence of him who had been the chief in the Commons or who had presided over and controlled the debates. This was felt so strongly by Lord Russell, that when Sir C. Wood was elevated, who tho' an eminent was still a subordinate Minister, Lord Russell counselled your Majesty to make him a Viscount,[1] otherwise in the House of Lords he would have been in an inferior position

[1] Halifax.

to Sir B. Hall,[1] Mr. V. Smith,[2] and others who in the House of Commons were immeasurably his inferiors both in political rank and public reputation.

Mr. Disraeli might say that, at his time of life and with the present prospects, it is a dreary career again to lead and form an Opposition party: but he does not say so, because in truth, if in that post he could really serve your Majesty and your Majesty really felt that, it would be a sufficient object and excitement in public life, and he should be quite content even if he were never Minister again.

But next to your Majesty there is one to whom he owes everything, and who has looked forward to this period of their long united lives as one of comparative repose and of recognised honor. Might Mr. Disraeli therefore, after 31 years of Parliamentary toil, and after having served your Majesty on more than one occasion, if not with prolonged success at least with unfaltering devotion, humbly solicit your Majesty to grant those honors to his wife which perhaps under ordinary circumstances your Majesty would have deigned to bestow on him ?

It would be an entire reward to him, and would give spirit and cheerfulness to the remainder of his public life, when he should be quite content to be your Majesty's servant if not your Majesty's Minister. He would humbly observe that no precedents are necessary for such a course, but there are several.

When his friends on the formation of a new Govt. wished that the elder Pitt, who only filled a subordinate office, should not leave the House of Commons, his wife was created a peeress in her own right as Baroness Chatham. When in very modern times—indeed in your Majesty's own reign—Lord Melbourne wished to induce Sir John Campbell to remain in the House of Commons, and only as Attorney-General, his wife was created Baroness Stratheden.

Mr. Disraeli is ashamed to trouble your Majesty on such personal matters, but he has confidence in your Majesty's gracious indulgence and in some condescending sympathy on your Majesty's part with the feelings which prompt this letter.

Mrs. Disraeli has a fortune of her own adequate to any position in which your Majesty might deign to place her. Might her husband then hope that your Majesty would be graciously pleased to create her Viscountess Beaconsfield, a town with which Mr. Disraeli has been long connected and which is the nearest town to his estate in Bucks which is not yet ennobled ?

[1] Created Lord Llanover.   [2] Created Lord Lyveden.

From Queen Victoria.

WINDSOR CASTLE, *Nov.* 24, 1868.—The Queen has received Mr. Disraeli's letter, and has much pleasure in complying with his request that she should confer a peerage on Mrs. Disraeli, as a mark of her sense of his services. The Queen thinks that Mr. Disraeli, with whom she will part with much regret, can render her most useful service even when not in office; and she would have been very sorry if he had insisted on retiring from public life.

The Queen can indeed truly sympathise with his devotion to Mrs. Disraeli, who in her turn is so deeply attached to him, and she hopes they may yet enjoy many years of happiness together.

The Queen will gladly confer the title of Viscountess Beaconsfield on Mrs. Disraeli.

The Queen cannot conclude without expressing her deep sense of Mr. Disraeli's great kindness and consideration towards her, not only in what concerned her personally, but in listening to her wishes—which were however always prompted by the sole desire to promote the good of her country.

To Queen Victoria.

Nov. 25, 1868.—Mr. Disraeli at your Majesty's feet offers to your Majesty his deep gratitude for your Majesty's inestimable favor and for the terms—so gracious and so graceful—in which your Majesty has deigned to speak of his efforts when working under a Sovereign whom it is really a delight to serve.

Though there was some ill-mannered comment in a portion of the Radical press, public opinion in general accepted Mrs. Disraeli's peerage as a graceful and appropriate recognition of her husband's eminence and her own devotion. Derby wrote: ' Pray let me be among the first to congratulate " Lady Beaconsfield " on her new honour. She will, I am sure, receive it as a graceful acknowledgment, on the part of the Crown, of *your* public services, unaccompanied by the drawback of removing you from the House in which (*pace* Sir R. Knightley) your presence is indispensable.' And Gladstone concluded a formal letter to Disraeli about the Speakership with a pleasant reference: ' I also beg of you to present my best compliments on her coming patent to (I suppose I must

still say, and never can use the name for the last time
without regret) Mrs. Disraeli.' By a happy thought,
or a happy chance, the Secretary of State, who signed
the warrant for the issue of the patent of the new peeress,
was an old friend, Stanley.

To Lord Stanley.

10, DOWNING STREET, *Nov.* 27, '68.—She was very much
pleased with your note; and still more, that you were destined
to be the Secretary of State, who performed the function.

There seemed a dramatic unity and completeness in the
incident; bringing her memory back to old days, wanderings
over Buckinghamshire commons, when, instead of a great
statesman, you were only a young Under-Secy

CHAPTER III.

Reserve in Opposition.

1868–1871.

The concentration of the Liberal party, which had been a marked feature of the elections, was reflected in the composition of the new Government. Gladstone was able to combine in his Cabinet both Whigs and Radicals, Reformers and anti-Reformers, Clarendon and Goschen, Bright and Lowe. Clarendon went to the Foreign Office as of right; Lowe was very infelicitously placed at the Exchequer; Granville was of course restored to that leadership of the Lords which he had held with general acceptance under Palmerston. No sooner was the Ministry constituted than the Prime Minister set himself to work out in detail and reduce to legislative form his Irish Church policy; with such success that he was in a position to introduce his measure within a fortnight of the reassembling of Parliament in February.

Meanwhile Disraeli's attention, almost immediately after his retirement from office, was claimed by a family loss. His youngest brother James, whose health had been failing for some time, died very suddenly. He had been for ten years a Commissioner of Excise. Disraeli described him to Corry as 'a man of vigorous and original mind and great taste,' and mentioned that he had left 'a collection of French pictures of Louis Quinze period, and bricbracquerie, very remarkable; and of drawings by modern artists of the highest class.' Disraeli inherited a substantial sum, about £5,000, from his brother; but he did not enjoy the duties of executor.

To Lord Beauchamp.

GROSVENOR GATE, *Dec.* 24, '68.—I was most distressed at missing to write to you by yesterday's post: but the death was so sudden, everything so unprepared, everybody away, I finding myself executor without having had the slightest hint of such an office devolving on me, and having to give orders about everything, and things which I least understand, and most dislike—that I was really half distracted, and lost the post.

Amid sorrow, and such sorrow, one ought not to dwell upon personal disappointments, but it is a great one to Lady Beaconsfield and myself, not to pass our Xmas with friends we so dearly love, as Lady Beauchamp and her lord.

To Lord Stanley.

GROSVENOR GATE, *Jan.* 11, 1869.—Your letter was very welcome, and very interesting, as your letters generally are. Events affect the course of time so sensibly, that it came to me like a communication from some one I had known in another life, perhaps another planet. It seemed such long ages, since we used to see each other every day, and communicate almost every hour.

Here I have remained; and probably shall until the end of the month, when we shall re-enter life by going to Burghley. I have seen no one, and been nowhere, not even to a club: I have in fact realised perfect solitude: but I have found enough to do, and regular hours are the secret of health. . . .

The General Election of 1868 sent Disraeli back once more to that seat facing the box on the Speaker's left, in which he had already spent so much of his Parliamentary life. He had no doubt as to what must be the immediate course of the Opposition. Just before the session was resumed, he wrote to Stanley, declining an invitation to a public dinner in Lancashire, and giving as his reason, ' I think on our part there should be, at the present, the utmost reserve and quietness.' Even when, in opposition to Palmerston, he commanded a formidable minority not much short, in voting strength, of the forces of the Government, he often practised tactics of the kind. Now that he was facing a Minister who had behind him a large and enthusiastic majority such as Parliament had not seen

since the fall of Peel, reserve was all the more imperative.
Kicking against the pricks was neither dignified nor useful.
Plenty of rope, to vary the metaphor, was what a wise
Opposition would extend to a Premier of boundless eager-
ness and activity.

Accordingly the resistance which Disraeli offered to
Gladstone's Irish Church Bill, though strenuous, was not
prolonged. Nor was his speech on the second reading a
very successful effort. Salisbury in retrospect described
it as much below the orator's usual level; Hardy at the
time characterised it as 'sparkling and brilliant, but far
from earnest.' Perhaps the most interesting passage in
it was one protesting against the confiscation by the
State of corporate property, and especially of Church
property, which was 'to a certain degree an intellectual
tenure; in a greater degree a moral and spiritual tenure.
It is the fluctuating patrimony of the great body of the
people.' The constant sense of the anomalous position
of the Irish Church rather paralysed Disraeli's efforts in
its defence; and in this second reading debate the Opposition speaker who roused the enthusiasm which can only
be produced by conviction as well as eloquence was
Gathorne Hardy.

But no conviction and no eloquence were of any avail
against a majority returned by the newly created constituency to deal with this very question, and against a
Minister who conceived himself to be entrusted with
a mission to pacify Ireland. The second reading was
carried by 118. Though Disraeli told Archbishop Tait
that it was 'a mechanical majority,' which 'created no
enthusiasm,' and gave the Archbishop the impression that
he hoped to be able to set the Liberal party by the ears,
he realised that it was impossible to resist the Bill with
effect in the Commons. He discouraged blind opposition
to every clause in Committee, urged his followers to concentrate on a few vital amendments, and made no attempt
at delay. The Bill, therefore, in spite of its complexity,
passed easily through its various stages with the support

of an undiminished majority, and on the last day of
May was read a third time by 114. Disraeli's speech on
that occasion, though Hardy was again dissatisfied and
called it ' wretched,' contains at least one passage which
was highly prophetic. All who remember what the state
of Ireland was at the moment of the outbreak of the
Great War in August, 1914, will realise that Disraeli
had grasped the essentials of the Irish position, which
Gladstone and his followers glozed over with optimistic
sentimentalism. ' It is very possible,' he said, ' that
after a period of great disquietude, doubt, and passion,
events may occur which may complete that severance
of the Union [between England and Ireland] which to-
night we are commencing.'

What I fear in the policy of the right hon. gentleman [Glad-
stone] is that its tendency is to civil war. I am not surprised
that hon. gentlemen should for a moment be startled by such
an expression. Let them think a little. Is it natural and
probable that the Papal power in Ireland will attempt to
attain ascendancy and predominance ? I say it is natural;
and, what is more, it ought to do it. Is it natural that the
Protestants of Ireland should submit without a struggle
to such a state of things ? You know they will not; that is
settled. Is England to interfere ? Are we again to conquer
Ireland ? Are we to have a repetition of the direful history
which on both sides now we wish to forget ? Is there to be
another Battle of the Boyne, another Siege of Derry, another
Treaty of Limerick ? These things are not only possible,
but probable. You are commencing a policy which will
inevitably lead to such results.

Disraeli looked to the Lords to secure better terms for
the Irish Church than Gladstone and the Commons were
disposed to accord. Directly the second reading was
carried he had written to the Archbishop urging him to
call a meeting at Lambeth of leading peers of various
shades of opinion, in order that the Upper House, whatever it might ultimately decide to do, should not act on
party lines or under party leaders. ' Every day,' he
added, ' will make us comprehend more clearly what is
the real feeling of England. It is on a just appreciation

of that that the right decision will depend.' The Archbishop, who had already at the Queen's instance accepted a mediatory position, was only too glad to do what he was asked. ' I saw the Archbishop of Canterbury to-day,' wrote Disraeli to Cairns on April 10, ' a long interview. He is in favour of reading the Bill a second time, I think, tho' he does not wish to decide on that prematurely; and he accedes to my suggestion of summoning a preliminary meeting of peers at Lambeth to consult.' There is reason to believe that Disraeli agreed with the Archbishop's tactics. But he was in a difficult position, as his authority with the Conservative peers was very far short of what it ultimately became, and Derby, to whom they looked, absolutely refused to attend the Lambeth meeting, on the ground that ' no consideration on earth ' would induce him to enter into any compromise on a measure of the kind. The meeting was accordingly a failure, Cairns, the leader in the Lords, showing, in view of Derby's attitude, great reserve, though Salisbury and one or two others agreed with the Archbishop. The Conservative peers met at the Duke of Marlborough's house, and disregarded the hesitations of their leaders. It was resolved to oppose the second reading, in spite of the certainty that the rejection of the Bill, immediately after a decisive General Election, would provoke a constitutional crisis of the first magnitude. Happily some of the leaders, acting we may well believe with Disraeli's sympathy, were able, in conjunction with the Archbishop, to effect by influence behind the scenes what they had failed to carry at the party meeting; so the Bill, owing to many abstentions and thirty-six Tory votes in its favour, was carried on second reading by the respectable majority of thirty-three.

There followed a series of somewhat drastic amendments making ampler pecuniary provision than the Bill allowed for the Church about to be disestablished, and inserting the principle of concurrent endowment by applying some of the surplus to the needs of Roman Catholic priests

and Presbyterian ministers instead of converting it
altogether to secular use.   Concurrent endowment still,
as in the previous year, divided the friends of the Church;
for Disraeli and the majority of his colleagues were in
favour, and Cairns and some others strongly against.   It is
unnecessary here to describe the game of battledore and
shuttlecock which was played over these amendments
during June and July between Lords and Commons,
Ministers and ex-Ministers, as the whole story has been
set out in full in the *Life of Archbishop Tait*, ch. 19,
and Lord Morley's *Gladstone*, Book VI., ch. 1, and
Disraeli was hardly a protagonist.   That an arrangement,
by which the Church obtained a considerable slice of what
her friends thought to be her right, was finally arrived
at was due mainly to the tireless efforts of the Queen
and the Archbishop, maintained in spite of Gladstone's
unconciliatory attitude, and to the willingness of Cairns
to assume at the last moment, without possibility of due
consultation, an onerous responsibility.   Disraeli's letters
to Cairns show that it was the question of concurrent
endowment which gave him most trouble.

To Lord Cairns.

Confidential.   GROSVENOR GATE, *June* 27, 1869.—. . .   What
I hear of the state of your House and of the Cabinet alarms
me; both conditions seem to me rather anarchical.

Your followers want a meeting, that they should be advised,
according to custom, as to what amendments they should
support.   But this I apprehend, might be embarrassing to
you, from your hesitation as to your course respecting the
appropriation of the surplus.   The Government's truly
idiotic scheme on that head will not hold water.   It is universally condemned, while the general principle of some concurrent endowment seems to gain ground, in both Houses,
daily.   It is thought that many would support a liberal treatment of our own Church, if something were simultaneously
done for presbyter and priest.

There can be little doubt I conceive, abstractedly, of the
wisdom of such an arrangement.   But what alarms me is
the possibility of your being put in the situation of supporting
the Government with a fraction of your followers, and that

not the most influential, and dividing against the bulk of your friends.   This would be serious.

July 12.—What I originally apprehended occurred last night, and it will be now necessary to arrange our course with respect to ' concurrent endowment ' in the House of Commons.   With all our late colleagues there favorable to it, except perhaps Hardy, this will not be a very easy business, looking to future consequences as well as present results. . . .

Concurrent endowment was eventually abandoned. Disraeli sent his wife early intelligence of Cairns's arrangement:

To Lady Beaconsfield.

July 22, '69.—The Irish Church Bill is settled.   Cairns has made a compromise with Lord Granville; which saves the honor of the Lords, and will satisfy all moderate men. I don't think the more decided spirits on either side will like it as much.

I am obliged to hold my tongue even to my colleagues, as Cairns is to announce the terms.   They may be known soon after this reaches you, but it will be prudent not to send the news to anyone.

Perhaps the Archbishop's comment in his diary best sums up the net result:

We have made the best terms we could, and, thanks to the Queen, a collision between the two Houses has been averted; but a great occasion has been poorly used, and the Irish Church has been greatly injured, without any benefit to the Roman Catholics.

The most strenuous opponent of the Irish Church Bill in the Lords was the old Tory leader, Derby; it was he who made the most stirring speech in the debate on the second reading; and, when the compromise over the Lords' amendments was announced, he was so angry, Malmesbury tells us, that he left the House.[1]   It was the final scene of his political life, and his natural life lasted only three months longer.   But, though his strength was failing, he was for some weeks without actual illness, and

[1] Mr. Alfred Gathorne Hardy, in *Cranbrook*, Vol. I., p. 271, records ' on Lord Cairns's authority ' that Lord Derby, though at first startled and annoyed, ultimately expressed satisfaction with what was done.

Disraeli's last letter to his old 'chief' was apparently
written without any premonition of the approaching end.

To Lord Derby.

HUGHENDEN MANOR, *Sep.* 15, 1869.

MY DEAR CHIEF,—I was delighted at hearing from Knowsley, which recalled old times: not that I mean to say I was
insensible to the charms of your red venison, which I particularly appreciate.

We have been here three weeks, and have literally not seen
a human being, beyond the dwellers on the soil. After the
session we visited for a few days some of our friends, and among
other places we found ourselves at Alton Towers. It pleased
me very much. Though in Staffordshire, it is on the Derby-
shire border, and combines the character of both counties:
the scenery is romantic and rich. As for the house, it is the
only thing I have ever seen that gave me an idea of the castle
of Barbe Bleu in Madame D'Aulnois's wondrous tale. It is
so various and fantastic.

We are now literally stepping into the carriage to pay a
visit of a couple of days to Bulstrode. The late Duke of
Somerset bought the park from the Minister Portland, who
pulled down the mansion where lived Judge Jeffreys, and
began building a castle, but, being turned out of office, he
fancied he was ruined, and sold the place. The present Duke
of Somerset has built a fair and convenient dwelling, in the
Tudor style, in the park, which is undulating and well-
timbered : but I dare say you may remember it when you were
at Eton.

Pray make our kindest remembrances to Lady Derby.
I shall take the liberty of writing to you sometimes, if I have
anything to say, and you, perhaps, will not entirely forget
Your devoted D.

Early in October the last illness began, and on the
23rd the end came. To Disraeli Derby's death was the
severance of the most momentous political connection
of his life, a connection which had survived Derby's
resignation and his own succession to the first place. The
long and intimate association with one of a social position
so much higher, and a political reputation so much longer
and at first so much greater, had tended to habituate
Disraeli to the part of inspirer of measures and policies
for which Derby bore the main public responsibility; and

there is probably some truth in Fraser's assertion that Disraeli's ' fixed idea ' was ' that he was to be the mysterious wirepuller; the voice behind the throne; unseen, but suspected. That he should rise to be the absolute monarch, which he was at last, does not seem to have been anticipated by him.' So far as Fraser's view is correct, Derby's death was the emancipation of Disraeli.

To Lord Stanley.

HUGHENDEN, *Oct.* 25, '69.—It is with reluctance, that I intrude on you at this moment, overwhelmed, as you must be, with sorrows, cares, and duties; the memory of the past and the responsibility of the future. But I cannot refrain from expressing to you the sympathy of friendship.

As for the great departed, there existed, between him and myself, relations wh. have rarely been maintained between two human beings; twenty years, and more, of confidential public life, tried by as searching incidents as can well test men. I remember at this moment, not without solace, that there never was any estrangement between us; and that I have to associate with his memory no other feelings, than those of respect and regard.

How well justified was Disraeli's claim, in spite of occasional misunderstandings, has been shown throughout this biography. Lennox wrote to him from Paris: ' I fear you will have felt Lord Derby's death much. He was, with all his peculiarities, very true to you.' Disraeli, too, for his part, was ' very true ' to Derby; even in the deferential manner with which he used, as his secretaries noticed, to clinch disputed matters when in office by the phrase, ' Lord Derby wishes it.' He paid a worthy tribute to his old chief when, as Prime Minister, he unveiled in 1874 the statue of the ' Rupert of debate ' in Parliament Square; but he observed on that occasion a dignified reticence as to their personal relations. The qualities which he singled out for eulogy were ' his fiery eloquence, his haughty courage, the rapidity of his intellectual grasp '; ' his capacity for labour and his mastery of detail, which never were sufficiently appreciated because the world was astonished by the celerity

with which he despatched public affairs.' He summed
up Derby's share in the great transactions of the previous
fifty years in a noteworthy sentence: ' He abolished
slavery, he educated Ireland, and he reformed Parliament.'[1] It was not for him to say what history records,
that one of Derby's claims to the interest of posterity
was his intimate association with the career of Benjamin
Disraeli.

Derby's death sensibly affected the evolution of a
question which, during the first year and more of opposition, caused Disraeli some trouble—the leadership of the
party in the House of Lords. Malmesbury, who had
filled the post during 1868, was indisposed to continue
after the General Election. In Disraeli's view, Cairns,
the ablest man on the Conservative front bench in that
House, ought to be the successor. But so great was the
impression that Salisbury's character and abilities had
created that, in spite of his secession from, and denun-
ciation of, his colleagues over the Reform Bill, there
was a movement among the peers to choose him; and
even Cairns sounded him on the subject. Disraeli
promptly made it clear that he could concur in no such
arrangement.

To Lord Cairns.

Confidential. GROSVENOR GATE, *Dec.* 14, 1868.—Taylor
came to me yesterday, much perplexed and alarmed about
a conversation, between Colville and yourself, as to the leading
in the Lords. I told him I had seen you on the matter, and
would see you again, if necessary. He thinks, unless we act
with some decision, we may injure our position.

The Leader in the Lords must be one who shares my entire
confidence, and must act in complete concert with myself.
I do not know whether Lord Salisbury and myself are even
on speaking terms.

You contemplate making a man leader of a party of which
he is not even a member. If we show strength in Parliament
and the country, it is probable, in due time and course, he
will join us. If we try to force the result, we shall only subject
ourselves to humiliation.

[1] ' Every word of your admirable speech went to my heart, you understood my dearest husband so well,' wrote the widowed Lady Derby.

Parliament will not virtually meet till the middle of February, and you ought to meet it as the leader of the party in the Lords.

Salisbury himself realised the impropriety of the suggestion, urged Cairns to accept, and promised him cordial and earnest support. Accordingly Cairns, though very reluctant owing to his semi-judicial position as ex-Chancellor and his recent creation as a peer, consented, and was elected unanimously. One session, however—but that session an exceptionally trying one, owing to the controversy over the Irish Church Bill—convinced him that his objections were sound and should prevail; and he wrote to Disraeli on September 27 that he had made up his mind to resign. Not only was he anxious to devote considerable time to the judicial business of the House of Lords, but he had felt in the recent debates that his authority had not been duly regarded by the party. 'The more anxious part of the labours of the session has been, not the resisting the measures of our opponents, but the endeavouring to avoid the appearance of disunion among our friends. I have little capacity for either operation, but for the latter I have absolutely none.' The state of Lady Cairns's health, he added, had made it necessary for him to pass the entire winter abroad, so that in any case there would be a temporary interruption of his leadership; and he considered this a fitting opportunity for his permanent withdrawal from it.

To Lord Cairns.

Private. HUGHENDEN MANOR, *Sep.* 29, 1869.—The receipt of a letter, like yours, ought immediately to be acknowledged.

At present, I can only say, that I have read it with consternation. When I recover from its contents, if I ever do, I will endeavor to consider the perplexities of our sad situation. now so much aggravated, and will communicate with you.

There was no need to come to any decision in the early months of the recess; and the death of Derby, by transferring Disraeli's friend and political pupil, Stanley, to the Lords, seemed to open out a satisfactory solution. But the new head of the house of Stanley was slow to move and to take risks; and friends and colleagues found it impossible to obtain any definite promise during the autumn.

To Lord Derby.

CARLTON CLUB, *Nov.* 20, 1869.—We came up from Strathfieldsaye yesterday, and I found your kind recollection of your old comrade.

Never was a present more opportune; and I dined off a Knowsley hare yesterday, and breakfasted off a Knowsley pheasant this morning: both first-rate.

I am sorry to hear, that the House of Lords is to meet, so far as our friends are concerned, as *acephali*. It will, of course, at first, produce great scandal; but I have witnessed so many ' breaks-up ' of the party, that I have come to view them as Talleyrand did his ' revolutions '—with sanguine indifference.

To Lord Cairns.

Private. HUGHENDEN MANOR, *Dec.* 12, 1869.—. . . I saw Stanley when in town, and he is coming to stay here on our return from Blenheim, which I suppose will be about the sixteenth or so.

Nothing could be more cordial or more satisfactory, than the expression of his relations towards myself, but I could not expect any man to walk into a House of Parliament for the first time, and at once offer to take the conduct of affairs. Certainly I could not expect such a course from a man of the cautious and usually reserved habit of the present Lord Derby.

The arrangement you have decided on,[1] tho' I regret the personal inconvenience it may entail, appears to me the most judicious to be pursued; at once prudent and conciliatory.

I trust that all will develop satisfactorily, and I count on your continued counsel and support. . . . .

To Lord Derby.

HUGHENDEN MANOR, *Dec.* 16, 1869.—. . . We shall be delighted to receive you next Tuesday, the 21st. Although the shortest day, it is my birthday, wh: will be a sort of hedge, and I shall look out, in consequence, for a bottle of the best Falernian.

---

[1] To come over from Mentone for the meeting of Parliament, hold the usual Peers' dinner, and then formally resign.

I met Hardy at B[lenheim] and had much gossip about the H. of Lords with the Duke, but this and many other things will keep.   Excuse a frozen hand.

The choice of a leader in the Lords did not, of course, rest with the party chief who sat in the Commons or even with the party as a whole, but with the Conservative peers themselves; as Disraeli explained to a correspondent who suggested a joint meeting of the Conservatives in both Houses to make the election.

To William Johnston of Ballykilbeg.

HUGHENDEN MANOR, *Dec.* 8, 1869.—The leader of a party in a House of Parliament is never nominated: the selection is always the spontaneous act of the party in the House in which he sits.   It was so in the case of Lord Cairns, who yielded most unwillingly to the general wish, Lord Salisbury being one of the warmest of his solicitors.   It was so in my own case.   Lord Derby never appointed me to the leadership, but the party chose to follow me and the rest ensued.

The same jealousy of interference with an arrangement in which their own feelings and even tastes should pre-eminently be consulted would no doubt be felt, if the leadership of a House was to be decided by the votes of those who did not sit in it.

I make no doubt our friends in the House of Lords will in due season find their becoming chief; but our interposition will not aid them, they will be better helped to a decision by events. . . .

The claims of Salisbury were once more advocated by a section, but there was a general feeling that the man best able to unite the party would be Derby.   Would he accept ?   Hardy described him in his diary in December as 'not quite willing, but showing symptoms of persuadability.'   He was elected unanimously at the beginning of the session of 1870, Salisbury seconding the nomination, which was proposed by the Duke of Richmond. He took a day to consider, and then declined; as Hardy in retrospect wrote, 'He knew himself better than he was known.'   Thereupon Carnarvon put forward the impracticable plan that Salisbury should take an in-

dependent lead in and for the Lords, without holding
any confidential communication with the leader in the
Commons, who happened also to be the leader of the
party. The plan was not merely impracticable; it
would also have been not far short of an insult to
Disraeli. This absurdity was avoided, and finally Richmond, who had joined the Cabinet in 1867 when the
three seceded, accepted the 'uncoveted position,'[1] being
proposed by Salisbury and seconded by Derby. Salisbury
manifested throughout a disposition to resume friendly
working relations with his old friends—except with
Disraeli.

How unchanged was his attitude to Disraeli had been
shown in an article which he wrote in the *Quarterly Review*
in the autumn of 1869, on 'The Past and the Future
of Conservative Policy.' This renewed attack formed
the logical sequel of the articles in 1860 and 1867,[2] and
like them condemned severely the tactics of selecting
the Whigs for hostility and the Radicals for alliances.
In the Reform Act the party had committed a 'great
Parliamentary suicide.' A lurid picture was drawn of
the degradation and danger of office without power, as
revealed in past history. Though Disraeli's name was
never mentioned, it required only the most superficial
knowledge of politics to understand that it was he who
was portrayed as the 'dishonest man,' the 'mere political
gamester,' to whom office in a minority afforded too
tempting a field; that it was his 'baseness' and 'perpetual political mendicancy' that the writer was chastis-
ing; that he was the parliamentary leader whose conduct
was described as worthy of unmitigated contempt.

To Sir Anthony de Rothschild.

HUGHENDEN MANOR, *Dec.* 30, 1869.—A battalion of
pheasants, and some hares, arrived here yesterday, without
any label, but the porter said, that, tho' it had been lost,

---

[1] See Gathorne Hardy, Vol. I., pp. 294, 295.
[2] See Vol. IV., pp. 285-293, 556, 557.

there was no doubt that the game was for Hughenden and that it had come from Aylesbury.

No one in that direction cd. be so magnificent except yourself. You not only send many pheasants, but you send pheasants worth eating; nothing could be finer than those wh. preceded the last arrivals.

There is no middle state in this bird. A pheasant is ' aut Cæsar, aut nihil.' . . .

To Lord Derby.

GROSVENOR GATE, *Feb.* 1, 1870.—Will you come and dine at a large House of Commons dinner—forty—here on Wednesday the 16th ?

And if you will. wh. will please them much, shall I ask some swells to meet you, K.G.'s and that sort of thing—or would you prefer being the sole swell, like a big boy to the old school for a day ? I think that would be more characteristic, but just as you please.[1]

The disestablishment of the Irish Church did less than nothing for the moment to promote that pacification of Ireland towards which it was to be the first step; a tempest of sedition and crime swept in 1869 over the island which Abercorn and Mayo, the Tory Viceroy and Chief Secretary, had brought into comparative order. Gladstone, though he admitted, in the language of the Queen's Speech of 1870, that ' the recent extension of agrarian crime in several parts of Ireland ' had caused the Government ' painful concern,' held it to be all the more imperative to proceed with his second Irish measure, a Land Bill; and Disraeli, in his speech on the Address, promised a candid consideration for Ministerial proposals, though he pointed out that the tenure of land in Ireland was an old grievance, and could not possibly be the immediate cause of the present disorder. That disorder he attributed mainly to the extravagant hopes which the policy of the Government and the language of their supporters had encouraged. The Irish people reasoned: ' Is it not a natural consequence that if you settle the

[1] Derby accepted the second alternative; but the dinner had to be abandoned, as Disraeli, when the time came, was confined to his room by illness.

question of the Irish Church by depriving the bishops and rectors of their property, you will settle the question of the land by depriving the landlords of their property?' Disraeli called attention to a recent election for Tipperary in which the Government candidate, who had been Law Adviser at Dublin Castle, pledged himself to an extreme policy, and yet was beaten by a convicted Fenian, O'Donovan Rossa. ' The people of Ireland had to choose between a sham Fenian and a real Fenian, and it is astonishing what a preference is always given to the genuine article.' Then the Government, long so tolerant of disorder, at last took action.

Horrible scenes of violence had been occurring in Ireland, but the Government would never move. Landlords were shot down like game, respectable farmers were beaten to death with sticks by masked men; bailiffs were shot in the back; policemen were stabbed; the High Sheriff of a county going to swear in the grand jury was fired at in his carriage and dangerously wounded; households were blown up, and firearms surreptitiously obtained. All this time the Government would not move; but the moment the Government candidate was defeated at the hustings—a Government candidate pledged to confiscation, pledged to a course of action which would destroy all civil government—the moment that occurred there was panic in the Castle, there was confusion in the Council; the wires of Aldershot were agitated; troops were put in motion, sent across from Liverpool to Dublin, and concentrated in Waterford, Tipperary, and Cork. . . . I remember one of Her Majesty's Ministers [Bright] saying, I think last year, ' Anyone can govern Ireland with troops and artillery.' So it seems; even that right honourable gentleman.

The speech appears to have been generally admired. Malmesbury wrote to Cairns : ' Lady Tankerville says that at the opening of the session Bright had become dizzy, and Dizzy had become bright.'

To Sir Joseph Napier.

Confidential. GROSVENOR GATE, *Feb.* 21, 1870.—It is eighteen years since you and I first conferred together about an Irish Land Bill. It was a great thing then for me to have

such an adviser, and it would have been a wise thing if our
friends had adopted the result of our labors.

Now I am in a very different situation.   Not a single Irish
lawyer in the H. of Commons, at least on our benches, except
Ball, who is of course in the diocese of Armagh; even Cairns
has departed for Mentone.   On the 7th I have to express
my views on the Government Bill.   What a situation for the
leader of a party; as Bright says, 'still a great party!'

Under these circumstances I write to you, my old confederate.   Can you find time from your ecumenical council
to give me the results of your reflections on the Government
scheme, and such materials as may be opportune and profit-
able to me ?

I don't even know whether the Ulster right can be enforced
in a court of law, and there is nobody here to tell me !   I
must therefore summon 'Napier to the rescue.'

Gladstone's Bill was directed to the security of the
Irish tenant, who, contrary to the usual practice in
England, had generally received his land in a prairie
condition from the landlord, and had done all the draining,
reclaiming, fencing, farm-building, and other improvement himself.   By custom in Ulster and in some other
parts of Ireland, so long as the tenant paid his rent he
could not be evicted; and on giving up his farm he could
claim compensation for unexhausted improvements and
sell the goodwill for what it would fetch in the market.
Where no custom prevailed, the landlord was at liberty
to raise the rent in proportion as the tenant improved the
land, and to evict him at will without compensation.
Roughly speaking, Gladstone's Bill turned the Ulster
custom into law and extended it throughout Ireland,
thus giving the Irish tenant an estate in the land he
farmed.   So far as the measure provided for compensation,
and retrospective compensation, to the tenant, Disraeli
was heartily in its favour, as this was one main principle
of the Bills which Napier prepared under his auspices in
1852; and he therefore announced on the second reading
that some legislation was necessary and that he should
support the Bill in principle.   But he had his doubts about
the wisdom of turning custom into law.

The moment you legalise a custom you fix its particular character; but the value of a custom is its flexibility, and that it adapts itself to all the circumstances of the moment and of the locality. All these qualities are lost the moment you crystallise a custom into legislation. Customs may not be as wise as laws, but they are always more popular. They array upon their side alike the convictions and the prejudices of men. They are spontaneous. They grow out of man's necessities and invention; and, as circumstances change and alter and die off, the custom falls into desuetude and we get rid of it. But if you make it into law, circumstances alter, but the law remains, and becomes part of that obsolete legislation which haunts our statute-book and harasses society.

Disraeli deplored the interference with freedom of contract effected by the Bill; but Gladstone asked with some force whether Disraeli would allow the tenant to contract himself out of its benefits. By far Disraeli's shrewdest and most incisive criticism was that the Bill terminated 'at one fell swoop all moral relations between the owner and occupier,' and endeavoured to establish a purely commercial relation between them. Yet, if ever there was a state of society where the relations should be paternal, where forbearance should be shown to the tenant who from vicissitudes of seasons is in arrear with his rent, it was Ireland, where there were farmers holding only one acre. Hitherto small tenants had not appealed in vain 'to the distinguished facility and good nature of the Irish landlord.' But why should forbearance be shown when the tenant in arrear is a co-partner, in getting rid of whom the landlord has a direct interest, and when the payment of rent is the only bond? Disraeli developed this point in Committee, when he reduced the majority of the Government to seventy-six on an amendment limiting compensation to unexhausted improvements. The landlord would say to the tenant in future, argued Disraeli, 'We must both stand upon our rights. This new-fangled law, which has given you a contingent remainder to the third of my freehold, has at least given me this security, that if you do not pay me

your rent I may get rid of you.' Evictions would naturally follow; there would be a new grievance, the payment
of rent; and the non-payment of rent would become a
principle asserted by the same rural logic which had
produced the crimes and horrors of the past year. There
would be great complaints of vexatious and tyrannical
evictions, and the occupiers would assert their supposed
rights by the most violent means. 'So far from the
improvement of the country terminating all these misunderstandings and heartburnings, which we seem now
so anxious on both sides of the House to bring to a close,
you will have the same controversies still raging, only
with increased acerbity, and under circumstances and
conditions which must inevitably lead to increased bitterness and increased perils to society.'

It was a speech of extraordinary prescience, predicting
with exactness the course which the agrarian movement
followed in Ireland during the next ten or fifteen years.
In painful contrast was Gladstone's optimistic reply, insisting that the measure was an exceptional one to meet
a temporary need, and expressing the hope that the time
would come when it would be no longer necessary and freedom of contract would be restored. Though he anticipated
the failure of Gladstone's scheme, Disraeli did not realise,
any more than Gladstone, that the creation by the aid of
the State of a peasant proprietary was, as Bright with
real vision maintained, and subsequent history has shown,
the true remedy for agrarian discontent in Ireland. To
placate Bright, Gladstone did indeed frame some inadequate clauses with this object, but he laid no stress on
them, and Disraeli even singled out these clauses for disapproval. However, having recognised the necessity of
legislation, Disraeli discouraged divisions on both second
and third readings; and, the Opposition in the Lords
following the example of the Commons, the experiment
which Gladstone sanguinely advocated was duly tried—
and proved so inadequate that in ten years its author had,
with unabated optimism, to set his hand once more to the
same task.

The other great measure of the session, the one whose passage was perhaps the foremost distinction of Gladstone's Ministry, Forster's Education Bill, was actively assisted by the Conservative party, under Disraeli's direction. He had claimed at Edinburgh, in the autumn of 1867, that from his entry into public life he had done his best to promote the cause of popular education. He had given it a prominent place in his address when first elected for Bucks in 1847; one of the outstanding features of his scheme for administrative reform in 1855 was the constitution of education as a separate Ministry with a Secretary of State as its head; the Derby - Disraeli Government of 1858 appointed the Newcastle Commission on the subject; and, while the last Palmerston Government had persistently neglected to take any steps in consequence of the Commission's Report, save to enforce the very questionable recommendation of payment by results, Disraeli's first Ministry in 1868 prepared and submitted, through the Duke of Marlborough, to the House of Lords, a comprehensive scheme which, at least in the importance attached to the Education Department, was even in advance of Forster's measure. But Forster introduced the principle of a local rate which Disraeli's Ministry had shirked, and his scheme, while increasing the Government grants to denominational schools, mainly belonging to the Church of England, already in existence, provided for supplementing their deficiencies by the creation of school boards all over the country, which should establish and conduct rate-aided schools, so that elementary education should be ultimately provided for every English child. The great difficulty, then as subsequently, proved to be the religious teaching. The general sense of the House and of the country was that the Bible should be read and that there should be religious education in all schools, guarded by a conscience clause; but the Radicals and the bulk of the Dissenters pressed for an entirely secular system. This the Government could not concede; but they ultimately accepted a compromise, proposed by Cowper Temple, a Whig, providing that, while the Bible should be read and explained, no catechism or other distinctive formulary should be taught in a board school. Disraeli immediately fastened on the weakness of this arrangement. The schoolmaster could not, he pointed out, teach, enforce, and explain the Bible without drawing some conclusions, and what could those be but dogmas ? ' You will not entrust the priest or the presbyter,' he said, ' with the privilege of expounding the Holy Scripture to the scholars; but for that purpose you are inventing and establishing a new sacerdotal class. The schoolmaster who will exercise these functions . . . will in the future exercise an extraordinary influence upon the history of England and upon the conduct of Englishmen.' In a speech in the autumn at a Bucks diocesan meeting he described the new Act, though it was a step in advance, as but a measure of transition, with which the English people would not be satisfied in the long run. They would require richer and more various elementary education, and, when they obtained that, they would require a religious education, because as their intelligence expanded and was cultivated they would require information as to the most interesting of all knowledge—the relations which exist between God and man. The various subsequent modifications in our education policy, culminating in the Act of 1902, and in Mr. Fisher's Bill of the current year (1918), testify to Disraeli's foresight. With one immediate result of Forster's policy he must have been well content—the opening of a rift between the Gladstone Ministry and its erstwhile devoted supporters, the political Dissenters. He was careful to avoid inconsiderate attacks which might draw his opponents together.

Not merely the policy of reserve which he had deliberately adopted, but ill-health of a continued character greatly restricted Disraeli's activities during the session; and on several occasions he had to rely upon Hardy, his

'sword-arm,' to take his place.   Writing to Lennox in
July he said: 'I have been unwell all this year, and am
afraid I have thought too much of myself.   Illness
makes one selfish and disgusts one's friends.'   A letter
to Northcote, who had gone to Canada, as Chairman of
the Hudson Bay Company, in connection with disputes
between the company and the Canadian Government,
gives a picture of the work of the session up to May.

To Sir Stafford Northcote.

GROSVENOR GATE, *May* 14, 1870.—. . . The Land Bill
after Easter moved; and then, like a ship on the stocks, moved
rapidly.   I think the Lords will certainly have it before Whitsun.   It has been greatly modified in Committee—much by
the Govt. yielding to Roundell Palmer and Co.; and much
by our friend Ball, who has shown as much resource and knowledge as on the Irish Church Bill, and with a happier result.
We must be cautious in not over-altering it in the Lords. . . .
    There is a hitch about the Education Bill.   Gladstone,
I apprehend, is prepared to secularise, if he were only convinced he could keep his majority together by that process.
But the elements of the calculation are various and discordant, and every possible result, therefore, doubtful.
    The Ballot bothers me.   Cross and the Lancashire men are
all in favor of it, and say that at this moment we should carry
every great town in the North, were it adopted.   But I apprehend the great body of our friends would not like to see it
applied to counties; and then there are Ireland and Scotland
and Wales also to be remembered.   We are going to have a
council in a day or two; the leading members of both Houses,
and some representative men.   I miss you sadly on these
occasions, and indeed always.
    The great social event is Derby's approaching marriage.
He is radiant with happiness.   Literally you would not know
him.
    I can't say much for myself.   I have been to the seaside;
but it has brought me no relief, and I still suffer, which is
disheartening. . . .

Derby was about to marry Salisbury's stepmother,
who had long been a friend of Disraeli's, and had frequently entertained him at Hatfield during the last
twenty years.   To his sister he described her in 1851 as

' an admirable hostess and a very pleasing woman; great simplicity, quite a Sackville.' [1]

To Lord Derby.

GROSVENOR GATE, *May* 7, 1870.—Next to yourself, by what you tell me, no man, perhaps, will be happier, than I am. Under this roof, we have long, and fondly, wished, that this shd. happen. The lady I have ever loved; and if fine intelligence, a thoughtful mind, the sweetest temper in the world, and many charms, can make a man happy, your felicity is secured.

Marriage is the happiest state in the world, when there is, on each side, a complete knowledge of the characters united. That you have secured—and to all the many blessings wh. distinguish you in life, rank, wealth, and, above all, great abilities, you have had the wisdom to add the only element, wh. was wanting to complete the spell.

Lady Beaconsfield sends you her congratulations thro' her tears—of joy.

To Gathorne Hardy.

GROSVENOR GATE, *May* 22, '70.—I am sorry—very—to say, that you must not count on me to-morrow to support and assist you in the debate on University Tests, as was my hope, and firm intention. My medicos declare that I must not attempt anything like public speaking at present, and refrain, indeed, as much as possible, from private.

Tho' I hope I shall get it all straight, my right lung is seriously affected, and it is no use any longer to tamper with it. Remedies, and quiet, and this hot weather, may put all to rights, and in a short time, but I must try them.

It pains me to leave a faithful colleague to struggle alone with a difficult question—but you will do all that man can do, which is my consolation, tho' not a sufficient one.

Hardy's own account of Disraeli's health and views is given in his diary for May 22: ' Called on Disraeli, who remains poorly and dreads the east wind. He is desponding, but looks forward to Gladstone becoming useless to the Radicals, and a disruption. Gives two years or more.'

[1] See Vol. III., p. 336.

MARY COUNTESS OF DERBY.

From a portrait after J. Swinton, at Hughenden.

To Lord Stanhope.

GROSVENOR GATE, *July* 17, '70.—. . . I quite agree with you about the division in the House of Lords:[1] avowedly to regulate that assembly by the prejudices, or convictions, of the University of Oxford, cannot be wise. Some think, however, that the great event of the last eight and forty hours may bring about a state of affairs more suitable to a policy of resistance, tho' that was not contemplated by the instigator in the present instance.

I dined at York House, Twickenham, yesterday: a curious and interesting moment to be a guest there. It was not wonderful, that my host[2] should be somewhat excited. It is an important break in the existence of himself and his brother colonists. One of the guests, however, did not think so; and said they were forgotten, and had done nothing to make themselves remembered. We shall see! They may be wanted. Nobody is forgotten, when it is convenient to remember him.

' The great event of the last eight and forty hours ' was indeed calculated to alter men's views and affect their policies. The relations of France and Prussia had caused the statesmen of Europe, and Disraeli among them, grave anxiety ever since 1866; and when he wrote this letter to Stanhope a sudden dispute between the two countries over the offer of the Spanish throne to a Hohenzollern prince had, in spite of the prince's withdrawal, been aggravated, by Bismarck's unscrupulous manipulation and Napoleon's fatal folly, into a quarrel which only the sword could decide. A despatch from Ems, describing the diplomatic proceedings between Benedetti, the French Minister, and the King of Prussia, had been so dexterously edited by Bismarck as to prove, as he hoped and expected, a red rag to the Gallic bull. French mobilisation had been ordered ; the Parisians were shouting ' To Berlin '; a declaration of war was inevitable within a few days. Bismarck's share in provoking the explosion was not then known; and Disraeli was at one with public opinion in

[1] On a motion by Salisbury, the recently elected Chancellor of the University of Oxford, which defeated the second reading of the University Tests Bill.
[2] The Comte de Paris.

England in casting all the blame on Napoleon's ambition
and French recklessness. Moreover, in expressing the
view that a Sovereign who trusted to melodramatic
catastrophes, such as military surprises and the capture
of capitals, would have to meet ' a more powerful force
than any military array,' namely, ' the outraged opinion
of an enlightened world,' he showed that he was not
himself entirely emancipated from the sentimental
optimism about international relations which was rampant among his political opponents.

For a quarter of a century Disraeli had preached that
a good understanding with France should be the basis of
British foreign policy; and when in office, both in 1852
and in 1858-1859, had acted throughout in the spirit of
that creed.   It was not without great reluctance, and only
after mature consideration and the experience of Napoleon's ambition and instability gained during his two
years and a half of office in 1866-1868, that, like Palmerston in his latter days, he abandoned the theory as no
longer practicable; and, in spite of a profound distrust
of Bismarck's policy, began to incline rather to the Court
view that the more natural affinity of Great Britain was
with the Germans, who had often been our allies and never
our enemies.   The behaviour of the French Government
and people in July, 1870, confirmed him in his new faith;
and so too did the calculated revelation, by Bismarck,
at this critical moment, of the overtures made to (and
perhaps perfidiously provoked by) him, in 1866 and
subsequently, to abet a French conquest of Belgium in
return for compensations to Prussia in South Germany.

But, though Disraeli considered that the orientation of
our European policy must be changed, he was as determined as the Government that Great Britain must preserve a strict neutrality in the war.   Only he insisted,
in a speech on August 1, that it must be an armed
neutrality, a neutrality which on the right occasion might
speak with authority to the belligerents.   In such a
neutrality he hoped we might be able to secure the co-

operation of Russia.   But, he asked, were our armaments
in a condition to enable us to adopt this policy ?   This,
though he omitted to claim the credit, was a question he
had every right to put, as the additions to the navy and
army estimates which his own Government had wisely
sanctioned were fiercely denounced by the Liberals during
the General Election of 1868; and the Gladstone Ministry,
in spite of the unstable European equilibrium, had
boasted of the economies and reductions they had effected
during their two years of office.   Disraeli had made careful inquiries, as the Beaconsfield correspondence shows,
into the actual condition of our armed forces, and
warned the Government that there were defects urgently
requiring to be supplied.   Let them remember the
humiliation the country suffered at the time of the
Crimean War, because of the failure of the Aberdeen
Government to come to a decision in time.   Let them
speak to foreign Powers with that clearness and firmness
which could only arise from a due conception of their
duties and a determination to fulfil them.

In this speech Disraeli dwelt upon the vital importance
of securing the neutrality and independence of Belgium,
guaranteed by the Treaty of 1839.   Here he was forcing
an open door, as Ministers, moved by Bismarck's revelation, negotiated a fresh treaty with France and Prussia,
by which, in the event of the violation of Belgian neutrality by either of the belligerent Powers, England bound
herself to co-operate with the other to ensure its observance.   This satisfied public opinion both in England and
in Belgium; and, though Disraeli expressed a doubt
whether a fresh treaty was required and whether a notice
of England's firm determination to uphold the Treaty of
1839 would not have been sufficient, he accepted the
resolve to maintain the independence of Belgium as a
wise and spirited policy.   ' It is of the highest importance
to this country that the whole coast from Ostend to the
North Sea should be in the possession of flourishing
communities, from whose ambition, liberty, or independ-

ence neither England nor any other country can be menaced.'

From Disraeli's correspondence of the autumn we can obtain glimpses into his feelings as to the rapid and startling German victories; the announcement of the impending marriage of a daughter of the Sovereign to a subject, Lord Lorne; and the progress of Conservatism among the electorate.

To Lord Derby.

GROSVENOR GATE, *Aug.* 17, 1870.—I am here, the focus of all intelligence, and where we get news sooner, than at Berlin or Paris.

I do not much believe in the great battle, wh. they say is going on. The French are in full retreat on their whole line, and the Prussians, as is usual under such circumstances, are following them up and harassing them. Being strong in cavalry, the Germans have an additional advantage.

This collapse of France has all come from the Emperor's policy of nationality. That has created Italy and Germany; wh. has destroyed the French monopoly of Continental compactness. The Emperor started this hare in order that he might ultimately get Belgium. Belgium is safe and France is smashed ! . . .

England is busy at mediation, but Prussia thinks the Gauls are not yet sufficiently humiliated. Russia jealous of Prussia, yet hating France—England strong in words, but a mediation of phrases won't do.

P.S.—I never was better: quite, quite myself.

To Lord Cairns.

Oct. 9, 1870.—. . . I have entirely cured mine [gout] by giving up sugar, burgundy, and champagne—almost as great a surrender as Sedan !

To Montagu Corry.

HUGHENDEN, *Oct.* 9, '70.—We go to-morrow to Lord Bathurst's, and I expect to be in town on Friday night and on the following Monday to Knowsley. We have refused almost every invitation this year, and particularly those at a distance: but found it impossible to say *no* to Lord and Lady Derby: the first gathering of their friends. I look forward to the journey with fear and trembling: having scarcely ever left this delicious place in this delicious weather. . . .

To Queen Victoria.

[*Oct.*, 1870.] Mr. Disraeli with his humble duty thanks your Majesty for your gracious kindness in communicating to him through Lady Ely the very happy news of the approaching marriage of the Princess Louise.

The engaging demeanor of Her Royal Highness, her beauty, her sensibility and refined taste had always interested him in her career and made him desirous that her lot should not be unworthy of a nature so full of sweetness and promise.

What is about to happen seems to him as wise as it is romantic. Your Majesty has decided with deep discrimination that the time was ripe for terminating an etiquette which has become sterile, and the change will be effected under every circumstance that can command the sympathy of the country.

Mr. Disraeli has the pleasure of knowing Lord Lorne. The gentleness of his disposition and the goodness of his temper are impressed upon his countenance, which, while it is bright with cultivated intelligence, could not, he feels sure, express an evil passion.

Knowing the depths of your Majesty's domestic affection, which the cares of State and the splendor of existence have never for a moment diminished or disturbed, Mr. Disraeli feels that he will be pardoned if he presumes to offer your Majesty his sincere congratulations on an event which will consolidate the happiness of your hearth.

There is no greater risk perhaps than matrimony, but there is nothing happier than a happy marriage.

Though your Majesty must at first inevitably feel the absence of the Princess from the accustomed scene, the pang will soften under the recollection that she is near you and by the spell of frequent intercourse. You will miss her, Madam, only like the stars: that return in their constant season and with all their brightness.

Lady Beaconsfield thanks your Majesty for your Majesty's gracious enquiries after her. She is, I am happy to say, quite well and singularly interested in the subject of your Majesty's communication.

To Lord John Manners.

HUGHENDEN MANOR, *Oct.* 30, 1870.—. . . France can neither make peace or war. No country in modern times has been placed in such a predicament, nor she herself at any time except under Charles the 7th, whose reign she is fast reproducing. She has no men now, as then. Will she have a maiden ?[1]

---

[1] The reference is, of course, to Joan of Arc.

I am glad to hear of your working-man's meeting. My hope in them hourly increases. How well for the country that we settled the suffrage question ! The trading agitators have nothing to say, or, if they open their mouths, are obliged to have recourse to European Jacobinism. . . .

The Franco-German War had two by-products, both distasteful to Disraeli. The Italian Government seized the opportunity offered by the withdrawal of the French garrison and the serious plight of the French armies to enter and occupy Rome, the last remnant of the Papal States, and to restrict the Pope's temporal jurisdiction to St. Peter's and the Vatican. Disraeli regretted the abasement of anything that represented, as the Pope did, the spiritual order; but Protestant and Italophil England rejoiced. The country, however, was as disturbed as was Disraeli when Russia—instead of combining, as he had hoped, with Great Britain in a watchful and armed neutrality to impose peace at a suitable moment on the belligerents—took advantage of France's critical position and of Britain's comparative helplessness to notify the European Powers, that she would no longer hold herself bound by the Black Sea neutralisation clauses of that Treaty of Paris, which France and Britain, as victorious allies in the Crimean War, had forced her to accept. Granville, who on Clarendon's death in the summer had succeeded him as Foreign Secretary, strongly protested; and the Government, by allowing their agent to threaten a war with Russia which the Prime Minister never seriously contemplated, obtained Bismarck's aid in getting Russia to submit her claim to a Conference of the Powers in London, with the understanding that the modifications she desired would receive European assent.

To Lord Derby.

HUGHENDEN MANOR, *Nov.* 27, 1870.—. . . The Govt. appear to be in trouble, and probably will continue to be so. What[eve]r their ultimate decision, these matters take time. But, no doubt, how[eve]r they may act, their embarrassment must be great, for they can hardly avoid proposing increased armaments.

Gladstone wished a paragraph to be inserted in *The Times* intimating, in dark and involved sentences, that he was not the writer, only the inspirer, of the *Edin. Rev.* Art.—that is to say, I suppose, dictated it to Mr. W. H. Gladstone or, perhaps, to dr. Catherine herself—but Delane refused his columns to the *communiqué* and suggested a distinct letter from the Premier himself, wh. never came.[1]

Dorothy Nevill says that Lowe impressed on her to preach the only gospel, ' Peace at any price,' and that she goes about society preaching accordingly.

Lorne, who has been here for a couple of days, is for cross benches in the House of Commons: significant. . . .

To the Hon. Algernon Egerton.

[? *Dec.* 27, 1870.]—I am honored by the wish of my Lancashire friends that I should pay them a visit and very proud of it.   But in the present critical state of public affairs I doubt the expediency of political gatherings.

I regret that Her Majesty's Ministers did not feel it consistent with their duty to advise the summoning of Parliament before Christmas, but that meeting cannot now be long delayed and our position will then be ascertained from authority, and we shall be better enabled to consider our prospects.   Unquestionably they are serious, and I fear not likely to diminish in gravity: but the people of Lancashire will be more qualified to form an opinion upon them after the Speech from the Throne; and if at a fitting season in the course of next year they continue to care to hear my views of the condition of the country I shall feel it a great and gratifying distinction to be their guest.

To Lord Stanhope.

HUGHENDEN, *Jan.* 22, '71.—. . . I think the avoidance of Parliament, at such a crisis, is highly to be condemned: but I doubt, whether delays will mend their position.

Next to Gambetta, the most wonderful man of the day is John Russell, who raises armies by a stroke of his pen, and

---

[1] Lord Morley writes in *Gladstone*, Bk. VI., ch. 5: ' It was about this time that Mr. Gladstone took what was, for a Prime Minister, the rather curious step of volunteering an anonymous article in a review, upon these great affairs in which his personal responsibility was both heavy and direct.   The precedent can hardly be called a good one, for, as anybody might have known, the veil was torn asunder in a few hours. . . .   The article . . . was calculated to console his countrymen for seeing a colossal European conflict going on, without the privilege of a share in it.   One passage about happy England—happy especially that the wise dispensation of Providence had cut her off by the streak of silver sea from Continental dangers—rather irritated than convinced.'

encourages the country almost in ' Cambyses' vein.' What energy ! At least in imagination.

To Lord Derby.

GROSVENOR GATE, *Jan.* 25, 1871.—My views respecting French affairs are the same as expressed in our talks at Knowsley in the autumn, except that they are stronger. I can conceive nothing more fatal, than our entering into the contest, or assuming an anti-German position; and I deeply regret the inveterate manner in wh. Ld. Salisbury works the *Q*[*uarterly*] *R*[*eview*], and inspires the *Standard*, in that direction. No one has recognised his powers more readily than I have done at all times, but he is always wrong.

It is unnecessary for me, therefore, to say, that I entirely agree with all you have written about France, and I shall be careful to use no word in a contrary spirit.

I am not, however, sorry to see the country fairly frightened about foreign affairs. 1st, because it is well, that the mind of the nation should be diverted from that morbid spirit of domestic change and criticism, which has ruled us too much for the last forty years, and that the reign of priggism should terminate. It has done its work, and in its generation very well, but there is another spirit abroad now, and it is time that there shd. be.

2nd, because I am persuaded that any reconstruction of our naval and military systems, that is practicable, will, on the whole, be favorable to the aristocracy, by wh. I mean particularly the proprietors of land: and 3rdly because I do not think the present party in power are well qualified to deal with the external difficulties wh. await them.

I cannot believe, that the conference, tho' peaceable, will be satisfactory, because I understand we are to relinquish all we fought for; and because I am persuaded that Russia will make another move on the board in about six months' time.

Moreover, tho' I do not believe in an American war, I think the U.S. are going to worry us. Their reduction of their over-moderate armaments means nothing. Were there hostilities bet[wee]n U.K. and U.S., they trust to privateering mainly for their naval offence, and their military institutions are of such a character, that they can create a powerful army as quickly as Germany. The Militia system of U.S. was always first-rate, or, in the revolt, our Generals would not have been beaten by a Militia Colonel !

I think the Government, with the information wh. they possessed, were not justified in their reductions; that they

completely blundered the business when the crisis arrived;
and that they do not comprehend our present position. On
all these points I shall attack them, and I shall not discourage
the country. And I hope you will not. With all your admirable prudence, I always maintain you were really the
boldest Minister that ever managed our external affairs.
Witness the Luxemburg guarantee! the way in wh. you
baffled Russia about Crete, when you were left alone; and the
Abyssinian expedition—all successful and eminently successful, but daring. *Macte tuâ virtute!*

When Parliament met, Disraeli attacked the Government on the lines of his letter to Derby. While he promised full support for any measures they might propose to
increase our military strength, he repeated that an armed
neutrality might have prevented war and would certainly
shorten it. But how could such a policy be adopted
by a country without armaments? An armed neutrality
was a very serious thing for a nation that for a year and
a half had been disbanding its veterans; a nation with
skeleton battalions and attenuated squadrons, bat-
teries without sufficient guns, and yet more guns than
gunners; a nation without a military reserve; a nation,
moreover, which had left off shipbuilding, reduced its
crews and its stores, and failed to furnish artillery for
its men-of-war. This was our plight when we were faced
with an upheaval, the magnitude of which was fully
realised by Disraeli's vivid imagination.

Let me impress upon the attention of the House the character of this war between France and Germany. It is no
common war, like the war between Prussia and Austria,
or like the Italian war in which France was engaged some
years ago; nor is it like the Crimean War. This war represents
the German revolution, a greater political event than the
French revolution of last century. I don't say a greater, or
as great a social event. What its social consequences may
be are in the future. Not a single principle in the management of our foreign affairs, accepted by all statesmen for
guidance up to six months ago, any longer exists. There is
not a diplomatic tradition which has not been swept away.
You have a new world, new influences at work, new and
unknown objects and dangers with which to cope, at present
involved in that obscurity incident to novelty in such affairs.

We used to have discussions in this House about the balance of power. Lord Palmerston, eminently a practical man, trimmed the ship of State and shaped its policy with a view to preserve an equilibrium in Europe. . . . But what has really come to pass ? The balance of power has been entirely destroyed, and the country which suffers most, and feels the effects of this great change most, is England.

The result of this destruction of the balance of power was Russia's repudiation of the Treaty of 1856. Russia had a policy which, if inevitably disturbing, was legitimate and not blameworthy. She wished to get to the sea. Disraeli maintained that she had already accomplished her object, and had admirable harbours. But her further policy, to obtain Constantinople, he pronounced to be illegitimate, like the French claim to have the Rhine. She had no moral claim to Constantinople; she did not represent the race to which it once belonged; she had two capitals already, and a third would produce a dislocation of the general arrangement of her population. This was the policy which we fought the Crimean War to frustrate; and now the object for which we made serious sacrifices of valuable lives and treasure was to be treated as moonshine and given up in the Conference.

The line which Gladstone and the Government took in answer to this argument was to assert that Palmerston and Clarendon never believed that the neutralisation of the Black Sea could last long, that they said so at the time to diplomatists and in private conversation with friends, and that in consequence they did not attach serious value or importance to that part of the treaty. Lord Morley seems to accept these stories as credible and conclusive. Disraeli, however, powerfully pointed out in a subsequent debate[1] that England could have obtained all the other stipulations of the Treaty of Paris at the Conference of Vienna in the spring of 1855; but that Palmerston and Clarendon, supported by the country, did not hesitate to fight for another year rather than make peace without

[1] Feb. 24.

obtaining the neutrality of the Black Sea. And yet
Ministers were prepared ' to impute to statesmen of great
eminence, and now unfortunately departed, opinions
not only which they did not hold, but which were contrary to their convictions, which contradicted their
whole policy, and which would intimate that public
men of the highest distinction who proposed a policy,
in enforcing which the treasure of the country was
expended without stint, and the most precious lives of
the country were sacrificed, were laughing in their
sleeves at the excitement of the nation.' Disraeli suggested that those who took Palmerston's private remarks
about public affairs too seriously forgot that that eminent
man was a master of banter, and disliked discussions of
grave matters when not in his cabinet or in the House of
Commons.

Gladstone, with a deplorable lack of humour, had
adduced the fact that he had himself expressed in the
House in 1856 the confident conviction that it was impossible to maintain the neutralisation of the Black Sea,
as evidence of the view taken by the country at the
time. Disraeli reminded him that he was then not a
Minister, nor even leader of Opposition, but the most
unpopular member of ' a minute coterie of distinguished
men who had no following in the country,' and whose
lukewarmness and hesitation were supposed to have been
responsible for the Crimean War. It is no wonder that
Gladstone winced under this attack. ' The Premier
was like a cat on hot bricks,' wrote a looker-on, ' and
presented a striking contrast to Disraeli; for Disraeli cuts
up a Minister with as much *sang-froid* as an anatomist cuts
up a frog. Gladstone could hardly keep his seat. He
fidgeted, took a quire of notes, sent for blue books and
water, turned down corners, and " hear-heared " ironically,
or interrupted his assailant to make a denial of one of his
statements, or to ask the page of a quotation so frequently
that Disraeli had to protest once or twice by raising his
eyebrows or shrugging his shoulders. And when Glad-

stone rose, you could see that every stroke of Disraeli's had gone home.   He was in a white passion, and almost choked with words, frequently pausing to select the harshest to be found.'

Disraeli satisfactorily vindicated Palmerston and Clarendon, and the *bona fides* of British policy in 1855 and 1856, but he observed a discreet silence about his own personal opinion at the time, which he did not indeed obtrude in those years in debate, but to which he had given frequent vent in the *Press*.   As may be remembered[1] he, like Gladstone, then thought that too much stress was laid on Black Sea neutralisation, and that restrictions on the amount of naval force to be maintained by a Sovereign Power were illusory guarantees.   So they had proved in this case to be, and the Conference of London buried them decently to the accompaniment of a special protocol recording that it was ' an essential principle of the law of nations that no Power can liberate itself from the engagements of a treaty, nor modify the stipulations thereof, unless with the consent of the contracting Powers by means of an amicable arrangement.'   But the example of Russia's success proved more powerful than a paper protocol.   In 1908 Austria, one of the signatories of the protocol, repudiated an integral portion of the Treaty of Berlin, just as Russia in 1870 had repudiated an integral portion of the Treaty of Paris; and, under the threat of Germany in shining armour, Russia, the Power disregarded in 1908, and Europe acquiesced, without even providing a conference to give the repudiated clauses decent burial.

What Disraeli said in the debate on the Address about America was almost as noteworthy as what he said about the Franco-Prussian War and the Russian thunderbolt. The claims of the United States against Great Britain, arising out of the American Civil War, were still unsettled; and, in consequence, the then customary licence of American public men in speaking of this country had

[1] See Vol. IV., ch. 1.

exceeded all bounds, even the President himself and the
Chairman of the Foreign Affairs Committee of the Senate
having joined in it. As Gladstone gracefully confessed
in the debate, ' the course of forbearance and prudence '
that Disraeli pursued during the Civil War entitled him,
if any man, to be a critic in this matter without offence;
and his criticism was very plain and timely. The American tone towards Great Britain, he said, was not, as he
once thought, an instance of ' the rude simplicity of Republican manners '; because the American Government
could be courteous enough to other Powers, such as
Russia or Germany. It was only to Great Britain that
they were insolent and offensive; and it was because
they believed that they could adopt this attitude with
impunity. It might be a mere electioneering game;
but Disraeli uttered an impressive warning.

The danger is this—they habitually excite the passions of
millions, and some unfortunate thing happens, or something
unfortunate is said in either country ; the fire lights up, it is
beyond their control, and the two nations are landed in a
contest which they can no longer control or prevent. . . .
Though I should look upon it as the darkest hour of my life
if I were to counsel or even support in this House a war with
the United States, still the United States should know that
they are not an exception to the other countries of the world;
that we do not permit ourselves to be insulted by any other
country in the world, and that they cannot be an exception.
If once . . . it is known that Her Majesty's dominions
cannot be assaulted without being adequately defended,
all this rowdy rhetoric, which is addressed to irresponsible
millions, and as it is supposed with impunity, will cease.

Gladstone had come triumphantly through the first two
sessions of the 1868 Parliament, and had carried three
great Acts—the Irish Church Act, the Irish Land Act, and
the Education Act—in such a manner as to enhance
even his Parliamentary reputation, and to confirm the
position of his Government. The session of 1871
saw a change. Russia's high-handed action appeared
to show that Great Britain under Gladstone enjoyed
no particular consideration in Europe, and his acqui-

escence in Russian demands, thinly disguised under the paraphernalia of a conference, hurt British self-respect and disposed people to look critically upon the other proceedings of his Government. And partly through ill-luck, but mainly through Ministerial ineptitude, there was much to criticise. Disraeli accordingly became more active, and began those mordant and deftly aimed attacks which were eventually to bring the Ministry to the ground.

First of all, the Minister who had persuaded Parliament to discard the principles it cherished for England in order to pacify Ireland, and who had in the winter testified to his belief in the success of his policy by releasing the Fenians still in prison, came nevertheless to Parliament, for the third year in succession, for repressive legislation. The motion which the Chief Secretary made was for a secret Committee to inquire into the condition of an Irish county, Westmeath, where life was rendered intolerable by gross and constant outrages. Disraeli's taunts went home.

The right hon. gentleman [Gladstone] persuaded the people of England that with regard to Irish politics he was in possession of the philosopher's stone. Well, Sir, he has been returned to this House with an immense majority, with the object of securing the tranquillity and content of Ireland. Has anything been grudged him ? Time, labour, devotion— whatever has been demanded has been accorded, whatever has been proposed has been carried. Under his influence and at his instance we have legalised confiscation, consecrated sacrilege, condoned high treason; we have destroyed churches, we have shaken property to its foundation, and we have emptied gaols; and now he cannot govern a county without coming to a Parliamentary Committee ! The right hon. gentleman, after all his heroic exploits, and at the head of his great majority, is making government ridiculous.

To Sir Stafford Northcote.[1]

GROSVENOR GATE, *Mar.* 10, '71.—We have had some disquietude since you left us, and nearly a ministerial crisis.

[1] Who was at Washington, as one of the Commissioners to negotiate the *Alabama* treaty.

Gladstone astonished us all by proposing a secret Committee on some Irish counties, where anarchy is rampant and spreading. It seemed, for four and twenty hours, that the Government must have been beaten: and I was obliged to leave the House with Hardy and between 50 and 60 of our friends to prevent a catastrophe, or something approaching one. However, affairs now are calm again, tho' the unpopularity of the Government, both in and out of the House, [is] daily increasing. If we only had fifty more votes, I could and would turn them out, but in the present state of affairs, they must remain.

Politics seem also interesting in your part of the world, and the expulsion of Sumner [1] from the seat of his ceaseless mischief and malice seems to promise for the success of your mission.

If U.S. would give in their adhesion to the Paris Declaration,[2] my objections to that unwise document would certainly be mitigated, tho' I shall always regret that shallow surrender to waning Cobdenism. I could not however sanction the principle of private property at sea, and I do not believe, in the present state of the public mind, it would go down. There is a rising feeling that stringent maritime rights are the best, perhaps only, check and counterpoise against the military monarchies of the Continent. . . .

The Army Bill does not get on; the Radicals begin to think that, after doing away with purchase, they will have as aristocratic an army as before.

In the next place Lowe, whose Budgets Disraeli scornfully qualified as ' harum-scarum,' produced his most harum-scarum Budget of all. Having an estimated deficit, due to additional military expenditure, of £2,700,000, Lowe proposed to meet it by a tax on matches, an increase of the succession duties, and an increase of 10s. 8d. per cent. (slightly over $1\frac{1}{4}$d. in the pound) in the income tax. Rich and poor were alike disgusted. Popular discontent compelled the Government incontinently to drop the match-tax; the Whigs brought pressure to bear to prevent the increase of the succession duties; and finally Gladstone announced that Ministers would put the whole burden on the income tax, which would be increased by 2d.   On ' the

[1] Sumner was deposed this spring from the chairmanship of the Committee of the Senate on Foreign Relations.
[2] The Declaration of Paris in 1856 about maritime war.

sweet simplicity ' of this proposal Disraeli was justifiably severe, and in many felicitous speeches held up
the Budget, the Chancellor of the Exchequer, and the
Government, to scorn and ridicule. The income tax was
essentially an emergency or war tax; it was monstrous,
when your proposed indirect taxes had proved unpopular,
to fall back on direct taxation for the whole amount of
the deficiency. It was equally monstrous to charge the
Opposition, who had the support of only one newspaper
in London, with ' hounding on ' the country, and to
attribute to their machinations the pecuniary difficulties
in which the Government were involved.

The mortality among Government Bills was prodigious.
Out of more than 130, the chronicler in the *Annual
Register* tells us, the University Tests Bill alone, with
some trifling exceptions, passed into law in its original
shape. Two Bills of first-class importance—Bruce's
Licensing Bill and Goschen's Local Government Bill—
proved so unpopular, the one in the boroughs, the
other in the counties, that they were withdrawn before second reading. Confidence in the administration of the navy was shaken by the capsizing of our
newest battleship, the *Captain*, and in that of the
army by the postponement of manœuvres owing to the
anticipation of rainy weather ! Important business
was thrust aside in order to push forward a Ballot Bill,
to which Gladstone was a very recent convert. ' Why,'
asked Disraeli, ' is all this old stuff brought before us ?
Only because the Prime Minister has been suddenly
converted to an expiring faith, and has passionately
embraced a corpse.' It was all, he said, part of a system,
the object of which was to oppress and alarm the public
mind by constant changes. New methods of Government, new principles of property, every subject that could
agitate the mind of nations, had been brought forward
and patronised until the country, anxious and harassed,
knew not what to expect. There might have been a
plausible case, he maintained, for the ballot in the past,

in the days of Old Sarum and Gatton.   But now that
the franchise was recognised to be a privilege and not
a trust, it was a retrograde step to divorce political life
from publicity.   The Bill, obstructed by Conservative
free-lances—Beresford Hope, James Lowther, and the
Bentincks—in the Commons, was defeated in the Lords.

The principal measure of the session, Cardwell's Army
Regulation Bill, was indeed passed into law in a truncated
form; but not until the Prime Minister, irritated by a
dilatory resolution in the Lords, had invoked the prerogative to effect the main alteration proposed, the abolition of
the system by which officers purchased their promotion.
The system had grown up under Royal Warrant, and the
Queen was in the end advised to terminate it by Royal
Warrant, but only after the greater part of the session
had been occupied in the effort to terminate it by the
clauses of a Bill.   So far as Cardwell's measure was
calculated to effect a reorganisation of all our military
forces, and to create a reserve by short service, Disraeli
supported it; and he did not even oppose the abolition of
purchase; though he rather doubted whether there was a
really strong feeling on the subject in the country, and
whether a system of selection would give us the officers
we wanted.   But he unhesitatingly disapproved the *coup
d'état* by which Ministers attained their object.   It was
part of ' an avowed and shameful conspiracy against the
privileges ' of the House of Lords.   He did not dispute
the prerogative of the Crown; but the prerogative should
not be used to cut the Gordian knots that have to be
encountered in dealing with popular assemblies.   ' No
Minister acts in a wise manner who, finding himself
baffled in passing a measure, . . . comes forward and
tells the House that he will defy the opinion of Parliament,
and appeals to the prerogative of the Crown to assist
him in the difficulties which he himself has created.'
Public opinion supported Disraeli in this protest against
the manner in which an otherwise popular reform was
carried.

To Montagu Corry.

HUGHENDEN, *Sept.* 17, '71.—. . . I am sorry to find we shall not have you for our harvest home, which is on the 26th. Lancashire hangs fire. They themselves only propose the end of January, or the first week in February. I would not, under any circumstances, involve myself in such distant engagements, and I am still very doubtful, whether affairs are yet ripe enough for the move: in spite of Truro.[1] I have answered Lancashire in your name, not extinguishing all hope.

We have never left Hughenden for a moment. Enjoying a summer of unbroken brilliancy: Miladi very well indeed. . . .

Meyer de Rothschild continues his year of triumphs,[2] and Bucks is proud of having the first stable in the country. . . . Lord Russell is going abroad for a year, and shall not return for Parliament 'unless,' he adds, ' Mr. Gladstone attempts to abolish the House of Lords.' He has become quite deaf, but my informant tells me most agreeable and entertaining, because, as he can hear no one talk, he never ceases to talk himself. But when he is exhausted, he is bored, and you must go. . . .

In the course of this year 1871, as Lord Morley tells us, ' a wave of critical feeling began to run upon the throne.'[3] The seclusion which the Queen had practised since the death of her husband was not unnaturally resented by her people; and her Prime Minister repeatedly pressed her to increase the number of her public appearances. Neither Minister nor people quite realised the physical weakness which at this period made it impossible for Her Majesty to add, to the unceasing and laborious duties which she was bound to perform of government behind the scenes, those ceremonial displays which make much more demand upon the strength than can be easily understood by private individuals, whose modest position exempts them from the tiring experience. Disraeli had the knowledge and insight which others lacked; and he took the opportunity of the harvest festival at Hughenden to explain what the state of the Queen's health was, and how conscientiously in spite of weakness she carried on the most material part of her work.

---

[1] The Conservatives won a seat at Truro in a by-election this month.
[2] On the turf.   [3] *Gladstone*, Bk. VI., ch. 10.

The health of the Queen has for several years been a subject of anxiety to those about her, but it is only within the last year that the country generally has become acquainted with the gravity of that condition.   I believe I may say that there is some improvement in Her Majesty's health, but I fear a long time must elapse before it will reach that average condition which she has for some time enjoyed, and I do not think we can conceal from ourselves that a still longer time must elapse before Her Majesty will be able to resume the performance of those public and active duties which it was once her pride and pleasure to fulfil, because they brought her into constant and immediate contact with her people.   The fact is we cannot conceal from ourselves that Her Majesty is physically incapacitated from performing those duties, but it is some consolation to Her Majesty's subjects to know that, in the performance of those much higher duties which Her Majesty is called upon to perform she is still remarkable for a punctuality and a precision which have never been surpassed, and rarely equalled, by any monarch of these realms.

A very erroneous impression is prevalent respecting the duties of the Sovereign of this country.   Those duties are multifarious; they are weighty, and they are unceasing. I will venture to say that no head of any department in the State performs more laborious duties than fall to the Sovereign of this country.   There is not a despatch received from abroad nor one sent from this country which is not submitted to the Queen.   The whole internal administration of this country greatly depends upon the sign manual; and of our present Sovereign it may be said that her signature has never been placed to any public document of which she did not know the purport and of which she did not approve.   Those Cabinet Councils of which you all hear, and which are necessarily the scene of anxious and important deliberations, are reported and communicated on their termination by the Minister to the Sovereign, and they often call from her critical remarks, necessarily requiring considerable attention.   And I will venture to add that no person likely to administer the affairs of this country would treat the suggestions of Her Majesty with indifference, for at this moment there is probably no person living in this country who has such complete control over the political traditions of England as the Sovereign herself.   The last generation of statesmen have all, or almost all, disappeared: the Sir Robert Peels, the Lord Derbys, the Lord Palmerstons have gone; and there is no person who can advise Her Majesty, or is likely to advise Her Majesty in the times in which we live, who can have such a complete mastery of what has occurred in this country, and of all the great and important affairs of State, foreign and domestic, for the last thirty-four years, as the Queen herself.   He, therefore, would not be a wise man who would not profit by Her Majesty's judgment and experience. . . .

I would venture, in conclusion, to remind those whom I address that, although Her Majesty may be, and often is, of great service and assistance to her servants, there never was a more Constitutional Sovereign than our present Queen. All who have served her would admit that, when Ministers have been selected by her in deference to what she believed to be the highest interests of the State in the opinion of the country, she gives to them a complete confidence and un-deviating support.   But although there never was a Sove-reign who would more carefully avoid arrogating to herself any power or prerogative which the Constitution does not authorise, so I would add there never was a Sovereign more jealous, or more wisely jealous, of the prerogatives which the Constitution has allotted to her, because she believes they are for the welfare of her people.

The effect of Disraeli's words was unfortunately marred by a slip which he made in speaking—a slip which party malice magnified and distorted.   He said that the Queen was ' physically *and morally* incapacitated ' from perform-ing her duties of ceremonial and pageant.   It was not a happy phrase and he immediately recalled it; but it gave no real foundation for the legend that was promptly circulated, to the effect that the Opposition leader had declared the Queen to be mentally incapacitated for her work.   Even the Queen herself was disturbed, and Disraeli had to explain.

To Sir William [Jenner].[1]

[*Oct.,* 1871.]—. . . I need not assure you that the epithet *moral* involves *mental* no more than the epithet *physical* does.   What I meant to convey was that neither Her Majesty's frame nor feelings could at present bear the strain and burthen of the pageantry of State.

After I had used the word it was suggested to me that it might be misinterpreted by the simple, and I requested the reporters to omit it.   I understood they willingly agreed to

---

[1] The letter is printed from a draft, but it is fairly clear that Jenner, Her Majesty's physician, is the ' Sir William ' to whom it was addressed.

do so; but it seems the *Daily Telegraph* could not resist the opportunity of attempting a sensation.

The whole Press of authority, *Times, Post, Standard, Pall Mall, Daily News, Spectator, Saturday Review, Echo,* have denounced, or utterly disregarded, the interpretation of the *Telegraph*, which the country have not accepted and have felt to be quite inconsistent with the whole tenor of my observations.

I need not say how deeply I regret that any expression of mine should have occasioned pain to Her Majesty, especially when my only object in speaking was an humble endeavor to assist the Queen. . . .

A selection from Disraeli's letters throws some light on his interests during the autumn and winter of this year, the later weeks of which were a period of acute anxiety, owing to the dangerous illness of the Prince of Wales from typhoid fever.

To the Duke of Wellington.

[? *Oct.*, 1871.]—. . . I was detained in town for three days with my time greatly to myself, and I spent it in examining and then partly perusing these 3 volumes [of the Wellington Despatches and Memoranda]—with such keen interest, with so much delight, I may say, that I cannot refrain from expressing to you, however imperfectly, my sense of their inestimable value. They form out-and-out much the most interesting political book that has been published in this century. Indeed I know of no memoirs of a great leading character, either in civil or military life, in any age or language, that I can place above them. The importance of the subjects treated, their immense variety, the striking events, the marked and historic character of the correspondents, the towering greatness of the chief actor, make a whole, so far as my knowledge can guide me, unrivalled.

It would be useless to select portions or passages, yet if I had to name a composition which, alike in conception and execution, may vie with anything in classic pages, it is the letter of the Duke recommending the appointment of Mr. Canning to the King. Nothing more noble and nothing more skilful was ever penned by man, and one feels, as one reads it, that it must have raised and re-established, at least for the moment, the lax and shattered moral tone of the individual to whom it was addressed.

All about Canning subsequently, all about poor Castlereagh's sad and I fear disgraceful end, are most dramatic.

That is the character of the volumes. They are full of life, and stirring life. The papers on the campaign, on the state of Spain and so on, all beyond praise.

The effect of reading these volumes on me is this: that although my time for the past is now very limited, I shall certainly read the whole of your great father's works: a volume will always be at hand when I have time to recur to what has gone before us.

The country owes you a debt of gratitude not easily to be repaid for the publication of this book.

To Lord Henry Lennox.

GROSVENOR GATE, *Nov.* 3, '71.—I thought your speech thoroughly capital: out-and-out, the star of the recess. I have not read Gladstone's.[1] I tried, but I could not get on with it: not a ray of intellect or a gleam of eloquence. They tell me that, if I had persevered, I should have been repaid, by encountering a quotation from the Hyde Park Litany; either a burlesque of the Athanasian Creed or of the National Anthem; equally appropriate in the mouth of our most religious and loyal ruler. . . .

To Montagu Corry.

HUGHENDEN, *Dec.* 4, '71.—. . . Our camp is struck, and, probably in 8 and 40 hours, we shall be settled permanently at G.G. The stable goes up to-morrow. The severe and savage weather, that prevents all outdoor employment, quite sickened my lady, who had trusted to planting and marking trees to amuse her. Now she sighs for Park Lane, and twilight talk and tea. The Canford party rather precipitated her resolve, but the prospect even of that being put off will not now change affairs here. . . .

We have received telegrams from Sandringham every morning, and generally speaking Francis Knollys[2] has written by post with details which telegrams cannot convey. Our telegram this morning the most favorable we have yet received, and the second post, which brought your letter, brought also one from F. K.

They are still very nervous at Sandringham, and very cautious in their language, but it is evident to me, that they think they have turned the corner. . . .

[1] Gladstone's famous speech of two hours in the open air at Blackheath, in the course of which he quoted, with approval, from a republican and secularist book of poems, a parody of the National Anthem.
[2] Private Secretary to the Prince of Wales, and subsequently to King Edward and King George; now Viscount Knollys.

To Gathorne Hardy.

GROSVENOR GATE, *Dec.* 23, 1871.—I had seen Noel[1] before I received your letter, and had given him the same answer as you had done.   Great wits, etc.

The proposition is absurd.   We cannot modify the position we have taken up on the Ballot, tho' many of our friends may wish to do so.   It wd. break up the party, which is in a tolerably robust state at present.

What we shd. do, is to get the Bill thro' our House with as much promptitude as decency permits.   The Govt. wd. like to keep it there and distract attention from other matters. Our policy is the reverse.

There must be a discussion on the principle, but it need not be a prolonged one, and, in Comm[itt]ee, we shd. confine ourselves to *bona fide* improvements of its machinery, wh. may be the foundation, if fortune favored us, of a future compromise.

We are here rather unexpectedly, having been stopped in our progress to country houses by the impending calamity, and being too anxious to return to Hughenden; and now, in a few days, we shall have to fulfil some of these engagements, so I don't think we shall return to Bucks. . . .

[1] One of the Whips.

CHAPTER IV.

LOTHAIR.

1869–1870.

In 1869 Disraeli had some real leisure, for the first time for many years. When he led the Opposition against Russell, Aberdeen, and Palmerston, it had been in Parliaments where parties were fairly balanced, and a change of Government was always a possibility. In these circumstances the labours of leadership were nearly as onerous in opposition as in office. But, with the large and compact majority of 1868, Gladstone's Government was for the time impregnable; and Disraeli's mind therefore naturally turned to his early love, literature. It was more than twenty years since the publication of his last novel, *Tancred*, in March, 1847; it was nearly twenty years since his last book, *Lord George Bentinck*, in December, 1851; it was more than a dozen years since he had ceased active journalism in the *Press*, in February, 1856. *Tancred* and *Lord George Bentinck* and the articles in the *Press* had still breathed, though not to the extent of his earlier political writing, the spirit of combat and propaganda; they had been the work of one who, though he had risen high, was still fighting for his ideas and for his place. Now he had arrived; he had carried a great historical measure; he had held the highest position under the Crown; his ambition was largely satisfied; and when he began to write again, in his sixty-fifth year, it was in a somewhat different vein. He surveyed the great world of his day, now intimately known by him, and he drew a picture of aristocratic and political society, and of the

ideas animating it, together with the currents of thought
and action which were moulding the history of Europe.
Like the great trilogy of *Coningsby*, *Sybil*, and *Tancred*,
Lothair was a political novel, and a political novel dealing
with the events of the day; unlike them, its underlying
purpose seems to have been subordinated to a desire to
mirror and satirise the passing show.   Unlike them, too,
it observes a reticence, becoming in an ex-Premier, with
regard to the leading figures in the political arena and to
the immediate subjects of acute political dissension.

Different as it was from the trilogy in its outlook, it
was different also in the secrecy in which it was conceived
and written.   ' I make it a rule never to breathe a word
on such matters to anyone,' Disraeli told a literary friend
in 1872.   ' My private secretary, Mr. Montagu Corry,
who possesses my entire confidence in political matters,
who opens all my letters, and enters my cabinet and deals,
as he likes, with all my papers in my absence, never knew
anything about *Lothair* until he read the advertisement
in the journals.'   This was a new practice for Disraeli, as
in regard to the trilogy and to *Lord George Bentinck* he
made confidences about his progress from time to time
to his sister, and to his close friends such as Manners,
Smythe, and Lady Londonderry.   No such sources of
information are available in regard to the composition of
Lothair.   But the incident which suggested the main
action of the story, the reception of the third Marquis of
Bute into the Church of Rome, only took place on Christmas Eve, 1868.   Disraeli had then just resigned office;
and we may therefore confidently look upon the book as
the firstfruits of his retirement.   The stimulus to write
it may well have been provided by the offer of £10,000
for a novel, which was made to him by a publisher
immediately on his resignation, but declined with
thanks.   The book was finished in the spring of 1870.
The arrangement with Longmans for its publication was
made in February of that year, and it appeared at the
beginning of May.

The story of *Lothair* covers almost exactly the period of Disraeli's third tenure of office; it is all comprised between the August of 1866 and the August of 1868; and yet, though a great number of his English characters are more or less politicians, there is no reference to the Reform struggles or to the passage of the Reform Bill, or (save as a matter involving urgent whips) to the debates on the Irish Church; nor is there any personal allusion to the Prime Ministers of the time, first Derby and then Disraeli himself. The political and social movements, the intellectual and spiritual problems, which form the background of Disraeli's story, had in truth little relation with actual proceedings in Westminster Palace. Secret societies and their international energies, the Church of Rome and her claims and methods, the eternal conflict between science and faith : these are the forces shown to be at work beneath the surface of that splendid pageant of English aristocracy in which most of Disraeli's characters move, and which he never described with more brilliance and gusto than in *Lothair*. So brilliant is that description that Froude even asks us to see the true value of the book in its perfect representation of patrician society in England flourishing in its fullest bloom, but, like a flower, opening fully only to fade.

The plot is simple. The hero, one of those fortunate beings whom he loved to paint, an orphan peer—apparently a marquis—of fabulous wealth, brought up and educated quietly in Presbyterian fashion in Scotland, is thrown, as he reaches adolescence, fresh upon the world, first of Oxford, and then of London and the great country houses. The priggishness born of his early education leads him at the outset to say, ' My opinions are already formed on every subject; that is to say, every subject of importance; and, what is more, they will never change.' But he is in reality very impressionable, and anxious to discover, like Tancred, what he ought to do and what he ought to believe. All the influences and all the teachers of the day are naturally concentrated upon one whose adhesion might be expected so materially to benefit any cause which he espoused.   The main struggle is between three forces, represented by three women, with all of whom Lothair falls successively in love.   These forces are, first, the Church of Rome; secondly, the international revolution and what may be called free religion; and thirdly, the Church of England and the round of duties and occupations natural to Lothair's birth and station. Clare Arundel, the representative of the first force, is an attractive and ardent saint; Theodora Campian, the representative of the second force, has great personal charm, lofty character, and high purpose.   But Theodora dies and Clare enters a convent; and the victory is won in the end by the Lady Corisande, the representative of the third force, whose principles are indeed immaculate but who is a somewhat uninteresting heroine.   The action takes place mainly in London and in three English country houses; but the autumn and winter of 1867 are occupied with Lothair's experiences in Rome and the neighbourhood; and the spring of 1868 finds him in those scenes of the Mediterranean and the Holy Land which Disraeli visited as a young man and afterwards lovingly reproduced in so many of his novels.

Nothing in the book is more carefully drawn or more delicately finished than the chapters which deal with the Roman Catholic group of priests and laymen who conspire —the word is hardly too strong—to entrap Lothair into the Roman Church.   The old Catholic English family— Lord St. Jerome, devout and easy in his temper, but an English gentleman to the backbone, who gave at his ball suppers the same champagne that he gave at his dinners; Lady St. Jerome, an enthusiastic convert, ' a woman to inspire crusaders,' who received Lothair at a party ' with extreme unction'; and their beautiful niece, Clare Arundel, who could only be weaned from the convent in which her hopes had centred by the vision of attracting Lothair through marriage into the true fold: and then the priests—Father Coleman, whose devotion to gardening masked his skill as a controversialist; Monsignore Catesby, the aristocratic and fashionable missionary of the Church to convert the upper classes; Monsignore Berwick, the priest as statesman, the favourite pupil of Antonelli; and Cardinal Grandison, a wonderful study of asceticism, devotion, high breeding, tact, delicacy, and unscrupulousness, whose appearance and manner were copied from Manning, though some of his mental and moral characteristics may be referred to Wiseman. ' It seemed that the soul never had so frail and fragile a tenement' as his attenuated form; 'I never eat and I never drink,' he said in refusing an invitation to dinner. One marked feature in his character was that he was ' an entire believer in female influence, and a considerable believer in his influence over females.'

Disraeli was at once attracted and repelled by Rome. Her historical tradition and her sensuous and ceremonial worship appealed strongly to one side of his nature; but he was even more keenly alive to the bondage which she imposed upon the spirit of man, and he had been of late particularly impressed by the stealthy and indirect methods which her propaganda in England had assumed. He had had a personal experience of a disagreeable but revealing character in the ' stab in the back' which Manning and the Roman party had given him over the question of University education. Both the attraction and the repulsion are brought out in *Lothair*. The description of the service of *Tenebrœ* in Holy Week at Vauxe, the St. Jeromes' country house, is such as to satisfy the emotions of a devout Roman Catholic; the St. Jerome family life and Clare's aspirations are sympathetically treated; and there is no lack of appreciation of the enormous support the Roman Church affords to that religious element in man which he held it to be essential to foster.

On the other hand, a large portion of the book is occupied by a merciless dissection of the various arts employed by Cardinals and Monsignori to entangle

Lothair so deeply in the meshes of Roman influence that conversion might appear to him to be the only honourable outcome.   Begun in London and at Vauxe, continued during the coming-of-age festivities at Muriel Towers, and brought to a climax at Rome after the battle of Mentana, these machinations were so cleverly contrived that their object was within an ace of accomplishment.   Moved by the overpowering personality of Theodora, Lothair had temporarily thrown off their trammels, and had even ranged himself by Garibaldi's side in the advance on Rome in the autumn of 1867.   The return of the French garrison had wrecked the hopes of the enterprise; Theodora was killed; and Lothair himself fell, badly wounded, at Mentana.   A kindly Italian peasant woman of handsome mien brought news of his plight to Clare Arundel, who was in Rome for the winter and occupied in caring for the faithful wounded.   She found him all unconscious in a hospital and nursed him back to life. During his illness a pious legend was evolved; the peasant woman was discovered to be the Virgin Mary, recognised as such by the halo round her head; and it was claimed that Lothair had been fighting, when he fell, on behalf of the Pope instead of against him.   He was induced in his weak state to support Clare in an ecclesiastical function which he believed to be merely one of thanksgiving for recovery, but which the official Papal journal treated as a solemn recognition on his part of the special favour shown by the Mother of God to her chivalrous defender.   The mendacities of the official account drove Lothair, still suffering, and almost a prisoner of the Church in a Roman palace, to a mixture of indignation and despair; but he thought he might rely on Cardinal Grandison as an English gentleman and a man of honour to put the matter right.   He was mistaken; and the description of the conversation between the two is inimitable.

To Lothair's protestations against ' a tissue of falsehood and imposture,' the Cardinal opposed confidence in an ' official journal ' drawn up by ' truly pious men.'   It

was, he said, the ' authentic ' story of what happened at
Mentana; Lothair's own statement, he airily suggested,
had neither confirmation nor probability; ' you have been
very ill, my dear young friend, and labouring under much
excitement.' Such hallucinations were not uncommon,
and would wear off with returning health.

King George IV. believed that he was at the Battle of
Waterloo, and indeed commanded there; and his friends
were at one time a little alarmed; but Knighton, who was a
sensible man, said, ' His Majesty has only to leave off curaçao,
and rest assured he will gain no more victories.'

Lothair must remember, the Cardinal continued, that he
was in the centre of Christendom, the abode of truth.
' Divine authority has perused this paper and approved
it. . . . It records the most memorable event of the
century.' The appearance of the Virgin in Rome had
given the deathblow to atheism and the secret societies;
Lothair must return to England and reconquer it for
Rome. The eye of Christendom was upon him. He
might be bewildered like St. Thomas, but like him
he would become an apostle. The Holy Father would
personally receive him next day into the bosom of the
Church.

In spite of all the Cardinal's arts, a vision of Theodora
at night in the Coliseum—Disraeli was partial to visions
as a melodramatic resource—saved Lothair from the
priests; and the Cardinal, when he met him afterwards
in London, affected complete unconsciousness as to the
intrigue in Rome, and even suggested to him that he
should attend the approaching Ecumenical Council as an
Anglican !

The revolutionary characters in *Lothair* are almost as
closely studied, in themselves, and in their setting, as the
Roman. With the Revolution as with Rome Disraeli,
who claimed once that he had a revolutionary mind, had
a certain sympathy, which, though it did not blind him to
the impossible nature of the creed, enabled him to understand it. Theodora herself is certainly his most elabor-

ately conceived heroine. Seen by Lothair first at an evening party, her face is thus described: ' It was the face of a matron, apparently of not many summers, for her shapely figure was still slender, though her mien was stately. . . . The countenance . . . pale, but perfectly Attic in outline, with the short upper lip and the round chin, and a profusion of dark chestnut hair bound by a Grecian fillet, and on her brow a star.' She had sat for the head of ' La République Française ' in 1850, as a girl of seventeen, and was therefore well over thirty when she met Lothair in the autumn of 1866. She was the wife of an American Colonel, with a villa at Putney. An Italian by birth, she was an ardent sympathiser with movements for freedom throughout the world; but for the unity of her native country and the destruction of Papal govern- ment in Rome she was prepared to give her life. Dr. Garnett has happily observed that ' she impersonates all the traits which Shelley especially valued in woman,' and that she was also her creator's ideal. ' There is not a single touch of satire in the portrait; it plainly represents the artist's highest conception of woman.' A hater of priests and priestcraft, Theodora is yet strongly religious in her idealistic way. Orthodoxy, she holds, has very little to do with religion; ' I worship,' she tells Lothair, ' in a church where I believe God dwells, and dwells for my guidance and my good: my conscience.' The romantic adoration, free from all sensual taint, with which she inspires Lothair is drawn with great delicacy. Indeed ' the exquisite and even sublime friendship, which had so strongly and beautifully arisen, like a palace in a dream, and absorbed his being,' was a sentiment of which the author was himself capable, at all stages of his life.

As Theodora represents the ideal side of the revolu- tionary movement, so Captain Bruges embodies the practical side. His career corresponds to, and may have been copied from, that of General Cluseret, the military commander who was so prominent in the Paris Commune. Bruges's common sense and resolution shine amid the

mouthings of the revolutionary council in Soho and the
turmoil of the Fenian meeting in Hoxton; and when he
takes command of the camp in the Apennines he appears
as a true leader of men, bold, wary, and unscrupulous.
His mission is to be the sword-arm of the secret societies,
Mary Anne of France and Madre Natura of Italy.

From a very early date, Disraeli had been deeply
impressed by the widespread activities of the secret
societies in Europe. He drew special attention to the
danger in *Lord George Bentinck* and in his speeches in the
House of Commons on the Italian question. During his
recent term of office, Irish and Irish-American Fenianism
had to be met and defeated; and the information that
then poured in upon the Government confirmed and
extended his previous knowledge of revolutionary con-
spiracies. Of all this he made full use in *Lothair*.
Reviewers accused him of gross exaggeration, of conjuring
up imaginary perils; Mary Anne, though referred to in the
protocols of Paris in 1856, was treated as a bogey. But
within a year the outbreak of the Paris Commune, with
its revelation of the malign workings of the International
Society, showed how thoroughly well justified were the
apprehensions of Disraeli's Monsignori and diplomatists,
and the boasts of his revolutionaries. Catesby says of the
secret societies: ' They have declared war against the
Church, the State, and the domestic principle. All the
great truths and laws on which the family reposes are
denounced. Their religion is the religion of science.'
The French Ambassador declares that the Mary Anne
associations in France were all alive and astir. ' Mary
Anne,' he explains, ' was the real name for the Republic
years ago, and there always was a sort of myth that these
societies had been founded by a woman. . . . The word
has gone out to all these societies that Mary Anne has
returned, and will issue her orders, which must be obeyed.'
And Bruges, the revolutionary general, confirms the
representatives of authority. ' There are more secret
societies at this moment than at any period since '85,

though you hear nothing of them; and they believe in
Mary Anne, and in nothing else.' He anticipates, moreover, and defends the policy of arson which the Commune
employed, to the world's horror, in Paris in the spring of
1871. He is speaking of Rome. 'Those priests! I
fluttered them once. Why did I spare any ? Why did
I not burn down St. Peter's ? I proposed it.' There was
something to be said for Monsignore Berwick's ejacula-
tion: 'It is the Church against the secret societies. They
are the only two strong things in Europe, and will
survive kings, emperors, or parliaments.'

When Disraeli dealt with his third set of influences, those
springing from English society and the Anglican Communion, he painted with some boldness from people he knew
and personal and family circumstances which had come
directly under his observation. The plot was suggested by
Lord Bute's recent conversion to Rome; and Bute's history was faithfully followed in Lothair's vast fortune and
long minority, in his elaborate coming-of-age festivities,
in his relations with Monsignore Capel (called in the book
Catesby, but 'Capel' appeared by a slip in one passage
in the original issue), and even in the ducal family where
he went to seek a bride. But Lothair was not received
into the Church of Rome, and Bute in the end married a
lady who was not a daughter of 'the duke' of the novel.
Nor did Lothair resemble Bute in appearance, character,
or tastes. Indeed Lothair is given so little character,
save that of general candour, openness, and desire to do
right, coupled with a trifle of priggishness, that Sir Leslie
Stephen is almost justified in his remark that 'Lothair
reduces himself so completely to a mere " passive bucket "
to be pumped into by every variety of teacher, that he is
unpleasantly like a fool.'

If the hero's circumstances almost directly reproduced
Bute's, there is a still closer resemblance between 'the
duke' of *Lothair* and his family, and a duke and his
family who were numbered among Disraeli's friends.
'Lord Abercorn has thirteen children,' wrote Disraeli in

1863 to Mrs. Willyams after meeting the Abercorns at
Hatfield; ' and looks as young as his son who is an M.P. . . .
His daughters are so singularly pretty that they always
marry during their first season, and always make the most
splendid matches.' So of the ducal family described in
the early pages of *Lothair* we are told that the sons and
daughters reproduced the appearance and character of
their parents, and the daughters ' all met the same fate.
After seventeen years of a delicious home, they were
presented and immediately married.' The Duke of
Abercorn, who obtained his dukedom on Disraeli's recommendation, was one of the handsomest men of the day;
and society enjoyed the gentle raillery which wrote of
' the duke ': ' Every day when he looked into the glass,
and gave the last touch to his consummate toilette,[1] he
offered his grateful thanks to Providence that his family
was not unworthy of him.'   That the family so graciously
characterised by Disraeli was not unworthy has since
been abundantly shown by the distinguished place its
members have occupied in the political and social world.
But Disraeli has dowered the dukedom of Abercorn with
all, and more than all, the then possessions of that of
Sutherland.   Brentham must be Trentham, and Crecy
House in London Stafford House.

From Montagu Corry.

Admiralty, *Sept.* 22, 1868.—. . . He (Lord Bute)
is going to Baronscourt next month, it is evident rather as a
claimant of his bride than as a suitor.   Evidently the whole
matter is already arranged.   But still, I fear, that his joining
himself to the ' scarlet woman '—and soon too—is equally
certain.

Fergusson says that no ingenuity can counteract the influence which certain priests and prelates have over him,
chief among them being Monsignore Capel. The speedy
result is inevitable, and the consummation is only delayed
till he has won his bride. . . .

---

[1] Disraeli eldom committed the artistic mistake of reproducing the
character and habits of his original in every de ail. The Duke of Abercorn
was careless about the fit of his clothes.

The Anglican Bishop is clearly taken from Wilberforce; and considering the licence which the Bishop since the autumn of 1868 had permitted himself to use in speaking and writing of Disraeli, is a not unflattering portrait. The Bishop in *Lothair* is described as ' polished and plausible, well-lettered, yet quite a man of the world. He was fond of society, and justified his taste in this respect by the flattering belief that by his presence he was extending the power of the Church; certainly favouring an ambition which could not be described as being moderate.' We are told of his ' gracious mien,' his ' honeyed expressions '; that he was ' a man of contrivance and resolution '; while in his lighter moments he was capable of 'seraphic raillery,' ' angelic jokes,' and ' lambent flashes.' It was when he had made some particularly deadly lunge or parry, in the secret duel for Lothair's soul which was carried on between him and the Cardinal at Muriel Towers, that these playful characteristics were displayed.

The minor characters are as distinctive and amusing as they are wont to be in Disraeli's novels. There is St. Aldegonde, heir to the wealthiest dukedom in the kingdom, but ' a republican of the reddest dye. He was opposed to all privilege, and indeed to all orders of men, except dukes, who were a necessity. He was also strongly in favour of the equal division of all property, except land. Liberty depended upon land, and the greater the landowners the greater the liberty of a country.' He comes down to breakfast in a country house on Sunday morning in a ' shooting jacket of brown velvet and a pink shirt and no cravat,' and, in the presence of the Bishop of the diocese, exclaims ' in a loud voice, and with the groan of a rebellious Titan, " How I hate Sunday !" '

Then there is Mr. Phœbus, the painter, who belongs rather to the revolutionary group than to the panorama of society; a descendant of Gascon nobles, and brilliant, brave, and boastful as they; the prophet of Aryan art against Semitism. ' When Leo the Tenth was Pope,' he says, ' popery was pagan; popery is now Christian, and

art is extinct.' What he admires about the aristocracy
is that they 'live in the air, that they excel in athletic
sports; that they can only speak one language; and that
they never read.' It was the highest education since the
Greek. Nothing could induce him to use paper money;
but he carried about with him on his travels 'several
velvet bags, one full of pearls, another of rubies, another
of Venetian sequins, Napoleons, and golden piastres. "I
like to look at them," said Mr. Phœbus, "and find life
more intense when they are about my person. But bank
notes, so cold and thin, they give me an ague."' He
rented an island in the Ægean where, in the company of his
beautiful Greek wife and her equally attractive sister, he
'pursued a life partly feudal, partly Oriental, partly
Venetian, and partly idiosyncratic'; but, in spite of his
Aryanism, he consented to go to the Holy Land on a commission from the Russian Government to paint Semitic
subjects, moved partly by the reflection, 'They say no one
can draw a camel. If I went to Jerusalem a camel would
at last be drawn.' It was Phœbus who refurbished and
launched the ancient gibe at the critics, as 'the men who
have failed in literature and art.'

Mr. Pinto is another capital sketch; the middle-aged,
oily Portuguese who was one of the marvels of society.
'Instead of being a parasite, everybody flattered him; and
instead of being a hanger-on of society, society hung on
Pinto.' 'He was not an intellectual Crœsus, but his
pockets were full of sixpences.' Here is one of his 'sixpences' in conversation with St. Aldegonde. 'English
is an expressive language, but not difficult to master. Its
range is limited. It consists, as far as I can observe, of
four words: "nice," "jolly," "charming," and "bore."'

Then we have Lord and Lady Clanmorne, 'so good-
looking and agreeable that they were as good at a dinner-
party as a couple of first-rate entrées'; and Apollonia, the
wife of Putney Giles, the prosperous solicitor, whose
principal mission it was to destroy the Papacy and her
lesser impulses to become acquainted with the aristocracy

and to be surrounded by celebrities. Sir William Stirling Maxwell, in congratulating Disraeli, happily singled out ' your remarkable power of painting a character by a single stroke.'

Nor must we forget Mr. Ruby, the Bond Street jeweller, whose conversation with his eminent clients is delightful. He holds forth to Lothair on pearls.

Pearls are troublesome property, my Lord. They require great care; they want both air and exercise; they must be worn frequently; you cannot lock them up. The Duchess of Havant has the finest pearls in the country, and I told her Grace, ' Wear them whenever you can, wear them at breakfast;' and her Grace follows my advice, she does wear them at breakfast. I go down to Havant Castle every year to see her Grace's pearls, and I wipe every one of them myself, and let them lie on a sunny bank in the garden, in a westerly wind, for hours and days together. Their complexion would have been ruined had it not been for this treatment.

Visitors to Hughenden in the latter years of Lady Beaconsfield's life remember how faithfully Disraeli followed Mr. Ruby's advice; how he was wont himself, on sunny days, to bring out his wife's pearls and lay them carefully on the grass by the terrace, so that they might not fail to get the ' air ' which was so important for their complexion.

Scattered here and there throughout the book are many shrewd political appreciations. Take this, of Scotland: ' The Establishment and the Free Kirk are mutually sighing for some compromise which may bring them together again; and if the proprietors would give up their petty patronage, some flatter themselves that it might be arranged.' Disraeli himself was to abolish the ' petty patronage,' and now for several years Presbyterian reunion has been drawing visibly nearer. About Ireland there is naturally more. A revolutionary leader says of the Irish: ' Their treason is a fairy tale, and their sedition a child talking in its sleep '; while a Roman Monsignore tells us that ' the difficulty of Ireland is that the priests and the people will consider everything in a purely Irish point of

view.   To gain some local object, they will encourage the
principles of the most lawless Liberalism, which naturally
land them in Fenianism and atheism.'   The aspirations of
Germany after a fleet are again noted.   In the revolutionary meeting in London the German delegate says: ' The
peoples will never succeed till they have a fleet. . . .   To
have a fleet we rose against Denmark in my country. . . .
The future mistress of the seas is the land of the Viking '—
an odd paraphrase for Germany.   Of Austria Monsignore Berwick says: ' Poor Austria !   Two things made
her a nation : she was German and she was Catholic, and
now she is neither.'   A French diplomatist suggests
to the Monsignore the very settlement of the Roman
question which was actually effected in a few months :
' I wish I could induce you to consider more favourably
that suggestion, that His Holiness should content himself with the ancient city, and, in possession of St.
Peter's and the Vatican, leave the rest of Rome to the
vulgar cares and the mundane anxieties of the transient
generation.'   And the Disraeli of *Sybil* and of the Artisans'
Dwellings Acts speaks through the mouth of Lothair
when he says: ' It seems to me that pauperism is not an
affair so much of wages as of dwellings.   If the working
classes were properly lodged, at their present rate of wages,
they would be richer.   They would be healthier and
happier at the same cost.'

There are of course the oddities of grammar, absurdities
of expression, and exaggerations of fact and of phrase,
which no novel of Disraeli's is without; and in *Lothair*
some readers are put off by the occurrence of a large
proportion of these in the early pages.   But we have also,
what is more to the purpose, an abundance of those apt
phrases, half aphorism half paradox, into which Disraeli
distilled his worldly and other-worldly wisdom.   The
hansom is ' the gondola of London '; Pantheism is
' atheism in domino '; a member of the Church of England
appears to a Roman convert to be ' a Parliamentary
Christian '; an agreeable person is ' a person who agrees

with ' you; at the end of the season ' the baffled hopes
must go to Cowes, and the broken hearts to Baden '; ' the
originality of a subject is in its treatment '; ' the world,
where the future is concerned, is generally wrong ';
' patriotism was a boast and now it is a controversy ';
' to revive faith is more difficult than to create it.'

The joy which Disraeli evinces in the material world, in
natural and artistic beauty, in the dignity and even in the
gauds and tinsel of wealthy and aristocratic life, should
never blind the reader to the fact that the story of the
book is a spiritual conflict, and that the author puts here,
as in *Tancred* and all his more serious writing, the soul
above the body.   It is Lothair's soul for which the various
forces have been contending.   The somewhat shadowy
Syrian Christian, Paraclete, whom Lothair meets towards
the end of his wanderings, seems to speak the author's real
mind.   What is his teaching ?   ' Science may prove the
insignificance of this globe in the scale of creation, but it
cannot prove the insignificance of man. . . .   There is no
relation between the faculties of man and the scale in
creation of the planet which he inherits.'   ' There must
be design, or all we see would be without sense, and I
do not believe in the unmeaning.'   ' A monad of pure
intelligence, is that more philosophical than the truth . . .
that God made man in his own image ?'   Science can no
more satisfy the soul than superstition or revolt.   But
Disraeli's practical advice is that which the revolutionary
General gave as his parting word to Lothair.   ' Whatever
you do, give up dreams. . . .   Action may not always
be happiness, but there is no happiness without action.'
These are the things in the knowledge of which Disraeli
declares the salvation of our youth to consist.   ' Nôsse
omnia hæc salus est adolescentulis ' is the motto from
Terence prefixed to the book.

Beyond this motto, Disraeli, who revealed in the
General Preface to the novels in the autumn the origin
and intention of his earlier romances, declined to give any
hint about the purport of *Lothair*.   But Longmans, his

publishers, circulated, presumably with his consent, as an advertisement of the new edition, a letter which Professor John Stuart Blackie had addressed to the *Scotsman* on the significance of the work.   It was undoubtedly, Blackie maintained, ' what the Germans call a *tendenz-roman*,' showing how certain intellectual agencies, prominent in the world at the time, act upon a hero of the Wilhelm Meister type, and how the illusions of Romanism may be dispelled in favour of rational liberty and rational piety. Count Vitzthum, Disraeli's old friend in the diplomatic world, also noted the resemblance to *Wilhelm Meister*, both novels treating of ' the development of a human being by the working of life and experience.'   But he thought Goethe's hero looked 'pale, narrow-minded, little, a poor bourgeois,' by the side of Lothair, ' a real prince, a citizen of the world.'   Vitzthum, moreover, selected for praise the facility of giving the formulas of all the philosophical schools of the age so that a child might understand them.   But perhaps the appreciation of James Clay, a friend from the days of the Mediterranean wanderings, pleased Disraeli most: ' You are a wonderful fellow to have retained the freshness and buoyancy of twenty-five.'

Seldom has a book been anticipated with such interest or produced such a sensation on its first appearance. There was no occasion for Longman to employ the puffing tactics by which Colburn in Disraeli's youthful days had heralded the publication of *Vivian Grey*.   A novel by an ex-Premier, and an ex-Premier of so strange and fascina-ting a type, was enough in itself to set the town, if not the world, agog.   ' There is immense and most malevolent curiosity about Disraeli's novel,' wrote Houghton.   ' His wisest friends think that it must be a mistake, and his enemies hope that it will be his ruin.'   The book was actually published, in three volumes, on Monday, May 2. But the advance demand had already kept Longman's printers busy.   On April 22, he told Disraeli that the subscription list would be about 2,000, and that a third

thousand was ready; on the 27th that 3,000 were bespoken
and a fourth in hand; and on the 29th, three days before
publication, that they had gone to press with a fifth.
Four days after publication he humorously described to
Disraeli the run upon his ' bankers in Paternoster Row.'

From Thomas Longman.

FARNBOROUGH HILL, HANTS, *May* 6, 1870.—There has
been a run upon your bankers in Paternoster Row, and our
last thousand is nearly gone ! We shall have another thousand in hand on Wednesday next. This will be the *sixth*
thousand, and I do not feel quite certain we shall not be
broken before Wednesday ! I am not sure that it would not
do good, now we have nearly 5,000 in circulation. On Monday
morning Mr. Mudie's house was, I am told, in a state of siege.
At an early hour his supply was sent in two carts. But real
subscribers, and representative footmen, in large masses were
there before them. Mr. Mudie has had 700 more copies. . . .

All the world read the book; every journal reviewed it.
It was the principal topic of polite conversation during the
London season: a pretty woman was even heard to bet a
copy of *Lothair* on a race at Ascot. Horses, songs, and
ships were named after the hero and heroine; a scrap in
Disraeli's handwriting gives the following list:

Lothair. Mr. Stevens' colt, Mr. Molloy's song by Mme.
Sherrington, Greenwich ship, Lothair Galloppe, Lothair Perfume, Lothair Street.
Corisande. Baron Rothschild's filly,[1] Mr. Martin's song
by Mme. Montserrat, Durham ship, Corisande Valtz.

Edition followed edition. The circulation was greatly
helped by the publication of an abusive letter from one
who conceived himself to be the original of the Oxford
professor described in the book as ' of advanced opinions
on all subjects, religious, social, and political '; ' clever,
extremely well-informed,' but with ' a restless vanity and
overflowing conceit '; ' gifted with a great command of

---

[1] Lady Beaconsfield preserved among the Beaconsfield papers the telegram by which Baron Meyer de Rothschild announced to her and Disraeli
the victory of the famous filly Corisande in the Cesarewitch.

words, which took the form of endless exposition, varied by sarcasm and passages of ornate jargon '; and—unkindest cut of all—' like sedentary men of extreme opinions, . . . a social parasite.'

From Goldwin Smith.

CORNELL UNIVERSITY, ITHACA, STATE OF NEW YORK, *May* 25, 1870.—In your *Lothair* you introduce an Oxford professor, who is about to emigrate to America, and you describe him as a social parasite. You well know that if you had ventured openly to accuse me of any social baseness, you would have had to answer for your words; but when, sheltering yourself under the literary form of a work of fiction, you seek to traduce with impunity the social character of a political opponent, your expressions can touch no man's honour; they are the stingless insults of a coward.

This was, indeed, as a journalist said, ' 'Ercles' vein '; and it is no wonder that Longman could write on June 9: ' The Oxford Professor's letter is doing its work well. So much so that we shall print again as soon as I have your corrections.' Disraeli never answered Goldwin Smith; but in a letter to an American literary friend he threw an interesting sidelight on the outburst.

To Robert Carter.

Confidential. HUGHENDEN MANOR, *Aug.* 13, 1870.— . . . I know nothing personally of Mr. Goldwin Smith. I never saw him. More than twenty years ago, the Peelite party, who had purchased the *Morning Chronicle*, mainly to decry me and my friends, engaged a new hand who distinguished himself by a series of invectives against myself, wh. far passed the bounds of legitimate political hostility. I cared nothing, and have never cared anything, about these personal attacks, to which I have been subject all my life and wh. have never, in the least, arrested my career; but the writer, I found out many years afterwards, was Mr. Goldwin Smith, who was well paid for his pains. I don't, and never did, grudge him that: but this is hardly the person to inveigh against personalities and anonymous writing. I have sometimes brushed him aside, as I would a mosquito, but am always too much occupied to bear him, or any other insect, any ill-will. . . .

The outbreak of the Franco-German War caused the demand, for the moment, somewhat to slacken; but with the appearance in November of a collected edition of Disraeli's novels, at 6s. a volume, having *Lothair* as the first volume, the ' Lothair-mania,' as Longman wrote, broke out again ' with all its virulence. Twice we have printed 5,000 copies, and now we have another 5,000 = 15,000, at press.' The book was translated into every European language, and the demand in Germany so far exceeded expectation that Baron Tauchnitz, the publisher, as Longman noted, ' doubled, *more suo*, his tribute-money.' In America the sale was even greater than in England. Messrs. Appleton began by printing 25,000 copies, which were sold out in three days; and in July the demand was still a thousand copies a day. By October 80,000 copies had been sold there. Disraeli proudly claimed, in the General Preface which he wrote for the collected edition, that the book had been ' more extensively read both by the people of the United Kingdom and the United States than any work that has appeared for the last half-century.'

But if the public devoured the novel, the reviewers for the more critical journals and magazines were, as a rule, unfavourable. *The Times* was, indeed, highly appreciative; and the *Pall Mall Gazette* called it an ' admirable novel ' which ' must have cost the author, we cannot help fancying, no effort whatever; it was as easy and delightful for him to write as for us to read.' But the *Saturday Review* was captious, and the *Edinburgh* patronising; the *Athenœum* maintained that the book would have passed unnoticed if written by anyone else; while both *Blackwood*, a representative of Scottish Conservatism, and the *Quarterly*, true as ever to its anti-Disraeli attitude, condemned it with the utmost severity. The latter dubbed it a ' failure,' an ' outrage,' ' a sin against good taste and justice,' ' a vast mass of verbiage which can seldom be called English '; and even had the hardihood to call a book which contains some of Disraeli's

liveliest and most satirical writing, ' as dull as ditchwater
and as flat as a flounder.'   Abraham Hayward, always a
malignant critic of Disraeli, wrote the *Quarterly* article;
Houghton, a 'good-natured' friend, the *Edinburgh;* the
Blackwood attack[1] was from the incisive pen of the
soldier-critic, Hamley.   In the General Preface Disraeli
hit some shrewd blows back; and one can recognise at
least Houghton and Hayward in the following passage:

> One could hardly expect at home the judicial impartiality
> of a foreign land.   Personal influences inevitably mingle in
> some degree with such productions.   There are critics who,
> abstractedly, do not approve of successful books, particularly
> if they have failed in the same style; social acquaintances also
> of lettered taste, and especially cotemporaries whose public
> life has not exactly realised the vain dreams of their fussy
> existence, would seize the accustomed opportunity of wel-
> coming with affected discrimination about nothing, and
> elaborate controversy about trifles, the production of a friend;
> and there is always, both in politics and literature, the race
> of the Dennises, the Oldmixons, and Curls, who flatter them-
> selves that, by systematically libelling some eminent personage
> of their times, they have a chance of descending to posterity.[2]

At least one later critic of undoubted competence has
endorsed the condemnation of the contemporary reviewers.
Sir Leslie Stephen, who showed much appreciation of the
earlier novels, has left on record the opinion that the
easiest assumption to make about *Lothair* is ' that it is a
practical joke on a large scale, or a prolonged burlesque
upon Mr. Disraeli's own youthful performances.'   Nevertheless, the judgment of the world is decisive against
Stephen, and holds that *Lothair* is among the best, if not
the absolute best, of Disraeli's novels.   Mr. George
Russell expressed a growing opinion when he declared it
the author's masterpiece; ' a profound study of spiritual
and political forces at a supremely important moment in
the history of modern Europe.'   Lord Russell saw deep

[1] Manners wrote on Nov. 10: ' Did I ever tell you that in consequence
of that abominable article in the summer I renounced *Blackwood ?* Though
you would not care for his ribaldry, perhaps you may like to know that
your friends did.'
[2] General Preface to the novels, Oct., 1870.

'CRITICS'

(WHO HAVE NOT EXACTLY 'FAILED IN LITERATURE AND ART.'
SEE MR. D.'S NEW WORK).

MR. G–D–S–NE: 'H'M—FLIPPANT!'   MR. D–S–R–LI: 'HA'—PROSY!'

Reproduced, by kind permission of the Proprietors, from 'Punch,' May 14, 1870.

significance beneath the gaudy trappings, and held it to be
the work of a political seer. Froude regarded it as 'immeasurably superior' to anything of the kind which
Disraeli had previously produced; adding, '*Lothair* opens
a window into Disraeli's mind, revealing the inner workings of it more completely than anything else which he
wrote or said.' This last appreciation is, perhaps, excessive; *Tancred* and *Lord George Bentinck* are more self-
revealing, if only because of their insistence on the
Jewish standpoint, which is not obtruded in *Lothair ;*
but *Lothair* takes rank beside *Coningsby*, and these two
are the novels on which Disraeli's literary reputation
rests with the general reader of to-day.

The pecuniary return of *Lothair* was considerable. For
the original edition of 2,000 copies Longmans paid
Disraeli £1,000; and together with royalties on subsequent copies and on the one-volume edition, and with
the foreign rights of the book, he had received in all by
the end of 1876 over £6,000. The large sales of *Lothair*
increased the demand for its predecessors, from *Vivian
Grey* to *Tancred*. On these in the new edition Disraeli
had already received over £1,000 in royalties, when, in
1877, he came to a new arrangement with his publishers
by which they paid him a further sum of £2,100 for the
copyright of the whole ten volumes of novels. He was
so much encouraged by his success that he soon made a
start upon a new novel, *Endymion ;* which, however,
owing to the renewal of his political activity and his
subsequent return to office, was not completed and
published till ten years later.

The publication of *Lothair*, like that of *Tancred*, was
politically a hindrance rather than a help to Disraeli.
The serious politician, like Gladstone in the *Punch* cartoon,
pronounced it flippant. How could Parliamentarians
be expected to trust an ex-Premier who, when half-
way between sixty and seventy, instead of occupying
his leisure, in accordance with the British convention,
in classical, historical, or constitutional studies, pro-

duced a gaudy romance of the peerage, so written as
to make it almost impossible to say how much was
ironical or satirical, and how much soberly intended?
It may be taken for granted that Disraeli's old colleagues
did not know what to think of the book, as among the
congratulatory letters preserved in the Beaconsfield
correspondence their handwriting is markedly absent.
This political distrust was increased by the resuscitation,
in the General Preface in the autumn, of all the peculiar
doctrines about English history and politics, about
Christianity and Judaism, and about religion and science,
which the English people had found difficult of assimila-
tion when propounded in *Coningsby*, *Sybil*, and *Tancred*,
in *Lord George Bentinck* and in the Sheldonian speech,
and many of which were even now *caviare* to the general.
The whole literary performance of the year made Disraeli,
the man, a more interesting figure than ever; but it only
deepened the doubts about Disraeli, the statesman, which
the heavy defeat of 1868, and the apparent hopelessnes
of the Conservative cause in opposition, had aroused.

CHAPTER V.

THE TURN OF THE TIDE.

1872–1873.

'There are few positions less inspiriting than that of the leader of a discomfited party.' The words are Disraeli's own, from the first chapter of *Lord George Bentinck*, and they were written in reference to Russell's position in the Peel Parliament of 1841. But they apply with at least equal force to the situation which Disraeli had himself occupied since the General Election of 1868. Opposite him there had sat an overwhelming and enthusiastic majority, who, with few exceptions, had steadily acted on the principle that it was their duty ' to say ditto to Mr. Gladstone ' as the Prime Minister pursued his strenuous career; and though in the session of 1871 there had been many Ministerial mishaps, with the corollary of some Opposition victories in by-elections, yet all the efforts of the Conservative party and the adroitness of their leader had hitherto been unavailing materially to improve their position and prospects. *The Times*, in a judicial leading article towards the close of 1871,[1] pronounced that anything like a permanent tenure of office for the Conservatives was impossible. ' The leaders of the party do not believe in it. The country gives them no confidence. The majority is against them. All the forces of the time are strained in an opposite direction.' It was as true of Disraeli from 1869 to 1872, as of Russell from 1841 to 1845, that

he who in the Parliamentary field watches over the fortunes of routed troops must be prepared to sit often alone. Few care to share the labour which is doomed to be fruitless, and

[1] Nov. 20.

none are eager to diminish the responsibility of him whose course, however adroit, must necessarily be ineffectual. . . . A disheartened Opposition will be querulous and captious.   A discouraged multitude have no future; too depressed to indulge in a large and often hopeful horizon of contemplation, they busy themselves in peevish detail, and by a natural train of sentiment associate their own conviction of ill-luck, incapacity, and failure, with the most responsible member of their confederation.[1]

The discontent reached a climax in the winter of 1871–1872.   The policy of reserve in opposition which Disraeli had on the whole maintained, and which had produced satisfactory results in alluring ministers into indiscretions, was galling to eager and impetuous spirits; and in the previous session the ' Colonels ' had got out of hand in their violent opposition to the Army Bill, and the anti-Disraeli clique in their obstruction of the Ballot Bill. Complaint was made that, in spite of tempting opportunities afforded by Ministerial blunders, Disraeli had avoided political speaking during the recesses, putting off from year to year the demonstration in Manchester which his Lancashire friends pressed him to accept.   His own excuse to Matthew Arnold, who met him at a country house party at Latimer in January, 1872, was that ' the Ministers were so busy going about apologising for their failures that he thought it a pity to distract public attention from the proceeding.'   Further, the publication of *Lothair* and of the General Preface to the novels had revived all the former doubts as to whether a Jewish literary man, so dowered with imagination, and so unconventional in his outlook, was the proper person to lead a Conservative party to victory.   Would it not be better to go into battle under the old Stanley banner ?   Derby had gained golden opinions as Foreign Secretary, and had that plain common sense, love of peace, and moderation of political faith which appealed to the middle classes in the rapidly growing urban communities, and which might be expected, were he

[1] *Lord George Bentinck*, ch. 1.

the party leader, to attract considerable Liberal support
to the Conservative cause. The rival claims of Disraeli
and Derby were widely discussed by politicians throughout the party and the country, in newspapers, clubs, and
debating societies; though Derby made no sign whatever,
and there is not the smallest reason to suppose that he
would have consented to play the part his admirers
allotted to him.

Even Disraeli's colleagues were infected with the rising
spirit of dissatisfaction; and no less intimate a friend than
Cairns was the first to give it expression at a gathering of
Conservative leaders at Burghley just before the session;
from which gathering not only Disraeli himself, but also
Derby, Richmond, and Malmesbury were absent. Hardy's
diary is our authority for what took place.

At our meeting (February 1) Cairns boldly broached the
subject of Lord Derby's lead, and the importance of Disraeli
knowing the general feeling. We all felt that none of his old
colleagues could, or would, undertake such a task as informing
him. John Manners alone professed ignorance of the feeling
in or out of doors. I expressed my view that D. has been
loyal to his friends, and that personally I would not say that
I preferred Lord D., but that it was idle to ignore the general
opinion. Noel [1] said that from his own knowledge he could
say that the name of Lord Derby as leader would affect 40
or 50 seats. . . .   For my own part I do not look forward with
hope to Derby, but I cannot but admit that Disraeli, as far
as appears, has not the position in House and country to
enable him to do what the other might.[2]

Northcote is not mentioned in this account; but he
has recorded in his diary under a subsequent date that
he and Manners were the only two present who were
stanch to their chief, and that he wondered if Disraeli
knew of their loyalty. It may be taken for granted that
none of Disraeli's colleagues informed him of the opinions
expressed at Burghley. Apparently, however, some representation of the discontent of a section of his followers in
the House of Commons was conveyed to him, and in

---

[1] One of the Whips.   [2] Gathorne Hardy, Vol. I., p. 305.

reply he intimated that he would be quite ready to give place to Derby if the party wished it, but in that case he would himself retire below the gangway—a contingency which the most recalcitrant follower would hardly face.

In any case so shrewd a judge of party feeling could not fail to be aware of the prevailing uneasiness; accordingly, while his lieutenants were discussing his shortcomings at Burghley, he, as his correspondence shows, was gathering in his hands all the strands of a complicated political situation, and preparing to demonstrate that he was as indispensable as he had ever been since he had imposed himself on his party in 1849. A rap over the knuckles for his colleague, the duke who led the Opposition in the Lords, was a clear reminder of his claims as leader—especially if the censure was, as Hardy thought, unjust. Incidentally the high tone he takes shows how little disposed he was to that adulation of dukes, which some who misread *Lothair* have attributed to him. ' Talk not to me of dukes,' he burst out on one occasion when a duke had disappointed him; ' dukes can be made !' He had made one himself.

To the Duke of Richmond.

Confidential. BURGHLEY HOUSE, STAMFORD, *Jan.* 11, 1872. —I have been much engaged during the last six weeks, in correspondence with our supporters in the Ho. of Commons, as to their course, in the next session, respecting the ballot. The Lancashire members, our most powerful friends, are particularly embarrassed by this question: the members for the boro[ugh]s, in some instances, being hard pressed by their constituents to support it, while, on the other hand, Mr. Cross, the M.P. for South Lancashire, who defeated Mr. Gladstone, moved, at his own request, the absolute rejection of the Bill during the last session.

This gentleman, uneasy on the matter, and requesting my advice, informed me, some time ago, that Lord Skelmersdale had assured him, that he might depend on the Whig peers giving the measure an uncompromising opposition. Not being myself certain of this, I advised him, in our perplexity, not to change his front, but not unnecessarily to dwell on the subject.

In this state of affairs, I took advantage of being in the West to arrange to meet Lord Cairns at Ld. Malmesbury's, and to confer with him on matters in general, wh. daily assume a more critical character.   To my astonishment, I learned from Lord Cairns, that your Grace had received a communication from Lord Russell, that our party in the House of Lords must no longer count on him, the Duke of Somerset, and others, as opponents to the ballot.   Lord Cairns naturally assumed that your Grace had immediately apprised me of this information, so necessary to me for the satisfactory conduct of business.[1]

I am sure your Grace will not misconceive my meaning, when I express my deep regret at the habitual want of communication, which now subsists between the leaders of our party in the two Houses.   If my individual feelings only were concerned, I should not touch upon the matter, but, with the responsibility of conducting difficult affairs for the common good, it is my duty to remark on circumstances, wh., I am sure, are fraught with injurious consequences to the cause wh. we are anxious to uphold.

From the Duke of Richmond.

Goodwood, Chichester, *Jan.* 12, 1872.—I hope that ere this you will have recd. a letter which I wrote a few days ago, and directed to Hughenden.   I enclosed a letter from Lord Russell.

I will not conceal from you how very much annoyed I am to find from your letter that you consider there has been habitual want of communication subsisting between the leaders of our party in the two Houses.

This wd. imply that I had studiously avoided acting with you.   If this was so I should have been justly liable to censure, for I quite concur that, unless the leaders in both Houses act in concert and with cordiality, it is quite impossible that the business can be carried on in a satisfactory manner.

I think, if you reflect, you will recollect that I was in constant communication with you during the last session of Parliament.   You will recollect Cairns and I met you in the Carlton to discuss the American question.   I also saw you frequently about the Army Bill and the ballot, and communicated to you at once all the negotiations which were then pending between me and Lord Russell.

I did not think it necessary to trouble you with the letter I recd. fr. Lord Russell after I got to Scotland, but always

---

[1] 'I shall certainly tell the Duke of R.,' wrote Malmesbury to Disraeli on Jan. 8, ' my opinion as to his want of concert with you.'

intended to do so before the meeting of Parliament. It is possible that it would have been better had I sent it to you sooner, but for some time past I have been very busy with my own affairs.

I have deemed it right to enter into these details, because I am most anxious that you should be satisfied that I have not been guilty of any want of courtesy towards you. Indeed I should have hoped that our long acquaintance would have been sufficient to have prevented you from imagining such a thing. I quite appreciate the responsibility and difficulty of your position, and always wish to assist you by all means in my power.

To the Duke of Richmond.

Latimer, Chesham, *Jan.* 16, 1872.—I have received both your letters, and have read the last in the spirit in wh. it is written.

I return herewith the letter of Lord Russell, and the copy of his letter to Lord Lyveden. They do not appear to me to bear altogether the interpretation, wh. Lord Cairns placed upon them, or, rather, wh. I apprehended he placed upon them.

The intimations of Lord Russell seem to me to be altogether hypothetical, and to rest upon a basis, wh. he contemplated as probable, but wh. has not occurred, viz., ' That the country would support the House of Commons in asking for the ballot.'

The country during the recess has been silent on the subject, and tho' many important elections have happened, and are about to take place, the question of the ballot seems to have no influence upon their result.

Lord Russell and his friends, therefore, on the reassembling of Parliament, are free to recur to their old grounds of opposition to the measure, and may even do so.

Whether such a course on their part should regulate ours, is another question, and wh. I would rather leave to personal deliberations when we are better acquainted with the exact propositions of the Ministry.

We must not conceal from ourselves, that the Tory party in the Ho. of Commons is not united on the question, and tho' I am not myself prepared, under any circumstances, to concede the principle of secret voting, as at present advised, I fear our ranks may be broken.

I wish I could see the practical elements of that compromise wh. Lord Russell seems to contemplate. Any provision to secure scrutiny and prevent personation, will, according to the Radical view, destroy the Bill.

Richmond showed this correspondence to his principal colleagues, who, while they gave him their sympathy, could not fail to draw their own conclusions as to the disposition of their chief. Cairns's comment was that after two years of apathy Disraeli was beginning to wake up, and fancy all beside were asleep. What Cairns called apathy might perhaps be more truly described as calculated and successful reserve; but at any rate there is no doubt that Disraeli was awake now.

The public question which gave him and his political friends at the moment most concern was the difficulty with the United States over the *Alabama* question. Disraeli and his Foreign Secretary, Derby, had been the first British statesmen in office to admit the principle of arbitration; and accordingly Northcote, as a leading Conservative statesman, had consented to take a share in negotiating in the previous year the Treaty of Washington which carried the principle into practical effect.[1] Disraeli was not satisfied with the conduct of the negotiations; but, at any rate, the terms of the treaty were so limited by the British Commissioners as to render it in their opinion *ultra vires* for the tribunal to admit and adjudicate upon those indirect claims, making this country responsible for the prolongation of the Civil War, which spread-eagle politicians in America like Sumner put forward, but which Derby had expressly excluded in 1868. Great was the shock, therefore, when it was discovered that the American case to be submitted to the arbitrators embraced and insisted upon these very far-reaching claims as well as those specifically ' growing out of the acts committed ' by certain vessels.

---

[1] Lord George Hamilton in his *Reminiscences* says that Northcote accepted the task without consulting Disraeli; but this appears to be a mistake, as Lord Morley in his *Gladstone*, Bk. VI., ch. 9, quotes a contemporary letter from Granville, then Foreign Secretary, to Gladstone: ' I asked Northcote. . . . He said he must ask Lady Northcote, and requested permission to consult Dizzy. The former consented, ditto Dizzy.'

To Lord Cairns.

Private. GROSVENOR GATE, *Jan*. 27, 1872.—. . . Affairs
here are most critical and anxious. All is absorbed in the
Alabama question. Hayward told Exmouth yesterday, that
unless they withdraw from the arbitration, the Cabinet must
break up. Would that they would withdraw! But can
they ? After having advised their Sovereign to ratify the
treaty—and in such haste !

I have not seen the foreign case, nor has Lord Derby, but
we know its scope from those who have—Cockburn, Delane,
Ld. Stanhope and others speak of it as most masterly. Northcote, who has it, speaks of it disparagingly: can easily be
answered, crushingly, and all that. But this is not the point.
Our complaint is, that it opens the indirect issue, the relin-
quishment of which by U.S. was our consideration for consenting to express regret, and dealing with the law of nations
ex post facto. In the initiated quarters, there is no confidence
in, at least two of, the arbitrators. They are supposed to be
manageable by an unscrupulous Government. Altogether I
never knew public feeling so disturbed and dark.

I am most anxious to see you Tuesday at 12. Perhaps
Northcote may be here. It was impossible for me to go to
Burghley, as I had previously declined Belvoir. At this
moment I must be at headquarters.

To Sir Stafford Northcote.

Private. GROSVENOR GATE, *Jan*. 30, '72.—. . . Cairns has
been with me this morning. A long, but not a satisfactory,
visit. He holds, in this with me, that the Government scheme
of protesting to the arbitrators, and awaiting their judgment
on the protest, [is] quite futile.

They are not bound to adjudicate on the point and they will
decline. Arbitrators, he says, always avoid unnecessary
decisions, and details; and he is quite prepared, if the arbitration is concluded, that they will give their verdict for a sum
without apportioning the amount.

2. He holds withdrawal from the arbitration, a clear *casus
belli*.

3. He is of opinion that the treaty justifies the American
demand, and, he says, he said as much in House of Lords
last year.

In such a mess of difficulties all I can see at present, is to
counsel direct and friendly application to the Government of
Washington. This will not be a *casus belli*, but I fear must
end in that.

The Americans will not go to war—at least at present—for
there are many reasons to deter them, but they will keep the
question open, and we shall still, after our sacrifices, have the
Alabama claims, but in a worse form. . . .

When Parliament met, Disraeli described the indirect
claims as ' preposterous and wild,' and equivalent to ' the
tribute of a conquered people.'   If the Government held
that there was no doubt that the treaty excluded these
claims, they must speak out calmly, frankly, and firmly,
avoiding ' the Serbonian bog of diplomacy,' and tell the
United States Government plainly that it was impossible
to accept their interpretation, and that, if they maintained
it, the treaty must be cancelled.   Gladstone responded
in a like spirit, acknowledging Disraeli's patriotic and
discreet treatment of American questions, and insisting
first that the terms of the treaty were absolutely clear,
and secondly that no nation with any spirit could submit
to the American demands.   There is no doubt that the
strong support which Disraeli gave to the Government
materially contributed to the cause of arbitration by
convincing the American people that Great Britain was
in earnest.   The United States, however, made it a point
of honour not to waive the indirect claims; and the
British Government on its side determined to adjourn
the arbitration until these were abandoned.   But what
the United States would not do as a Government their
arbitrator, Charles Francis Adams, did for them.   He
persuaded his colleagues summarily to rule these claims
out; and the arbitration accordingly proceeded.   Disraeli
raised himself decidedly in public estimation by his conduct of this question.   It was seen that there had been
serious mismanagement by the Government to bring
matters to such a pass, and that it was highly patriotic of
Disraeli to dwell but lightly on these shortcomings, and
to strengthen Gladstone's hands at a critical moment.

In other respects he did not spare the failures of
Ministers.   They had lived, he said in the debate on the
Address, during the last six months ' in a blaze of apology.'

They would have further opportunities for defending themselves in the House. 'If it is in the power of the Government to prove to the country that our naval administration is such as befits a great naval power, they will soon have an occasion for doing so; and if they are desirous of showing that one of the transcendental privileges of a strong Government is to evade Acts of Parliament which they have themselves passed, I believe, from what caught my ear this evening, that that opportunity will also be furnished them.' The last sentence referred to two pieces of the Prime Minister's patronage, one legal, the other clerical, which required a good deal of apology. In one case, Sir Robert Collier, the Attorney-General, had been appointed a paid member of the Judicial Committee of the Privy Council, although by statute such appointments were limited to those who had held judicial positions in the superior courts. A technical compliance with the law was effected by making Collier a Judge of the Common Pleas for a couple of days. In the other case, the rectory of Ewelme, which by statute could only be held by a member of Oxford Convocation, had been conferred upon a Cambridge graduate, who was thereupon technically qualified by being admitted to an *ad eundem* degree at Oxford. There was no suggestion in either case that an unfit person had been appointed; but the evasion of the plain meaning of the law was rendered all the more flagrant by the fact that the statutes regulating the two appointments had both been passed at the instance of Gladstone's Government in the preceding session of Parliament. Disraeli, who seldom in his maturer years mixed himself up in personal squabbles, took no part in the angry debates which were raised in both Houses on these strange proceedings; though he noted with satisfaction that the Collier appointment only escaped condemnation in the Commons by twenty-seven votes—a number almost exactly corresponding with the number of Ministers voting—while in the Lords the rescue had to be effected by the Chancellor's own vote.

To Montagu Corry.

H. of C., *Feb.* 16, '72.—. . . On Wednesday, the Government had not even made a whip in the H. of C. for next Monday, and last night, the Ministers thinking they were going to be beaten by a whacking majority, like damned fools, did nothing but abuse the House of Lords, and deride their judgment and influence.

The old Whigs, without an exception almost, came to their rescue on this occasion, there having been a meeting at Brooks's anent, and either our men purposely stayed away from fear of disturbing the Ministry or were shockingly whipped, as is the commoner opinion: the abuse of Skelmersdale being very rife.

He told me, the day before, the majority would be 60. Yesterday evening, about 8 o'clock, that it would be between 30 and 40, and at 12 o'clock, that it would be only ten. At ½ past 12 he was beaten apparently by two: but there was an error of one in the counting, and the majority was only an unit: described really by the Lord Chancellor, who voted for himself! Our friends are chapfallen, but, for myself, I think the affair was well enough. . . .

Disraeli's resolute and ambitious character was not the only thing with which the dissatisfied pundits of the party, whether colleagues, members of Parliament, or wire-pullers, forgot to reckon; there was also the profound impression which his personality had made among the British people. For the goodwill of the democracy he had never laid himself out, even when enormously extending their privileges. No British statesman of recent years was ever less of a demagogue. With few, if striking, exceptions, it was only in Parliament and in Bucks that he opened his lips. ' I have never in the course of my life,' he said at Manchester in April, 'obtruded myself upon any meeting of my fellow-countrymen unless I was locally connected with them, or there were peculiar circumstances which might vindicate me from the imputation of thrusting myself unnecessarily on their attention.' But the admiration and confidence which he had never courted came to him spontaneously, and even for a while unperceived. Gladstone had been extraordinarily popular in 1868 with an electorate which had been taught

to believe that they owed to him that which they had
received from Disraeli. His inexhaustible and lofty
eloquence, his insistence on the moral law in politics, the
specious cries with which he garnished his electoral
campaign, took captive an inexperienced constituency.
But the constantly destructive nature of their favourite's
energies, his arrogant demeanour, his apparent indifference
to his country's prestige, the un-English casuistry which
was inwoven in his moral texture, and the inexplicable
vagaries of some of his colleagues, had alienated public
sympathy; and that enthusiastic nature of the English
people, on which it was Disraeli's wont to insist, led
them to seek another object for their trust, as different as
might be from him who had so failed them. Disraeli had
for years excited an amused curiosity and interest; but
it was as often an interest of repulsion as of attraction.
There was now an awakening to the fact that his patience,
his courage, his genius, his experience, and his patriotism
constituted a character round which popular feeling,
disappointed in its idol, might safely rally.

The first outward sign of this development of opinion
was shown in the autumn of 1871, when the youth
of Liberal Scotland recognised Disraeli's eminence by
electing him, in preference to Ruskin, as the Lord Rector
of Glasgow University. But London politicians, and
probably Disraeli himself, first realised how strong was
the popular interest in him, on February 27, 1872, when
the Prince of Wales went to St. Paul's to return thanks
for his recovery from typhoid fever, and when the people
had in consequence an unusual opportunity of singling
out its favourites as they passed in succession along the
streets. The reception of Gladstone was indifferent or
hostile;[1] but that of Disraeli was so enthusiastic that Sir
William Fraser maintains that it changed his destiny.
Fraser writes:

On returning from St. Paul's, Disraeli met with an overpowering ' ovation '; I should say ' triumph,' for he was in

[1] See *Life of Dean Church*, p. 291.

his chariot. This not only continued from the City to Waterloo
Place; but his carriage, ascending Regent Street, turning to
the right[1] along Oxford Street, and thence back to the Carlton
Club, the cheers which greeted him from all classes convinced
him that, for the day at least, a more popular man did not
exist in England. Soon after his return I happened to pass
into the morning room of the Carlton Club. Disraeli was
leaning against the table immediately opposite to the glass
door, wearing the curious white coat which he had for years
occasionally put on over his usual dress. Familiar as I was
with his looks and expression, I never saw him with such a
countenance as he had at that moment. I have heard it
said by one who spoke to Napoleon I. at Orange in France,
that his face was as that of one who looks into another world:
that is the only description I can give of Disraeli's look at the
moment I speak of. He seemed more like a statue than a
human being: never before nor since have I seen anything
approaching it: he was ostensibly listening to Mr. Sclater
Booth, now Lord Basing. In the afternoon I said to the
latter, ' What was Disraeli talking about when I came into
the room ?' He replied, ' About some county business; I
wanted his opinion.' I said, ' I will tell you what he was
thinking about: he was thinking that he will be Prime Minister
again !' I had no doubt at the time; nor have I ever doubted
since.[2]

The principal demonstration of Disraeli's popularity
with the masses and of the reviving power of Conservatism
was made at Manchester at Easter, when he and his wife
paid that visit to his Lancashire friends which was so
long overdue. It was, as Disraeli wrote, a ' wondrous
week.' It opened on Easter Monday with a rousing
reception by a holiday crowd of workers who promptly
extemporised a human team to draw the visitors' carriage.
But perhaps its most striking feature was an immense
parade next day, undaunted by pitiless rain, of deputations from all the Conservative Associations of the county,
between two and three hundred in number. For each deputation the leader had an apt word, as one after another,
with banners flying and laudatory addresses in their

---

[1] ' Right ' is apparently a mistake for 'left.' The carriage was presumably going to drop Lady Beaconsfield at Grosvenor Gate before taking
Disraeli to the Carlton Club.
[2] Fraser, pp. 374-376.

hands, they defiled before Disraeli and Lady Beaconsfield, filling the vast dancing hall of the Pomona Gardens, a building reckoned to hold thirty or forty thousand people.

Well might Disraeli be proud of the show, as it was the direct result of his own labours behind the scenes. During these years of reserve in opposition, when he appeared to colleagues and followers to be apathetic, he had been quietly working at Conservative reorganisation, and creating a machine which was to lead to the victory of 1874, and to be the forerunner of the great party organisations of to-day. The arrangements for party management which he had originally made in the early fifties with Rose, his lawyer and confidential agent, and which had been continued, after Rose's withdrawal, with Spofforth, a member of Rose's firm, had been a great improvement on the chaos which existed before Disraeli's accession to the leadership. But, even with the assistance and supervision of that shrewd politician the late Lord Abergavenny, and of a special committee appointed *ad hoc* in 1868, they were wholly insufficient, as had been shown in the last election, for an age of household suffrage and large popular constituencies. An entirely new system must be set up; and Disraeli looked about for a young and ambitious Conservative who would be ready to devote the best years of his life to working out a scheme. His choice fell upon John Eldon Gorst,[1] a barrister, who had had a distinguished career at Cambridge, and had sat for a year or two in Parliament, but was now no longer a member. An authentic statement of what was done by Disraeli in this important sphere is furnished in a short political life of him written by Gorst's son.[2] What was most wanted, Disraeli told his new manager, was that every constituency should have a suitable candidate ready in advance. To secure this desirable object a Central Conservative Office was established in Whitehall under the party manager and furnished with a capable

[1] Afterwards Sir John Gorst, Q.C., Solicitor-General, and subsequently Under Secretary for India.
[2] See Harold Gorst's *Earl of Beaconsfield*, ch. 13.

staff. Then the influential Conservatives in each constituency were persuaded to form local associations on a substantially democratic basis; the interest and co-operation were sought and obtained, not merely of the aristocratic and professional and trading classes, but also of the local artisans. In Lancashire, where several Conservative working men's societies already existed, the idea was taken up with special enthusiasm. Communication was regularly maintained between the central office and the provincial associations. The central office kept a register of approved candidates; but instead of supplying these at its discretion to the constituencies, it endeavoured to get the local people to make their own selection. 'In registering candidates care was taken to note down their peculiar qualifications. . . . A constituency, in applying for a candidate, was asked to state the kind of man wanted. The party manager declined to make the selection himself, but requested some of the leading men in the constituency to come up and make their own choice. Meanwhile a list of likely men was compiled from the register; and, if desirable, personal interviews were arranged. By this means each place was provided with a candidate suitable to its political needs.' Finally, mainly at the suggestion of Henry Cecil Raikes, a coping stone was put on the edifice by the affiliation of all these Conservative associations to a comprehensive National Union.

Though, in entrusting the business to Gorst, Disraeli left him a free hand, he paid nevertheless constant personal attention to all that was being done, and was ready to give his manager the benefit of his sagacity and experience at every stage. And when the machine was established and was proving its utility by the satisfactory results of the by-elections from 1871 onwards, he kept a careful watch on its working in each particular instance. Writing to a friend in October, 1873, he mentioned that 'after every borough election, an expert visits the scene of action, and prepares a confidential despatch for me, that, so far as is possible, I may be thoroughly acquainted with the facts.' One point he made clear from the outset, as might be anticipated from his insistence on accompanying his great measure of Reform by a Corrupt Practices Act. He was resolved that no countenance whatever should be given by his new organisation to the practice on which both parties had too often relied in the past, the winning of elections by bribery.

Disraeli was thus responsible for starting the first great party machine, and he reaped the harvest in the victory of 1874. But, though experience here and elsewhere seems to prove that party organisations are essential to democratic government, Disraeli's judicious admirers are hardly likely to claim much credit for him on the score of this feat. As might have been expected, the Liberals bettered the Conservative example by perfecting the Birmingham caucus, and extending its operations to the whole country; and the machine soon became so highly organised on both sides as to make increasingly difficult the entry into the House of Commons, and the continuance there, of those independent politicians to secure whose adhesion it was necessary for Governments in the past to look beyond party. Hence there has come a serious decline of Parliamentary control over Ministers; and a great accession of power to the statesman or the party committee who may happen to have commanded at the preceding election the support of a majority in the constituencies.

The full importance of the parade of Conservative associations at Manchester was hardly realised at the time; and attention was mainly fixed on the great meeting on the Wednesday evening[1] in the Free Trade Hall, where, with Derby by his side and the numerous Conservative members for the county on the platform, Disraeli spoke to an enthusiastic audience with unflagging spirit for three hours and a quarter. In this effort, so tremendous for a man never very robust and in his sixty-eighth year,

[1] April 3.

he was sustained, H. C. Raikes tells us, by two bottles of white brandy, indistinguishable by onlookers from the water taken with it, which he drank in doses of ever-increasing strength till he had consumed the whole !

The speech was an answer to the Liberal taunt that the Conservatives had no programme. Their programme, said Disraeli, was to maintain the Constitution of the country, because political institutions were the embodied experience of race. It was the cue of his critics to say that our great institutions, such as the Monarchy, the House of Lords, and the Church were as dear to Gladstone and the Liberals as to the Conservatives, and so their defence could not be appropriated by any one party. But the left wing of the Liberal party was in full cry both against the Church and against the House of Lords; and individual Radicals, who could not be dismissed as nobodies, Dilke and Auberon Herbert, were declaiming against the heavy cost of Monarchy, and comparing it unfavourably with the supposed cheapness of a republic. Moreover, on all these questions, as Disraeli pointed out, Gladstone sent forth an uncertain sound, avoiding, as far as might be, a distinct breach with even extreme followers. On each of the three threatened institutions Disraeli had something to say which arrested attention. He maintained that the continuous prosperity of the country and its advance in civilisation were very largely due to the Throne.

Since the settlement of [the] Constitution, now nearly two centuries ago, England has never experienced a revolution, though there is no country in which there has been so continuous and such considerable change. How is this ? Because the wisdom of your forefathers placed the prize of supreme power without the sphere of human passions. Whatever the struggle of parties, whatever the strife of factions, whatever the excitement and exaltation of the public mind, there has always been something in this country round which all classes and parties could rally, representing the majesty of the law, the administration of justice, and involving, at the same time, the security for every man's rights and the fountain of honour.

Disraeli proceeded to explain, in language which, though of course general, recalled his speech about the Queen in the autumn, that it was a mistake to suppose that the personal influence of the Sovereign was absorbed in the responsibility of the Minister: and that such influence must increase, the longer the reign and the greater the experience of the Sovereign. That, it may be added, was certainly, in the opinion of competent statesmen, the case with Queen Victoria, whose influence, in spite of the increasing democratisation of the country, was never greater than in the twenty years by which she survived her favourite Minister. As to the cost of Monarchy, Disraeli pointed out how cheap it was, compared with the Continental scale; and even compared with America, when you added together the salaries of the Federal Legislature and those of all the sovereign legislatures of the different states that went to form that greatest of republics—an argument, by the way, which has been weakened since members of Parliament here have accepted payment.

With regard to the House of Lords, experience showed a Second Chamber to be necessary; but with the exception of the American Senate, composed of materials not possessed by other States, no other country had solved successfully the problem of its constitution, whereas the House of Lords had developed historically, and periodically adapted itself to the necessities of the times. That House had the first quality of a Second Chamber, independence, based on the firmest foundation, responsible property. Would life peerages be as satisfactory ? A peer for life could exercise the power entrusted to him according to his own will; and nobody could call him to account. But a peer whose dignities descend to his children had every inducement to study public opinion, ' because he naturally feels that if the order to which he belongs is in constant collision with public opinion, the chances are that his dignities will not descend to his posterity.'

There are some philosophers who believe that the best substitute for the House of Lords would be an assembly formed of ex-Governors of Colonies. . . . When the Muse of Comedy threw her frolic grace over society, a retired governor was generally one of the characters in every comedy; and the last of our great actors . . ., Mr. Farren, was celebrated for his delineation of the character in question. Whether it be the recollection of that performance or not, I confess I am inclined to believe that an English gentleman—born to business, managing his own estate, administering the affairs of his county, mixing with all classes of his fellowmen, now in the hunting field, now in the railway direction, unaffected, unostentatious, proud of his ancestors, if they have contributed to the greatness of our common country—is, on the whole, more likely to form a senator agreeable to English opinion and English taste than any substitute that has yet been produced.

Disraeli's defence of the Church followed the lines which he had adopted in the sixties. He dwelt on the vital importance of connecting authority with religion, and maintained that ' to have secured a national profession of faith with the unlimited enjoyment of private judgment in matters spiritual is the solution of the most difficult problem, and one of the triumphs, of civilisation.' As a practical answer to the disestablishers he pointed out how powerful and highly organised and wealthy a corporation the Church was, and must remain, whatever the conditions of disestablishment; and asked whether the severance of the controlling tie which bound such a body to the State could be favourable to the cause of civil and religious liberty. He had a great respect for the Nonconformists, and expressed his mortification that, from a feeling of envy or pique, they should have become the partisans of secular education, instead of working with the Church for religious education, which was ' demanded by the nation generally and by the instincts of human nature.'

While expressing his belief that the working classes both in town and country had shared in that advance of national prosperity which had been favoured by the stability of our political institutions, he pointed to social reform as a sphere in which no inconsiderable results might be obtained, and gave his party a famous catchword.

A great scholar and a great wit, 300 years ago, said that, in his opinion, there was a great mistake in the Vulgate, which as you all know is the Latin translation of the Holy Scriptures, and that, instead of saying ' Vanity of vanities, all is vanity '—*Vanitas vanitatum, omnia vanitas*—the wise and witty King really said, *Sanitas sanitatum, omnia sanitas*.[1] Gentlemen, it is impossible to overrate the importance of the subject.   After all, the first consideration of a Minister should be the health of the people.

So far Disraeli's discourse had been rather a constitutional lecture[2] than a party speech.   But now he turned on the Government and in biting words summed up the pith of his charges against their proceedings.   It was an Administration avowedly formed on a principle of violence. Their specific for the peace and prosperity of Ireland was to despoil churches and plunder landlords, with the result of sedition rampant, treason thinly veiled, and the steady return to Parliament of Home Rulers ' pledged to the disruption of the realm.'   ' Her Majesty's new Ministers proceeded in their career like a body of men under the influence of some deleterious drug.   Not satiated with the spoliation and anarchy of Ireland, they began to attack every institution and every interest, every class and calling in the country.'   After giving some instances he proceeded in a passage which Lord Morley calls ' one of the few pieces of classic oratory of the century.'

As time advanced it was not difficult to perceive that extravagance was being substituted for energy by the Government.   The unnatural stimulus was subsiding.   Their paroxysms ended in prostration.   Some took refuge in melancholy, and their eminent chief alternated between a menace and a sigh.   As I sat opposite the Treasury Bench the Ministers

---

[1] Disraeli had given this watchword of *Sanitas*, etc., at Aylesbury on September 21, 1864, without much notice being taken of it.

[2] Cairns, in congratulating Disraeli on the speech, wrote: ' It will live and be read, not only for its sparkling vigour, but also for the deep strata of constitutional thought and reasoning which pervade it.'

reminded me of one of those marine landscapes not very unusual on the coasts of South America. You behold a range
of exhausted volcanoes. Not a flame flickers on a single
pallid crest. But the situation is still dangerous. There are
occasional earthquakes, and ever and anon the dark rumbling
of the sea.

Before concluding, Disraeli turned to foreign affairs,
prefacing what he had to say with a few introductory
sentences whose truth will be more generally acknowledged now than they were in the early seventies, in spite
of the then recent lesson of the Franco-German War.

I know the difficulty of addressing a body of Englishmen
on these topics. The very phrase ' foreign affairs ' makes an
Englishman convinced that I am about to treat of subjects
with which he has no concern. Unhappily the relations of
England with the rest of the world, which are ' foreign affairs,'
are the matters which most influence his lot. Upon them
depends the increase or reduction of taxation. Upon them
depends the enjoyment or the embarrassment of his industry.
And yet, though so momentous are the consequences of the
mismanagement of our foreign relations, no one thinks of
them till the mischief occurs, and then it is found how the
most vital consequences have been occasioned by mere in-
advertence.

Disraeli proceeded to condemn the weakness of the
Government in its dealings with Russia over the Black
Sea, and its negligence and blundering in regard to the
difficulties with the United States over the indirect
claims; and he finished on the imperial note.

Don't suppose, because I counsel firmness and decision
at the right moment, that I am of that school of statesmen
who are favourable to a turbulent and aggressive diplomacy.
I have resisted it during a great part of my life. I am not
unaware that the relations of England to Europe have undergone a vast change during the century that has just elapsed.
The relations of England to Europe are not the same as they
were in the days of Lord Chatham or Frederick the Great.
The Queen of England has become the Sovereign of the most
powerful of Oriental States. On the other side of the globe
there are new establishments belonging to her, teeming with
wealth and population, which will, in due time, exercise their
influence over the distribution of power. The old establish-

ments of this country, now the United States of America,
throw their lengthening shades over the Atlantic, which mix
with European waters. These are vast and novel elements
in the distribution of power. I acknowledge that the policy
of England with respect to Europe should be a policy of
reserve, but proud reserve; and in answer to those statesmen,
those mistaken statesmen, who have intimated the decay of
the power of England and the decline of her resources, I express here my confident conviction that there never was a
moment in our history when the power of England was so
great and her resources so vast and inexhaustible. And yet,
gentlemen, it is not merely our fleets and armies, our powerful
artillery, our accumulated capital, and our unlimited credit
on which I so much depend, as upon that unbroken spirit of
her people, which I believe was never prouder of the Imperial
country to which they belong.

The speech and the Manchester reception at once placed
Disraeli's leadership beyond question, and proved the
reality of Conservative reaction. Sidonia's familiar words
—' The age of ruins is past. Have you seen Manchester ?'
—had acquired a fresh significance. That Conservatism
should have taken such a hold of Lancashire and that
Manchester should welcome Disraeli with such enthusiasm
was indeed a portent. There was no more industrial
district in England, and none where the working man was
more independent. Manchester was the home of Free
Trade, and the hall in which Disraeli spoke was the
favourite platform of Cobden and Bright during the
struggle against the Corn Laws. Lancashire was the
native county of both Gladstone and Bright, the pillars
of Liberalism at this period; and Gladstone, by political
progresses through its towns in the sixties, had made an
impassioned bid for its support. Both Gladstone and
Bright had sat for a while for Lancashire seats; but both
had been defeated and gone elsewhere. The great
territorial Conservative influence in Lancashire was that
of the house of Stanley, whose present head was designated
by the discontented as Disraeli's supplanter. But even
in Lancashire Derby was ready to yield Disraeli place,
to speak of him not merely as his ' old political colleague '
and ' a personal friend of more than twenty years' stand-

ing,' but as his ' chief,' and to bear striking testimony to his high qualities. ' Few leaders of men have ever been more successful in securing the personal confidence and sympathy and goodwill of those with whom they act, and no one has ever shown himself more faithful both to the obligation of private friendship and to the honourable tie of party connection.' Another passage in Derby's speech at the meeting in the Free Trade Hall showed that the Conservative leaders were determined not to snatch prematurely at power, but to wait till the disgust of the country with Gladstonian policy was complete. It might be the tactics of the Radical party to put a Conservative Government in office in a minority; ' but just because it is their game it ought not to be ours.' The course which Disraeli took when Gladstone resigned over his defeat in the following spring on the Irish University Bill was clearly foreshadowed in this sagacious advice.

To W. Romaine Callender, jun.[1]

GROSVENOR GATE, *April* 6, 1872.—I am sure you and kind Mrs. Callender will be glad to hear of our safe and agreeable arrival at Grosvenor Gate; cheered, as far as the Potteries, by your enthusiastic population, which calmed, by degrees, as we entered less busy lands, and which, when we traversed my own country, was as still as became a true prophet.

One is little disposed to do anything to-day, but it is impossible to refrain expressing to you our sense of all your kindness, delicate attentions, and munificent hospitality.

We have talked of them ever since, and shall often do so; and, from all I hear, this wondrous week will have no ordinary influence on public opinion and future history. . . .

Disraeli took another opportunity in June to review and inspirit his new party machine and to elaborate the policy which he proposed to the country. This time the body which he addressed was the National Union, the central society to which the Conservative and Constitutional associations throughout the country were affiliated.

[1] Disraeli's host at Manchester and chairman of the Free Trade Hall meeting. He won a seat at Manchester in 1874, was selected by Disraeli to second the Address, and was offered by him a baronetcy at the close of 1875; but he died, prematurely, early in 1876, before the baronetcy had been gazetted.

Speaking, on June 24, to this representative audience at a banquet at the Crystal Palace he laid it down that the Tory party had three great objects: to maintain our institutions, to uphold the Empire, and to elevate the condition of the people. On the first he had dwelt at considerable length at Manchester, and he added little that was fresh at the Crystal Palace. With regard to social reform, Liberals had scoffed at his proposals as a 'policy of sewage'; but to a working man, Disraeli maintained, it was a policy of life and death. It was, he said, a large subject, with many branches.

It involves the state of the dwellings of the people, the moral consequences of which are not less considerable than the physical. It involves their enjoyment of some of the chief elements of nature—air, light, and water. It involves the regulation of their industry, the inspection of their toil. It involves the purity of their provisions, and it touches upon all the means by which you may wean them from habits of excess and of brutality.

But the part of his speech which struck the highest note was that which associated Conservatism with the maintenance of Empire. His Reform Act of 1867, he said, was founded on the confidence that the great body of the people were conservative in the purest and loftiest sense; that the working classes were proud of belonging to a great country, and wished to maintain its greatness; that they were proud of belonging to an Imperial country, and resolved to maintain their Empire. What was the record of Liberalism in regard to Empire, and what ought to be Conservative policy?

If you look to the history of this country since the advent of Liberalism—forty years ago—you will find that there has been no effort so continuous, so subtle, supported by so much energy, and carried on with so much ability and acumen, as the attempts of Liberalism to effect the disintegration of the Empire of England. And, gentlemen, of all its efforts, this is the one which has been the nearest to success. Statesmen of the highest character, writers of the most distinguished ability, the most organised and efficient means, have been employed in this endeavour. It has been proved to all of us that we have lost money by our Colonies. It has been shown with precise, with mathematical demonstration, that there never was a jewel in the Crown of England that was so truly costly as the possession of India. How often has it been suggested that we should at once emancipate ourselves from this incubus! Well, that result was nearly accomplished. When those subtle views were adopted by the country under the plausible plea of granting self-government to the Colonies, I confess that I myself thought that the tie was broken. Not that I for one object to self-government; I cannot conceive how our distant Colonies can have their affairs administered except by self-government.

But self-government, in my opinion, when it was conceded, ought to have been conceded as part of a great policy of Imperial consolidation. It ought to have been accompanied by an Imperial tariff, by securities for the people of England for the enjoyment of the unappropriated lands which belonged to the Sovereign as their trustee, and by a military code which should have precisely defined the means and the responsibilities by which the Colonies should be defended, and by which, if necessary, this country should call for aid from the Colonies themselves. It ought, further, to have been accompanied by the institution of some representative council in the metropolis, which would have brought the Colonies into constant and continuous relations with the Home Government. All this, however, was omitted because those who advised that policy—and I believe their convictions were sincere—looked upon the Colonies of England, looked even upon our connection with India, as a burden upon this country; viewing everything in a financial aspect, and totally passing by those moral and political considerations which make nations great, and by the influence of which alone men are distinguished from animals.

Well, what has been the result of this attempt during the reign of Liberalism for the disintegration of the Empire? It has entirely failed. But how has it failed? Through the sympathy of the Colonies for the Mother Country. They have decided that the Empire shall not be destroyed; and in my opinion no Minister in this country will do his duty who neglects any opportunity of reconstructing as much as possible our Colonial Empire, and of responding to those distant sympathies which may become the source of incalculable strength and happiness to this land.

That is the famous declaration from which the modern conception of the British Empire largely takes its rise. In it Disraeli struck a chord that immediately echoed round the Colonies, India, and the Dependencies; and the reverberation has never ceased. The time could not be far distant, he prophetically told his hearers, when England would have to decide between national and cosmopolitan principles. In their fight against Liberalism or the Continental system Conservatives would have against them those who had enjoyed power for nearly half a century; but still they could rely, he said in sonorous Disraelian language, on ' the sublime instincts of an ancient people.'

The issue is not a mean one. It is whether you will be content to be a comfortable England, modelled and moulded upon Continental principles and meeting in due course an inevitable fate, or whether you will be a great country, an Imperial country, a country where your sons, when they rise, rise to paramount positions, and obtain not merely the esteem of their countrymen, but command the respect of the world.

Lord Morley remarks of Disraeli's watchwords of Empire and Social Reform, that ' when power fell into his hands he made no single move of solid effect for either social reform or imperial unity,'[1] whereas it was Gladstone's wont to embody policy in Parliamentary Bills. The statement is very far from being accurate, and subsequent chapters of this biography will show what a material contribution both to social welfare and to imperial con-solidation was made by the Beaconsfield Government of 1874. But it is, of course, true that many of Disraeli's most fertile ideas did not issue in Bills; and as a practical politician he must in this respect yield place to Gladstone. It is, however, precisely the fact that Gladstone seldom or never played with political ideas which could not be enclosed within the compass of a Bill that marks his inferiority as a statesman and explains his diminishing hold on the present generation; and it is precisely the fact that Disraeli did allow his mind such free play that is his greatest praise in our eyes and that will insure his fame with those who come after us.

[1] *Gladstone*, Bk. VI., ch. 8.

Between Manchester and the Crystal Palace Disraeli had another proof of his growing popularity. He attended, along with a crowd of distinguished personages, the Literary Fund dinner, in order to support a reigning Sovereign in the chair, Leopold II., King of the Belgians. Writing to Corry a day or two afterwards, he said: ' The demonstration at the Literary Fund meeting was equal to Manchester. The mob consisting of Princes, Ambassadors, wits, artists—and critics !' His speech in proposing the King's health was one of his happiest. It was a charming and delightful inconsistency, he said, that the republic of letters should be presided over by a monarch; let them meet it by an inconsistency as amiably flagrant, and give their Sovereign Chairman a right royal welcome. His description of Belgium, and of the policy which guaranteed its independence and neutrality, has a special interest to-day.

Forty years ago a portion of Europe, and one not the least fair, seemed doomed by an inexorable fate to permanent dependence and periodical devastation. And yet the conditions of that country were favourable to civilisation and human happiness; a fertile soil skilfully cultivated, a land covered with beautiful cities and occupied by a race prone alike to liberty and religion, and always excelling in the fine arts. In the midst of a European convulsion, a great statesman resolved to terminate that deplorable destiny, and conceived the idea of establishing the independence of Belgium on the principle of political neutrality. The idea was welcomed at first with sceptical contempt. But we who live in the after generation can bear witness to its triumphant success, and can take the opportunity of congratulating that noble policy which consecrated to perpetual peace the battle-field of Europe.

Disraeli's political activities in this spring of 1872 were almost entirely confined to his two great extra-Parliamentary appearances. He was much shocked in February to receive the news of the murder of his friend Mayo, the Viceroy of India, in the Andaman Islands.

To Lady Beaconsfield.

Feb. 12, '72.—Horrible news from India! Lord Mayo assassinated and dead! The enclosed telegram is from Robert Bourke!

Shall be home pretty early.

Quite shaken to the centre. Gladstone announced it: I said a few words.

G. GATE, *April* 26, '72.—Last night was very damaging to the Government :[1] a family quarrel, in which we did not interfere, except on the part of Ball, who could scarcely be silent. Bouverie in fierce opposition; and though the affair ended without a vote, as was inevitable, the Government most unnecessarily blundered into a signal defeat at the end of the night. . . .

May 7.—Last night the Government received a great, and unexpected, blow: Gordon's resolution[2] having been carried to the surprise of both sides! The cheering exceeded even that on the Ballot Clause. . . .

To Lord Derby.

GROSVENOR GATE, *May* 3, 1872.—My suggestion of identical subscriptions from [Mayo's] colleagues found no favor. It was thought to be an idea, perhaps, suited to colleagues in a Ministry, who then can frame a tariff according to their salaries, but was not deemed applicable to existing circumstances. Our late colleagues are like Martial's epigrams—some rich, some poor, some moderate; so they prefer subscribing according to their means, or their inclination. . . .

The ballot was again seriously damaged in Ho. of Comm. last night, and we supported the Govt. and the Whigs against an infuriated Mountain. . . .

The Ballot Bill was the main occupation of the session; and as Disraeli's object, in view of divided opinions in his party, was to get the question settled, he maintained a rigorous silence while it was running a troubled course through the House. His policy was to take care that the Liberals should not have a popular grievance to exploit, a popular cry on which to dissolve, either through the

---

[1] A debate on a University Tests (Dublin) Bill, in which independent Liberals like Fawcett, Playfair, and Bouverie strongly attacked the Government.

[2] On the Scottish Education Bill. The Government was defeated by 7; 216 to 209.

failure of the Bill in the Commons owing to Tory obstruction or through its rejection on second reading by the Lords. But he hoped that amendments making the Bill optional would be secured in the Lords by the pressure of a unanimous Tory party aided by Russell and the old Whigs. This programme was duly carried out, and when the Bill was returned amended to the Commons Disraeli broke his silence to defend the fantastic plan of optional secrecy. But the Commons would have none of it; and in the Lords, the Duke of Northumberland, at the head of a body of independent Conservatives, averted a struggle between the two Houses by supporting the motion not to insist upon the amendment. Disraeli was rather put out at the way in which the matter had been bungled.

To Lord Derby.

GROSVENOR GATE, *June* 20, 1872.—I was in hopes I might have met you somewhere yesterday, and had a few minutes' conversation with you *re* Ballot Bill (H. of Lords) wh. seems to me in an unsatisfactory position.

When the Duke of Richmond called on me to confer on his alternative propositions—to throw out the Bill on the 2nd reading, or to make it permissive in Committee, I assented to the latter scheme on the very distinct conditions that it shd. be sanctioned by the unanimous assent of the party, and especially of yourself. The Duke subsequently wrote to me, that he had conferred with you, Ld. Salisbury, and others, and that you had unanimously adopted the latter scheme.

But it seems there must have been some terrible mistake on this head, as I observe you did not vote on the occasion, and it is now rumored, that you disapprove of the proposal.

Unless the Duke is supported, the Ballot Bill will pass, wh. neither the House of Comm. nor the country desire. It is impossible for the Duke to recede from his position; it would make him ridiculous and totally unable in future to pretend to control affairs. Lord Russell sanctioned the move, and still is of opinion, that we shd. not recede from the ground we have, after deliberation, occupied. Whether the Duke is beaten or not, his character and the repute of the party demand that he shall be firm. All that important and influential section who were in favor of throwing out the Bill on the 2nd reading, at least on our side, would be outraged, if there were any transaction or compromise, wh. secured the virtual passing of the Government measure.

I hope, therefore, you will gravely consider these critical circumstances, for, tho' the Duke of Richmond, publicly and privately, must make every effort to rally his forces for the occasion, there is no doubt those exertions will be considerably neutralised if you are the avowed opponent of his proceedings.

July 12.—Thanks for your letter, wh. is full of good stuff; I think we may raise a flame, wh. will well occupy the lieges during the recess, and sustain the unpopularity of the Ministry.

The ballot in your house was a sad business. Nothing but unanimity could justify our course. I think it was the right one, and that throwing out the Bill on the second reading (even if it cd. be done) would have raised an agitation against the House of Lords on the ground of their purely obstructive policy.

The Duke of Northumberland shd. be asked why, after having attended the two meetings at D. of Richmond's in silence, interpreted as assent, he shd. have led the defection ? Had he spoken out at the meetings and been supported, the course might have been changed.

The truth is, I fancy, he, and his following, and all others, were satisfied enough at the time, but got frightened afterwards by the articles in *The Times*, wh. laughed at them the next day for their pains.

However, the mischief is done, and our only consolation must be, that the Government wh. first appeals to the country on the secret suffrage will, in all probability, be cashiered.

One serious rebuff which the Government received in this session must have given Disraeli peculiar satisfaction. When he had assumed the leadership in the spring of 1849 he had made it his principal object to endeavour to convince Parliament of the injustice suffered by the landed interest in having charged upon it the whole of the local rates. Rates, he had pointed out, were raised for national as well as for local objects, and benefited the whole community and not merely the owners and occupiers of real property. Now that the State had withdrawn protection from the landed interest, they had a right, he had argued, to have this injustice redressed. The argument impressed the House at the time, and the majorities against Disraeli's motions became smaller with succeeding years. But little or nothing had been actually done in this direction in Parliaments where Disraeli never had a majority; and fresh charges had been constantly put upon the rates, while the actual administration was largely withdrawn from local control. Sir Massey Lopes, a substantial county member who had made a special study of the question, carried this session against the Government, by a majority of no less than a hundred, a motion that £2,000,000 worth of these charges, dealing with the administration of justice, police, and lunatics, should be placed on the Consolidated Fund. Disraeli strongly urged that the reform was five and twenty years overdue, while the burdens on real property had greatly increased, and, with the urgent claims of public education and public health, must increase still further. In spite of the adverse vote, the Government shirked their responsibility; accordingly, the relief which Disraeli had pleaded for in his first days of leadership he was himself to be the Minister to grant.

The Government were damaged less by their defeat on Lopes's motion than by their success in carrying a much-needed measure, the Licensing Act, which irritated a powerful trade and interfered with the habits of countless individuals. Their unpopularity was increased in the autumn by the blow to British pride involved in the swingeing damages awarded to the United States by the Geneva arbitrators in respect of the *Alabama* dispute. The loss of Ministerial seats at by-elections continued. Consequently, though Disraeli, absorbed by domestic sorrow,[1] did not resume his pungent attacks between the close of the 1872 session and the opening of the next, Ministers met Parliament in February, 1873, with a tarnished reputation and clouded prospects, and promptly received a stunning blow from which they never pro-

[1] See below, ch. 6.

perly recovered. The task before them in the session was obviously a perilous one. Gladstone, who had already carried, with the full force of an unimpaired majority, two great Irish Bills, was about to venture, with his majority much less under control, on a third. This time he was to deal with that University question which his rival had in hand when he himself overtrumped him with disestablishment. Once again Manning was deep in the counsels of a British Premier hopeful of finding a solution; and he was to mislead Gladstone as he had misled Disraeli. Disraeli's letters show us the hopes and fears of the Opposition.

To Montagu Corry.

H. OF C., *Feb.* 10, '73.—Lord Derby on Saturday seemed to think a crisis was at hand, and rather regretted going away (which, by the bye, Cairns is also doing). D. said ' You can telegraph for me.' . . .

Feb. 11.—I wrote you a wretched scrawl yesterday from H. of C. in a miserable state, and am not much better to-day.

From what I gathered from Robert Montagu, coached by Manning, I should think Gladstone's scheme will do. I infer something like this. Trinity Coll. to be no longer a University, but to retain a considerable endowment. The Romans not to be endowed. The Peel Colleges to be abolished. An Examining Board ½ Catholic and ½ Protestant; but Cath. under-grads. to be examined only on those subjects and in that manner the priesthood approves and, of course, by the Cath. moiety of examiners.

They say G. is to make the greatest speech to-morrow he has yet accomplished. . . .

Feb. 15.—I have been in a state of coma for the last few days—and have been unable to write. Indeed, it is only the recollection that it is Saturday, which forces me to this feebleness. Everything seems to have calmed down again, and I see no movement for the next fortnight. . . .

I conclude there will be no attempt to oppose the 2nd reading of the Bill, though there will be a considerable debate thereon: and in Committee, though nothing ever succeeds in Committee, there will be an effort to establish the Professorships of Philosophy and History, and perhaps to reconstruct the Governing Council. . . .

Feb. 18.—There is to be a council at my rooms on Saturday *re* Ir. Univ. Bill. . . .

Feb. 22.—We had our meeting this morning; it was very long and very troublesome. We came to a conclusion, as a Home Ruler has given notice of opposing 2nd reading, to encourage and carry on a great debate—for three nights, if possible, and, in the course of it, to announce, that we should move resolutions on going into Committee.

I should not be surprised if Fawcett gives notice of resolutions at once in much the same spirit, speculating on the Home Ruler relinquishing his purpose. . . .

Feb. 25.—. . . There is a feeling in the air, that the 3rd branch of the Upas-tree will still blast Celtic society. As Ball says, if the Bill is got rid of, no party in the country, and neither side of the House, will ever hear of the question again: for, in fact, it is all humbug. . . .

12, GEORGE ST., *Feb.* 27.—I had an interesting letter from Lord Derby yesterday, anxious about the Irish Bill, and impressing upon me, that, if wanted, he could be here in 4 and 20 hours. He dined with Thiers, whom he found very old, feeble, with a cracked voice, but warming up into animation as he talked on; never alluding even to domestic affairs, but expatiating on every point of foreign. . . . He seemed to think dissensions must soon break out between Prussia and Bavaria, and repeatedly said that the first and, indeed, only object for France was the reorganisation of her army: ' not that we wanted war, etc., but nobody knew what might happen, and we must be prepared.' . . .

I am now going down to the House, walking; as the air is clear and the wind westerly. . . .

March 1.—. . . There is no news, except a general impression that Gladstone will withdraw his Bill. So Lord Stanhope told me this morning at British Museum: but I doubt it. He will not like losing the opportunity of self-vindication in many speeches.

To Gathorne Hardy.

Saturday, March 8, 1873.—I thought your speech excellent, and so, I observe, does the *Spectator* to-day; no mean Parliamentary critic.

It was a hard trial to get up at midnight, as I know from experience—but all the things you omitted to say will come into another speech, and had you not demonstrated, the effect wd. have been most injurious.

I was very glad that you alluded to a Gladstone dissolution as ultimately inevitable, and that you spoke out to Knightley.

[1] Sir Rainald Knightley (afterwards Lord Knightley), of Fawsley, M.P. for South Northants, a squire of long descent, high honour, many prejudices, and some Parliamentary capacity, was an irreconcilable member of the

He belongs to a clique, who think we have no single object in the world but place and patronage; little suspecting, that for four years we have, for the sake of the country, and especially for the Tory party, unceasingly labored to prevent a premature change.

The fever of my attack seems to have subsided, but I am very feeble.

As the letters suggest, Gladstone's scheme sounded very plausible when set forth by himself in one of those exegetical discourses in which no other Parliamentarian could compare with him; but it would not stand critical examination. Protestant feeling was offended by the constitution of the governing body of the new University, which was such that, in Lord Morley's euphemistic words, ' it did not make clerical predominance ultimately impossible.' In spite of this prospect, the Irish Bishops were offended by the maintenance of the principle of mixed education, in which Protestant colleges and students were to stand side by side with Roman Catholic colleges and students; and ultimately Cardinal Cullen refused and denounced the offer. Those who realised what a University meant and cared for the interests of higher education, of whom Fawcett was the most prominent representative, were disgusted by the prohibition of any University teacher in theology, modern history, or mental and moral philosophy; and by the liability of all teachers to suspension or deprivation for giving offence to religious convictions.

---

anti-Disraeli Tory clique, and only supported the Opposition leaders by his vote on this occasion because he was satisfied from Hardy's speech and conversation that they would not take office till after a dissolution. A story which Lady Knightley tells, in her *Journals*, p. 240, of the origin of her husband's feeling towards Disraeli, suggests that a plentiful lack of humour had much to do with Tory mistrust of their witty and sardonic chief. ' I asked Rainald to-day,' writes Lady Knightley on March 15, 1873, ' when he first began to distrust [Disraeli]. He said, " Very soon after I came into Parliament, I was desired by the Whip to do all I could to get our men to vote against the Government on some question—not a very important one—on which they seemed to me to be in the right. However, I trusted our leader, and thought he probably knew more about it than I did, so I did as I was bid. When we got into the lobby, we found ourselves in a minority, upon which Disraeli said, ' There ! we've sacrificed our characters, and voted wrong, and haven't beat the Government after all !' " Comment, I think,' adds Lady Knightley, ' is superfluous.' It is indeed.

The impracticability of the scheme as it stood was so patent that Ministers were reduced to endeavouring to obtain support by suggesting that large amendments could be made in Committee, and by dwelling on the threat that they would treat the second reading as a vital matter.

Disraeli in his speech on the last night of the debate declined to put any confidence in these unconfirmed hints of Committee amendments, and protested against the threat of resignation. No one wished to disturb Gladstone in his place, but it was the duty of members to say distinctly whether they could approve this particular measure. It proposed to found a University which was not universal, and in an age when young men prattled about protoplasm and young ladies in gilded saloons unconsciously talked atheism, to prohibit the teaching of philosophy! He chaffed Gladstone about the 'anonymous persons' who were to constitute the council of the new University. He vindicated his own policy of concurrent endowment in 1868, a policy which had been steadily pursued by statesmen of all parties down to that date, but had then been killed by Gladstone. 'The right hon. gentleman says I burnt my fingers on that occasion, but,' said Disraeli, holding out his hands across the floor of the House amid general amusement, 'I see no scars.' He continued:

The right hon. gentleman, suddenly—I impute no motive, that is quite unnecessary—changed his mind, and threw over the policy of concurrent endowment, mistaking the clamour of the Nonconformists[1] for the voice of the nation. The Roman Catholics fell into the trap. They forgot the cause of University education in the prospect of destroying the Protestant Church. The right hon. gentleman succeeded in his object. He became Prime Minister of England. . . . The Roman Catholics had the satisfaction of destroying the Protestant Church—of disestablishing the Protestant Church. They had the satisfaction before the year was over of witnessing the disestablishment of the Roman Catholic Church at

[1] Another reading has 'the *Nonconformist*'—the newspaper organ of the Dissenters.

Rome. As certain as that we are in this House, the policy
that caused the one led to the other. . . . The Roman
Catholics, having reduced Ireland to a spiritual desert, are
discontented and have a grievance; and they come to Parliament in order that it may create for them a blooming Garden
of Eden.

And then Disraeli proceeded to one of those attacks on
the general tendency of Gladstonian policy which were
beginning to sink deeply into the national mind.   Gladstone, he said, had substituted a policy of confiscation
for the policy of concurrent endowment:

You have had four years of it. You have despoiled
churches. You have threatened every corporation and endowment in the country. You have examined into everybody's affairs. You have criticised every profession and
vexed every trade. No one is certain of his property and
nobody knows what duties he may have to perform to-
morrow.

Gladstone, in reply, urged Parliament to go on in its
work of bringing justice to Ireland in spite of the perverse-
ness of those whom it was attempting to assist; but the
House realised the absurdity of proceeding with proposals
repudiated by Catholics as well as by Protestants.   The
division was taken after two o'clock on the morning of
Wednesday, March 12.   Ministers were beaten by 3 votes,
the numbers being 287 to 284.   They had a small majority
among the English members, and a large majority among
the Scotch; but the Irish voted 68 to 15 against them.
'The Irish Romans,' wrote Hardy in his diary, ' voted
against Gladstone in a body, but it was utterly wrong of
Gladstone to taunt us, for our opposition long preceded
theirs, and there was no compact whatever. And now
what will follow ? I doubt not Gladstone will try to
force us in, but in vain. It is neither our duty nor our
interest to dissolve Parliament for him, and I cannot
admit the right of any Government to make any question
they please vital, and, if a combination negatives, to force
upon one portion of it all the responsibility.'

Hardy's opinion, thus recorded decisively at the first

moment in his diary, was the one which prevailed with Disraeli and his colleagues. In truth the situation had been anticipated; and, though two of Disraeli's most important colleagues, Derby and Cairns, were abroad, he had ascertained from them before they went their unwillingness to accept office in the event of such a contingency as had occurred. The Beaconsfield papers contain the following scrap in Derby's handwriting:

If it is only contended that Mr. D. before announcing his decision, ought to have maturely considered the circumstances and consulted with his friends, the answer is that he had done so already in anticipation of what for the last six weeks was a possible and not improbable contingency.

Hardy and Richmond went to see their chief on the morrow of the division, and there was an agreement between them all in this sense, though apparently Disraeli's Socratic method suggested to Hardy that he had a doubt on the subject. The upshot of the talk of the three colleagues was that the impracticability of office was so clear that Disraeli might decline without further consultation.

Meanwhile there was some hesitation in the Ministerial camp, and it required a couple of Cabinet Councils, one on the Wednesday and one on the Thursday, to bring them to resignation.

To Lord Beauchamp.

Thursday, March 13.—I have had a good night, except disturbed too much by my cough, which must be again attended to. I neglected remedies in the anarchy of yesterday.

What is going to take place ? And what is the 2nd Cabinet about ? Our friend cannot even resign in the usual manner, I was in hopes yesterday that the Q. had not accepted his resignation as in my case, which would have solved many knots, and that we should have an early dissolution on his part; but the ambiguous voices of the oracles this morning perplex me.

The second Cabinet, however, decided for resignation; Gladstone saw the Queen in the early afternoon of the Thursday, and announced the fact in Parliament at 4.30.

Disraeli was stopped in the lobby, as he was entering the House of Commons, by a message from the Palace.

From Queen Victoria.

BUCKINGHAM PALACE, *March* 13, 1873.—Mr. Gladstone has just been here and has tendered his resignation and that of all his colleagues in consequence of the vote of the House of Commons on Tuesday night—which the Queen has accepted. She therefore writes to Mr. Disraeli to ask him whether he will undertake to form a Government.

The Queen would like to see Mr. Disraeli at 6 or as soon after as possible.

She sends this letter by her private secretary, Colonel Ponsonby, who can be the bearer of any written or verbal answer from Mr Disraeli.

The Queen herself drew up a memorandum to describe what passed at the audience which followed.

Memorandum by Queen Victoria.

BUCKINGHAM PALACE, *March* 13, 1873.—Mr. Disraeli came at a little after 6. After expressing my feeling for him in his sorrow and shaking hands with him, I said I had sent for him in consequence of last night's vote; and he asked whether I wished him to give a categorical answer, or to say a few words on the present state of affairs. I said I should willingly hear what he had to say.

He then went on to say that he had not expected the vote; he had thought, after Mr. Cardwell's speech, the Government would have a majority. That the Conservative party never was more compact or more united; that there was the most perfect understanding between him and all those who had served with him, and especially named Ld. Derby, Ld. Cairns, Mr. Hardy, and Sir S. Northcote. That he was perfectly able to form a Government at once, perfectly fit to carry on the administration of the country to my entire satisfaction; that he could command 280 votes; that since, as he said, ' I had left your Majesty's *immediate* service, for I never consider myself out of your Majesty's service,' the party had gained considerably, about thirty seats; that he had laboured to keep the party as much together and in as efficient a state as possible; but that it would be useless to attempt to carry on the Government with a minority in the House of Commons, and that he must therefore state his inability to undertake to form a Government in the present Parliament.

What was then to be done ? I asked. 'Mr. Gladstone ought
to remain in and continue to carry on the Government.'
This, I said, I thought he very likely would object to, having
declared his views so strongly on this measure. This was a
mistake, Mr. Disraeli replied, and he ought never to have
done so. That might be so or not, I said, but anyhow Mr.
Gladstone *did* feel this, and did not ask for a dissolution,
therefore I thought it doubtful whether he would consent
to resume or continue in office, feeling he could not submit
to this vote. ' But he has *condoned* for it by his resignation
and readiness to give up power,' was the answer; that he
should not throw up office merely for this vote; it would not
be a good return to the present Parliament, which had supported him so warmly, and in which he had carried 3 great
measures, for so he must call them, though he might not agree
with them. I again asked him what I was to say to Mr.
Gladstone, and he repeated that ' I decline to form a Government in the present Parliament, and I do not ask for a dissolution.'

Of course, he said, there were instances where a Sovereign
had been left without a Government, and in such a case he
would, of course, be ready to serve me. I said that I would
at once let Mr. Gladstone know, but that I might have to
call upon him again.

Disraeli, in giving Hardy afterwards an account of his
audience, added that the Queen's ' cordiality was *marked*,'
and that ' she manifested, as he thought, a repugnance
to her present Government.' To Beauchamp he wrote:
' I had a more than gracious reception; and, if Her
Majesty were leader of the Opposition, I believe this
morning she would be First Lord of her own Treasury.'
The Queen at once sent Ponsonby to Gladstone with
an account of what had passed, adding, ' She considers
this as sending for you anew.' But Gladstone suspected
a trick and told Ponsonby that he ' thought Mr. Disraeli
was endeavouring, by at once throwing back on me an
offer which it was impossible for me at the time and under
the circumstances to accept, to get up a case of absolute
necessity founded upon this refusal of mine, and thus,
becoming the indispensable man and party, to have in his
hands a lever wherewith to overcome the reluctance and
resistance of his friends, who would not be able to deny

that the Queen must have a Government.'   To Gladstone
Disraeli was the wily mystery-man, and the simple reasoning which had led his rival to decline did not appear at
all adequate to one who was determined to find some
deep calculation in all that rival did.   Accordingly,
Gladstone asked, through Ponsonby, that Disraeli's reply
might be put in writing.

Memorandum in Colonel Ponsonby's Handwriting.

March 13, 1873.—Colonel Ponsonby called on Mr. Disraeli
in the evening with a message from the Queen, asking him
to give Her Majesty, in writing, the substance of his conversation with the Queen.

Mr. Disraeli willingly complied with Her Majesty's wishes,
and wrote down roughly the chief points on which he had
spoken.

Colonel Ponsonby asked Mr. Disraeli if he might assume
that this meant an unconditional refusal.   Mr. Disraeli
replied that such was the meaning in the present state of
affairs.

Colonel Ponsonby asked, if the Queen was ready to sanction
a dissolution as soon as possible, whether Mr. Disraeli could
then accept office, taking, of course, the responsibility of
giving the advice to Her Majesty to dissolve.

Mr. Disraeli replied that he could not accept office with such
an understanding, and that his refusal was absolute.

He hoped in some future day, when another Parliament
assembled, to find an opportunity of serving the Queen, but
with the present House of Commons with a large majority
opposed to him, he could not undertake the Government.

Such was the official report, certified by Disraeli to be
correct, which Ponsonby made to the Queen.   But
Ponsonby drew up a longer and more detailed account of
what took place, which shows more clearly Disraeli's
position, while it also amusingly brings out the secretary's
Whig distrust of the Tory leader.[1]

[1] Disraeli, subsequently, during his great Ministry, bore striking testimony to the absolute impartiality with which Ponsonby carr ed out his
duties as private secretary to the Queen.   He said to a political friend:
' I believe that General Ponsonby used to be a Whig, but, whatever his
politics may once have been, I can only say that I could not wish my case
better stated to the Queen than the private secretary does it.   Perhaps I
am a gainer by his Whiggishness, as it makes him more scrupulously on
his guard to be always absolutely fair and lucid.'   See article on 'The
Character of Queen Victoria,' *Quarterly Review*, April, 1901.

Her Majesty sent me to see Mr. Disraeli in Edwards's Hotel, George Street, Hanover Square.[1] He at once acceded to the Queen's wish, and getting pens and ink said, ' There, let me see, I can easily put down what is wanted; that is very nearly what I said.' I observed that I did not quite understand it, and hoped he would forgive me if I asked him whether he meant it as a refusal to take office while this Parliament sat, or whether he refused entirely, whether the Queen consented to dissolve or not. He said he meant it as a refusal, that he could not carry on the Government in a Parliament where there were 80 votes of majority against him. ' But,' I said, ' would you take office and dissolve ?' He said, ' I thought the Queen would not agree to this.' I replied I thought she would not object, in fact, I felt certain she would not. ' But,' he said, ' there is an idea that this, being my Parliament, cannot be dissolved by me.' ' But,' I remarked, ' the Queen could offer you a dissolution, though, of course, you would be responsible for advising her to do so.' ' Of course,' he said, ' I well understand that; but I decline altogether to accept office.'

He went on, ' How could I proceed ? For two months at least Parliament must continue, while the regular estimates, Mutiny Act, etc., are passed. The Conservatives are gaining favour in the country, but these two months would ruin them. They would be exposed in a hostile House to every insult which the Opposition might choose to fling at them, and the party would be seriously damaged, while the business of the country would suffer. The only possibility of carrying any measure would be by allying myself to the Irish lot, whom I detest and disagree with, and who would throw me over whenever it suited their purpose.' I said, ' You have defeated the Government; ought you not therefore to under-take the responsibility of forming one ?' ' No,' he replied; ' we did not defeat the Government. We threw out a stupid, blundering Bill, which Gladstone, in his *tête montée* way, tried to make a vote of confidence. It was a foolish mistake of his; but he has condoned for it by resigning. He can now resume office with perfect freedom.'

During the first part of the interview Disraeli sat at a table, and as he spoke with eagerness, there was something in his over-civil expressions about the Queen or ' my dear Colonel,' which made me think he was playing with me, and I felt once or twice a difficulty in not laughing; but when he developed the reasons of his policy he rose and stood much more upright than I have ever seen him, spoke in a most frank and straight-forward manner, and with a sharpness and decision which

[1] See below, p. 233.

was different from his early words.   Yet probably he had
measured the length of my foot, and had been more sincere
and honest in his message to the Queen than when he made me
believe in his frank exposition of policy.

He was far easier to speak to than Gladstone, who forces
you into his groove, while Disraeli apparently follows yours
and is genial, almost too genial, in his sentiments. . . .

In accordance with Her Majesty's desire, Disraeli
embodied in a couple of sentences the reply which he had
already given:

In answer to the gracious inquiry, whether he would undertake to form a Government, Mr. Disraeli said he was prepared
to form an Administration which he believed would carry
on Her Majesty's affairs with efficiency, and would possess
her confidence, but he could not undertake to carry on Her
Majesty's Government in the present House of Commons.

Subsequently, Her Majesty having remarked that Mr.
Gladstone was not inclined to recommend a dissolution of
Parliament, Mr. Disraeli stated, that he himself would not
advise Her Majesty to take that step.

The language was perhaps not as categorical as it might
have been, and Gladstone's ingenious mind found a
discrepancy between the two sentences, which led him on
the Friday to make a further inquiry of the Queen.   To
Her Majesty's common sense it was clear that, if Disraeli
would neither take office in the existing Parliament nor
advise a dissolution, his attitude amounted, as Ponsonby
put it in his memorandum, to an ' absolute refusal '; and
she accordingly answered that Disraeli had unconditionally
declined to form a Government.   After such a reply, it
might have been thought that a Minister who still
possessed for the ordinary purposes of government a
majority of eighty or ninety would have considered the
immediate resumption of office, with or without the intention of an early dissolution, to be his obvious duty.   But
Gladstone, indignant at Disraeli's avoidance of responsibility, embarrassed the Queen by discovering an alternative
course—the drafting of a detailed memorandum to show
that Disraeli's action was neither justifiable in itself nor

in accordance with precedent. He urged that the proceeding between the Queen and Disraeli could not be regarded as complete, as the vote had been the result of concerted action by the Opposition on a matter declared to be vital by Ministers; and therefore Disraeli ought by counsel and inquiry among his friends to have exhausted all practicable means to form a Government. He recited the history of previous Parliamentary crises to show that there was no precedent for Disraeli's summary refusal. He could not call his colleagues together and ask them to resume their offices were he not able 'to prove to them that according to usage every means had been exhausted on the part of the Opposition for providing for the government of the country, or at least that nothing more was to be expected from that quarter.'[1]

It was a lame conclusion. Gladstone had already been told that nothing more was to be expected from that quarter. The Queen felt this strongly, when the memorandum was presented to her on the Saturday. But as her constitutional duty was to obtain a Government, and as it was plain that the only way in which this could be done was to persuade Gladstone to return, she consented to humour him so far as to become the medium of communication for the rival leaders. Her secretary put on paper an explanation of her views.

Memorandum in Colonel Ponsonby's Handwriting.

BUCKINGHAM PALACE, *March* 15.—The unusual course followed by Mr. Gladstone of asking the Queen for further explanations before he could call the Cabinet together, made it necessary for Her Majesty to consider how she could meet his request.

The Queen could not refuse to take any notice of it, as this would have retarded the progress of the negotiations which Her Majesty was anxious to bring to a satisfactory termination. Besides which, Her Majesty desired there should be no misunderstanding.

The Queen could not assure Mr. Gladstone that Mr. Dis-

---

[1] The text is given in Lord Morley's *Gladstone*, Book VI., ch. 12, where the crisis is narrated and examined at length.

raeli's refusal to accept office was complete, as Her Majesty would then have undertaken the responsibility of answering for the Opposition party.

The Queen could not herself have called on Mr. Disraeli for further explanations, as Her Majesty would then have assumed the view taken by Mr. Gladstone of Mr. Disraeli's conduct.

The Queen therefore, with Mr. Gladstone's knowledge and consent, forwarded his letter entire to Mr. Disraeli.

From Queen Victoria.

BUCKINGHAM PALACE, *March* 15, '73.—The Queen communicated, as Mr. Disraeli is aware, the substance of his refusal to undertake to form a Government in the present Parliament, to Mr. Gladstone, and she thinks it due to Mr. Disraeli to send him the accompanying letter (with Mr. Gladstone's knowledge), and will be glad to receive a reply from Mr. Disraeli which she can show Mr. Gladstone.

The Queen allows this communication to be made through her in order to prevent as much as possible any misunderstanding.

On receipt of this letter on Saturday afternoon, Disraeli told Ponsonby that he could easily write a short reply at once, but he ' felt sure it would meet with your Majesty's wishes and his own inclinations if he consulted Lord Derby and other members of his party before writing to your Majesty.' Derby had returned on the Friday, but Cairns remained abroad. Disraeli's memorandum was not ready till the middle of Sunday, and he sent it down in the afternoon to the Queen, who had retired to Windsor.

To Queen Victoria.

GEORGE STREET, HANOVER SQUARE, *March* 16, 1873.—Mr. Disraeli with his humble duty to your Majesty.

He thanks your Majesty for communicating to him Mr. Gladstone's letter, with Mr. Gladstone's knowledge.

He is grateful to your Majesty for deigning to allow these communications to be made through your Majesty, and humbly agrees with your Majesty that it is a mode which may tend to prevent misunderstanding.

The observations of Mr. Gladstone, generally considered, may be ranged under two heads: an impeachment of the conduct of the Opposition in contributing to the vote against the Government measure, when they were not prepared, in the event of success, to take office; and a charge against the Leader of the Opposition, that, when honored by the commands of your Majesty, he gave a 'summary refusal' to undertake your Majesty's Government, without exhausting all practicable means of aiding the country in its exigency.

The argument of Mr. Gladstone, in the first instance, is that the Opposition, having, by 'deliberate and concerted action,' thrown out a Bill, which the Government had declared to be 'vital to their existence,' is bound to use all means to form a Government of its own, in order to replace that which it must be held to have intentionally overthrown.

It is humbly submitted to your Majesty, that though, as a general rule, this doctrine may be sound, it cannot be laid down unconditionally, nor otherwise than subject to many exceptions.

It is undoubtedly sound so far as this: that for an Opposition to use its strength for the express purpose of throwing out a Government, which it is at the time aware that it cannot replace—having that object in view, and no other—would be an act of recklessness and faction, which could not be too strongly condemned. But it may be safely affirmed that no conduct of this kind can be imputed to the Conservative Opposition of 1873.

If the doctrine in question is carried further; if it be contended that, whenever, from any circumstances, a Minister is so situated that it is in his power to prevent any other Parliamentary leader from forming an Administration which is likely to stand, he acquires, thereby, the right to call upon Parliament to pass whatever measures he and his colleagues think fit, and is entitled to denounce as factious the resistance to such measures—then the claim is one not warranted by usage, or reconcilable with the freedom of the Legislature.

It amounts to this: that he tells the House of Commons, ' Unless you are prepared to put some one in my place, your duty is to do whatever I bid you.'

To no House of Commons has language of this kind ever been addressed: by no House of Commons would it be tolerated.

In the present instance, the Bill which has been the cause of the crisis, was, from the first, strongly objected to by a large section of the Liberal party, and that on the same grounds which led the Conservative Opposition to resist it, namely, that it seemed calculated to sacrifice the interests of Irish education to those of the Roman Catholic hierarchy.

A protracted discussion strengthened the general feeling of the House of Commons as to the defects of the measure: the party whom it was, apparently, intended to propitiate, rejected it as inadequate; and, probably, if the sense of the House had been taken on the Bill, irrespective of considerations as to the political result of the division, not one-fourth of the House would have voted for it. From first to last, it was unpopular, both inside and outside Parliament, and was disliked quite as much by Liberals as by Conservatives.

It is humbly submitted to your Majesty that no Minister has a right to say to Parliament, ' You must take such a Bill, whether you think it a good one or not, because, without passing it, I will not hold office, and my numerical strength in the present House is too great to allow of any other effective Administration being formed.'

The charge against the Leader of the Opposition personally, that, by his ' summary refusal ' to undertake your Majesty's Government, he was failing in his duty to your Majesty and the country, is founded altogether on a gratuitous assumption by Mr. Gladstone, which pervades his letter, that the means of Mr. Disraeli to carry on the Government were not ' exhausted.' A brief statement of facts will at once dispose of this charge.

Before Mr. Disraeli, with due deference, offered his decision to your Majesty, he had enjoyed the opportunity of consulting those gentlemen, with whom he acts in public life; and they were unanimously of opinion, that it would be prejudicial to the interests of the country for a Conservative Administration to attempt to conduct your Majesty's affairs, in the present House of Commons. What other means were at Mr. Disraeli's disposal ? Was he to open negotiations with a section of the late Ministry, and waste days in barren interviews, vain applications, and the device of impossible combinations ? Was he to make overtures to the considerable section of the Liberal party who had voted against the Government, namely, the Irish Roman Catholic gentlemen ? Surely Mr. Gladstone is not serious in such a suggestion. Impressed by experience, obtained in those very instances to which Mr. Gladstone refers, of the detrimental influence upon Government of a ' crisis ' unnecessarily prolonged by hollow negotiations, Mr. Disraeli humbly conceived that he was taking a course at once advantageous to the public interests and tending to spare your Majesty unnecessary anxiety, by at once laying before your Majesty the real position of affairs.

There are many observations in Mr. Gladstone's letter which Mr. Disraeli, for convenience, refrains from noticing. Some of them are involved in an ambiguity not easy to encounter in a brief space: some of them, with reference to Mr. Disraeli's conduct in the House of Commons, Mr. Disraeli would fain hope are not entirely divested of some degree of exaggeration. 'The deliberate and concerted action of the Opposition' would subside, Mr. Disraeli believes, on impartial investigation, into the exercise of that ordinary, and even daily, discipline of a political party, without which a popular assembly would soon degenerate into a mob, and become divested of all practical influence. In the present instance, Mr. Disraeli believes he is correct in affirming, that his friends were not even formally summoned to vote against the Government measure, but to support an amendment by an honorable gentleman, which was seconded from the Liberal benches, and which could only by a violent abuse of terms be described as a party move.

Then, again, much is made of the circumstance that the existence of the Government was staked on this measure. Mr. Disraeli has already treated of this subject generally. But what are the particular facts ? No doubt, more than a month ago, the Prime Minister, in a devoted House of Commons, had, in an unusual, not to say unprecedented, manner, commenced his exposition of an abstruse measure by stating that the existence of the Government was staked on its success. But inasmuch as, in the course of time, it was understood that the Government were prepared to modify, or even to withdraw, most of the clauses of this measure, these words were forgotten or condoned, and could not be seriously held as exercising a practical influence on the ultimate decision.

From Queen Victoria.

WINDSOR CASTLE, *March* 16, 1873.—The Queen thanks Mr. Disraeli for his letter. She has sent it to Mr. Gladstone, and asked him whether he will undertake to resume office.

Gladstone was at last convinced, to use his own language, that no 'further effort' was to be expected from the Opposition 'towards meeting the present necessity.' He and his colleagues accordingly resumed their offices. But in writing to the Queen he recognised that the political position had been 'seriously unhinged by the shock,' and that neither the Administration nor the Parliament could again be what they were; and he did not disguise in his explanation to Parliament the damage that had been sustained, and the disadvantages necessarily attaching to a returning or resuming Government.

The best opinion, both of the public and of the Conservative party, approved of Disraeli's decision. *The Times* had advised that course throughout. Its editor's view was sent to Disraeli by Lennox.

From Lord Henry Lennox.

Private. 19, GROSVENOR GARDENS, S.W., *March* 16, 1873.—Delane dined with me last evening, and I cannot forbear letting you know what he said.

First, that you now stand in the highest position in which any statesman has stood for many years past; that you had by your decision given proof of the very highest order of statesmanship, both unselfish and patriotic; that he is convinced your statement of to-morrow will produce the very best effect throughout the country, and will earn for you the gratitude of your followers and the respect and admiration of your opponents; and lastly that in this matter you have displayed a judgment and a spirit of which Gladstone would be utterly incapable.

I need not tell you with what pleasure I heard his remarks, especially as they were made in presence of the P. of Wales, the Duke of Edinburgh, and many others.

So strong a party man and competent a manager as Lord Abergavenny held that 'Dizzy has acted most wisely in refusing to form a Government.' But there was of course a disappointed section of the party, who clamoured for the bold policy of forcing a dissolution and forming a Government, and maintained that any hesitation to seize the helm would have as discouraging and dispiriting an effect as Derby's refusal in 1855. It was mainly to the satisfaction of these impatient partisans that Disraeli addressed himself in his Parliamentary explanation on March 30. Some parts of an unnecessarily elaborate speech were not very happy; and Hardy rightly criticised his chief's remarks about the impossibility of a matured and complete policy in opposition. But there was a large amount of necessary financial and other business which a new Government would have had to get through before the session could be wound up and dissolution accomplished, and there was no answer to the passage in which Disraeli pointed out what would during the intervening period be the certain lot of an Administration with a majority of ninety against them.

I know well—and those who are around me know well—what will occur when a Ministry takes office and attempts to carry on the Government with a minority during the session, with a view of ultimately appealing to the people. We should have what is called ' fair play.' That is to say, no vote of want of confidence would be proposed, and chiefly because it would be of no use. There would be no wholesale censure, but retail humiliation. A right hon. gentleman will come down here, he will arrange his thumbscrews and other instruments of torture on this table. We shall never ask for a vote without a lecture; we shall never perform the most ordinary routine office of Government without there being annexed to it some pedantic and ignominious condition. . . . In a certain time we should enter into the paradise of abstract resolutions. One day hon. gentlemen cannot withstand the golden opportunity of asking the House to affirm that the income tax should no longer form one of the features of our Ways and Means. Of course a proposition of that kind would be scouted by the right hon. gentleman and all his colleagues; but, then, they might dine out that day, and the Resolution might be carried, as Resolutions of that kind have been. Then another hon. gentleman, distinguished for his knowledge of men and things, would move that the diplomatic service be abolished. While hon. gentlemen opposite were laughing in their sleeves at the mover, they would vote for the motion in order to put the Government into a minority. For this reason. ' Why should men,' they would say, ' govern the country who are in a minority ?' totally forgetting that we had acceded to office in the spirit of the Constitution, quite oblivious of the fountain and origin of the position we occupied. And it would go very hard if on some sultry afternoon, some hon. member should not ' rush in where angels fear to tread,' and successfully assimilate the borough and the county franchise. And so things would go on until the bitter end—until at last even the Appropriation Bill has passed, Parliament is dissolved, and we appeal to those millions, who, perhaps, six months before, might have looked upon us as the vindicators of intolerable grievances, but who now receive us as a defeated, discredited, and degraded ministry, whose services can neither be of value to the Crown nor a credit to the nation.

The Tory party, Disraeli maintained, occupied a most satisfactory position. It had divested itself of excrescences and emerged from the fiscal period. In order to deal with the more fundamental questions which were rapidly coming to the front, it was of the utmost importance that there should be ' a great Constitutional party, distinguished for its intelligence as well as for its organisation, which shall be competent to lead the people and direct the public mind.' That there might be no obstacle to its future triumph, he, as the trustee of its honour and interests, declined to form a weak and discredited Administration.

To the Duke of Richmond.

Friday, March 21, 1873.—I thought what you said was most judicious and *à propos*, and will have a good effect, and encourage the country. You spoke too highly of your colleague and correspondent, but it proved our union; and I must try to deserve your praise.

I don't think the Prime Minister greatly distinguished himself in our House.

We shall all of us be glad to see Cairns again. How much has happened in his absence, and ripe, I think, with the seeds of the future.

The seeds of the future were indeed germinating. To an Opposition which, little more than a year before, was discredited, discontented, factious, and hopeless, Disraeli had given organisation, policy, popular respect, the assurance of high and unselfish leadership, and the expectation of early and definitive success.

CHAPTER VI.

BEREAVEMENT.

1872–1873.

While Disraeli's political prospects grew daily brighter, a heavy cloud fell upon his domestic life. After thirty-three years of unbroken happiness and affection, he lost the wife who was in very deed his chosen helpmate,[1] to whom he attributed, in a speech at Edinburgh in 1867, all the successes of his life, 'because she has supported me by her counsel and consoled me by the sweetness of her mind and disposition.' The world might laugh at her queernesses and *gaucheries*, which became more marked with age; might find it difficult to decide which were the odder, her looks or her sayings, the clothes she wore or the stories she told. In externals, she might seem a strange wife for a statesman. But, besides the obvious kindness and genuineness of her nature, and the shrewd judgment which underlay her inconsequent words, she had qualities peculiarly becoming in her place: absolute trustworthiness and discretion in political secrets, which Disraeli never seems to have hid from her; a constancy and heroism which matched his own, and which, on one notable occasion, enabled her to bear the jamming of her finger in a carriage door in smiling silence so that his equanimity on the way to an important debate might not be disturbed.

Lady Beaconsfield was now an old woman of eighty, and of late years had experienced much ill-health; on one occasion, in 1868, her life was for some days in

---

[1] See Vol. II., ch. 2.

peril. In the spring of 1872, after the fatigue and excitement of the Manchester demonstrations, she once more showed signs of breaking down; but for a time performed, and was encouraged by her physician to perform, her social duties as usual.

To Montagu Corry.

G. Gate, *May* 7, 1872 —Sir William [Gull] examined me this morning and has decided that though one of the bronchial tubes is clogged, there is nothing organically wrong, or which may not soon be put right.

Miladi is suffering less. She went to Lady Waldegrave's last night, but was obliged to come home almost immediately. But, as she boastfully says, her illness was not found out. She delighted Fortescue[1] by telling him that she had heard him very much praised. He pressed her very much when and where. She replied, ' It was in bed.'

Sir William gives a good account of her to-day, and seems to think he has remedied the pain, which is all we can hope for, and has sanctioned, and even advised, her to go to Court: but I don't think he allows enough for her extreme weakness. However, I shall be with her to-day; last night she was alone, which I think fearful.

H. of C. *May* 9, '72.—The visit to Court was not successful. She was suffering as she went, and was taken so unwell there, that we had to retreat precipitately; but without much observation. Knowing the haunts of the palace a little, I got hold of some female attendants who were very serviceable. . . .

Carlton Club, *May* 14, '72.—I have been, and am, so harassed, that I have been quite unable to write a line—and this will be sad stuff.

Nothing encouraging at home. To see her every day weaker and weaker is heartrending. I have had, like all of us, some sorrows of this kind: but in every case, the fatal illness has been apparently sudden, and comparatively short. The shock is great under such circumstances no doubt, but there is a rebound in the nature of things. But to witness this gradual death of one, who has shared so long, and so completely, my life, entirely unmans me.

For herself, she still makes an effort to enter society: and Sir William approves and even counsels it: but it is impossible the effort can be maintained.

---

[1] Chichester Fortescue, afterwards Lord Carlingford, was Lady Waldegrave's husband.

I know not what are our movements. If the weather were genial, I think she is disposed to try Hughenden, but I leave everything of this sort to her fancy and wish. She once talked of going down on Thursday. I can't believe that after her return, she will attempt society any more: the break of a fortnight will produce some effect in this way. . . .

Lady Beaconsfield was taken to Hughenden for the Whitsuntide recess; but the malady did not yield to the change and country air.

To Montagu Corry.

HUGHENDEN, *May* 22, 1872.—. . . I have no good news. Her sufferings have been great here: but the change of weather has brought a ray of distraction.

She moves with great difficulty and cannot bear the slightest roughness in the road, which sadly limits our travels. She enjoyed yesterday going to the German Forest, ascending from the Lady's Walk, but suffered afterwards. Antonelli pushes her about in a perambulator a little, and seems to amuse her. He heard a nightingale ' whistling ' about the house. She thinks ' whistling ' a capital term for bird noises. . . .

With indomitable pluck, Lady Beaconsfield, after her return to town, refused to accept the confinement of an invalid; but resumed her social life, until on July 17, at a party at Lady Loudoun's house to meet the Duchess of Cambridge, she suddenly became very seriously ill and had to be taken home at once. The hostess and the guests were struck by her wonderful courage, ' and indeed heroism,' and by the unselfishness with which she seemed to think more of the inconvenience which her illness might cause her hostess than of her own acute pain. She was never able to go out in London society again.

To Lady Beaconsfield.

July 25, 1872.—I have nothing to tell you, except that I love you, which, I fear, you will think rather dull. . . .

Natty[1] was very affectionate about you, and wanted me to come home and dine with him; quite alone; but I told him that

---

[1] The late Lord Rothschild, at this time M.P. for Aylesbury.

you were the only person now, whom I could dine with; and only relinquished you to-night for my country.

My country, I fear, will be very late; but I hope to find you in a sweet sleep.

From Lady Beaconsfield.

July 26.

MY OWN DEAREST,—I miss you sadly. I feel so grateful for your constant tender love and kindness. I certainly feel better this evening. . . . Your own devoted BEACONSFIELD.

This is the last letter of his wife's which Disraeli preserved—probably the last she wrote him. She was not able to be moved to Hughenden until the end of September; so he and she passed, as he expressed it, their ' first summer in London.'

To Lord Cairns.

Private. GROSVENOR GATE, *Aug.* 17, 1872.—Many, many thanks. The birds were capital and pleased the fastidious palate of my invalid.

The prospect of reaching Hughenden seems every day fainter. Lady Beaconsfield has had more than one return of her hemorrhage, and, sometimes, I feel, and fear, that even her buoyant and gallant spirit will hardly baffle so many causes of exhaustion.

We have not been separated for three and thirty years, and, during all that time, in her society I never have had a moment of dullness. It tears the heart to see such a spirit suffer, and suffer so much ! May you, my dear Cairns, never experience my present feelings ! . . . .

From the Duchess of Cleveland.

RABY CASTLE, DARLINGTON, *Sept.* 12, '72.—. . . One privilege you have which is not granted to all. No two people surely can look back upon a life of such loving and perfect companionship. One of my sons once spoke to Lady Beaconsfield in wonder of the youthful energy and high spirits she preserved, and said something of the courage and force of character it showed. ' No,' she said, ' it is not that. It is that my life has been such a happy one. I have had so much affection, and no troubles—no contradictions: that is what has kept me so young and well.' . . .

To Gathorne Hardy.

Private. GROSVENOR GATE, *Sept.* 16, 1872.—We are much touched by yr. kind letter, which I mentioned to my wife. She sends her very kindest regards to Mrs. Hardy and yourself, but she does not see this letter, so I will say that her condition occasions me the greatest disquietude, tho' they tell me there is some improvement. Her illness, under wh. she has, to some degree, been suffering for many months, is a total inability to take any sustenance, and it is to me perfectly marvellous how she exists, and shows even great buoyancy of life.

We have never left Grosvenor Gate, tho' as everything has been tried in vain, Lady Beaconsfield now talks of trying change of air, and endeavouring to get down to Hughenden. As for myself, I have never been into the town during the whole of August and the present month, so, when business commences, Pall Mall and Whitehall shall be as fresh to me as to my happier comrades, who are shooting in Scotland or climbing the Alps. One has the advantage here, when we wake, of looking upon trees, and bowery vistas, and we try to forget, that the Park is called Hyde, and that the bowers are the bowers of Kensington.

We take drives in the counties of Middx. and Surrey, and discover beautiful retreats of wh. we had never heard; so we have the excitement of travel. What surprises me, more than anything, is the immensity and variety of London, and the miles of villas wh. are throwing out their antennæ in every suburban direction. . . .

I should like to hear from you again as to your own health. All depends on you. I am only holding the reins during a period of transition, and more from a feeling of not deserting the helm at a moment of supposed difficulty and danger, than any other. . . .

A note in Disraeli's handwriting, apparently intended for the Queen, gives some further particulars of these drives round London.

What miles of villas! and of all sorts of architecture! What beautiful churches! What gorgeous palaces of Geneva![1]
One day we came upon a real feudal castle, with a donjon keep high in the air. It turned out to be the new City prison in Camden Road, but it deserves a visit; I mean externally.

[1] In letters to friends written at this time the 'gorgeous palaces of Geneva' became more prosaically 'gin-palaces.'

Of all the kingdoms ruled over by our gracious mistress, the most remarkable is her *royaume de Cockaigne*, and perhaps the one the Queen has least visited. Her faithful servants in question, preparing their expeditions with a map, investigated all parts of it from Essex to Surrey, and Lady Beaconsfield calculated that from the 1st of August to the end of September she travelled 220 miles.

To Lord Cairns.

GROSVENOR GATE, *Sept.* 26, 1872.—You have expressed so much sympathy for us, and it has been so highly appreciated, that I must tell you that, to-day, we hope to reach Hughenden. There has been, within the last week, a decided, and, I hope now. a permanent improvement in my wife's health, and she is resolved to try change of air. I am a little sorry, that we go home in the fall of the leaf, and that too in a sylvan land, but home only can insure her the comforts and the ease, which an invalid requires.

If she could only regain—not appetite—but even a desire for sustenance, I should be confident of the future, the buoyancy of her spirit is so very remarkable. However, there is a streak of dawn. . . .

What Disraeli called ' our hegira from Grosvenor Gate ' proved at first a success; and on October 3 he could write more cheerfully to Corry: ' Lady Beaconsfield has been here a week, and has improved daily; there seems a sustained revival of appetite, which had altogether ceased.' In answer to the Queen's sympathetic inquiries through Lady Ely he was able to report ' continuous improvement. You know her buoyancy of spirit. She says she is now convinced that everybody eats too much; still at the same time she would like to be able to eat a little.'

The improvement was fallacious; and though Lady Beaconsfield occasionally received visitors and even apparently paid a call on near neighbours, her husband's letters show that her strength was waning during the following two months, till the final attack came upon her in the second week of December.

To Montagu Corry.

HUGHENDEN, *Oct.* 13, '72.—. . . Things here very bad.

Nov. 8. —. . . Affairs have been going very badly: so badly, that I telegraphed, yesterday, for Leggatt and he came down immediately: but he took a different view from us, I am glad to say: and persisted that, if sustenance could be taken, no immediate danger was to be apprehended. But how to manage that ? The truth is, she never has even tasted any of the dishes, that the Rothschilds used to send her in London, and anxious as she was to partake of the delicacies you so kindly provided for her, and which touched her much, it has ended with them as with the feats of Lionel's *chef !*

Shall you be disengaged for three or four days on the 21st ? The John Manners are to come here on that day, if all goes well. A party is impossible, but perhaps we might manage a couple of men.

Nov. 13.—Things go on here much the same: some improvement which I ascribe to the weather—not in the appetite, but in continued absence of pain, and consequently enjoyment of life. . . .

To Philip Rose.

HUGHENDEN MANOR, *Nov.* 13, 1872.—. . . Lady Beaconsfield intended to have called at Rayners to-day, and to have hoped that Mrs. Rose and yourself would be able to dine with us on Friday the 22nd. I trust we shall find you disengaged. The snow frightened me, tho' my wife was inclined to face it.

The temporary improvement lasted long enough to enable the patient to enjoy her little party from November 21 to 25, including, besides the John Manners, Lord Rosebery for the first two days, and Harcourt and Lord Ronald Gower for the last two; and to justify one of those guests in writing her a jocular letter of thanks.

William Vernon Harcourt to Lady Beaconsfield.

TRIN. COLL., CAMBRIDGE, *Nov.* 26, 1872.—I have all my life made efforts (apparently destined to be unsuccessful) to appear what Falstaff, or is it Touchstone ?, calls ' moderate honest.' But here I am actually a felon *malgré moi*. Joseph's butler was not more alarmed and shocked than I was when, on opening my sack, the first thing I discovered in its mouth was the French novel you had provided for my entertainment in my charming bedroom at Hughenden. Whether the act was one of accidental larceny by my servant or whether it was insidiously effected by Lord J. Manners in order to ruin my public and private reputation, I do not feel sure. I did however return it by this morning's post before I left London, and so I hope to be forgiven.

I have already taken measures to secure a consignment to you of Trinity audit ale. Delicious as it is, I doubt whether there really exists anyone except a Cambridge man who can drink it with impunity. . . .

And now a truce to nonsense. I must offer you one word of serious and sincere thanks for the true and genuine kindness which I have received at your hands and those of Mr. Disraeli. It was no language of compliment but of simple truth which I spoke when I told you that, of all visits which it was possible to pay, there was none of which I should have been more ambitious than that which I owed to your hospitality last Sunday. There are things in the world which one not only enjoys at the time but which one remembers always—and these are of them. . . .

Disraeli told Harcourt that a glass of the Trinity audit ale was almost the last thing which passed Lady Beaconsfield's lips before she died. Lord Ronald Gower, writing of this visit in his *Reminiscences*, vividly depicts Disraeli's distress in talking of his wife's sufferings. ' His face, generally so emotionless, was filled with a look of suffering and woe that nothing but the sorrow of her whom he so truly loves would cause on that impassive countenance.'

To Montagu Corry

Nov. 29.—. . . My lady's appetite has been sustained; indeed I think I may say it is restored: but her sufferings are increased, and I have just been obliged to send to Leggatt to beg him to come down to-morrow.

She got over her visit and visitors, notwithstanding this, with success and great tact: showing little, but always to effect. . . .

To Philip Rose.

HUGHENDEN, *Dec.* 6, 1872.—Affairs are most dark here— I tremble for the result, and even an immediate one. My poor wife has got (it matters not by what means) congestion on her lungs, and with her shattered state, it seems to me almost hopeless, that, even with her constitution, we should again escape. I entirely trust to your coming to me, if anything happens. *I am totally unable to meet the catastrophe.* . . .

The last stage was mercifully not prolonged. She died on December 15, after a week's acute illness, during which her husband seldom left her room. A note which he sent out to Corry on one of these days is preserved: ' She says she must see you. Calm, but the delusions stronger than ever. She will not let me go out to fetch you. Come. D.'

There was a great outpouring of public and private sympathy with Disraeli in this severe trial. The terms of close affection on which he had lived with his wife, long familiar to his intimates, had of late years become widely known to the country. Letters of condolence poured in, not merely from friends and colleagues, but from perfect strangers of all classes and parties; and the public journals manifested appreciation and respect. The Queen, whose telegrams and messages of inquiry had been constant throughout the illness, wrote:

From Queen Victoria.

WINDSOR CASTLE, *Dec.* 15, 1872.—The Queen well knows that Mr. Disraeli will *not* consider the expression of her heart-felt sympathy an intrusion in this his first hour of desolation and overwhelming grief, and therefore she at once attempts to express what she feels. The Queen knew and admired as well as appreciated the unbounded devotion and affection which united him to the dear partner of his life, whose only thought was him. And therefore the Queen knows also *what* Mr. Disraeli has lost and what he must suffer. The only consolation to be found is in *her* present peace and freedom from suffering, in the recollection of their life of happiness and in the blessed certainty of eternal reunion.

May God support and sustain him is the Queen's sincere prayer.

Her children are all anxious to express their sympathy. *Yesterday* was the anniversary of her great loss.

The Prince and Princess of Wales and other members of the Royal Family were among the first to send their sympathy. Queen Sophia of the Netherlands wrote: ' It is given to few to have a character like hers '; the King of the Belgians, on behalf of the Queen and himself: ' Toute notre sympathie est avec vous dans ce cruel moment'; the Duc D'Aumale: 'Personne mieux que moi ne comprend pas l'étendue de votre douleur. . . . Mon cœur est tout avec le vôtre'; and the Empress of Austria, through Count Bernstorff: 'She knows how deeply Lady Beaconsfield was devoted to you and how you returned her devotion by touching affection and gratitude.' Her great personal kindness was what the old Whig leader, Russell, among many others, dwelt on in a sympathetic note. Lord Rosebery, who had been one of the last visitors at Hughenden, wrote: 'I can hardly now realise that my kind hostess whom I saw full of life and spirit a few days ago has passed away. . . . I suppose no one ever came near her without admiring her goodness, her unselfishness, and her magnificent devotion.' The Prime Minister's letter and an American tribute may be given more at length:

From William Ewart Gladstone.

10, Downing Street, Whitehall, *Jan.* 19, 1873.—. . . You and I were, as I believe, married in the same year. It has been permitted to both of us to enjoy a priceless boon through a third of a century. Spared myself the blow which has fallen on you, I can form some conception of what it must have been and be. I do not presume to offer you the consolation which you will seek from another and higher quarter. I offer only the assurance which all who know you, all who knew Lady Beaconsfield, and especially those among them who like myself enjoyed for a length of time her marked though unmerited regard, may perhaps render without impropriety; the assurance that in this trying hour they feel deeply for you, and with you. . . .

To William Ewart Gladstone.

Hughenden Manor, *Jan.* 24, 1873.—I am much touched by your kind words in my great sorrow. I trust, I earnestly trust, that you may be spared a similar affliction. Marriage is the greatest earthly happiness, when founded on complete sympathy. That hallowed lot was mine, and for a moiety of my existence; and I know it is yours.

From John Lothrop Motley.

MENTMORE, LEIGHTON BUZZARD, *Feb.* 21, '73.—. . . I shall never forget the most agreeable visit which my wife and I enjoyed at Hughenden a little before we left England nor any of Lady Beaconsfield's acts of charming and graceful hospitality united to your own. I always admired her ready wit, her facility and charm in social intercourse, her quick perception of character and events, and it was impossible not to be deeply touched by her boundless devotion to yourself, which anyone, allowed the privilege of your acquaintance, could see was most generously and loyally repaid. . . .

I never met her in society without being greeted by a kindly smile and a sympathetic word, and I have frequently enjoyed long and to me most agreeable conversations with her. She knew well how thoroughly I appreciated and shared in her admiration for the one great object of her existence. . . .

Disraeli was, for the time, overwhelmed by his loss. Two of his letters will show his feeling. He used the same or very similar expressions to all his friends. That she had appreciated them was their great merit in his eyes. 'Of character,' he wrote to one of them, 'she was no mean judge. I must ever regard those who remember her with tenderness and respect.'

To the Prince of Wales.

HUGHENDEN MANOR,
Dec. 22, 1872.

SIR AND DEAR PRINCE,—I will attempt to thank Her Royal Highness and yourself for the sympathy which you have shown to me in my great sorrow, a grief for which I was unprepared, and which seems to me overwhelming.

A few days before her death, she spoke to me of the Princess and yourself, Sir, in terms of deep regard, and, if I may presume to say so, of affection. I took, therefore, the occasion of mentioning the invitation she had received to Sandringham, and she was gratified. She said 'It would have been a happy incident in a happy life, now about to close. I liked his society, I delighted in the merriment of his kind heart.'

I shall always remember with gratitude the invariable kindness shewn by Her Royal Highness and yourself, Sir, to one who for 33 years was the inseparable and ever interesting companion of my life.

To Lord Cairns.

GROSVENOR GATE, *Dec.* 28, '72.—Kind and much loved friend! I thank you for all your sympathy in my great sorrow, and for all your goodness to one, who was my inseparable, and ever-interesting companion for a moiety of my existence. She always appreciated you, and thought me fortunate in having such a friend.

Altho' you are the one, whom I should wish first, and most, to see, I will not precipitate our interview, for I have not yet subdued the anguish of the supreme sorrow of my life.

I am obliged to be here on business, and shall remain here till Friday, when I go out of town for a day or two, but not to Hughenden. On Monday, *i.e.*, to-morrow, week, I must return here. It will be my last visit to a house, where I have passed exactly half my days, and, so far as my interior life was concerned, in unbroken happiness. . . .

Among Lady Beaconsfield's papers was found a touching letter of farewell to her husband, written many years before, in view of the high probability that she, who was the elder by twelve years, would be the first to die.

June 6, 1856.

MY OWN DEAR HUSBAND,—If I should depart this life before you, leave orders that we may be buried in the same grave at whatever distance you may die from England.[1] And now, God bless you, my kindest, dearest! You have been a perfect husband to me. Be put by my side in the same grave. And now, farewell, my dear Dizzy. Do not live alone, dearest. Some one I earnestly hope you may find as attached to you as your own devoted MARY ANNE.

Accordingly, Lady Beaconsfield was buried in Hughenden churchyard in the vault in which her husband was himself to be laid, and by the side of their benefactress, Mrs. Brydges Willyams. Directly the simple funeral was over, Disraeli, as appears from his letter to Cairns, was plunged in business. His wife's death made a vast change in his circumstances; he lost thereby £5,000 a year and a house in town; though his generous friend, Andrew

---

[1] This was written shortly before Disraeli and his wife were about to leave England for a cure at a Continental watering-place on account of his health. See Vol. IV., p. 51.

Montagu, gave him material assistance by reducing the interest on his debts from 3 to 2 per cent. He had to move all his possessions from Grosvenor Gate, and find a new abiding-place in London. 'Corry seems his factotum,' wrote Hardy in his diary, ' and he needs one, for he is quite unfit for that sort of business.' He took refuge for a time in an hotel—Edwards's Hotel, in George Street, Hanover Square. ' It was, in the days of my youth,' he told Northcote, ' the famous house of Lady Palmerston, then Lady Cowper; and at least I shall labour in rooms where a great statesman has been inspired.'

There had been some fear amongst his colleagues, whom the events of the past year had quite converted from their heresies on the leadership, lest the loss of one so intimately associated with the triumphs of his political career should incline Disraeli to withdraw from active politics. On the contrary, he turned to them as a welcome distraction. He asked two of his leading colleagues, Cairns and Hardy, to come to him at Hughenden in the middle of January. Their presence, he wrote, would be ' a source of strength and consolation,' and would make him ' much more capable of re-entering public life.' With them he discussed the political situation and the vagaries of the Government; and to them he declared his intention of being present and speaking when the session began.

When he went up to town he was deprived of the comfort of Corry's presence, owing to the serious illness of Corry's father.

To Montagu Corry.

EDWARDS'S HOTEL, *Feb.* 4, '73.—I left you with a bleeding heart yesterday, amid all the sorrows, which seemed to accumulate around our heads: but your telegram has a little lifted me out of the slough of despond. I had just energy enough to send a paragraph to the papers, and messages to Northcote and Derby. The former was with me at 11 o'clock, and has undertaken to communicate with Gladstone about the speech, and the latter has just left me. . . . Barrington has also paid me a long visit. Hardy is to be with me to-morrow morning, and has sent me a memorandum from Cairns, which contains all I required. Hardy gives a dinner to the party to-morrow : Cairns to-day to Lords and Commons.

Give my kind regards to your father and sister. I hope every hour to have another telegram that his amendment has become convalescence.

All my friends admire my rooms. I cannot say I agree with them, but things may mend.

Fortunately for Disraeli the political crisis which resulted in Gladstone's abortive resignation immediately supervened. He had something therefore to distract his thoughts; but his loneliness in his hotel weighed heavily upon him, and in his letters to Corry he constantly harped on his ' miserable state,' his ' melancholy,' ' the heaviness and misery ' of his life. Corry could not return to him, as the elder Corry's illness became increasingly serious and ended fatally in March. Disraeli said to Malmesbury with tears in his eyes, ' I hope some of my friends will take notice of me now in my great misfortune, for I have no home, and when I tell my coachman to drive home I feel it is a mockery.' His friends responded to his appeal, and did their best to cheer him up by asking him to dine with them quietly.

To Montagu Corry.

HOUSE OF COMMONS, *Feb.* 10, 1873.—. . . All yesterday, rumors of a crisis were in the air. At Lionel's[1] where I was asked to a family circle I found, to my annoyance, not merely Charles Villiers and Osborne, whom I look upon as the family, but Lords Cork and Houghton. The political excitement was great, and not favorable to the position of Ministers : but Lionel told me afterwards, that he had seen the Bill (Delane had shown it him). Would you believe it, I was so *distrait*, and altogether embarrassed, that I never asked him a question about it?

This morning I was obliged to go to Middleton's about the picture,[2] which is virtually finished. He has altered the expression, but not hit the mark. I have made some suggestions, but am not sanguine about them. . . .

Adieu ! *mon très cher.* I never wanted you more, but it is selfish to say so.

Feb. 17.—. . . I was much pleased with the portrait,

[1] Baron Lionel de Rothschild.   [2] Of Lady Beaconsfield ; see Frontispiece.

and the frame, which is exquisite. He has succeeded in giving to the countenance an expression of sweet gravity, which is characteristic. . . .

Feb. 18.—. . . I dined yesterday at the Carlton: latish and was not annoyed. The John Manners asked me again for to-morrow, but I declined. On Thursday I am to dine with the Cairns and meet the Hardys, and on Friday alone with the Stanhopes: Saturday alone with my Countess:[1] so all my plans of absolute retirement are futile. I regret this, for every visit makes me more melancholy—though hotel life in an evening is a cave of despair.

I was with Brunnow an hour to-day—and Madame would come down, and kiss me!

March 1.—Your letter greatly distressed me, and I have been in hopes of receiving a telegram.

I have been dining out every day, but only with my host and hostess alone—and sometimes a very friendly fourth. Yesterday, at the John Manners', with Duke of Rutland; and on Thursday at the Stanhopes' with dear Henry,[2] who received two despatches from Marlboro' House, during the dinner. I dine with dear Henry to-day to meet B. Osborne alone: and to-morrow with the Malmesburys; it is better than dining here alone, which is intolerable, or at a club, which, even with a book, is not very genial. . . .

March 7.—Your silence, my best and dearest Montagu, was ominous of your impending woe. What can I say to you, but express my infinite affection? Death has tried you hard during the last few months, but you have shown, in the severe proof, admirable qualities, which all must admire and love.

I should be glad to hear some tidings of your sister: as for myself, I am a prisoner, and almost prostrate, with one of those atmospheric attacks which the English persist in calling ' colds,' and, for the first time in my life, am absent from House of Commons in the midst of a pitched battle.

But these are nothings compared to your sorrows. Though I cannot soften, let me share, them.

April 4.—. . . To-day I went by appointment to New Court, expecting to do business: nothing done. Lionel there, but not well: a terrible luncheon of oysters and turtle prepared, and after that nothing settled. This was disgusting. I dine with the Stanhopes to-day. On Wednesday last a rather full party at Grillion's: the last dinner at the bankrupt Clarendon [hotel]. Salisbury was there, and Lowe. . . .

---

[1] Apparently Lady Chesterfield, or perhaps Lady Cardigan.
[2] Lord Henry Lennox.

To the Duchess of Abercorn.

12, George Street, Hanover Square, *May* 18, '73.—
It is most kind of you, and of his Grace, to remember me:
but I am, really, living in seclusion, so far as general society
is concerned, and therefore, I am sure you will permit me to
decline your obliging invitation for the 24th.

Your ' boys ' deserve kindness and encouragement, because they are clever and, above all, industrious, and perhaps,
also, because they inherit the agreeable qualities of their
parents.

CHAPTER VII.

LADY BRADFORD AND LADY CHESTERFIELD.

1873–1875.

To Disraeli the rupture of a union so complete as was that between him and his wife meant more than it would have meant to most affectionate husbands. His temperament was such that he could not be happy, and could not bring out the best work of which he was capable, without intimate female association and sympathy. 'My nature demands that my life should be perpetual love,' had been a glowing outburst of his youth; and that love, for all his wealth of men friends and the affection which he lavished on them, must be the love of woman. In *Henrietta Temple* he wrote: 'A female friend, amiable, clever, and devoted, is a possession more valuable than parks and palaces; and, without such a muse, few men can succeed in life, none be content.' Throughout his whole life he had been blessed with devotion and sympathy of this kind in ample measure. Two women, first his sister and then his wife, had made him and his ambitions the centre of their existence; to both of them his own affection and devotion had been unstinted; there had been between him and them a constant communion of thoughts and hopes and sympathies. In a lesser degree Mrs. Brydges Willyams, in her later years, shared in this close intimacy. There were, moreover, other ladies whose sympathetic appreciation had cheered and helped his career—such as Mrs. Austen, Lady Blessington, and Frances Anne Lady Londonderry. 'I feel fortunate,' he wrote[1] in 1874, 'in serving a female Sovereign. I owe everything to woman; and if, in the sunset of life, I have still a young heart, it is due to that influence.' With all the women who influenced him he kept up a constant correspondence of a romantic and sentimental kind, in which he revealed, not merely his doings, but his thoughts and his character. 'A she-corre-spondent for my money,' was the exclamation of one of his exuberant youthful heroes; and it is to the fact that he carried on throughout his life a copious correspondence with women that our knowledge of the real Disraeli is largely due.

With Lady Beaconsfield's death the last of the women with whom he had hitherto enjoyed this sympathetic intercourse passed away; and he was left for the time widowed indeed. Few men at his age—sixty-eight—would have had the freshness of heart to form new attach-ments, and to resume with others the sentimental and romantic intimacy which had proved so stimulating an influence; and of those who still possessed sufficient youth-fulness for the adventure, most would have been pre-vented, especially if public men, by the fear of incurring censure and ridicule. But Disraeli's affections were still warm, and craved sympathetic understanding; nor was he to be deterred by possible ridicule from following their dictates. He spoke for himself when he wrote a few years earlier in *Lothair*:[2] 'Threescore and ten, at the present day, is the period of romantic passions. As for our enamoured sexagenarians, they avenge the theories of our cold-hearted youth.'

Among those who showed him special kindness in his early months of loneliness and desolation were two sisters, whom he had long known in society, Lady Chesterfield and Lady Bradford. Anne Countess of Chesterfield was the eldest, and Selina Countess of Bradford was the youngest, of five sisters, daughters of the first Lord Forester, the head of an ancient Shropshire family. Of

---

[1] To Lady Bradford.   [2] Ch. 35.

ANNE COUNTESS OF CHESTERFIELD.

From a portrait after Sir E. Landseer, R.A., at Hughenden.

the other sisters one married Lord Carrington's eldest son, Robert John Smith, and died young in 1832, before her husband succeeded to the title. She was of course a neighbour of the Disraelis after they established themselves at Bradenham in 1829; and it was at Wycombe Abbey, but apparently after Mrs. Smith's death, that Disraeli first met Lady Bradford. 'Mr. D. will tell you,' wrote Lady Bradford to Mrs. Disraeli in March, 1868, 'that our first acquaintance was 100 years ago in poor Lord Carrington's house, before he [Disraeli] knew you.' Another sister married General Anson, who was Commander-in-Chief in India when the Mutiny broke out ;[1] and the remaining sister married Lord Albert Conyngham, afterwards the first Lord Londesborough. In their youth the five sisters were prominent in the world of fashion, gaiety, and sport—the world that revolved round Almack's, of which their mother Lady Forester was an eminent patroness; and at least Lady Chesterfield, Mrs. Anson, and Lady Bradford had been reigning beauties. Disraeli, in his days of dandyism, was naturally thrown in their company. In 1835 he went to a specially gorgeous fancy dress ball with a party which included the Chesterfields and the Ansons, and told his sister that ' Lady Chesterfield was a sultana.'[2] In 1838 he met at Wycombe Abbey a whole family party of the Foresters—'rather noisy, but very gay '—' Lady Chesterfield, George and Mrs. Anson, the Albert Conynghams, Forester,' and ' made the greatest friends with all of them,' he told Mrs. Wyndham Lewis.[3] The second brother, General ' Cis ' Forester, who sat for Wenlock in Parliament for nearly half a century and succeeded to the title in 1874, had been a friend of Disraeli's from early years.

Of the five sisters only Lady Chesterfield and Lady Bradford were still living. Lady Chesterfield, who was a couple of years older than Disraeli, was the widow of the sixth Earl of Chesterfield who had died seven years before.

---

[1] See Vol. IV., p. 87.   [2] See Vol. I., pp. 302, 303.
[3] See Vol. II., p. 49.

Her daughter had married one of the Reform Bill dissentients, Carnarvon. Lady Bradford was the wife of the third Earl of Bradford, a sporting peer, and a man of character and consideration, who had been Disraeli's colleague as Lord Chamberlain from 1866 to 1868, and was again to be his colleague as Master of the Horse from 1874 to 1880. She was seventeen years younger than her sister; but both ladies were by this time grandmothers. When Lady Bradford's eldest son, Lord Newport, was married in 1869, Disraeli had written him what his mother called, we learn from a note of Corry's of that date, ' the nicest letter in the world, and *such* a clever one.'

With both these sisters Disraeli became, during the spring and summer of 1873, on terms of intimate friendship. In them he found that female sympathy and companionship without which life was for him an incomplete thing. That they were ladies influential in the fashionable and aristocratic Tory society which had shown some reluctance to admit his undisputed sway as leader counted, no doubt, for something with him. That they recalled the memories and attachments of his youth, when to be taken up by Lady Forester and the bright particular stars of Almack's was of importance to him, counted for more with one whose gratitude was lifelong. But, over and above all these considerations, his personal affection for, and devotion to, both ladies were quite unmistakable. Of the circumstances in which the intimacy arose he wrote to Lady Chesterfield in the autumn, ' Altho', from paramount duty, I attended Parliament this session, I have never been in society, except that delightful week when, somehow or other, I found myself in the heart of your agreeable family.' The first letter to Lady Chesterfield which has been preserved was written in June, 1873, and he was already on such terms with her that he addressed her as ' Dearest Lady Ches.' and subscribed himself, ' Your most affectionate D.' The first letter of the series to Lady Bradford was written in July, and in the second, in August, she too was ' Dearest Lady Brad-

ford.' He went to stay in the autumn with the one at
Bretby and with the other at Weston; and these visits
were constantly repeated to the close of his life, and were
returned by the ladies and by Lord Bradford at Hughenden. There have been preserved some 500 letters to
Lady Chesterfield in these eight years, and no fewer than
1,100 to Lady Bradford; while the twelve years of his
acquaintance with Mrs. Brydges Willyams only produced about 250. This Bradford-Chesterfield correspondence is absolutely invaluable for a due understanding of Disraeli's final period; like the letters in
earlier times to his sister and his wife, it both reveals
his intimate hopes and feelings, and also describes
in brilliant fashion, from day to day, at times almost
from hour to hour, his political and social experiences.[1]
The ladies' letters were destroyed, by their desire, after
his death.

So necessary to Disraeli's life was the intimacy thus
established—'the delightful society,' as he told Lady
Chesterfield in March, 1874, 'of the two persons I love
most in the world'—that he endeavoured to make it
permanent by asking Lady Chesterfield to marry him, so
that he might grapple one lady to his heart as his wife,
and the other as his sister. She not unnaturally refused.
Even had she been willing, when she had passed her
seventieth birthday, to marry once more, she must have
speedily realised that she did not occupy the first place
in Disraeli's affections. For though it was to Lady
Chesterfield, as the only sister who was free, that he
proposed marriage, it was to Lady Bradford that he was
most tenderly attached. He wrote to her more than
twice as many letters as he did to her sister, sometimes, when in office, sending her two, or even three,
in one day, by special messengers from Downing Street
or from the Treasury bench. Such messengers, he
wrote, ' may wait at your house the whole day, and are

[1] The Duke of Richmond told Cairns on July 27, 1876, that Lady Bradford ' seems to know everything, down to the most minute details of everything that passes.'

the slaves of your will.   A messenger from a Prime
Minister to a Mistress of the Horse cannot say his soul
is his own.' Romantic devotion breathes in Disraeli's
language to both sisters; but the Oriental extravagance
of his sentiments is beyond a doubt more marked when
he is addressing Lady Bradford. The correspondence with
Lady Chesterfield, in spite of the offer and refusal, preserves
on the whole an even tone of deeply affectionate friendship. But Lady Bradford was often taken aback by
Disraeli's septuagenarian ardour, and embarrassed by
his incessant calls at her house in Belgrave Square and
his unending demands on her time; though she, as well
as her sister, could not but be flattered by the assiduous
attentions of one who was for the greater part of the
last eight years of his life the most famous and admired
man in the country.

The relation between Disraeli and these sisters can
hardly fail to recall the relation between Horace Walpole,
in the last decade of his long life, and the two Miss Berrys.
There was the same affection in each case for two sisters;
the same desire to marry one, in order to insure the
constant society of both. The Miss Berrys, however,
were in the twenties when Horace Walpole made their
acquaintance; whereas Lady Chesterfield was over seventy
and Lady Bradford was in her fifty-fifth year when
Disraeli's attachment began. But Disraeli's chivalrous
devotion to women was independent of physical attraction and the appeal of youth. Otherwise his elderly
wife—not to speak of Mrs. Willyams and others—would
hardly have influenced him as she did to the day of
her death. Though the Russian Ambassador might
sneer at the society which Disraeli in his latter years
affected as *toutes grand'mères*, it is a most honourable
feature in his composition that, in his relation to women,
as in his relation to the problems of life and eternity, he
rejected absolutely any physical or sensuous standard,
and poured out his devotion before an ideal, regardless
of the ravages of care and time.

The characters of the two sisters were complementary; Lady Chesterfield had more strength and constancy, Lady Bradford more sweetness and gaiety ; both were sympathetic in a high degree.   Lady Bradford, as befitted the mother of marriageable daughters, was in the full whirl of society, a constant attendant at the functions of the London season, and at the principal race meetings, moving in the autumn from one country house party to another. Lady Chesterfield, a much older woman, though taking a fair share of social pleasures, was more often to be found, surrounded by friends, in her own home at Bretby.   Lady Bradford had perhaps a quicker appreciation of Disraeli's moods and aspirations, but was by no means so certain to respond to them as her sister. Writing to Lady Bradford, in January, 1874, he said of Lady Chesterfield that ' the secret of her charm is the union of grace and energy; a union very rare, but in her case most felicitous.' Of Lady Bradford's own character he wrote to herself in May of that year: ' A sweet simplicity, blended with high breeding; an intellect not over-drilled, but lively, acute, and picturesque; a seraphic temper, and a disposition infinitely sympathetic—these are some of the many charms that make you beloved of D.'

The fervid nature of Disraeli's devotion will be realised from a letter which he wrote to Lady Bradford three weeks after becoming Prime Minister for the second time. She and Lady Chesterfield were leaving London for the country; and a separation which was only to last from the middle of March till the first week of April filled him with consternation.

To Lady Bradford.

10, DOWNING STREET, WHITEHALL, *March* 13, 1874.—The most fascinating of women was never more delightful than this afternoon. I could have sat for ever, watching every movement that was grace, and listening to her sparkling words—but alas ! the horrid thought, ever and anon, came over me—' It is a farewell visit.' It seemed too cruel ! I might have truly said,

> Pleased to the last, I cropped the flowery food,
> And kissed the hand just raised to shed my blood.

Constant separations !   Will they never cease ?   If anything could make me love your delightful sister more than
I do, it is her plans for Easter, which realise a dream !

I am certain there is no greater misfortune, than to have
a heart that will not grow old.   It requires all the sternness
of public life to sustain one.   If we have to govern a great
country, we ought not to be *distrait*, and feel the restlessness
of love.   Such things should be the appanage of the youthful
heroes I have so often painted, but alas ! I always drew from
my own experience, and were I to write again to-morrow,
I fear I should be able to do justice to the most agitating,
tho' the most amiable, weakness of humanity.

Writing to Lady Chesterfield of the same farewell visit
Disraeli said : ' The matchless sisters, as I always call them,
were never so delightful as yesterday afternoon,' and he
proceeded to use to her much the same language as to
Lady Bradford.   Lady Chesterfield, the widow, accepted
the compliment without demur : but Lady Bradford, the
wife, was offended by the extravagance of his expressions.
Disraeli assumed, in return, the airs of a despairing lover.

To Lady Bradford.

10, DOWNING STREET, *March* 17, 1874.—I sent you a hurried
line this morning, as I thought it my only opportunity of
writing, and I did not wish you to think I was silent, because
I was ' tetchy.'   I have just come back from W[indsor],
and I send you this, because I think it may prevent misapprehension.

Your view of correspondence, apparently, is that it should
be confined to facts, and not admit feelings.   Mine is the
reverse ; and I could as soon keep a journal, wh. I never
could do, as maintain a correspondence of that kind.

The other day you said it was wonderful that I cd. write
to you, with all the work and care I have to encounter.   It is
because my feelings impel me to write to you.   It was my
duty and my delight : the duty of my heart and the delight
of my life.

I do not think I was very unreasonable.   I have never
asked anything from you but your society.   When I have
that, I am content, which I may well be, for its delight is
ineffable.   When we were separated, the loneliness of my life
found some relief in what might have been a too fond idolatry.

The menace of perpetual estrangement seemed a severe
punishment for what might have been a weakness, but scarcely

an unpardonable one. However you shall have no cause to inflict it. I awake from a dream of baffled sympathy, and pour forth my feelings, however precious, from a golden goblet, on the sand.

'I thought all was over between us,' he wrote in his next letter; but two days afterwards the difference was made up; 'I found a letter, which took a load off my heart, and I pressed it to my lips.' This lovers' comedy was repeated with Lady Bradford over and over again during the early years of the 1874 Administration. The septuagenarian, who had the governance of the Empire and the conduct of the Commons on his shoulders, and who necessarily was leading a public life of incessant and laborious occupation, nevertheless traversed in his private life the whole gamut of half-requited love—passionate devotion, rebuff, despair, resignation, renewed hope, reconciliation, ecstasy; and then traversed it *da capo*. One such crisis occurred in connection with a masked ball in the height of the season of 1874.

To Lady Bradford.

H. OF C., *June 29*, 1874.—I am distressed at the relations which have arisen between us, and, after two days' reflection, I have resolved to write once more.

I went to Montagu House on Friday with great difficulty, to see you, and to speak to you on a matter of interest to me. I thought your manner was chilling: you appeared to avoid me, and when—perhaps somewhat intrusively, but I had no other chance, for I saw you were on the point of quitting me— I suggested some mode by which we might recognise each other at the ball, you only advised me not to go !

Your feelings to me are not the same as mine have been to you. That is natural and reasonable Mine make me sensitive and perhaps *exigeant*, and render my society in public embarrassing to you, and therefore not agreeable. Unfortunately for me, my imagination did not desert me with my youth. I have always felt this a great misfortune. It would have involved me in calamities, had not nature bestowed on me, and in a large degree, another quality—the sense of the ridiculous.

That has given me many intimations, during some months; but, in the turbulence of my heart, I was deaf to them   Reflection, however, is irresistible; and I cannot resist certainly the conviction that much in my conduct to you, during this year, has been absurd.

On Friday night, I had written to you to forget it, and to forget me. But I linger round the tie on which I had staked my happiness. You may deride my weakness, but I wished you to know my inward thoughts, and that you should not think of me as one who was ungrateful or capricious.

2, Whitehall Gardens, *Wedy.* [? *July* 1].—Your note has just reached me. It was unexpected and delightful. I am touched by your writing so spontaneously, for my stupid words did not deserve a response. . . . I am glad you think I am ' better and wiser of late.' I feel I am changed, but I am much happier.

Thursday [*July* 2, 1874].—. . . I regret to tell you that my enemy attacked me in the night, and I am obliged to go down to the Ho. of C. in a black velvet shoe, of Venetian fashion, part of my dress for that unhappy masqued ball, my absence from wh. causes such endless inquiries wh. exhaust even my imagination for replies. . . .

Lady Chesterfield was in the secret of this misunderstanding, and to her Disraeli humorously explained how he had obtained a pleasant revenge for Lady Bradford's treatment of him.

To Anne Lady Chesterfield.

2, Whitehall Gardens, *Thursday* [*July* 9, 1874].—. . Yesterday was very agreeable at the Palace. I found a seat next to Selina, and I took her to supper. She was standing by me in the royal circle, when the P. of Wales, Princess, Princess Mary, and others, came up in turn, and asked why I had not been at the masqued ball. I said to some, ' It was a secret, and that I was bound not to tell.' I said to the Princess of Wales, that I was dressed in my domino and about to go, when a fair Venetian gave me a goblet of aqua tofana, and I sank to the ground in a state of asphyxia. Selina heard all this ! . . .

Here is another self-revealing letter after a rebuff:

To Lady Bradford.

2, Whitehall Gardens, *Aug.* 3, 1874.—. . . To love as I love, and rarely to see the being one adores, whose constant society is absolutely necessary to my life; to be pre-

cluded even from the only shadowy compensation for such a
torturing doom—the privilege of relieving my heart by expressing its affection—is a lot which I never could endure,
and cannot.

But for my strange position, wh. enslaves, while it elevates,
me, I would fly for ever, as I often contemplate, to some beautiful solitude, and relieve, in ideal creation, the burthen of
such a dark and harassing existence. But the iron laws of
a stern necessity seem to control our lives, and with all the
daring and all the imagination in the world, conscious or unconscious, we are slaves. . . .

This is rather a long scribblement: pardon that, for it is
probably one of the last letters I shall ever send you. My
mind is greatly disturbed and dissatisfied. I require perfect
solitude or perfect sympathy. My present life gives me
neither of these ineffable blessings. It may be brilliant, but
it is too fragmentary. It is not a complete existence. It
gives me neither the highest development of the intellect or
the heart; neither Poetry nor Love.

And here, from the correspondence of 1875, are letters
betraying various moods of jealous and unsatisfied
affection:

To Lady Bradford.

2, WHITEHALL GARDENS, *Feb.* 24, 1875.—I should grieve
if the being to whom I am entirely devoted shd. believe for
a moment that I am unreasonable and capricious. Therefore I will condense in a few lines a remark or two on a topic
to which I hope never to recur.

You have said that I prefer your letters to your society.
On the contrary, a single interview with you is worth a hundred even of your letters, tho' they have been, for more than
a year, the charm and consolation of my life. But I confess
I have found a contrast between yr. letters and yr. general
demeanor to me, which has often perplexed, and sometimes
pained, me: and it is only in recurring to those letters that
I have found solace.

Something happened a little while ago, wh., according to
my sad interpretation, threw a light over this contrariety;
but it was a light wh. revealed, at the same time, the ruin of
my heart and hopes. I will not tell you how much I have
suffered. I became quite dejected, and could scarcely carry
on public affairs.

But the sweetness of your appeal to me yesterday, and the
radiant innocence of yr. countenance, entirely overcame me;
and convinced me that I had misapprehended the past,

and that the mutual affection, on wh. I had staked the happiness of my remaining days, was not a dream.

March 21.—. . . It [a letter Disraeli wished to show Lady Bradford] will keep till my next visit after yr. return from France, if you ever do return, and if ever I pay you another visit. These things much depend on habit, unless there is a very strong feeling such as sincerely actuated me when, last year, I said I cd. not contemplate life without seeing you every day. I feel very much like poor King Lear with his knights; half my retinue was cut down before you went to Kimbolton: 'three times a week' was then accorded me. When you return from your foreign travel, wh. wonderfully clears the brain of former impressions, there will be a further reduction of my days; till, at last, the dreary and inevitable question comes, 'Why one?'

Don't misunderstand this. This is not what you call a 'scolding.' It is misery: that horrible desolation wh. the lonely alone can feel. . . .

I have given this morning the Constableship of the Tower to General Sir Chas. Yorke, G.C.B. I keep the Isle of Man still open: open till you have quite broken my heart.

July 4.—. . . I hardly had a word with you to-day, and cd. not talk of to-morrow! I wonder if I shall see you to-morrow! Not to see you is a world without a sun. . . .

I wonder whom you will sit bet[wee]n to-day, and talk to, and delight and fascinate. I am always afraid of your dining at houses like Gerard's, in my absence. I feel horribly jeal[ous]; I cannot help it.

In such moods I sometimes read what was written to me only a year ago—tho' that's a long time—words written by a sylph, 'Have confidence in me, believe in me, believe that I am true—oh! how true!'

Even if one cannot believe these words, it is something to have them to read—and to bless the being who wrote them.

Make what discount we may for Disraeli's tendency to extravagance and exaggeration, especially in his address to women, it is impossible, after reading his letters to Lady Bradford, to doubt the reality and depth of his attachment. During one year, 1874, we find such expressions as the following: 'To see you, or at least to hear from you, every day, is absolutely necessary to my existence.' 'I have lived to know the twilight of love has its splendor and its richness.' 'To see you in society is a pleasure peculiar to itself; but different from

SELINA COUNTESS OF BRADFORD.

From a portrait after Sir F. Grant, P.R.A., at Hughenden.

that of seeing you alone; both are enchanting, like moon-light and sunshine.' 'It is not "a slice of the moon" I want; I want it all.' Playful references of this kind to the meaning in Greek of Lady Bradford's Christian name Selina—'the moon'—are plentiful in the corre-spondence. In one letter Disraeli explained the different nature of his feelings towards the two sisters.

To Lady Bradford.

2, WHITEHALL GARDENS, *Nov.* 3, 1874.—. . . I am sorry your sister is coming to town. She will arrive when I am absorbed with affairs, and will apparently be neglected and will probably think so. This will add to my annoyances, for I have a great regard for her. I love her, not only because she is your sister and a link between us, but because she has many charming qualities. But when you have the govern-ment of a country on your shoulders, to *love* a person and to be *in love* with a person makes all the difference. In the first case, everything that distracts your mind from yr. great purpose, weakens and wearies you. In the second instance, the difficulty of seeing your beloved, or communicating with her, only animates and excites you. I have devised schemes of seeing, or writing to, you in the midst of stately councils, and the thought and memory of you, instead of being an obstacle, has been to me an inspiration.

You said in one of yr. letters that I complained that you did not appreciate me. Never! Such a remark, on my part, wd. have been, in the highest degree, conceited and coxcombical. What I said was: You did not appreciate my love; that is to say, you did not justly estimate either its fervor or its depth.

The affection between Disraeli and Lady Chesterfield had none of the alternations of hot and cold that marked his relation with her sister. Here there was steady warmth and steady devotion; and he could always count upon consolation from her when, as often happened, he was rebuffed by what he called Lady Bradford's 'irre-sistible, but cold, control.' Though his passion was less, yet in his method of address he was more ardent to Lady Chesterfield than to the other. The letters to Lady Bradford generally start without any prefatory endear-ments; but Lady Chesterfield was 'dearest, dearest Lady Ches.,' 'dearest of women,' 'charming playfellow,' and

finally, in most of the letters after the first year or two,
' dear darling '; and we find such expressions as ' whatever happens to me in the world I shall always love you ';
and after an attack of gout at Bretby, ' Adieu, dear and
darling friend, I have no language to express to you my
entire affection.'   It might not always suit Lady Bradford
to have him at Weston or Castle Bromwich; but Bretby
was constantly open to him, and his table in London and
at Hughenden was regularly furnished with the produce
of its gardens, its dairy, its poultry farm, and its coverts.
' My dearest, darling friend,' he wrote on one occasion
to Lady Chesterfield, ' you literally scatter flowers and
fruit over my existence.'

To Anne Lady Chesterfield.

2, WHITEHALL GARDENS, *March* 6, 1875.—. . . It is a long
time since [*Contarini Fleming*] was born—some years before
I had the pleasure of meeting you at Wycombe Abbey, and
fell in love with your brilliant eyes flashing with grace and
triumph—and wh. cd. hardly spare a glance, then, to poor
me.   But now I am rewarded for my early homage, and, amid
the cares of empire, can find solace in cherishing your sweet
affections. . . .

Such was the nature of the attachments that gave
brightness and colour to the last eight years of Disraeli's
life.   It must not be supposed that there was in them any
unfaithfulness to the memory of a wife who had herself
laid on him her injunctions to find consolation in others.
He never forgot her and his happiness with her; his
poignant regret and his loneliness without her are the
frequent theme of his letters.   On one Queen's birthday
during his great Ministry he was looking with Lord
Redesdale at the elaborate preparations for his official
banquet, ' when all of a sudden,' his companion tells us,
' he turned round, his eyes were dim, and his voice husky,
as he said, " Ah ! my dear fellow, you are happy, you have
a wife." '   He always maintained the signs of mourning;
the whole of his correspondence with the sisters, as with
others, save on a few occasions when, being away from

home, he had to fall back on local stationery, was written on paper with a deep black edging; nor did he feel that there was any incongruity in inscribing protestations of devotion to the living on pages which recalled by their very appearance the memory of the dead.

To Lady Bradford.

HUGHENDEN MANOR, *Sept.* 27, 1875.—. . . You said you were glad to see 'white paper' the other day. It is strange, but I always used to think that the Queen, persisting in these emblems of woe, indulged in a morbid sentiment; and yet it has become my lot, and seemingly an irresistible one. I lost one who was literally devoted to me, tho' I was not alto-g[ethe]r worthy of her devotion; and when I have been on the point sometimes of terminating this emblem of my bereavement, the thought that there was no longer any being in the world to whom I was an object of concentrated feeling overcame me, and the sign remained.

Once—perhaps twice—during the last two years, I have indulged in a wild thought it might be otherwise; and then something has always occurred, wh. has dashed me to the earth. . . .

These new sentimental relations were springing up during the second portion of the session of 1873, after the reluctant return of the discredited Ministers to their places. In the House of Commons Disraeli continued on the whole his policy of reserve, assured that his opportunity must come before long. His main political activity was behind the scenes, preparing with his whips and his party manager for a dissolution which could hardly be postponed beyond the next year, rather than in the House itself where there was not much contentious business.

To Montagu Corry

April 5, '73.—It will be impossible to get a Tory majority, if lukewarmness, or selfishness of those who have a safe seat, prevent contests. There are more than 30 seats in this pre-dicament, and I have appointed a small committee of men of social influence to take them in hand: Lord J. Manners, Barrington, Chaplin or Mahon.

I hope you are better. I am well enough, but wretchedly low-spirited. . . .

To William Hart Dyke.

HUGHENDEN MANOR, *April* 15, 1873.—. . . Lady Derby writes to me this morning, that she means to give assemblies on 29th inst. and 6th May, and if somebody could send her a list of names to St. Jas. Sqre., marked to be forwarded, she would work at the list. If, therefore, you could forward her a catalogue of the M.P.s, their wives and dau[ghte]rs, that ' she would do well to invite,' business wd. be advanced.

I think, from what Miladi said to me when I last saw her, that she wished a little discretion to be exercised in the transaction. An overplus of quizzes neutralises the distinction, and it is better that she shd. be encouraged to give more parties than to swamp her good intentions and make her feel her receptions are a failure.

To Montagu Corry.

May 17, '73.—The Government continues in a discredited state, but we have not availed ourselves, as much as we ought to have done, of several recent opportunities. The causes, or probable causes, of this, I must keep till we meet. It seems that the Ministry will totter through the session, though at present, the decomposition of ' the great Liberal party ' is complete. It still keeps, on the surface, together, from the hope, I think a vain one, that ' something will turn up ' for them : the last resource of imbecility and exhaustion.

I am not particularly well, and sent for Leggatt to-day, and am now a prisoner, besieged by this scathing easterly wind. . . .

Such incursions as Disraeli made in debate had a distinctly electioneering flavour. When the Budget was discussed, he delivered a lively attack on Lowe's finance, partly with a view to deride that eminent anti-Reformer's pose as the friend of the working man, and partly in the interest of that relief of local taxation which the party had championed with success in the previous year. But his most interesting speech was made in opposition to Osborne Morgan's Burials Bill, which proposed to open the parish churchyards to Dissenting funerals. His view was that by refusing to pay church rates the Dissenters had publicly recognised that the churches and churchyards belonged to churchmen; and therefore if they wished to use the parish churchyards,

that use must be, by every principle of law and equity,
upon the conditions imposed by those to whom they
belonged. He ended his speech by some earnest words
of advice to his Nonconformist fellow-countrymen.   Lord
Grey's Reform Act, he said, had given them great power,
which in many cases they had used wisely.

So long as they maintained toleration, so long as they
favoured religious liberty, so long as they checked sacerdotal
arrogance, they acted according to their traditions, and those
traditions are not the least noble in the history of England.
But they have changed their position.   They now make war,
and avowedly make war, upon the ecclesiastical institutions
of this country.[1] I think they are in error in pursuing that
course.   I believe it not to be for their own interest.   However
ambiguous and discursive may be the superficial aspects of the
religious life of this country, the English are essentially a religious people. . . . They look upon [the Church] instinctively
as an institution which vindicates the spiritual nature of man,
and as a city of refuge in the strife and sorrows of existence.
I want my Nonconformist friends to remember that another
Act of Parliament has been passed affecting the circumstances
of England since the Act of 1832.   It appeals to the heart of
the country.   It aims at emancipation from undue sectarian
influence; and I do not think that the Nonconformist body will
for the future exercise that undue influence upon the returns to
this House, which they have now for forty years employed. . . .
Let them not be misled by the last General Election.   The
vast majority arrayed against us was not returned by the
new constituencies.   It was the traditional and admirable
organisation of the Dissenters of England that effected the
triumph of the right hon. gentleman.   They were animated
by a great motive to enthusiasm.   They saw before them the
destruction of a church.   I do not think that, at the next
appeal to the people, the Nonconformist body will find that
the same result can be obtained.   I say not this by way of
taunt, certainly not in a spirit of anticipated triumph.   I
say it because I wish the Nonconformist body to pause and
think, and to feel that for the future it may be better for
them, instead of assailing the Church, to find in it a faithful
and sound ally.   There is a common enemy abroad to all
churches and to all religious bodies.   Their opinions rage on
the Continent.   Their poisonous distillations have entered
even into this isle.

[1] Miall, the Nonconformist spokesman in Parliament, regularly introduced motions for the disestablishment of the English Church.

The Dissenters, distracted by the controversies over the Education Act, were not a determining force in the 1874 election.   But their enthusiastic support of Gladstone's bag and baggage policy went far to settle the result in 1880, and, a quarter of a century later, their campaign of passive resistance was certainly one of the causes which helped in the decisive overthrow of the Unionists under Mr. Balfour.   On the other hand, the life seems to have gone out of the disestablishment movement, save in regard to Wales; and it is noteworthy that the Dissenters have never been able to secure, during many years of Parliaments in which their friends have always had a considerable majority, that educational arrangement with a view to which they exerted themselves so strenuously in 1906.

As the session drew to a close there was a painful outcrop of administrative scandals mainly affecting mail contracts and telegraphic extension.   Disraeli, true to his practice of avoiding personal squabbles, took little or no part in the discussion of matters which reflected seriously on three important members of the Government.   The principal achievement of Ministers was the Judicature Act for the reorganisation of the Courts of Law and Equity.   A curious question of privilege arose during the passage of this measure.   The Commons made an amendment which no less an authority than Cairns declared to be a breach of the Lords' privileges.   It was rather a storm in a teacup, but it gave Disraeli an opportunity to show his quality.

To Lord Cairns.

12, GEORGE STREET, HANOVER SQUARE, *July* 15.—Misled by Gladstone, who bewildered me in the most Jesuitical manner, I dined at Grillion's, and lingered there, and was going home when I heard Frdk. Cavendish, G.'s private secretary, say to Hardy ' about this time the privilege is on.'   Hardy seemed astonished, and maintained it was impossible.   However I thought I would go down to the House.   I found it on, and nearly finished, and G. was concluding when I entered, with my wits scarcely collected. However, I went at it, and tho' I should have spoken much better, if I had remained at the House, and went almost breathless into battle, I still got the materials of the case fairly out, and am now going down to the House to resume the fight if G. chooses.

From Lord Cairns.

5, CROMWELL HOUSES, W., *July* 15, 1873.—I think the dinner at Grillion's must have been a most happy preparation for the speech: at all events, nothing could, in my opinion, have been more successful in at once putting before the House the substance and truth of the precedents; in maintaining the proper attitude of the House of Commons on such an occasion; and in covering the Govt. with ridicule for their terror-stricken and undignified attitude.

As soon as the session was over Gladstone effected a very considerable reconstruction of his Government. The Ministers chiefly concerned in the Post Office irregularities, of whom Lowe was one, could not remain longer in their existing places; and, in the course of the shuffle, Gladstone took himself the Chancellorship of the Exchequer in addition to his previous office, and Bright, who had a year or two before left the Cabinet owing to ill-health, re-entered it as Chancellor of the Duchy. But nothing could stem the unpopularity of the Government. They continued during the autumn to lose seat after seat at by-elections: in August, at Shaftesbury, East Staffordshire, and Greenwich; in September, at Dover and in Renfrewshire; in October, at Hull; and in December, at Exeter. Many of the vacancies were caused by Ministerial promotions, so that the verdict of public opinion was particularly marked and particularly galling.

Disraeli went down to Hughenden before the end of July, and spent a quiet time in examining and sorting his own papers and his wife's; burrowing among those treasures which have formed the basis of this biography. His letters to old and new friends show both how he felt his loneliness in the country home of his wedded life, and the way in which he regarded the political scene, in which, for many weeks, he refused to take an active part.

To Montagu Corry.

HUGHENDEN, *July* 30.—I came down here with a resolve to get the house in complete order, and worked yesterday to my satisfaction.   This morning I determined, with all the keys, to grapple with the bird's nest imbroglio.   The first thing I wanted were her private papers, etc., which I thought were stowed in one of the new tin boxes.   I have opened four, all there, but cannot find them : nothing, apparently, but scraps and chaos.   I am now exhausted, and have given up the task, for the day at least.

Can you throw any light on the matter ? . . .

Aug. 1.—. . . The Government really seems on its last legs.   They can gain no laurels in the recess.   That must be spent in apologies, and explanations; especially of the discomfitures and imbroglios of the last fortnight of the session They will, probably, also lose every election, that occurs before the reassembling of Parliament.

The weather here is delicious, and I have also plenty to amuse me in the house, in trying to get the library into perfect order, arranging pictures and so on; but my great business must be the papers, and I am about to set at them again forthwith.   I shall not be content until the house is in perfect order. . . .

Aug. 3.—. . . I found the missing papers, and continue at work at their companions between two and three hours each day.   I cannot manage more.   The progress is not encouraging, but I feel, if I missed this opportunity in my life, I should probably never have another.

She does not appear to have destroyed a single scrap I ever wrote to her, before or after marriage, and never to have cut my hair, which she did every two or three weeks for 33 years, without garnering the harvest; so, as you once asked for some of an early date, I send you a packet, of which I could not break the seal.

There are missing at present two Russian sabres, which Lord Strangford left me, and a long yataghan in a crimson velvet scabbard.   These arms were too long to be packed up with the other daggers.   Can you throw any light on them ? You can on most things.

Aug. 10.—Hardy writes ' What does it all mean ?   Dissolution, or a more radical policy ?'

My opinion is, that instead of dissolution, it is merely a

diversion to escape dissolution, which was inevitable, had they not done something. But their reconstruction is only a sham, and the idea of being saved by the return of that hysterical old spouter, Bright, is absurd. As for a policy, they are much too flustered to have any.

These great events are exciting, especially the elections, and one wants something. The business of my life is a most melancholy one. I only finished arranging her personal papers yesterday: and she has died for me 100 times in the heartrending, but absolutely inevitable, process.

To Lord John Manners.

HUGHENDEN MANOR, *Aug.* 28, '73.—A letter from a friend is like the sight of a sail to one on a desert isle; but when it comes from the best and dearest of friends, it is cheering indeed.

I have been here since the last days of July, and have never been out of the grounds. With one or two casual exceptions, I have never spoken to a human being. Among the casuals, between ourselves, was Sir Arthur Helps, on his way to Balmoral: a royal reconnaissance. It is a dreary life, but I find society, without sympathy, drearier.

As for my health, it is perfect. I have been often told, and I have sometimes thought, that the bronchial disturbance from which I suffered, was a gouty symptom: and so, two years ago, I left off sugar, and with advantage. For a month and more I have now lived without wine, and my cure seems complete. Some stimulus is requisite, but the Lord Rector of a Scotch University has not far to seek for the necessary restorative, tho' it must be kept a secret from the more delicate Southrons.

I am greatly amused with the fast-drifting incidents of the political scene, and so, I suspect, are some others of higher mettle. I don't suppose, that Gladstone, at present, has decided on any course whatever, but he will not go out without attempting something. I hear he is deeply mortified by the utter destruction of the prestige of his Administration, and that his only thought now is to, what they call, re-habilitate it, before it disappears. He will find this a hard task. . . .

To Lady Bradford.

HUGHENDEN MANOR, *Aug.* 29, 1873.—. . . I hope your visit to Windermere has been enchanting. They say the weather has been fitful in England generally, but here we have had a summer of romance. . . .

On Wednesday last, I received from the lady an announce-

ment of the immediately impending event,[1] ' as you have
always taken so kind an interest in my welfare.'   One can
scarcely congratulate, but may sincerely wish her every happiness.   It sounds very bad. . . .

To Anne Lady Chesterfield.

HUGHENDEN MANOR, *Sept.* 8, 1873.—. . . I expected,
when I saw the Queen in March, the decomposition of the
Ministry, but it has been more complete than I contemplated.   Had Gladstone then gone out, uncommitted on either
Church or education, and the squabbles of his colleagues
unknown, he would have gone out with almost undiminished
prestige, and would soon have rallied.   The firm is now
insolvent, and will soon be bankrupt.   When the Tories
return, it will be their own fault if their reign be not long and
glorious. . . .

To Sir Stafford Northcote.

Confidential.   HUGHENDEN MANOR, *Sept.* 11, 1873.—You
cannot take too decided a line about Ashantee, barring pro-
phecies, like Lowe, of the indubitable failure of the expedition.
The great point to insist on, after indicating the dangers and
the chances of failure, is the want of analogy between the
Ashantee and the Abyssinian cases.   What is the cause of
quarrel ?   If the Ash. want commercial access to the coast,
wh. they always used to have, their claim does not seem unreasonable : a matter certainly that ought to admit of arrangement. . . .

The country is deadly to Europeans.   Black troops may

---

[1] Lady Cardigan's marriage to the Count de Lancastre. Lady Cardigan's story in her *Recollections* that Disraeli himself made her an offer of
marriage may safely be disregarded.   Apart from the improbability of a
statesman in Disraeli's position desiring to marry a woman of a somewhat
equivocal reputation, there were only eight months—between December,
1872, when he became a widower, and August, 1873, when she married a
second time—in which a proposal of marriage was possible from him to
her; and these were months when he was forming other attachments.
She narrows the time still more by placing the occurrence in the hunting
season—in other words, very shortly indeed after Lady Beaconsfield's death.
By way of corroboration she states that she asked and obtained the advice
of the then Prince of Wales, whom she encountered at a meet at Belvoir,
whether she should accept; but, when the book was published, King
Edward told his personal friends that no such conversation had taken
place.   It is, of course, possible that there was a question of marriage
between Lady Cardigan and Disraeli in the sense that she proposed to him
and he declined.   There is, certainly, in the *Recollections* a striking exhibi-
tion of spite against Lady Bradford, as well as a tendency to disparage
Disraeli.   Moreover, there is reason to believe that there were other ladies
of wealth and position who gave Disraeli to understand, at this period, that
they were ready to unite their lot with his.

live in it, but, then, they won't fight.   But above all there are no prisoners to rescue.   If we get there, what is the gain? If we are beaten by the climate, wh. is on the cards, are we to sit down with a defeat, or is there to be another expedition; more lives thrown away and more money ?

There cannot be a more unprofitable, and more inglorious quarrel.   All the motives of the Abyssinian expedition are wanting, and all the circumstances are different.   Lord Derby writes me that he met Lowe, who made no scruple of saying that he had not been consulted, and did not know what his colleagues were about !   So much for Ash. !

As to general politics, I think it highly desirable that you should notice the misconception of my expression of the necessity of our knowing the situation and engagements of the Govt. before we could decide on our policy on several foreign subjects of pressing importance.   Nothing can be better than what you propose to say on this head.   As to our general policy, it is to uphold the institutions of the country, and to arrest that course of feverish criticism and unnecessary change, too long in vogue.   I would not too much insist on our policy being essentially defensive, because they always make out that means being stationary.   If pressed about reduction of county suffrage, or unable to avoid it, take the ground that constant change in the distribution of power is in itself an evil; that the measure of 1868 is only just digested; that it has been followed by the ballot, hardly yet tried; that we have no reason to fear extension of the franchise to properly qualified classes, but that any large increase of either the boro' or the county constituency cannot be considered alone; that the latter must lead to a considerable disfranchise-ment of the towns from 30,[000] to 10,000 inhab.; that, tho' this may not be immediately unfavorable to the Cons. cause, you are not prepared, without deep consideration and clear necessity, to diminish, to a great extent, the influence of urban populations in our system of Govt., being one favor-able to public liberty and enlightenment. . . .

For the last month, I have not interchanged a word with a human being.   It is a dreary life, but I find society drearier. I have realised what are the feelings of a prisoner of State of a high class: the fellow in the Iron Masque, and so on. I have parks and gardens, and pictures and books, and every-thing to charm and amuse, except the human face and voice divine.   I really have never been out of my own grounds. However, my imprisonment is nearly at an end, for towards the close of this month I am going to the Bradfords in Shrop-shire.   I hope I shall be able to behave myself in civilised society. . .

To Montagu Corry.

HUGHENDEN, *Sept.* 14, 1873.—. . . All that we have seen, or I have told you, of the correspondence, is nothing to what has since transpired. I am amazed! I should think at least 5,000 letters in addition to all I had examined: and apparently, more important and interesting than any. Nothing seems to have escaped her. Many letters of Metternich, Thiers, Brougham. I should say 100 of Bulwer: as many of Stanley, beginning with Trinity College, Cambridge; enough of George Smythe for three volumes, and I dare say not a line in them not as good as Horace Walpole. The whole of Lady Londonderry's correspondence—I dare say 100 letters! Among them, I saw a packet—more than a doz.— from Butt. Many of D'Orsay: his last letter written in pencil, just before his death, on hearing that I was C. of E[xcheque]r and leader of the H. of C. The last letter received from Lady Blessington—a most interesting one. It is the only one I have read: if I had once indulged in reading them, I never should have licked them into any form.

To Lady Bradford.

BEDFORD, BRIGHTON, *Sept.* 24, 1873.—. . You will be a little surprised at my date; but after two months of solitude, with everything to charm except the greatest of charms, the human face and voice divine, I thought London might be a relief. It was intolerable, so I came down here. It might have succeeded, for I found our friends, the Sturts,[1] here, and in the same hotel. She is ever pleasing, and his wondrous rattle is as good as champaign [*sic*]; but alas! she fell ill, and fancied it was the fault of Brighton, and they went off at a moment's notice.

Yesterday the Brunnows found me out, and took me home to dine with them, quite alone. I sate between the Ambassador and Madame. No other guest, not even a *sous-secrétaire* of embassy. We had six servants in the room, and a wondrous repast, which, as I live on a ' spare radish,' was rather embarrassing. They were kind but it was not lively, tho' I was amused by the great excitement of Brunnow as to English politics, which he flattered himself he concealed. He was always recurring to the Dover election which made a great sensation here. We had telegraphs of the poll every hour, and at ten o'ck. they gave me a serenade, or a chorale, the most beautiful thing I ever heard. No one knows who were the serenaders; they say a private musical society. Not, certainly, the Christie [*sic*] minstrels, who all take off

[1] Afterwards Lord and Lady Alington.

their hats to me when I pass: which is awkward, as I was told
I should be as unnoticed here in September, as in the woods
of Hughenden.

My kind remembrances to Lord Bradford.

I cannot express to you the delight I anticipate from seeing
you again. It seems to me that the only happy hours I have
had in this melancholy year are due to your charming society.

The visits to Lord and Lady Bradford at Weston and
to Lady Chesterfield at Bretby followed, and confirmed
him in his devotion to both ladies, though he protested to
a friend that he did not really enjoy this country-house
visiting.

To Lord Henry Lennox.

WESTON, SHIFNAL, *Oct.* 2, '73.—. . . I hope you have
not given up your Bretby visit, and that we shall meet on
Monday. I am not very much inclined to it, and rather
count on your help. The fact is, visiting does not suit me,
and I have pretty well made up my mind, after this year,
to give up what is called society, and confine myself solely
to public life. The only consolation I have is, that my health
is good; as, doubtless, we have some coming scenes, that
will try both our nerves and muscle.

I linger on here, boring and bored, notwithstanding a
charming hostess, on whom I feel myself a tax. I could
not make my other visits[1] fit in without postponing my arrival
at Bretby for a couple of days. And this, I thought, under
all circumstances, would be too great a liberty.

The Weston visit was notable for Disraeli's last experiment in riding to hounds. He never rode at all at
Hughenden, and, indeed, is only recorded to have crossed
a horse twice in the past quarter of a century: once when
Lord Galway's guest at Serlby in 1853, and again when
Lord Wilton showed him the Belvoir hounds in 1869.[2]
In these circumstances it argued great pluck in a man
nearly sixty-nine to accept an invitation to go cub-hunting
at Chillington, five miles from Weston. He rode a little
chestnut hack, remained in the saddle three or four hours,
and was so exhausted that he actually reeled against the
stable wall when he dismounted.

While Disraeli was at Weston, there was an election

[1] One of these was to Knowsley.
[2] See Meynell's *Disraeli*, Vol. I., p. 177.

contest proceeding at Bath, the third in the course of the year. At the beginning of the Parliament Bath had been represented by two Liberals. Both had died, one after the other, this spring, and each seat in turn had been won for the Conservatives. Now one of the new members, Lord Chelsea, had succeeded to the peerage; and to Lord Grey de Wilton, the Conservative candidate for the vacancy, a personal friend of his own, Disraeli wrote for publication from Weston on October 3:

For nearly five years the present Ministers have harassed every trade, worried every profession, and assailed or menaced every class, institution, and species of property in the country. Occasionally they have varied this state of civil warfare by perpetrating some job which outraged public opinion, or by stumbling into mistakes which have been always discreditable, and sometimes ruinous. All this they call a policy, and seem quite proud of it; but the country has, I think, made up its mind to close this career of plundering and blundering.[1]

It was a full-blooded letter, conceived in the hustings spirit, but it only restated, in pointed fashion, charges which Disraeli had often brought against Ministers in public speeches and across the table of the House of Commons. A vehement outcry was, however, raised against its tone and language; and even many of his own party attributed to this indiscretion Grey de Wilton's failure by a small majority to retain the seat which Chelsea had won by a majority somewhat similar. Disraeli, at any rate, was quite impenitent.

To Anne Lady Chesterfield.

HUGHENDEN MANOR, *Oct.* 24, 1873.—. . . The storm against my letter to Grey was quite factitious; got up by a knot of clever Liberal journalists, who had, they thought, an opportunity. It has quite evaporated, and from the number of letters I daily receive about it, from all parts of the country, and from the quotations from it daily cropping up in the press, I have no doubt it will effect the purpose for which it was written.

---

[1] Disraeli had used the phrase before, in *Coningsby*, Bk. II., ch. 4.

I wished to give a condensed, but strictly accurate, summary
of the career of the Gladstone Ministry. There is not an
expression which was not well weighed, and which I could
not justify by ample, and even abounding, evidence. Lord
Salisbury,[1] and the Hull election, together, will effectively
silence my critics. . . .

Disraeli went in the following month to Glasgow,
and there defended himself in detail. Ministers might
sigh, he said, and newspapers might scream, but the
question was, Was the statement a true one ?   It was no
answer to say ' Oh, fie ! how very rude !'   He maintained that he had written the history of a Ministry that
had lasted five years and had immortalised the spirit
of their policy in five lines.

The occasion of Disraeli's visit to Glasgow was that
he might be installed Lord Rector of the University,
and might thereupon deliver his address to the students
who had elected him two years before, but who had
been deprived of the treat of seeing and hearing him
in the previous autumn by Lady Beaconsfield's last illness. Many other functions, however, were planned to
welcome the man of the hour to the Clyde. Writing
to Lord Barrington a few days beforehand he said the
expedition was ' assuming colossal proportions. . . .
My plans assume that I shall return to England alive;
when I see the programme of the Glasgow week, it seems
doubtful. Nothing can be more inhuman; and if there
were a society to protect public men, as there is to protect
donkeys, some interference would undoubtedly take place.'

Few statesmen were more qualified by sympathy and
experience to give advice to youth. He had never
ceased to be young in feeling, and to feel for the young;
and he himself was a dazzling example of what resolute
and aspiring youth could achieve. He impressed upon
his hearers at Glasgow the necessity, in order to succeed
in life, for two kinds of knowledge—first self-knowledge,
and then knowledge of the spirit of the age. Self-know-

[1] Who had written an article in the current number of the *Quarterly
Review*, strongly criticising ' The programme of the Radicals.'

ledge, he told them, could not be obtained with certainty either in the family circle, or from the judgment of one's fellows, or from that of one's tutors; but from self-communion. The young would make many errors and experience much self-deception; it was their business to learn the lesson of their mistakes, and to accept the consequences with courage and candour. Only by severe introspection could they obtain the self-knowledge they required and make their failures the foundation of their ultimate success.

But self-knowledge was not enough. Without a knowledge of the spirit of the age life might prove a blunder; a man might embrace a profession doomed to grow obsolete, or embark his capital in a decaying trade. It did not follow that the spirit of the age should be adopted; it might be necessary to resist it; but it was essential to understand it. He considered the spirit of the mid-Victorian age in which he spoke to be one of equality. So far as the word stood for civil equality—equality of all subjects before the law—it was the only foundation of a perfect commonwealth, and had been largely responsible for British patriotism and security. But there was also social equality, which had been established by the Revolution in France, but which recent events, in 1870 and 1871, showed not to be a principle on which a nation could safely rely in the hour of trial. And, further, there was the demand of a new school for physical and material equality. 'The leading principle of this new school is that there is no happiness which is not material, and that every living being has a right to share in that physical welfare.' The school substituted the rights of labour for the rights of property, and recognised no such limitation of employment as resulted from the division of the world into states or nations. 'As civil equality would abolish privilege and social equality would destroy classes; so material and physical equality strikes at the principle of patriotism, and is prepared to abrogate countries.' Against this theory he appealed to the

Creamus Te Legum Doctorem

MR. DISRAELI AT GLASGOW UNIVERSITY, 1873.

From a drawing by Mrs. Blackburn at Hughenden.

traditional patriotism of his Scottish audience, and proceeded, in a peroration which sums up his teaching on
spiritual matters in *Tancred, Lord George Bentinck*, the
Sheldonian speech, and *Lothair*:

It is not true that the only real happiness is physical happiness; it is not true that physical happiness is the highest happiness; it is not true that physical happiness is a principle on
which you can build up a flourishing and enduring commonwealth. A civilised community must rest on a large realised
capital of thought and sentiment; there must be a reserved fund
of public morality to draw upon in the exigencies of national
life. Society has a soul as well as a body. The traditions
of a nation are part of its existence. Its valour and its discipline, its venerable laws, its science and erudition, its
poetry, its art, its eloquence and its scholarship are as much
portions of its life as its agriculture, its commerce, and its
engineering skill. . . .
If it be true, as I believe, that an aristocracy distinguished
merely by wealth must perish from satiety, so I hold it equally
true that a people who recognise no higher aim than physical
enjoyment must become selfish and enervated. Under such
circumstances, the supremacy of race, which is the key of history, will assert itself. Some human progeny, distinguished
by their bodily vigour or their masculine intelligence, or by
both qualities, will assert their superiority, and conquer
a world which deserves to be enslaved. It will then be found
that our boasted progress has only been an advancement in
a circle, and that our new philosophy has brought us back to
that old serfdom which it has taken ages to extirpate.[1]
But the still more powerful, indeed the insurmountable,
obstacle to the establishment of the new opinions will be
furnished by the essential elements of the human mind.
Our idiosyncrasy is not bounded by the planet which we
inhabit. We can investigate space, and we can comprehend
eternity. No considerations limited to this sphere have
hitherto furnished the excitement which man requires, or the
sanctions for his conduct which his nature imperatively
demands. The spiritual nature of man is stronger than codes
or constitutions. No Government can endure which does not
recognise that for its foundation, and no legislation last
which does not flow from that fountain. The principle may
develop itself in manifold forms, in the shape of many creeds
and many churches; but the principle is divine. As time

[1] A profound passage, which the history of the world since 1914 enables
the men of to-day to appreciate.

is divided into day and night, so religion rests upon the Providence of God and the responsibility of man. One is manifest, the other mysterious; but both are facts. Nor is there, as some would teach you, anything in these convictions which tends to contract our intelligence or our sympathies. On the contrary, religion invigorates the intellect and expands the heart. He who has a due sense of his relations to God is best qualified to fulfil his duties to man.

Disraeli brought to a close an address which had contained many references to Greek and Latin authors by a quotation, in the original Greek, of four lines from the *Ajax* of Sophocles, containing the poet's acknowledgment of Divine Providence. Other quotations from Greek plays are found in *Lord George Bentinck*. Disraeli has been accused of pretending, in these and other passages, to a classical erudition which he did not possess. But, as was shown in Vol. I., ch. 3, he had attained while at school, and in the year or more of private study which followed, to a wide knowledge of Latin and a moderate acquaintance with Greek; and it is reasonable to assume that a man of letters who, like Disraeli, rather ignored contemporary literature, would refresh his mind throughout life by recurring to his favourite authors of antiquity. He was at any rate sufficiently familiar with classical literature, Greek as well as Latin, to sustain a whole evening's conversation on the subject in the summer of 1880 with Northcote, a lifelong scholar, upon whom he could not hope to impose with sham knowledge, and who records the talk in his diary without a suggestion that his chief was discussing matters which he did not understand. Sophocles, in particular, he told Northcote, he used at one time to carry about in his pocket.

So satisfied were the Glasgow students with the brilliancy of their Rector's address and the lustre of his career that, having originally elected him in 1871 by a large majority in each of the four 'nations' into which they were divided, they paid him the unusual compliment of re-electing him in 1874, in the same handsome fashion, for a second term.

The Glasgow festivities included, besides the Uni-

versity function, a municipal banquet with the Lord
Provost in the chair, the conferment of the freedom
of the city, and the presentation of an address by the
local Conservative association. Every mark of respect
and consideration was shown Disraeli; and the warmth
of the popular reception was unmistakable. He told
Rose that ' Glasgow, without exaggeration, was the
greatest reception ever offered to a public man: far beyond
Lancashire even !' At the banquet he touched with
some grace on the question of the leadership, now a
purely academic one. He had led his party in the Commons, he said, for twenty-five years, the longest period
of leadership on record. Peel had led the Conservative
party there for eighteen years, though unfortunately
it twice broke asunder; and Russell's leadership of the
Liberals had lasted seventeen years, till at last it slipped
out of his hands.

Do not suppose for a moment that I am making these
observations in a vain spirit of boasting. The reason that
I have been able to lead a party for so long a period, and
under some circumstances of difficulty and discouragement,
is that the party that I lead is really the most generous and
most indulgent party that ever existed. I cannot help smiling
sometimes when I hear the constant intimations that are given,
by those who know all the secrets of the political world, of
the extreme anxiety of the Conservative party to get rid of
my services. The fact is, the Conservative party can get
rid of my services whenever they give me an intimation that
they wish it. Whenever I have desired to leave the leadership of the party they have too kindly requested me to remain
where I was; and if I make a mistake the only difference in
their conduct to me is that they are more indulgent and more
kind.

A declaration at once modest, generous, and politic,
but giving perhaps a somewhat idealised version of the
relationship between leader and party. His political
address to the local Conservatives was largely occupied
with the defence of the Bath letter; but in his peroration
he sounded a warning note as to the contest that was
proceeding in Europe between the spiritual and the temporal power. It would be the greatest danger to civili-

sation if in this struggle the only representatives of the two sides should be the Papacy and the Red Republic. England could hardly stand apart. ' Our connection with Ireland will be brought painfully to our consciousness; and I should not be at all surprised if the visor of Home Rule should fall off some day, and you beheld a very different countenance.' It might be the proud destiny of England to guard civilisation ' alike from the withering blast of atheism and from the simoom of sacerdotal usurpation.' Finally he adjured Scotsmen to ' leave off mumbling the dry bones of political economy, and munching the remainder biscuit of an effete Liberalism.'

From Montagu Corry.

WESTON, SHIFNAL, *Nov* 28, '73.—The Duke of Richmond tells me that nothing but regard for your time has prevented his obeying his impulse to write to you his warm appreciation of the great speech of Saturday. He asked me to tell you this at our next meeting, and also that all his correspondents agree in declaring the satisfaction which it has given the party.

He further told me that none of your words at Glasgow had afforded him so much pleasure as your remarks on your leadership, which he thought well timed and in excellent taste. He hopes the mouths may now be shut of those who, ' whenever Lord Derby goes about starring at Mechanics' Institutes, etc.,' . . . cry out ' Here is *the* man !' With such the Duke does not agree, nor seems to deem the Earl better qualified to lead in his own Chamber ! . .

To Lady Bradford.

KEIR, DUNBLANE, N.B., *Nov.* 26, 1873.—You were right in supposing that your letter was more precious to me than ' loud huzzas.'

It has been a great week—without exaggeration.

What pleased me, personally, most was the opportunity, *forced* on me, of shattering all the hypocritical trash about my letter to Grey. I call it the Weston manifesto, for it was written under the roof that you inspire and adorn.

I rather long for rest, but have no prospect of it. I live on the railroad and am now going to Cochrane's for a day, for I could not resist his reproachful countenance any more. . . .

To Gathorne Hardy.

BLENHEIM PALACE, WOODSTOCK, *Dec.* 12, 1873.—. . . We have a very gay and gorgeous party here, but the frost has stopped all the hunting, and the fog has marred the shooting.

I attended the Princess yesterday on a visit to yr. constituents, but the fog was so great, that we could neither see, nor be seen.

We lunched at the Dean of Xchurch, and I saw in the flesh Jowett, M. Müller, and Ruskin![1] That was something. M. Bernard was also there, tho' I wonder he had an appetite for any meal, even luncheon, after the quantity of dirt he has eaten.[2]

The Whigs here did not like Exeter. . . .

To Anne Lady Chesterfield.

HUGHENDEN MANOR, *Dec.* 15, 1873.—. . . What with Glasgow, Keir, Lamington, Gunnersbury, Ashridge, Sandringham and Blenheim, I have lived in such a whirl during the last month, that I can hardly distinguish the places where I met persons, and attribute the wrong sayings to the wrong folk.

I think the Government has quite relapsed into the miserable condition they were in at the end of the session, and from which the accession of Mr. Bright, and his sham programme, had, for a moment, a little lifted them out. There will be no measures about reform, or land, or education, and I continue of the opinion I expressed when I was at Bretby, that they will have to dissolve in March. . . .

I was agreeably disappointed with Sandringham. It is not commonplace; both wild and stately. I fancied I was paying a visit to some of the Dukes and Princes of the Baltic; a vigorous marine air, stunted fir forests, but sufficiently extensive; the roads and all the appurtenances on a great scale, and the splendor of Scandinavian sunsets.

Disraeli interrupted his merely social visits to attend a gathering of the party chiefs just before Christmas, at Hardy's house in Kent. 'It is a meeting,' he told Lady Chesterfield, 'that usually takes place at Hughenden,

---

[1] In a letter of the same date to Sir Arthur Helps, Disraeli wrote of these three eminent men: "The first does not look like a man who could devise or destroy a creed, but benignant; the second all fire, and the third all fantasy' (*Correspondence of Sir Arthur Helps*, p. 360).

[2] Professor Mountague Bernard had been one of the British Commissioners at Washington.

but I am not equal to the affair this year, with a
broken household, and with no organising spirit;' to
Lady Bradford he protested, ' It is the sort of thing
I abhor.'   The date originally suggested was December 15, but Disraeli wrote to his ' dearest Hardy ':
' Pardon me all the trouble I am giving you, but,
as far as I am concerned, it must be the 16th.   The
preceding day is the anniversary of my great sorrow.'
Besides Disraeli and Hardy, Cairns, Northcote, Manners,
Ward Hunt, Taylor (the Whip), and Montagu Corry
were present.   No definite conclusions were come to,
Hardy tells us; and indeed the next move must necessarily
be with the Government.   But there was, no doubt, much
interchange of opinion on a subject which had for months
formed the topic of Conservative correspondence; namely,
how to deal, when the session opened, with the question
whether the Prime Minister, since his acceptance of the
additional office of Chancellor of the Exchequer, was
any longer a Member of Parliament, seeing that he had
not, in compliance with the statute of Anne, submitted
himself to his constituents for re-election.   It is a question
on which much can be, and has been, said on both sides;
but which was deprived of all actuality by the unexpected
course which Gladstone took before Parliament could
meet.

To Lady Bradford.

HEMSTED PARK, STAPLEHURST, *Dec.* 19, 1873.—. . .
[Corry] leaves me, I am sorry to say, on Monday for
Savernake, so I shall pass my Xmas alone. That is, however, not a great grief to me beyond losing his society, as I
never was a great admirer of a merrie Xmas, even when a
boy. I always hated factitious merriment, in the form of
unnecessary guzzlement, and those awful inventions, round
games, worse even than forfeits, if that be possible ! . . .

HUGHENDEN MANOR, *Dec.* 28, 1873.—. . . I passed my
Xmas at Trentham in the enemy's camp, where I was taken
captive; but they treated me with great humanity, and spared
my life, which was valuable to me, as I had a prospect of
seeing you. They wished me to remain a week, but I gave
them only two days. I do not stay a week, except with those
I love. The page of human life is quickly read, and one does
not care to dwell upon it, unless it touches the heart.

CHAPTER VIII.

POWER.

1874.

The opening of the New Year found Disraeli still pursuing a round of visits in country-houses, Crichel, Heron Court, and Bretby; strengthening the ties which bound him to Lady Chesterfield and Lady Bradford; and busying himself apparently almost as much about securing a permanent residence in London as over the favourable political outlook. By-elections continued to herald the doom of the Government. Stroud and Newcastle-on-Tyne, both with a long record of Liberal representation, polled in the early days of the year, with the result that a Conservative took the place of a Liberal at Stroud by a substantial margin, while the Liberal majority at Newcastle sank from 4,000 to 1,000.

To Anne Lady Chesterfield.

CRICHEL, WIMBORNE, *Jan.* 10, 1874.—Lady Bradford gave me your congratulatory message on the Stroud election; much the most important event of the kind that has yet occurred. I observe then the *Spectator* acknowledges that to deny the ' reaction ' now is impossible and absurd.

I enclose you a letter on the subject from Sir Michael Beach, a very able and rising man, and who threw himself into the Stroud contest as Sir Stafford Northcote did into that of Exeter. I agree with Sir Michael that, after Stroud, nothing ought to astonish us. . . .

To Lady Bradford.

BRETBY PARK, BURTON-ON-TRENT, *Jan.* 20, 1874.—. . . I arrived here yesterday at tea twilight, and the first words I heard were ' Selina is ill, and they are going to Bournemouth.' This so knocked me up that I could scarcely perform the offices of civility to my delightful hostess, and her guests who loomed in the chamber, of ambiguous light, in the shapes of Wilton, the Dick Curzons, and your friend the great General.[1] I ought not to forget Carnarvon, whom I absolutely did not recognise. . . .

I have not yet received an answer about Duchess[2] Eleanor's house. What do you think of your sister's house in Hill St.? She wants to let it. Would that do for me? They seem to think that Whitehall Gardens has such a strong recommendation in being near the Ho. of Commons. I doubt that Hill St. would secure a walk, which is something. Certainly I might find a substitute, if in Whitehall, by walking to the House of C. *via* Belgrave Square,[3] which would not only secure health, but also happiness, which is something also.

To-day's post informs me that I have succeeded in getting rooms at Edwards's Hotel from Friday next, and I shall keep them on till my plans for the season are matured. They are miserable; merely a couple of rooms on the ground floor, but they are a sort of headquarters, until I get a house, or commit some other folly. . . .

Accordingly on Friday, January 23, Disraeli came up from Bretby to his London hotel with the view of attending on the Saturday a meeting of the trustees of the British Museum, and also of deciding finally on his future house. It still wanted nearly a fortnight to the date fixed for the opening of the session; and his intention was to return after a week-end in town to his home at Hughenden. When, however, he woke on the Saturday morning, he was greeted by the momentous news that the Queen had been advised to dissolve Parliament immediately, and that Gladstone, in appealing to the electors to give him a new lease of power, had dangled before their eyes a surplus of several millions, and promised therewith to abolish the income tax. 'I saw the necessity,' Disraeli told Lady Bradford, 'of immediately accepting the challenge of Gladstone, which of course he counted on my not being able to do. But a political manifesto is the most responsible of all undertakings, and I had not a human being to share that responsibility.' It was a Saturday in the recess;

---

[1] J. Macdonald.   [2] Of Northumberland.
[3] Where the Bradfords lived.

he had only such conveniences at his disposal as two 'miserable' hotel rooms provided; he was without secretary, papers, or books; and his colleagues were all scattered. But, in spite of these disabilities, his indomitable resolution and industry enabled him to issue his reply to Gladstone's appeal on the following Monday morning. A letter to Lady Chesterfield tells how it was done.

To Anne Lady Chesterfield.

EDWARDS'S HOTEL, *Jan.* 27, 1874.—I was quite taken by surprise. Luckily, I was in London: as you perhaps remember, I curtailed my visit to dear Bretby, and lost a day of your charming society, in order to attend a meeting of the Trustees of the Brit. Museum, whom the Government threatened with some harassing legislation.

I was not up when my servant brought me *The Times.* Be sure I did not go to the Brit. Museum, but, after carefully studying the manifesto, instantly commenced a draft of answer, as I felt everything depended on an immediate reply. Then, I telegraphed to my secretary, Montagu Corry, who was at his uncle's, Lord Shaftesbury, in Dorsetshire! to Ld. Derby, Lord Cairns, Mr. Hardy, and Sir Stafford Northcote. Lord Cairns and Mr. Hardy[1] soon appeared, my secretary at night; and working hard all the next day we got copies prepared for *all* the Monday morning's papers. Our friends are much pleased with my reply, and are full of courage.

It is too soon to speak with confidence either of details, or probable result, of the election; but, generally speaking, we are well prepared, for there had been, during the last six months, two occasions when dissolution seemed inevitable, so, with the exception of five or six men abroad, all our candidates are at work.

I have never had three days of such hard work in my life as the three last; writing, talking, seeing hundreds of people, encouraging the timid and enlightening the perplexed.

I will let you know, however roughly, how things go on. But be of good heart!

The Derbys arrived on Sunday night, too late to assist me with his counsel with my address. I dined with them yesterday alone. . . .

[1] Hardy did not arrive till after the address had been settled by Disraeli in conjunction with Cairns. 'I only had the advantage,' Disraeli told Lady Bradford, 'of the critical counsel of my Lord Chancellor, but he is a host.' Hardy suggested a few changes 'rather verbal than of substance' which Disraeli accepted. See Gathorne Hardy, Vol. I., p. 334.

Think of me, and write to me, whenever you can, for I like, in this great struggle, to feel I have friends whom I love.

Mem. I agree with Carnarvon that G[ladstone]'s manifesto is very ill-written, but I do not agree with Carnarvon that it is not in his usual style. I think his usual style the worst I know of any public man; and that it is marvellous how so consummate an orator should, the moment he takes the pen, be so involved, and cumbersome, and infelicitous in expression.

Many considerations had converged to drive Gladstone to dissolution, of which the almost unbroken series of defeats in by-elections was perhaps the most operative, though the outside world, and especially the Opposition, were disposed to attribute most importance to the difficulty about his seat in Parliament. But the immediate occasion was a serious difference of opinion with Cardwell and Goschen, the Ministers responsible for the defence of the country. To realise his grandiose scheme of total abolition of income tax Gladstone wanted, he told Granville, from three-quarters of a million to a million off the naval and military estimates jointly; and the two Ministers concerned sturdily resisted his demands. There was no way out of the deadlock save by dissolution; but in the *verbosa et grandis epistola*, occupying more than three columns of *The Times*, which Gladstone issued to the electors of Greenwich, the country was never told that, in order to realise the promised boon, it would be necessary not merely to have an 'adjustment,' which Disraeli interpreted to mean an increase of taxes, but also to cut down the naval and military estimates seriously below what the Admiralty and the War Office thought requisite for national safety.

If Gladstone's manifesto was, as Disraeli said, ' a prolix narrative,' Disraeli's answering address to the electors of Bucks was rather of a negative character. Remission of taxation, he observed, would be the course of any party or any Ministry in possession of a large surplus; and as for Gladstone's principal measures of relief, the diminution of local taxation and the abolition of the income tax, these were 'measures which the Conservative party have always favoured and which the Prime Minister and his friends have always opposed.' For the rest, the improvement of the condition of the people had been Disraeli's aim throughout, in or out of office, but not by 'incessant and harassing legislation.' It would have been better if, during the last five years, 'there had been a little more energy in our foreign policy, and a little less in our domestic legislation.' After blaming the Ministry for their diplomatic action in regard to the Straits of Malacca—an obscure and intricate matter, of little serious importance, which loomed largely in election speeches and then disappeared—and deprecating further extension of the suffrage at the moment, Disraeli repeated his charge that our national institutions were not safe in Liberal hands, and ended on the imperial note.

Gentlemen, the impending General Election is one of no mean importance for the future character of this Kingdom. There is reason to hope, from the address of the Prime Minister, putting aside some ominous suggestions which it contains as to the expediency of a local and subordinate Legislature, that he is not, certainly at present, opposed to our national institutions or to the maintenance of the integrity of the Empire. But, unfortunately, among his adherents, some assail the Monarchy, others impugn the independence of the House of Lords, while there are those who would relieve Parliament altogether from any share in the government, of one portion of the United Kingdom. Others, again, urge him to pursue his peculiar policy by disestablishing the Anglican as he has despoiled the Irish Church; while trusted colleagues in his Cabinet openly concur with them in their desire altogether to thrust religion from the place which it ought to occupy in national education.

These, Gentlemen, are solemn issues, and the impending General Election must decide them. Their solution must be arrived at when Europe is more deeply stirred than at any period since the Reformation, and when the cause of civil liberty and religious freedom mainly depends upon the strength and stability of England. I ask you to return me to the House of Commons to resist every proposal which may impair that strength and to support by every means her imperial sway.

There is no doubt that Disraeli was well advised in basing his main appeal on the desire of the electorate for rest, and on their sense of wounded pride at the disrepute of their country abroad. Great sections of the community were in arms against the Government, moved either by resentment at past treatment, or by fears for the future; not merely the landed interest, always Conservative in tendency, but also, on the one hand, the clergy and an overwhelming proportion of the laity of the Church of England, together with those outside her pale who desired religious education in elementary schools, and, on the other hand, the brewers and the licensed victuallers, whom Ministers had threatened with even more stringent regulation than that which they had carried through; a fortuitous but powerful combination, which Liberals might deride as ' beer and the Bible,' but which they realised would be very difficult to defeat. Moreover, some of the classes upon which the Liberals usually relied were far from enthusiastic for the cause; the Dissenters were sore over the Education Bill, and the working men were inclined to believe that their social aspirations would meet with at least as much sympathy from a democratic Tory Government as from a politico-economic Liberal Administration. In external affairs, the disregard with which British representations had been treated in 1870 by France and Prussia, Russia's contemptuous repudiation of treaty obligations, and the humiliations of the *Alabama* negotiations and award, had sunk deeply into the mind of the country, and made men of different opinions unite in a resolve to have a Government which should insure respect for Britain among the nations of the world. The bait of abolition of income tax was offered in vain to the classes who would mainly benefit by it, as they were the very classes who had most reason to be dissatisfied with Ministers, and they did not believe that abolition could be secured without readjustments of taxation which would hit them equally hard. To many even among the Liberals the mere offer of such a bait seemed a discreditable electioneering manœuvre; and the supporters of the Government, as a body, were irritated by what appeared to them to be a capricious and premature dissolution. The Conservatives had the advantage both in organisation and in leadership; Gorst's machine was in full working order, while the Liberal caucus had not yet been developed; the popularity of the 'People's William'[1] had temporarily waned, and the eyes of the country were fixed on his rival, who had given utterance at Manchester, the Crystal Palace, and Glasgow to the ideas which were beginning to stir the nation's heart.

It seemed probable, therefore, that the General Election would follow the lines of the by-elections and result in a Conservative success. But the best judges on that side dared not, in view of the long predominance of the Liberals at the polls, place their expectations very high. Gorst's estimate just gave them a majority, but so small a majority as to have left a Conservative Government at the mercy of any malcontent section.

From John Eldon Gorst.

CARLTON CLUB, *Jan.* 30, 1874.—Our estimate is as follows:

	Cons.		Rad.
England ..	.. 271	..	189
Wales ..	.. 10	..	20
Scotland ..	.. 12	..	48
Ireland ..	.. 35	..	68
	328		325

Thompson thinks this is fair and reasonable: Taylor says we have underestimated. We have been rather hard upon the boroughs, but we have taken a sanguine view of the counties.

One feature of the elections, which disturbed the calculations of wirepullers, was the introduction of the ballot; but Disraeli's prediction in 1872 was absolutely verified that 'the Government which first appeals to

[1] This was the popular sobriquet for Gladstone in the early seventies; afterwards superseded by the 'Grand Old Man,' or ' G.O.M.'

the country on the secret suffrage, will, in all probability, be cashiered.' Disraeli's expectations during the contest appear from his letters to Lady Bradford.

To Lady Bradford.

CARLTON CLUB, *Jan.* 27, 1874.—. . . It is impossible to form any opinion at present of the result of a General Election. There has not yet been time to learn the feeling of the country. But I see no signs of enthusiasm on the part of the Liberals, and their press is hesitating and dispirited.

So far as the surprise is concerned, we are as prepared as our opponents. There is no possible seat without a candidate. . . .

Wednesday [*Jan.* 28]—. . . I think things look well. What sustains me is the enthusiasm among the great constituencies. This was never known before. I shall be disappointed if we do not carry both seats for Westminster and two for the City. Chelsea even looks promising, and there are absolutely spontaneous fights in Finsbury and Hackney. Nothing like this ever occurred before.

I am making no sacrifice in writing to you. It relieves my heart; and is the most agreeable thing to me, next to receiving a letter from you. Yours, this morning, gave me the greatest pleasure. In the greatest trials of life, it sustains one to feel that you are remembered by those whom you love.

I can truly say that, amid all this whirl, you are never, for a moment, absent from my thoughts or feelings.

Thursday.—. . . With two sons candidates, you certainly ought to write to their chief every day. . . .

HUGHENDEN MANOR, *Feb.* 1.—Yesterday was a complete success; to my content—and you know that, as regards my own doings, I am very rarely content. I think the Malacca Straits will now be pretty well understood by all England—and Mr. Gladstone too.

I found on my table on my return at night tels. telling me of three seats *gained*—Guildford, Andover, Kidderminster; and two, which I thought *lost, saved*—Eye and Lymington. That looks well; but I will not indulge in hopes till I have more information: much must be known which is not known to me, for the telegraph will not work on Sunday.

Thursday [*Feb.* 5].—. . . This morning, I hear from the Managing Committee that they now absolutely contemplate obtaining a majority. I think it must greatly depend on this day, which was always the critical one. If London and West[minste]r follow Mary[le]bone, the situation will be grave. . . .

Polling began at the end of the last week in January; and before the close of the first week in February the borough returns were known and were decisive of the general result. The grant of household suffrage in boroughs, which Salisbury had condemned as 'Parliamentary suicide' for the Conservatives, had been justified, as Disraeli always maintained that it would be justified, even from a party point of view. Gorst reported on February 6: 'If all the elections were to go as we estimated at the time when we made out a majority of 3, we should have a majority of 27.' The city of London swung over to the Conservatives, Goschen only coming in as the minority member, and Disraeli's Liberal friend Rothschild suffering a final defeat; Westminster followed the City; and seats were won at Chelsea, Greenwich, Marylebone, Southwark, and Tower Hamlets. At Greenwich Gladstone was only returned second on the poll, below a Conservative; 'more like a defeat than a victory,' he wrote. Striking Conservative victories were recorded in the great manufacturing towns, such as Manchester, Leeds, Bradford, Sheffield, Oldham, Newcastle-on-Tyne, Nottingham, Stoke-on-Trent, Wakefield, Wigan, Warrington, Stalybridge, and Northampton. In the English boroughs as a whole there was a net Conservative gain of over thirty seats. No wonder the Liberals were in despair at this revelation of the impression produced on the working man by five years of Gladstonian government.

From Montagu Corry.

CARLTON CLUB, *Feb.* 6, '74.—. . . There is a panic, I am told at Brooks's: there *was*, I should say, for all is now bitterness and despair. Wolverton[1] has fled from town in horror, and the cry is 'They are in for years.' Gladstone is prostrate and astounded, and his colleagues (in two cases at least which have come to my knowledge) announce in their offices that the next is their last week of power.

Wolverton's advice has caused the whole catastrophe, which has caught a Cabinet in a fool's paradise.

[1] The Liberal Whip.

The Carlton is crowded till midnight: all the dear 'old lot' whom we know so well—all the *frondeurs* and the cynics, professors, *now*, of a common faith—cry for 'The Chief,' as young hounds bay for the huntsman the day after the frost has broken up.

You will have to come, next week.

We meet so soon that I say no more—except to record what I hear on every side, that the Newport Pagnell speech has immeasurably influenced the events of the last 48 hours.

During the elections there was an oratorical duel between Greenwich and Bucks; and little attention was paid to any other speeches save to the thrusts and parries of the rival leaders. These orations were not in themselves very remarkable; though Disraeli's at least served their purpose of heartening his party, and received cordial praise from that one of his colleagues on whose judgment he most depended. 'A splendid effort,' Cairns wrote of the first; of another, 'your Newport Pagnell oration must certainly stand at the head of all the election speeches of this, and perhaps of any, crisis'; and the last he described as 'the fitting topstone of the series.' One passage may be rescued in which Disraeli distinguished between true and false economy.

All Ministers of all parties are in favour of economy, but a great deal depends upon what you mean by economy. I venture to say, that I do not believe you can have economical government in any country in which the chief Minister piques himself upon disregarding the interests of this country abroad, because such neglect must inevitably lead us into expenditure, and an expenditure of the kind over which we have the least control. We are in the habit of hearing it said (and nothing is more true) that the most economical Government we ever had was the Duke of Wellington's—and why was it? It was because the Duke of Wellington paid the greatest possible attention, more than any Minister who ever ruled in this country, to the interests and position of England abroad. . . .

But Mr. Gladstone's view of economy, or rather the view of his own party and of the school which he represents, is of another kind. He says—'The English people do not care for their affairs abroad. I don't much care for them

myself, but I must have economy. I must discharge dock-
yard workmen. I must reduce clerks. I must sell the
Queen's stores. I must starve the Queen's services. I must
sell the accumulations of timber in the dockyards and ar-
senals. I must sell all the anchors belonging to the navy.
I must sell '—which we were selling for the first year or two—
' half the ships in the navy.' And this is economy !

The county elections emphasised the tendency of the
borough returns. The home counties followed the lead
of London; the Liberals were swept out of Middlesex, Surrey, Essex, and Sussex, where the representation
had hitherto been divided. In the whole of this area,
including, besides the four counties already mentioned,
Kent, Herts, Bucks, and Berks, there were only three
Liberal candidates returned for county seats, the minority members for Herts, Bucks, and Berks. Disraeli
was for the first time at the head of the poll, his old
colleague Du Pré having retired. The figures were:
Disraeli (C) 3004, Harvey (C) 2902, Lambert (L) 1720—
all these elected, and Talley (LC) 151. Though the
verdict of the metropolitan area was perhaps the most
outstanding feature of the elections, victories were
reported from counties in all parts of England, despite
the fact that the Conservatives already held the majority
of the county seats.

The Conservative majority in England was over 110;
and substantial gains were even made in Liberal Scotland
(9) and in Liberal Wales (2). In Ireland a new situation
arose, more disquieting for the Liberals than for the
Conservatives, though it involved the nominal loss of
a few seats to the latter. The first response of Ireland
to Gladstone's remedial legislation had been a violent
recrudescence of crime; the second, a revival in a more
specious form of the Repeal agitation, on the plea that
the British Parliament was incompetent to remedy
Irish grievances. This movement was started by Isaac
Butt, a distinguished Irish lawyer, who had won popularity by his exertions in defending Fenian prisoners. He
christened his new policy ' Home Rule,' and invited all

Irishmen, independently of party, to join him. He had sat himself at Westminster in past years as a Conservative, and had been one of the original writers in Disraeli's *Press ;* and Disraeli, at first, mistaking the movement as merely one for local government, expressed a wish to have in Parliament Conservative, as well as Liberal, Home Rulers. The rapid spread of Butt's organisation, and the disintegrating doctrines which it preached, speedily enlightened him as to its tendency, and he offered it a strong opposition. Butt returned to Parliament at a by-election in 1871 as a Home Ruler; and the new party, under his guidance, took a material share in the rejection of Gladstone's Irish University Bill. When the General Election came, they won seats all over Ireland, heavily defeating Chichester Fortescue, who had been Gladstone's Chief Secretary and right-hand man in Irish policy; and at a meeting in Dublin they formally severed themselves from connection with any British party. Ireland, which in 1868 had sent to Parliament 67 Liberals and 38 Conservatives, was represented in 1874 by only 12 Liberals and 34 Conservatives, while there were 57 Home Rulers, constituting an actual majority of the Irish representation. The final figures of the whole election were: Conservatives, 350; Liberals (including two representatives of Labour), 245; Home Rulers (among whom an appreciable minority claimed to be Conservative), 57. While the Conservatives, therefore, had a majority of about fifty over all other parties, they could boast, as compared with the Liberals alone, of a balance of over a hundred: a position of extraordinary strength and security.

As the returns came in, Disraeli's letters naturally became more jubilant, in spite of his disgust at being forced into an unnecessary contest in Bucks.

To Lady Bradford.

HUGHENDEN MANOR, *Friday* [*Feb.* 6, 1874].—Amid 1000 affairs, I write to you one line. I have written to Lady Ches: I am detained here by my *contested !!* election. No danger, but great trouble when I have so much to think of and do, and great and vexatious expense, for nothing.[1]

My last accounts are that we have gained 40 seats, equal to 80 on a division, and have now a majority of 14 over Gladstone. That majority will increase.

Amid all this, I continually think of you and of your grief, and should like to wipe the tears from your eyes, for I feel they flow. Bear up! Francis[2] is young, and if we prosper he will soon have his way.

I think of going up to town on Monday, but on Tuesday or Wednesday I must be at Buckingham and speak.[3] This is horrid!

Feb. 8.—. . . Myself, I do not think the crisis so near as the world does. I think he will meet Parliament, if only not to imitate me. . . .

Our gains up to last night were $46 = 92$; more than Peel gained in 1841, and more than Gladstone gained in 1868.

I am very well, but sigh for moonlight. I think I could live, and love, in that light for ever!

Thursday [*Feb.* 12].—. . . I hear from high authority that the crisis is at hand, and that G.'s colleagues will not support him in his first idea of meeting Parliament.

The Fairy[4] will be here on the 17th.

We shall have 50 majority; the strongest Government since Pitt. . . .

If Ministers were about to follow the precedent of 1868 and resign at once without meeting Parliament, and if a strong and representative Conservative Administration was to be ready to take their place, no time must be lost on the Opposition side in healing the breach caused by the Reform policy of 1867. General Peel had retired from Parliament and public life in 1868, and so had no longer to be reckoned with. With Carnarvon Disraeli had just re-established amicable relations through the

[1] The expenses were subsequently met by a spontaneous movement among Disraeli's constituents, anxious to show their 'pride and gratification' at the eminent position which their representative had attained.

[2] The Hon. F. Bridgeman, afterwards General Bridgeman (1846-1917), was defeated at Stafford.

[3] It was in this speech that Disraeli, with office looming in the immediate future, congratulated Bucks on having supplied four, or (in some reports) five, Prime Ministers out of thirty in all. They were George Grenville, Lord Shelburne, Duke of Portland (twice), and Lord Grenville. Disraeli was himself a Bucks man by adoption.

[4] Disraeli's romantic imagination conceived of his Royal Mistress as the Faerie Queene of Spenser; and to his intimates he wrote of her as 'the Fairy,' or 'Faery.' See Vol. VI., ch. 'Beaconsfield and the Queen.'

good offices of Lady Chesterfield, Carnarvon's mother-in-law. There remained Salisbury, at once the most distinguished and powerful, and the most bitter, of the secessionists. He had, indeed, been working in general harmony with his old colleagues in the House of Lords throughout the Gladstone Administration; and had given cordial support to Disraeli's lieutenant there, the Duke of Richmond. But his distrust of Disraeli himself had apparently not abated. No direct communication whatever had passed between them since they parted in March, 1867; the overture about office in February, 1868, having been made through Northcote, and rejected in so summary a fashion as to close the door upon amicable intercourse. Disraeli, who had been ready throughout for reconciliation, had taken advantage of his visit in December to Hardy's house in Kent to pay a friendly call on Salisbury's sister, Lady Mildred Beresford-Hope, whose husband's antagonism to him rivalled Salisbury's; and, for a final healing of the breach, he now made use of the kindly offices of the lady who was at once Derby's wife and Salisbury's stepmother. Salisbury's main objections of a public character had been met by Disraeli's refusal to take office in a minority in 1873, and by the fact that a Conservative Government in 1874 would have a secure majority. Nevertheless, before consenting even to meet Disraeli, Salisbury, we are told, went through a severe mental struggle; but public spirit and a noble ambition prevailed. Disraeli was so well aware both of the strength of Salisbury's distrust and of his vital importance as a colleague in office that until the meeting, which was at first accidentally delayed, had been satisfactorily effected and agreement reached, he did not disguise his anxiety.

To Lord Salisbury.

2, Whitehall Gardens, *Feb.* 16, 1874.—Lady Derby tells me, that she thinks it very desirable, and that you do not, altogether, disagree with her, that you and myself should have some conversation on the state of public affairs.

The high opinion which, you well know, I always had of your abilities, and the personal regard which, from the first, I entertained for you, and which is unchanged, would render such a conversation interesting to me, and, I think, not disadvantageous to either of us, or to the public interests.

I should be very happy to see you here, at your convenience, or I would call on you, or I would meet you at a third place, if you thought it more desirable.

From Lord Salisbury.

BEDGEBURY PARK, CRANBROOK, *Feb.* 16, 1874.—It would certainly be satisfactory to me to hear your views upon some of the subjects which must at present be occupying your attention—the more so that I do not anticipate that they would be materially in disaccord with my own. I am much obliged to you for proposing to give me the opportunity of doing so. In conformity with your suggestion I called on you this afternoon; but I was not fortunate enough to find you at home. . . .

Just in the nick of time Disraeli found a house to suit him in Whitehall Gardens,[1] within a short walk both of Downing Street and of Westminster Palace; and so he was able to escape the inconveniences of an hotel, and, as he told Lady Bradford, 'live again like a gentleman.' To Whitehall Gardens he came up before the close of the second week in February, and in private conferences with his principal counsellors, Derby, Cairns, Northcote, and Hardy, settled the general plan of his Ministry, so that he was fully prepared when General Ponsonby arrived with the expected message on the evening of Tuesday, the 17th. Ponsonby found him 'much more open, lively, and joyous' than at the crisis in the preceding year; not concealing his delight at the astonishing majority, which had shown, he claimed, how correct was the information on which he wrote the Bath letter.

From Queen Victoria.

WINDSOR CASTLE, *Feb.* 17, '74.—The Queen has just seen Mr. Gladstone, who has tendered his resignation and that of

---

[1] No. 2, Whitehall Gardens, has in recent years become, very appropriately, the office, first, of the Committee of Imperial Defence, and, afterwards, of Mr. Lloyd George's War Cabinet.

his colleagues, which she has accepted. She therefore writes to Mr. Disraeli to ask him to undertake to form a Government.

The Queen would wish to see Mr. Disraeli here at ½ past 12 to-morrow morning.

To Lady Bradford.

¼ to 7 o'ck., Tuesday, Feb. 17.—General Ponsonby, who brought me a letter from the Queen, has just left me. I go down to Windsor to-morrow morning at 11 o'ck.

I have seen Lord Salisbury, who joins the Government.

Disraeli knew that a cordial welcome awaited him at Windsor. Lady Ely had written to him on the Monday: 'My dear mistress will be very happy to see you again, and I know how careful and gentle you are about all that concerns her. I think you understand her so well, besides appreciating her noble fine qualities.' The Queen was in sympathy with the country in desiring a less harassing time in domestic legislation, and a prouder outlook in foreign affairs; and she had a pleasant recollection of the care for her wishes and her honour which had marked Disraeli's short Administration in 1868.

Memorandum by Queen Victoria.

Feb. 18.—Mr. Disraeli came at ½ p. 12. He expressed great surprise at the result of the elections. He had thought there might have been a very small majority for them; but nothing like this had been anticipated, and no party organisation cd. have caused this result of a majority of nearly 64. Not since the time of Pitt and Fox had there been anything like it. Even in '41 when such a large majority had been returned for Sir R. Peel, it had not been so extraordinary, because he had had a small majority. It justified, he said, the course he had pursued last March in declining to take office. . . . Sir J. Pakington Providence had disposed of,[1] as he amusingly said. . . . He was anxious to bring as much new talent and blood into the Govt. as possible. . . . He repeatedly said whatever I wished shd. be done—whatever his difficulties might be !

Disraeli returned from his audience of the Queen with his Cabinet fully matured and provisionally approved,

[1] Pakington was defeated at Droitwich, and raised to the peerage as Lord Hampton.

and he gave an account of his arrangements to the colleague who had now for four years led the Conservative party in the Lords.

To the Duke of Richmond.

Private. WHITEHALL GARDENS, *Feb.* 18, 1874.—I had an audience of the Queen to-day at Windsor, from which I have this moment returned, when Her Majesty directed me to form an Administration and invited my views, how the Cabinet was to be constructed.

I said, that I thought it ought not to be too large, that it should not exceed 12 members and that they might be divided equally between the two Houses.

I proposed that your Grace should take the lead and management of the House of Lords, in which you have been successful, with the post of Lord President, supported by the Lord Chancellor, and three Secretaries of State, namely Foreign, Indian, and Colonial, filled by Lords Derby, Salisbury, and Carnarvon respectively; that these secretaryships, not being departments connected with the great branches of expenditure, might fairly be placed in the Lords: and, with the Privy Seal, that would account for a moiety of the Cabinet.

In the Commons, [that] the Treasury would be represented by myself, and Sir Stafford Northcote as Chancellor of Exchequer, and that the two great spending departments of Army and Navy I proposed to entrust to Mr. Hardy and Mr. Hunt, as it was impossible to sustain debate in the Commons, if these great offices were represented by little men.

It would be necessary to introduce a stranger to public, or rather official, life for the office of Home Secretary, and I mentioned for Her Majesty's consideration the name of Mr. Cross, the Member for Lancashire.

Lord John Manners would, as Postmaster-General, complete the other moiety.

The Queen will consider all this, and I shall hear from her probably this evening, but Her Majesty viewed the scheme favorably, and I am now going to communicate it to my contemplated colleagues. I earnestly hope that you, and they, may also favorably receive it, as I count much upon your support. . . .

This is rather a rough epistle, but I have had rather a rough day. Excuse its shortcomings, and believe me, that it is written with a sincere and anxious desire, to secure for the Queen a valuable servant, and for us all a colleague, whom we greatly regard, and highly respect and esteem

The formation of the Cabinet proceeded without friction amongst Disraeli's colleagues. Malmesbury, who became Privy Seal, expressed a very general feeling in his letter of acceptance. ' In the almost unexampled importance of your present position you *must*, at any sacrifice of your personal predilections, look, not to the past services, but to the future usefulness of your colleagues.' The Cabinet accordingly was constituted as follows:

First Lord of the Treasury	B. DISRAELI.
Lord Chancellor	LORD CAIRNS.
Lord President	DUKE OF RICHMOND.
Lord Privy Seal	EARL OF MALMESBURY.
Home Secretary	RICHARD A. CROSS.
Foreign Secretary	EARL OF DERBY.
Colonial Secretary	EARL OF CARNARVON.
War Secretary	GATHORNE HARDY.
Indian Secretary	MARQUIS OF SALISBURY.
Chancellor of the Exchequer	SIR STAFFORD NORTHCOTE.
First Lord of the Admiralty	G. WARD HUNT.
Postmaster-General	LORD JOHN MANNERS.

Wisely restricted to the very manageable number of twelve persons,[1] it was as strong and capable a Cabinet as has ever taken over the government of this country. In its chief it had the most arresting figure in politics since the death of Pitt; in Salisbury a man who was destined to hold in the future a place in history little less than his chief, and who was even then recognised as of unlimited promise. Besides these two there were four statesmen, not unequal to the first place if fortune should accord it to them—Cairns, Derby, Hardy, and Northcote; five more who had given proofs, either of character or of cleverness or of administrative ability beyond the common—Richmond, Malmesbury, Carnarvon, Hunt, and Manners; and one new man—Cross, who was to administer the Home Office in such fashion as to set a shining example to future Governments. Little difficulty was found in allotting the departments. Cairns, Malmesbury, Derby, Carnarvon, and Salisbury went

[1] Gladstone's Cabinet had numbered fifteen.

naturally back to the offices which they had filled in one
or other of the Cabinets of 1866-68, and where Cairns
and Derby at least had served with much distinction.
For Richmond, as leader of the Lords, the Presidency of
the Council was a suitable post. Northcote, the only
financier in the Commons capable of coping with Gladstone, was in his right place at the Exchequer, where,
but for the Abyssinian War, he would have been sent in
1868; and it was wise to allot to Hardy, perhaps the
most successful administrator as well as the most fervid
orator of the party, the delicate task of conducting the
military forces of the Crown through the transition period
inaugurated by the Cardwell reforms, with a view to
their transformation into an army of modern type.
There was, indeed, no particular reason why Ward Hunt,
whose reputation had been gained at the Treasury,
should have been sent to administer the Admiralty; and
there may be some who, remembering Hunt's enormous
size and physical weight, will suspect Disraeli of having
had a double meaning when he wrote to Richmond that
a great office like that of First Lord should not be represented by a little man. Manners, too, was perhaps a
square peg in a round hole with a business department
like the Post Office; and he told Disraeli he was 'rather
apprehensive' of not fulfilling expectations. Cross's appointment was the natural outcome of the substantial
support given by his native Lancashire to the Conservative cause; his qualifications, as lawyer and man of
affairs, were vouched for by the Lancashire magnate,
Derby, and had been recognised by Disraeli on his Manchester excursion.

A galaxy of ability in a Cabinet does not always promote efficiency. Unless Ministers are deeply imbued
with loyalty to a cause or a chief, their individual cleverness may indeed tend to resolve them into a chaos of
jarring atoms. But this Cabinet was bound together by
strong confidence in its chief. There were only two men,
Salisbury and Carnarvon, who entered it with any mis-

giving; and there is evidence that Salisbury, at any rate, having once, though with difficulty, brought himself to come in, sought loyally from the first for points of agreement rather than of difference, and did his utmost to make the combination a success. For the rest of the Cabinet, four of them—Derby, Manners, Malmesbury, and Northcote—were bound to Disraeli by ties of long-standing personal friendship and political companionship; and though the intimacy with Cairns and Hardy was more recent, the friendship and mutual confidence were almost equally strong. With Richmond as leader in the Lords there had been four years of harmonious working; and Hunt and Cross owed their promotion to their chief's appreciation of their ability.

If the Cabinet was capable and united, there were men of note in responsible positions outside. The most rising of the new men, Sir Michael Hicks Beach, whose exclusion from the Cabinet was almost accidental, became Chief Secretary for Ireland. A first-class man of business, William Henry Smith, was appointed Secretary of the Treasury; and in Lord George Hamilton Disraeli discovered a young man who justified his discernment, and who proved adequate to the heavy task of representing India in the House of Commons. Lord George had been offered the Under-Secretaryship for Foreign Affairs, but had been doubtful of his French: Disraeli assured him that at the India Office there would be no necessity of speaking either Hindustani or Persian. Sir John Karslake and Sir Richard Baggallay were the law officers; not perhaps quite so admirable a combination as that which succeeded them in the later years of the Government, Sir John Holker and Sir Hardinge Giffard. In Hart Dyke Disraeli had a most efficient Chief Whip. The Lord-Lieutenancy of Ireland proved a difficulty, as often before and since. The Duke of Abercorn, who had filled the post with such distinction from 1866 to 1868, at first refused it; but after ineffectual attempts had been made to obtain the services first of the Duke of Marlborough, and then of the Duke of Northumberland, he was pressed to reconsider his decision and ultimately consented. The government of Scotland was placed in the capable hands of Lord-Advocate Gordon, whose mettle Disraeli had already proved.

No statesman ever succeeded in forming a Ministry without giving more or less serious offence in some quarter. There was a clever friend of Disraeli's, who as a young man had been one of his discoveries, but who, owing to a certain instability of character, had hardly fulfilled anticipations. Him Disraeli approached in the most tactful and conciliatory manner, making him an offer somewhat above his deserts, but decidedly below his hopes.

To Lord Henry Lennox.

WHITEHALL GDNS., *Feb.* 19, '74.—The Queen said to me yesterday, that there was one office which she was always anxious about, and that was the President of the Board of Works: it touched her more personally than most.

When I told Her Majesty, that I contemplated recommending her to appoint you, she appeared relieved, and pleased.

It is an office with a great deal of work; but agreeable work. It gives room for the exercise of your taste and energy. The parks, the palaces, and the public buildings of London, under your rule, will become an ornament to the nation, and a credit to the Government, of which, I trust, you will thus become a member.

Lennox, who had set his heart on Cabinet rank—very unreasonably, considering that his brother, the Duke of Richmond, was bound to be of the number—was deeply hurt. Though he accepted the post and kept up the forms of the old affectionate friendship with Disraeli, he ' never forgave the indignity,' and spoke of his chief to others with ' venomous acerbity.' Such is the testimony of Lord Redesdale, who, as Bertram Mitford, served as Secretary to the Board of Works under Lennox's presidency, and who was himself deeply attached to Disraeli. Lennox's administration was not a success, caused Disraeli frequent worry, and came to a premature end.

'The first thing after the Cabinet is formed is the
Household,' remarked a magnate in *Coningsby*.   To this
delicate part of his task, so interesting to the great
people among whom he moved, Disraeli's mind was
directed on his very first audience of the Queen; as he
hoped by a Household appointment to gratify the wishes
of his dearest friend.

To Lady Bradford.

WINDSOR CASTLE, *Feb.* 18, 1874.—It is doubtful whether
I shall see you to-day, for a tremendous pressure awaits me
when I get back to town; which I think may be about $\frac{1}{2}$ past
4 or 5; but I hope to try in the evening.

What you suggested in your note of this morning had already
occurred to me some days ago; but the difficulties are immense,
as you will see when we meet.   Yet they will, I trust, be overcome, for I am influenced in this matter by a stronger feeling
even than ambition.

To Anne Lady Chesterfield.

2, WHITEHALL GARDENS, *Feb.* 21.—Yesterday I kissed
hands, and to-day I take down Carnarvon to Windsor and
make him a Secy. of State, which, I hope, will please you.

Bradford is Master of the Horse, and Selina will ride in
royal carriages, break the line even in the entrée, and gallop
over all Her Majesty's lieges.   I see a difference already in
her demeanor. . . .

It was in the course of the formation of the Household that Disraeli was first brought face to face with a
thorny problem, which was to divide his Cabinet in their
first session, and to range against the Government a
section of the community who should have been among
the firmest upholders of Conservatism.   The spread of
Ritualism was a marked feature of the day, and one
specially repugnant to the Queen; who refused to admit
advanced High Churchmen into that personal service to
herself which the Household involved unless they undertook not to take a prominent part in Church politics.
Disraeli turned in this difficulty to the leading High
Churchman in his Cabinet.

To Lord Salisbury.

2, WHITEHALL GARDENS, *Feb.* 22, 1874.—You were very right in saying, that the only obvious difficulties we should have in our Govt. would, or rather might, be religious ones.

Last night, the Queen, while accepting the appointment of Beauchamp as a favor to myself, requires that there shall be an undertaking from him, that he will take no prominent part in Ch. politics.

It is very desirable, Her Majesty adds, that this condition should be clearly understood, as she looks upon the views of the Ch. party with wh. Ld. B. is connected, as detrimental to the interests of the Ch. of England, and dangerous to the Protestant religion.

The Queen, therefore, could give no countenance to that party by admitting a prominent member of it into the Royal Household.

This morning comes another letter. She hears with regret, that Lord Bath is as bad, as Lord Beauchamp: consequently, the same restrictions must be put upon him as on Lord Beau., etc., etc.

I shall say nothing to Beauchamp myself, lest he throw up his appointment in an ecclesiastical pet, wh. would be only cutting his own throat, and whatever may be his faults of manner and temper, he is a thorough good fellow, as, I believe, we both feel.

But I wish you would consider all this, and give me your advice. You might perhaps say things as a friend to him, wh. might be harder to bear from an official chief. I think with tact, and a thorough understanding between you and myself, the ship may be steered thro' all these Church and religious sandbanks and shallows, but I see that vigilance is requisite. Greater trials will arise than the appointment of a Lord Steward or a Lord Chamberlain.

From Lord Salisbury.

Confidential. 20, ARLINGTON STREET, S.W., *Feb.* 22, '74.— I will speak, if you think it desirable, to both Bath and Beauchamp on this point. I am sure they will feel it a matter of duty not to put themselves forward in Church matters in a sense disapproved of by the Queen, so long as they are so closely connected with her immediate service. The argument —if I may venture to suggest it—which will weigh with her most strongly, I believe, against too decided measures, is that this Ritualist party, though not preponderant in numbers, is numerous enough, if it goes against the Establishment,

to turn the scale. It is earnest, to fanaticism: it sits loosely
to the Establishment, as matters stand: and if driven by any
act of serious aggression, will listen to its most reckless advisers
and throw itself on the Free Church side. A disruption in
England will not perhaps take place for so light a matter
as that which took place in Scotland. But, if it does take
place, it will bring the whole fabric of the Church down about
our ears.

Of course this applies to graver matters than Household
places. Mere discountenance will do little harm: but I should
look with the gravest alarm to any action on the part of the
Legislature. The Bishops are at some work which may be
dangerous—moved by Ellicott,[1] who is an unsafe guide. I
hope in such matters you will take counsel with the Bishops
whom you and Lord Derby placed upon the Bench. They
are all I think sound men.

Salisbury's advice was in the main judicious, and for the
moment Disraeli was apparently disposed to accept it,
as he passed it on to his royal mistress, to whom it was
extremely unpalatable.

To Queen Victoria.

2, WHITEHALL GARDENS, *Feb.* 23, 1874.—Mr. Disraeli with
his humble duty to your Majesty:
Your Majesty may rest assured, that your Ministry will do
everything in their power to discountenance the Ritualist
party. Much may be done in that way, particularly if done
by a Ministry that is believed to be permanent. Any aggressive act of a legislative character will only make martyrs
and probably play the game of the more violent members of
the party. . . .

Feb. 28.—. . . Your Majesty's Household is now complete
and need not fear competition with the Royal Household
formed by any Ministry, either in your Majesty's happy reign,
or in those of your royal predecessors.

Mr. Disraeli thinks it of importance, that the high nobility
should be encouraged to cluster round the throne.

'To change back the oligarchy into a generous aristocracy round a real throne' had been one of the aims of
'Young England'; and Disraeli no doubt felt he was
fulfilling at least part of his earlier aspirations when he

---

[1] Bishop of Gloucester and Bristol.

placed round the person of his Sovereign the heads of
the houses of Cecil (elder branch), Seymour (younger
branch), Bridgeman, and Lygon, the heir of the Percies,
a Wellesley, and a Somerset; while in the Cabinet and in
important positions outside there were the representatives of the Stanleys, Hamiltons, Lennoxes, Herberts, and
Cecils (younger branch), besides a Manners, a Lowther, a
Bentinck, and a Bourke; the house of Churchill failing
to be represented only because its head had declined for
family reasons the Lord-Lieutenancy of Ireland.

Hardy describes Disraeli during the process of Ministry-
making as ' in a whirl, much excited and tired of all his
disagreeable duty.'   But though the business tired him,
and drove him at its close to Brighton to recruit his
strength, there can be no doubt that he took a keen and
justifiable pleasure in his first uncontrolled exercise of
the patronage of the Crown, and especially in the opportunity it gave him of finding suitable positions for those
of his friends whom he knew to be competent.   We get an
insight into his feelings from his letters to Lady Bradford.

To Lady Bradford.

2, WHITEHALL GARDENS, S.W., *Feb.* 27, 1874.—What with
the drawing-room yesterday and a crowd of interviews
afterwards in Downing St., and endless letters, I could not
find time to write the only lines which really interested me—
to her, who is rarely absent from my thoughts and never from
my heart.

It has been an awful affair altogether, but it is now done,
and on Monday next there will be a Council at Windsor,
when we shall appoint the Lord Lieut[enan]t of Ireland, and
swear in, and sanction, all the remaining members of the Govt.
The Queen did not settle about the Chamberlainship till
midnight on Wednesday.   I had retired when the box arrived,
but was roused at 6 o'ck. a.m. with the news of the capture of
Coomassie,[1] which I sent on to H.M. immediately with three
dashes under the word ' Important ' on the label.   She had
been very low the night before about the first news.

The Government is a very strong Government, and gives
much satisfaction.   I have contrived, in the minor and

---

[1] The Ashantee capital.

working places, to include every ' representative ' man, that
is to say every one who might be troublesome.   Clare Read
and Sir Massey Lopes have enchanted the farmers, and I have
placed Selwin Ibbetson, Jem Lowther, Cavendish Bentinck,
and all those sort of men who would have made a Tory cave.
There are some terrible disappointments, but I have written
soothing letters, which on the whole have not been without
success.

I am not very well.   I rather broke down yesterday, having
had some warnings, but I can keep quiet now till Monday. . . .

Montagu [Corry] is with me here as much as he can, but, between dead and living sisters, not as much as I wish.   Since you
left town, I have never dined out.   There is plenty to occupy
me in the evening, for my table is covered with despatch
boxes, all of which must be attended to.   In ordinary affairs,
these can be managed, even with a Ho. of Commons, but there
is nothing so exhausting as the management of men—my
present life—except perhaps the management of women;
and I make little progress at night.

I shall always consider it most unfortunate, I would almost
say unkind, that you quitted town at this conjuncture—the
greatest of my life.   I do not think I could have deserted you;
but I will only say, Adieu.

March 1.—The Queen is delighted with the Household
appointments in the Commons; Ld. Percy, Treasurer; Ld.
Henry Somerset, Comptroller; Barrington, V.-Chamberlain.
She says I ' *rejoice* ' they have accepted these posts. . . .

I am a prisoner to-day, but I hope I shall be all right to-
morrow and get to Windsor : then my indisposition will not
transpire.   I have had a great many visitors to-day, among
them the Master of the Horse.

I have been writing consolation letters all the morning—
among them to Cochrane.[1]

I should not be surprised were the Und. Secy. of War to
be—the Earl of Pembroke ! [2] but this is a *real* secret, known
only to me, himself, and you.

Tuesday night [*March* 3].—. . . I am not as well as I
could wish to be.   The truth is forming a Government is a
very severe trial, moral and material.   I have never, until
to-day, had air or exercise, tho' I have had to make five
journeys to Windsor.

I was thinking of getting to Brighton for a couple of days
after the Cabinet to-morrow, but I shall come up if I hear of
your arrival.

[1] The first Lord Lamington.
[2] Son of Disraeli's old opponent, Sidney Herbert. The appointment
was made.

The P. of Wales has written me a most affectionate letter from St. Petersburg; he was so touched by my note telling him that the Queen had sent for me ! You know all about that. . . .

The Countess of Cardigan and Lancastre called here the other day, and has since written—a wondrous letter ! These are some of the things that have happened to D.

BEDFORD HOT[EL], BRIGHTON, *March* 8.—. . . How very unlucky I should have left town—but for the first time in this great affair I felt dead beat ; always, almost, in the same room, unceasing correspondence or endless interviews. But to have seen you would have been a much better and more beneficial change, than even these soft breezes and azure waters. . . .

H.R.H. paid me a visit on Friday morning, before noon— a very long one; and he asked me to dine with him *en petite* [*sic*] *comité* on Sunday. I was obliged to decline and gave him the reason. . . .

If affairs were not at this moment so *pressing*—the Queen's Speech to prepare, and frequent Cabinets, I should come down to Bournemouth. I cannot do that, tho' my thoughts will be ever there. . . .

To Anne Lady Chesterfield.

WHITEHALL GARDENS, *Mar.* 16, 1874.—I was interrupted while writing to you late yesterday, by the unexpected call of the Duc d'Aumale. . . . Next to Lord Orford, the Duc d'Aumale is my greatest friend—I dedicated *Lothair* to him. I do not know his equal. Such natural ability, such extreme accomplishment, and so truly princely a mind and bearing. Between the Comte de Chambord and the Comte de Paris, he has been ' sat upon ' in life, and has had no opportunity. He looks extremely well and says he is, ' tho',' he added with much melancholy, ' I am now alone in the world.' . . .

Corry, of course, resumed his position of principal private secretary to the new Prime Minister—with two Treasury clerks to assist him: Algernon Turnor, after- wards Financial Secretary to the Post Office, and James Daly, who succeeded later to the peerage of Dunsandle. There was no suitable place on Disraeli's staff for Rose, who was intimately associated with his private fortunes; and who had long been in the closest touch with his political career, until the work of agent to the Conserva- tive party outgrew the capacities of a busy firm of solicitors. But Disraeli was never ungrateful; and one of his earliest recommendations for honours was that of Rose for a baronetcy.

Philip Rose to Montagu Corry.

Feb. 21, 1874.—What a pleasure it is to see D. so really great ! You can understand some of my feelings at witnessing the complete realisation of my early predictions, attributed at that time to boyish enthusiasm, but which only strengthened as time went on, and which I have never let go even in the darkest times. You will not wonder that at times it cost me a pang at being shut out from all share in those triumphs of political life with which at one time I was actively associated, and for the main object of which I have toiled and striven for 30 years, and with which my life has been identified; but in the lottery of life some are destined to climb the ladder, and others to remain obscure.

To Queen Victoria.

10, DOWNING STREET, *April* 17, 1874.—. . . Mr. Philip Rose is the son of a burgher family of Bucks, which has existed in repute for more than two centuries. Mr. Rose is now the possessor of a fine estate in that county, of which he is a magistrate. He is a man of education, but entirely the creator of his own fortune. His life has been one of singular prosperity; mainly owing to his combined energy and integrity, and to a brilliant quickness of perception.

Disraeli, from first to last, regarded his life as a brightly tinted romance, with himself as hero. Now the third volume[1] had been opened. By genius and resolution, in spite of a thousand obstacles, the ' Jew boy,' the despised adventurer, the Oriental mystery-man, had reached the summit of place and power. Not only was he once again the First Minister of what Englishmen may be forgiven for thinking the leading nation in the modern world, but his countrymen had unmistakably expressed their desire to be governed by him; he was supported by a large majority in both Houses of Parliament, all signs of disaffection in the party to his leadership having dis-

---

[1] The present generation may need to be reminded that, in mid-Victorian days, novels—and Disraeli's among them—were wont to appear in three volumes.

SIR PHILIP ROSE, FIRST BARONET.

From a portrait by Van Havermaet, at Hughenden.

appeared. He was surrounded by a capable and unusually homogeneous band of colleagues. He was
regarded with peculiar favour by his Sovereign; and he
rapidly came to hold in society, strictly so called, a place
of distinction such as few Prime Ministers have aspired
to and fewer attained.

It was a triumph of romance, but it was also a tragedy.
The hero had all that he had played for; but fruition had
been delayed till he was in his seventieth year and had
lost the partner of his life and of his ambition. Even
on his first attainment of the Premiership in 1868, he
had said to W. F. Haydon in reply to congratulations,
'For me it is twenty years too late. Give me your age
and your health.' How much more fervently did he
echo that cry of 'Too late' to those who congratulated
him six years afterwards ! 'Power !' he was heard once
to mutter in his triumphal year of 1878; 'it has come
to me too late. There were days when, on waking, I
felt I could move dynasties and governments; but that
has passed away.' That youth was the period for action;
that to be granted adequate scope for your genius when
young was the supreme gift of Heaven, had always been
his creed. Now, however much he might call in art to
assist nature, he was indubitably becoming old; though
he might still be fresh in spirit, he was not physically
comparable to Palmerston when he reached the Premiership at a similar age in 1855, or to Gladstone when he
took up the burden a second time at the age of seventy
in 1880. Tough as Disraeli's fibre had proved through the
struggles of nearly fifty years, he had never been really
robust, and indeed in early manhood had undergone a
prolonged period of grave debility. His intimate notes
to his wife from the House of Commons form a constant
record of indisposition, and of requests for pills and
other remedies or prophylactics. Then in 1867 he had
had a serious attack of gout, and he had suffered in-
termittently since, notably from bronchial trouble in
1870. The labours of the Premiership in the Commons

almost immediately brought on renewed attacks; first
in the spring and then in the autumn of 1874 he was
pursued by gout, gouty bronchitis, and asthma; and
finally in 1876 he was driven to choose between definite
retirement and a retreat to the House of Lords. Even
the relief afforded by the conduct of business in the less
laborious House, though great, was not sufficient; and
the unwearied service which he rendered to his country
was accompanied by a persistent undercurrent of pain
and physical debility, down to his last illness in 1881.

Without the stimulus given not merely by his honourable ambition but by the intimate and endearing relations which he had established with Lady Bradford and
Lady Chesterfield, he could hardly have borne the principal burden of government during years of difficulty and
danger. But even the intimacy with his new friends
could not dull the sense of loneliness and desolation
caused by the absence of the wife to whom, as Hardy
noted in his diary, the ' long reign ' of 1874-1880 would
have been a ' true joy.' Had Lady Chesterfield accepted
him, or had it been possible for him to marry Lady
Bradford, the vacancy by his hearth, which so keenly
affected him, would have been filled. But, as things
were, he experienced only too vividly through all his last
eight years that melancholy which prompted the bitter
cry of his friend the Duc d'Aumale, ' I am now alone in
the world.' Sir William Fraser's fussy obtrusiveness and
misplaced egotism often mar the effect of his Disraelian
stories; but he was inspired by a true discernment in the
message which he sent to his chief in the beginning of the
1874 Administration.

The only communication which I made to Disraeli at the
time of his last Premiership was one which I was told he felt
deeply. I asked a common friend to tell him that I was
sure that the feeling in his heart which dominated all others
was, that one who had believed in him from the first, whose
whole life and soul had been devoted to him, who had longed
and prayed for his ultimate success, was, now that his success
had come, no more—his wife.[1]

[1] Fraser, pp. 270, 271.

CHAPTER IX.

POLITICAL SUCCESS AND PHYSICAL FAILURE.

1874.

'I am only truly great in action. If ever I am placed in a truly eminent position I shall prove this.' So in a moment of exaltation wrote Disraeli in his thirtieth year; now, in his seventieth, at long last, he was to show that he had not misjudged his own capacity. Social improvement at home and the enhancement and consolidation of our imperial position abroad were to be the task of the Ministry under his guidance; but in both respects Ministers proceeded with caution and deliberation, with the unexpected result that the interest of their first session was predominantly ecclesiastical. On the domestic side, in compliance with the general desire for a respite from incessant legislation, they determined to do no more than lay this year a foundation for their policy. They appointed a Royal Commission to investigate the subject of the relations of master and servant; and proposed to deal at once with only a few minor matters, including an amendment of the Factory Act and certain modifications of the new licensing law. On the imperial side, in order to show that the new Government hoped to infuse some spirit and dignity into foreign policy, Disraeli suggested to Derby the introduction into the Queen's Speech of 'a phrase which, without alarming, might a little mark out our policy from our unpopular predecessors'.' The phrase actually used was: 'I shall not fail to exercise the influence arising from these cordial relations [with foreign Powers] for the maintenance of

European peace, and the faithful observance of international obligations.'

To Queen Victoria.

10, DOWNING STREET, *March* 14, 1874.—Mr. Disraeli with his humble duty to your Majesty:

He encloses a draft of the Royal Speech for your Majesty's consideration.

Your Majesty will observe, that he has somewhat deviated from the routine paragraph respecting foreign affairs. He thought the accession to office of a new Ministry was not a bad occasion to call the attention of Europe to that respect for treaties which your Majesty's present advisers, with your approbation, are resolved to observe.

In case news of the treaty being signed do not arrive, the paragraph respecting the Ashantee War will require modification.

Parliament will open on Thursday the 19th. Whether your Majesty will be graciously pleased to open it, shall be a matter, always, for your Majesty alone to decide.

Mr. Disraeli has too high, and genuine, an opinion of your Majesty's judgment, and too sincere an appreciation of your Majesty's vast political experience, to doubt that, whatever your Majesty's decision on this important subject, it will be a correct one. He will not, therefore, presume to dwell [on], only to glance at, the peculiar circumstances of the present occasion: a new Parliament; a ballot Parliament; a new Ministry; a Ministry recommended to your Majesty by an extraordinary expression of Conservative opinion; the great and deep popularity of the Royal House at the present moment, and the especial, and even affectionate, reverence for your Majesty's person; the presence of illustrious strangers, at this moment, at your Majesty's Court, and the most interesting cause of that presence [1]—all these considerations, Mr. Disraeli feels sure, will be duly weighed by your Majesty, and decided upon with dignified discretion.

Disraeli's insinuating pleading did not prevail to secure the Queen's presence at the opening of Parliament; and accordingly there was nothing dramatic about the first public appearance of his Ministry. He had the wisdom and magnanimity to suggest the re-election of the Liberal Speaker chosen towards the close of the last

---

[1] The recent marriage of the Duke of Edinburgh to a daughter of the Emperor of Russia.

Parliament, Henry Brand.   The depression of the beaten
Liberals was augmented by Gladstone's announcement
that he only proposed to attend occasionally during the
present session, and reserved to himself the right to
resign absolutely the leadership of the Opposition in the
following spring.   It was, Disraeli said on one of the
occasions when he met his rival on the neutral ground
of Marlborough House, 'the wrath, the unappeasable
wrath, of Achilles.'

To Anne Lady Chesterfield.

WHITEHALL, *March* 17, 1874.—. . . Yesterday we had a
grand banquet at Marlboro' House, which was agreeable
enough.   I had not very lively neighbours at dinner. . . .
However, I do not dislike what Macaulay called some 'flashes
of silence,' and unless I sit next to you, or somebody as interesting and charming, I find a pleasant repose in a silent
banquet, particularly with a good band.

After dinner we had conversation enough, and I could
amuse you for hours, if we were walking together alone at
Bretby, but alas ! the pressure of business, wh. is now getting
intense, can only spare time for a snatch.

The Dss. of Edinburgh was lively as a bird.   She does not
like our habit in England of all standing after dinner, and I
must say I find it exhausting.   In Russia the Court all sit.

She asked me who a certain person was, talking to a lady.
I replied, ' That is my rival.'   ' What a strange state society
is in here,' she said.   ' Wherever I go, there is a *double*.   Two
Prime Ministers, two Secretaries of State, two Lord Chamber-
lains, and two Lord Chancellors.' . . .

To Lady Bradford.

WHITEHALL, *March* 19, 1874.—. . . I had a very hard day
yesterday.   A great personage,[1] a favourite of yours and of
mine, was with me all the morning at this house with difficult
and delicate affairs; then without luncheon, I had to run to
D[owning] S[treet] to keep my appointments with the mover
and seconder of the Address, each of whom I had to see
separately; then a long Cabinet, and then the banquets !
Mine was most successful, and I believe also Derby's.   Everybody said they never saw a more brilliant table.   I gave
Gunter *carte blanche*, and he deserved it.   He had a new service of plate.   Baroness Rothschild sent me six large baskets
of English strawberries, 200 head of gigantic Parisian

[1] The Prince of Wales.

asperges, and the largest and finest Strasburg *foie gras* that ever was seen. All agreed that the change of nationality had not deprived Alsace of its skill. . . .

To-day I am to take my seat at four o'ck., introduced by *Cis*[1] and Mr. Henley. . . .

' Things went off very quietly in the House,' was Disraeli's description of the opening day to Lady Bradford. ' Gladstone made a queer dispiriting speech, and, in short, told his party that the country had decided against them, and that they were thoroughly beaten.' The one urgent topic was the famine in India; and the vigorous measures which, in spite of Anglo-Indian opposition, the Liberal Viceroy, Northbrook, was taking to cope with it received warm support from Salisbury and the new Government. The occasion gave Lord George Hamilton an opportunity to show that Disraeli had not been mistaken in singling him out for responsible office. ' This is a triumph for me,' he wrote to Lady Bradford.[2]

To Queen Victoria.

HOUSE OF COMMONS, *March* 20, 1874.—Mr. Disraeli with his humble duty to your Majesty: . . .

Mr. Disraeli was very inadvertent in not reporting the proceedings of the House of Commons last night to your Majesty. He will to-night *ab initio*, so that your Majesty's record of the new Parliament shall be complete.

He is now writing hurriedly in his place, in the midst of business and not wishing to keep the Windsor messenger.

10, DOWNING STREET, *March* 20, 1874.—. . . An interesting evening in the House of Commons. The Home Rule debate was actively, but not forcibly, sustained by the Irish members. Mr. Gladstone spoke early in the debate, and well. Sir Michael Beach with great force and success.

The night was favourable to the young Ministers. Lord George Hamilton greatly distinguished himself in his Indian statement. Both sides of the House were delighted with him: with his thorough knowledge of his subject; his fine voice; his calmness, dignity, and grace. He spoke for exactly

---

[1] General Forester, Lady Bradford's brother, who shortly afterwards succeeded as 3rd Lord Forester, was in March, 1874, Father of the House of Commons.

[2] Lord George, in his interesting *Parliamentary Reminiscences*, has given in full the flattering description of his speech in the letter to Lady Bradford.

an hour.   Mr. Disraeli has rarely witnessed so great a success
—and, what is better, a promise of greater.

There were only ten days of the Parliamentary session
before the Easter recess; and the new Minister had a vast
amount both of work and of society to pack into his
early days of power.

To Anne Lady Chesterfield.

WHITEHALL, *March* 24, 1874.—. . . Yesterday was a gal-
loping day. . . .

I had to see Sir Garnet Wolseley[1] at one, and find out what
he expected, or wished, as a reward: not a very easy or pleasing
task.   It often happens, in such cases, that Governments
put themselves much out of the way to devise fitting recognition of merit, and then find they have decided on exactly
the very thing that was not wanted.

Then I had a great deputation in D.S. at ½ past 2 o'ck.;
then the Ho. of Comm. at ½ past four, and then, keeping my
brougham ready, I managed to steal away to Belgrave Sqre.
at ½ past 6, and see somebody I love as much as I do yourself.
Then I had to get home to dress for one of the great wedding
banquets; at Gloster House: all the royalties there—Marlboro'
House, Clarence House, and Kensington Palace; and a host of
Abercorns, Ailesburys, Baths, Barringtons, etc., etc., not
forgetting the hero of the hour, Sir Garnet again.

He is a little man, but with a good presence, and a bright
blue eye, holds his head well, and has a lithe figure: he is only
40; so has a great career before him. . . .

I am very well, altho' the work is increasing and it seems
a dream.   I told *somebody* that I was well because I was
happy, and she said ' Of course you are, because you have got
all you wished.'

But I assure you, as I assured her, it is not that.   I am
happy in yr. friendship and your sister's.   They are the charm
and consolation of a life that would otherwise be lonely.
You are always something to think about; something that
soothes and enlivens amid vexation and care. . . .

5 o'ck., *March* 29.—. . . We have had a busy week, social
and otherwise: a drawing-room and a levée.   Selina presented
her daughter, Lady Mabel,[2] as you know.   Selina was in mourning, but it particularly becomes her, and, in my opinion, she

---

[1] Who had commanded the Ashantee expedition and taken Coomassie;
afterwards F.M. Viscount Wolseley.

[2] Now Lady Mabel Kenyon-Slaney.

was much the most distinguished person at the Palace. I dined in Belgrave Sqre. aft[erwar]ds and met the Baths, and one or two agreeable people: a little round table; not more than the Muses and not less than the Graces. . . .

10, DOWNING ST., *March* 31.—I have just adjourned the Ho. of Commons for a fortnight. I begin to feel the reality of power. . . .

To Lady Bradford.

10, DOWNING STREET, *March* 31.—. . . I spoke last night[1] quite to my own satisfaction, which I rarely do, but did not produce any great effect on the House, which expected something of a more inflammatory kind in all probability. I gave them something Attic. Your friend *The Times* again assailed me, wh. I disregard and shd. not notice if you did not. . . .

Disraeli spent the Easter recess at Bretby. Two sentences, one from a letter to Corry, and the other from a letter to Lady Bradford, give us pictures of his afternoon drives and his evening relaxations. 'We came home in an open carriage—a break—in pelting rain; but my fascinating hostess covered me with her umbrella, so that I was as comfortable as in a tent, and wished the storm to last.' 'We play whist every evening, and I have never once revoked; more than that, Lady Ches. says I play a "really good game."'

The immediate business before the Government was the Budget—a particularly crucial issue, as it was on the financial cry of abolishing the income tax that Gladstone had gone to the country. From Bretby, in answer to an appeal from Northcote, who had kept him fully informed of the development of his schemes, he wrote a decisive letter.

To Sir Stafford Northcote.

BRETBY PARK, *April* 4, 1874.—If we don't take care, we shall make a muddle of the Budget. It is indispensable that we should take 1d. off the income tax. . . .

I was always in favour of introducing a rating bill, provided we could deal largely with local taxation. If you pass a rating bill, relieve the ratepayers from police and lunatics, and

---

[1] In moving the vote of thanks to the General and the troops for the Ashantee expedition.

abolish the Government exemptions, I consider the local taxation question virtually settled. The rating bill would run pretty easily with such adjuncts. You will have, by this mode, satisfied a large party in the House, and largely consisting of our friends.

The repeal of the sugar duties will satisfy the free traders and the democracy.

The reduction of one penny in the income tax will be a golden bridge for all anti-income tax men in our own ranks. They will grumble, but they will support us.

With these three great objects accomplished, I think you may count on success.

If you can do more, do it, but that would not be necessary. The repeal of the horse duty was necessary, when you contemplated dealing so partially, and, comparatively speaking, slightly, with the local burthens. Now it will range itself if necessary with the taxes on locomotion, the consideration of which may keep. It seems to me, however, that you might repeal the horse duty in addition; and I am clear that you had better not recede in any considerable degree from the original estimates. . . .

I hope I have made my views pretty clear. I send this by messenger, as I don't like the post as a means of conveyance, when the repeal of taxes is concerned.

It pleased the Opposition to describe a Budget drawn on these large lines as frittering away the Liberal surplus of over five millions; but subsequent history has shown how utterly impracticable was Gladstone's showy policy of complete abolition of the income tax. Had he prevailed for the moment, the increasing demands of armaments on the one hand, and of social legislation on the other, must have led to its reimposition within a very few years; and it is creditable to Disraeli, that, though he dallied long with the hope of abolition, yet when he attained power in 1874 he declined, with the prospect of progressive expenditure, to abandon so powerful an engine of revenue. He was able, in this halcyon period of abounding trade and political quietude, to reduce the rate to twopence, to abolish the sugar duties and the horse tax, and to relieve local rates of the burden of police and lunatics; boons which, save in comparison with total relief from income tax, would have been regarded as eminently praiseworthy, and which were accepted by Parliament as satisfactory.

Within a few days of his return from Bretby Disraeli was seized by the first of a series of attacks of gout which crippled him, at intervals, for the remainder of the year.

To Anne Lady Chesterfield.

WHITEHALL GARDENS, *April* 16, 1874.—. . . After five years' truce, the gout attacked my left hand on Monday last. I have borne up against it as well as I could, for I don't think the world likes sick Ministers, but I am afraid it has beaten me. After a long Cabinet yesterday, I was obliged to send my excuses to the Speaker, to decline dining with him; and tho' I must manage to appear in the H. of C. to-day for the Budget, I fear my arm must be in a sling. . . .

WHITEHALL, *April* 18. —. . . I have seen my hand to-day for the first time for a week, and tho' not exactly fit for a Lord Chamberlain, it would do for a morganatic marriage, wh. is always rather an ugly affair. . . .

To Lady Bradford.

W[HITEHALL GARDENS], *April* 18, 1874. — . . . The Budget is very successful.[1] . . . .

If I can I must go to the Salisbury banquet to-day, but I will not decide till six o'ck. . . . I was in the House last night till midnight, and only left because I was assured there cd. be no more divisions. There was one, however, and Mr. Secy. Cross talked, I see, of the Prime Minister's absence on account of the *state of his health ! ! !* What language! . . .

April 19.—. . . It won't do for me to go down to Brighton, and give up the dinners I have accepted, or they wd. make out I was very ill and all that. I have refused every invitation that has arrived since I returned to town. I mean to fashion and frame my life into two divisions: the public life, wh. speaks for itself; and the inner, or social life, wh., so far as I can arrange, shall be confined to the society of those I love and those who love them.

Life, at least so much of it as may remain to me, is far too valuable to ' waste its fragrance on the desert air.' I live for Power and the Affections; and one may enjoy both without being bored and wearied with all the dull demands of conventional intercourse. . .

---

[1] In reporting to the Queen Disraeli wrote that 'the Budget was extremely well received by the House. The speech was artistically conceived and the interest skilfully sustained till the end.'

Yesterday was one of those cumbrous banquets wh. I abhor, and wh. in my present condition was oppressive—French Ambassadors, and Dukes and Duchesses of Marlboro' and Cleveland, and all that. It did me no harm, however, for I was resolved and firm, asked for seltzer water, did not pretend to drink wine, or to eat. I had the honor to sit by the great lady of the mansion, so long, and so recently, my bitter foe. She feasted me with, sometimes skilful, adulation. If I were not really indifferent to it, wh. I think I am, I certainly appeared to be so yesterday, for with the depression of my complaint, and the want of all artificial stimulus, I felt I was singularly dull and flat. I could scarcely keep up the battle-dore; the shuttlecock indeed frequently fell.

I am told by another great lady, that all this homage is sincere. It is the expression of ' *gratitude* '; not so much for the offices I have showered on them,[1] as for the delicate manner in which I spare them the sense of ' humiliation.'

April 25.—. . . Last night[2] was most amusing. Gladstone stagey, overdone, and full of false feeling and false taste; trying to assume the position of Scipio Africanus, accused by a country which he had saved.

But, between Smollett and Whalley, it was a provincial *Hamlet* bet[wee]n clown and pantaloon.

To Anne Lady Chesterfield.

W.G., *May 6.*—Yesterday was the first party division of the session, and the Ministry won triumphantly.[3] The battle came off on a different issue from that which I had apprehended when I dined out, wh. was almost as rash as the Duke of Wellington's ball at Brussels. But I had made all my preparations, tho' I had contemplated a different point of attack.

The majority of 63 may be looked upon as our working majority—to be raised to 80 on very critical occasions. Our friends are in high spirits and have quite forgotten the mis-

---

[1] Besides Lord Salisbury, his brother, Lord Eustace Cecil, held office in Disraeli's Administration; as well, of course, as Lord Exeter, the head of the elder branch of the Cecils.

[2] Smollett (C.) moved and Whalley (L.) seconded an abortive vote of censure on Gladstone for advising the recent dissolution. On the debate on the Address, Disraeli had generously said: ' If I had been a follower of a parliamentary chief as eminent, even if I thought he had erred, I should have been disposed rather to exhibit sympathy than to offer criticism. I should remember the great victories which he had fought and won; I should remember his illustrious career; its continuous success and splendour, not its accidental or even disastrous mistakes.'

[3] The question at issue was the educational standard to be reached by the children of out-door paupers.

adventure of the other night.[1]   Forster, Lowe, Goschen, and
Co. looked dreadfully crestfallen. . . .   All the Home Rulers
voted against us.

The humdrum course of hardly contentious Government business was little to the taste of eager spirits on
the Opposition benches.   Mr. (now Sir George) Trevelyan,
accordingly, pushed into the foreground the question of
the county franchise.   But a newly elected Conservative
Parliament could hardly be expected to welcome an
immediate prospect of further constitutional change, and
Mr. Trevelyan's motion was decisively rejected.

To Anne Lady Chesterfield.

W. Gardens, *May* 14, 1874.—We had a capital division
on a capital subject—the extension of the household franchise to counties.   There were rumors that the Liberal
party was to be reorganised on this ' platform,' and amazing
whips were made by both sides.   The result surprised both.
Lord Hartington . . . and other Whigs left the House without
voting; and Mr. Lowe actually voted with us !   There were
five hundred, and more, in the House during the debate, and
we had a purely Conservative majority, with the exception
of Mr. Lowe, of 114 ! .

Disraeli's opposition to the motion was of an oppor-
tunist character.[2]   While pointing out that the distribution of political power in the community was an affair
of convention, and not of moral or abstract right, he
expressly disclaimed any objection in principle to the
enfranchisement of the county householder.

I have no doubt that the rated householder in the county
is just as competent to exercise the franchise with advantage
to the country as the rated householder in the town.   I have
not the slightest doubt whatever that he possesses all those
virtues which generally characterise the British people.   And
I have as little doubt that, if he possessed the franchise, he
would exercise it with the same prudence and the same benefit
to the community as the rated householder in the town.

[1] When the Government was beaten during the dinner hour on an
Irish question by two votes.
[2] ' The measure will not be passed for ten years; and when ten years are
over it will be harmless.'—*Letter from Corry for Beaconsfield to C. S. Read*
Dec. 27, 1877.

But, as the enfranchisement would enormously increase the county electors, causing them considerably to outnumber the borough electors, it would be necessary to have a great redistribution of seats at the same time, with the result of the erasure from the Parliamentary map of the important class of boroughs of 20,000 or 25,000 inhabitants. He was not prepared to strike a fatal blow at the borough constitution of the United Kingdom. It was an unwise thing for an old country to be always speculating on organic change. In that matter their course of late years had been very rapid and decisive. He was confident in the good sense of the people. But they had had a great meal to digest, and he was not sure that it had as yet been entirely assimilated. The mind of the agricultural class was occupied not with political change, but rather with the elevation of their social condition. ' When the disposition of the country is favourable, beyond any preceding time that I can recall, to a successful consideration of the social wants of the great body of the people, I think it would be most unwise to encourage this fever for organic change.'[1] Here was sounded clearly the note of social reform, which honourably distinguished all the domestic legislation of the Government.

To Anne Lady Chesterfield.

2, WHITEHALL GARDENS, *May* 19, 1874.—. . . Last night was critical. Gladstone reappeared with all his marshals, Lowe and Childers and Goschen, and others of the gang. They were to make an attack on our Supplementary Estimates for the navy. But a traitor had apprised me of their purpose, and my benches were full to overflowing. They dared not attack the master of 100 legions, and they took refuge in a feeble reconnaissance by Childers, who was snuffed out by the Chanr. of the Excr.

The elections continue to go well for the Ministry, wh. shows that the Conservative reaction was not a momentary feeling. . . .

[1] This was Disraeli's last statement of policy on Parliamentary Reform. He had, it may be added, when still in opposition, announced his adhesion in principle to the extension of the suffrage to women.

To Queen Victoria.

2, WHITEHALL GARDENS, *May 22, 1874.*— . . . To-night, there was an amusing debate respecting making Oxford a military centre.   Mr. Hall, the new Conservative member for Oxford City, made a maiden speech of considerable power and promise: a fine voice, a natural manner, and much improvisation.   While he was sitting down, amid many cheers, Lord Randolph Churchill rose, and, though sitting on the same side of the House, upheld the cause of the University against the City, and answered Mr. Hall.

Lord Randolph said many imprudent things, which is not very important in the maiden speech of a young member and a young man; but the House was surprised, and then captivated, by his energy, and natural flow, and his impressive manner.   With self-control and study, he might mount. It was a speech of great promise. . . .

The Whitsuntide recess was a period of great refreshment to Disraeli, as he had the Bradfords to stay with him at Hughenden, the party to meet them comprising Maria Lady Ailesbury, the Wharncliffes, and Pembroke. It was ' the fulness of spring,' he wrote to Lady Chesterfield, while awaiting their arrival: ' thorns and chestnuts and lilacs and acacia, all in bloom, and the air still and balmy. . . . I am as restless as if I were as young as the spring.'   Unfortunately he came back to town with a suspicion of trouble in his throat; and the remedies given him to restore his voice brought out the gout once more.   ' I left the H. of C. on Monday night at 10 o'ck.,' he wrote to Lady Bradford on June 10, ' all the difficulties about the Licensing Bill being triumphantly over, with the view of going to Montagu House; but when I began to dress I found I hobbled, and a P. Minister hobbling wd. never do, so I gave it wisely up.'   ' The enemy has entirely overpowered me,' he wrote in another note.   ' After a night of unceasing suffering I have been obliged to send to Hardy to take the reins, as it is physically impossible for me to reach the Ho. of C.'

MONTAGU CORRY.　　LORD BRADFORD.　　LORD WHARNCLIFFE.　　BENJAMIN DISRAELI.

LADY BRADFORD.　　LADY WHARNCLIFFE.　　LORD PEMBROKE.

GROUP AT HUGHENDEN, WHITSUNTIDE, 1874.

From a photograph by H. W. Taunt, Oxford.

To Lady Bradford.

2, WHITEHALL GARDENS, *June* 12.—. . . Yesterday, about six o'ck., I was invaded by the Cr. of the Exr., John Manners, Barrington, with pale faces and distracted air, bearing me a paper signed by all the Irish members of both sides announcing that they must vote against the Ministry on the Factory Bill, unless Ireland was excluded from its provisions. In their alarm, they seemed inclined to yield.

I said that such a representation, if it were a just one, ought to have been made to me long ago, not when my Secy. of State was moving the 2nd reading of this Bill. 2ndly that the representation was unjust and absurd. That to exempt the flax spinners of Belfast from the restrictions on labor placed on the flax spinners of Yorkshire would be in fact establishing a system of Protection in favor of Ireland.

My friends were much alarmed, but I was clear as to our course; and that it was better to be beaten than to yield to such remonstrances.

You see the result. We had 200 majority. . . .

To Anne Lady Chesterfield.

2, WHITEHALL GARDENS, *June* 16.—. . . It was a very rash venture yesterday, but it was successful. The House was cordial, they cheered me when I rose, and I knocked up the terrible Lyon Playfair in no time, tho' a few days ago it was said that, on the question of a Minister of Education, the Opposition would certainly beat us.

I got away by eight o'ck., not materially injured by the exertion: but I am now to be quiet for 8 and 40 hours, and then I shall be more than quite well. . . .

Last Sunday Bradford came on a social visit, and was so shocked at finding me knocked up, that he directed Selina to pay me a visit, wh. she did yesterday before her departure. . . .

Handicapped in this way by illness, Disraeli had to face, in the last portion of the session, the most critical stage of a delicate and difficult question. ' There is not a rock ahead or a cloud,' he told Lady Chesterfield; but, as he remembered when writing to Lady Bradford, there was one exception, ' the Church Bill, which is not our child, and of which the fortunes are very obscure.' It was an unmerited misfortune for Disraeli that his accession to power should have coincided with the transference of the Ritualistic controversy from the stage of public discussion to that of legislative action. He had been a party to the appointment of a Royal Commission in 1867 to investigate the problem, and might reasonably have hoped that it would have been taken in hand by Parliament before 1874. The Commission had been issued after a condemnation of Ritualistic excesses by Convocation; it contained a full representation of the High Church party, Bishop Wilberforce, Beauchamp, Beresford-Hope, J. G. Hubbard, Canon Gregory, and Sir Robert Phillimore; and in August of 1867 it issued its first and practically unanimous report, affirming the expediency of restraining variations of vestments, and pronouncing that this should be done by providing aggrieved parishioners with easy and effectual process for complaint and redress. Gladstone, a devoted son of the Church of England, had held office, with a large majority at his back, for five subsequent years; and yet, beyond expressing strongly in the House of Commons in 1872 his belief that there was an urgent case for legislation, he had taken no step whatever to deal with the extravagance which he deplored. Shaftesbury, as Evangelical as he was philanthropic, had endeavoured year after year to obtain support in the Lords for a drastic Bill of his own; but a man of his extreme views could hardly expect support from the bench of Bishops. Meanwhile the situation had become worse, owing to the rapid extension of the Ritualistic party on the one hand, and, on the other, to a striking discrepancy among the oracles of the law. In the Purchas case the use of Eucharistic vestments, of the eastward position by the celebrant, of wafer-bread, and of the mixed Chalice —the four points to which most importance was attached by both the contending parties—had first been affirmed to be lawful by the Dean of Arches and then, on appeal to the Privy Council, had been condemned as unlawful. By these judgments each party in turn was exalted and depressed; and the reversal of the first by the second

rallied to the Ritualistic side no small following among
the moderate High Churchmen.   In these circumstances
the Bishops, under the guidance of Archbishop Tait,
came to the conclusion that legislation must be promoted to prevent the further spread of anarchy and the
possible disruption of the Church.   But they concerned
themselves solely with the machinery for enforcing the
law, ignoring the patent fact, which the Purchas judgments advertised, that that law was capable of very
different interpretations.

When, in January, 1874, the episcopal decision was
taken, Gladstone was in power; before the session opened,
there was a new Government, and one in which both
High and Low Church had eminent representatives—
Salisbury, Hardy, and Carnarvon on one side, and Cairns
on the other.   Disraeli himself, much impressed, as
Lothair showed, by the recent successes of Roman propaganda in England, and believing also, as he wrote in
the General Preface to the Novels, that the ' medieval
superstitions,' which Ritualism revived, were ' generally
only the embodiment of pagan ceremonies and creeds,'
was averse from the new development; in private letters
he disrespectfully referred to Ritualistic practices as
' high jinks.'   But, with a vivid recollection of the Ecclesiastical Titles fiasco in 1850-51, he was much too
shrewd to wish to embark on ecclesiastical legislation;
and in his correspondence over Beauchamp's appointment to the Household had been quite ready to accept
Salisbury's standpoint.

But hardly was he installed in office before pressure
was applied to him.   Within the first week he received,
along with the Archbishop's congratulations, a notification that the Bishops were contemplating a Bill and looked
to the Government for advice and support.

From Archbishop Tait.

Private and Confidential.   ADDINGTON PARK, *Feb.* 23, '74.—
First let me express my congratulations, if indeed it be a
subject of congratulation to have won the most influential

post in Europe by a most honorable manifestation of the regard of a great people, even though that post brings the heaviest burden that any one man can be called to bear. May God sustain you and help you to use all your influence for the best interests of the country!

Secondly will you allow me in my own department to proceed to add to your burden? May I ask you to read the enclosed memorandum? It has been drawn up after full consultation with the Queen. Her Majesty is much interested in it, thinking, I believe rightly, that, unless something of the kind indicated is done, the Church of England will go on the breakers. The Bishops also have almost unanimously approved.

If, after talking over the matter with the Queen, you see your way to help us with the force of Government in some necessary legislation, I shall feel very grateful for your advice.

The great body of moderate persons will I think approve, unless some cannonade is opened against us in the newspapers and they are frightened from their guns.

Lords Salisbury and Carnarvon, B[eresford] Hope and Hubbard must be persuaded that we do not mean to persecute their friends, only to make them act reasonably. Lord Shaftesbury and his following must be convinced that there is no danger of weapons intended for other purposes rebounding against themselves, unless in such cases as are obvious violations of the law.

I trust you may be able and willing to help us. I am sure there is a well-grounded alarm caused by the lawlessness which has sprung up of late, and which is sure to go on and increase, if we wait for a general amendment of the administration of the ecclesiastical law, which may I fear be expected to be accomplished about the Greek Kalends. . . .

The Archbishop of York is thoroughly with me in the matter on which I write.

The Queen had already shown her antipathy to the Ritualistic movement by her protest against receiving extreme High Churchmen into her Household; and before the end of February she talked earnestly to Derby about 'the duty of the Government to discourage Ritualism in the Church.' The Archbishop's memorandum dwelt on the lawlessness of selfwilled incumbents, the complicated and cumbrous proceedings of the ecclesiastical courts, and the necessity for 'some simple, summary, and inexpensive process, for securing obedience to the law.'

The Bishops, Disraeli was told, suggested that summary
effect should be given to a monition issued by the Ordinary,
the Bishop, on the advice of a diocesan board, half clergy,
half laity, to be enforced by sequestration, subject to an
appeal to the Archbishop of the Province.   Disraeli at
once, as on the Household difficulty, consulted Salisbury,
who put the capital objection in a nutshell: ' I sympathise
with you sincerely in having this trouble put upon you.
The Archbishop is asking for an impossibility: that it
shall be as easy to apply a much-disputed law, as if it were
undisputed.'   Salisbury proceeded to detail his criticism
in a note.

Note by Lord Salisbury.

March 2, 1874.—Most people will sympathise with the Archbishop's desire to prevent 'rash innovations which destroy
the peace of parishes.'   The difficulty is to devise the legislation that will do this without producing a civil war in the
Church of England.   The memorandum is vague: and upon
the most essential point ambiguous.   I cannot help thinking
that the acquiescence of the Bishops is due to that cardinal
ambiguity.

It proposes to give to a Bishop, acting with a council of
clergy and churchwardens, a power of forbidding under pain
of sequestration—*something*—but what ?   May they forbid
anything they please ?   or only anything illegal ?   The distinction is vital: but there is nothing in the memorandum to
indicate which kind of power they are to have.   I must,
therefore, examine both alternatives.

1. Let us assume that they are to have the power of forbidding anything they please.   I cannot conceive that so
despotic a proposal would pass. . . .

I pass to the second alternative.   Let us assume that the
Bishop and his council are, by the new legislation, to have power
of forbidding, not what they please, but what is illegal.   I
cannot see what advantage such an enactment would bring.
Its object is to avoid costly litigation.   But the question would
still remain—what is illegal: and that question can only be
decided in a court of justice. . . .

I conclude therefore that the proposals of the memorandum,
if understood one way, would be contrary to the whole tenor
of English law, and would certainly break up the Establishment: if understood the other way, they would not attain
the cheapness and the simplicity they have in view.

Disraeli was very reluctant to meddle with a thorny question which must necessarily divide his Cabinet. But events rapidly forced his hand. Within a few weeks an indiscretion of the press revealed the intentions of the Bishops, whereupon public feeling began to kindle, the Protestant party demanded legislation of an even more stringent kind, and Pusey in a series of letters to *The Times* marshalled High Churchmen in general to take their stand by the Ritualists. It was clear that a hornets' nest was being stirred; and the Queen seized the occasion to bring strong pressure to bear on Disraeli to support the Archbishop.

From Queen Victoria.

WINDSOR, *March* 20, '74.—Mr. Disraeli is aware, the Queen believes, that the Archbishop of Canterbury intends to introduce a Bill after Easter to check the prevalence of Ritualism in the Church of England, which is becoming very alarming.

No measure so important affecting the Established Church should be treated as an open question, but should have the full support of the Government.

As far as the Bill may be directed against practices so lately declared illegal, little difficulty can arise. But the Queen wishes to express further that she warmly sympathises with the laity in general and with those of the clergy, who wish to carry on the service according to long-established usage.

The Queen therefore earnestly hopes that her Government may equally support any dispensing powers in the Bill that may be added for their protection or suggest others to meet the same object. Her *earnest* wish is that Mr. Disraeli should *go as far as he can without embarrassment* to the Government, in *satisfying* the *Protestant* feeling of the country in relation to this measure.

The Queen's proposal, which was in effect that those clergy who erred on the side of excess of ceremony should be restrained and punished, but those who erred on the side of defect should be protected, provoked very naturally a strong protest to Disraeli from Salisbury.

From Lord Salisbury.

INDIA OFFICE (*Undated*).—A very unpleasant state of things. Of course I cannot—and I suspect other members of the Cabinet could not—support such a Bill as is here sketched out.

But I hope that no serious difficulty is really impending. I saw the Bishop of Peterborough on Thursday. He assured me that the Bishops had as a body approved of no Bill; and that the majority of them were opposed to any Bill giving them despotic powers. All he wanted was power to stop practices which he thought illegal, *pending* the decision of the proper court.

This is a perfectly reasonable proposal—and at the same time it might be made to satisfy the Queen.

Such a unilateral Bill as she proposes would be simply impossible to draw. If you gave a dispensing power to Bishops they would use it on both sides; and you cannot name the excepted practices in an Act of Parliament.

I have seen Liddon. He was very moderate: promised me that he and Pusey would write to the chief Ritualists in the most earnest terms to warn them of the danger of their proceedings. This has been done. But he told me that he was being treated as a renegade by a large section of his party. . . .

Salisbury further pointed out that the procedure suggested by the Archbishop's Bill involved a fundamental change in the status of the clergy. At present the beneficed clergy were freeholders so long as they obeyed known conditions; under the Archbishop's scheme they would be subjected to a purely discretionary power. But Salisbury was anxious to find a *modus vivendi ;* and had various talks with Cairns to that end. Cairns was as little disposed to accept the Archbishop's proposal as Salisbury.

From Lord Cairns.

5, CROMWELL HOUSES, S.W., *March* 25, 1874.—This is a very embarrassing question.

I have a strong opinion that if it were attempted to carry or support a Bill like this, *as a Government*, it would lead to a secession of several members of the Cabinet.

I doubt much whether the Evangelical and ' Protestant ' division of the Church would be willing to give to Bishops and Archbishops as much power and discretion as this Bill does.

The Bill is full of crudities and unworkable provisions, and the alterations in some of its leading features shew that its framers are not decided as to what they mean.

By the Bill the Archbishop and his Vicar-General could decide the most knotty point of law as to ecclesiastical ritual or practice without appeal.

I should, individually, much prefer an enactment by which six household parishioners (without any fantastic council), declaring themselves members of the Church, might, on giving security for costs, complain of any breach of the law . . .; the complaint to be made in a summary way to the Bishop, and an appeal from him to the Queen in Council, to be referred to the Appellate Court, with ecclesiastical assessors, under the Act of last year.

Something like this passed a select committee of the H. of L. a few years ago, and was assented to by, *inter alios*, Lord Salisbury.

With Cairns's help Disraeli set himself to make the Archbishop's Bill a more workable and practicable measure; substituting for the brand-new diocesan board the assessors provided under the Church Discipline Act, and providing that the ultimate appeal should be to the Privy Council instead of the Archbishop. Disraeli was well aware of the pitfalls, and therefore, while lending his aid to the Archbishop, was careful to do so as a layman of influence rather than as Prime Minister.

To Lady Bradford.

WHITEHALL, *March* 26, 1874.—. . At twelve to-day, the Archbishop comes. There falls to me the *hardest nut* to crack, that ever was the lot of a Minister. A headstrong step, and it is not only Ministries that wd. be broken up, but political parties altogether, even the Anglican Church itself.

I have no one really to consult with. I can listen to my colleagues, and all they say is worth attention, but they are all prejudiced, one way or other. . . .

To Queen Victoria.

2, WHITEHALL GARDENS, *April* 18, 1874.—Mr. Disraeli with his humble duty to your Majesty:

He has just had an interview with the Archbishops of Canterbury and York.

They informed him of the result of the meeting of the Bishops yesterday at Lambeth, when they submitted to them the new Bill, framed on the lines suggested by Mr. Disraeli and the Lord Chancellor. These new propositions have at least secured unanimity on the part of the Bench of prelates: the High Church Bishops, especially Salisbury[1] and Oxford,[2] though still expressing their opinion that legislation

---

[1] Moberly. [2] Mackarness.

is unnecessary, assenting to the proposed measures. This is something.

It is clearly understood, that the Prime Minister, and the Lord Chancellor, have assisted in these deliberations, and in this correspondence, only as two Churchmen, not without influence, but in no way or degree binding on your Majesty's Government.

The only object of Lord Cairns and Mr. Disraeli has been to further your Majesty's wishes in this matter, which will always be with them a paramount object.

After the statement of the Archbishop of Canterbury in the House of Lords next Monday, and the first reading of the Bill, Mr. Disraeli will summon a Cabinet, probably on Wednesday, for its consideration.

Mr. Disraeli refrains from being sanguine as to this appeal, but he is supported by the conviction, that his efforts, which have been unceasing, have at least prevented some mischief from occurring, and he can only assure your Majesty, that in this, as he hopes in all things, your Majesty may rely on his efforts for the advantage of your realm and Church.

So strong was the public feeling of the necessity for legislation to prevent anarchy that, in spite of the growing opposition of High Churchmen and of the doubts as to the machinery suggested, the Bill passed both its first and its second reading in the Lords without a division; and Salisbury appeared as the Government mouthpiece on the latter occasion. The Government, he said, occupied an independent position. He admitted that a check to lawlessness was desirable; but he dwelt strongly on the danger of jeopardising the spirit of toleration on which the stately fabric of the Establishment reposed. The three great schools in the Church, the Sacramental, the Emotional, and the Philosophical, must be frankly accepted; no attempt must be made to drive any of them into secession. Cairns grumbled to Disraeli that he should be sorry if this speech ' was to continue to be the expression of the manner in which, as a Cabinet, we looked at questions of this kind.' But Disraeli was manœuvring with great skill to preserve the unity of his Cabinet in a difficult position. Here is his account of a critical moment in the Committee stage in the Lords.

To Lady Bradford.

2, WHITEHALL GARDENS, *June* 5, 1874.—The proceedings of yesterday in the H. of Lords were the most important in the history of the present Government.   You saw, then, the result of all my anxious deliberations with the Archbishops for the last three months and more; of my long counsels with Lord Cairns; and of the anxious discussions of many Cabinets.

Nothing could be more triumphant: the Archbishops deferring entirely to the Ministry; and Ld. Salisbury himself supporting the masterly, and commanding, exposition of the Lord Chancellor.   Every arrangement was brought about, and every calculation succeeded.

You were in the secret which even the Fairy[1] was not, tho' I shall now tell her all; but the admirable *sangfroid* with which our amendments were divided between Ld. Shaftesbury and the Bp. of Peterboro' must have been amusing to you. I think the whole affair, in conception and execution, one of the most successful, as it certainly is one of the most important, events in modern political history.   I don't think Bismarck really could have done better; and I believe the Church will be immensely strengthened, notwithstanding Beauchamp will probably resign and, I fear, our friend Bath is furious. I fear, too, we are doomed not to meet at Longleat.

I cannot give you a good account of myself.   I was well yesterday, and in good spirits considering I had not had the solace of seeing you; I looked after affairs in both Houses, guided the Licensing Bill in the Commons thro' some quicksands, and frequently visited the Lords, conferring with D. of Richmond, Bishops of Peterboro' and Winchester, Ld. Derby, and Beauchamp during the crisis.   The latter came to me twice while under the Throne, to assure me the Lord Chancellor had ruined everything, and when I mildly mentioned that Ld. Salisbury approved, he said 'the High Ch. thought nothing of Lord Salisbury.'   But, as Derby said, ' if Beauchamp disapproves, we must be right.'

Our House sate till two o'ck.; and it was critical to the last, so I cd. not leave my place.   And then I had to write to the Fairy on the proceedings of both Houses, as I had promised her.   I did it in my room in the H. of C., but when I rose from my seat, I found the enemy had attacked my left foot.   I was obliged to send a policeman, ov— ..... our quarter of the town, to find me a cab: and here I am with the D. of Manchester, Ld. Fitzwalter, and Andrew Montagu, with three different appointments bet[wee]n 12 and 2, and the absolute necessity of being in the H. of C. at $\frac{1}{2}$ past 4. . . .

[1] Queen Victoria. See above, p. 283, and Vol. VI., ch. ' Beaconsfield and the Queen.'

[*Same date*].— . . . I look upon the affair in the Lords as the greatest thing I have ever done. . . .

Shaftesbury's amendment, which was supported by the High Churchmen Salisbury, Selborne, and Bath, and inserted in the Bill, was the vital one which established a single lay judge, to be appointed by the two Archbishops, as the sole tribunal of first instance. The Bishop of Peterborough's proposal was to constitute a 'neutral zone' of practices—some affected by High Church, some by Low, some by Broad—which should not be liable to prosecution. Its exact value in the tactics of the campaign is shown by a sentence in a letter from Cairns to Disraeli on June 12:

You may be interested to know that the Bishop of Peterborough's clause seems to have perfectly done its work as a 'red herring' across the scent; and the probability is that with the thankful approval of both Archbishops, most of the Bishops, Shaftesbury, Salisbury, Harrowby, Beauchamp and the Ritualists, it will be withdrawn on Monday, and the remodelled Bill pass out of Committee with universal consent, if not applause !

Cairns's expectation was fulfilled. So adroitly had Disraeli pulled the wires behind the scenes that the Bill was read a third time in its amended form without a division and sent down to the Commons. Neither the Government nor the Prime Minister had as yet taken any overt responsibility for it; and it was a respected private member, Russell Gurney, the Recorder of London, who moved the second reading on Thursday, July 9. On the eve of the debate the Archbishop of Canterbury wrote to urge, in the Queen's name, as well as in his own, that it would be highly inexpedient to allow the Bill to fail, and so to encourage a perilous agitation in the autumn. Its progress was at once seriously threatened by the greatest orator in the House. Gladstone emerged, by no means for the first time, from his retirement, delivered an impassioned speech of strong opposition on the broad ground of liberty, and announced that he would move six voluminous Resolutions defining the whole

position of the Established Church. For the moment
he carried his hearers away, but a powerful argument from Harcourt, who reminded the House that
the Church was based on successive Acts of Uniformity,
broke the spell of the great enchanter; and when Hardy
appeared to support Gladstone's case, he was met by
noisy demonstrations of disapproval. Disraeli watched
the rising temper of the House and of the public, and drew
the conclusion that his own sentiments about Ritualism
were shared by the great body of his countrymen, and
that therefore it was now the moment to come into the
open and associate himself and the Government with
the national resolve. He was no doubt confirmed in his
decision by the insistence of his Sovereign.

From Queen Victoria.

WINDSOR, *July* 10, '74.—. . . She [the Queen] is deeply
grieved to see the want of Protestant feeling in the Cabinet;
Mr. Gladstone's conduct is much to be regretted though it is
not surprising: but she wrote to him in the strongest terms of
the danger to the Church and of the intention of the Archbishop
to bring forward a measure to try and regulate the shameful
practices of the Ritualists.

He [Disraeli] should state to the Cabinet how strongly the
Queen feels and how faithful she is to the Protestant faith,
to defend and maintain which, her family was placed upon
the Throne ! She owns she often asks herself what has become of the Protestant feeling of Englishmen. . . .

July 11.—The Queen thanks Mr. Disraeli for his letter
which is very reassuring. It is a *most* important question.
Mr. Disraeli must have managed his refractory Cabinet most
skilfully.

(*Telegram in cypher*) *July* 13.—Pray show that you are in
earnest and determined to pass this Bill and not to be deterred
by threats of delay.

Accordingly Disraeli announced that Gladstone's Resolutions amounted to a challenge of the whole Reformation
settlement, and must be brought to an early issue; and
on the resumption of the second reading debate, he
urged that the Bill should be passed, and passed during
the current session. Its object was, he said—adopting
a phrase from Gladstone's speech which has ever since

been fathered on himself—'to put down Ritualism.'
He protested that he considered all three parties in the
Church, characterised respectively by ceremony, enthusiasm and free speculation, to be perfectly legitimate;
but he wished to discourage ' practices by a portion of
the clergy, avowedly symbolic of doctrines which the
same clergy are bound, in the most solemn manner, to
refute and repudiate.' He was prepared to treat with
reverence Roman Catholic doctrines and ceremonies,
when held and practised by Roman Catholics; what he
did object to was the ' Mass in masquerade.' The speech
elicited the sympathy of the whole House with insignificant exceptions. The second reading, in spite of Gladstone's vehement opposition, was carried without a
division; and a Gladstonian of proved fidelity urged his
leader to withdraw Resolutions for which not twenty
men in his own party would vote—a suggestion which
Gladstone was too experienced a Parliamentarian to
disregard. ' An immense triumph: Gladstone ran away,'
was Disraeli's complacent report to Lady Chesterfield.
The enthusiasm which carried the second reading without a division was prolonged throughout the Committee;
the members were ' mad,' said the protesting Hardy;
and all the important clauses were passed by vast majorities. Only one point of detail needs notice. The
Archbishops had been careful to give the Bishop a veto
so as to prevent frivolous and irresponsible prosecutions
of devoted clergymen. In the teeth of Gladstone's remonstrances there was inserted a clause permitting
appeal against the veto to the Archbishop of the Province,
and, in spite of Gladstone's renewed assault, and of a
plea 'from both front benches against disturbing the
settlement reached in the Lords, the House maintained
its amendment by a majority of twenty-three.

The right of a Bishop to uncontrolled rule in his diocese
at once became the war-cry of High Churchmen, and
was warmly taken up by Salisbury and their other representatives in the Cabinet. ' Affairs are very critical,
and I believe that wrongheaded Marquis will bolt after

all,' wrote Disraeli late in July to Lady Bradford. In the first days of August it looked as if the Bill would fail and the Cabinet might be broken up. Disraeli was urgent with the Archbishop to get the Lords to acquiesce in the Commons' amendment, without which, in his opinion, the Commons would refuse to proceed with the Bill. The Archbishop himself was inclined to share Disraeli's fears, but could not persuade his suffragans to surrender what they held to be their unquestionable episcopal rights. Salisbury urged the House of Lords to disregard the kind of bluster which was always used when the Peers showed a disposition to insist on a disputed point. He for himself repudiated the bugbear of a majority in the House of Commons. The Lords accordingly struck out the appeal to the Archbishop of the Province; and Disraeli was in despair.

To Anne Lady Chesterfield.

Private. 2, WHITEHALL GARDENS, *Aug.* 5.—Things are as bad as possible: I think the Bill is lost, but worse things will happen in its train.

I found Carnarvon at the Carlton, dining in a tumultuous crowd of starving senators. He not only voted against the Archbishops, Ld. Chanr., and D. of Richmond, but spoke against them; and did as much harm as Salisbury: more, they say. . . .

Eventually, however, owing largely to the Archbishop's unwearied diligence in bringing his personal influence to bear, Disraeli managed to induce the Commons to surrender the amendment rather than lose the Bill; and to be content with a little strong language in the place of destructive action. The Bill, therefore, passed; but the final stage, on Wednesday, August 5, just before prorogation, was of dramatic quality. Salisbury's stinging phrase about bluster provoked an outbreak. Harcourt, long Disraeli's friend in private, made from the front Opposition bench his most notable approximation to him in public. Amid general cheers, he appealed to him, as ' a leader who is proud of the House of Commons and

of whom the House of Commons is proud,' to vindicate
its dignity 'against the ill-advised railing of a rash and
rancorous tongue, even though it be the tongue of a Cabinet Minister, a Secretary of State, and a colleague.' The
speech provoked a satirical rebuke from Harcourt's
leader, Gladstone; but Disraeli responded sympathetically.
The necessity of putting down a 'small but pernicious
sect' was, he said, urgent. The House, therefore, would
do wisely to pass the Bill, even without the amendment;
and members should not be diverted from the course
which, as wise and grave men, they thought it right to
follow, by any allusions to a speech in the other House of
Parliament.

My noble friend was long a member of this House, and is
well known to many of the members even of this Parliament.
He is a great master of gibes and flouts and jeers; but I do
not suppose there is anyone who is prejudiced against a Member
of Parliament on account of such qualifications. My noble
friend knows the House of Commons well, and he is not
perhaps superior to the consideration that by making a speech
of this kind, and taunting respectable men like ourselves with
being 'a blustering majority' he might probably stimulate
the *amour propre* of some individuals to take the course which
he wants, and to defeat the Bill. Now I hope we shall not fall
into that trap. I hope we shall show my noble friend that
we remember some of his manœuvres when he was a simple
member of this House, and that we are not to be taunted into
taking a very indiscreet step, a step ruinous to all our own
wishes and expectations, merely to show that we resent the
contemptuous phrases of one of our colleagues.

It was no doubt chaff, but it was chaff with a sting in
it; nevertheless Disraeli, having conspicuously asserted
himself, and vindicated the Commons, was anxious that
a public difference should not degenerate into a private
quarrel.

To Lord Salisbury.

2, WHITEHALL GARDENS, *Aug.* 5, 1874.—Harcourt attacked
your speech in H. of Lords last night. I conceived a playful
reply to his invective, but what was not perhaps ill conceived was, I fear, ill executed, and knowing what figure that
style of rhetoric makes in 'reports,' I write this line to

express my hope, that you will not misconceive what I may have been represented as saying, or believe, for a moment, that I have any other feelings towards you but those of respect and regard.

Salisbury wrote a good-humoured reply, and took an opportunity before the prorogation to explain in the Lords that he had never used the expression ' blustering majority,' and that when he talked of ' bluster ' he was referring to the argument that, when there was a difference of opinion between the two Houses, it was the privilege of the Commons to insist and the duty of the Lords to yield. There was accordingly no lasting soreness between Disraeli and his colleague—a happy result, creditable to both men, which many of the public and some even of their friends were slow to believe.

From Lady Derby.

Private. 23, ST. JAMES'S SQUARE, S.W., *Aug.* 7, 1874.— ... I thought you might like to have some private report of the wild man of your team.[1] I have just seen him, and all is right for the moment; he seems much pleased with a letter he has had from you; he was hard at work at his chemistry and experiments, which the state of the atmosphere was interfering with, and he will be off to Dieppe to-night. I have had some anxious moments this week, and dread a recurrence of difficulties from that quarter in November when Cabinets recommence.

To Lord Carnarvon.

LONGLEAT, *Aug.* 8.—. . . I had never seen the newspapers, and of course took it for granted that Harcourt was strictly accurate in his quotation of Lord Salisbury's speech, particularly as Cairns had complained to me, the night before, of S.'s violent speech. It was a mess; but Salisbury has behaved like a gentleman, and I earnestly trust that we shall all manage to keep together. No effort, for that object, will be spared on my side. . . .

For the moment, and from the Parliamentary standpoint, Disraeli's championship of the Public Worship Regulation Bill was an enormous success, and riveted his

[1] Here Lady Derby was almost certainly quoting a playful phrase of Disraeli's own coinage.

hold on his Sovereign, the legislature, and public opinion, without even dislocating seriously his hesitating Cabinet. But subsequent experience of the scandals of imprisoned clergymen—men of high character if doubtful judgment— has shown that he would have done better, in the interest both of the Church and of his party, to adhere to his original position, and to discourage and postpone legislation which certainly brought to the Church not peace but a sword. No one could blame an ordinary Prime Minister for fixing his attention almost exclusively on a growing lawlessness which seemed to demand prompt abatement, and ignoring delicate points of Church tendency and feeling to which Archbishops and Bishops and a large number of High Church laymen were equally blind. But a deeper insight might have been expected from Disraeli, who never failed to recognise the profound importance of the spiritual in human nature, whose historical studies had made him thoroughly familiar with the inflammability of High Churchmen, as shown in Dr. Sacheverell's case, and who had had personal experience, in the Irish Church controversy, both of their detachment from political party, and of their electoral weight. He had warnings both from ecclesiastics and from wirepullers. The Bishop of Brechin (Alexander Forbes) told him in June that three-fourths of the clergy —a class whom the Bishop called 'proverbially vindictive' —regarded the Bill with extreme discontent. 'That the great mass of the clergy, who have no sympathy with the *effrenata licentia* of the younger men, should make common cause with them against the Bill shows how strongly they feel, and I put it to you whether 15,000 discontented men of education scattered thro' the country is not a thing to be dreaded by any Government.' The gross exaggeration of this statement probably blinded Disraeli to the substratum of truth which it contained. But his party manager, Gorst, reported in the same general sense. 'The potential electoral strength of the High Church party,' he wrote on July 29, 'is generally underestimated on our side. If they became actively hostile, as the Dissenters were to Gladstone before the dissolution, we should lose many seats both in the counties and boroughs.' It has always been the opinion of some of the shrewdest judges that resentment at Disraeli's action on the Public Worship Regulation Bill counted for much in the readiness of the High Church leaders to think evil of his policy on the Eastern Question and to throw themselves ardently into the support of Gladstone's whirlwind propaganda.

In one of his letters to Archbishop Tait at a critical moment in the history of the Bill,[1] Disraeli described himself as ' one who, from the first, has loyally helped you, and under immense difficulties.' There is no reason to doubt that, over and above the political game, Disraeli was, in his conduct of this awkward business, sincerely anxious to promote the interests of religion in the Church. It is a shallow cynicism that refuses to see earnestness as well as insight—coupled unfortunately with an inadequate sense of the historic continuity of the Church— in such a passage as the following from his second reading speech in the House of Commons.

I have never addressed any body of my countrymen for the last three years without having taken the opportunity of intimating to them that a great change was occurring in the politics of the world, that it would be well for them to prepare for that change, and that it was impossible to conceal from ourselves that the great struggle between the temporal and the spiritual power, which had stamped such indelible features upon the history of the past, was reviving in our own time. . . . I spoke from strong conviction and from a sense of duty. . . . When I addressed a large body of my countrymen as lately as autumn last, I said then, as I say now— looking to what is occurring in Europe, looking at the great struggle between the temporal and spiritual power which has been precipitated by those changes of which many in this House are so proud, and of which, while they may triumph in their accomplishment, they ought not to shut their eyes to the inevitable consequences—I said then, and say now, that

---

[1] For a detailed history of the controversy on this measure, see chapters 21 and 24 of the *Life of Archbishop Tait.*

in the disasters, or rather in the disturbance and possible disasters which must affect Europe, and which must to a certain degree sympathetically affect England, it would be wise for us to rally on the broad platform of the Reformation. Believing as I do that those principles were never so completely and so powerfully represented as by the Church of England; believing that without the learning, the authority, the wealth, and the independence of the Church of England, the various sects of the Reformation would by this time have dwindled into nothing, I called the attention of the country, so far as I could, to the importance of rallying round the institution of the Church of England, based upon those principles of the Reformation which the Church was called into being to represent.

A private letter in the autumn provoked by a magazine article of Gladstone's on Ritualism further elucidates Disraeli's position.

To Lady Bradford.

2, WHITEHALL GARDENS, *Oct.* 5.—. . . I have read G., but with difficulty. He is a cumbrous writer. Now for the substance, however. Nothing. He does not meet the great question, wh. every instant is becoming greater.

All—at least all civilised beings—must be for the ' beauty of holiness.' No one stronger than myself. In ecclesiastical affairs I require order, taste, ceremony. But these are quite compatible with a sincere profession of the estab[lishe]d religion of the country. What I object to is the introduction of a peculiar set of ceremonies, wh. are avowedly symbolical of doctrines wh. that Established Church was instituted, and is supported, to refute and to repudiate. This is what the people of England are thinking of. His article is mere ' leather and prunella.' . . . .

If Disraeli's well-intentioned efforts had not materially contributed to strengthen the Church of England, he had the satisfaction this session of settling the affairs of the Church of Scotland on a generally acceptable basis. The question of patronage had agitated Scottish churchmen for 300 years. There was a strong feeling in Presbyterian Scotland, thoroughly conformable to its special type of Christianity, that the congregation was the proper authority to select the minister; and it was largely because this privilege was denied in the Establishment and the patronage rested to a great extent in the Crown and in the hands of laymen that there had been the momentous secession of the Free Kirk in the forties. But even in the Establishment there had been several variations of custom, and on the advice of Lord-Advocate Gordon on the one hand, and of the Duke of Richmond, a great lay patron, on the other, Disraeli determined to settle the vexed question by a universal transfer of lay patronage to the congregations. The Bill passed the Lords with ease, being blessed by that eminent Presbyterian Liberal, the Duke of Argyll; but Gladstone, enticed by the lure of ecclesiastical controversy, appeared in the Commons to make a vigorous protest, mainly on the strange ground that it would be an injustice to the Free Kirk to remedy a grievance in the conditions of establishment which caused them to secede! He further expressed a fear lest the measure should hasten on disestablishment, a policy of which he professed himself ' no idolater,' though he was willing that his memory should be judged by his dealings with the Church of Ireland. Disraeli, in reply, naturally expressed the hope that upon Gladstone's tombstone there would not be inscribed the destruction of another Church. It was not Gladstone's fault that his epitaph lacked this additional embellishment. In later years he gave in his adhesion to the policy of disestablishment for Scotland which in 1874 he professed to dread; but the removal of the grievance of patronage, which had been effected in his despite by Disraeli's prudence, had by that time so strengthened the Church of Scotland in the affections of the Scottish people that the assault was repulsed without serious difficulty; and the whole current of Scottish opinion has now for many years set in the direction, not of disestablishment, but of reunion of all Presbyterians in one national Church. Should this desirable consummation be reached, Scotsmen should not forget Disraeli's important share in creating the predisposing conditions.

There was one other ecclesiastical measure, introduced by Ministers in July, which gave Disraeli some trouble, and did not enhance the reputation of the Government. This was an endowed Schools Bill, which modified the policy of Gladstonian legislation, by restoring to the Church of England certain schools on which their founder had impressed a specially Church character, but which had been thrown open indiscriminately by the last Parliament. However theoretically defensible, it was hardly an act of wisdom to disturb an arrangement accepted by Parliament and already in force; and the Liberals, under Gladstone's lead, came together with some animation to protest. Disraeli saw that it was desirable to abandon a course which Salisbury had pressed upon his colleagues; so he amusingly assured the House that the clauses of the Government Bill were so obscure as to be unintelligible to him, and he must therefore withdraw them for reconsideration. The Bill was accordingly reduced to a measure merely to substitute Charity Commissioners appointed by the Tory Government for Endowed Commissioners appointed by their predecessors.

To Queen Victoria.

HOUSE OF COMMONS, *Wednesday*, 1 a.m. [*July 25, 1874*].—Mr. Disraeli with his humble duty to your Majesty:

The debate on endowed schools has ended with a good majority for the Government; between 60 and 70.

What is of equal importance, with a much better tone in the House: everything good-tempered and conciliatory.

The Cabinet agreed to many concessions yesterday, though with difficulty: Lord Salisbury stood almost alone, but he was very unmanageable. It is entirely his Bill, but had Mr. Disraeli refused to sanction it, which he only did after many great alterations by himself and Lord Derby, Lord Salisbury would never have consented to your Majesty's Government passing the ' Public Worship Bill '; and that was all-important.

From Queen Victoria.

Confidential. OSBORNE, *July* 27, '74.—The Queen has received Mr. Disraeli's letter of yesterday. She sees *all* the difficulties and herself has regretted that the Church Regula-

tion Bill could not have been delayed till next year, on account
of the inconvenience and difficulty it caused to the new
Government: but it was impossible.

As however Mr. Disraeli always likes to have the Queen's
opinion, she will state to him openly what she thinks it most
important for him and his government to avoid, in order to
enable them to carry on the government for a length of time,
and thus to save the country from frequent crisises.

He will recollect that when he left office in '68 the Queen
urged upon him the importance of keeping the Conservative
party to what it really ought to be, viz.: *Conservative*, and not
to attempt to be *more liberal* than the Liberal party, which
the passing of the Reform Bill (which was forced no doubt
upon the late Lord Derby) rather led them to appear to be.

Now, while being decidedly still of this opinion, which the
Queen considers to be essential to the wellbeing of the British
Constitution and safety of the Crown, it is at the same time
equally important that there should be no attempt at a *retrograde* policy which would alarm the country and injure the
present Government. The country has great confidence
in Mr. Disraeli, but not so much in those of his adherents,
not to say colleagues, who show a disposition to urge such a
policy as she has named above. This would be, the Queen
need not say to Mr. Disraeli, *very* dangerous; and while improvements, modifications and alterations may no doubt in
many cases—where new systems have not worked well—
be very desirable and even necessary, any reversal of principle
ought to be avoided, even for the sake of precedent. The
Queen feels sure that, with Mr. Disraeli's very enlightened
views, he would be as much against this as any one; still this
Endowed Schools Bill has been by many looked at in this
light and she trusts that Mr. Disraeli will take any opportunity he may have to show that this is *not* the policy of the
Government.

Disraeli's letters to his intimate friends give a kaleido-
scopic view of the ups and downs of the Parliamentary
session at its height. Here, first of all, are some extracts
which show his own personal exertions in order to aug-
ment the art treasures of the nation.

To Lady Bradford.

H. OF COMM., *June 2, 1874.*—. . . I mean to rise early
to-morrow and go to Christie's. If the Barker pictures are as
rare and wondrous as I hear, it shall go hard if the nation does
not possess them. I always remember with delight that in

1867-8, on my own responsibility, I bought for the nation the Blacas collection of gems—£50,000 !

If I could give our gallery some pictures of equal quality, one wd. not have lived in vain.

2, WHITEHALL GARDENS, *June* 4.—. . I have been closeted the whole morning with Mr. Burton, the Director of the National Gallery, concocting my plans for Saturday's sale. I believe it will end in the H. of Comm. repudiating my purchase, and I shall have to appeal to Rothschild, Lord Bradford, and some other great friends, to take the treasures off my hands, and relieve me, by a raffle, from my æsthetical embarrassments. We must be very silent till Saturday, as I don't want any one to know the Government is a purchaser. . . .

10, DOWNING STREET, *June* 17.—. . . When the debate over the pictures comes off, there will be some fun. . . .

July 28.—. . . After all, the great attack, so long threatened, about my pictures, ended in vapor. I thought once the vote wd. have passed unchallenged, and in silence; but Mr. Hankey forced me up, and the purchase[1] was sanctioned amid cheers from both sides. . . .

To Anne Lady Chesterfield.

H. OF COMM., *June* 20, 1874.—A hurried line. Yesterday was a very hard day in the House. The Opposition got so irritated at all our new proposals in the Licensing Bill, which are very popular, that they waxed factious, and resolved to delay business, and throw over the Bill till next Monday. I had a great force and beat them throughout the night by large majorities.

My new troops got blooded, and begged me to sit up dividing till 5 o'ck. in the morning; and I am not sure I shd. not have done so, had I not found out that I could appoint a morning sitting without notice. This quite turned their flank. We met this morning accordingly, and have carried the Bill through. A great triumph ! . . .

To Lady Bradford.

2, WHITEHALL GARDENS, *July* 3.—. . . Yesterday's debate was satisfactory. I think Home Rule received its *coup de grâce*.

Hartington had spoken in a manner worthy of the subject, and his own position, on the previous night. Yesterday Beach quite confirmed his rising reputation in the House,

[1] The pictures bought included a Piero della Francesca, a Pinturicchio, a Luca Signorelli, and two Botticellis.

and the public confidence in my discrimination of character
and capacity.   Lowe was very good; terse, logical, and
severely humorous; and your friend was not displeased with
himself, wh., for him, you know is saying a great deal. . . .
The most effective passage in my speech was the reference to
the three Irish Prime Ministers I had known, *the three Irish
Viceroys*, etc., etc.   All this in the synopsis in *The Times*
appears; but in the report it is a hash, and the 3 Irish Viceroys
are turned into three judges.   A curious piece of ignorance
is ' morbid sentiment ' turned into a ' mere bit of sentiment,' [1]
wh. is a feeble vulgarism. . . .

Disraeli's speech on the Home Rule debate was one
of his very happiest performances.   Its keynote was a
bantering protest against the absurd insistence of the
Irish in proclaiming to the world that they were a subjugated people, a conquered race.   The House seized the
point with immediate sympathy and punctuated the
sentences in which he elaborated it with frequent cheers.
' I have always been surprised,' he said, ' that a people
gifted with so much genius, so much sentiment, such
winning qualities, should be—I am sure they will pardon
my saying it; my remark is an abstract and not a personal
one—so deficient in self-respect.'   He denied that the
Irish were conquered; ' they are proud of it; I deny that
they have any ground for that pride.'   England had been
subjugated quite as much, but never boasted of it.   Both
the Normans and Cromwell had conquered England,
before they conquered Ireland.   He was opposed to
Home Rule in the interests of the Irish themselves.
' I am opposed to it because I wish to see at this important crisis of the world—that perhaps is nearer arriving
than some of us suppose—a united people welded in one
great nationality; and because I feel that, if we sanction
this policy, if we do not cleanse the Parliamentary bosom
of this perilous stuff, we shall bring about the disintegration of the Kingdom and the destruction of the Empire.'

---

[1] A natural, almost excusable, mistake.   In the shorthand note ' morbid '
would be written ' mrbd,' and ' mere bit ' ' mr bt '—a difference of only
one letter and a space.

To Lady Bradford

2, WHITEHALL GARDENS, *July* 31.—A most severe day yesterday, the Irish members having announced their determination, whatever might happen, not to allow the continuance of what are called their ' Coercion Acts ' to pass; and their success was inevitable with an adequate quantity of staying power.

I was in my seat 12 hours—from 4 to 4 ! [1] a most exciting scene, with many phases of character. At first they were in serried rank, and very firm and resolute: our men the same, and Dyke ordered, in the great dining-room, a grilled bone and champagne supper at 2 o'ck. to be ready for the Tories.

As the evening advanced, the Liberal party, who had ostentatiously informed us that nothing in the world wd. induce them to act with the Home Rulers, could no longer resist the opportunity of embarrassing, or defeating, the Government, and joined the rebels in force; but were defeated —our smallest majority being 61.

Then about two, the Irishry began quarrelling among themselves, the more respectable, Butt himself, Sullivan, a clever fellow, who wants to be the leader, and Mitchell Henry, an English millionaire tho' an Irish member, and who supplies the funds of the party, getting ashamed of the orgies of faction in wh. they found themselves being steeped; and about three o'ck., when they left the House, when the factious divisions took place, they were absolutely hissed by their own assumed creatures. And a little before 4 o'ck. we tired out, or shamed, even these rapscallions, and the Bill went thro' Committee amid loud cheers.

I broke their ranks by keeping my temper and treating Butt and his intimate colleagues as gentlemen, wh. they certainly are not; but their vanity is insatiable, and these fierce rebels did nothing but pay me compliments. . . .

10, DOWNING STREET, *Aug.* 1.—. . . We have had a long Cabinet, and I have had many deputations and interviews; business gets thick the last days, and gentlemen get audiences wh. they asked for months ago. You wd. have been amused if you had seen and heard all I have done since the Cabinet closed at three o'ck.: Sir Henry Rawlinson and the President of the Royal Society and Admiral Sherard Osborn, who want a new polar expedition; and Owens College, with a *posse* of professors and M.P.'s, who want 100 thousand pounds and to become a University; and Mr. —— who says his brother (late M.P.) is low-spirited that, after 40 years of

---

[1] ' The hardest life I ever went thro',' Disraeli told Lady Chesterfield.

Parly. service, 'there is nothing now attached to his name'—
would like to be a Privy Councillor, or baronet, and wd.
not refuse an Irish peerage, and so on. . . .

The tone of complacency which Disraeli adopts with
reference to his achievements during the session is fully
justified by the comments of the chief Parliamentary
observer of the day.

Foremost in official position, as in personal success, is the
Premier. Never did the peculiar genius of Disraeli (it is a
sublime sort of tact) shine more transcendently than during
the past session.   He has at no period of his career risen higher
as a Parliamentary speaker, while his management of the House
is equalled only by that of Lord Palmerston. Not in the
zenith of his popularity after the election of 1868 did Gladstone
come near his great rival in personal hold upon the House
of Commons. . . . Disraeli's slow, deliberate rising in the
course of a debate is always the signal for an instant filling up
of the House and a steady settling down to the point of attention, the highest compliments that can be paid to a speaker.
At the outset of his current Premiership, Disraeli fixed upon
a policy of polite consideration, to which he was the more
drawn as certain members of the Ministry he succeeded
were notorious for the brusqueness of their manner. The
addition of a bit of banter and of a dash of serio-comicality
lent a spiciness to his speech which was always relished, and
was never allowed to reach the proportion at which the
mixture left an unpleasant taste upon the Parliamentary
palate. . . . Suffering acutely from gout, Disraeli has
stuck to his post with Spartan-like patience; and one of his
most successful speeches, if not, on the whole, his best speech
of the session—that on the Home Rule question—was delivered
after he had been sitting for four hours with folded arms on
the Treasury Bench, visibly tortured by twinges from his
slippered and swollen feet.[1]

The somewhat acute difference which had arisen between Disraeli and the High Churchmen did not prevent
him from fulfilling an engagement to pay a visit to his
friend, Lord Bath, a conspicuous member of that party,
at Longleat, immediately after the close of the session.
He came direct from Osborne, experiencing on the journey
the embarrassing attentions which await popular states-

[1] Sir Henry Lucy's *Diary of Two Parliaments*, Vol. I., p. 40.

men at the hands of their admirers.   Bath told Mr. George
Russell that Disraeli was the dullest guest he ever entertained at Longleat; and Disraeli's own accounts suggest
that he did not find himself in congenial society.

To Lady Bradford.

LONGLEAT, WARMINSTER, *Aug.* 7. — . . . Osborne was
lovely, its green shades refreshing after the fervent glare of
the voyage, and its blue bay full of white sails.   The Faery
sent for me the instant I arrived.   I can only describe my
reception by telling you that I really thought she was going
to embrace me.   She was wreathed with smiles, and as she
tattled, glided about the room like a bird.   She told me it
was 'all owing to my courage and tact,' and then she said
'To think of your having the gout all the time !   How you
must have suffered !   And you ought not to stand now.
You shall have a chair !'

Only think of that !   I remember that *feu* Ld. Derby,
after one of his severest illnesses, had an audience of Her
Majesty, and he mentioned it to me, as a proof of the Queen's
favor, that Her Majesty had remarked to him 'how sorry she
was she cd. not ask him to be seated.'   The etiquette was so
severe.

I remembered all this as she spoke, so I humbly declined the
privilege, saying I was quite well, but wd. avail myself of her
gracious kindness if I ever had another attack. . . .

I have very bad stationery here,[1] but I have sent for some
official stores from D.S. to-day, and shall then get on better.
If you find this a stupid epistle, it is the stationery.   Their
paper, muddy ink, and pens, wh. are made from the geese
on a common, entirely destroy any little genius I have, and
literally annihilate my power of expression. . . .

My travelling from S.hampton to Warminster was very
fatiguing.   I had to wait at S. and also at Salisbury; an hour
at each place.   They had telegraphed along the line to keep
compartments for me, so wherever I stopped there was an
enthusiastic group—'Here he is ' being the common expression,
followed by three times three, and little boys running after
me.   You know how really distressed I am at all this.   And
I had a headache, and wanted a cup of tea, and made fruitless
efforts to get one.   I always found outside of my chamber,
wh. had been lent me by the manager, a watchful band.   I
got a cup of tea at Salisbury, however, from apparently a most
haughty young lady; but I did not do her justice.   She not
only asked me for an autograph, but to write it in her favorite

[1] At Longleat.

work, *Henrietta Temple !*   I could have refused the Duchess of Manchester, but absolutely had not pluck to disobey this Sultana.   I never felt more ashamed of myself in my life.

At Salisbury, I found Lady Paget, who was going to Longleat with her son, a very young Etonian.   Sir Augustus had travelled by an earlier train with the luggage.   I cd. not avoid giving her a place in my compartment, and she talked, and with her usual cleverness, the whole way: an hour of prattle on all subjects. . . .

We did not get to L. till 9, and tho' we dressed in ten minutes, people who dine at 8 don't like dining at 9.   We were seven at table. . . .   I sate by Lady B. but with a racking headache, rare with me, and not in very good spirits, for if Bath was rather furious for your defalcation, I cannot say it added to my happiness.   A more insipid, and stupid, and gloomy dinner I never assisted at, and I felt conscious I added my ample quota to the insipidity and the stupidity and the gloom. Lady P[aget] tried to rally the scene, but she had exhausted her resources bet[wee]n Salisbury and Warm[inste]r.

It was only two hours before we all retired, and had I been younger, and still in the days of poetry, I shd. have gone away in the night, wh. I used to do in my youth, when I was disgusted.

This morning things are a little brighter.   The Baths are appeased. . . .

Perhaps, and probably, I ought to be pleased.   I can only tell you the truth, wh. I always do, tho' to no one else.   I am wearied to extinction and profoundly unhappy.

Aug. 8.—. . . Of all the people here, I like best the *châtelaine*.   She is very kind and has offered more than once, and unaffectedly, to be my secretary, and copy things for me. Bath says she writes an illegible hand.   I rather admire it.   It reminds me somewhat of missals and illuminated MSS. . . .

Aug. 11.—. . . Monday (yesterday) Lady Bath drove me to Frome to see Bennett's famous church, with a sanctuary where ' lay people ' are requested not to place their feet, and among other spiritual pageantry, absolutely a Calvary—and of good sculpture.   The church is marvellous; exquisitely beautiful, and with the exception of some tawdriness about the high altar, in admirable taste. . . .

The priest, or sacristan, or whatever he was, who showed us over the church, and exhibited the sacred plate, etc., looked rather grimly upon me after my anti-ritualistic speeches; and, as Lady Bath observed, refrained from exhibiting the ' vestments.'   But I praised everything, and quite sincerely; and we parted, if not fair friends, at least fair foes.   The world found out who was there, and crowded into the church.   They evidently were not Bennett's congregation; however, they capped me very much, wh. pleased Lady Bath, who would drive me, in consequence, round the town in triumph. . . .

After leaving Longleat and spending a couple of days at Fonthill and one in London, Disraeli passed the early part of the autumn, with the exception of a week at Balmoral, as the guest of Lady Chesterfield at Bretby; though he made a short excursion to the Bradfords at their villa on Lake Windermere, and would have visited them at Weston in October but for the death of Lord Forester, the brother of the two ladies. Although he was seemingly not attacked by gout till the middle of September, his letters suggest that he was in poor health and in poor spirits.

To Lady Bradford.

10, DOWNING STREET, *Aug.* 14.—. . . You seem surprised I went to Fonthill. I went for distraction. I cannot bear being alone, and when I join others, I am wearied. I do not think there is really any person much unhappier than I am, and not fantastically so. Fortune, fashion, fame, even power, may increase, and do heighten, happiness, but they cannot create it. Happiness can only spring from the affections. I am alone, with nothing to sustain me, but, occasionally, a little sympathy on paper, and that grudgingly. It is a terrible lot, almost intolerable. . . .

BRETBY PARK, *Aug.* 20.—. . . I came down here very much out of sorts, but the kindly methodical life here—the regular hours, the tranquillity of the sylvan scene, and a delightful companion, who has the sweetness and simplicity of a flower, have combined much to restore me. And increased tone brings that serenity of mind, wh. ought to content one, instead of those romantic thoughts that tear the heart and spirit, wh. ought to vanish with youth, and certainly ought not to be cherished by any being who pays rates and taxes.

Southey wrote a very remarkable poem on the falls of Lodore, wh. imitates the rush and crash and splashing and hissing of the waters. It is difficult to find his poems anywhere nowadays, but, if they can be found, I should think it must be at Windermere. Consult John Manners anent.

Southey was a poet, but he could not condense or finish. He was gifted with a fatal facility. He was in fact an improvisatore. And this is strange, because as a prose writer he is almost without a rival, and has none superior to him in polish and precision. . . .

Bretby Park, *Aug.* 21.—[My letters] are weak, inconsistent, incoherent, and, without meaning it, insincere: the reflex of a restless, perplexed, hampered, and most unhappy spirit. . . . Your sister has thrice, in five days, drawn me aside, to ask if anything had happened, I looked so unhappy. . . .[1]

To Anne Lady Chesterfield.

St. Catherine's, Windermere, *Aug.* 30.—. . . I visited with interest, the scene of Wordsworth's life and poetry. I shall recur to his, perhaps, not hitherto sufficiently appreciated volumes with much interest after gazing on the mountains, the woods, and waterfalls of Rydal.

All has gone here, on the whole, pretty well: Selina charming, tho' fitful, and my Lord absolutely friendly.

Whatever happens to me in the world I shall always love you.

To Lady Bradford.

Bretby, *Sept.* 1.—My journey was not very successful, for my train was always too late to fit in with Bradshaw, so I had to wait an hour at Staff[ord] and at Lichfield. But after all, this is not a mischance that ever much disturbs me: one can always think. I got in good time, and they were congratulating me on having a quiet dinner (wh. by the bye I wanted), . . . when, lo and behold, as we were about to sit down to table, Mr. Scott[2] in an affected whisper, audible to everybody, and looking very pompous, announced a messenger from the foreign office on very urgent business. I was obliged to go out; and found matters as he described. Had I been at Weston or Windermere I don't know whether the secret wd. have been kept exactly, for I have told you one or two before this, and I know the Master of the Horse to be very discreet; but here things are different. I read the despatch, and found it utterly impossible to reply to it offhand: it required, however urgent, much deliberation. So I made up my mind to sleep upon it, and send a telegram for the moment. But then I had to telegraph in cypher, and you know what that is, from George Paget, who was a whole morning over one line. However I managed it at last, and tried to return with a smiling and easy mien to my dinner. But, hungry as I was, having touched nothing but my St. Catherine's

---

[1] In answer to this letter, it appears that Lady Bradford called Disraeli ' a humbug.'

[2] Lady Chesterfield's servant.

sandwich, and that before noon, my appetite was nothing to the ravenous eyes of Lady A.,[1] who exhausted all her manœuvres to obtain an inkling of what had occurred.

I had a good dinner all the same, and indulged in some good claret, convincing myself it was a wine favorable to judgment: then we had a rubber which I lost as usual, and my wits were so woolgathering that it was fortunate I did not revoke, as I did at Weston.

I slept very well till five o'ck., when I woke, but with my mind quite clear, and what, at night, had seemed difficulties were all removed; so I opened my shutters and wrote my despatch in pencil in bed. By the time my fire was lit, it was done, and I had nothing left to do but to write it in ink with very few alterations; and the messenger was off by the very earliest train. . . .

You will say 'Here is much ado about nothing. Who cares for his despatches and his telegrams ?'

That is true in a certain sense; but everything interests, if you are interested in a person. I assure you I like to know very much how you are all getting on. You need never want matter in writing to me if you will only give me a bulletin of the sayings and doings of your circle—the one, after all, wh. interests me more than any other family in England. . . .

To Anne Lady Chesterfield.

[AT BRETBY] *Sept.* 2.—A piece of great social news ! Don't tell them directly, but make them guess a little. A member of the late Government, of high rank, and great wealth, has gone over to the Holy Father !

Who is it ? No less a personage than the Marq. of Ripon, K.G. ! ! !

Shall not be able to come down to breakfast, as bag very heavy, and if I don't work now, I shall not get my walk with my dear companion.

From Bretby Disraeli went for his second and final visit to Balmoral, stopping for a week-end with the John Manners at Birnam on the way.

To Lady Bradford.

BALMORAL CASTLE. *Sept.* 10.—. . . The Faery here is more than kind; she opens her heart to me on all subjects, and shows me her most secret and most interesting corre-

---

[1] Maria Lady Ailesbury, a friend both of Lady Chesterfield's and of Disraeli's, was generally known in society as 'Lady A.'

spondence. She asked me here for a week, but she sent to-day to say that she hoped I wd. not so limit my visit, and that I would remain at least to the end of next week, and so on. . . .

The Derbys dined here yesterday, and with Princess Beatrice and Lady Churchill made up the 8[1]. . . . The Dss. [of Edinburgh] was full of life,[2] asked the Queen at dinner whether she had read *Lothair*. The Queen answered, I thought, with happy promptitude, that she was the first person who had read it. Then the Duchess asked her Gracious Majesty, whether she did not think Theodora a divine character; the Queen looked a little perplexed and grave. It wd. have been embarrassing, had the Dss. not gone on, rattling away, and begun about Mr. Phœbus and the 'two Greek ladies,' saying that for her part she shd. like to live in a Greek isle. . . .

Sept. 12. —. . . I have not been well here, and had it not been for Sir William Jenner, might have been very ill. All is ascribed to my posting in an open carriage from Dunkeld to Balmoral, but the day was delicious, and I was warmly clothed and never apprehended danger. I felt queer on Wednesday, tho' I dined with the Queen on that day. Thursday Sir William kept me to my room. I have never left the Castle once. On Friday I paid Prince Leopold a visit, who wanted to see me, and, later in the day, the Queen sent for me, and I had a very long and most interesting audience. She told me that Sir Wm. had reported to her that I had no fever, and therefore she had sent for me; otherwise she wd. have paid me a visit. She opened all her heart and mind to me, and rose immensely in my intellectual estimation. Free from all shyness, she spoke with great animation and happy expression, showed not only perception, but discrimination, of character, and was most interesting and amusing. She said I looked so well that she thought I cd. dine with her.

But when Sir William came home from his drive with P. Leopold and paid me his afternoon visit, he said the symptoms were not at all good; put me on a mustard poultice on the upper part of my back, gave me some other remedies and said I must not think of dining, or of leaving my room. The remedies have been most successful; an incipient congestion of the lung seems quite removed, and he does not doubt of my being able to travel on Tuesday.

[1] The other four being the Queen, the Duke and Duchess of Edinburgh, and Disraeli.

[2] Writing to Lady Chesterfield, Disraeli described the Duchess at dinner on the previous day as 'most lively,' and as breaking through 'all the etiquette of courtly conversation. Even the Queen joined in her vivacity, and evidently is much influenced by her.'

This morning the Queen paid me a visit in my bedchamber. What do you think of that ? [1]

The G. Duchess [2] is in despair at not seeing me : she is reading Froude, and wanted to talk it over with me   The Derbys also came to see me to-day. . . .

You will understand from all this that I am a sort of prisoner of state, in the tower of a castle; royal servants come in and silently bring me my meals; a royal physician two or three times a day to feel my pulse, etc., and see whether I can possibly endure the tortures that await me.   I am, in short, the man in the Iron Masque. . . .

To Lord Salisbury.

BALMORAL CASTLE, *Sept.* 13.—Being here, I attended to your business at once. . . .

Our royal mistress is well, and looks extremely so.   She takes the greatest interest in the Ripon incident, and is most curious to ascertain, who was the artist, who cooked so dainty a dish.   H.M. believes neither Manning, nor Capel. . . .

The Ld. Chan[cello]r is only a short distance from me, as the crow flies, but a day's journey, from the mountainous ranges.   He wants to see me before I return to the South, but it is difficult.

The Derbys seem quite delighted with Abergeldie and its birchen groves.   Not that the Court see much of them—' they are so devoted to each other.' . . .

From Balmoral Disraeli went back, still unwell, to Bretby, and there on Saturday, September 19, to use his own words, ' fell into the gout, and that very badly.' The attack came in time to prevent his committing a great imprudence.   Zealous to perform his high duties with efficiency, and realising the importance to the Prime Minister of having some first-hand knowledge of a country which, like Ireland, was necessarily so constantly in his mind, he had proposed to spend part of his first vacation after accepting office in a visit to the island.   The arrangement was that he was to arrive in Dublin as the Viceroy's guest on Saturday, October 24, and then visit Killarney, Cork, Waterford, Derry, Giant's Causeway, and Belfast, delivering speeches in the three capital cities,

[1] ' What do you think,' Disraeli wrote to Lady Chesterfield, ' of receiving your Sovereign in slippers and a dressing-gown ?'
[2] **The Duchess of Edinburgh, who was a Russian Grand Duchess.**

and only returning to England just in time for the autumn Cabinets in the middle of November. It was an anxious undertaking for a man in his seventieth year, full of gout, and therefore needing rest between two arduous sessions instead of a wearisome progress of this kind; and the nearer the date approached, the more serious the difficulties appeared. 'What am I to speak about, as politics are out of the question?' he wrote to Corry on September 10 from Balmoral. A few days later Derby, with sound common sense, wrote to dissuade his friend and leader from carrying the mad scheme through.

From Lord Derby.

ABERGELDIE, ABERDEEN, *Sept.* 15, 1874.—More I think of your Irish tour, less I like it: and for various reasons.

First you are overdoing yourself. No man can go through two years of such work as yours, leading the H. of C. and all the rest of it, without an interval of complete repose. You are depriving yourself of yours without any strong reason for so doing that I can see: and in the interest of the party and the public, I think you are wrong. We ought to be in for 3 or 4 years, and neither you nor anyone else can keep up the pace at which you have started for that length of time.

Everybody would understand the case and nobody would consider you as either invalided or indolent if you put off your Irish expedition on that ground alone. Indeed a quiet interval is in your position almost necessary in order to consider what shall be proposed to the Cabinet. When Cabinets begin it is too late for any other work than discussion of details.

But, apart from personal reasons, what are you to say to the Irish? Every question in Ireland whether of the past, present or future, is a party question. It is not in the power of man to deal with topics of public interest in such a way as to please Ultramontanes and Orangemen. The moderates are few and feeble—what the press is you know. You must be pressed to do local jobs which you must refuse—to release political prisoners—to give fixity of tenure in land—and to receive deputations suggesting, with the utmost loyalty, some perfectly impracticable modification of Home Rule. You cannot be decently civil to Catholics without offending Protestants, and *vice versa*. The only point upon which both parties agree is the duty of spending more English money on Irish soil.

Your knowledge will fill up the rough outline which I am

drawing of your difficulties.   And why incur them ?   We are
doing very well.   A moderately extensive programme of well-
considered measures will satisfy Parliament for next year.
There is absolutely not a cry of any kind that has attracted
the least public attention of late.   The only strong feeling that
I can trace in the public mind is anti-Catholic feeling: and that
you cannot gratify and may possibly have to run against in
the course of an Irish progress.

Pray excuse unasked advice: though in fact you did partly
ask for it when we met.   If you modify the large programme
which has been marked out for you, is it not worth considering
whether the postponement of the whole affair, leaving hopes
for another year, will not give less offence than the curtail-
ment of parts ?

Derby's reasoning may have shaken Disraeli's purpose;
in any case the gouty attack at Bretby put the Irish
visit out of the question.   The Queen expressed a hope
that he might 'some other year be able to go there, when
he is quite well, for it would do good '; but the opportunity never recurred.   Consequently Disraeli never set
foot in Ireland; Gladstone was once there, for three
weeks, in October, 1877.   To those who reflect upon the
prolonged contentions of the rivals over Irish policy and
the dominating hold which Ireland obtained over Gladstone's later career, these facts must seem incredible,
were they not true.

To Lady Bradford.

(*In pencil.*) BRETBY PARK, *Monday* [*Sept.* 21].—I am too
ill to write even to you.   A severe attack of gout has been
the culmination of my trials, and tho' it has removed, or
greatly mitigated, dangerous symptoms, it adds to my suffering
and my prostration.   The dear angel here is more than kindness, but that only makes me more feel what an enormous
outrage on her hospitality is the whole affair. . . .

I sit in silence quite unable to read, musing over the wondrous 12 months that have elapsed since this time last year.
I have had at least my dream.   And if my shattered energies
never rally, wh. considering that these attacks, more or less,
have been going on for 6 months, is what I must be prepared
for, I have at any rate reached the pinnacle of power, and
gauged the sweetest and deepest affections of the heart.
Adieu !

It was nearly a fortnight before Disraeli was able to be moved, and then, after passing through town to consult Sir William Gull, he went home to remain quietly at Hughenden till the November Cabinets were approaching.

To Anne Lady Chesterfield.

HUGHENDEN MANOR, *Oct.* 23.—. . . There is no repose. The Court is a department in itself.

However the Ministry are in great favor. The adieu of the Queen, after the Council, to the Duke of Richmond, was 'I wish you to remain in as long as you possibly can.' He had quickness eno' to reply 'That is exactly, Madam, what I and my colleagues intend to do.'

This letter *really* must be for your own eye and ear. . . .

To Lady Bradford.

HUGHENDEN MANOR, *Oct.* 26.—. . . I like him [M. Corry] very much, better than any man: but, as a rule and except upon business, male society is not much to my taste. Indeed I want to see only one person, whom I never see, and I want to see her always. Otherwise I would rather be alone. Solitude has no terrors for me, and when I am well, has many delights. But one can't be always reading and thinking; one wants sympathy, and the inspiration of the heart. . . .

I have not seen Chas. Greville's book, but have read a good deal of it. It is a social outrage. And committed by one who was always talking of what he called 'perfect gentlemen.' I don't think he can figure now in that category. I knew him intimately. He was the vainest being—I don't limit myself to man—that ever existed; and I don't forget Cicero and Lytton Bulwer;[1] but Greville wd. swallow garbage, and required it. Offended selflove is a key to most of his observations. He lent me a volume of his MS. once to read; more modern than these; I found, when he was not scandalous, he was prolix and prosy—a clumsy, wordy writer. The loan was made *à propos* of the character of Peel, which I drew in George Bentinck's *Life*, and which, I will presume to say, tho' you may think me as vain as Greville for saying so, is the only thing written about Peel wh. has any truth or stuff in it. Greville was not displeased with it, and as a reward,

---

[1] In the corresponding letter of the same date to Lady Chesterfield this phrase takes the more clear-cut form: 'I have read Cicero, and was intimate with Lytton Bulwer.'

and a treat, told me that he wd. confide to me his character
of Peel, and he gave me the sacred volume, wh. I bore with
me, with trembling awe, from Bruton St. to Gros[veno]r Gate.
If ever it appears, you, who have taste for style and expression,
will, I am sure, agree with me that, as a portrait painter,
Greville is not a literary Vandyke or Reynolds: a more
verbose, indefinite, unwieldy affair, without a happy expression, never issued from the pen of a fagged subordinate of the
daily press.[1]

With regard to myself, what I am suffering from is not
gout, but incipient affection in my throat, tho' I doubt not
real gout is at the bottom of it all.   I have more confidence
in Leggatt than the other gentlemen you mention.   L. says
I ought to go to Buxton, or at least to the sea, and so on, and
not live, as I am doing, among decomposing woods.   That
is very true, and I have generally managed to avoid the fall
of the leaf.   But the total absence of all comfort or comforts,
that one encounters at an hotel, countervails the happier
atmosphere.   One must be at home; and I am going to town,
where I am not surrounded by mighty beeches brown with
impending fate, and limes of amber light, and chestnuts of
green and gold—and every now and then an awful sou'-wester
that brings, in whirling myriads, their beauties to the ground.

In the meantime, I am like Crusoe on his isle, taking infinite
delight in many silent companions.   My mittens are a ceaseless charm. I fear they will wear out sooner than you expected,
for they are never off my hands.   They keep the hand warm
and yet free.   My aneroid is at my side at this moment; not on
my dressing-table, as originally projected, but my writing-
table.   I manage it now with the same facility, as Herschel
or Ld. Rosse did their colossal telescopes.   If, in my loneliness,
one is tempted sometimes to feel or fancy that some characters
and things we remember are merely a dream, my pencil case
in my waistcoat pocket proves their reality, and if I still
doubted, something is singing, all day long, which is called
' Selina.' [2]

Disraeli's verdict on the Greville Memoirs was endorsed
with great vigour from Balmoral.   It is not surprising
that the Queen should have been horrified at the relentless

[1] Greville's character of Peel appears in Part II., Vol. III., ch. 31, of the
Memoirs : Disraeli's character of Peel appears in *Lord George Bentinck*,
ch. 17, and is quoted in Vol. II., ch. 11, of this biography.   The loan of
part of Greville's MS. to Disraeli is mentioned in *Memoirs*, Part II.,
Vol. III., ch. 32.

[2] The mittens, aneroid, pencil case, and singing bird were, of course, all
presents from Lady Bradford.

exposure of the vices and foibles of her royal uncles contained in the first part, which was all that was published in 1874.   But Reeve, the editor, was quite impenitent under royal and Ministerial displeasure.   Sir Arthur Helps, Disraeli told Lady Bradford, read to Reeve some passages of a letter from the Queen.   ' The Queen said, " the book degraded royalty."   " Not at all," rejoined Reeve, " it elevates it, by the contrast it offers between the present and the defunct state of affairs," and so on, fighting every point with smiling impudence !'

From Queen Victoria.

BALMORAL, *Nov.* 12,[1] '74.—The Queen thanks Mr. Disraeli for his letters received to-day. She hopes that he is quite well and taking care of himself. But she would strongly advise him not to accustom himself to very hot rooms, for nothing gives people more cold than sitting over a large fire and then going out.

The Queen omitted in her last letter saying how *horrified* and *indignant* she is at this dreadful and really scandalous book of Mr. C. Greville's, who seems to have put down all the gossip which he collected and which, as we well know from the experience of the present day, is totally unreliable. His indiscretion, indelicacy, ingratitude towards friends, betrayal of confidence and shameful disloyalty towards his Sovereign make it *very important* that the book should be severely censured and discredited. The tone in which he speaks of royalty, is unlike anything which one sees in history even, of people hundreds of years ago, and is most reprehensible.

Mr. Reeve however is almost as much to blame considering that he is a servant of the Crown and ought never to have consented to publish such an abominable book.

To Queen Victoria.

WHITEHALL GARDENS, *Nov.* 10,[1] 1874.—Mr. Disraeli with his humble duty to your Majesty:

He thinks your Majesty's critique on the Greville publication, ought to be printed. It condenses the whole case—no, not the whole—' indiscretion, indelicacy, ingratitude.' The book is a social outrage, but what is most flagrant is, that it should be prepared, and published, by two servants of the Crown !

---

[1] There must be some mistake in the dates of these letters. The second is clearly the answer to the first.

Mr. Disraeli has been revolving in his mind, how some public reprobation of such conduct could be manifested. For this purpose he has wanted to confer with various people— and, unhappily, he has never been able to leave his house since he arrived in town, so he has not been able to go to clubs, or talk with men, who, as Dr. Johnson used to describe them, are ' clubable.' . . .

Mr. Disraeli humbly thanks your Majesty for your Majesty's ever gracious interest in his health.

He assures your Majesty he endeavors to obey all your Majesty's commands in this respect.   He never sits over a fire, and he has a thermometer in every room, with instructions never to exceed 63.   He fears he is suffering from a gouty habit, which has broken out late in life, but which, now understood, may be conquered with care and diet.

What details for a servant of the Crown to place before a too gracious mistress!   His cheek burns with shame.   It seems almost to amount to petty treason.

Disraeli had a further attack of gout in Whitehall Gardens in the early part of November, and it was with considerable difficulty that he managed to appear at the Guildhall banquet and to hold the autumn Cabinets. At Guildhall he vindicated, against Gladstone's scepticism, the existence and indeed inevitability of the Conservative working man.

I have been alarmed recently by learning, from what I suppose is the highest Liberal authority, that a Conservative Government cannot endure, because it has been returned by Conservative working men, and a Conservative working man is an anomaly.   We have been told that a working man cannot be Conservative, because he has nothing to conserve—he has neither land nor capital; as if there were not other things in the world as precious as land and capital ! . . .   There are things in my opinion even more precious than land and capital, and without which land and capital themselves would be of little worth.   What, for instance is land without liberty ? And what is capital without justice ?   The working classes of this country have inherited personal rights which the nobility of other nations do not yet possess.   Their persons and their homes are sacred.   They have no fear of arbitrary arrests or domiciliary visits.[1]   They know that the adminis-

[1] It was suggested that Disraeli was indirectly reflecting upon Bismarck, who was employing methods of this kind in his quarrel with Count Arnim, German Ambassador in Paris.   Disraeli thought it worth while to dis-

tration of law in this country is pure, and that it is no respecter of individuals or classes. They know very well that their industry is unfettered, and that by the law of this country they may combine to protect the interests of labour; and they know that though it is open to all of them to serve their Sovereign by land or sea, no one can be dragged from his craft or his hearth to enter a military service which is repugnant to him. Surely these are privileges worthy of being preserved! Can we therefore be surprised that a nation which possesses such rights should wish to preserve them? And if that be the case, is it wonderful that the working classes are Conservative?

The exertion of holding the Cabinets was too much for Disraeli, and in the end of November he had another attack, almost as severe as that which had prostrated him at Bretby.

To Lady Bradford.

2, WHITEHALL GARDENS, *Nov. 23.* — . . . I called in Jenner on Saturday, suffering much in my chest, I believe from the fogs, wh. have been very bad here. He insisted on Bournemouth, but I had intended first to pay a little visit to you all, wh. wd. have been a consolation in my loneliness; but last night attacked by gout in my right foot, and cannot move.

If you write to me sometimes, when you have time or inclination, I shall be grateful: but I do not press it or expect it—hardly think it reasonable to wish it. I can make no return. Long suffering—for this has gone on more or less for many months—and exhaustion, and some chagrin of the heart, have done their work on me. Our correspondence has always been so essentially spontaneous, that I do not wish it to degenerate into forced sentences or the bulletins of an invalid, which, I know, you do not like, and there we resemble each other I cannot write; all my spring is gone. . . .

(*In pencil.*) *Dec. 1.*—Amid my daily reveries and nightly dreams, it seemed to me I had only one purpose—to write to you, and try to convey to you some conclusions, at wh. I had arrived, as to this strange illness, wh. has harassed me, more or less, for nine months, and now has reached its climax. But when I take up my pencil (your pencil), my mind deserts me, and I am utterly incapable of expressing thought or

---

claim this interpretation by a *communiqué* in *The Times*: whereupon he was absurdly accused by the Liberals of subserviency to Bismarck. 'No man in his senses,' wrote Delane to Corry, 'will blame the Premier for removing a cause for irritation he had not intended to excite.'

feeling when, only a moment before, the thoughts seemed so
deep, and the feelings so just and vivid.

But I can be silent no more, if I write only to thank you
for your letters. They have always had for me an ineffable
charm; being both gay and affectionate, like yr. own happy
disposition.

Mine have been different: unreasonable, morose, exacting,
discontented. I feel all this now. I will not defend them.
I wd. rather leave their vindication to your seraphic idiosyncrasy.

What is exactly to become of me, I don't know. Whether
I can rally must be doubtful. To get out of this *repaire* is a
necessity, but how I can bear travelling for hours when writing
this makes me fall back exhausted on my pillow, I cannot
comprehend.

After this last attack Disraeli went, on the recommendation of the Queen as well as of his physicians, to try what
Her Majesty called 'the very salubrious air of Bournemouth' for the midwinter weeks. The physicians declared
that the sea-air would gradually 'burn the gout poison'
out of his blood. Unfortunately, it was a particularly
bitter season. 'How damnable,' wrote Corry on December
19, 'that we should be having the most inclement winter
of the decade!' 'The cold is intense here,' Disraeli
replied: 'deep snow, and I can't get my rooms up to 60.'
Nevertheless the change was successful. He was decidedly better when he left Bournemouth early in January
for Crichel; and he was able to tell Rose on January 15:
'I am pretty well; not quite; but much better than I was
any day last year.'

To Queen Victoria.

B-mouth, *Dec.* 10, 1874.—Mr. Disraeli with his humble
duty to your Majesty:

He cannot refrain from thanking your Majesty for your
gracious inquiries as to his health.

It is difficult to decide on atmospherical influences under a
week, but he thinks he can venture to say, that the visit to
this place, which your Majesty yourself deigned to recommend, will turn out a great success.

The weather has been too variable; one day it was like the
Corniche, so soft and sunny, the Isle of Wight looming, and

yet not distant, and the waters glittering in the bay-like coast.
But storm has prevailed, and nothing but the bending pines
could have withstood its violence. Mr. Disraeli is on the cliff,
which is a great advantage to him.

He has received the Prince's *Life*,[1] which he is reading with
much interest, particularly as it reaches a period, when he
himself began to take some part in public affairs. Much
of the earlier part he was familiar with from General Grey's
volume. This, however, will be all fresh to the public, and
Mr. Disraeli has no doubt the work will produce a deep, a
pleasing, and an enduring impression. . . .

Dec. 18, 1874. — . . . He began the *Life* towards the
end, being interested in the new matter; then he turned to
other parts to compare the different treatment in the
present, and in the volume compiled by General Grey.
Then he got so interested in the treatment of the subject,
that he began the work regularly from the beginning, and he
can truly say, that it is a most able book, and one that will
endure. There is in the general treatment of the theme an
amenity worthy of the subject. Your Majesty most truly
and justly observes, that the contrast between Mr. Martin's
volume and a too notorious publication is striking; but it is
also beneficial. This book will rally the public tone. After
the turbulent and callous malignity of the Greville Memoirs,
one feels as if an angel had passed through the chamber.
He may be invisible, but one feels, as it were, the rustling of
his wings.

To Lady Bradford.

2, WHITEHALL GARDENS, *Jan.* 30, 1875.—. . . I am going
to Hughenden to-day with Monty; and on Tuesday I am going
to Osborne, and to stay there till the Council is held on the
4th. The *Alberta* is to be placed at my disposal, wh. can go
alongside the pier, so I am not to get into an open boat, and
there is a cabin closed in on the deck, where I am to sit during
the passage.

Mr. Corry is to accompany me, and I am forbidden to make
any change in my usual evening costume, as it might give
me cold.

Everything is to be made comfortable for me, and it is hoped
I may stay for two days, in order that I may rest, and, having
the *Alberta*, I may choose my own time.

What do you think of this? And when will you be so
kind to me? Fancy Monty a recognised courtier! The
first private secretary whose existence has been acknowledged
by royal lips. . . .

[1] Sir Theodore Martin's *Life of the Prince Consort*.

It was while he was at Bournemouth that Disraeli
completed the arrangement for one of the most picturesque
features of his first year of office—the offer to Thomas
Carlyle of the G.C.B. and a pension. He had been corresponding with Derby in the autumn as to what could
be done to honour men of science. ' I wish,' he wrote
on October 9, ' we had some comprehensive order like
the Legion of Honor. I am sorry that society persists
in cheapening a simple knighthood. It satisfied Sir
Isaac Newton and Sir Walter Raleigh. Would it satisfy
Stokes?'[1] The Government gratified the scientific world by
promoting the Arctic Expedition under Sir George Nares.
' Can we do anything for Literature?' wrote Derby on
November 28. He suggested that Tennyson and Carlyle
were the only conspicuous names; and in pressing
Carlyle's claims mentioned that he was, ' for whatever
reason, most vehement against Gladstone. . . . Anything that could be done for him would be a really good
political investment. What it should be you know best.'
Disraeli caught at the idea; he realised the splendour of
Carlyle's genius and the reproach of its total neglect by
the State; and his imagination supplied the unique distinction[2] which might not unfitly be offered to the *doyen*
of English letters.

To Queen Victoria.

B-MOUTH, *Dec.* 12, 1874.—Mr. Disraeli with his humble
duty to your Majesty:

As your Majesty was graciously pleased to say, that your
Majesty would sometimes aid him with your advice, he presumes to lay before your Majesty a subject on which he should
much like to be favored with your Majesty's judgment.

Your Majesty's Government is now in favor with the
scientific world. The Arctic Expedition, and some small
grants which may be made to their favorite institutions, will
secure their sympathy, which is not to be despised.

Can nothing be done for Literature?

Eminent literary men are so few, that there would be no

[1] Professor George Gabriel Stokes, the mathematician and physicist,
1819–1903. He was created a baronet in 1889.
[2] The Order of Merit was not founded until the Coronation of King
Edward VII.

trouble as to choice, if any compliment in the way of honor was contemplated. Mr. Disraeli knows only of two authors, who are especially conspicuous at this moment: Tennyson and Carlyle. He has no personal knowledge of either, and their political views are, he apprehends, opposed to those of your Majesty's Government, but that is not to be considered for a moment.

He has an impression, that Mr. Tennyson could sustain a baronetcy, and would like it. Sir Robert Peel offered that distinction to Southey.

Mr. Carlyle is old, and childless, and poor; but he is very popular and respected by the nation. There is no K.C.B. vacant. Would a G.C.B. be too much ? It might be combined with a pension, perhaps, not less than your Majesty's royal grandfather conferred on Dr. Johnson, and which that great man cheerfully accepted, and much enjoyed.

These thoughts are humbly submitted to the consideration of your Majesty, with, Mr. Disraeli hopes, not too much freedom.

The Queen, in Disraeli's words, 'entered into the spirit of the affair'; and he conveyed the offer to Carlyle in a letter conceived in the grand manner, to the composition of which, it is evident from the interlined draft found among his papers, he had devoted considerable labour. As a proffer of State recognition by a literary man in power to a literary man in (so to speak) permanent opposition, it would be difficult to excel it either in delicacy or in dignity. Fully to appreciate its magnanimity, it must be remembered that Carlyle had always treated Disraeli as a 'conscious juggler,' 'a superlative Hebrew conjurer.' 'He is the only man,' Carlyle wrote to John Carlyle, 'I almost never spoke of except with contempt; and if there is anything of scurrility anywhere chargeable against me, he is the subject of it; and yet see, here he comes with a pan of hot coals for my guilty head.'

To Thomas Carlyle.

Confidential. BOURNEMOUTH, *Dec.* 27, 1874.—A Government should recognise intellect. It elevates and sustains the tone of a nation. But it is an office which, adequately to fulfil, requires both courage and discrimination, as there is a chance of falling into favoritism and patronising mediocrity, which, instead of elevating the national feeling, would eventually degrade and debase it.

In recommending Her Majesty to fit out an Arctic expedition, and in suggesting other measures of that class, her Government have shown their sympathy with science. I wish that the position of high letters should be equally acknowledged; but this is not so easy, because it is in the necessity of things that the test of merit cannot be so precise in literature as in science.

When I consider the literary world, I see only two living names which, I would fain believe, will be remembered; and they stand out in uncontested superiority. One is that of a poet; if not a great poet, a real one; and the other is your own.

I have advised the Queen to offer to confer a baronetcy on Mr. Tennyson, and the same distinction should be at your command, if you liked it. But I have remembered that, like myself, you are childless, and may not care for hereditary honors. I have therefore made up my mind, if agreeable to yourself, to recommend Her Majesty to confer on you the highest distinction for merit at her command, and which, I believe, has never yet been conferred by her except for direct services to the State. And that is the Grand Cross of the Bath.

I will speak with frankness on another point. It is not well that, in the sunset of life, you should be disturbed by common cares. I see no reason why a great author should not receive from the nation a pension as well as a lawyer and a statesman. Unfortunately the personal power of Her Majesty in this respect is limited; but still it is in the Queen's capacity to settle on an individual an amount equal to a good fellowship, and which was cheerfully accepted and enjoyed by the great spirit of Johnson, and the pure integrity of Southey.

Have the goodness to let me know your feelings on these subjects.

The letter to Tennyson reproduced the phraseology of the early portion of that to Carlyle, though it naturally did not draw a distinction between a 'real' poet and a 'great' one. Both authors refused. Tennyson had had a similar offer from Gladstone nearly a year before, and explained to both Prime Ministers in succession that he could not accept a baronetcy for himself, but would be grateful if such an honour could be secured for his son. Nine years later the poet was raised to the peerage on Gladstone's recommendation. Carlyle's answer was reported to Derby by Disraeli.

To Lord Derby.

B-MOUTH, *Jan.* 1, '75.—. . . Alas! the Philosopher of Chelsea, tho' evidently delighted with the proposal, and grateful in wondrous sentences, will accept of nothing—' Titles of honor, of all degrees, are out of keeping with the tenor of my poor life,' and as for money—' after years of rigorous and frugal, but, thank God, never degrading poverty,' it has become ' amply abundant, even super-abundant in this later time.'

Nevertheless the proposal is ' magnanimous and noble, without example in the history of governing persons with men of letters' and a great deal more in the same highly-sublimated Teutonic vein.

I have not received any reply from Tennyson, but this is a secondary affair.

I think of getting away from this on the 4th and shall stay a week at Crichel and then to Westminster. Northcote is with me for a day or two, preparing for the Cabinets; and the Ld. Chan[cello]r is a great assistance to me. . . .

For the moment Carlyle recognised that he had mis-judged Disraeli. Lady Derby, whom Carlyle credited, perhaps rightly, with the origination of the idea, wrote to Disraeli on January 15: ' I saw old Mr. Carlyle to-day, and he scarcely knew how to be grateful enough for the mark of attention you had paid him. I assure you it was quite touching to see and hear his high appreciation of the offer.' But, save that he continued to prefer Disraeli to Gladstone, the feeling was transient; and when, a few years later, he dissented from Ministerial policy in the East, he reverted once again to his earlier language, and was not ashamed to talk of the Prime Minister as ' a cursed old Jew, not worth his weight in cold bacon,'[1] ' an accursed being, the worst man who ever lived.'[2]

[1] *Life of James Macdonell*, p. 379.
[2] *Some Hawarden Letters*, p. 15.

CHAPTER X.

Social Reform.

1874-1875.

The main Government programme of Social Reform was definitely entered upon in the second session of the Parliament. ' In legislation,' wrote Disraeli to Hicks Beach in December, 1874, 'it is not merely reason and propriety which are to be considered, but the temper of the time.' The time was propitious. Though there were disquieting symptoms underlying the situation abroad, the surface was undisturbed, and there was no immediate reason to anticipate any foreign complication; while at home the defeated Opposition showed as yet no sign of cohesion or recovery. Social improvement and not revolutionary change was what people demanded; and, to give effect to this desire, Labour members, Alexander Macdonald and Thomas Burt, the forerunners of a mighty political force, had been returned for the first time to Parliament. The general tendency of the projected legislation was settled, on Disraeli's initiative, early in the history of the Government; and as the autumn Cabinets of 1874 approached, the Prime Minister asked his principal colleagues for further suggestions. The letter which he wrote to Salisbury is typical.

To Lord Salisbury.

HUGHENDEN MANOR, *Oct.* 12, 1874.—I hardly know, whether you have left your *château sur la Manche,*[1] but doubt not this will reach you, somehow or other.

[1] Salisbury had a villa at Dieppe, where he spent the autumn.

In about a month we ought to commence our November Cabinets. It would be of great service to me, and very agreeable also, if you would favor me, some time previously, and confidentially, with your general views as to our situation, and any suggestions you can make as to our future course.

I saw the French Ambassador,[1] as I passed thro' town—an intimate acquaintance, and more, of forty years. He is, as you know, experienced in English politics. He said, ' In your internal situation, I do not see a single difficulty.' I trust he is correct.

The position of affairs in Ireland must, however, demand our attention. The group of laws, called the Coercion Acts, are on the eve of expiring—but we could scarcely arrive at a definite resolution on the subject until the meeting of Parliament.

Is there any question connected with home affairs that occurs to you, wh. has not been touched on in our councils ? I believe, that Mr. Secy. X[2] is working at a Dwellings Bill. . . .

The Cabinets were very harmonious, the only measure, a *remanet* from the past session, which might have caused friction being judiciously shelved in a manner which showed that Salisbury bore no lasting grudge against either chief or colleagues.

To Queen Victoria.

2, WHITEHALL GARDENS, *Nov.* 12, 1874.—Mr. Disraeli with his humble duty to your Majesty :

The Cabinet met to-day, and sate two hours, and did a great deal of work, and all satisfactory.

In the first place, not in order, but in importance, the question of the endowed schools was brought forward, so that there might be no future misconception on the subject.

Lord Salisbury spoke with much moderation and said, that he would be satisfied with a compromise, which Mr. Hardy had suggested in the Cabinet at the end of the session. This was conciliatory, but not satisfactory to those, who deprecated any further legislation at all.

To our great surprise and relief, Mr. Hardy said that he thought it, on the whole, best, not to take any further action in the matter, particularly as there was a new Commission, whose views we ought to become acquainted with.

The Lord Chancellor strongly supported Mr. Hardy, and,

---

[1] The Comte de Jarnac. See Vol. III., p. 172.
[2] R. A. Cross, the Home Secretary.

ROBERT, THIRD MARQUIS OF SALISBURY.

From a portrait at Hughenden.

no one then speaking, Lord Salisbury said, that neither in this, nor any subject, did he wish to urge his views against a majority of the Cabinet, and one apparently unanimous. He was prepared, therefore, to do nothing.

Upon which Lord Derby exclaimed ' Thank God, we have got rid of the only rock a-head !' . . .

Nov 15.—. . . The Cabinet was engaged yesterday in considering the measure for the Improvement of the Dwellings of the People.   This is likely to be a very popular and beneficial measure, but will require great care.   Your Majesty's Ministers must be cautious not to embark in any building speculation : but nothing of this kind is contemplated.   This, and some other measures completing the code of sanitary legislation, took up the whole sitting. . . .

These meetings have been eminently satisfactory : unanimous and friendly, and never the slightest indication of there being two parties in the Cabinet.

The path of the Government was still further smoothed, as the session approached, by Gladstone's definite retirement from the Opposition leadership, and the choice in his place, as leader of the Liberal party in the House of Commons, of a politician of weight and judgment rather than of aggressive force—Lord Hartington, the heir of the Whig house of Cavendish. Disraeli told Lady Chesterfield ' the new joke about the Whigs. . . You know Ld. Derby, *père*, said the Whigs were *dished;* they say now they are Caven*dished*.'

To Lady Bradford.

2, WHITEHALL GARDENS, *Feb.* 2.—. . . The political world was never mo e amusing : I am glad that Harty-Tarty has won the day.   Never was a party in such a position, and, tho' I never would confess it to anybody but yourself, never was a man in a prouder position than myself.   It never happened before, and is not likely to happen again.   Only those who are acquainted with the malignity of Glad[stone] to me thro' a rivalry of 5 and 20 years, can understand this. . .

To Queen Victoria.

2, WHITEHALL GARDENS, *Feb.* 5, 1875, *Friday night.*— Mr. Disraeli with his humble duty to your Majesty :

The House of Commons reassembled to-day, in unusual numbers, the benches on both sides being thronged.

Lord Hartington took his seat at the last moment; ½ past four; and was cheered by both sides. Mr. Forster[1] and your Majesty's humble correspondent were also received by their friends with great cordiality.

The Address was moved by Hon. Edward Stanhope in a speech of striking ability. Instead of a mechanical comment on each paragraph of the Royal Speech, Mr. Stanhope generalised on two great subjects, your Majesty's Colonial Empire, and the Health of your People. He produced a great effect. He commenced by an allusion to the illness of H.R.H. Prince Leopold, and to your Majesty's anxiety, than which few things could be more graceful and felicitous.

The Member for Glasgow, who seconded the Address, unfortunately spoke in the language of his country, and, so, soon lost the House; but all his observations were sensible and acute, and worthy of a descendant of Bailie Nicol Jarvie. The new houses in Glasgow for the artisans, and the polluted state of the famous Clyde, gave him a becoming position in the business of the evening.

Lord Hartington, well-prepared and thoughtful, made a reputable appearance, and the general impression on both sides was favorable to the effort.

Mr. Disraeli closed the debate, as no one would rise, though there had been rumors that Mr. Fitzgerald was about to call the consideration of the House to the contemplated invasion of Holland by Prince Bismarck. The House was in good spirits and good temper, and there seems the prospect of an active, but serene session.

Writing to Lady Chesterfield, Disraeli described Hartington's *début* as leader more familiarly. ' Harty-Tarty did very well; exactly as I expected he would; sensible, dullish, and gentlemanlike. Lowe said, " At last I have heard a proper leader's speech; all good sense, and no earnest nonsense." '

In the favourable atmosphere thus created, the Ministerial programme of social legislation was auspiciously launched. *Sanitas sanitatum, omnia sanitas* had been Disraeli's watchword. ' A policy of sewage,' the Liberals had sniffed in reply. Even if limited to sewage, such a policy was praiseworthy; but, as Disraeli pointed out

[1] W. E. Forster, afterwards Chief Secretary for Ireland, had refused to let his name be submitted in competition with Hartington's for the Liberal leadership.

at the close of the session, sanitary reform, ' that phrase so little understood,' included ' most of the civilising influences of humanity.' Disraeli had given the artisans the vote in 1867. Gladstone had prevailed on them to use it in effecting great political changes in the institutions of the country, and particularly of Ireland. What they really wanted, in Disraeli's opinion, and what in the General Election of 1874 they set themselves to obtain, were better, healthier, more humanising conditions in their own daily life. They wanted sanitary and commodious homes; they wanted regulation of their occupations so as to minimise risk to life and health and to prevent excessive toil for their women and children; they wanted freedom of contract and equality before the law with their employers; they wanted encouragement and security for their savings; they wanted easy access to light and air and all the beneficent influences of nature. These were their principal wants in the sphere of material sanitation; but they had no less need of what may perhaps be called mental and spiritual sanitation—a sphere which Disraeli was little likely to overlook; they wanted the provision of sound education and the enlargement of religious opportunity.

With one conspicuous exception, these direct and obvious needs of the working population had been neglected by the Liberals, still dominated as a party by the doctrines of *laisser faire*. Elementary education, indeed, they had taken comprehensively in hand; but Forster's great Bill would never have passed into law, in view of the bitter hostility of Radicals and Dissenters, had it not received the general support of Disraeli and the Conservatives. The other working-class problem which Gladstone's Ministry had touched, that of the relations between employers and workmen, they had conspicuously failed to solve. In one single session, 1875, Disraeli and his colleagues vigorously attacked the ' condition of the people ' question in three main branches, housing, savings, and relations of master and man, effecting in each case a

striking improvement in the law; and there was none of
the working-class needs enumerated above that was not
to a large extent supplied before the Tory Government
were expelled from office.

The Minister chiefly responsible for this social
legislation was the Home Secretary, Richard Cross, the
shrewd Lancashire lawyer and man of business who
frequently figures in Disraeli's correspondence as 'Mr.
Secy. X '; and, after him, Northcote, the Chancellor
of the Exchequer. The homes of the poor were dealt
with first of all; and an entirely new departure was
made in the Artisans' Dwellings Bill, which for the
first time called in public authorities to remedy the
defects of private dwelling-houses. By its provisions
local authorities in large towns were empowered to remove
existing buildings for sanitary reasons and replace them
by others, the new buildings to be devoted to the use
of artisans. True to his rigid economic doctrine, the
eminent Radical, Fawcett, scoffed at the proposal; and
asked why Parliament should facilitate the housing of
working men and not that of dukes ? But the artisans
themselves and the public at large welcomed this honest
attempt to deal with the rookeries which disgraced our
urban civilisation, and which made decent life almost
impossible for those who dwelt in them. When excessive
demands for compensation impeded the working of the
scheme, the Government passed in 1879 an Amending Bill
providing that, if overcrowding had created a nuisance,
compensation should be fixed on the value of the house
after abatement of the nuisance, so that grasping and
callous owners should not profit by their misdeeds.

Savings were promoted and secured by a Friendly
Societies Bill, in Northcote's charge. This struck a
mean between the extremes of too great State interference
and of insufficient protection. It left the Societies a
wide measure of self-management, but insured the
adoption of sound rules, effective audit, and rates of payment sufficient to maintain solvency. It established

the Friendly Societies, and with them the people's savings,
on a satisfactory basis.

But the most important legislation of the session
dealt with the relation of master and man.   Hitherto
the workman had been severely handicapped in his contentions with his employer about wages and conditions
of service by two rules of law coming down from a state
of society antecedent to the industrial epoch.   In the
first place, breach of contract by the workman was regarded, and punished, as a criminal offence, while the
employer in a like case was only liable in the civil courts;
and, in the second place, the doctrine of ' conspiracy '
among workmen was applied in such a way as to cover
the normal actions of trade unions, and to bring their
promoters within reach of the criminal law.   By two Bills
which Cross introduced, in pursuance of the report of
the Royal Commission of the previous year, both these
wrongs were righted.   The one made employers and
workmen equal before the law as regards labour contracts, constituting breach of contract merely a civil
offence on the part of a workman as it had always been
on the part of an employer.   The other made ' conspiracy ' as applied to trade disputes no longer a crime,
except when it was for the purpose of committing what
would be a crime if done by one person.   These two Acts,
said a Trade Union Manual of Labour Laws of the day,
were the charter of the social and industrial freedom of
the working classes; and the Labour member, Alexander
Macdonald, in the House, and the Labour Congress
formally in the autumn, thanked the Government
warmly for passing them.

The Acts which have been already described were
by no means the whole crop garnered by the Government
in this fertile session of constructive social legislation.
The interests of agricultural tenants were not forgotten,
but Disraeli himself piloted a Bill through the House of
Commons by which the tenant obtained compensation for
unexhausted improvements, a presumption of law being

created in his favour, while at the same time freedom of contract between landlord and tenant was preserved. Moreover, the protection of merchant seamen from the dangers of unseaworthy ships was undertaken in circumstances to which we shall recur. Finally, Cross in this same session consolidated and improved the whole sanitary code in the Public Health Act—the foundation on which all subsequent amendment in detail has been built.

After 1875 there was never again, during the lifetime of the Government, a session untroubled by serious foreign or imperial complications; but, though the pace was necessarily slower, steady progress was made throughout with social reform. The greatest and most important work of all was to put the coping-stone on that edifice of factory legislation which Shaftesbury had gradually reared, with the steady support of Disraeli and of 'Young England,' in the teeth of the bitter opposition of Bright and the Manchester School. In their very first session, 1874, the Government had remedied the wrong done in 1850, when the ten hours' day which Parliament had decreed in 1847 for women and children was for administrative reasons enlarged, in face of strong opposition by Disraeli and John Manners, to a ten-and-a-half hours' day.[1] Fifty-six hours a week, or ten hours on five weekdays and six on Saturday, was the total allowed by the Act of 1874; and even this modification was opposed by the individualist Fawcett, and, in the division lobby, by 79 Liberals. Then in 1878 the whole intricate series of factory laws were brought under review, improved, and codified by a Consolidation Act, of which Shaftesbury spoke in the Lords with unbounded satisfaction. He said that he was lost in wonder at the amount of toil, of close investigation, and of perseverance involved in its preparation; two millions of people in this country would bless the day when Cross was appointed Home Secretary. Nor were the Factory Acts the only measures passed by this Government ameliorating the circum-

[1] See Vol. III., p. 254.

stances of labour. Hosiery manufacture was brought under the Truck Acts in 1874; provision for inspecting and regulating canal boats was made in 1877; and in 1876 permanent and humane conditions were laid down for merchant shipping.

In these ways the Government effected a notable improvement in the conditions of labour; but it was on the old lines of Shaftesbury's movement. In another field they broke new ground. They reversed the old policy of the Enclosure Acts, which encouraged the conversion of common land into private and therefore presumably productive occupation; and, in view of the rapid development of the urban population and the necessity of securing for it the enjoyment of grass and light and air, prevented by an Act of 1876 any further enclosure save where it would be a public as well as a private benefit, and promoted free access to commons and their use as public playgrounds. In a similar spirit, in 1878, Ministers secured, by the Epping Forest Act, the unenclosed portion of that wild tract on the verge of East London to the use of the public for ever. In these acts they were putting into effect a policy in which Mr. Shaw Lefevre, who (as Lord Eversley) is still with us, and Henry Fawcett, so often a foe to Disraeli's social legislation, were pioneers; but both these reformers opposed the Enclosure Bill, because it was not, in their opinion, sufficiently drastic. With the like object of preserving the bounty of nature free and uncontaminated for the people's enjoyment Ministers passed in 1876 the Rivers Pollution Act, absolutely prohibiting the introduction of solid matter into rivers, securing them from further pollution by sewage, and imposing upon manufacturers the liability to render harmless the liquid flowing from their works. Here, as so often in their sanitary legislation, the strongest opposition with which Ministers met was from an eminent Radical—in this instance Dilke.

While passing these measures of material sanitation,

the Government in no way neglected the mental and spiritual health of the people. Indeed, their record in the promotion of education was a substantial one. In 1876 they widely extended the benefit of elementary education by a Bill amending Forster's Act of 1870; in 1877 they reformed by the agency of statutory commission the Universities of Oxford and Cambridge, making the revenues of the Colleges more available for educational purposes: while in 1878 and 1879 they materially improved Irish education—university, secondary, and elementary— first, by establishing an examining and degree-giving Royal University to meet in some degree the claims of the Roman Catholics; next, by taking a million from the Irish Church fund to encourage secondary education by means of exhibitions to successful students and of grants to managers of efficient schools; and finally by establishing out of the same fund a proper system of pensions for national school teachers. In the sphere of spiritual sanitation, besides the respect for the religious needs of the people which a critical body of Dissenters and secularists in Parliament found only too clearly expressed in the terms of the English educational Bills, the Government encouraged the Church of England to extend her usefulness by extending her episcopate as advocated by Disraeli himself in 1864; passing Bills for the creation of new dioceses of St. Albans and Truro in 1875 and 1876, and a more general Bill in 1878, under which no fewer than four additional sees, Liverpool, Newcastle, Wakefield, and Southwell, were authorised. It was the greatest ecclesiastical reform since the Reformation, said Tait, the Archbishop of Canterbury, in the House of Lords.

Such in general scope was the code of social and sanitary legislation which Disraeli's great Ministry established for the people of this country. It took the practical pressing needs of the working population one by one, and found a remedy for them, without inflicting hardship on any other class, or affecting our historical institutions in any way, save to strengthen their hold on popular affections.

'The palace is not safe, when the cottage is not happy,' Disraeli had said at a Wynyard Horticultural Show in 1848; and he did his best in the 1874-1880 Ministry to make the one safe by making the other happy. Well might Alexander Macdonald tell his constituents in 1879, 'The Conservative party have done more for the working classes in five years than the Liberals have in fifty.' The work then done has had of course to be extended and supplemented in many respects, but in its main out-lines it has stood the test of time. The aspirations of *Sybil* and 'Young England,' the doctrines in which Disraeli had 'educated' his party for thirty years, the principles laid down in the great speeches of 1872, were translated into legislative form; it was Tory democracy in action. Gorst, who, owing to his position as party organiser, was in close touch with Disraeli during these years, has expounded in an impressive passage[1] what he understood the domestic policy of his 'ancient master' to be.

The principle of Tory democracy is that all government exists solely for the good of the governed; that Church and King, Lords and Commons, and all other public institutions are to be maintained so far, and so far only, as they promote the happiness and welfare of the common people; that all who are entrusted with any public function are trustees, not for their own class, but for the nation at large; and that the mass of the people may be trusted so to use electoral power, which should be freely conceded to them, as to support those who are promoting their interests. It is democratic because the welfare of the people is its supreme end; it is Tory because the inst tutions of the country are the means by which the end is to be attained.

It is a proof of Disraeli's greatness, and of the sound-ness of his conception, that the stamp printed by him on Tory policy has persisted, though it has sometimes been obscured by accretions of class and party interest. Gorst, indeed, whose relations with his party became increasingly uncomfortable until he finally quitted it,

[1] In a letter in *The Times* of Feb. 6, 1907.

held that only Randolph Churchill and his immediate comrades carried on the Tory democratic tradition. This tradition was perhaps not the aspect of Disraeli's work that specially appealed to his successor, Salisbury. But circumstances drove Salisbury into a close alliance with Chamberlain and Chamberlain's school of social reformers, and thus powerfully reinforced all the progressive elements of the Tory party. The result has been, to take only four conspicuous instances, that it is to that party that the people of this country owe the popular reconstitution of county government and of London government, the freeing of elementary education, the final consolidation of the Factory Acts in 1901, and the enormous educational advance of Mr. Balfour's Act of 1902. It may be added that the intimate association of Tory leaders with Labour representatives in Mr. Lloyd George's Ministry is an arrangement which largely carries into effect the ideals of *Sybil*.

It has sometimes been suggested that because Disraeli left the conduct of the Ministerial measures of social reform mainly in the very competent hands of Cross and Northcote, therefore his own share in this beneficent legislation was little or none, and all the credit should be given to his lieutenants. In view of the facts, this is an untenable theory. Disraeli was no *roi fainéant* in his Cabinet; on the contrary, by the testimony both of colleagues and of opponents, he was, in matters which interested him, himself the Government, to a greater degree even than Gladstone had been from 1868 to 1874. But from his first experience of Ministerial leadership in 1852 he had adopted the practice of leaving his colleagues to manage by themselves the conduct of Bills affecting their own departments, and of not intervening himself save at critical moments. A system of Ministerial devolution, deliberately adopted when he was in the prime of manhood, would be all the more strictly followed at a time when approaching old age and recurrent gout made it imperative for him to husband his physical

resources. His correspondence with the Queen and with
his friends confirms in detail what was already sufficiently
apparent from his public speeches, especially those at
the close of the 1875 session: that the carrying into effect
of the programme of social policy outlined in 1872 was
not less his work than the programme itself.

We have seen how he wrote of the Artisans' Dwellings
Bill to the Queen; to Lady Bradford he boasted of his
social reforms as 'a policy round which the country
can rally.' He showed his personal interest in housing
problems by attending, as Prime Minister, in June, 1874,
the opening by Shaftesbury of a 'workmen's city,' at
Lavender Hill, built by a limited company having shareholders of all ranks from dukes to bricklayers; and then
he had said that the best security for civilisation was the
dwelling. ' It is the real nursery of all domestic virtues,
and without a becoming home the exercise of those virtues
is impossible.' He had added that the experience gained
at Lavender Hill might ' guide the councils of the nation
in that enterprise which I believe is impending in this
country on a great scale, of attempting to improve the
dwellings of the great body of the people.' With the
labour legislation of the 1875 session his personal connection was especially close. He had been studying the
labour laws at Hughenden in the autumn of 1873, and
had asked Hardy at that time for a memorandum on the
law of conspiracy as being a subject that ' will press
us.' We have his own definite statement that on this
subject he converted to his policy a hesitating Cabinet.

To Lady Bradford.

2, WHITEHALL GARDENS, *June* 29.—. . . I cannot express
to you the importance of last night. It is one of those measures, that root and consolidate a party. We have settled
the long and vexatious contest bet[wee]n capital and labor. It
will have the same effect on the great industrial population
' on the other side Trent ' wh. the Short Time Bill had in the
West Riding and Lancashire.

I must tell you what I will tell to no other being, not even
the Faery, to whom I am now going to write a report of the

memorable night, that when Secy. X explained his plan to
the Cabinet, many were agst. it, and none for it but myself;
and it was only in deference to the P. Min[iste]r that a decision was postponed to another day. In the interval the thing
was better understood and managed.

To Queen Victoria.

2, WHITEHALL GARDENS, *June* 29, 1875.—Mr. Disraeli with
his humble duty to your Majesty:
   The proceedings in the House of Commons were so important
last night, that he feels it his duty to furnish your Majesty
with a memorandum of them.
   The ' Labor Laws ' of the Government, contained in two
bills, were read a second time with not only approbation, but
with general enthusiasm.   The representative working men,
like Macdonald, and the great employers of labor, represented
by Mr. Tennant, the member for Leeds, and others, equally
hailed these measures as a complete and satisfactory solution
of the greatest question of the day; the relations between
Capital and Labor.
   Mr. Lowe and Mr. Forster spoke in the warmest terms of
the measures, and the latter said that, after passing such
Bills, Her Majesty's Government need have no apprehension
of their reception during the recess, and that all their opponents must join in the general commendation of the country.
   Mr. Disraeli believes, that this measure, settling all the long
and long-envenomed disputes between ' master and servant,'
is the most important of the class, that has been carried in
your Majesty's long and eventful reign: more important, he
thinks, because of more extensive and general application,
than even the Short Time Acts, which have had so beneficial
an effect in softening the feelings of the working multitude.
   He is glad, too, that this measure was virtually passed on
your Majesty's Coronation Day. . . .

   As the Prime Minister took little or no personal part
in recommending to the House of Commons the social
legislation which owed so much to his initiative, the
dramatic scenes of the session were few, and were mostly
concerned with issues of very secondary importance.
Questions of privilege, in lieu of more vital matters,
loomed large, and the Opposition coquetted with the
discontented Irish in raising difficulties where Disraeli's
strong sense of the dignity of the House of Commons led

him to hold a straight course. The House supported him
in refusing to allow John Mitchel, an unpurged felon,
elected for an Irish constituency, to take his seat; in
allowing Kenealy, the counsel whose outrageous methods
in conducting the defence of the Tichborne claimant
had caused his profession to cast him out, to advance,
as a duly elected and unconvicted member, to the table
of the House and take the oath—in spite of his inability
to get any fellow-member to introduce him; in condemning Kenealy's unworthy agitation against the judges who
decided against him, and in declining to pay the smallest
attention to his ridiculous contention that a private jest
of Lord Chief Justice Cockburn's at a dinner-table was
evidence of a fixed determination to condemn the plaintiff;
and, further, in refusing to abandon offhand, because of
an indiscreet enforcement of privilege claims, the ancient
privilege of Parliament, as against the press. His letters
to the Queen and his friends give some idea of the vicissitudes of the session.

To Lady Bradford.

2, WHITEHALL GARDENS, *Feb.* 17, 1875.—. . . Yesterday,
when I could well have been spared such trifling trouble, was
taken up with a struggle betn. Parliamentary privilege and
semi-royal prerogative.

I was engaged to dine with the Speaker, whom I threw over,
as the phrase is, for the P. of W., alleging *command*. The
Speaker wd. not take my excuse, alleging that there was no
' command ' except from the Sovereign; that a dinner to the
Ministry without the P.M. was a mockery, and that he must
vindicate the authority of the Chair.

The Prince behaved very well. I was rather afraid, and
prepared he wd. be annoyed. Monty, who was pretty well,
was of great use to me. He saw Knollys and explained the
painful situation, and after saw the Prince, who had been
hunting. The Prince said it was a grand party; all the Ambassadors and the Derbys, etc., and that he wanted the Prime
Minister; that he thought the Speaker always dined on Saturday (in wh. he was right; this is an innovation) but he felt
the importance of the occasion and so released me. Monty
was with him twenty minutes or so, and he was amiable
and agreeable. In the evening came a large card, and a note

from Knollys, saying the Prince thought I cd. be represented
at the dinner by no one better than by my faithful Secy.
Monty is quite in his stirrups, and has no doubt that all
the Prince's banditti, at the Marlboro' Club, will be very
jeal[ous]. . . .

To Anne Lady Chesterfield.

2, WHITEHALL GARDENS, *Feb.* 19.—. . . I could not
write yesterday, for it was a day of great trouble and anxiety.
The Opposition chiefs had signified their intention to support
my resolution against the rebel, Mitchel; but only just before
the meeting of the House I heard that Harcourt and Lowe
had got round Ld. Hartington, and persuaded him to support,
as an amendment, a committee to inquire. This, if carried,
would have been a great blow, and it was supposed, that there
was a chance, and not a bad one, of its being carried.

If I had accepted the amendment, in lieu of my own uncompromising Resolutions, the humiliation of the Government would have been very great.

The result showed that I had not miscalculated the spirit
of the Ho. of Commons, and the Opposition chiefs, while taking
an unpatriotic course to please the Irish rebels, sustained an
ignominious overthrow. There has seldom been a greater
triumph for a Minister than yesterday. After dividing on
the pretence of adjourning the debate, and getting beaten by a
majority of more than 160, they allowed my Resolutions to
pass *nemine contradicente.* . . .

To Lady Bradford.

W[HITEHALL], *Feb.* 26.—. . . We did well in the House
last night, and carried the second reading of our Friendly
Societies Bill. That, with the Artisans' Dwellings Bill, is the
second measure of social improvement that I think we shall
now certainly pass. It is important, because they indicate
a policy round wh. the country can rally.

The question who shall be Serg[ean]t-at-Arms in the House
of Commons, is agitating political society, and is in a strange
quandary. . . . In brief, Ld. Hertford nominated his son-
in-law (Erskine[1] I think), and sent in his name to the Queen.
The House of Commons signed a Memorial to Her Majesty,
praying the Queen to bestow the office on Gosset,[2] wh.
they intended the Speaker to present. He disapproved the
Memorial, as an interference with the prerogative, but said

---

[1] Sir H. D. Erskine, Sergeant-at-Arms from 1885 to 1915.
[2] Then the Deputy-Sergeant, who was, Disraeli told Lady Chesterfield,
' a great favorite with all parties,' and had served for thirty-five years.

he wd. represent the unanimous feeling of the House to the Primo, etc., etc.

So I wrote to the Queen and put the matter before her, never anticipating what wd. happen. Last night, I received her reply. She has thrown over Ld. Hertford, and leaves me to communicate her gracious favor to the Commons, the son-in-law of Ld. Hertford to have the deputy place. I have not told a human being except you, as I wish, if possible, to spare Ld. H. and give him a golden occasion to be gracious. . . .

To Queen Victoria.

2, WHITEHALL GARDENS, *March* 5, 1875.—Mr. Disraeli with his humble duty to your Majesty:

The large majority of your Majesty's Government, on the Army Exchange Bill, was sustained last night, and it is rumored, that the future opposition will be slight.

There is a strong party, in both Houses, which desires the restoration to the House of Lords of their position as Court of Ultimate Appeal.

An Act to abolish this function, so far as England is concerned, has already passed, but does not come into force until next November.

The House of Lords is still the Court of Ultimate Appeal for Ireland and Scotland, and it is not probable that the Bills introduced, to assimilate those countries to England, will pass.

The anomaly, then, will be established of separate Courts of Final Appeal for different parts of your Majesty's dominions.

To remove this anomaly, it is understood that Mr. Walpole will bring the matter before the House of Commons, with the view of practically rescinding the English Act, that comes into play in November. The circumstances are rather critical.

Mr. Disraeli attended, yesterday, a meeting of the peers, at the Duke of Richmond's, and succeeded so far as to induce them to take a prudent and moderate course for the moment, but their spirit was high and somewhat unmanageable. Peers, who, two years ago, showed the greatest apathy on the subject, have become quite headstrong. . . .

March 17.—. . . Yesterday was a great day in the House of Commons. In consequence of the tactics of delay on the part of the Opposition, Mr. Disraeli was obliged to have recourse to a morning sitting; unprecedented before Easter—so yesterday the House was sitting all day.

But the greater event was—the return from Elba: Mr. Gladstone not only appeared, but rushed into the debate. The House, very full, was breathless. The new members

trembled and fluttered like small birds when a hawk is in the
air.   As the attack was made on Mr. Secretary Hardy and his
department, Mr. Disraeli was sorry not to be able to accept
the challenge, but he had nothing to regret.   Mr. Hardy, who,
suffering under a great sorrow,[1] has been languid this session,
was inspired by the great occasion, and never spoke with more
force and fire.   The Bill[2] was carried through Committee
by large majorities, and without alteration. . . .

To Anne Lady Chesterfield.

HUGHENDEN MANOR,[3] *March* 30.—I returned here yesterday
with a cold, notwithstanding all my care: but I had to pace
the corridor at Windsor, wh. I think can't be less than 1,000
feet long, five times a day (that was exercise) with blasts from
every opening in my progress (that was air).

I did not return smothered with flowers, tho' the Faery
was most gracious, and is going to give me her portrait for
Hughenden. For a long time I wrote, almost every day, to
three ladies: one of them has given me her portrait; another
has promised me her portrait; the third has not only not given
me her portrait, but has prevented another person from
giving it to me.   I shd. have placed the two sisters in the
saloon, each on one side of our Sovereign. . . .

Confidential. 2, WHITEHALL GARDENS, *May* 5.—Public
affairs are so grave and pressing that I can hardly command
my mind to write a private letter—even to you.

I am now going to the Faery, who has much to make her
disquieted.   Bismarck is playing the game of the old Buona-
parte.[4]

Then I must go to the Ho. of Commons, and blow into the
air the conspiracy of the Liberals, the Fenians, and *The Times*
newspaper, their organ, to discredit, and eventually to destroy,
H.M. Government.   They will find both results a little more
difficult than they imagine.   I have no doubt I shall baffle
and beat them down, but I have got a little gout, wh. is not
very agreeable under such circumstances. . . .

To Lady Bradford.

2, WHITEHALL GARDENS, *May* 7, 1875.—. . . We got
on capitally last night in the House of C. after my lecture.
The Irish withdrew all their opposition, and we nearly got

---

[1] Hardy's eldest daughter died on Jan. 8.
[2] Regimental Exchanges Bill.
[3] Disraeli spent the Easter Recess at Hughenden, with the exception of
a short visit to Windsor.
[4] See below, ch. 11.

thro' Committee with one of our sanitary Bills, all of wh. I am resolved to carry.

Gladstone, I am told, is furious, tho' a greater bully than himself never ruled the Ho. of Comm. The plot was to waste the sess[ion] and then hold the Government up to scorn, for their imbecility, during the recess.

Late at night on Tuesday, without anybody being aware of it, we passed the 3rd reading of the Artisans' Dwellings Bill, our chief measure, wh. now goes to the Lords. They have got the Army Exchange Bill already, and before many days they will have the Irish Bill;[1] so we have not done so very badly.

The Agricultural Holdings Bill, which has passed the Lords, I intend to bring in myself; nor shall they have a moment's rest. . . .

Northcote's Budget for 1875 raised the reputation of the Government. He established a new sinking fund, setting aside for the service of the National Debt a fixed annual sum, in excess of what was required for payment of interest; an admirable plan, under which more than 150 millions of debt were paid off in the last quarter of the nineteenth century. Gladstone once more rushed out of his retirement into the fray, but, says a Liberal historian,[2] ' did not even succeed in dispelling the notion that if he had been in office he would have done much the same thing himself.'

---

[1] Irish Peace Preservation Bill. Disraeli's speech on the second reading contained a well-known passage: ' There was once a member of this House, one of its greatest ornaments, who sat opposite this box, or an identical one, and indeed occupied the place which I unworthily fill. That was Mr. Canning. In his time, besides the discovery of a new world, dry champagne was invented. Hearing everybody talking of dry champagne, Mr. Canning had a great desire to taste it, and Charles Ellis, afterwards Lord Seaford, got up a little dinner for him, care of course being taken that there should be some dry champagne. Mr. Canning took a glass, and after drinking it and thinking for a moment, exclaimed, " The man who says he likes dry champagne will say anything." Now I do not want to enter into rude controversy with any of my hon. friends opposite who doubt the existence of Ribbonism; but this I will say, that the man who maintains that Ribbonism does not exist is a man who—ought to drink dry champagne.' Ribbonism was the form that Irish conspiracy had assumed for the time.

[2] Mr. Herbert Paul in his *History of Modern England*.

To Lady Bradford.

2, WHITEHALL GARDENS, S.W., *May* 8, 1875.—Last night
was to have witnessed the destruction of the Govt: an attack
on our whole line, led on by Achilles himself. Never were
assailants so completely overthrown.

There was really a flutter of fear along our benches, which
were crowded, when Gladstone rose. We have many new
members, and they had heard so much of G. that they
trembled.

The great man spoke for two hours, but it was the return
from Elba. The Chancellor of the Exr. our little Northcote,
originally G.'s private secretary, followed him, and I can truly
say annihilated him, in one of the most vigorous speeches
that ever was made by a man master of his subject.

Lowe tried to rally the affair, and I put up Hunt to answer
him. It did not require great gifts to do that, for Lowe
made a stammering affair of it—a dead failure.

Then the most curious part of all—every finance authority
on the Liberal side spoke for the Government, and by the time
I had intended to rise to sum up the question, the House had
nearly vanished. Enough members however remained to
help us to get thro' a great deal of business; and, whether it
be what I said in the House or not, all I know is that we have
done more business during the last 8 and 40 hours than for
the last fortnight. . . .

HUGHENDEN MANOR, *May* 19.—. . . I have been here
nearly a week,[1] and have not interchanged a syllable with
any human being. My personal attendant (Baum), tho'
sedulous, and, sometimes I believe, even honest, is of a
sullen and supercilious temperament, and never unnecessarily
opens his mouth. This I think a recommendation. Work
has been brisk, especially foreign. . . .

I am very much like Robinson Crusoe on his island, before
he found Friday. Talking of which immortal work reminds
me how I have passed my evenings here: in reading *Gil Blas*.
What a production! It is human life. I read it when
a child, and was charmed with its unceasing adventure; but
could not realise its real meaning. I read it now with a very
large experience of existence, and I relish every line.

HOUSE OF COMMONS, 6 *o'ck.* [? *May* 27, 1875].—Gladstone
has come down like the Dragon of Wantley breathing fire and
fury on some of our financial Bills. . . .

---

[1] For the Whitsuntide recess.

To Queen Victoria.

HOUSE OF COMMONS, *May* 31, 1875.—Mr. Disraeli with his humble duty to your Majesty:

He has, generally speaking, been a little remiss, this session, in reporting the operations of the House of Commons to your Majesty, but there have been more interesting topics to trouble your Majesty about.

To-night, however, has been one of a signal character.

For nearly a month, the Opposition, by every means the press could afford, have endeavoured to impress upon the country, that your Majesty's Government have made a great mistake in their management of the ' privilege question '; that they have lost a golden opportunity of settling these difficulties; and have given that opportunity to Lord Hartington to establish himself in the confidence of the country.

Mr. Disraeli was perfectly aware, that the whole of the representation was a delusion, and knew that the advice he had given to his party, on the subject, was the sound and right one: that which had been adopted, or followed, on similar occasions, by all the great leaders and members, who preceded him: Peel, Lord Russell, Graham, Lords Eversley and Ossington, Sir George Grey, Bouverie.

To-day and to-night, after many delays, the great occasion arrived, ' one of the decisive battles ' not of the world, but of the session.

There was a meeting of the supporters of the Ministry in the morning in Downing Street, when [? whom] Mr. Disraeli addressed. There were 248 present. The hour, in consequence of the levée, was changed from two to noon: otherwise, as the telegrams showed, there would have been 333 members present. Sir Robert Peel never could assemble such a number, even in his palmiest day.

The battle commenced at five o'clock; at ½ past seven the House divided on Lord Hartington's chief resolution, when he was beaten by a majority of *107 :* then he threw up his cards, and said he would leave it to Mr. Disraeli to do what he thought best. And he did it.

This immense victory will have an incalculably beneficial effect on the progress of public business.

To Anne Lady Chesterfield.

2, WHITEHALL GARDENS, *June* 1, 1875.—Before you get this you will have known the result of the great Opposition plot, scheme, confederacy, of wh. poor Hartington was the tool, and the victim.

For more than a month, there has been an organised agitation, to subvert the privileges of the House of Commons, showing that I was totally incapable of dealing with these great questions, self-confessedly incompetent, and ought to be deprived of the leadership, not only because I was of opinion that no change was desirable, but had also given my rival such a golden opportunity of distinguishing himself and his party.   They had engaged every newspaper in the plot; even the *World*, and of course Carnarvon's favorite, the *Spectator*.   *The Times* began it before Whitsun with announcing in a series of articles that the Ho. of Commons was in a state of chaos from my disinclination, or inability, to settle these inevitable changes.   Even 4 and 20 hours ago, they said the Cabinet Council of Saturday was to receive my resignation, and to listen to the address in wh. it was to be communicated to the House of Commons.

Yesterday morning I held a meeting of the party in Downing St., and soon saw they were troops with wh., as the D. of Wellington sd. of his Peninsular legions, that they were men with whom he cd. march anywhere [*sic*].   I addressed them in a speech of 55 minutes, and spoke to my satisfaction.

Then, after a long levée, I went to the House of C.; and at ½ past seven Ld. Hartington, ' the coming man,' was beaten by a majority of 107 ! ! ! threw up the reins, and begged me to settle the matter as I liked; wh. I did.   There never was such a smashing defeat.   The House in the most signal manner confirmed my policy, that no change in our privileges shd. take place, and it was only owing to my personal influence that I cd. get them to assent to a slight alteration in one of our rules,[1] wh. will keep the Irish ruffians in order. . . .

I can't get rid of my cough; but I am stronger, and Sir William [Jenner] maintains every day that I am better.   He says he has to write to the Queen every day he sees me: but that her great anxiety about my health is occasioned, he thinks, not so much from love of me, as dread of somebody else. . . .

To Queen Victoria.

HOUSE OF COMMONS, *June* 11, 1875.—. . . With respect to compulsory education, it was defeated on Wednesday by a majority of more than 90, and though the majority was even much larger last year, Mr. Disraeli attributes this diminution only to casual and social causes; principally Ascot races, always perilous to the Tories.

---

[1] At that period strangers, including reporters, were ordered to withdraw whenever any individual member called attention to their presence; and the Irish Extremists had made use of the rule to obstruct business. The alteration provided that a division should first be taken, without debate.

Mr. Disraeli had scores of supporters away: the Opposition only their leader, the Marquess of Hartington.

Lord Henry Somerset, the Controller of your Majesty's Household, was absent, and entertaining his friends; among them, several of your Majesty's Government. Mr. Disraeli was, however, ruthless; he kept the wires of the telegraph vibrating alternately with menaces and entreaties, and exactly five minutes before the division, a special train arrived with the Controller of the Household, and all his wassailers.

Lord Sandon spoke well: and was completely master of his subject.

To Lady Bradford.

2, WHITEHALL GARDENS, *June* 13, 1875.—. . . I had a Cabinet at 12, and I gave them a good ' wigging,' I believe that is the word, for the treatment of the Sultaun of Zanzibar at Ascot. They sate still and silent, like schoolboys; but my observations told, for, in the course of the afternoon I received the enclosed letter from one of the most powerful of our daimios. You know what those animals are in Japan ?

About four o'ck. by appointment, I paid my visit to the Sultaun myself. He received me at the door, or rather in the hall, of his hotel, with all his chiefs. They were not goodlooking, but he himself is an Arab with a well-favored mien, good manners, a pleasing countenance, and the peculiar repose of an Oriental gentleman. Being used, from my travels, to these interviews and gentry, I addressed him directly, looking in his face as I spoke, and never turning to the interpreter. This greatly pleases them, but it is very difficult to do. The audience was successful. I took Monty (just arrived) with me, and Mr. Bourke the Under Sec. for For. Affairs. . . .

The article is certainly Gladstone's; I have not seen it, but I never read anything he writes. His style is so involved, so wanting both in melody and harmony, that it always gives me a headache.

The most dramatic moments of the session arose out of the Merchant Shipping Bill, an apparently prosaic measure, which, however, resulted in an explosion, dangerous to the existence of the Government. For some years there had been a growing movement, headed by Plimsoll, member for Derby, in favour of legislation to bring merchant shipping under further control, so as to minimise loss of life among seamen. The movement was in accord with the social policy of the Government;

and accordingly, the Board of Trade prepared a Bill. But the subject was a thorny one, and the Government found it difficult to steer a middle course between shipowners and humanitarians; while the difficulties were increased by the inadequacy of Adderley, the President of the Board of Trade, and his uneasy relations with the permanent officials of the Board.   Disraeli's interference became necessary at an early stage.

To Lady Bradford.

2, WHITEHALL GARDENS, *April* 10.—. . . This has been a week of immense labor, and some anxiety, tho' of more excitement. . . .   The Mercht. Shipping Bill, a measure necessarily of great importance, was the cause.   Before I left town, I was confidentially informed that there were rocks ahead, that Adderley had quarrelled with all his office, that he was disliked by his own party in the House, that they wd. not support the Government measure but Plimsoll, who is a Moody and Sankey in politics: half rogue and half enthusiast — that is to say, one of those characters who live by pandering to passion, and fall into an enthusiastic love and admiration of themselves.   I took certain measures to put things right before I left town, and delegated the rest to Northcote, who generally succeeds.   But alas ! not in this case.

I had a bad despatch at Hughenden, and when I got to town—the Bill being fixed for 2nd reading on Thursday ensuing—I found perfect anarchy. . . .   I was obliged to undertake the management of the whole case: a vast and most complicated case, and of wh. then I knew little.   Besides this I have had to give constant interviews to the confused, the refractory and the vacillating.   After the Cab. on Wednesday, I was obliged to give myself to this work, instead of writing to the Queen as I had promised; and I did not get things really right—in order—until 4 o'ck. on Thursday afternoon, so that they were painting the scenes as the curtain drew up.

But the result was most triumphant.   Adderley, who is after all a gentleman, and who has been, and may be yet, the victim of a cabal, behaved very well, and made a discreet opening address.   We not only carried the second reading, but carried it without a division, and Plimsoll had to leave the House, being desperately ill, probably from chagrin. Then the enemy, finding they cd. not successfully oppose the Bill, tried to adjourn the debate, wh. wd. have been most injurious to us, but I coaxed the House into carrying my point. . . .

It is perhaps not surprising that, after this troublesome experience, Disraeli and the Cabinet should have preferred, when a choice had to be made late in July, to drop the Merchant Shipping Bill in order to proceed with the Agricultural Holdings Bill. But when Disraeli made the announcement, on July 22, Plimsoll lost patience, moved the adjournment in order to protest against the abandonment of the shipping measure, vehemently denounced ' shipknackers,' shouted that he would unmask the ' villains ' who sent seamen to their graves, pirouetted in the middle of the floor, shook his fist at Disraeli, and, defying the authority of the Speaker, flung himself out of the House. Disraeli, as leader of the House, moved that Plimsoll should be reprimanded; but he eventually accepted the plea of the offender's friends that he was in a state of intense excitement and would, when he was calmer, express regret for his conduct; and substituted a motion merely requesting him to attend in his place on that day week.

The Opposition, who had been on the lookout for a cry against the Government, thought that they had now found an excellent opportunity for working upon the humanitarian feelings of the people. Disraeli's private letters give a highly coloured story of the proceedings of the next few days, and show how he turned his difficulties to good account and finally passed a Shipping Bill after all.

To Lady Bradford.

2, WHITEHALL GARDENS, *July* 27.—I was up till 3 o'ck., and have a terrible day (days !) before me, but I have risen early, that, if possible, I might write to you.

The ——[1] was an anxious one. A certain person violent, treating the whole agitation with contempt—would not sacrifice our dignity as a Government, wh. he saw wd. be the result.

Strange to say, he was supported by one of a totally different temperament, who had proved by inexpugnable logic on

---

[1] The dash appears in the original letter. The word omitted is obviously Cabinet.'

a previous occasion that the course then adopted was ' the only one,' and he stuck to it.

At one moment I thought nothing cd. be effected; but at last, and *with unanimity*, there was a decision.

That has had immediate effect—at least in the H. of C. There was ' a meeting ' in the morning of yesterday, as last year, of an expectant Cabinet. Gladstone was brought up, and Carlingford, who had been President of the B. of Trade, and then a great opponent of Plimsoll, was consulted. There was to have been a fierce attack on the Government on the order of the day, but Sir C. Adderley's announcement stopped all this, and we went quietly into Committee on the Agri-[cultura]l Bill, and made immense progress, so that I really expect to conclude the Committee to-day, for I have got the whole morning late from 2 to 7, and then from 9 till the usual hour.

I *entreat* you not to breathe a word of what I have written above to any human being. I don't mean Bradford, of course, from whom I have no secrets, and who is a Privy Councillor, and whom I wd. trust were he not a P.C.

The Cabinet meets in an hour. We have to settle our measure; and what is of not less importance my answer this morning at 2 o'ck. to Dillwyn, as to whether we will give a day immediately to P[limsoll]'s Bill. I think as much depends on my reply as on our measure. . . .

I sadly miss you all, tho' I could not go and see dear Ida,[1] even if she cd. receive me. I had a talk with Newport in the lobby, who seems now my only link to domestic life and private happiness. .   .

J[ohn] M[anners], who has just come from O[sborne], says that the Faery only talked on one subject, and that was her Primo. According to him, it was her gracious opinion that the Govt. shd. make my health a Cabinet question. Dear John seemed quite surprised at what she said; but you are more used to these ebullitions. . . .

A certain person, the great logician, made, among many other sharp remarks, a good one yesterday. He said he had not only not changed his opinion, but believed that the with-drawment of the Mercht. Ship. Bill wd. have passed without notice by the country, had it not been for two unexpected incidents—wh. we cd. not have counted on—the Plimsoll scene, and the verdict against a wicked shipowner in the Irish Courts.

The first showed, he said, what a dangerous man P. was to trust to in legislation, and the second proved that the

---

[1] Then Lady Newport, now the Countess Dowager of Bradford.

existing law was an efficient one; and yet these two incidents, fanned of course by faction, have agitated the country. . . .

P.S.—What do you think of yr. new friend, Delane ? I believe he was at the meeting of the new Cabinet. . . .

July 28, 6 *o'ck.*—I send a rapid line after a morning of great excitement, of endless and terrific rumors, and all possible events and combinations—Plimsoll, to-morrow, not to appear; Plimsoll, to-morrow, to appear and re-defy the House; to get into the custody of the Sergt.-at-Arms at all events, but to come down first with four brass bands, open carriage with four white horses, and twenty thousand retainers !

Then our Bill to-day was not to be permitted to be brought in, and other mischances and difficulties and humiliations. However, our Bill *has been* brought in, and I have fixed its second reading for Friday morning—and remain, ostensibly at least, perfectly calm, amidst a sea and storm of panic and confusion. My position is difficult in one respect, for the Queen, devoted to me, can't help me; for if I were defeated in the House, I cd. not dissolve, for, in the present fever, I shd. probably get worsted; and I can't prorogue, for I have not got my money, the Estimates not yet being concluded.

All I have got to look to are my friends. If they stand by me, I shall overcome everything, and greatly triumph, but does friendship exist in August ? Does it not fly to Scotland, and Norway, and the Antipodes—or Goodwood ? I have seen some wonderful long faces, that used to smile on me. I neither love them more nor less. The only beings in the world I care for are away—and Heaven knows even if they spare a thought to me and my agitated fortunes.

July 29, 10 *o'ck.*—I got your letter an hour ago; a great consolation to me in my fierce life. . . .

Now I know exactly what a General must feel in a great battle—like Waterloo for example — with aide-de-camps flying up every moment with contrary news; and spies, and secret agents, and secret intelligence, and all sorts of proposals and schemes.

The Plimsollites, in and out of Parliament, are at me; now cajoling, now the reign of terror. Their great object is to get Plimsoll into the custody of the Sergt.-at-Arms, and on my motion. That, they consider, from what they have been told, is inevitable if he does not appear to-day; and they are right according to precedent. But I am the person to make the motion, and I will make a precedent too. After the declarations of his authorised friend in the House, that ' he was off his head,' etc., I shall hold him as a man not responsible for his conduct, and move the adjournment of his case for a month.   This will sell them if they try the scheme of his absence—*i.e.*, disobedience to the commands of the House.

I shd. not be surprised if, after all his bluster, he gives in and makes an unconditional apology.   Every intriguer is trying to make some fortune by the crisis.   Plimsoll has a wonderful number of enthusiastic friends, very suddenly.   I only wish they had supported our Bill when it was before them, instead of throwing every obstacle in its way.   Horsman is very busy; asked Monty to luncheon yesterday, told him it was all over with the Government, tho' he once thought he cd. save them; advised, as a last resource, that I should deliver a panegyric to-day in favour of P. and accept his Bill *pure et simple.*

My own judgment of the House of Commons is that a considerable, and the most reputable, section of the Opposition is against Plimsoll, and believes, wh. is the truth, that his Bill wd. injure, not to say destroy, our mercantile marine, and that, if my friends are firm to me, I shall certainly triumph.

As far as I can hear, I have no reason to doubt their devotion.   Many of our most considerable men have told me that they are prepared, if necessary, to alter all their plans and remain by my side. . . .

Tell Bradford I was greatly disappointed that his horse came in second.   I cannot understand why a great noble, with his brains and knowledge of horses, does not command the turf.   I don't want him to have a great stable, but I want him to have a famous one; that he shd., at any rate, obtain some first-rate blood, and then carefully, and sedulously, breed from it, as Rothschild did with King Tom.   I saw the beginning of his plan at Mentmore, and people turned up their noses at his scheme and his sire for a while; and yet eventually that blood gave him the Derby, the Oaks, and the St. Leger in one year.   I shd. like to see that done at dear Weston.

For aught I know, while I write of these pleasant things, the mob may be assembling wh. is to massacre me.   I have several letters threatening assassination.   I shall take no pre-cautions, but walk down alone with Monty, and meet my fate, whatever comes.   I feel sure, at least almost, that there will be one family in England who will cherish my memory with kindness and indulgence.

July 30.—Everything went off quietly yesterday out of doors, and triumphantly inside.

Mr. Secy. X, who is naturally a brave and firm man, got so frightened about his chief, that I believe there were 1000 constables hid in the bowers of Whitehall Gardens and about. But I had no fear, and principally from this, that Monty, who has been everywhere and doing everything, ascertained that

Bradlaugh and Co. had completely failed in getting up a
Clerkenwell mob, as the people said they wd. not go agst. me,
who had passed the Labor Laws for them.

All the meetings in the provinces were held by tel. orders
from the Reform Club; but before they cd. hold their meetings,
at least generally speaking, the announcement of the Govt.
measure had taken the wind out of their sails.

Plimsoll also got restive and did not like the brass bands
and flags, etc., and said he wd. not be made a party tool,
and that he had received more support from the Tories than
the Whigs. The consequence of all this was very much fiasco.

The papers will tell you what took place in the House.
The campaign opened unfortunately for the foe. They
tried to stop public business and failed ignominiously. Adam,
the Whig Whip, who is a gentleman, told Dyke that ' the
Plimsoll business was a flash in the pan.' They did not think
so 8 and 40 hours ago.

Then after the failure I got into Committee on my Bill,
and absolutely at one o'ck. concluded it amid loud cheers. I
never had more continuous, and greater, majorities than thro'-
out this Bill.

I am very glad Harry C[haplin] was not at Goodwood. He
has never left my side, and his aid has been invaluable. He
is a natural orator, and a debater too. He is the best speaker
in the H. of C., or will be. Mark my words.

I have a Cabinet at noon: the H. of C. at two, when we
have the 2nd reading of our Ship. Bill. I shd. not be surprised
if it passed without a division. The battle of Armageddon,
howr., will be on Monday, when in Committee they will try
to substitute Plimsolliana for our proposals. I am sending
all over the world for votes. Chaplin has a house full for
Brighton races, but remains here. *O ! si sic omnia !* or rather,
omnes.

Aug. 3.—We pulled thro', but not triumphantly; had the
Opposition had a leader adequate to the opportunity, we might
have been much humiliated. As it was, it needed much
tact and vigilance to mitigate, or conceal, our concessions;
but the enemy made so many mistakes, and played their
cards so ill, that it all ended better than was once hoped.

Adderley committed an awful blunder ! . . .

These political excursions and alarums did not prevent
Disraeli from making frequent appearances in society.
He always set a high value on social influences in con-
solidating a political connection, and often lamented
the backwardness of Tory magnificoes and great ladies

in providing counter-attractions to Whig hospitalities.
He was determined to do his own part as Prime Minister;
and accordingly, in the spring of 1875, when he had for
a while thrown off his gout, he gave a series of political
and Parliamentary dinners, mixing Royal Princes and
Ambassadors with his peers and Members of Parliament.
In this experiment he was following the counsels of his
own Vivian Grey, uttered fifty years earlier: ' I think a
course of Parliamentary dinners would produce a good
effect. It gives a tone to a political party. The science of
political gastronomy has never been sufficiently studied.'
The dinner-parties proved a great success; and, when
Granville started a somewhat similar series, Disraeli
flattered himself that this time it was the Whigs who
were the imitators.

To Anne Lady Chesterfield.

WHITEHALL GARDENS, *Feb.* 24.—. . . I have asked an
Ambassador to each of my dinners, a new feature. . . .
Ct. Schouvaloff[1] is a most agreeable man, and very good-
looking, and very clever. When he had his first audience
of me in the spring on his arrival, he cd. not speak or comprehend a word of English. Yesterday at the levée he said to
me, ' I want to have the honor of another interview some day,
but *here* I will not talk shop.' And so I found that he now
not only speaks English, but English slang, quite idiomatic. . . .

To Lady Bradford.

H. OF COMM., *Feb.* 25, 1875.—. . . The dinner, wh. I
expected to be a failure, turned out to be a great success.
The physical part was good. It was really a dinner of high
calibre and quite hot, which is wonderful when you have to
feed forty. I sate betn. the German Ambassador and D. of
Manchester, who is silly, but not dull. Next to him was
Lothair,[2] who had travelled up from the wilds of Scotland
to show his gratitude for his Thistle. He had other hardships
to endure, for it is Lent! and, of course, he could eat nothing
but fish. He managed pretty well, for he instructed his
attendant to secure for him a large dish of well-sauced salmon,
and that sustained him during all the courses. Claud Hamilton sate next to Lothair, and talked well, and made him

---

[1] The new Russian Ambassador.   [2] See above, ch. 4.

talk. But everybody talked. I think it was the most noisy
party, without being boisterous, I well recollect. These
affairs, generally, are solemn, not to say dull. To make up
for the lack of brilliant furniture, I gave them *carte blanche* for
plants and flowers; and they certainly effected marvels. . . .

I found Münster a very capable man, with great conversa-
tional powers. The cold proud Duke of Northumberland
sate next to him, but was grim and acid. . . .

2, WHITEHALL GARDENS, *March* 15.—. . . My new dean
preached: Monty liked him, he never charmed me. What
was good was his length; twenty minutes, tho' a charity
sermon. The plate brought to me was disgraceful: there were
so many sixpences, that it looked like a dish of whitebait. . . .

It is mentioned to me, and it is true (look in the newspapers)
that Granville, my rival in more senses than one, has copied
my scheme and system of banquets, wh. was quite original.
He started on Saturday, with an Ambassador or two, ½ a
dozen peers (with one Duke at least) and a batch of commoners,
tho' he can only manage 'covers for 26.' I can 42. . . .

To Anne Lady Chesterfield.

2, WHITEHALL GARDENS, *April* 17.—. . . Affairs are very
heavy—in weight, I mean, not in spirit, for there is no want
of that in external affairs; but I hope to prevent war. It
is a proud position for England if she can do this.[1] . . .

I have got a banquet to-day, and H.R.H. the Duke of
Cambridge comes to me: the Duke of Edinburgh on the 28th,
and the Prince of Wales, I believe, on the Birthday. I have
now dined 242 members of the House of Commons and sixty
peers. I had hoped to have finished this campaign by the end
of April; but I shall hardly be able to do it, as there are 112
members of the Commons to be invited, and they are not
contented unless they meet a certain portion of swells. . . .

Besides giving many dinners himself, Disraeli constantly dined out, often attended evening parties, and
even sometimes, until he was scolded out of his imprudence by Lady Chesterfield, finished up his night at a
ball. If the dinner or the party involved a meeting and
a talk with Lady Bradford, it counted with him as a
success.

To Anne Lady Chesterfield.

2, WHITEHALL GARDENS, *July* 3.—. . . On Wednesday
I dined at the Malmesburys'—a Duke of Cambridge banquet,

[1] See below, ch. 11.

good company. I took down Lady Tankerville, who is joyous. On my other side an Australian, who has beguiled foolish and very young Ld.——into marrying her, on the pretence she is a great beauty. All the relations are by way of vowing she is so now, tho' they were very squeamish about the match at first. I thought her an underbred minx, affecting artlessness, and trying it on me ! I cd. only see Selina at a distance, but after dinner, when the D. of Cambridge had done with her, I got my turn, and she was delightful—made a rather dull dinner a success. Lady A. was there. Three great houses were open that night, Grosvenor, Apsley, and Stafford. But I was firm and went home at once. This getting to bed before midnight answers very well. . .

Yesterday I dined at 43, Bel. Square—a brilliant and amusing party. I took down the Dss. of Westminster to dinner and sate next to Pss. Mary. The Duchess said as we walked in, 'You are going to sit between the two fattest women in London.' That might be true; and yet they have both grand countenances, and are agreeable and extremely intelligent. Indeed Princess Mary has wit. The Abercorns were there also: the beautiful Viceroy in goggles ! having been struck on his eyes by a cricket ball. He excels in the game, as in everything. I never saw such roses as S. had on her dinner-table. I suppose other people have as good, but she arranges them, or inspires their arrangement, with peculiar taste. Her party was very successful, the guests wd. not go, but stayed till nearly midnight, the test of an agreeable dinner party.

I wd. not go to Dorchester House, where there was a great festival. I told S. I shd. tell you this, and it wd. please you. She also was prudent and did not go either.

July 25.—. . . Yesterday I dined at Holland House; a banquet, 4 and 20 at least. As they were all grandees, I went out, as usual, last, and feared I shd. be as badly off as at Lady A.'s, and dine, as I did there, between two men; but, as I entered, a faithful groom of the chamber took me under his care, and deposited me, by the instructions of the lady of the house, next to—S. ! She had been taken out by Lord Stanhope. It was a most delightful dinner, and a most charming evening. We had Mr. Corney Grain to amuse us, with his songs and mimicry, and some were quaint and good. S. immensely enjoyed them. The Grand Mecklenburgs were there, the blind Duke in fits of laughter; Duke of Sutherland; the Ilchesters who, by an arrangement, accede to Holland House on the demise of its present genial lady; the Malmesburys; some distinguished foreigners, of course, who knew me years ago.

I had a dreadful accident to my brougham in the evening, and I fear I shall lose my beautiful horse, the Baron, for whom I gave 300 gu[ine]as, four years ago, and who has never been ill a single hour.

Bradford was most kind, as, I must say, he always is to me, and took me home with S. and Mabel. It was such a happy day that I did not care much for any accident.

I have 8 and 40 hours' distraction from heavy and anxious affairs. I shall manage them, but they are hard.

I meet S. at dinner to-day at the Sturts, her great friends; and then the curtain falls.

July 28.—I can't write letters, not even tels. I live in a storm—at the House morning and night; glad to get off for 12 hours a day; Cabinets early in the morning; called out for ceaseless interviews: much fright and confusion—but I am cool and have no fear.

I see, as from a tower, the end of all.

Never mind *The Times;* it will soon change. I will beat even your *Times*, wh. I know you are always afraid of; so is dear S.

Amid all this, the servant perpetually comes in, and announces, ' fruit from Bretby,' ' flowers from B.', ' butter from B.' Blessed Bretby ! and I can only send you in return my love.

It was the cue of the Opposition to represent the legislation of the session as petty and valueless, because in two of the principal measures, the Artisans' Dwellings Bill and the Agricultural Holdings Bill, the principle of compulsion was not admitted. In both cases a new departure was made in English legislation, and Disraeli strenuously upheld the wisdom of proceeding at first by way of permission, rather than of compulsion. ' Permissive legislation,' he said on the Agricultural Bill, ' is the character of a free people. It is easy to adopt compulsory legislation when you have to deal with those who only exist to obey; but in a free country, and especially in a country like England, you must trust to persuasion and example as the two great elements, if you wish to effect any considerable changes in the manners of the people.' And again, in the House at the close of the session : ' It is only by persuasion—the finest persuasion in the world, which is example—persuasion in action, that you can influence, and modify, and mitigate habits which you disapprove.' The other charge against Government, which resounded through the Liberal press, and was even echoed by *The Times*, was one of Parliamentary mismanagement, largely based on Disraeli's refusal to accept the press view of Parliamentary privilege. Sir Henry Lucy draws a strong contrast between Disraeli's success in the Commons in the early part of the session, and what he considers his failure and feebleness after the privilege question had been raised. It is possible that Disraeli's regular participation in the social events of the season may to some extent have exhausted the energy which should have been directed to Parliamentary management; it is also possible that Sir Henry, whose contrast on this point is too much heightened to be convincing, was biassed both by his Liberalism and by his sympathy with the press. In any case a great mass of beneficent social legislation was enacted amid the plaudits of the working classes; what Disraeli called a ' crucial session ' was successfully surmounted; and the attempt of the Opposition just before the prorogation to enforce their apocryphal version of events was easily repelled. Disraeli himself, in replying to Hartington, was, says Hardy, ' full of fire, force, and energy, and wound up our sessional career admirably.'

To Lady Bradford.

2, WHITEHALL GARDENS, *Aug.* 7, 1875.—. . . I was indeed sorry I cd. not reach Bel. Sqre. last night, but Harty-Tarty could not rise till nearly eleven. Had he given me 10,000 pounds he cd. not have done me a greater service than making his attack. I am rarely satisfied with myself, but I was last night—almost as much as my friends, who were literally in a state of enthusiasm. I think I left Harty-Tarty in a state of syncope. He sate quite opposite to me, and I cd. see his face—the look of wooden amazement and the blush of proud confusion. Gladstone was by him, having been kept in town for the occasion; but the bottleholder was Lowe, who made copious notes to answer me, but did not dare to rise! They all deserted him. *The Times* has not even a leading article ' to cover his retreat ' !

Aug. 8.—. . . You will be rather pleased to hear that when we met yesterday [1] Derby said, ' Our first act ought to be to thank our chief for closing the campaign by a victory.'

Aug. 9.—. . . N. Rothschild, who knows everything, told me yesterday about the coming art. in *The Times*. It was written by Lowe, and shd. have been his answer to me.

Aug. 10.—. . . Notwithstanding the House of C. I ventured in trembling, for a division was impending, to call on Lady Holland, whom I had not seen since the very happy day when she called me ' naughty boy.'

The servant informed me that her L[adyshi]p had ' gone to town '; she always went on Monday, the only day in the week she did not receive. ' I thought you wd. know that, Sir,' he added. ' I did not,' I replied, ' nor did I know this was Monday.' And I left him staring.

But my disappointment was fortunate, for the division came on instantly on my arrival, and I had the pleasure of supporting Geordie Hamilton, who is deservedly a great favorite of mine, and who, yesterday, as usual, much distinguished himself. . . .

We have done capital business, both in Lords and Commons, these few last days; and several most important measures, wh. they pressed me so eagerly to give up a month ago, have been passed.

Some capital measures of the Chr. of the Exr. wh. Harty-Tarty taunted me with having to give up, and wh. I thought then were virtually surrendered, have been carried: but above all, the Trade Marks Bill, a measure of the utmost gravity and importance, a subject wh. Parlt. has been hammering at for years, and no Govt. cd. settle, has been passed triumphantly and will give profound satisfaction to the whole manufacturing and commercial world. After the approval of the Speech by the Queen this has happened, and I have been obliged this morning to insert a fresh paragraph in the great document,

The Times may scold; it may rave and rant; but it will not daunt me. I know it greatly influences you, and it rules Anne, and that the confidence of you both in me is greatly shaken: but you will see that I am right, and very soon see it, and that public opinion will decide in my favor. The Queen's Speech is a document of such weight and authenticity, dealing only with facts, that the nation is always influenced by this sovereign summary. . . .

[1] In Cabinet.

Ministers, at any rate, were satisfied with themselves, and celebrated their successful session with a more than usually hilarious fish dinner at Greenwich.

To Lady Bradford.

OSBORNE, *Aug.* 13, 1875.—Bradford has told you all about the fish dinner; therefore I need not dwell on it. I put Geordie Hamilton in the chair, the youngest member of the Ministry. They were all astonished and charmed by him: I was not astonished, but charmed. I knew my man. It was a perpetual flow of wit, and playful humor, and grace; a due mixture of the aplomb of the statesman and the impertinence of the page.

You know he is authorised by me, while he is in the chair, to do anything he likes, and say anything he chooses He is a sort of Abbot of Misrule; 'tis a carnival, a saturnalia; the Roman slave freely criticising his masters; and Cabinet Ministers trembled in their shoes before the audacious sallies of this brilliant stripling and subordinate. Part of the hilarious ceremony is the investiture of an illustrious order. The decoration is a wooden spoon of rather gigantic and pantomimic size. It is strictly to be given to the member of the Ministry who has been in the least number of Ho. of Commons divisions; practically it ought to be the appanage of our stupidest member. Geordie had the impudence to award it to me, who sate on his right hand ! his lord and master, and who had helped him a little in his wonderful summary of the session. Ungrateful youth !

In bygone days, I remember this decoration being awarded to an eminent gentleman, who has filled great posts, and is now a member of the Upper House: he was so indignant that he could not smother his rage and mortification, and actually rose from his seat and left the room. I was not quite such a fool as that, but wore my decoration, suspended round my neck by a piece of cord for the whole evening, and even dared to vindicate, as well as I cd., the order of Spooneys.

I expected to find that the remaining one of the three ladies, to whom hitherto I have written for some time every day of my life, had also lost her confidence in me; but that was not so. She looks extremely well; ten years younger than when I saw her last. She almost deigned to say the same of me, and I tried to cough, lest I shd. be commanded to Balmoral, but could not. . . .

The Queen, I ought to tell you, had ordered the *Fairy* for my special use, in order that I shd. not get into boats; but

Monty, by tel. to Ponsonby, declined this, as I think it makes
an injudicious distinction from my colleagues, who have been
to me faithful and devoted colleagues.

It is decided that Adderley shd. leave the Board of Trade,
and be succeeded by Sir Michael Beach, and that H. Chaplin
shall succeed Beach and go to Ireland as Secretary. Little
George Bentinck also must leave the Board of Trade, but I
have been able, I think, to provide for him. These are great
secrets, unknown to any of my colleagues, and perhaps will
not be announced for a month. I need not impress upon
you the most profound secrecy, always excepting Bradford
of course. . . .

The changes which Disraeli foreshadowed to Lady
Bradford as imminent at the Board of Trade were never
carried out, save for the removal of Bentinck from the
Parliamentary Secretaryship. Both Disraeli and his
principal colleagues, especially Cairns and Northcote,
felt, after the experience of the session, the advisability
of strengthening the Board, but serious difficulties arose
in the way of the suggested shuffle of offices. Northcote,
with characteristic unselfishness, offered to step down
from the Exchequer and take the Presidency himself,
but Disraeli would not hear of the idea. ' I think your
proposition monstrous,' he wrote on August 3. ' You
are, and ever have been, my right hand, my most trusty
counsellor; and I look to your filling a higher post than
that which you admirably discharge.' The discussions
occupied several months of the autumn; and finally
Adderley was left in possession of his post, but the Board
was strengthened by the appointment, as Parliamentary
Secretary, of Edward Stanhope, the historian's son, one
of the most promising of the younger Tories, whose death
some years later in the prime of manhood was a real
loss to his country.

To Sir Stafford Northcote.

2, WHITEHALL GARDENS, *Sept.* 23, 1875.—. . . Adderley
has mistaken a letter, which I thought was clear. I lost no
time, after seeing the Queen, in informing him of my intentions, because I thought, if they reached him from any other

source, he might think himself the victim of an intrigue, which he certainly is not.

But I have done nothing in the matter, tho' I have labored much. I have conferred greatly about it with the Lord Chancellor, and with Dyke and Sclater Booth, and the result has been nothing.

There are great objections to our increasing the number of the Cabinet. It is thought, that Adderley might remain, if George Bentinck were removed, and Ibbetson, who has studied the railway question, were put in his place, and there is a great objection to any great change of any kind.

The difficulty about an Irish Secretary is immense. George Hamilton could not go there with his father V.Roy. Chaplin, whom I thought of, is not experienced enough for this nest of corruption, intrigue, and trickery.

I did write to Beach, but after corresponding with the Lord Chancellor and conferring with Sclater Booth, the letter remains in my red box, six weeks old, and I will break the seal when we meet. . . .

To Lady Bradford.

2, WHITEHALL GARDENS, *Nov.* 12.—. . . Adderley's business still teases me, tho' I have sent word to-day that all must be settled in 4 and 20 hours, or everybody concerned shall go out. Monty is of use to me, being resolute as well as sharp; but his interference is *my* interference, and I don't want to appear unnecessarily in these matters. The Cr. of the Exchequer, to whom I look to arrange these things, tho' very clever, is a complete Jesuit, and proceeds always by innuendo, wh. coarse natures do not understand. . . .

It was during this autumn of 1875 that events occurred —the insurrection in Herzegovina, the visit of the Prince of Wales to India, the purchase of the Suez Canal shares—which made, in ever-increasing measure, the foreign policy and the imperial position of Great Britain the dominating considerations in the mind of the Prime Minister and in the counsels of the Government. But Disraeli was also not without worries in domestic affairs. The Admiralty, after consultation with the Foreign Office, issued a fugitive slave circular, drafted by the Law Officers, which roused public indignation by its apparent reversal of British anti-slavery policy; it directed the surrender on demand, within territorial limits, of a

fugitive slave who had sought the protection of a British
ship. When the storm arose, Disraeli acted with promptitude and decision. Derby was about to speak at a
banquet at Liverpool, and his chief telegraphed his
wishes.

To Lord Derby.

(*Telegram*) *Oct. 6, 1875.*—The affair is grave. Many letters
to-day. It should be stated that there is not the slightest
change in our policy, that the instructions have been referred
to the Law Officers, who do not agree in the public interpretation, but that as there should be no ambiguity on such a subject
the instructions are at present suspended. Answer if you
agree.

Derby replied that he entirely agreed, and he made
an announcement in the sense of Disraeli's telegram.
Disraeli called the Cabinet together a few days earlier
than had been intended, to take action.

To Queen Victoria.

Confidential. HUGHENDEN MANOR, *Oct. 28, 1875.*—Mr.
Disraeli with his humble duty to your Majesty:
He finds it necessary to call the Cabinet together on the
4th November. The immediate cause is the Admiralty
Resolutions, respecting slavery.
Although the expressions of Lord Derby at Liverpool,
and the suspension of the instructions—and Mr. Disraeli
is responsible both for the expressions and the suspension—
arrested mischief, they have not terminated a state of public
opinion, with reference to this unfortunate affair, which may
be dangerous. It has got hold of the public mind more than
the newspapers would convey, of which, indeed, your Majesty
is aware, for your Majesty has already called Mr. Disraeli's
serious attention to the subject. . . .
2, WHITEHALL GARDENS, *Nov. 5.*—. . . The consideration of the Cabinet yesterday was entirely confined to the
slave circular and Admiralty circumstances. The Lord
Chancellor, as arranged with Mr. Disraeli, put the whole question of the instructions before the Cabinet, and showed,
that they were as wrong in law as in policy. The Cabinet
came to an unanimous resolution to cancel immediately the
already suspended instructions, and requested the Lord
Chancellor himself to draw up those, which are to be substituted for them.

A strange affair altogether ! That all the Law Officers should blunder, and that the indiscretion in policy should have been committed by the Earl of Derby ! ! ! . . .

After this muddle, it is not surprising to find Disraeli writing next day to the Queen that he ' suffers terribly from the want of capable law officers. The unfortunate break-up of Sir John Karslake's health broke the chain, and we have never been able to find an adequate link.' Within a fortnight, however, he had secured a team on which he could rest with much greater confidence.

To Queen Victoria.

2, WHITEHALL GARDENS, *Nov.* 17, 1875.—. . . In conse-quence of the promotion of Sir R. Baggallay, it would be desirable, that your Majesty should sanction that of Sir John Holker to the Attorney Generalship.

As high legal talent is wanted in the House of Commons, Mr. Disraeli recommends your Majesty to appoint Mr. Har-dinge Giffard [1] to the office of your Majesty's Solicitor-General. Mr. Giffard is not at present in Parliament, but Mr. Disraeli can arrange to bring that about.[2] There is no lawyer in the Ministerial benches, at present, equal to the post. . . .

To Lady Bradford.

2, WHITEHALL GARDENS, *Nov.* 17.—. . . Hardinge Giffard is Solicitor-General. . . . I don't know whether he will turn out as strong a man as his friends suppose, but at any rate I shall have a lawyer of high reputation, who will be able to state his opinions with effect. . . .

Further worry was entailed on Disraeli, and much correspondence with the Court and with the Admiralty, by a misadventure in the Solent in August. The royal yacht *Alberta*, when crossing from the Isle of Wight with the Queen on board, had the ill-fortune to run down the sailing yacht *Mistletoe* with fatal results. Her Majesty was immensely distressed by the accident, and was dis-satisfied both with the public comments and with the

---

[1] Now Earl of Halsbury.

[2] The arrangement did not prove easy to bring about, and the Solicitor-General did not appear in Parliament till the spring of 1877, when he was elected for Launceston.

incidents and outcome of the various inquiries which
were instituted. But, with all his burdens and responsibilities, Disraeli was able to enjoy a number of country
visits, and even to attend the Doncaster St. Leger, where
he betted and lost his money. When he went subsequently to Sandringham, he had to put up with plenty of
chaff on this adventure from the Prince of Wales. He
told Lady Bradford that he denied his losses at first,
' having really forgotten that I had been so unlucky and
so foolish.' ' Sir,' he protested, ' a sweepstakes with some
ladies.' ' Oh no,' replied the Prince, ' I hear a good round
sum; paid in bank notes, a rouleau. I always thought
Bunny was sharp, but I never thought he would top all
by putting the Prime Minister on a dead horse !'

To Lord Bradford.

HUGHENDEN MANOR, *Aug.* 18.—I am most obliged to you
for your kind proposal. If I might, I would offer to come at
once, I mean next Monday the 23rd, for several reasons—
1st I shd. be glad to see Weston with unshrivelled leaf; 2nd
because I am never happier than under your roof, and with
you and yours; and 3rdly because it would save me some
terrible local functions, opening a Cottage Hospital for the
hundred of Desborough, and wh. I wish to foist on the
shoulders of Charley Carington,[1] etc., etc., the impending
sense of wh., I believe, is the cause of my horrible despondency, wh. does not become a Minister, who has, I believe,
less cause for care and anxiety than any man, who ever had
his hand upon the helm.

You will never see *The Times* go wrong for any length of
time, tho' it is managed by those who are personally our foes.
It is managed in this way. They receive daily, I am well
informed, about 300 letters from all parts of the country, and
it is from these spontaneous, unpaid and unsolicited, correspondents that they, after due reflection, derive their cue.
The Times thought it had caught us napping, and attacked
us, animated by their own personal feeling, and the passions
of their social patrons, but the 300 letters have poured in
since, and they find, wh. I believe is a fact, that the present
Ministry is popular with the country. This is the explanation wh. was given to me by Baron Rothschild, who is a
Liberal and who knows everything.

[1] Now the Marquis of Lincolnshire.

Here our harvest is *splendid !* Nothing less, after all our fears and trials; wages high and rising; our local manufacture, the chair trade, exporting everywhere, to ' China and Peru' ! I get 2s. per foot for my beech, and can't supply them with the raw material. My father got 6d. . . .

To Montagu Corry.

HUGHENDEN, *Sept.* 30, '75.—. . . After a short, but satisfactory, visit to Osborne, leaving my royal mistress in the highest health and spirits, little anticipating the months of mortification and anxiety that were then impending over her, I went to this place for a week. I crossed the Solent in the now too celebrated yacht, which was accorded to me as a particular attention, and it was commanded by Welsh !

From Hughenden, I went to Weston for a week or so, and, they[1] then going to Longshawe, I made my visit to Bretby, and joined them again at Wortley, where I passed two or three agreeable days, and then I went with the Bs. to Sandbeck, where I had a long engagement for the Race week. I left Sandbeck and S. on the 18th, when our party broke up, and then I went to Duncombe, a place of high calibre. Returning, I passed a day with Harlowe[2] at Gopsal ! S. was jeal.

I am well, and the old attack once menacing me, I treated it, determinately, on my own system, and completely baffled it. I have not had much repose: foreign affairs are troublesome, and between them and ' the collision,' it has rained telegrams, sometimes, as the diplomatic phrase is, ' in figures.' S. helped me in this, and is very clever at it. She says ' it is immense fun.' H.M., I think, has written to me every day, until she went to Inverary. You really must put the royal correspondence in some order.

I have had a function to open my new church, and on the whole, I got through it with less annoyance, than I expected. I got the Cheshams, without the prize ox himself, and Carington and Harcourt and N. Sturt to meet the Bishop. Lady Ely was to have been with us, but continual, and contradictory, telegrams about her departure for Balmoral prevented her, to her and our great vexation, for now she does not depart until to-night.

I shall see her this afternoon, for I am now going to London, preliminarily to a visit to-morrow to Sandringham, a farewell visit p evious to his departure for India: and I am asked till the 6th, but this is too long. I was about to enjoy some

---

[1] The Bradfords.　　　　　　　　[2] Lady Howe.

repose, when this command arrived, and on the 9th, the North-cotes come here.

There is a great deal of business, official and personal, rather pressing, to attend to, and he is the best of my colleagues for that sort of work. He can put his hand to anything. . . .

The prodigality of contributions for my local entertainments was remarkable. Bretby and Weston vied with each other in cases of roses and nectarines, and peaches and grapes: haunches of venison, and mighty hams. When I had got all this, the Rothschilds must have stripped one of the glass-houses at Gunnersbury, and all their gifts provided a public dessert. But what will surprise, and please, you was a cargo of grapes from Rowton !

The restoration of Hughenden Church had been taken in hand by Disraeli's new vicar, the Rev. Henry Blagden, a young and eager High Churchman, whom he had nominated in 1869. Mr. Blagden had not been the patron's first choice when the vacancy occurred. Disraeli had begun by offering the living to a Devonshire friend whose acquaintance he may have made in his visits to Mrs. Brydges Willyams at Torquay, the Rev. Reginald Barnes, father of the accomplished ladies known on the stage as Violet and Irene Vanbrugh. The offer was at first accepted, and the presentation was even made out on December 14, 1868; but Mr. Barnes never actually entered upon the living, apparently because he found that the highlands of Bucks would not suit a delicate man who had long basked in the more genial climate of Devon-shire. Mr. Blagden's energy, and the generosity of Mrs. Blagden's father, accomplished what Disraeli had long desired. The Church was a picturesque building, mainly Early English in style, with a massive tower containing Norman, if not Saxon, work; but the roof was unsound, the tower had a crack extending nearly from top to bottom, and the walls were so much out of the perpendicular as not to be safe. Blomfield, the archi-tect, recommended a new roof, a new aisle with the tower rebuilt at its west end, thorough repair of the walls, and a remodelling of the chancel. The patron took the altera-tions to the chancel as his share. The work was carried out, but not without friction, especially about the manorial right to a seat in the chancel, which Disraeli successfully asserted. Lady Beaconsfield was dead, and her husband was too much occupied as leader of Opposition and Prime Minister to exercise any personal superintendence over the operations.

To the Rev. Reginald Barnes.

GEORGE STREET, HANOVER SQUARE, *Wednesday, June* 11 [1873].—I am much touched by your letter, and shall, with satisfaction, insert your name in the list of our restorers; but as the accomplishment of my wishes is not so near, as I had hoped, you will, I am sure, not misinterpret my returning to you, for a time, your obliging cheque.

Hughenden, in a parochial sense, is no longer the Paradise it was, for nearly twenty years, under the gentleman[1] to whom I wished you to succeed. Parties have arisen among us, the unhappy Education Act[2] has brought affairs to a crisis, and, among other evils, it delays, and may even prevent, my consolatory intention of connecting the restoration of the church with the memory of her, whom I have lost. I thought at Whitsun I had settled these differences, but, since my return to town, they have broken out afresh; and having a great pressure of public affairs on me, and being deprived of the wise and skilful energy, that used to regulate my home interests, I sometimes almost despair of accomplishing my wishes.

I trust your health is good in the Favonian atmosphere of your lovely county. I always remember Devon with delight and affection.

Neither the difficulties hinted at in this letter, nor the fact that the new vicar felt it to be his duty to protest to his patron and principal parishioner against the policy of the Public Worship Regulation Bill, prevented the steady maintenance of friendly relations between the manor-house and the vicarage or the cordial encouragement by the squire of the parochial activities of the vicar and his wife. But Disraeli wrote of his parson to Lady Bradford, half in jest and half in earnest, as a ' rebellious priest,' and he was by no means pleased with the elaborate

---

[1] The Rev. C. W. Clubbe.   [2] Mr. Forster's Act of 1870.

ceremonial with which the restored church was opened. In his speech at the subsequent luncheon, after expresing his satisfaction that it could no longer be said of Hughenden that the house least honoured in the parish was the house of God, he significantly added: ' I trust that we shall show to the country that it is possible to combine the " beauty of holiness " with the profession of the pure Protestant faith of the Church of England.'

To Lady Bradford.

HUGHENDEN MANOR, *Sept.* 30, 1875.—. . . The sacerdotal procession was tremendous; not only a banner, but the Bishop's crosier, borne, and certainly nearer a 100 than 50 clergymen in surplices and particolored scarves. I was resolved not to be betrayed into a speech, and especially an ecclesiastical speech; but I was obliged to bring in a Protestant sentiment by way of protest. Everything was intoned, and the high altar and its rich work absolutely emblazoned with jewels. One lady in Warwickshire absolutely sent a string of pearls, and not mean ones, to enrich the altar cloth.

Nothing cd. be more stupid and misapprehensive than *The Times* remark on Harcourt's speech; wh. was perfectly playful and goodhumored, and very happy. It helped us on; he was so goodtempered that he wd. not allude to the rather ritualistic display, tho' he was glad of my Protestant phrase, wh. saved us. . . .

Disraeli had hoped for the pleasure of a visit from Lady Bradford at Hughenden in October; but she disappointed him at the last moment, and Bradford came alone.

To Anne Lady Chesterfield.

HUGHENDEN MANOR, *Oct.* 14, 1875.—I have been very busy, in many ways, and out of sorts a little, wh. is awkward when people are in the house. So I was not in a vein to write—even to you.

The Northcotes came here on Saturday, and depart to-morrow: a long visit, but there was much to do. There never was such an indefatigable worker as the Chanr. of the Exr.[1] Yesterday he went up to town, to clear up some points, but returned for dinner.

Bradford arrived on Monday, in a very good humor. By

[1] ' He is quite " a little busy bee," ' Disraeli wrote to Lady Bradford.

dining late, and retiring early, the day dies. We also managed a couple of rubbers. I can't, myself, get beyond that. In the third rubber my wits are woolgathering; in Downing St., Pekin, the Herzegovina, and the Admiralty. . . .

Your picture at Hughenden was much admired. Bradford admired it, and said he wd. have one of S. copied for me, and offered me his own. I accepted everything, but as S. wd. not come here, I do not know whether she wd. care to have her portrait here; or rather I do believe that she cares nothing about the matter.

I was very busy the morning of Tuesday, and have been so all the time, but we managed pretty well. . . . B[ernal] O[sborne] came down for dinner, and was, of course, immensely amusing, and Bradford seemed really pleased. They played whist in the evening, I sitting out, and Brad[for]d went off to Weston yesterday morning. B. O. departed this [morning], and the Ns. go to-morrow. . . .

The portraits which Bradford promised reached Hughenden early in the New Year.

To Lord Bradford.

Private. HUGHENDEN MANOR, *Jan.* 11, '76.—Lady Bradford arrived at Hughenden last night; a most charming picture; and you have signally added to the many kindnesses for which I am indebted to you and to your house.

It will be the greatest, and most treasured, ornament of my Gallery of Affection; for I shall have no portraits in it, except Byron, but of those who have personally influenced my heart and life. Those [? that] of Her Majesty, after her favorite and famous new painter, Herr von Angeli, and that of yourself, will soon arr ve, and you will find them, I trust, on your next visit to Hughenden.

Here is a pleasant picture of Disraeli's working day, when alone, as Prime Minister, at Hughenden:

To Lady Bradford.

HUGHENDEN MANOR, *Oct.* 18, 1875.—. . . I do not breakfast in public: I only did that, in the summer, to see you, as I thought it was perhaps the only opportunity (and it often was) of seeing you in the course of the day, or of speaking to you, wh. you always seemed to grudge me.

I always rise at ½ pt. 7, go thro' my bag, and after my

THE LIBRARY AT HUGHENDEN.

toilette, saunter on the terrace, if the sun shines, and review
the peacocks; then I go up to my little room (my cabinet),
for my correspondence, and work at that till one.   Then
déjeûner; and at ½ past one, the messenger arrives, and as now
I am not at home to any human being, I change the scene
after *déjeûner*, and work at my boxes in the library.   It is a
favorite room of mine, and I like to watch the sunbeams on
the bindings of the books.

Now that you are more knowing in such things, I shd.
like to show you some of my Renaissance books.   My
Guicciardini and my Machiavelli are, as becomes such writers,
modern editions; but there are many volumes, of less use no
doubt, but of more rarity, wh. wd. charm your eye and taste.

Some day when I have time, wh. I really have not now,
for only to you cd. I write this, I will tell you about *Somnium
Poliphili*, the dream of Poliphilus, one of the most beautiful
volumes in the world, and illustrated throughout by Giovanni
Bellini, as only in the Renaissance they could illustrate.   But
I was delighted yesterday, as I have been delighted before
and after, by a thin folio of the sacred time   It is a letter from
Cardinal Bembo to Giulio de' Medici, opening the Cardinal's
grand scheme for the nation to renounce writing in Latin and
dead languages, and dare to form a popular style in their own
beautiful vernacular.   The subject, the author, the beautiful
printing, the pages, 400 years old but without a stain—all
these are interesting circumstances; but then the exquisite
binding with the tiara and the keys, and the arms of the
Medici, boldly tooled on the side of the book—for Giulio had,
in the interval, become Pope Clement 7 !   This was his
own copy, and must have been captured and secured in the
famous sack of Rome by the Constable of Bourbon. . . .

2, WHITEHALL GARDENS, *Nov.* 20.—. . . I agree with you
in liking him [Lord Hartington].   Indeed, I think he is
exactly the man to suit you; having all he qualities you
require and appreciate; a certain distinction, only made up
of fashion, rank, intelligence, and personal influence, and
none of that imagination and surplus sensitiveness, wh.
disturb the cream of existence, and wh., tho' for a moment
interesting from novelty, are ultimately found to harass and
embarrass life.   ' He is easy to get on with because he is not
spoilt.'   We know who is constantly said to be ' spoilt,' tho'
perhaps most unjustly, and who, therefore, is not easy to get
on with. . . ,

CHAPTER XI.

An Imperial Foreign Policy.

1874–1875.

It was as an ' imperial country ' that Disraeli, when laying down his programme in 1872, invited his hearers to regard Great Britain; to maintain and heighten its imperial character was the special work at which he laboured as Minister. During the early months of his Administration the process was mainly silent and almost unperceived, though the diplomatic world soon began to realise that the atmosphere of British diplomacy under the inspiration of Disraeli was different from that to which they had grown accustomed since 1869; that observance of European treaties, respect for British rights, and consideration for British opinion in matters of European concern, were expected and would, if necessary, be enforced. The veil was a little lifted in May, 1875, when it was discovered that a wanton renewal by Germany of her attack on France would be resented not only by Russia but, under Disraeli, by England also; that England, with Disraeli Prime Minister, was not prepared to regard with indifference Continental complications which, though they might not affect her directly, yet would grievously upset the European balance. A sudden opportunity in November, 1875, revealed in a flash the new spirit, and immediately arrested the attention of the world.

The situation of Great Britain when Disraeli was called to power was in many ways unsatisfactory. There was, indeed, great prosperity at home. Though the social improvement of the mass of the people had not kept pace with the increase of wealth, and though there had been so many years of abounding trade and good harvests that, in the normal cycle, bad 'times were nearly due, still the immediate prospect was good. Abroad, however, the reputation of the country had sunk. Looked up to for half a century as the leading power in Europe, she had been treated as a negligible quantity at the time of the Franco-German War; she had permitted Russia to tear up, no doubt under the guise of due diplomatic formalities, the Black Sea clauses of the Treaty of Paris; she had so mismanaged her relations with the United States as to have to put up with a judgment which condemned her to pay preposterously exaggerated damages for her negligence during the Civil War. Germany under Bismarck dominated the European field; but for the moment a more serious domination for the British Empire was that of Russia in the Near Eastern and Asiatic field. While Russian influence in this sphere extended from year to year, the direct connection of England with her great Asiatic dependency of India and with her Australasian dominions had been rendered less secure. Since the discovery of the Cape of Good Hope, the main route from Europe to India, and, indeed, the only one, with the exception of tedious caravan tracks across deserts and mountains under Turkish control, had been for generations by the open sea round Africa. In the middle of the nineteenth century competition had been set up by the establishment of the overland route across Egypt from Alexandria to Suez; this involved breaking bulk and was only suitable for passengers, mails, and light wares. But in 1869 the journey had been absolutely revolutionised by the opening of the Suez Canal, which provided the means of a short, and uninterrupted, sea voyage from England and Europe to India, Australia, and the East. Palmerston had realised what a change the Canal would make in the defensive position of the British Empire, and had therefore opposed the project from the first. Disraeli also had opposed it, relying, however, mainly on what he believed to be its engineering impracticability. Gladstone had supported it in the name of progress, ridiculing the possibility of danger arising from it to British interests. As the English followed Palmerston's lead and refused co-operation, the Canal had been built by French enterprise and French money; it was managed by a French company, whose head office was in Paris; and the shares were held, roughly speaking, half by Frenchmen, and half by the Khedive of Egypt, the ruler of the country through which it passed, who was himself a more or less independent feudatory of the Sultan of Turkey. The Eastern trade was diverted at once to the new route, and, from the first, 75 or 80 per cent. of the shipping which used the Canal was British. Accordingly what became, as soon as it was completed, a vital link in British imperial communications was under the control of a foreign company and at the mercy of a foreign ruler. Gladstone, who held office during the first five years of the Canal's existence, refused, in spite of several opportunities and of the representations of some of his colleagues, to take any steps to remedy this unsatisfactory position and to secure British interests in the new waterway.

Meanwhile Russia was pressing on, both in Europe and in Asia. In Europe she had restored her power in the Black Sea, had started a menacing Pan-Slavonic propaganda, and was becoming as formidable as ever to the Sublime Porte. In Asia, in spite of repeated assurances from the Tsar and his Ministers to the contrary, her proconsuls were rapidly advancing her frontiers by annexing, one after another, the decadent Tartar and Turcoman States which occupied the country between Siberia on the north, and Persia, Afghanistan, and India on the south. General Kaufmann, who became Governor of Turkestan in 1867, captured Samarkand and subdued Bokhara in 1868, and reduced Khiva in 1873, proceeding in 1875 to the conquest of Khokand north of the Syr Darya. In 1870 he opened friendly communications with the Ameer of Afghanistan, into whose immediate neighbourhood Russian power had now penetrated. The Indian Government, to whom the Ameer referred this new development, treated it with indifference, relying on the assurances of the St. Petersburg Government that they regarded Afghanistan, the frontier State across which an invader from the north-west must advance to attack India, as completely outside the sphere of Russian influence. Kaufmann was therefore able to proceed without interference in a persistent policy of tampering with the Ameer's fidelity to the British connection. After the fall of Khiva, Sher Ali, the Ameer, felt that the advance of Russia made it indispensable for him to know where he stood between the two great European forces in Asia. He asked for a definite promise of aid from the British Government in case of Russian attack; and one of the last acts of Gladstone's Ministry was to refuse, in adherence to the Lawrence policy of avoiding all intermeddling with Afghanistan, any definite engagement beyond vague assurances of support. From this time Sher Ali steadily gravitated to the Russian side.

For dealing with difficulties of this kind Disraeli was especially fitted by the bent of his mind and the experiences of his career. It was the fortune of Great Britain, at a time when the British Empire in Asia and the highway to the East were threatened, to have a Prime Minister of Oriental extraction and imagination, whose whole outlook had been coloured at the most impressionable period of his life by his travels in the Levant, and who had played a large and decisive part in the affairs of India in the troubled fifties. Disraeli's personal and anxious attention to the problem was therefore assured; but he necessarily relied much on two colleagues, his Foreign Secretary and his Indian Secretary, Derby and Salisbury. The intimate political and personal relations which had bound him to Derby from the first made their confidential co-operation, in spite of serious differences of temperament, easy and natural; but with Salisbury, just converted from critic into colleague, the beginnings of mutual trust had to be created. Disraeli, guided by good feeling no less than by his knowledge of men, set himself to win confidence by giving it; showing abundantly the reliance he felt on his colleague's capacity to administer rightly the great affairs entrusted to his care, and his own anxiety to help and support him in all difficulties; and recurring, as we have seen, to his advice on many important matters outside departmental work. Approximation was aided by the mutual realisation of a great community of aim in imperial affairs, and of a considerable similarity of temper and method in dealing with them. A lover of peace, Salisbury was never afraid on fitting occasion to assume serious responsibilities which might lead to war; resembling in this respect his chief, and having none of that tendency to hesitation and procrastination which often afflicted Derby at a critical moment.

In the very first days of the Government we find Disraeli making arrangements for combined working with Derby and Salisbury, and following with keenness the Russian advance in Central Asia.

To Lord Salisbury.

BRIGHTON, *March* 7, 1874.—Lord Northbrook's letter is dated Feb. 5th. He had then received Sir Henry Rawlinson's mem. but does not seem to have received a copy of Lord Granville's despatch to Ld. A. Loftus dated Jan. 7th; but wh. as I learn, was not sent off till the 17th.

Lord Northbrook cd., therefore, know nothing of the subsequent assurances of the Russian Government; that no such expedition, as he referred to, was to take place.

The despatches of Lord A. Loftus in consequence of Lord Granville's despatch, and the concluding despatch of Prince Gortchakoff to Comte Brunnow, of wh. a copy was left with H.M.'s Government (communicated to Granville by Brunnow on the 17th Feb.), contain, on the part of the Russian Govt., a complete disclaimer of the intentions, wh. it was supposed to entertain at the time when Lord Northbrook's letter was written; this information is, therefore, superseded by what we have since heard.

The Russians may be lying, but we cannot do more, so far

as diplomacy is concerned, than obtain from them such pledges as they have given.

But the question arises, have you seen these despatches ? I have in MS.; and they are, now, in that form, I believe, circulating thro' the Cabinet—but it strikes me, that the system of communicating such information among ourselves is not a very convenient one.

The whole correspondence is in print at the F.O. by this time, and a copy will, of course, be sent to each Cab. Minister. This by the way.

It seems to me, that a private communication to you from the Viceroy should be treated as a private letter from an Ambassador to the For. Secy. of State. It is always forwarded to the P. Minister, but not circulated, unless it leads to questions of instant business and responsibility.

In the instance of Northbrook's letter, had it been sent on to me immediately, I should have requested you and Lord Derby to have met me at D. S. and then we would have ascertained exactly how we stood. There ought to be some system, especially in these times, when the Secretaries of State for F.O. and India should be able to communicate with more promptitude, and, if necessary, reserve, than at present seems the habit. I do not, at this moment, see any better system, than that which I have intimated—but we will talk the matter over together, and I doubt not will arrive at a sound conclusion.

I question, also, the expediency of sending despatches, like Lord Northbrook's, in a common circulation box, except marked 'strictly confidential.' In these days, every private secy. has a Cabinet key, I believe—perhaps I might add, I fear; and we should encourage some processes of reserve.

I feel confident you will not be offended by the frankness of these remarks. They are literally *currente calamo*, and are jotted down rather for our future joint consideration, than in any spirit of pedantic over-regulation. . . .

Not merely the Central Asian question, but also that of the Suez Canal, was forced on Disraeli's attention immediately on assuming office. Ferdinand de Lesseps, the great Frenchman who had conceived and executed the work, had hitherto failed to make it remunerative, and had in consequence given the Gladstone Government those opportunities of securing British interests in the Canal which they had neglected to utilise. His latest resource had been to increase the tonnage duties from which the company derived its revenue by levying them on a novel basis which the maritime nations, and especially Great Britain, considered not to be warranted by the terms of the concession, and which, early in 1874, had been condemned as illegal by an International Commission. Lesseps defied the Commission and the British Admiralty, insisted that no ship should be let through the Canal which did not pay on the higher scale, and was only reduced to reason by the mobilisation by the Khedive of 10,000 men to evict the company.

To Lord Derby.

WHITEHALL G., *April 23, 1874.*—The Lesseps affair is getting serious; he has gone to Jerusalem to get out of the way, but there is little doubt he intends mischief, at least what we call mischief, for, so far as I can judge, the law is on his side.

I do not like to contemplate the Canal being shut up for months, wh. will probably be the case.

Could we advise the Porte to postpone the enforcement of their regulations for one month; and, in the interval, make an arrangement? Lesseps is 'toujours prêt de negocier sur la base du droit.' His self-love would be spared and soothed, if you took the matter in hand, and you would gain European glory.

My own opinion is that the ultimate and proper solution would be an International Commission, like that of the mouths of the Danube.

From Lord Derby.

Private. F.O., *April 24, 1874.*—Read Col. Stokes's mem. on the Suez Canal. . . . You will see in this the true explanation of Lesseps's conduct. The surtax question is little more than a pretext. Our engineers were right as to the difficulty of keeping up the Canal when made. Port Said is silting up, and cannot be maintained in a state of efficiency without an outlay greater than the company can afford, except at an absolute sacrifice of profit for years to come. In fact, the undertaking is all but bankrupt: and M. L[esseps] is probably well pleased at having an excuse to get out of it.

We cannot let the Canal go to ruin: it is too useful to us. Stokes suggests buying out the shareholders, by guaranteeing them a fixed dividend, and working the Canal through the agency of an International Commission. There are difficulties in the way, obvious and grave; but things really look as if this were the only way out of the scrape. . . .

Our course is plain. Lesseps has put himself in the wrong, all the Powers are agreed in saying so (even France): and we must maintain our decision. That does not preclude his being fairly, and even generously, treated. But you must bear in mind, in considering his recent sayings and doings, that the thing is a commercial failure, utter and hopeless, and that he knows it.

Disraeli did not rest content with solving the immediate difficulty. He made up his mind to secure British interests in the new waterway by obtaining some control over the company, whose ' bankrupt ' state seemed to provide an opportunity. He went to work, not through the regular diplomatic agency, but by the private methods which he had used in the Government of 1858–1859, when he had sent Earle on a mission to Napoleon III. It was, on one side, a financial matter, and he invited in May the aid of the prince of financiers, his old friend Baron Lionel de Rothschild; with the result that Rothschild's eldest son, M.P. for Aylesbury, and afterwards Lord Rothschild, went over to Paris to intimate to Lesseps that the British Government were prepared to purchase the Canal if suitable terms could be arranged. The mission was a failure. French patriotic feeling, then reviving after the disasters of the war of 1870, was not disposed to tolerate any surrender of French rights over a French canal; and Lesseps, after his repeated rebuffs by England in past years, and his quarrel with the British Government and British shipowners over the tonnage question, was in no mood to renew his previous offers. Disraeli was disappointed, but waited his time, keeping constantly in touch with the Canal authorities. ' On more than one occasion,' he told the House of Commons in 1876, ' M. de Lesseps came over here himself, and entered into communication with us as he had before with our predecessors, but there was no possible means of coming to any settlement which would be satisfactory to the proprietary.'

In the comparative calm of the first eighteen months

of the Disraeli Administration, a few episodes in foreign
affairs attract attention, and may serve to indicate the
Prime Minister's aims and methods.   A visit to London,
during the first session, of the Tsar Alexander, whose
daughter had just been married to Queen Victoria's
second son, the Duke of Edinburgh, was the occasion of
a difficulty with the Court, which Disraeli was able to
settle in such a fashion as to command the admiration
of his colleagues, and to contribute materially to the
maintenance of friendly relations with Russia.   The
Emperor's visit was to be prolonged for a couple of days
beyond the date fixed by the Queen for entering upon
that spring sojourn at Balmoral which her physicians
prescribed for her health; and Her Majesty refused at
first to modify her plans.

From Lord Derby.

Private.   F.O., *May* 4, 1874.—The more I think of the
matter, and the more I hear what is said, the stronger becomes
my conviction that the Queen's going away during her guest's
stay in England will really make a serious trouble.   It will
be talked of everywhere as an instance of incivility so marked
as to appear intentional: it will be resented by the Russians,
who are as touchy as Yankees, and for the same reason: it
will entirely destroy whatever good result may be expected
from the marriage and the visit: in India it will be taken up
by the native press—much of which is nearly as seditious as
that of Ireland—as a proof that the two countries are not
really on good terms; and what possible excuse can we make ?
Not health, for if the great lady can bear 5 days of ceremonies
she can bear 7: not public business, for what has she to do at
Balmoral ?   It is . . . the less excusable because, of all
persons connected with the reception, she will have the least
personal trouble.
   As a rule, I try always to keep matters which concern the
Government, and matters which concern the Court, as far
apart as possible : but it is not always possible: and if there
is a row, part of the blame will fall on us.
   Do try what you can to set this business right.   Nobody
can have managed the lady better than you have; but is
there not just a risk of encouraging her in too large ideas of
her personal power, and too great indifference to what the
public expects ?   I only ask: it is for you to judge.

To Lady Bradford.

Ho. OF COMM., *May 5.*—My head is still on my shoulders. The great lady has absolutely postponed her departure! Everybody had failed, even the Prince of Wales; but she averted her head from me—at least I fancied so— at the drawing room to-day, and I have no doubt I am not in favor. I can't help it. Salisbury says I have saved an Afghan War, and Derby compliments me on my unrivalled triumph. . . .

From Queen Victoria.

May 7.—. . . [The Queen] feels much the kindness of Mr. Disraeli as expressed to herself and Sir William Jenner on the occasion of the delay of her departure for Scotland. . . . It is for Mr. Disraeli's sake and as a return for his great kindness that she will stop till the 20th. . . . The Queen thinks Lord Derby and Lord Salisbury have little knowledge of what is the etiquette between Sovereigns.

Disraeli took his full share in the festivities held in honour of the Russian visit.

To Anne Lady Chesterfield.

2, WHITEHALL GARDENS, *May 15, 1874.*—. . . Yesterday was the great festival at Windsor, and really not unworthy of the Crown of England. St. George's Hall was a truly grand scene, and cd. not be easily surpassed: at least I have never seen it equalled, tho' I have dined, in the great days of France, in the Gallery of Diana. . . .

The Emperor is high-bred: dignified, but soft in his manners, not that *ton de garnison* wh. offends me sometimes in the Russian Princes, particularly the Cesarevitch, and the Grand Duke Constantine.

I only arrived from Windsor to-day at noon. At 3 o'ck. I am to have an audience of the Emperor at Buckingham Palace. I dine at Marlboro' House to meet him; and I close with a ball at Stafford House in his honor! And at ½ past four I must be at the House of Commons! It is difficult to get thro' such a day, and I have to change my dress as often as an actor! . . .

May 16.—. . . At three o'ck. the Emperor held a levée of the Diplomatic Body and our Ministry at Buckingham Palace. There I had an audience, which was an audience rather of phrases, but nothing but friendliness to England and hopes that my Government wd. cherish and confirm those feelings. His mien and manners are gracious and graceful, but the expression of his countenance, wh. I now could very closely examine, is sad.

Whether it is satiety, or the loneliness of despotism, or the fear of violent death, I know not, but it was a visage of, I should think, habitual mournfulness. . . .

The Government and the Queen did not miss the opportunity to strengthen the bonds of amity between England and Russia. Under Derby's advice the Queen expressed to the Emperor on his departure her desire for a frank and free exchange of ideas at all times, so as to avoid misunderstandings between the two countries— a desire which Alexander reciprocated. Disraeli, how- ever, did not believe that in existing circumstances complete agreement was possible. He wrote to Salisbury on June 2: ' I have no great faith in a real " understanding with Russia " as to our Eastern possessions, but much faith, at this moment, in a supposed understanding, wh. will permit us to avail ourselves of the present opportunity of settling and strengthening our frontiers.'

Early in 1875 differences about the proper treatment of the Spanish Government brought out in high relief the characters of four individuals who were shortly to have a large share in moulding that Eastern policy by which the Beaconsfield Government is mainly remembered. The chaos of Republican administration in Spain had culmin- ated towards the close of 1874 in a strong movement for a Bourbon restoration; and in January, 1875, the young Alphonso, son of the ex-Queen Isabella, was proclaimed King. Queen Victoria, attracted by the romance of a youthful Prince restored by an unexpected turn of Fortune's wheel to his hereditary throne, and anxious to support the cause of Constitutional Monarchy in Europe, pressed for his immediate recognition, and for the observance by the British Government of a very sympathetic attitude to the new régime. Derby, the Queen complained, was ' so terribly impartial that he will never express interest one way or the other '; but it was surely wise, in regard to a country which

had gone through so many revolutions in the past
six years, to use the caution and circumspection by
which the Foreign Secretary was, above all men,
distinguished. Derby was confirmed in his waiting
attitude by the British Minister at the Spanish Court.
This was Austen Henry Layard, the excavator of Nineveh,
an old acquaintance of Disraeli's, nephew of the Austens
who had befriended the young author of *Vivian Grey*.
Layard, a Palmerstonian Liberal, had been Foreign Under-
Secretary in Palmerston's last Administration; and was
therefore more in sympathy with the Republican Government which had fallen than with the Conservative
Administration which Alphonso established and which
necessarily relied on Catholic support. But in any case
he was right in advising the Home Government to be
cautious, as a formidable Carlist insurrection on the one
hand and the discontent of the Republicans on the other
rendered Alphonso's prospects doubtful. The Queen was
impatient of these arguments, which Derby pressed on
her with more logic than sympathy, and wrote of him to
Disraeli as ' that very peculiar person Lord D.,' who was
' very difficult to manage.' It needed all Disraeli's tact,
and his loyalty to his Sovereign on the one hand, and to
his colleague and his colleague's agent on the other, to
steer through the difficulties. He was less disposed than
Derby to trust Layard entirely, and wrote to Derby on
January 12: ' It is unfortunate, at this crisis, we have
such a man as Layard there. Tho' of unquestionable
talents, he is prejudiced and passionate, and always—I
will not say misleads—but certainly misinforms us ';
on February 20; ' his tone is not diplomatic '; and on
March 2, he deprecated ' the exaggerated view Mr.
Layard takes of the Protestant party and interests in
Spain. They really are nothing,' Disraeli shrewdly
added, ' and tho', when the Republican and infidel
party is in power, the Protestants are permitted to hold
up their heads in order to mortify the Church, their
number and influence are alike contemptible.' But, as

he told Derby, 'I make it a rule to support everything which you have well considered,' and therefore sustained his policy against the royal remonstrances.

He was, however, especially anxious to promote a cordial and sympathetic feeling between his royal mistress and his colleague, and succeeded at any rate for the moment. The artist, the diplomatist, and the courtier in Disraeli are all brilliantly displayed in a letter which he wrote to the Queen describing his management of his uncourtly friend.

To Queen Victoria.

2, WHITEHALL GARDENS, *March* 21, 1875.—Mr. Disraeli with his humble duty to your Majesty:

He is grateful to your Majesty for your Majesty, amid all the cares and pressure of public business, graciously making him acquainted with the result of the audience of the Secretary of State. It much relieved Mr. Disraeli, for the disquietude of your Majesty on this matter has often greatly distressed him.

He had an interview with Lord Derby after the Cabinet, which was at 12 o'clock and lasted two hours. Mr. Disraeli spoke to him very seriously and earnestly about affairs, and adjured him, in the approaching audience, to do justice to himself, and step out of his icy panoply.

The necessary gulf, between a Sovereign and her Ministers, is no bar to confidence and sympathy, and, without these qualities, it is difficult to see how public affairs in England can be satisfactorily carried on.

Lord Derby did not speak a single word, but, when Mr. Disraeli closed the interview, he would accompany Mr. Disraeli, and when they reached the street door in Downing Street, instead of going into the Foreign Office, he offered Mr. Disraeli his arm, and would walk home with him, but in silence.

Mr. Disraeli invited him to enter his house, and lunch. He replied he never lunched; it prevented work. And, then, even with softness, he gave Mr. Disraeli his hand, which is not his habit, and said 'Good-bye, old friend.' 'Dear friend' Mr. Disraeli assumes Lord Derby would say to no one, but Mr. Disraeli had hopes, from this moment, that the impending audience might happily bear fruit. . . .

The points of view of the Queen and the Foreign Secretary were, however, too divergent to be permanently reconciled. The Queen pressed for the removal of Layard

to some other post, and Derby definitely appealed to his
chief for support. 'The question really is,' he wrote on
April 22, 'whether our representatives abroad are to
send statements of fact which seem to them true, or to
colour them and dress them up to suit what they suppose
to be the prevailing ideas at home. . . . I cannot agree
to any proposal for [Layard's] removal, unless it were to
give him a better post; and even then I do not think this
would be a convenient time.' Disraeli at once (April 24)
rallied to his colleague's side. 'As I do not think you
ought to bear all the brunt of the fray, I have written
to the great lady, I think, conclusively on the matter:
telling her that, in the opinion of her Govt., L. is
substantially correct in his views; that he cannot be
removed, as it would be a triumph to the *Parti Prêtre*.'

The Queen, according to her sound constitutional
practice, yielded to her Prime Minister and Foreign Minister; but her instinct was right as against Derby's caution
and Layard's prejudice. Alphonso XII. established his
position, to the advantage of Spain and of Europe, and
his son occupies his throne to-day with a granddaughter
of Queen Victoria as his royal consort. Layard was
retained at Madrid till he was promoted in 1877 to be the
convinced instrument, at the embassy at Constantinople,
of that Eastern policy which Beaconsfield forwarded with
the Queen's support, but which Derby resigned rather
than pursue at the risk of war.

The outstanding fact of the international situation in
Europe, as Disraeli found it on his return to power, was
the dominance of Germany, and of Germany's masterful
Chancellor, Bismarck. He had consolidated the German
people into a strong Empire under the Prussian kingship;
he had bound Austria to his chariot, though as yet only
informally; he had humbled and crippled France; he
was in friendly relation with Russia; and he was now,
by legislation subjecting the churches to the State, trying
a fall with the Pope. His experience of the Gladstone
Ministry inclined him to regard England as a negligible

factor in European affairs; but, until he had better assurances of the temper of the new Government, he showed them a benevolent friendliness, proffering them in particular his good offices in regard to the Eastern Question. 'I begin to think Bismarck means business,' wrote Disraeli to Derby on January 6, 1875, after reading a despatch from Lord Odo Russell, British Ambassador in Berlin; 'and, if so, the future may be less difficult.'

German policy in the spring made the position not less but more difficult. Catholic Belgium was stirred to its depths by the progress of Bismarck's campaign against the Pope; and things were said and done there by bishops and others which were made the excuse for grave warnings by the German Government. Belgium was told that, while it was incumbent upon every State not to allow its territory to be the basis of attacks against the peace of neighbouring States and against the security of their subjects, the doctrine applied with special force to a State enjoying the privilege of neutrality; that the perfect fulfilment of that duty was a tacitly presumed condition of its neutrality. Belgium promptly amended its penal laws in response to this threat to its neutrality and independence; but Disraeli began to realise that it would be necessary to stand up to Bismarck, if life in Europe for other, and particularly smaller, nations was to be tolerable. On reading the despatches from Brussels, he wrote on April 18 to Derby: 'We shall have no more quiet times in diplomacy, but shall be kept in a state of unrest for a long time: probably till the beginning of the next thirty years' war.' He gave a hint in the House of Commons.

To Queen Victoria.

HOUSE OF COMMONS, *April* 12, 1875.—. . . Mr. Disraeli has answered a question to-night about Germany and Belgium, which he hopes may do good, and will not displease your Majesty.

He endeavored to convey the impression, that cordial and confidential relations existed between your Majesty's Govern-

ment and that of Germany, which is flattering to Prince
Bismarck, and which he wishes to be believed, but at the same
time, struck a clear note about Belgium, which the House
understood, and cheered. A county member said to him
when he sate down, 'It was trust in God, and keep your powder
dry.'

From warning Belgium Germany passed to menacing
France. The German press was mobilised to call attention
to the rapid resurrection of French military power and
preparation, German diplomatists held language of a
similar character in the various European capitals,
Bismarck himself spoke serious words to Odo Russell;
and it looked as if he were endeavouring to force a
quarrel upon his recent victim before her recovery was
complete, in order to crush her once for all. France
turned for support to Russia and England, and her
Foreign Minister appealed to public opinion by communicating the facts to Blowitz, the famous Paris correspondent
of *The Times*. But even before Blowitz's article appeared
on May 6 and horrified a world desirous of peace, the
Tsar Alexander, who was about to pay a visit to the
German Emperor at Berlin, seems to have interposed
and sent an urgent message to his expectant host deprecating a hasty decision; and Derby was able on May 2 to
write, perhaps prematurely, to Disraeli: 'I believe the
alarm is over now, but nobody will answer for next year.'

Disraeli was fully alive to the danger, and resolved to
show Bismarck and Europe that England was to be
reckoned with; 'Bismarck is really another old Bonaparte
again, and he must be bridled,' he wrote to Lady Chesterfield. His former tendency to a political friendship with
France was revived. 'I had a rather long conversation
about French politics with Mr. Disraeli,' wrote Lord
Lyons, British Ambassador in Paris, on April 21, 'and
I found him thoroughly well up in the subject. He
wishes to encourage confidence and goodwill on the part
of France towards England, but sees the danger to
France herself of any such appearance of a special and
separate understanding as would arouse the jealousy of

Bismarck.' [1]   Disraeli was entirely in accord with the Queen, who wrote on May 5, that 'every means should be used to prevent such a monstrous iniquity as a war '; and Derby gave formal assurances in this sense to the French Government.

To Lord Derby.

2, WHITEHALL GDNS., *May* **6**, 1875.—I had an audience yesterday: she was very gracious, and, speaking entirely on foreign affairs, I thought very sagacious and intelligent.

She is much pleased with your letter which she praised highly; ' clear and full,' she said. She was ready to do anything, that you and I wished her to do in these matters; would write, if we wished it, to the Emperor of Russia, etc., etc. She said the Emperors met at Berlin on Monday, and they would be there two days. Then she threw out the idea, that Ld. Cowley might be sent there by you—and so on.

My own impression is that we shd. construct some concerted movement to preserve the peace of Europe, like Pam did when he baffled France and expelled the Egyptians from Syria.

There might be an alliance between Russia and ourself for this special purpose; and other powers, as Austria, and perhaps Italy, might be invited to accede. . . .

May 8.—I replied, that in all probability, Schou[valoff] [2] was with you at this moment, and that I wd. write to her at Windsor after I had seen you: also, that there was a Cabinet to-day at three, and, if necessary, I wd. write after that.

I have just got Odo's letter. It only makes me more anxious to pursue the course we contemplated yesterday. . . .

It was on a Saturday that the Cabinet was held, and the Tsar and his Chancellor, Gortchakoff, were due for the Berlin visit on the following Monday. Odo Russell was instructed by telegraph strongly to support the Tsar's movement for peace; and the Queen wrote to both Emperors in the same sense. Ministers felt fairly confident because, as Derby wrote to Disraeli on May 10, ' we know what the [Russian] Emperor is prepared to say and that it is in the sense we desire.' The next day they learnt that the British Ambassador had received all the requisite assurances.

[1] Lord Newton's *Lord Lyons*, Vol. II., p. 73.
[2] Russian Ambassador in London, who had just returned from St. Petersburg to his post, via Berlin.

Lord Odo Russell to Lord Derby.

(*Cypher telegram.*) BERLIN, *May* 11, 1875.—I have had a most satisfactory interview with Prince Gortchakoff at Prince Bismarck's house. They are both agreed that the peace of Europe shall not be disturbed, and co-operate for the maintenance of peace.

Confidential. Prince Gortchakoff has since called to tell me that he is so perfectly satisfied with the result we have achieved and the assurances given that he thinks we had better say no more for the present and allow the subject to drop.

To Anne Lady Chesterfield.

2, WHITEHALL GARDENS, *May* 12.—We shall have peace. . . . The news from Berlin came in the middle of the night on Monday, but they wisely did not wake me. However, it gave me an appetite for breakfast. . . .

The measures taken, first by Russia, and then by Great Britain, had been successful. Peace was for the time assured; and both the German Emperor and Bismarck strongly protested that Germany had never for a moment entertained the intentions attributed to her. The world, however, has made up its mind that the menace was real; the only question still in doubt is whether it proceeded from Bismarck himself, or from the military party forcing his hand. As England did not take action until after the Emperor of Russia had intimated to Berlin his strong disapproval, British intervention on this occasion has often been treated as of little account. In accordance with his temperament, the Foreign Secretary himself was one of the principal minimisers.

To Lord Derby.

HUGHENDEN MANOR, *May* 18, '75.—Your policy seems to be very popular, and very successful—I congratulate you heartily. It is encouraging. We must not be afraid of saying ' Bo to a goose.'

But we must get our forces in trim. We shall be able to do that next year. The revenue is coming in well.

From Lord Derby.

KNOWSLEY, *May* 20.—. . . We have been lucky in our foreign policy; for what we did involved no risk and cost no trouble, while it has given us the appearance of having helped, more than we really did, to bring about the result.

To Lord Derby.

2, WHITEHALL GARDENS, *May* 30, '75.—Let me earnestly impress upon you, in case Granville enquires or pushes you at all, to adhere to what I said in H. of C.: that it would not be expedient that our 'representation' shd. be produced at present. And I don't want it to be produced this sess. It is working well: *omne ignotum, etc.*

However Derby might seek to minimise what he and Disraeli had done, public opinion, both at home and abroad, recognised that England had reverted in a striking manner to the traditions of her foreign policy before Gladstone's premiership. The French Government expressed its gratitude; and Bismarck at once realised that he had to deal now in England with people who could make up their minds and act.

To Lady Bradford.

2, WHITEHALL GARDENS, *May* 14.—. . . P. Bis[marck] has sent a message to me and Derby, thanking us for our interference, and glad to see Eng[land] taking an interest in Cont[inental] affairs again. I believe, since Pam, we have never been so energetic, and in a year's time we shall be more.

Bismarck's compliments veiled a feeling of resentment at having unexpectedly to reckon once more with an international factor which he had come to think might be left out of account. A letter from the Crown Princess of Prussia, which her mother Queen Victoria forwarded to Disraeli, throws much light on the Chancellor's real views and position.

The Crown Princess to Queen Victoria.

POTSDAM, *June* 5, '75.—The Crown Prince saw the Great Man yesterday evening, who is going away into the country for some time. He assured him that he sees no cause any-

where for alarm on the political horizon—that he had never
wished for war, nor intended it—that it was all the fault of
the Berlin press, etc., etc. He said he deeply regretted
England being so unfriendly towards us, and the violent
articles in *The Times* against us. He could not imagine why
England suddenly took up a position against us. That you
had been much excited and worked upon against us, etc.
He even named the Empress Eugénie ! ! ! This seems so
foolish to me ! Certain it is that he did not intend (as you
will read in the little German *aperçu*) to alarm the world to
the extent he has done, and is now very much annoyed at the
consequences. He also fancies that in England there is yet
anxiety about India, and that England must therefore try
to make friends with Russia (*à nos dépens*). The P. of W.'s
journey to India is mentioned as a symptom ! This seems
to *me* very absurd, but that is what he thinks ! Lord Derby's
speech has also offended him, which I cannot understand.
I feel sure that all this irritation will blow over, but to us,
and to many quiet and reflecting Germans, it is very sad,
and appears very hard, to be made an object of universal
distrust and suspicion, which we naturally are, as long as
Prince Bismarck remains the sole and omnipotent ruler of our
destinies. His will alone is law here, and on his good or bad
humour depend our chances of safety and peace. . . .

Disraeli realised that the representations of the country
would not command respect abroad without a sufficient
backing of force. The Cabinet had already sanctioned
in the Budget of the current year additional expenditure
on the Navy and Army, and, after the anxious days of
April and May, even Derby reluctantly agreed that a
further increase was inevitable.

To Queen Victoria.

10, DOWNING STREET, *Jan.* 14, 1875.—Mr. Disraeli with
his humble duty to your Majesty :

Mr. Hardy was able to attend the Cabinet, which sate two
hours, and discussed the military expenditure. There must
be an increase, probably between £5[00,000] and £600,000, on
the Army and Navy. It is to be regretted, that it should
take place this year, as a Conservative Ministry, according
to their opponents, always increases expenditure. But it
cannot be helped, and Mr. Disraeli will be satisfied if the
expenditure, though increased, is not accompanied by fresh
taxation. But the government of the country becomes more

expensive every year. A great portion of the expenditure, too, is automatic, self-acting, as education for example, the amount claimed for which is this year enormous, but cannot be refused. . . .

From Lord Derby.

F.O. [*June*, 1875].—I should be more impressed by these papers if I could remember a time when the C.-in-Chief had not been seriously alarmed at the state of our armaments.

No doubt the Continent is arming; but with Germany and France watching one another, both are more likely to be civil to us than if they were on good terms.

It is a question, too, how long these enormous armaments will be endured by the masses who are compelled to serve.

But I do not suppose you want the question argued on abstract and general grounds. What we have to consider is what we can do.

The discussions in Cabinet left on my mind an impression that an increase of £300,000 or £400,000 is justifiable, because inevitable—I mean taking Army and Navy together. Beyond that we must not go. . . .

It should not be overlooked that during the crisis of May, 1875, as during the Tsar's visit to London in May, 1874, Disraeli's intervention was directed to the promotion of friendlier relations between Great Britain and Russia, an object which, in spite of acute antagonism at one period, he pursued throughout his career. While recognising that the interests of the two countries might well clash, he recognised also that it was the duty of statesmanship, so far as might be, to prevent such a clashing as would lead to war. Hence his anxiety during all these early months of his Ministry with regard to the position of Afghanistan, where he held that a system of drift would be fatal. Salisbury was convinced, and Disraeli agreed with him, that, with Russian emissaries at the ear of the Ameer, it was essential that the Indian Government on its side should have a duly established agent at his court. This policy Salisbury pressed upon Northbrook, the Viceroy; but was met by strong representations of its inexpediency in view of the certain unwillingness, and probable refusal, of the Ameer to accept such an agent.

To Lord Salisbury.

HUGHENDEN MANOR, *Oct.* 15, 1874.—. . . Persia and Afghan[ista]n are broken reeds—and I am sorry to see an inclination, on the part of Northbrook, to lean on them.

Our man in Persia, Thompson, the same. He is restless for arms, ammunition, officers, and, of course, subsidies, for the Shah !

Utterly useless for our object; indeed pernicious, as they would, and rightly, offend Russia. But the arms, the ammunition, discipline, and treasure, if used at all, would probably be used against us—at least, against the Turks.

Oct. 17.—The telegrams I receive from China this morning are very menacing; and I more than fear that war between that country and Japan is inevitable. This will increase your difficulties, for the East hangs together, and is wonderfully mesmeric.

You have a critical time before you in your department. I am sorry to hear that Northbrook disdains the only means by wh. safe intelligence can be obtained in Asia. This is a very serious point. However, I have the utmost confidence in your judgment, firmness, and resource.

CRICHEL, WIMBORNE, *Jan.* 6, 1875.—I had been thinking, for more than a month past, that it would be very satisfactory to me, were I, the moment I got to town, to have a full conversation with you on Indian affairs. They occasion me some disquietude, and would occasion me more, were it not for my firm, I might say unlimited, confidence in the colleague to whom those affairs are intrusted.

And now I receive your confidential and interesting despatch. . . .

I have always been strongly in favor of our Government being represented in Afghanistan, tho' not unaware of the difficulties and dangers. The necessity, however, outweighs everything. It is a question, whether we should not have an agent both at Candahar and Herat. . . .

To Lady Bradford.

10, DOWNING ST., *Jan.* 13, 7 *o'clock.*—. . . Ld. Salisbury called on me this morning at 12, and we had an interesting hour over Central Asia, and all its mysterious fortunes and perils. It is impossible for anyone to be more cordial ! . . .

While the question of the external security of India on its north-west frontier hung fire, Disraeli was deeply engaged in promoting its internal consolidation and

contentment by arranging for a personal visit of the heir
to the Throne. The original idea appears not to have
been his, but to have come from the Prince of Wales
himself, who had already visited the principal Colonies
and rightly thought it his duty now to proceed to India.
The Queen gave her assent; but, on reconsideration of
the many personal and political difficulties involved,
would gladly have recalled it. Her Prime Minister and
Indian Secretary, however, recognised the immense
political importance of establishing those personal relations between the British Throne and the princes and
peoples of India, on which Disraeli had insisted at the
time of the Mutiny. Disraeli, at the Queen's request,
undertook the management of the affair, with Salisbury's
assistance; and a thorny and anxious business he found
it. There was the critical question of expense. 'A
Prince of Wales must not move in India in a *mesquin*
manner. Everything must be done on an Imperial
scale,' as the Queen and her Minister agreed. 'The
simplicity of arrangement which might suit a visit to
our own fellow-subjects in the Colonies,' Disraeli said in
the House of Commons, would not equally apply in the
case of India. There was that remarkable and deeply
rooted characteristic of Oriental manners—the exchange
of presents between visitors and their hosts. Presents
of ceremonial could rightly be discouraged; but the Prince
would visit immense populations and be the guest, or
make the acquaintance, of many chiefs and rulers, and
he 'must be placed in a position to exercise those spontaneous feelings, characteristic of his nature, of generosity
and splendour, which his own character, and the character
of the country likewise, requires to be gratified.' Disraeli
accordingly proposed a vote, in addition to the charge
for the cost of the journey, of £60,000 for the Prince's
personal expenses during the visit.

The sum was felt by the country to be moderate; and
many of the Prince's personal friends and even some of
his Anglo-Indian counsellors advised him that he was not

being treated generously. The Prince himself was too amiable to bear any grudge—'the most amiable of mortals,' Disraeli wrote of him this year to Lady Chesterfield, but 'a thoroughly spoilt child,' who 'can't bear being bored. I don't much myself,' he added. Still, between the indignation of the Prince's entourage and the Queen's dislike of the whole expedition and desire to curtail it, Disraeli's social and official steering during the summer of the year 1875 was a delicate matter requiring a dexterous touch. He was justified in the end, as his estimate proved to be within the mark; and yet the Prince's progress was on a sufficiently imperial scale.

Disraeli's letters illustrate various phases of the controversy.

To Lord Salisbury.

2, WHITEHALL GARDENS, *June* 13, 1875.—I think you had better not report, to H.R.H., the Queen's approval.

One of his present grievances, is that Her Majesty does not communicate with him directly, but by her Ministers. . . .

I am now going to write to him fully on all the matters; worse than 'gathering samphire'; and to Her Majesty. . . .

To Lady Bradford.

2, WHITEHALL GARDENS, *July* 7.—. . . General Probyn and Mr. Ellis came to me about the eternal business and its ever-recurring difficulties. The Prince is at Newmarket.

I have had ceaseless correspondence with the Faery, who had refused Prince and Secy. of State, to permit H.R.H. to hold an investiture of the Star of India, and things looked very black indeed. I had to interfere. . . . She writes: 'As you recommend me to do it I consent, but I don't like it.' This is not pleasant. Then she summons me again for Sunday to the Château, wh. is most inconvenient. . . .

July 17, *Friday.*—All went well last night, but it was a very hard one. I made clear to the House and the country the *two* sorts of visits wh. the P. might make to India, and showed, I hope without offending him, how, after the second programme had been adopted by the Govt., his thoughtless parasites had substituted for it the first.

The letter in *The Times* signed 'A Conservative M.P.', was written by Randolph Churchill, under the dictation of Blandford and Bartle Frere. Under their inspiration he had

430 AN IMPERIAL FOREIGN POLICY   [CHAP. XI

prepared a Marlboro' House manifesto, and utterly broke down, destroying a rather rising reputation. The letter is a mass of absurdities. It assumes the P. is to make presents to the 95 reigning Princes. If he visited them all, his tour wd. be six years, not six months. He will visit only about five. . . .

Do you think I ought to dine at Stafford House on Tuesday to meet the P. of Wales ? or wd. it be better for me to write to the Duchess and get off ? Advise me. . . .

July 19.—. . . Yesterday, after work and church, I called on Sir Anthony de R[othschild], whom I cd. not see, and doubt wh[ethe]r I shall see again.[1] I saw, however, his wife. . . . I am sorry—very—for Sir Anthony; a thoro[ugh]ly good fellow, the most genial being I ever knew, the most kind-hearted, and the most generous. The P. of W. had called and would see him, and said he had seen one of the prettiest women in London that morning, and when he said he was going to call on Sir A., she replied, ' Then give him my dearest love.' Poor Sir A. was *intrigué*, and, pleased and perplexed, could not find out that the lady was the Pss. of Wales. . . .

Then I dined at Piccadilly Terrace[2] where I had invited myself (the day before), and where they then said, on Saturday, they were quite alone exc[ep]t Neilson. But I found a most amusing party, wh. they had scrambled up—Louise,[3] who was delightful tho' a little noisy, too shrieking in her merri-ment, and Harty-Tarty, and Count Corti, whom I had not seen for ten years, and the Peels, and B[ernal] O[sborne] and Chas. Villiers. . . . I took in to dinner Neilson, who pleased me, for she did not sing.

Did you hear how the Prince intrigued the Dss. of Suther-land at the masqued ball ? He addressed her, ' How do you do, Mrs. Sankey ? How is Mr. Moody ?' Very good, I think.

I dread my Stafford House dinner to-morrow. There was a Greenwich dinner on Friday or Saturday; the Prince there. The D. of Sutherland arrived, and said, ' What a shabby concern this vote is ! If I were you, Sir, I would not take it. I wd. borrow the money of some friends at five pr. ct.' ' Well, will you lend it me ?' sd. the Prince, wh. shut the Duke up.

If H.R.H. knew I had so successfully proved he was a wit, perhaps he wd. pardon me. . . .

Disraeli's apprehensions were, of course, rather of a mock-heroic character. At any rate, early in October

---

[1] Sir Anthony died in January, 1876.
[2] Baron Lionel de Rothschild's house.
[3] Duchess of Manchester.

the Prince, on the eve of departure, invited him to Sand-ringham for a long week-end visit, and treated his guest with high consideration.

To Lady Bradford.

HUGHENDEN MANOR, *Oct.* 13, 1875.—. . . I was so utterly overwhelmed by the disappointment of not seeing you[1] that I found it impossible on Sunday to write to the Prince (and cd. scarcely converse with my guests). I quite gave it up— I mean the letter; but I had a feeling of remorse at the last moment on Monday, at not following yr. suggestions, wh. I always wish to do, and sent a few lines, wh. he cd. not have received till past seven o'ck. on the eve of his departure. Nevertheless he found time to write me a touching letter and to send me his photograph with his signature, and the fatal date of his departure. . . .

From the Prince of Wales.

MARLBOROUGH HOUSE, *Oct.* 11, '75.

MY DEAR MR. DISRAELI,—I am much touched by your kind letter and good wishes on my long journey, and I thank you for your advice which I shall always be most ready to accept at your hands. I am fully alive to the importance of my visit to India and hope that neither you or any one else in my land will have cause to regret that the honour of my country has been placed in my hands whilst in India. Am I saying too much in stating this ? It will always give me the greatest pleasure to hear from you, and I know that you will always be a good friend to me.

Please accept the accompanying photograph and—Believe me, Yours most sincerely, ALBERT EDWARD.

The Prince's visit, which occupied the cold weather of 1875–1876, was eminently successful. In the midst of his progress, he wrote on January 9, with becoming modesty, to Disraeli: ' My tour through India continues to interest me in the highest possible degree. The work has been hard at times, but the reception from all classes of the natives has been most gratifying, and if on my return home I shall have met with the approval of the Queen and my countrymen, I shall have every reason to

---

[1] Lady Bradford had failed to fulfil her engagement to stay at Hughenden. See above, p. 403.

look back to my visit to this splendid country with the
feelings of the greatest possible satisfaction.' Apart from
his success in introducing the personal note into the
relationship between the Sovereign in England and the
subject in India, the Prince's good feeling and sense of
right led him to make, on one vital topic, generous and
fruitful representations.

To Lord Salisbury.

2, WHITEHALL GARDENS, *Dec.* 13, 1875.—I have just
returned from Windsor. . . .   Read extract from letter of
P. of W. to the Queen; and a passage I have marked in pencil.
Frequently I hear of this. Nothing is more disgusting, than
the habit of our officers speaking always of the inhabitants
of India—many of them descended from the great races—
as ' niggers.'
    It is ignorant, and brutal—and surely most mischievous.
We ought to do something. If you be in town, I should be
glad to see you. . . .

    It was natural that Disraeli should warmly welcome
and enforce representations so entirely in harmony with
what he had laid down in the fifties as the proper policy
of the British Government in India. ' Something ' was
done at once. Salisbury took the opportunity of an
address at Cooper's Hill, the Indian engineering college,
to warn the students against treating natives with
contumely and violence, or exhibiting race-arrogance in
any form. And Lytton, who succeeded Northbrook as
Viceroy in the spring of 1876, made the first case of native
ill-treatment and official condonation, which occurred
after his arrival in India, the occasion of a drastic minute,
which, though issued in defiance of current Anglo-Indian
opinion, had a far-reaching effect.
    It was while the final preparations were being made for
the Prince's departure from England that Disraeli learnt
that Northbrook, for private reasons, proposed to resign.
He was not entirely surprised, for he had written to
Salisbury on June 8: ' My own impression is that, somehow or other, Northbrook's reign will soon terminate,

and you and I must look out for the right man.'   For the
moment it was an awkward complication; but it provided
an opportunity for bringing the Government of India
into harmony with the Cabinet by placing at its head
someone who would receive in a more sympathetic
manner than the retiring Viceroy the anxious suggestions
of Disraeli and Salisbury for the strengthening of the
British position on the north-west frontier.

To Lord Salisbury.

HUGHENDEN MANOR, *Oct*. 15, 1875.—I think it unfortunate,
that Northbrook wishes not to fulfil his term.

If his intended resignation be announced at once, the public
mind, agitated at this moment about India, will impute his
withdrawal to any motive except the private one alleged,
and wh. indeed, under no circumstances, will ever be
credited. . . .

But, if the resignation be announced during the Prince's
visit, it will be still worse, for it will then certainly be imputed
to a misunderstanding with His Royal Highness.

I don't think he deserves an earldom—but you deserve
anything—and, therefore, if, on reflection, you wish it, he
shall have five balls.   Hardinge was only a viscount, and he
fought battles and gained victories.   Consider this.

Water, I trust, will not prove fatal to the Government.
Between Plimsoll, the *Vanguard*,[1] and the Admiralty Instruc-
tions and Minute, we seem in a leaky state: but it is only
October, and there is time, I hope, to caulk. . . .

Oct. 28.—I have called the Cabinet together, for the 4th
Novr., to confer, and decide, upon our course respecting
these accursed Admiralty Instructions. . . .

There is none of my coll. whose opinion I more value, than
your own.

Here I was going to end, but I can't resist telling you, that
I am anxious, and a little disquieted, about Central Asian
affairs.   Before you bring them, even indirectly, under the
consideration of the Cabinet, I think it would be better, that
we should confer together.

I am quite prepared for acting with energy and promptitude in the direction of Herat, if we could only come to a
bona fide understanding with Afghanistan.   But can we ?
If a movement on our part, wh. is not only to secure our

---

[1] H.M.S. *Vanguard* had sunk in Irish waters after collision in a fog
with H.M.S. *Iron Duke*.

Empire, but to preserve their independence, is actually used by Russia to create ill-feeling between us and Afghan[ista]n, that would be a deplorable result.

However, I have great confidence in you and a little in myself, and I trust, therefore, we may be equal to a critical occasion.

Can you suggest a good High Ch. Dean, who is not a damned fool, and won't make himself ridiculous ?

From Lord Salisbury.

Confidential. INDIA OFFICE, *Oct.* 31, 1875.—. . . Touching Central Asia: I should much like to talk the matter over with you: for the decision is one of great responsibility. The dilemma is simply this. It concerns us much to have an agent in Afghanistan. We want to guide the Ameer, and to watch; for there is the double danger that he may play us false, or, remaining true, may blunder into operations which will bring him into collision with Russia. It would also be a great security for peace, if we were able to keep the Czar, who wishes for peace, informed of the intrigues of his frontier officers, who do not. But on the other hand it is of great importance—I quite admit it—not to irritate the Ameer. But this is a sort of difficulty which the Indian Government has had constantly to meet. Diplomacy has been a real power in Indian history—because of the moral ascendancy which British officers have acquired over the Princes at whose Courts they were placed. I do not propose to send a mission to Afghanistan against the Ameer's wishes: but I propose to tell the Government of India to make the Ameer wish it. It cannot of course be done straight off—by return of post: but by the exercise of tact in the choice of the moment and the argument I feel sure that it can be done. The Ameer is genuinely frightened of the Russians: and every advance they make will make him more pliable, *until* their power on his frontier seems to him so great, and he is so convinced of our timidity, that he thinks safer to tie himself to them than to us. But on all this I should much like to talk to you.

The Queen has written to Lord Northbrook asking him to keep the secret till the close of the Prince's visit. I have telegraphed to him a similar message from her.

She told me that you proposed to make Lord Powis Viceroy. The intelligence rather startled me: for he has no experience of affairs, and I have noted in him no trace of practical ability. Your own judgment must of course guide you: but I hope you will not decide hastily, as there is plenty of time. The post is terribly important: a feeble occupant might bring about a great disaster.

I have put down in a separate note all that I know about possible High Church Deans—'who are not damned fools' —a formidable restriction !

Though the Queen, as well as Salisbury, was startled by the suggestion, Disraeli had excellent reasons for fixing on the third Earl of Powis [1] as his first choice for Viceroy. If Lord Powis never took a very active part in political life and so came little under the Queen's or Salisbury's notice, he was nevertheless an exceptionally able and well-read man, of sound judgment and tact, and of great reputation in local affairs in North Wales and Shropshire. Disraeli knew him in the House of Commons as one of the eager spirits attracted by 'Young England'; and he conceived that India would welcome as Viceroy the great-grandson, in the direct line, of Lord Clive.

To Queen Victoria.

2, WHITEHALL GARDENS, *Nov.* 5, 1875.—. . . The Cabinet meets again to-day, when Mr. Disraeli hopes to lay before them a general view of the probable business of next session.

After the Cabinet yesterday, at four o'clock, Mr. Disraeli had a long interview with Lord Salisbury.

There is no question now about Lord Powis. He had been sounded by Mr. Disraeli, without any unnecessary confidence, but said his health was too delicate for foreign service, and though he should have liked to have served the Crown earlier in life, he felt, now, it was too late for him to begin.

He is modest, for in presiding, somewhat recently, over the Royal Commission on Irish Education, he showed administrative powers of a high character.

The person whom Mr. Disraeli had fixed upon, for your Majesty's consideration, was Lord John Manners, a man of many admirable qualities, and unjustly under-rated by the public.

He is a statesman; with a large practical experience of public affairs; a student, as well as a practical statesman:

[1] 1818-1891: M.P. for North Shropshire, 1843-1848; High Steward of Cambridge University; first President of the University College of North Wales at Bangor; Lord-Lieutenant of Montgomeryshire and Chairman of Quarter Sessions.

thoroughly versed in all the great political questions of Eastern and European politics; an admirable administrator with a great capacity of labor; a facile pen; brave, firm, and a thorough gentleman. But Mr. Disraeli fears Lord John's health is breaking up.

Lord Salisbury and Mr. Disraeli agreed, that the resignation of Lord Northbrook should be kept quite close and confined to themselves and your Majesty. If imparted to the Cabinet, it will soon be babbled about by the wives. Indeed, the rumor is in the air, and has been more or less for a year. Yesterday Lady Derby mentioned it to Mr. Disraeli, who said ' That is an old story,' but anxious to find out whether it was the old story with her, he extracted, after a little while, her authority—Mrs. Morier.

Mr. Disraeli hopes your Majesty will approve of the Deanery of Chichester being conferred on Mr. Burgon. It will not be displeasing to the High Church party, who are very much offended with Mr. Disraeli, while Mr. Burgon is thoroughly sound on the great questions, being one of the ablest defenders of the union of the Church with the State : now the key-note of ecclesiastical politics, and which the pure Sacerdotalists are attempting to abolish.

Mr. Burgon is one of the most eminent of the resident Oxford clergy; eminent as a scholar, a writer, and a preacher : and a man of original and interesting character.

Mr. Disraeli will keep your Majesty perfectly informed of all that occurs; probably every day.

John Manners, as Disraeli feared when he wrote to the Queen, declined the Viceroyalty because he believed he had not sufficient health and strength for the post; Carnarvon, another colleague, to whom his chief next applied, declined because he was a widower with young children.   After this refusal Disraeli was rather at a loss, and Salisbury, who was ' in despair at the barrenness of the Tory land,' could only suggest names that seemed to him just ' tolerable.'   The Queen mentioned the name of a man who was afterwards a most successful Viceroy— Dufferin; but put it aside as ' he, she is afraid, has not health, and too large a " small family," as the High-landers say, to enable him to accept it.'   He was also a Whig.   Of another suggestion which Her Majesty made Salisbury wrote to Disraeli: ' The appearance of Derby's name is a charming touch of nature.   It reveals a world

of untold suffering—and desperate hope.' Finally,
Disraeli turned, with Salisbury's entire approval, to the
son of an old friend and colleague, the second Lord Lytton,
then British Minister at Lisbon, who combined the
practised deftness of a diplomatist with the imagination
of a poet. 'The critical state of affairs in Central Asia
demands a statesman,' wrote Disraeli on November 23,
'and I believe if you will accept this high post you will
have an opportunity, not only of serving your country,
but of obtaining an enduring fame.' Lytton, who was a
delicate man, had more claim than others who had pleaded
ill-health to exemption on that ground; but, after stating
the facts, he submitted to the decision of the Cabinet,
and, in Disraeli's words, accepted 'the superb but awful
post.' Derby was ready to release him at once from his
service under the Foreign Office, observing cheerfully
that he would die in India, but that to die Viceroy was
something.

To Lady Bradford.

HUGHENDEN MANOR, *Jan.* 5, 1876.—. . . We have been
obliged to announce the great Indian change somewhat sooner
than we intended, and rather suddenly, but it was leaking
out. There is always a traitor—except in the Suez Canal
business.[1] . . .

2, WHITEHALL GARDENS, ½ *past* 6 [*Jan.* 20, 1876].—. . . I
got from the Cab. at ½ pt. 5, and found Lytton waiting for
me; and now he has just gone. I knew him really before he
was born—a few months; and now I see him here, and a
Viceroy.

He told me his first remembrance of me was calling on him
at a little school he was at—at Twickenham, and I 'tipped'
him. It was the first tip he ever had; and now I have
tipped him again, and put a crown on his head! It's like
meeting the first characters of a play in the last scene! . . .

The Far East, as well as the Near East and India,
demanded Ministerial attention in 1875. There were
anxious negotiations with China arising out of the murder
of a British Consular official, A. R. Margary. A letter

[1] See below, ch. 12.

to Lady Bradford shows with what imaginative insight
Disraeli had grasped the essentials of Far Eastern development.

To Lady Bradford.

HUGHENDEN MANOR, *Sept.* 27, 1875.—. . . I have taken a
step in diplomacy, wh. I am sure never was taken before.   I
have induced the Japanese Minister in England to telegraph
to his Government, urging them to offer their mediation in
the event of serious difficulty arising bet[wee]n China and
England, and to declare that if China will not accept that
mediation, and act upon it, Japan will join England against
her, and place a Japanese contingent under the orders of
any British forces employed by us against the Celestial
Empire.   I know not why Japan shd. not become the Sardinia
of the Mongolian East.   They are by far the cleverest of the
Mongol race.   Now you know one of the greatest secrets of
State going !

Hence it appears that, only ten years after Japan had
definitely started on the path of progress, Disraeli
recognised her great qualities and possibilities, anticipated
that she would become ' the Sardinia of the Mongolian
East,' and proposed common action between her and
Great Britain on behalf of their common interests in that
region, thus initiating a policy which culminated, thirty
years later, in the Anglo-Japanese Alliance.

CHAPTER XII.

SUEZ CANAL AND ROYAL TITLE.

1875–1876.

It was while Disraeli's mind was full, on the one hand, of the Indian problems involved in the Russian advance in Asia, in the Prince of Wales's visit, and in the selection of a new Viceroy, and, on the other hand, of the threatened revival of the Eastern question owing to the outbreak in Herzegovina, that the opportunity came, for which he had been waiting, of striking an effective and resounding blow for the security of our imperial communications, and for the strengthening of the British position in the whole Eastern world. On Monday, November 15, 1875, Frederick Greenwood, a journalist of high distinction, who, as editor of the *Pall Mall Gazette*, gave Disraeli and his Government strong but independent support, called on Derby at the Foreign Office to tell him that the Khedive of Egypt, who held some 177,000 out of the 400,000 ordinary shares of the Suez Canal, was negotiating for their transfer to a syndicate of French capitalists, and to urge that the British Government should step in and purchase the shares itself. Greenwood's information was the result of meeting at dinner Henry Oppenheim, a financier largely interested in Egypt, and his political insight and enlightened patriotism prompted his mission to the Foreign Office.

It was a startling suggestion, and was naturally not at first welcomed by the cautious Derby. But Disraeli's imagination discerned at once the high political value of the purchase, and, while the Foreign Secretary reluctantly yielded to the necessity of preventing the great highway of British traffic with British India and British Australasia from passing into wholly French hands, the Prime Minister was eager for a transaction which should demonstrate the importance England attached to her Eastern Empire and sanguine of the immense benefit which would result. It is possible that Disraeli had got wind of the Khedive's negotiations from another quarter. Baron Lionel de Rothschild, to whose good offices Disraeli had already had recourse in connection with the Canal, was, like Disraeli himself and at Disraeli's request, on the lookout for an opportunity; and he may well have got early news from Paris or Cairo of what was in progress. It was Disraeli's frequent habit, when in town on official business out of the season, to offer himself to the Baron and Baroness for dinner, especially on Sunday evenings. At their house, he told Lady Bradford in a letter dated November 20—during the very week whose events we are describing—'there is ever something to learn, and somebody distinguished to meet.' M. Gavard, Chargé d'Affaires of France in London at this time, tells a story of a dinner at Rothschild's at which some such communication passed. As there was also a tradition in the Foreign Office that the information reached the Government from more sources than one,[1] it may well be that Disraeli heard on Sunday night from Rothschild something of what Derby was told by Greenwood on the Monday morning. This may explain the strange omission of Greenwood's name in the private correspondence of leading Ministers during the negotiations; unless indeed we are to attribute the omission to that dislike and contempt of newspapers and editors which have often underlain the outward flattery and deference exhibited by statesmen, but which could hardly be felt by one who,

---

[1] A short memorandum respecting the negotiations of the Khedive with a French group is understood to have reached the Foreign Office from Northcote at the Treasury on the day on which Greenwood called.

like Disraeli, had boasted in Parliament that he was himself a ' gentleman of the press.'

The information reached the Government only just in time. Turkey, the Empire of which Egypt was a semi-independent province, had gone bankrupt in the previous month; the effect had immediately been felt at Alexandria; and the Khedive Ismail, after many years of more than Oriental extravagance, found his credit on the point of collapse. By December 1, little more than a fortnight later, he had to meet the coupons on the Egyptian public debt, or else follow his Sovereign's example and default. From three to four millions sterling were wanted, and he was at the end of his resources. He was in negotiation with competing syndicates of French financiers, prepared, but on onerous terms, to furnish the needful funds. The principal asset he had to offer were these 177,000[1] shares in the Canal; the coupons on which, it should be added, he had already alienated in 1869 for twenty-five years. The proposals made to him involved either the mortgage of the shares or their sale outright. On the previous Friday, three days before Greenwood's call at the Foreign Office, he had consented to sell them for 92,000,000 francs, or £3,680,000, paying interest on them at 8 (afterwards changed to 11) per cent. till 1894, when the dividends would once again be payable by the Canal Company; the option to remain open till the following Tuesday. The holders of the option found serious difficulties in raising the money in Paris, owing to the opposition of the rival syndicate, and asked for, and obtained, an extension of time till the following Friday.

When, therefore, General Stanton, the British agent in Egypt, made, in consequence of orders from home,

---

[1] The number of shares was presumed throughout the negotiations to be 177,642; but on completion of the contract with the British Government they were found to be actually 176,602, or 1,040 less; and a corresponding deduction was made from the purchase price.

For the detailed history of the whole transaction, see *L'Achat des Actions de Suez*, by Charles Lesage, and an article in *The Times* of Dec. 26, 1905, by Mr. Lucien Wolf, with subsequent correspondence on Dec. 27, 28, and 29, 1905, and Jan. 13, 18, 26, 29, and 30, and Feb. 10, 1906.

inquiries on the Tuesday of Nubar Pasha, the Prime Minister, and of the Khedive himself, the sale had already been conditionally arranged, though Ismail characteristically protested that he had never thought seriously of the proposal of purchase, and had no present intention of disposing of his shares. But the intention to mortgage was admitted, as three or four millions must be obtained at once; and Nubar hinted that even by mortgage the shares might be lost, as the Egyptian Government might not be able to redeem their pledge. General Stanton told both Nubar and Ismail that the British Government could not view with indifference the transfer of the Khedive's interests in the Canal, and insisted on a suspension of negotiations in order to give that Government an opportunity of making a proposal —a suggestion which the Khedive welcomed.

Disraeli, on hearing Stanton's report, lost no time. The next day, Wednesday, November 17, the Cabinet, which was holding its usual autumnal sittings, took the matter into consideration, and determined in principle that England should acquire the shares. It is clear from Disraeli's reports to the Queen and from his private letters that the initiative was his, and that the Cabinet, though in the end unanimous, contained influential members who were reluctant to take such a very new departure. These included not only Derby, but Disraeli's special henchman, the Chancellor of the Exchequer, who loyally forwarded at the Treasury his chief's plans, but, even after they had been carried through, registered a protest, on November 26, against what he considered to be a policy wanting in magnanimity, adding emphatically, ' I don't like it.' Reconsideration, however, seems to have modified his views; and before the matter came to be debated in Parliament, he was able to write to Disraeli (January 25): ' So far as the purchase of the Suez Canal shares is in question, I think our case is perfect. Subsequent events have strengthened, rather than weakened, the arguments which induced us to decide on it.'

To Queen Victoria.

Confidential. 2, WHITEHALL GARDENS, *Nov.* 18, 1875.—Mr.
Disraeli with his humble duty to your Majesty:

The Khedive, on the eve of bankruptcy, appears desirous
of parting with his shares in the Suez Canal, and has communicated, confidentially, with General Stanton. There is a
French company in negotiation with His Highness, but they
purpose only to make an advance with complicated stipulations.

'Tis an affair of millions; about four at least; but would give
the possessor an immense, not to say preponderating, influence
in the management of the Canal.

It is vital to your Majesty's authority and power at this
critical moment, that the Canal should belong to England,
and I was so decided and absolute with Lord Derby on this
head, that he ultimately adopted my views and brought the
matter before the Cabinet yesterday. The Cabinet was unanimous in their decision, that the interest of the Khedive
should, if possible, be obtained, and we telegraphed accordingly.

Last night, there was another telegram from General
Stanton (not in reply), which indicated some new difficulties,
but the Cabinet meets again to-day (at two o'clock) and we
shall consider them.

The Khedive now says, that it is absolutely necessary that
he should have between three and four millions sterling by
the 30th of this month !

Scarcely breathing time ! But the thing must be done.

Mr. Disraeli perceives, that, in his hurry, he has not expressed
himself according to etiquette. Your Majesty will be graciously pleased to pardon him ! There is no time to rewrite
it. The messenger for Balmoral is waiting. He thought
your Majesty should know all this, and could not write last
night, as fresh intelligence was hourly expected.

Nov. 19.—. . . The Cabinet considered the affairs of the
Khedive yesterday for one hour and ½, and had, before them,
Lord Tenterden and Colonel Stokes, who has been engaged
by your Majesty's Government on the affairs of the Suez
Canal.

The pecuniary embarrassments of the Khedive appear to be
very serious, and it is doubtful whether a financial catastrophe
can be avoided. The business is difficult, but it is as important
as difficult, and must not be relinquished. We received
telegrams from General Stanton, who had personally seen the
Khedive, and we also returned telegrams.

The Khedive voluntarily pledged himself, that, whatever

happened, your Majesty's Government should have the refusal of his interest in the Canal. All that can be done now, is to keep the business well in hand. . . .

From Queen Victoria.

BALMORAL, *Nov.* 19, '75.—The Queen thanks Mr. Disraeli for his letters. She has telegraphed her approval of the course he intends pursuing respecting the Suez Canal, but fears it will be difficult to arrange. . . .

To Queen Victoria.

2, WHITEHALL GARDENS, *Nov.* 20, 1875.—Mr. Disraeli with his humble duty to your Majesty:

Received the telegram yesterday, which was most encouraging. Nothing very significant has happened on the subject during the last four and twenty hours—but communications between your Majesty's Government and Cairo are brisk. The affair will take time, but it must not be lost sight of for a moment; and can now be worked without the Cabinet, as they are unanimous as to the policy, and have given *carte blanche* to Mr. Disraeli to carry it into effect. Your Majesty's approbation greatly strengthens him. . . .

Stanton received the Cabinet decision of Wednesday in time to notify the Khedive the same night [1] that the British Government was ready, if satisfactory terms could be arranged, to purchase the shares. The Khedive expressed his contentment, but continued to protest that he had no present intention of disposing of them. He added that he was obliged to proceed with the mortgage, but, if he changed his views about sale, he would give the British Government the option of purchase. He immediately carried his project of mortgage into effect by signing next day a fresh contract with the owners of the previous option. British opposition and the difficulty of raising in Paris the money for purchase had put an end to the first negotiation. The present arrangement was an advance of 85,000,000 francs (£3,400,000) for three months at the exorbitant rate of 18 per cent. per

---

[1] The dates given in Stanton's despatch of Nov. 18 are not quite clear; and M. Lesage, apparently wrongly, places this notification on Thursday, Nov. 18, instead of Wednesday, Nov. 17.

annum. For this the Khedive pledged not merely the 177,000 shares but his right to 15 per cent. in the annual profits of the Canal. In default of payment, the shares and the 15 per cent. were to become the property of the syndicate, and the Khedive promised to pay 10 per cent. in lieu of the alienated coupons. The contract was to be ratified by November 26.

Presumably the Khedive was reluctant to place himself in the hands of the British Government; otherwise it is difficult to understand how he ever consented to a transaction so unfavourable to himself. It was called a mortgage, but the terms were so onerous that it was, in fact, a disguised sale. This was fully realised by the syndicate, and by Lesseps himself, who entered eagerly into the campaign in Paris to raise the money which should assure French domination over the Canal. Making use of this argument, he urgently prayed the French Government to interpose and remove all financial obstacles to the negotiation. But the Duc Decazes, the French Foreign Minister, was anxious to do nothing to alienate the British Government, who had intervened in a friendly and decisive manner on behalf of France at Berlin in the spring; and he must have realised that the great maritime Powers, and England at their head, could not view with indifference any arrangement by which the control of the main waterway between Europe and Asia would pass entirely into French hands. He sent the Chargé d'Affaires in London to sound Derby, and received the answer he must have expected. Derby pointed out that, as the Canal was our highway to India, and as nearly four-fifths of the shipping which used it was British, our interest in its maintenance and proper management was greater than that of any other European nation; that the possession by the Khedive of a large interest in the company was one of our main safeguards in dealing with Lesseps; and that 'we should certainly be opposed to these shares falling into the hands of another French company, so as to make the property in the Canal more French than it already was.' There possibly might not, he added, be the same objections to a mortgage, provided the Khedive had full power to redeem at any moment.

This categorical answer, which showed that Derby's initial hesitation had now given place to firm resolve, effectually prevented the French Government, though Disraeli seems still to have suspected them, from rendering any assistance to the French syndicates, and so brought the negotiations for a mortgage to naught. It was given on Saturday, November 20, and on the Tuesday, the Khedive, having learnt the failure of his negotiations with Paris financiers, and being encouraged by Derby's friendly assurances of anxiety to help him on reasonable terms, offered the 177,000 shares to the British Government for £4,000,000, with interest at 5 per cent. till the coupons were liberated. The offer was considered by the Cabinet on Wednesday, November 24, and accepted. On November 25 the contract was signed at Cairo, and on November 26 the shares were deposited there in the British Consulate. The whole transaction had been completed in ten days.

When once the policy of purchase had been accepted in principle, as it was at the Cabinet of November 17, it was essential to discover at once whether the £4,000,000 could be procured in time. Parliament was not sitting, and the affair would not wait. 'I am sure,' wrote Northcote to Disraeli on November 22, 'that there is no way by which we can raise the money without the consent of Parliament, and that the utmost we could do would be to enter into a treaty engaging to ask Parliament for the money, and then let the K[hedive] get it in advance from some capitalist who is willing to trust to our power of getting Parliamentary authority.' In these circumstances Disraeli's mind had naturally turned to his friends the Rothschilds, the magnitude of whose resources he knew, and whose aid he had already sought and obtained in connection with his Egyptian policy. Corry used to tell a story that Disraeli had arranged with him that he

should be in attendance—as was indeed his duty as
principal private secretary—just outside the Cabinet room
and, when his chief put out his head and said ' Yes,'
should take immediate action. On this signal being
given he went off to New Court and told Rothschild in
confidence that the Prime Minister wanted £4,000,000
' to-morrow.' Rothschild, Corry was wont to declare,
picked up a muscatel grape, ate it, threw out the skin,
and said deliberately, ' What is your security ?' ' The
British Government.' ' You shall have it.' We need not
take as gospel the whole of this picturesque detail; but
it is certain that at an early stage, the 17th or 18th of
November, Corry applied to Rothschild on Disraeli's
behalf, and obtained a promise of his co-operation. The
terms were finally settled with the Treasury at the beginning of the following week. ' I find,' wrote Northcote
to Disraeli on November 24, ' Smith and Welby a good
deal startled by the largeness of Rothschild's commission.
It will, I suppose, be criticised, but, if the business goes
right, a matter of that kind will not signify much.' Lowe
in the House of Commons was maladroit enough to base
his objections to the transaction largely on this point.
When it is considered that two millions were provided
by the firm for the Khedive on December 1, another
million on December 16, and the last million on January 5, the commission of 2½ per cent. will seem moderate
for so vast and prompt an accommodation. The withdrawal of four millions for a considerable period from the
resources even of so commanding a firm as that of the
Rothschilds necessarily entailed a large derangement of
the routine of its business; and they had obviously to
protect themselves against possible fluctuations in the
value of money, and against the conceivable, though
remote, risk that Parliament would refuse to vali-
date the purchase. It was a transaction entirely without precedent, as Rothschild pointed out to Corry in a
conversation at the time of the debates in Parliament.
In the same conversation Rothschild met another

criticism, often urged, that Ministers should have used the Bank of England, and not a private firm, as their agents.

. . . As to the question whether the Government should not have applied to the Bank of England, Baron Rothschild —giving no opinion as to the Bank's *power*—says that he understands the authorities to be about equally divided (even now) on the point of their *willingness* to have acted as the agents of the Government in this transaction. It is a point, moreover, which could only have been determined by the full Board, at the obvious sacrifice of despatch and secrecy. Mr. Hubbard, for one, is clear that the Bank could not, and would not, have acted (Mr. Hubbard tells me that he is prepared to say this in Parliament.—M. C.), while Mr. Gibbs and Mr. Thomson Hankey take the other view. Baron Rothschild imagines that the Government might, possibly, have *compelled* the Bank to find the four millions (and at a lower rate of commission). But this would have been a violent act, before the commission of which, he maintains, they were bound to use every endeavour to obtain the money from independent firms. He declares, too, without hesitation, that the Bank of England could not have found the required sum without grave disturbance of the money market.

It is upon the entire absence of such disturbance, under his operations, that he from a public point of view, rests his vindication of the commission charged, and is content that the matter should be judged by the results. . . .—M. C., *Feb.* 19, 1876.

It is no wonder that in his letters to the Queen and Lady Bradford after the final decision Disraeli should have sounded loudly the note of triumph.

To Queen Victoria.

2, WHITEHALL GARDENS, *Nov.* 24, 1875.—Mr. Disraeli with his humble duty to your Majesty:

It is just settled: you have it, Madam. The French Government has been out-generaled. They tried too much, offering loans at an usurious rate, and with conditions, which would have virtually given them the government of Egypt.

The Khedive, in despair and disgust, offered your Majesty's Government to purchase his shares outright. He never would listen to such a proposition before.

Four millions sterling! and almost immediately. There

BARON LIONEL DE ROTHSCHILD.

From a portrait at New Court.

was only one firm that could do it—Rothschilds. They behaved admirably; advanced the money at a low rate, and the entire interest of the Khedive is now yours, Madam.

Yesterday the Cabinet sate four hours and more on this, and Mr. Disraeli has not had one moment's rest to-day; therefore this despatch must be pardoned, as his head is rather weak. He will tell the whole wondrous tale to-morrow.

He was in Cabinet to-day, when your Majesty's second telegram arrived, which must be his excuse for his brief and stupid answer: but it was ' the crisis.'

The Government and Rothschilds agreed to keep it secret, but there is little doubt it will be known to-morrow from Cairo.

From Queen Victoria.

WINDSOR CASTLE, *Nov.* 25, '75.—This is indeed a great and important event, which, when known, will, the Queen feels sure, be most popular in the country. The great sum is the only disadvantage.

The Queen will be curious to hear all about it from Mr. Disraeli, when she sees him to-day.

To Lady Bradford.

2, WHITEHALL GARDENS, *Nov.* 25, 1875.—As you complain sometimes, tho' I think unjustly, that I tell you nothing, I will now tell you a great State secret, tho' it may not be one in 4 and 20 hours (still you will like to know it 4 and 20 hours sooner than the newspapers can tell it you)—a State secret, certainly the most important of this year, and not one of the least events of our generation.

After a fortnight of the most unceasing labor and anxiety, I (for between ourselves, and ourselves only, I may be egotistical in this matter)—I have purchased for England the Khedive of Egypt's interest in the Suez Canal.

We have had all the gamblers, capitalists, financiers of the world, organised and platooned in bands of plunderers, arrayed against us, and secret emissaries in every corner, and have baffled them all, and have never been suspected. The day before yesterday, Lesseps, whose company has the remaining shares, backed by the French Government, whose agent he was, made a great offer. Had it succeeded, the whole of the Suez Canal wd. have belonged to France, and they might have shut it up !

We have given the Khedive 4 millions sterling for his interest, and run the chance of Parliament supporting us

We cd. not call them together for the matter, for that wd. have blown everything to the skies, or to Hades.

The Faery is in ecstasies about ' this great and important event.' . . .

I have rarely been thro' a week like the last, and am to-day in a state of prostration—coma. . . .

WINDSOR CASTLE, *Nov.* 26, 1875.—A most hurried line to tell you that nothing cd. be more successful—I might say triumphant—than my visit. The Faery was most excited about Suez, said ' what she liked most was, it was a blow at Bismarck,' referring, I apprehend, to his insolent declarations that England had ceased to be a political power. This remark she frequently made, showing it was the leading idea of her mind.

I got here at ¼ to 6, and was summoned to the presence exactly at 6. . . . When I cd. get to general business, tho' I had an awful catalogue of demands and suggestions, they were comparatively soon exhausted: no difficulties made, every-thing granted, nothing but smiles and infinite *agaceries*. . . .

There were only courtiers at dinner. After din., altho' I had been in audience till ½ pt. 7, the Faery came up to me again, and was not only most gracious, but most interesting and amusing: all about domestic affairs. She shewed me, by the bye, at dinner, a couple of tels. she had received that morning from P. of W., and she wished me to write to him about Suez and all that. ' I wish it,' she sd., ' because he likes you.'

Lady Biddulph said after dinner she shd. resign if the Primo dined often there, as she cd. not stand while the Faery was talking to me. . . .

The Times has only got half the news, and very inaccurate, but it is evidently staggered. I believe the whole country will be with me. The Faery thinks so. . . .

Nov. 30.—. . . The Faery was in the 10th heaven, having received a letter of felicitations from the King of the Belges on ' the greatest event of modern politics.' ' Europe breathes again,' etc., etc.

It seems that P. Gortchakoff had arranged to call at Berlin on his way home and just catch P. Bismarck after his five months' retirement, and then confer together, and settle, or seem to settle, the Eastern question. It must have been during this meeting, or the day before it took place, that the great news arrived, wh., as it is supposed they were going to settle everything without consulting England, was amusing! Bismarck called on Odo Russell, but the latter unhappily was not at home. Odo called at the For. Office and saw Bülow, who handed him a tel. from Münster, saying ' the

purchase of the Suez Canal has been received by the whole
English nation with enthusiasm '; but not a word cd. be got
out of Bülow himself. . . .

I go this morning to Longleat. . . .

To Queen Victoria.

2, WHITEHALL GARDENS, *Nov.* 27, 1875.—. . . He thanks
your Majesty for the gracious note of last night.

He is assured, that there was only one opinion in the City
yesterday, and the accounts, from all the great centres of
your Majesty's kingdom, this morning, re-echo the same
feeling.

He believes it may, now, be looked on as a great, perhaps
unparalleled success.

But your Majesty predicted this when no one had given an
opinion, and when many great judges looked demure.

Sir Philip Rose to Montagu Corry.

1, CROMWELL ROAD, S.W., *Dec.* 1, 1875.—. . . Is it not
curious that the arrangement which I was urging upon Mr.
D. 18 months ago, to secure the Suez Canal for the English
Govt., should have been brought about, tho' in a much better
way, as my plan contemplated an arrangement with Lesseps
and his company, whereas they have now got a title from
the Sovereign, and have helped that Sovereign at the same
time ?

Disraeli did not exaggerate when he said that the
Ministerial stroke had been an unparalleled success.
Public opinion declared itself strongly on his side; and
even among leading Liberals there were many who
followed Hartington and Goschen in open or tacit
approval rather than Gladstone in indignant opposition.
Though there was naturally a little soreness in France,
Lesseps, having failed in his passionate attempts to prevent the transaction, had the cleverness and good sense
promptly to welcome in a letter to his shareholders the
acceptance by England of that share in the company
which she might have had at the first, and to point out
that the co-operation of the British Government was a
fortunate occurrence for the commercial success of the
Canal. From almost every European country except
Russia there came congratulations. Derby, after his

fashion, gave at Edinburgh in December a minimising account of what he had done; we had merely acted, he said, in order to prevent the great highway, over which we had three-fourths of the traffic, from being 'exclusively in the hands of the foreign shareholders of a foreign company.' This may have reassured some doubters, and certainly veiled, for some eyes at home, the vital significance of the Ministerial action; but in Berlin they were under no illusions.

From Queen Victoria.

WINDSOR CASTLE, *Dec.* 3, '75.—The Queen sends Mr. Disraeli the extract from a letter from her daughter the Crown Princess, which she thinks will gratify him. But Lord Derby tried to pour as much cold water as he could on the great success of the affair of the Suez Canal, though he seemed pleased at the feeling shown everywhere about it. . . .

[ENCLOSURE.]
The Crown Princess to Queen Victoria.

BERLIN, *Nov.* 30, 1875.—. . . I must congratulate you on the newest deed of your Government, the buying of half the shares of the Suez Canal; it sent a thrill of pleasure and pride, almost of exultation, through me ! It is a delightful thing to see the *right thing,* done at the *right moment.* Everybody is pleased here, and wishes it may bring England good; even the great man B[ismarck] expressed himself to Fritz in this sense yesterday evening ! Willy[1] writes from Cassel, 'Dear Mama, I must write you a line, because I know you will be so delighted that England has bought the Suez Canal. How jolly ! !'

The newspapers on the subject have been a pleasure to read (the English ones). The French and the Russians will be much annoyed it seems, but that will blow over, and they have no real cause to complain, so I fancy their irritation will not last.

This will rank in history among the many great, good and useful things done in your reign, and that makes me so proud and happy. I am sure Mr. Disraeli and Lord Derby must be quite delighted at the accomplishment of so important a measure, and at its popularity. The wisdom of it is so self-evident, that it *can* only be popular. . . .

[1] The German Emperor William II.

To Queen Victoria.

CRICHEL, WIMBORNE, *Dec.* 5, 1875.—Mr. Disraeli with his
humble duty to your Majesty:

He thanks your Majesty for your Majesty's most gracious
letter, and the gratifying and very interesting extract which
accompanied it.

He felt the shock of the ' cold water ' himself, though he
had endeavoured to guard against it, and had forwarded,
also, a letter from Lord Carnarvon, very well written, and in
the same vein.

Our consolation must be, that the deed is done, and it
must be an additional solace to your Majesty, that it was
greatly owing to the sympathy and support which Mr.
Disraeli received from your Majesty, and to the clear-
sightedness, which your Majesty evinced in the affair from
the outset. . . .

Derby protested, no doubt with perfect sincerity, that
nothing was further from his thoughts than the establishment of English authority in Egypt; that we merely
wanted a free passage for ourselves and for the rest of
the world, and nothing more. Disraeli's imagination
cannot have been so limited; but he used none but vague
phrases. Anyhow, immediately after the conclusion of
the bargain, in response however, no doubt, to a request
from the Khedive made before it, the British Government
took the first step towards intervention in Egypt by sending a British statesman, Stephen Cave, to inquire into
the tangled financial situation of the country. Thence
we came, as Mr. Lucien Wolf has well put it, ' by successive stages, to the Dual Control, the bombardment of
Alexandria, the "stricken field" of Omdurman, the
dramatic crisis of Fashoda, . . . the poetic *dénouement*
of the Lansdowne-Cambon Convention,' and, we may
add, finally to the establishment of a British Protectorate,
with a Sultan entirely independent of Turkey on the
throne. But Disraeli himself, having secured the British
hold on the Canal, was always careful of French
interests in Egypt, and sought French co-operation.
Accordingly, he never advanced throughout his adminis-

tration beyond the stage of Dual Control, resisting all suggestions to oust France from her share. The withdrawal of France was her own act, when, after Beaconsfield's death, she refused to join in the military operations which put down Arabi's revolt.

Disraeli well understood the kind of spirit in which British statesmen should attack Egyptian problems—the spirit afterwards displayed in such perfection by Lord Cromer.

To Lord Derby.

2, WHITEHALL GARDENS, *Nov.* 26, '75.—I can't approve of the employment of Mr. Lowe, and for this, among others, main reason. Throughout life, he has quarrelled with everybody. We want a calm, conciliatory spirit to deal with Egypt; not to oppose their first impressions and suggestions, but to correct, and change, them, in due time.

I think, that Cave, who has great financial and commercial knowledge, who, tho' ' an Oxford scholar,' has been a Bank director, and a Minister of State, is capable, under our guidance and instructions, of the office.

I think there ought to be no delay in the appointment of some one. . . .

The purchase of the Suez Canal shares promoted materially a better understanding between Disraeli and Salisbury, as what Derby regarded as an unfortunate necessity Salisbury, who, like his leader, possessed imagination, advocated as a stroke of high imperial statesmanship; and a visit to Hatfield in December contributed to the same end.

To Lady Bradford.

2, WHITEHALL GARDENS, *Nov.* 13.—. . . I went yesterday with ' Mary Derby,' whom I continue to call to her face ' Lady Salisbury '—most unfortunate—to Mr. Liebricht,[1] an oculist in Alb[emarl]e St., a famous man, who has only been here two years. I have seen double with my left eye for years, but wd. consult no one, for I assumed it was cat[arac]t, wh. my father and grandfather had, and did not wish to be convinced of the inevitable. But it was no such thing: a change in the focus of my eye, wh. a particular glass cured. Lady

---

[1] The proper spelling of the name seems to have been ' Liebreich.'

Derby had suffered from the same malady and he had cured
her.   That was why I went. . . .

    Dec. 17.—I go . . . to Hatfield.   Go I must, or there will
be all sorts of misunderstandings; but I would almost as lief
go to my execution.

Disraeli had the pleasantest recollections, extending
over many years of the fifties and sixties, of visits to
Hatfield during the time that his friend, who had now
become Lady Derby, was the gracious hostess.   It was
natural that he should be apprehensive of his first visit
under the new régime, considering how bitter had been
Salisbury's criticism and how recent the reconciliation.
Nor is it to be wondered at that, while he wrote afterwards to Salisbury, ' I remember my visit to H. with
great pleasure, and beg to be remembered to miladi and
Jem and Fish,' he should have told Derby at the time,
and through him Lady Derby, that he found it ' extremely
dull, strange people at dinner, and a great many little
boys of various families,' though paying in the same
letter a tribute to the ' ancient nobility ' and ' first-rate
intellect ' of his host.   Of the two descriptions of his
feelings, that given to Derby was probably for the moment
the more sincere; but the awkwardness and inapprecia-
tion on both sides soon passed away; and long before the
close of the Ministry Disraeli was thoroughly at home at
Hatfield, and in very friendly relations not only with his
host, but with his hostess and the family; while, to his
poignant regret, the intimate political and personal ties
which had bound him for thirty years to the Derbys had
been completely severed.

To Anne Lady Chesterfield.

    ·2, WHITEHALL GARDENS, *Dec.* 18, 1875.—. . . We had a
large and gay party at Ashridge, but I think the Pss. Mary
beat them all for her vigor and vivacity. . . .   There was a
concert to the county on Friday.   It was well done. . . .
Mme. Neruda played divinely—like an angel with a fiddle
in an old picture.   I witnessed her début at Orleans House,
9 years ago, and aft[erwar]ds sketched her in *Lothair*, for wh.

she was very grateful, and always reminds me of it.   I dare
say you remember the scene, as you have read all my works,
and often remind me of them.   S[elina] has read very few,
and does not remember a line she has read.

To Lady Bradford.

HUGHENDEN MANOR, *Dec.* 23, 1875.—. . . You revive the
controversy about reading my books. . . .   Those volumes
contain a multiplicity of characters and opinions, and yet I
don't remember your ever having referred to a single one in
all our frequent interviews. *Prima facie* therefore I had a
right to assume you were unacquainted with them.   If you
had read the books, the result is still more mortifying, as
their impression must have been very transient.   You will
exclaim ' Oh ! the vanity of authors !'   I dare say all authors
are vain, even if they be Ministers of State; but I don't think
it is entirely that.   I often feel my writing days are not over,
and there is nothing in life I so much appreciate as a female
critic.   Her taste, and tact, and feeling, and judgment are
invaluable and inspiring.   Therefore I confess I was grieved,
when I found one important and interesting tie between us
cd. not exist—and that, too, when our sources of sympathy
are, I often feel, not too numerous. . . .

From Montagu Corry.

EASTON, *Dec.* 29, '75.—. . . Münster says that we must
expect severe criticism of the Suez Canal affair, or rather
depreciation of the importance of the act.   He knows, he
tells me, that the game of the front bench opposite will be to
represent it to the nation at Lord D[erby]'s valuation.   They
expect that you will make the matter wear a different complexion, so (to quote Münster), ' they will uphold Lord D.
as the trumpet of common sense, and call Mr. D. a reckless
poet.'

The conferences at Hatfield were largely concerned
with the project of an addition to the Royal Title to
denote the new relation in which India, since the Act of
1858, which transferred its government from the company
to the Crown, had stood towards the Sovereign.   Disraeli
had insisted at the time on the vital importance of acting
upon the Indian imagination by establishing personal
contact between the Sovereign and the people; but it was
not thought, after consideration, that the morrow of the

Mutiny was an auspicious moment for Her Majesty to assume a new Indian title. The idea, however, had persisted both in Disraeli's mind and in the Queen's. Very shortly after assuming office he referred to it in a letter to her.

To Queen Victoria.

House of Commons, *April* 14, 1874.—. . . The official intelligence of the contemplated cession of the Fiji Islands has not yet arrived, and the Cabinet has not considered the question, but Mr. Disraeli must confess his impression, that your Majesty will feel it necessary to accept the sovereignty of this southern archipelago—as well as the Empire of India.

The Queen thought the present a suitable time for carrying the project through, and impressed her view upon her Minister. Disraeli, with the reopened Eastern question upon his shoulders, and the Suez Canal transaction as yet unsanctioned by Parliament, would gladly have postponed this particular undertaking to a later day; but could not resist Her Majesty's pressure to accomplish, as a pendant to the Prince of Wales's visit, what he considered to be in itself eminently desirable.

To Lord Cairns.

Confidential. Hughenden Manor, *Jan.* 7, 1876.—The Empress-Queen demands her Imperial Crown. Since our conference at Hatfield, I have avoided touching on the matter, but can do so no longer. Pray let me hear from you, and let me know how it is to be done. . . .

Turn in your mind the paragraph in the Speech from the Throne, which announces the Suez purchase. I have no wish to leave it to the tender mercies of Derby.

To Lord Salisbury.

Weston, Shifnal, *Jan.* 11, 1876.—. . . I am pressed much by the Empress about her Crown, and wrote to Cairns on it a few days back, but his answer, received here on my arrival yesterday, tells me nothing, wh. was not said in our conferences at Hatfield, and, in fact, he refers me to yourself, and, so, you came very *à propos.*

I doubt, whether it can be delayed or avoided, if practicable; and in that case, I would rather have the announcement in the Royal Speech after the Indian Visit paragraph. What then might have been looked upon as an ebullition of individual vanity, may bear the semblance of deep and organised policy: connected, as it will be, with other things.

I have told her that I have mentioned the Imperial matter only to the Ld. Chancellor and yourself: so you can speak to her on it, if you like.

From Lord Derby.

Private. Feb. 10, 1876.—. . . I wanted to mention to you at our last meeting, but had not an opportunity, that Delane has been making very friendly, and even pressing, overtures to Lady Derby; wanting information, and ready to back us up—as he says. You have many means of getting at him, but I think this worth your knowing.

To Lady Bradford.

2, WHITEHALL GARDENS, *Jan.* 28, 1876.—A most busy day, but I have written the Queen's Speech. . . .

There is to be war to the knife when the Houses meet—at least the Flea[1] told me so whom I met yesterday morn. Gladstone is to rush in to the arena; but Lowe is to be awful—crushing, overwhelming: a great invective agst. a stock-jobbing Ministry.

I told the Flea that I doubted not that there wd. be a great deal of noise, but that he might bet there wd. be no division. So he will say that all about town. . . .

Disraeli succeeded this year in persuading the Queen to open Parliament in person. Since the Prince Consort's death, she had only nerved herself to undertake three times, in 1866, 1867, and 1871, the task which she had regularly performed during all the earlier years of her reign. For some years after 1868, ill-health had made it necessary for Her Majesty to husband her resources; but that period of physical weakness was now happily over. Sympathetic as Disraeli was with the womanly feelings which made resumption of her public functions distasteful to the Queen, he was convinced that a Monarchy which was not seen could not continue to hold its place in the hearts of the people. Especially was it in his view

---

[1] Mr. Fleming, a man then well known in London society.

important, in order that the Crown might preserve its due weight in the British Constitution, that the Sovereign should show regularly, by personal association year by year, that Parliament consists of King, Lords, and Commons, and not of Lords and Commons only.   He was moreover, of course, not insensible to the political advantage which might accrue to him and his Government from the proof of confidence in her existing Ministers which the Queen's emergence from retirement on their advice and in their support would give.   One of his first official recommendations in 1874 was to suggest delicately to Her Majesty the resumption of this ceremonial; and though he did not prevail then, his tactful pleading would, but for the unexpected illness of Prince Leopold, have been successful in 1875, as is shown by the following letter:

To Queen Victoria.

B[OURNE]MOUTH, *Dec.* 10, 1874.—. . . He shall not breathe, even to his colleagues, a word as to the gracious contingency referred to in Lady Ely's note.   However interesting to Mr. Disraeli, it is a subject on which he had made up his mind never to press your Majesty, as he knows a long and impending engagement harasses and disquiets.   The gracious act, if it occur, should be quite spontaneous.

It was, of course, peculiarly becoming for the Queen to appear in person at Westminster at the commencement of a session which would have to deal with a Bill augmenting Her Majesty's style and title.   The royal ceremonial proved to be so attractive that Disraeli, who had compassed it, narrowly escaped serious maltreatment in the press of loyal members of Parliament struggling to get into their Sovereign's presence.

To Queen Victoria.

2, WHITEHALL GARDENS, *Feb.* 9, 1876.—Mr. Disraeli with his humble duty to your Majesty:

He offers his congratulations to your Majesty on yesterday: without sun, without joy-bells, everybody seemed excited and happy.   He himself followed the Speaker to the House of Lords, that he might have the satisfaction of seeing your

Majesty in your State, but the throng was so tumultuous, and
so violent, that he could not enter the House, and, in attempting to guard the Speaker, who was at one moment nearly
overcome, Mr. Disraeli himself was nearly borne down, when
he must have been trampled on. He believes that the mob,
which he never saw equalled in violence since the old Westminster elections, was, if not entirely, mainly of members of
the House of Commons. He saw the respectable Mr. Bass
absolutely fighting with a Conservative giant, the member
for Plymouth. And yet all this turmoil was, in a certain
sense, satisfactory; for it was occasioned by a desire to see
your Majesty, and indicates what an immense influence
your Majesty's occasional presence can produce.

Mr. Disraeli believes that, in both Houses, the proceedings
were eminently satisfactory.

In the Commons, the Address was moved, and seconded,
with rare, yet equal ability.

Lord Hartington made an elaborate criticism on the general
conduct of the Government, to which Mr. Disraeli replied:
on all the main points of coming struggle, especially the Suez
Canal, apparently to the satisfaction of a large majority in a
crowded house. As he found himself, necessarily, involved
in a sharp controversial speech, Mr. Disraeli thought it best
not to touch on the Indian visit and the intended alteration
of Imperial style, but reserve his remarks for the Bill, which
he is going to introduce, but, so far as he could collect from
the sympathy of the House with the observations on these
subjects which were made by the Mover and Seconder, under
his instructions, and from the general tone of the press this
morning, he feels persuaded that the Imperial assumption
will be most popular in the country.

Disraeli's prediction that there would be a great deal
of noise but no division on the Suez Canal purchase came
true. The four millions were voted, without challenge
in the lobbies, in the second week of the session, but it
was the prudence of Hartington which avoided a division,
in spite of carping and captious attacks by Gladstone and
Lowe. Disraeli defended the purchase as an act of
' high policy.' Why should we not wait, it was said, till
the French proprietary put obstacles in our way, as we
could always, in the last resort, obtain satisfaction by
the use of our naval force ? His answer was fine and
dignified.

If the government of the world was a mere alternation between abstract right and overwhelming force, I agree there is a good deal in that observation; but that is not the way in which the world is governed. The world is governed by conciliation, compromise, influence, varied interests, the recognition of the rights of others, coupled with the assertion of one's own; and in addition, a general conviction, resulting from explanation and good understanding, that it is for the interest of all parties that matters should be conducted in a satisfactory and peaceful manner.

England, Disraeli pointed out, was a great Mediterranean power, with strongholds upon those waters which she would never relinquish. But her policy was not one of aggression, and she would not interest herself in the redistribution of territory in that quarter, so long as the freedom of the seas and the dominion which she legitimately exercised were not imperilled. The Suez Canal would form a link in the chain of fortresses which we possess on the road to India; by the purchase we gained a great additional security, which we should prize, for the free intercourse of navigation. Disraeli left it to Northcote to justify the prudence of the investment of British money; but that has been amply vindicated by time. What, forty years ago, was bought for £4,000,000 was officially estimated, shortly before the great war, to be worth over £40,000,000.

To Queen Victoria.

2, WHITEHALL GARDENS, *Feb.* 22, 1876.—Mr. Disraeli with his humble duty to your Majesty:

He has had the honor to receive your Majesty's letter of yesterday. The subjects referred to, occupy his constant attention—but are full of difficulties; he means as regards the *Mistletoe;*[1] every effort will be made to fulfil your Majesty's wishes.

The great *Suez* business ended last night, and very satisfactorily. The House of Commons proved, that the opinion of the country on the measure was unchanged, and Mr. Gladstone produced no effect, though he spoke with more than his usual ability.

A fiercer struggle commences to-night, and will not terminate till Thursday.

[1] See above, p. 398.

The fierce struggle which this letter anticipated was on the Slave Circular;[1] a matter in which Disraeli had been the victim of departmental blundering. So strong and general was the anti-slavery feeling that the Government were only saved by a majority of forty-five. Disraeli had wisely deprecated a philanthropic agitation in regard to a delicate question of international law.

To the Lord Mayor of London (Alderman Cotton, M.P.).

Confidential. 2, WHITEHALL GARDENS, *Jan.* 20, '76.—It is of importance for the public interest, that there shd. be as little agitation as possible on the slavery question before the meeting of Parliamt.—otherwise, men get committed to views, which, if attempted to be put in practice, only aggravate the evils, wh. it is our common purpose to prevent.

Slavery is not a party question, and can't be made one. All parties, and all statesmen, have, upon it, the same policy. But we must remember, that resolutions at public meetings, and even Acts of Parliament, can't alter the law of nations. To that we must all bow, and the only consequences of our attempt to defy its omnipotence is,that our naval commanders are cast in damages, and the State itself suffers in the comity of nations.

A public meeting in the city of London, presided over by its chief magistrate, always produces an effect on opinion, and there is no doubt, that, if you can, without too great personal inconvenience, prevent, or postpone for a time, the proposed meeting at the Mansion House, it would be of public advantage.

The purpose of the meeting is wide and wild. It is not the criticism of an act of the Government that is contemplated, which wd. be a limited issue, and might be encountered; but it is to change the whole law of England on the most difficult of all subjects. There will be, as Lord Derby would say, a fine field for ' rant and cant.'

I shd. be glad, therefore, to hear, that the contemplated meeting, by your prudence and discretion, did not take place, and that the citizens will not be favored with the opinion and sentiments of the Lord Mayor on this interesting and difficult subject, until he expresses them as their representative in the House of Commons.

Over the Royal Titles Bill Ministers were much more successful than over the Slave Circular, though they were

---

[1] See above, pp. 396–398.

met at every stage by the devices of faction. A curious
omission on Disraeli's part contributed to inflame his
opponents. In matters affecting the dignity of the Crown,
it had been the practice for the responsible Minister, in
order to minimise controversy, to enter into communication with the leaders of Opposition. But Disraeli, in
spite of the easy social relations which he enjoyed with
both the official Liberal leaders, Granville and Hartington,
neglected this customary and courteous precaution until
the measure was already labouring heavily amid storms
of parliamentary criticism. The Queen took the blame
on herself. She wrote to Disraeli on February 10: ' She
is provoked at the conduct of the Opposition about the
Indian title, but thinks perhaps she ought (as was done
in the case of the Prince's title of Prince Consort) to have
herself informed Lord Granville of it, and thus have
prevented the disagreeable remarks. She could still do
this, and state how much *she* had urged this herself, if
Mr. Disraeli is of the same opinion.' [1] Her Majesty also
accepted the responsibility for a further omission, which
led the Prince of Wales to write to Disraeli from Seville
on April 22: ' As the Queen's eldest son, I think I have
some right to feel annoyed that . . . the announcement
of the addition to the Queen's title should have been read
by me in the newspapers, instead of having received
some intimation on the subject from the Prime Minister.'
Ponsonby wrote on the Queen's behalf to Disraeli on
May 3: ' She blames herself for not having written to
[the Prince] about the Titles Bill, adding, however, that
she certainly thought she had done so.'

The Bill was one to enable Her Majesty to add to the
royal style and title in order to mark the new relation
in which since 1858 she had stood towards India, its
sovereign Princes, and its many and various races. When
he introduced it, Disraeli did not say what the new title
would be; Her Majesty, he told the House of Commons,
would exercise her prerogative and assume that addition

[1] For the correspondence between the Queen and Granville, see *Fitzmaurice*, Vol. II., pp. 161-163.

to her style and title which she deemed expedient and proper. But he used the words ' Empire ' and ' imperial ' throughout his speech. The Prince of Wales's demeanour in India had qualified him, he said, for an ' imperial ' post; the new style would set the seal to the unanimous determination of the people of this country to retain our Indian ' Empire '; the House, by passing the Bill, would show their pride that India was a part of Her Majesty's ' Empire,' and was governed by her ' imperial ' throne. The public and Parliament at once assumed that 'Empress' was the title intended; and there was much indignation, partly real, partly affected, at what was described as tarnishing the grand old title of King or Queen, and introducing the associations of force, violence, and even debauchery which were alleged to attach to Emperor and Empress.

It was not until the debate on the second reading that Disraeli revealed what the new title was to be; and, in an adroit speech, he skilfully led up to the announcement by pointing out the remarkable circumstance that, to those desirous of objecting to the policy, one title alone had occurred; ' which *prima facie* is rather in favour of its being an apposite title.' It was not difficult to dispose of objections which can hardly be read with patience now. As for the ' bad associations ' of the title of Emperor, Gibbon had laid it down in an immortal passage that the happiness of mankind was never so completely assured or so long maintained as in the age of the Antonines—who were Emperors. Nor could the assumption of the title locally at all impair the title of King or Queen of Great Britain. Our Kings had always asserted an equality with Emperors, and the claim had been allowed. Nor was the title un-English; it was used of Queen Elizabeth in Spenser's dedication to her of the *Faery Queen*. The style of Empress of India so completely corresponded with notorious fact that, as Disraeli showed, to the amusement of the House, in a subsequent speech, it had been already attributed to Queen Victoria in a popular school geography of the day.

Disraeli justified the policy of the Bill in a weighty sentence. ' It is only by the amplification of titles that you can often touch and satisfy the imagination of nations; and that is an element which Governments must not despise.' In this and other speeches on the Bill he asked the House to turn from these paltry objections and look at the effect in India. There the Bill was anxiously expected. There the Princes and peoples knew exactly what it meant, and they knew that what it meant was what they wished. The Russian advance in Central Asia made the assumption of the new title peculiarly appropriate.

There is a country of vast extent which has been known hitherto only by its having sent forth hordes to conquer the world. That country has at last been vanquished; and the frontiers of Russia . . . are only a few days' march from those of Her Majesty's dominions in India. I venture to speak on this subject with some frankness, because I am not of that school who view the advances of Russia in Asia with those deep misgivings that some do. I think that Asia is large enough for the destinies of both Russia and England. But, whatever may be my confidence in the destiny of England, I know that empires are only maintained by vigilance, by firmness, by courage, by understanding the temper of the times in which we live, and by watching those significant indications that may easily be observed.

The population of India is not the population it was when we carried the Bill of 1858. There has been a great change in the habits of the people. That which the press could not do, that which our influence had failed in doing, the introduction of railroads has done; and the people of India move about in a manner which could never have been anticipated, and are influenced by ideas and knowledge which never before reached or touched them. What was the gossip of bazaars is now the conversation of villages. You think they are ignorant of what is going on in Central Asia ? You think they are unaware that Tartary, that great conquering power of former times, is now at last conquered? No; not only do they know what has occurred, not only are they well acquainted with the power which has accomplished this great change, but they know well the title of the great Prince who has brought about so wonderful a revolution. I have listened with surprise night after night to hon. gentlemen, on both

sides of the House, translating the title of Empress into all
sorts of languages, and indicating to us what name would
at last be adopted.   The nations and populations that can
pronounce the word Emperor, and that habitually use it,
will not be slow to accept the title of Empress.   That is the
word which will be adopted by the nations and populations
of India; and in announcing, as Her Majesty will do by
proclamation, that she adopts that title, confidence will be
given to her Empire in that part of the world, and it will be
spoken, in language which cannot be mistaken, that the
Parliament of England have resolved to uphold the Empire
of India.

The only objection to the measure of any real weight
was that the Colonies had as valid a claim as India to be
recognised in the royal title.   To meet this point, the
propriety of creating the Prince of Wales Prince Imperial
of India, and his second and third brothers Princes of
Canada and Australia, was canvassed between Ministers
and the Queen.   But it was a clumsy expedient, and was
very wisely dropped without ever being submitted to
Parliament; the Prince of Wales expressing strong
repugnance to the suggested addition to his style.   It
was pointed out by Disraeli in debate that the constant
intercourse and interchange of people between the Colonies
and the Mother Country entirely differentiated their case
from that of India; that the colonists were Englishmen
with relations to the Sovereign comparable to those of
Englishmen who remained at home.   India had a special
claim.   There was, at any rate, good reason for doing
one thing at a time; and the Dominions and Colonies
received their due when King Edward VII., on his accession, acting under the advice of Disraeli's colleague and
successor, Salisbury, and of the Imperial-minded Colonial
Secretary, Chamberlain, assumed the style of *Britan-
niarum Omnium Rex*, thus recognising the 'British
Dominions beyond the seas' as part of his realm.

Hartington's disposition was to leave the responsibility to the Government and let the Bill pass after a
moderate protest; and accordingly the second reading,
being resisted in the lobby by only a handful of Radicals,

was carried by 284 votes to 31, in spite of a speech of vehement opposition by Gladstone.

To Lady Bradford.

2, WHITEHALL GARDENS, *March* 10.—I am well satisfied with last night. When a crowded House ends in a dissolving view, and the Opposition, when the division is called, don't know what to do—run into holes and corners, rush out of the House, or vote against themselves, a Ministry is safe.

I had everything to make me nervous, for I had heard nothing for days but the danger of the situation, and that our own men cd. not be trusted, etc., etc., etc. When I got home from my dinner on Wednesday, I found a box, marked 'secret,' from a colleague on whom I mainly depend, counselling 'surrender.' It rather disturbed my night, I assure you, and I wanted a good one, instead of rising with shattered nerves.

This made me alter my tactics, and I resolved to open the ball with some remarks wh. might conciliate the House generally, and reanimate my friends. I think I succeeded, because I was told, when I sate down, that certain members on the other side of influence and independence, thought that there ought to be now no division, and the Speaker afterwards told me that Ld. Hartington was of that opinion too. But that wd. not satisfy Mr. G., who was brimful, took the reins in his own hands, and after a speech of vituperative casuistry, imagining every combination wh. cd. never happen, fled from his own motion, and left his party in a ditch. . . .

March 13.—. . . Gladstone is quite mad and I have no doubt that, by next Thursday, he will have prepared blowing up materials equal to Guy Faux. I understand it is to be something dreadful, but my friends are firm, and Harry Chaplin is going to give us a speech, out of love for me, and hatred of G. . . .

The measure was disliked by London society, and it had a bad press, *The Times* taking the lead in criticism and ridicule. Thus encouraged, Gladstone and Lowe, on the one hand, and Fawcett and the Radicals on the other, forced Hartington's hand; and the Opposition divided both against the motion to go into Committee and against the third reading, being beaten, however, in each case, by a large majority. This factious resistance puzzled and incensed the Queen. She lavished

her sympathy on her harassed Minister, and was fertile
in suggesting explanations which should smooth his path
and meet all reasonable objections to the policy.

From Queen Victoria.

WINDSOR CASTLE, *March* 11, '76.—The Queen thanks Mr.
Disraeli for his letter received yesterday and greatly rejoiced
at the successful 2nd reading of the Titles Bill, the opposition
to which still remains quite inexplicable to her ! . . .

March 15.—The Queen thanks Mr. Disraeli for his letter
and for all he said to General Ponsonby. She has no fear for
the result, but is sorry for the trouble it causes Mr. Disraeli
and for the ill-advised and mistaken conduct of the Opposition, which will not redound to the credit of the House of
Commons abroad.

There is clearly no feeling in the country against it and
delay might do much harm.

The Queen is really not worrying herself about it, for she
never wished anything that could impair her own old Unionist
title; and therefore her conscience is clear.

March 16.—. . . . Pray let telegrams be sent this evening.
Don't be anxious; all is sure to do well.

March 17.—The Queen is greatly rejoiced at the majority
last night, which she learnt on getting up this morning. She
heard twice during the evening. She cannot but regret the
extraordinary and to her incomprehensible and mistaken
course of the Opposition. She concludes that in the House
of Lords there will be little trouble.

The Queen cannot help taking this opportunity of impressing on Mr. Disraeli the importance of securing *some* newspaper as an organ for the Government. The *Globe* and *John
Bull* are very badly written and the latter so ultra and extreme
in its religious views as to prevent the Queen from taking it
in any longer, the last 3 years.

She hopes Mr. Disraeli is not the worse for all this excitement and annoyance.

March 18.—The Queen thinks, now that the Government
have so triumphantly carried the Titles Bill in the House of
Commons, it would be of great importance (as many really
excellent, loyal people will not understand it, and are full
of apprehension) if Mr. Disraeli, at the last stage of the Bill
in the House of Commons, would state strongly and clearly
that it was, and always had been, the Queen's wish that the
title of Empress of India which had been constantly colloquially used, should apply *only* to *India* and that the title of

Sovereign of the British Empire was *always* to remain what it was now, viz., Queen (or in future times King) of 'Great Britain and Ireland,' the other being added on at the end.

The Queen is very anxious that this should be done, for else she fears people (not the Opposition but the best disposed and ignorant ones) will continue to misinterpret the title, and she may be exposed to annoyance and misapprehension. She would also be glad if it were more generally known that it was *her* wish, as people *will* have it, that it has been *forced upon her!* If all this were once for all clearly put on record the Queen thinks there will be nothing more said about it and it will be completely understood. She would be glad if Mr. Disraeli would bring the purport of this letter before the Cabinet.

(*Same date.*)—The Queen has just received Mr. Disraeli's bag and hastens to answer it, that she fully authorises him to say that there never had been the *slightest intention* of giving the title of Imperial Highness to any of her children, or of making any change in the name of the Sovereign of Great Britain, which will remain precisely the same for all ages, but merely to legalise the name which had been colloquially always used—of Empress of her great Eastern Empire, and adding it on at the end. . . .

From Lady Ely.

Windsor Castle, *March* 21, '76.—. . . The Queen, quite *entre nous,* has been much upset by this debate, and has taken the opposition very badly to her title, personally, and for the sake of you, as the Queen says, ' her kind, good and considerate friend ';—she fears you have been much annoyed, but her displeasure is very great with those who have opposed it. . . .

For the moment, the royal explanations gave pause to the Opposition; and Disraeli became prematurely sanguine.

To Lady Bradford.

2, Whitehall Gardens, *March* 21.—. . . My interview with Harty-T. was satisfactory, tho' of course he could not answer for Gladstone, who gave us as much trouble as he could, being all the night in one of his white rages, and glancing looks at me, wh. wd. have annihilated any man who had not a good majority and a determination to use it.

Never was such a triumphant evening. I carried the Bill thro' Committee without a single amendment, tho' many were tried, and more threatened. This is a most unusual feat. When a Bill is carried thro' Committee without amendments, there is no 'Report' as it is termed—that is to say, a stage when all the old objections may be revived and repeated again; and you go to the 3rd reading and passing it, on the next stage, wh. we shall do on Thursday. I don't think there will be any attempt at a division then, and so I believe [the Bill] will after all pass unanimously. . . .

I look upon the Titles Bill to have proved more than anything the strength of the Ministry. I see no rocks ahead now; and I am going down to the House for the first time this session, without that tension of the nervous system, wh. I have had since Parlt. met. Never was a Government so unfortunate as we were during the recess, and we yet have extricated ourselves out of all our mischances !

To Anne Lady Chesterfield.

2, WHITEHALL GARDENS, *March* 22.—. . . All the hopes and schemes of the Opposition have now failed: Suez Canal, Slave Circular, *Vanguard* Minute, and royal titles. I begin to feel as if it were the end of the session, but I suppose the fires may yet burst out again. March is too early for despair, even for the desperate. . . .

The objectors pursued the Bill even in the House of Lords, where a formidable opposition developed under the lead of the independent Shaftesbury; but the attack was repelled, though not without difficulty. Nor did the outcry cease with the passage of the measure into law. Fawcett and the Radicals concentrated against the Proclamation which was to carry it into effect. In order to disable criticism, Ministers promised that that document should show on its face that the title would not be used in the United Kingdom. Accordingly it was therein set out that 'all charters, commissions, letters patent, grants, writs, appointments, and other like instruments not extending in their operation beyond the United Kingdom' should be excepted from the general use of the new title. This did not satisfy the objectors. Ministers were accused of a breach of faith, and Henry James moved on behalf of the Opposition a vote of censure, which, largely owing to a brilliant reply from Hardy, proved as great a fiasco as previous assaults on the new policy. Disraeli explained once more that the Queen would only assume the title of Empress externally; but for the whole internal Government of the United Kingdom it would not be used. It was really a very simple arrangement, and has worked excellently. The Sovereign's signature is decorated with an 'I' in addition to the familiar 'R'; in public proclamations 'Emperor of India' follows 'Defender of the Faith'; and the legend on our coins ends with 'Ind. Imp.' But the King has been King and nothing more in official and in ordinary use in these his Kingdoms; only in India, where the change has been heartily welcomed, is he King-Emperor. The fears of the Opposition of 1876 have proved to be chimeras. But the world understood that a new pledge had been given of the determination of the British Crown to cherish India; and her Princes and peoples understood that their Sovereign had assumed towards them a nearer and more personal relation.

'Greater nonsense was, I think, never spoken in both Houses of Parliament'; such was the Prince of Wales's terse and just appreciation, in a letter to the Queen, of the objections of the Opposition. But, nonsensical as it was, the factious controversy none the less bore heavily on the ageing Disraeli, as his private correspondence shows.

To Lady Bradford.

2, WHITEHALL GARDENS, *March* 30.—How is Juliet ? Our factions are not quite as fierce as the Montacutes and Capulets, but Shaftesbury, I really believe, wd. do anything. . . . He was invited to dine [at Windsor], and his denunciations of unutterable woe were his amusing small talk in the circle after dinner ! . . .

To Anne Lady Chesterfield.

10, DOWNING STREET, *March* 31, 1876.—. . . I am living in a fiery furnace. There never was such a factious Opposition. However, the Bill was read for the second time yesterday in the Lords without a division. The great struggle is on Monday, and I hope the faction will be overthrown.

The insolence of the D[uke] of —— surpasses belief. I will, some day, greatly chastise him. When I thought in the autumn that there would be a vacancy in the Cabinet, I recommended the Queen to appoint him ! I won't do that again in a hurry.

The weather is delicious: the spring of Ausonian lands. I walked to Selina in the morning and lunched at 43 [Belgrave Square]. In my walk, strolling up the shadowy walks of the Green Park, and lost in thought, somebody seized my hand, which was on my back. I started, and turned round—and it was S. !

2, WHITEHALL GARDENS, *April* 2.—To-morrow is the great Battle of Armageddon, when it will be decided, who governs England, I or the newspapers.[1] So far as I can judge, my friends will rally well. . . .

Some want us, if we have a good majority, to give up the title ' Empress.' They are the same people who wanted us, after the Slavery division, to give up our Circular and ' prevent agitation.' It would not; it wd. have been an act of weakness, not of conciliation. And now, whoever hears a word about the ' Circular ' ? Perfectly dead. If you want to govern the world you must know how to say ' Bo ' to a goose. And what is the use of power, if you don't make people do what they don't like ?

To Lady Bradford.

2, WHITEHALL GARDENS, *April* 4.—It was a substantial majority[2]—but with decent whipping might easily have been 60. . . .

April 6.—. . . Harty-Tarty has much disappointed me, for he lends himself to every device of faction—even when they are palpably violent and injudicious. After a council at Ld. Granville's on Tuesday, Gladstone present, they resolved to take up Fawcett, who was to move an Address to the Crown before the Proclamation cd. be issued, and they wished me to pledge myself that no Proclamation shd. be issued until the Address had been moved in the H. of C. Harty and Co. counted on the motion coming on after the recess, and the country being agitated during the holidays. I would not stand this and offered Fawcett Monday the 10th, wh. he pretended gratefully to accept; but I heard last night that there is disorder, and some discontent, in their camp, and that they will not fight on Monday. I think of giving the Commons as long a holiday as the Lords, for they have been much worked these two months. That would be to the

---

[1] Or, as Disraeli put the question in a letter to Lady Bradford, ' who shall rule the country, the Queen's Minister, or Printing House Square.'
[2] 137 to 91.

27th. In that, or indeed in any case, a Council could easily be held before Parliament reassembles, the Proclamation wd. be issued, and the affair finished. At present, the only apparent result of all this faction is that H.-T. has doubled my majority in the House of Commons, and ascertained that I have a majority, wh. I rather doubted, in the House of Lords. . . .

I dined in the evening at the Somers. . . . There were the Randolph Churchills; he glaring like one possessed of a devil, and quite uncivil when I addressed [him] rather cordially. Why? I thought at first it was something about the mysterious correspondence—but, perhaps, a simpler cause, that I gave the lordship of the Treasury to Crichton instead of himself. . . .

In the evening there was a reception, which is now a rare performance to me, but in which I distinguished more than one strata of society. While I was observing the world, the most impudent of women in it, a Mrs. —— of ——, addressed me. I never was introduced to her, and she once came to my house without an invitation. Now she said, ' It is delightful to meet an old friend,' and expatiated on her unhappiness in seeing so little of me. I escaped as soon as possible, and, this morning, she has asked me to dinner with her and her daughter next Sunday, *sans façon*! ! ! As Mr. Daly has not yet arrived from Belvoir, Mr. Turnor will have to reply to this impudence. . . .

April 7.—. . . Things have turned out well. The Liberal party—or a good section of them—rebelled agst. Harty-Tarty's alliance with Fawcett, and fairly wd. not march thro' Coventry, so he had to make yesterday an ignominious retreat, with many confused reasons. Then, their attack on the Budget entirely failed. They were beaten in preliminary divisions, and then they conveniently postponed their announced attack until after Easter, altho' Gladstone, and all his clerks, had come down arrayed with Hansards and blue books.

If I can only manage to mitigate the *Mistletoe* business on Monday, we shall have risen 50 per cent. There is good news from Egypt. . . .

I have had some touching letters from the Faery. She says ' The worry and annoyance to wh. Mr. D. is exposed by this unfortunate, and most harmless, Titles Bill, grieves the Queen deeply, as she fears she is the cause of it,' and so on. . . .

I hope to get down to Hughenden on Tuesday, when I shall be alone—but not more lonely than I feel here, since you and yours have gone. It was no doubt quite visionary—a mere delusion; but Belgravia had become to me a sort of home, a link between me and the domestic principle. Now life seems quite inhuman—nothing to soften or distract it: nothing but Parliaments, and Councils, and despatches, without a gentle thought or graceful deed! Alas! there was the daily letter always, and the little visit, to charm away cares and sometimes to solve difficulties; for in talking to those in whom we can confide, the knot often falls to pieces. Remember me to Bradford.

April 11.—. . . At four I go to Hughenden. . . .

The Faery has been greatly distressed about the *Mistletoe* business, but it was impossible to prevent its being brought forward, and it ended yesterday very well. She cannot understand that Captain Welsh is not merely her servant, but also an officer of the British Navy, who receives his pay and appointments from the House of Commons, who grant these in the Navy Estimates, wh. depend entirely on their vote. Altho' you say I spoil her, it has fallen to my lot to tell her these grave truths; but how they will be borne I do not know—very badly, I suspect. . . .

Carnarvon will find [the Queen] in great excitement about Captain Welsh, which she says is much more important to her than the ' Royal Titles.' I feel like a Minister disgraced, and as if I were going to be imprisoned in Hampton Court or Claremont.

HUGHENDEN MANOR,[1] *April* 12.—. . . I cannot read Whyte Melville, or anything of the kind; I cannot read now what are called ' works of fiction.' Such compositions entirely with me depend on their style; and that seems a quality quite unknown to the present generation of critics. Something very fine like *Wilhelm Meister*, or the earlier works of George Sand, might not only attract, but absorb, me: but I require nothing short of those great masters. Fiction must be first-rate or it is nothing. Second-rate histories and essays may go down, but when a self-announced magician waves the wand, we expect miracles.

April 13.—Snow, snow, snow! never-ceasing snow! A lonely house, and never-ceasing snow! and no letter from Weston—my solitary joy! . . .

April 15.—. . . It is a spring day again: the birds sing, and the peacocks, that were screaming all yesterday, and perched upon the pergola with their draggled trains, are magnificent again, reposing at full length on the terrace, or couched in the marble vases, glittering white against their purple gorges and their green and golden tails.

---

[1] Where Disraeli had gone for the Easter recess.

And in ½ an hour I shall leave them, in no very high spirits I can assure you, for the messenger, who has just arrived, brings me nothing but cares. I sometimes wish that they were at the bottom of the Red Sea, with the Suez Canal shares. I really am too old for ambition, and, except that I shall rarely see you again when my reign is over, the loss of my sceptre would not break my heart, I can assure you. But to you I am always the same.

2, WHITEHALL GARDENS, *April* 26.—. . . This inconvenient dying of the Dowager of Derby at this moment is sad. I have not seen the Sec. of F.O. yet! and so much going on, and the French Ambassador coming to me at ½ pt. 12!

It is also most injurious to the party. I quite counted on a series of F.O. receptions. With forty years of political experience, I never knew a party so deserted by all social influences as ours. I wonder how they are kept together— not a solitary dinner or a single drum!

If it were not for the mysterious letting of the house of my friend Lady Waldegrave, I think we must fall to pieces. It seems to me we have not a woman with the slightest ambition. All female movement seemed to have died out with poor Lady Carnarvon.[1] What is the use of the fine house of the Lonsdales? They might try something. It wd. not be fashionable, but it might be grand.

Talking of Carnarvon, I am extremely amused that, while all the Government are attacked in the metrop. papers for their blundering, etc., little Carnarvon, who feeds the Radical press, is always spared, and really he is the only one who has made mistakes, and committed a series of blunders.

(1) The Cape and Mr. Froude's agitation, and (2) the diplomatic mistake about the Gambia, and (3) the war in Malay-land, and now (4) the mysterious Barbados affair![2]

I had the satisfaction, last night, of extinguishing, I think, Mr. Fawcett and his faction, and forcing Harty-Tarty to throw him over. . . . Talking of Fawcett, yesterday morning all the papers had the most terrific leading articles on the subject of his impending motion, and you wd. have supposed the Govt. were already out. As for the *Daily Tel.*, or rather the *Delirium Tremens*, you wd. have supposed that I was the most abject and discomfited of men. I said 'Bo' to the goose, however, and this morning not a word! I mention this, as I know you and yours are ruled by newspapers, and believe every word that is written agst. me; you, I will admit, or hope so, with some pain, but still you believe. I shall say 'Bo' to a great many more geese before the session is over. . . .

[1] Carnarvon's first wife, Lady Chesterfield's daughter, died on Jan. 25, 1875.　　　　[2] See Vol. VI.

April 29.—I could not write yesterday, as it was an urgent and anxious day: that wretched Fawcett having given notice, on Monday night, tho' rather at 2 o'ck. on Tuesday morning, that, at the meeting of the Ho., on going into supply, he wd. bring forward a vote of censure on the Govt. As there was, so far as the order of business was concerned, a probability that he might have the opportunity, I had to make all the arrangements requisite, telegraph for absent members, etc., etc. —while I had myself to go to Windsor, instead of preparing for the combat. He did not, eventually, bring it on, but I had all the toil and anxiety.

The Prince has not exceeded his £60,000; which is rather a triumph, tho' a petty one, for me.

I have had a heavy Cabinet to-day, and many toilsome affairs, and can scarcely write this, and have to go to that most damnable ceremony, the Academy dinner, where 150 critics of the 'first water' expect me to give utterance to Attic sayings, when my brain has no Attic salt left in it. . . .

The only person whom you seem neither to care to see nor to please, is myself. And when you come to town, it will only, I fear, be to tell me, as you usually do, that you are going again into the country on some visit, or still more probably, even abroad. I fear our romance is over, if indeed it ever existed except in my imagination; but still I sometimes dreamed that the dream might last until I slumbered for ever.

2, Whitehall Gardens, *May* 2, 1876.—. . . There is some chance that the answers in our House, and the full reply of the Ld. Chan[cello]r, may check the hostile advance; and if checked, it may die, for the world is anxious, I rather feel, for a new subject. If the sun wd. only shine, and put the world in a better humor, we might have a chance, but gentlemen begin to despair of getting their rents. The farmers are really sulky, and vent their spite, not on nature, but the Ministry.

In the House of C. last night a round robin was in secret circulation among the Liberal party requesting a meeting of the party to consider the Royal Proclamation and do something. They are discontented with their chiefs, and Harcourt and Henry James and Fawcett want to force Harty-Tarty's hand. . . .

The Academy dinner was an hour shorter in consequence of F. Grant's health, and therefore was much improved.

May 5.—. . . I am tired and sad ! The session has been one of extraordinary exhaustion and anxiety, and the burthen has fallen on myself. . . . I dined at Sir N. Rothschild's on Wednesday: said to be the best dinner in London and always charming society. . . .

M[*ay*] 12.—Yesterday, as Cromwell said of the Battle of Worcester, was ' a crowning mercy.' Such a discomfiture has rarely been experienced by a party; and what is most delightful is that the numbers[1] were almost all our own. I don't think a Whig voted with us. The speech of Kenealy, wh. will be read by every rough in Britain, and wh. was well delivered, was *à propos*. Peel[2] spoke some time, and with great effect: without a thought or an argument. Such were the magic of a great name and a splendid voice ! I rose, past midnight, with a racking headache, and ought to have disgraced myself, but did not. . . .

In the debates on the Suez Canal purchase and on the Royal Titles Bill the most acrimonious, as well as the most petty, criticism had emanated from Lowe. He had dilated on the enormity of the Rothschild commission as a sufficient ground for rejecting the high policy of purchase ; and he had deprecated the introduction of India into the royal style and title on the ground that we ought to contemplate the contingency of losing our dominion there ! ' The right honourable gentleman is a prophet,' said Disraeli, ' but he is always a prophet of evil.' In a speech at East Retford during the Easter recess Lowe's recklessness and aversion to Disraeli led him to make a virulent personal attack both on the Queen and on the Minister. Her Majesty had frankly avowed to the Opposition leaders her personal interest and even initiative in the Royal Titles Bill. Hardy wrote to Disraeli from Windsor Castle on February 20: ' The Queen desired me to tell you that she had written to Lord Granville on the title; and that Forster, who had sent a corrected copy of his speech to General Ponsonby for her, had been told that she herself had initiated the proposal, which she thought would rather surprise him.' Lowe responded to Her Majesty's frankness by malicious insinuation. ' I strongly suspect,' he said, ' that this is not brought forward for the first time. I violate no confidence, because I have received none; but I am under a conviction that at least two previous Ministers have entirely refused

---

[1] 334 to 226.   [2] The 3rd Baronet, the Prime Minister's eldest son.

to have anything to do with such a change.   More pliant
persons have now been found, and I have no doubt the
thing will be done.'

   This was a very serious accusation for a Privy Councillor,
a former Chancellor of the Exchequer and Secretary of
State, to make; and Gladstone, Lowe's chief, felt that a
peculiar obligation lay upon him to repudiate, as he did
in the public press, the natural implication that he was
one of the previous Ministers referred to.   But even this
repudiation did not recall Lowe to a sense of what he
had done; and when, on May 2, the attention of Parliament was directed by a private member to the astonishing utterance, he treated the whole matter as trivial,
entirely declined to offer any explanation, and denied the
right of the House of Commons to call him to account
for words spoken out of doors, in a case where no breach
of privilege was involved.   Disraeli saw that his adversary
had been delivered into his hand.   'One of those
occasions,' he wrote next day to Lady Bradford, 'which
rarely, and yet in a certain sense always, come to the
vigilant, came to me, and I smashed that wretched
Lowe.'   He spoke, on his Sovereign's behalf and his own,
with a passion which, if rhetorically heightened, was yet
very real, and produced an electrical effect on the House.
Lowe's statements, he said, were monstrous if they were
true, and, if they were not true, must be described 'by
an epithet which I cannot find in my vocabulary.'

   Sir, did the right hon. gentleman or did he not—not merely
intimate, not insinuate, but I say broadly state to the people
of this country, that the Royal Titles measure was introduced
to the notice of Parliament by the unconstitutional and
personal influence of the Sovereign ?   Did he or did he not
take that occasion to hold up to public prejudice, and I will
say public infamy, the chief Minister, asserting, under circumstances detailed by the right hon. gentleman with minute-
ness, that after that gracious Sovereign had been balked and
baffled in her appeals to previous Ministers she had found a
pliant and a servile instrument who was now ready to do her
will ?

The words 'pliant Minister,' Fraser tells us, seemed
literally to choke Disraeli.[1] Of previous Ministers,
Gladstone, he proceeded, had already characterised the
allegation as ' false '; he himself could answer for Derby;
there only remained the venerable Russell and the
honoured Palmerston. To make the proof complete, and
stop the calumnies for ever, he asked and obtained leave
of the House to introduce the Sovereign's name in debate.
It was a short but conclusive message which he gave from
the Queen:

It is merely this statement on the part of Her Majesty,
that there is not the slightest foundation for the statement
that was made, that proposals, such as were described in the
Retford speech, were ever made to any Minister at any time.
Sir, the whole thing is utterly unfounded; merely that sort
of calumnious gossip which unfortunately, I suppose, must
always prevail, but which one certainly did not suppose
would come from the mouth of a Privy Councillor, and one
of Her Majesty's late Cabinet Ministers.

Nothing was left for Lowe but complete retractation
and apology. On May 5 Disraeli told Lady Bradford:
' Lowe appeared in a white sheet last night, holding a
taper of repentance. He was abject.' It was the last
blow to a Parliamentary reputation, which had attained
a great height during the Reform debates of 1867, and
had been rapidly sinking since. Never again did Lowe
count as a serious political force. ' He is in the mud,'
wrote Disraeli to Lady Chesterfield, ' and there I leave
him.'

It was in this session of 1876 that Joseph Chamberlain
entered Parliament as member for Birmingham. Though
in later life he was to maintain the same imperial cause
and use much the same imperial language as Disraeli,
he was regarded by the public then as an extreme Radical,
and in a speech at Birmingham in the spring made a
bitter attack on the Prime Minister's veracity. A
journalist who was present at Chamberlain's *début* in the
House writes: ' From the Gallery I saw the two great

[1] Fraser, p. 31.

imperial statesmen meet.   Chamberlain had said that
Disraeli never opened his mouth without telling a falsehood.   He stood, carefully groomed, eyeglass in eye,
recommending the Gothenburg system.[1]   Disraeli was
fetched, sat down, and put up *his* glass, which he seemed
to hold encircled with his forefinger, so that he might be
quizzing; and so the two surveyed each other, doubtless
exchanging telepathic defiance.'

Disraeli himself alluded to Chamberlain's attack, in a
letter addressed to Lady Chesterfield.   The letter was preserved among his papers, but was never sent, probably
because he thought better of the disparaging reflections
which it contained on Lady Bradford.   She, owing to the
proximity of Castle Bromwich to Birmingham, knew
something of the great qualities of the new member,
to which the crudity of his abuse of Disraeli did little
justice.

To Anne Lady Chesterfield (not sent).

2, WHITEHALL GARDENS, *June* 22, 1876.—. . . I dined at
Marlboro' House on Monday: a banquet given to the unfortunate Sir Salar Jung, who appeared, but in a wheeled chair:
I was amused, sitting next to the Duchess of Manchester,
who is an extremely clever woman, and very agreeable.
To-day, I meet the Prince and Princess at Stafford House:
and yesterday, I went to the concert at Buckingham Palace,
and sate next to S.; but she seemed very bored, and would
have preferred, probably, Mr. Chamberlain.

I thought his attack on me was one of the coarsest, and
stupidest, assaults I well remember.   No intellect, or sarcasm,
or satire, or even invective: coarse and commonplace abuse,
such as you might expect from the cad of an omnibus.   However, S., I believe, very much admired it, and seemed to be
rather glad, that I was attacked.   The House of Commons
were enraged, and I had the greatest difficulty in preventing
it being brought forward as a breach of privilege.   The
Speaker was evidently in favor of that course, but deferred
to me.

Are you aware, that Mr. Chamberlain recanted in a letter
to *The Times*—I think of Monday ?   A most abject apology:

[1] This is a mistake.   Chamberlain's maiden speech, to which the writer
was referring, was made on the Report stage of the Elementary Education
Bill on Aug. 4, just a week before Disraeli's last appearance in the
Commons.

I would sooner have made the speech than have written the letter, and that is saying a good deal. I said something like this to S., who fired up, admired the letter, and called him ' a great man '! Pleasant! . . .

As appears from the above letter, the return of the Prince of Wales from his Indian tour was the occasion of much festivity in London society; and the Prime Minister himself, though without a hostess to do the honours, gave a great dinner and reception to the Prince and Princess.

To Anne Lady Chesterfield.

2, WHITEHALL GARDENS, *June 25.*—Most dear, all your beautiful and bountiful presents came safe, and in good time, and added much to the lustre of my banquet. We sate down 42 : I had the Princess on my right, and the Dss. of Sutherland on my left; the Prince was opposite to me, with the Dss. of Beaufort, whom he took out, on his right, and the Dss. of Manchester on his left. Everybody was well placed, and, I think, everybody was pleased, as the party was rather noisy; and indeed, with plenty of music, flowers, and light, it is difficult to have a failure. A gentleman sent to me a bouquet for the Pss. wh. quite delighted. It was immense, but of graceful form; wondrous roses, with rare orchids, bright, sweet, and pendulous; and every now and then, studded with butterflies and humming birds. The Princess took one of the butterflies, and put it in her hair.

After dinner was the monster reception, where no one received. The Princess stood in a gallery overlooking the great staircase, surrounded by her Duchesses, and some other *grandes dames* who were equally an ornament, Lady Dudley, and I am glad to say also—S., who looked very well.

I never saw anyone more amused than the Princess watching the guests. She said it was better than a play, and it was so long since she had been out that it made it doubly diverting. I was obliged to trouble Her Royal Highness to make the tour of the apartments, that everybody might see her. But she always resisted a little, and asked for a few minutes more of her gallery. . . .

It was a fruitful session. Not only was the purchase of the Suez Canal shares sanctioned, and the royal title amplified; but, in spite of the time occupied with discussions on a situation in the Near East which grew daily more perplexing, the appellate jurisdiction of the

House of Lords was placed on a proper footing by the
addition to the tribunal of paid members, and the vivisection of animals for purposes of scientific experiment
was subjected to due regulation; moreover, the social
programme of the Government was further advanced by
a comprehensive Elementary Education Bill, a Merchant
Shipping Bill, and Bills putting a limit to the enclosure
of commons and the pollution of rivers. A hope that
Disraeli expressed to Lady Bradford on June 13 that
' our domestic reputation, at the end of July, will be equal
to our foreign ' was fulfilled.   A selection from his correspondence with the Queen enables us to regard the progress
of this legislation through his eyes.   Her Majesty, it may
be explained, was especially anxious for the Vivisection
Bill, which, she wrote to Disraeli on June 13, ' must be
passed if the nation is not to be disgraced by cruelty under
the shameful plea of humanity.'

To Queen Victoria.

2, WHITEHALL GARDENS, *July* 2, 1876.—Mr. Disraeli with
his humble duty to your Majesty:

The progress of the House of Commons, during the last
week, has on the whole been satisfactory. The necessity of
giving a Government night to the Irish Land Debate, has
rendered that progress less advanced, but it was absolutely
necessary, that the opinion of Parliament should be given
in an unmistakable manner on these schemes, in order to
prevent autumnal agitation, and to commit the leaders of
the Opposition to a public expression of sound views.

The prospect of the ensuing week looks well.

The debate on the government of Ireland, in the form of
Home Rule, on Friday, was highly interesting, from the
speech, in reply to Mr. Butt's motion, by Mr. Smyth, member
for the County of Westmeath, an avowed Repealer, and
something more.

The House of Commons has not witnessed, for many years,
a happier effort, combining, as it did, many of the higher
qualities of oratory: close reasoning, fine illustration, wit and
graceful sarcasm, in a style natural, though imaginative,
and highly finished. It tore up the banner of Home Rule to
shreds, and Mr. Disraeli does not believe that it will ever be
unfurled again in the House of Commons.

This speech of Mr. Smyth recalled to Mr. Disraeli what he

had read, and often fancied, of the style of the Irish House of
Commons; the House of Grattan and of Flood.

It was curious to see both sides cheering a member, who
avowed himself a Repealer, and once was a rebel.

It is a pity that this great oration was barely reported.
The Parliamentary reporters, who are mere machines, never
discovered till too late that a considerable Parliamentary
event was occurring. . . .

July 22.— . . . Mr. Disraeli was absent from the House on
Thursday night, and he regrets to say that the Ministry fell
into one of those messes of ecclesiastical weakness, which
seem inevitable, every now and then, for the Conservative
party. The whole of yesterday was consequently wasted on
an idle Education Clause, which conveyed a petty assault on
the Nonconformists.

Mr. Disraeli has called a Cabinet to-morrow morning again
on the winding up of the session, and he hopes he may rectify
this mistake. . . .

(Same date.)—. . . Mr. Disraeli proposed to Lord H.
Lennox[1] to move for a Committee of Inquiry and offered not
to accept Lord Henry's resignation unless the Committee
decided against him; but Lord Henry would not avail himself
of this offer. Mr. Disraeli could do no more with any regard
to public propriety and the character of your Majesty's
Government.

July 25.—. . . Mr. Disraeli deplores the mischance of Lord
H. Lennox, whom Mr. Disraeli had known intimately for
30 years, and whose very faults were not disagreeable.

July 29.—. . . There has been an agitating and anxious
week in the House of Commons with respect to the new
Educational Bill, which is a considerable measure; but all
has ended well. After a great struggle, by blended conciliation and firmness, the measure will be carried and the House
is now sitting (Saturday) to conclude the Committee. . . .

Mr. Disraeli made a strong appeal for Vivisection, and he
is still sanguine of carrying it. The great opponent is Mr.
Lowe, and if he persists in his opposition, it will be impossible
to attempt it: but there are good reasons to hope, that some
compromise may be effected. The great thing is to pass
some Act, and give evidence of the determination of the
Legislature to control this horrible practice. . . .

Aug. 3.—Mr. Disraeli . . . thanks your Majesty for your
Majesty's gracious letters, which always encourage, and, not
unfrequently, guide him. . . .

---

[1] Lord Henry Lennox resigned the office of First Commissioner of Works
owing to judicial animadversions on the conduct of the directors of the
Lisbon Steam Tramways Company, of whom he had been one.

Affairs have gone on rapidly in the House of Commons, and he thinks that the 12th will be the most convenient for the Council, though he will not speak positively till to-morrow.

The Education Bill may yet occasion a day's delay, but he more than hopes not.

It is no use attempting to conciliate the Dissenters. They take all you offer, and, the very next minute, will fly at your throat. The Education Bill, as introduced by the Government, was liberally conceived, and we made, in the course of discussion, several important further concessions to the Opposition. We could only induce our own friends to yield these on our promise that their amendments, or proposals, should also be considered; but the moment we granted anything to our own friends, there was a fierce cry of ' reaction,' which, under the conditions which Mr. Disraeli ultimately suggested, was not really well founded.

There was a stormy Cabinet one day, which required all Mr. Disraeli's experience to guide and assuage. And Lord Salisbury wrote to Mr. Disraeli a letter, which Mr. Disraeli intended to have forwarded to your Majesty, that your Majesty might comprehend the difficulties he had to contend against, which was really alarming. It was long and well written, and said: ' The men I was called upon to desert, were the very men who had stood by me on the Titles Bill'; an appeal difficult to withstand.

This letter has mysteriously disappeared, but when discovered, shall be forwarded to your Majesty.

The Nonconformist party in the country has been weakened by the last Reform Bill.

Mr. Disraeli encloses your Majesty a letter of a different kind from Mr. Secretary Hardy. It is a generous letter. All difficulties, on the subject to which it refers, are now removed, and there will be no unpleasant feeling in the Cabinet of any kind.[1] . . .

HOUSE OF COMMONS, *Aug.* 5.—. . . Vivisection seems quite safe.

The Education struggle has terminated by strengthening the Ministry, and by signally demonstrating the utter disintegration of the Opposition. What was really a point of administrative detail was so magnified and exaggerated by the Opposition, that it was elevated into a discussion, whether the primary education of the country should be religious or secular. . . .

[1] See Vol. VI., ch. 1.

To Lady Bradford.

2, Whitehall Gardens, *Saturday, Aug. 5,* 1876.—. . . I knew the storm that was brewing on Thursday night, a storm wh. periodically appears, and suddenly, like a white squall in the Mediterranean. I have had, in older and more factious days, some experience wh. guided me—so I left before one.

The Chanr. of the Exr., and Ld. Sandon, and Sir Willie Dyke, and Mr. Smith, and Monty, were with me next morning at eleven, for counsel, tho' they had not, what the *M. Post* calls, ' retired to their couches till past five.' They looked pretty fresh. I was, naturally, quite so, and had had time to consider their case. So we were all in our places at twelve for the renewed combat. Being an older hand than they, I did not expect one, and I was right. Our new moves all succeeded, and we carried the report of the Bill in its entirety by sitting last night also. Not that I was there for the final and easy stages. It is to be read a third time this morning. I don't think we have lost 4 and 20 hours by this burst of factious fight, and it has shown the utter demoralisation and rancorous breaking up of the Liberal party. It seems split into fragments: all working against each other. One night the whole of the Home Rulers deserted to us, and next day the Scotch Presbyterians joined them. Then Goschen answered Forster, and Rylands Mundella. Sullivan, the fiercest Ultramontanist, declared that he wd. sooner send his children to a Ch. of England school than to a secular. Where-upon Mr. Greene, the fiercest Protestant in the House, vowed that, in preference to a secular, he wd. certainly send his children to a Roman Catholic school: and then there was mutual cheering and embracing, always ending in increased majorities for Government. . . .

In spite of the pressure of the Eastern question, Disraeli followed during the summer and autumn with sustained interest the preparations made by the new Viceroy to celebrate worthily in India the assumption of the imperial title. ' All Lytton's proclamation schemes,' he wrote on September 3 to Salisbury, ' tho' they read like the 1,000 and one nights, I believe are judicious, and will be successful and beneficial—not only in India.' Not all of the imaginative Viceroy's schemes were accepted, but, even so, the effect was sufficiently striking. For the chiefs there were honours and decorations, increases in salary and pension; for the army increased pay and allowances; a new order was created for Anglo-Indians; food and clothing were distributed to the poor; there was a generous amnesty for prisoners; and a great Assemblage, collected from all parts of India and from the neighbouring East, and lasting fourteen days, from before Christmas till after the New Year, was held at Delhi. There, on Janaury 1, 1877, with Lytton, the Viceroy, presiding in state, and in the presence of the heads of all the Indian governments, of envoys from Siam, Burma, and Khelat, of representatives of the great Civil Service, of a picked force of British and native troops, of over seventy ruling chiefs and princes, of some three hundred native noblemen and gentlemen, and of a vast concourse of the Indian peoples, Queen Victoria was proclaimed, with all due solemnity and pomp, Kaisar-i-Hind, Empress of India, and was saluted by the Maharajah Scindia on behalf of the Indian princes as Shah-in-Shah Padshah, Monarch of Monarchs.[1] The Queen herself celebrated the occasion by asking her Minister to dine at Windsor.

To Lady Bradford.

HUGHENDEN MANOR, *Dec.* 28.—. . . On Monday I go to Windsor to dine with the Empress of India. It is New Year's Day, when she is proclaimed in Hindustan, and she wishes the day to be celebrated, and 'marked,' hereafter. . . . The Faery is much excited about the doings at Delhi. They have produced great effect in India, and indeed throughout the world, and vindicate triumphantly the policy of the measure wh. was so virulently, but so fruitlessly, opposed. It has no doubt consolidated our empire there. Our poetical Viceroy is doing justice to the occasion. The Faery is so full of the great incident, and feels everything about it so keenly that she sent me a Xmas card and signed her good wishes *Victoria Regina et Imperatrix.*

Beaconsfield, as he had then become, took down with him to Windsor Lord George Hamilton, Under-Secretary for India, who was responsible for the office while Salisbury, the Secretary of State, was attending the

[1] See *Lord Lytton's Indian Administration,* ch. 4.

Constantinople Conference.   Lord George tells us[1] that, with a fine dramatic sense, the Queen, usually so homely in attire, appeared at dinner that night 'a mass of Oriental jewellery, mostly consisting of very large uncut stones and pearls,' gifts from the reigning Princes of India in 1858 when the Crown took over the Government from the Company.   Beaconsfield, for his part, appreciating the unique character of the occasion, broke through all etiquette by rising and proposing the health of the Empress of India, ' with a little speech as flowery as the oration of a Maharajah'; to which the Queen responded with a 'pretty smiling bow, half a curtsey.'[2] Queen and Minister knew what Parliament and English society had not sufficient imagination to realise, that by the measure of the last session, translated into act at that day's Durbar, the British *raj* in India had received a significant accession of internal and external strength; that a new and durable link had been forged between the crowned democracy of the West and the immemorial Empire of the Middle East.

[1] *Reminiscences*, p. 120.
[2] Article on 'The Character of Queen Victoria,' *Quarterly Review*, April, 1901.

CHAPTER XIII.

FROM THE COMMONS TO THE LORDS.

1876–1877.

On Friday, August 11, 1876, a day or two before
the prorogation of Parliament, Disraeli replied, late in
the evening, to an attack on the Government for their
inaction over Bulgarian atrocities.[1] The speech was not
specially remarkable, though it contained a sly hit at the
Rhodian, or (according to some reports) Herodian, oratory
of his friendly opponent Harcourt, and though it closed
upon a thoroughly Disraelian note: 'What our duty
is at this critical moment is to maintain the Empire
of England.' The debate over, Disraeli walked slowly
down the House to the bar; there turned, and
stood for a minute carefully surveying the familiar
scene, galleries and all; and then, retracing his steps,
passed the Treasury bench and went quietly out behind
the Speaker's chair,[2] pausing to chat with Lord George
Hamilton on the prospects of a Liberal 'atrocity'
campaign in the autumn. He was noticed afterwards
in the lobby, 'in a long white overcoat and dandified
lavender kid gloves, leaning on his secretary's arm,' and
shaking hands with a good many people.[3] After that
night, he never entered the House of Commons again,
save as a visitor to the gallery. Unknown to all but one
or two present, he had made his last appearance in the
theatre of the labours and triumphs of nearly forty years.
The next morning it was announced that the Queen had

[1] See Vol. VI.. ch. 2.
[2] For these details I am indebted to the Right Hon. T. Burt, who was
present, and noted Disraeli's unusual procedure.
[3] See Dilke's *Life*, Vol. I., p. 211.

been pleased to create her Prime Minister an Earl. Some critics, notably Fraser, have expressed surprise that the supreme artist on the political stage should not have contrived a more spectacular exit. But here surely Disraeli showed a truer taste and a finer instinct than his critics. No formal leavetaking could have been more impressive than this silent withdrawal, which, without warning and without advertisement, transferred at a stroke the centre of political interest from the Commons to the Lords.

Disraeli's action was determined, of course, by considerations of health. Though during 1875 he had been on the whole free from the serious illnesses which had so frequently prostrated him in 1874, the respite proved to be only temporary. He spent the second week of January, 1876, at Weston, and on his return to town and work had an acute seizure. A pencil note from Whitehall Gardens to Lady Bradford, dated January 18, 12.30, says: 'I have had a very sharp attack, and nothing but remedies as sharp cd. have brought me to time—as I hope they have, for in an hour and ½ I must be at the Cab. It wd. not do to hold it here, it wd. be such a bad start; and the day is bland, and one must run risks in life, or else it wd. be as dull as death.' At half-past four the same afternoon, he reports, in ink: 'I have just come from the Cabinet. . . . I have been, and am, a great sufferer. I have had the illness of a month crammed and compressed into 8 and 40 hours.' His colleagues found him greatly pulled down: 'I judge,' he wrote two days later, 'from their expression and general mien, that they thought the Burials Bill, wh. we were discussing, was rather a fitting subject for their chief.'

This was a bad introduction to a session of worry and late hours. 'I wish the H. of C. was counted out oftener,' he wrote pathetically to Lady Bradford on March 1, 'that I might sometimes dine in the family circle. I think I shall retreat to the Elysian fields, where Bradford listened yesterday to Sandhurst and Cadogan, and then I might

a little more enjoy the society of my dear friends.' The
factious opposition to the Royal Titles Bill, and the
increasing gravity of the situation in the Near East, once
more strained the Minister's health almost to breaking-
point in the middle of May.

To Lady Bradford.

2, WHITEHALL GARDENS, [? *May* 16].—I could not call
yesterday and was very unwell with my throat. . . . I sate
through the debate in great suffering, scarcely mitigated by
our triumphant majority, and went home very late and rather
hopeless: but a compress has worked wonders, and if I cd.
have stayed at home, I shd. have been all right. But that
is impossible. Affairs are very grave. . . .

May 18.—The medico said I had a feverish catarrh—the
old story; and the remedies have already done me some good,
so far as the fever is concerned—but I am dreadfully weak
and out of cue. . . . The Faery keeps telegraphing for bulletins
with injunctions to see Jenner, who is going down to Windsor,
and will tell her exactly how I am, etc., etc. ' She is very
anxious.' . . .

[? *May* 19].—I shan't go into the City to-day, or to the H.
of Commons—but I ought to drive a little, or I shall become
a confirmed invalid. . . . I shd. like to know whether I might
call. . . .

May 25.—. . . Of all the duties and occupations wh.
devolve on me, letter-writing is that for wh. the sort of attack
I am now suffering from most unfits me. One can read, and
one can listen, and judge, and talk; but writing requires a
degree of energy and precision of wh. I am now quite incapable.
I am out of all pain this morning, and shd. have publicly
appeared—and may even yet—but the N.E. blast has returned,
and this is my direst foe. . .

I was obliged to hold the Cabinet yesterday under this roof.

May 26.—I can't give a good account of myself, as I had
a fresh attack last night. . . .

May 27.—The Cabinet is just over and under this roof !
I have had a good night and am quite free from pain. . . .

HUGHENDEN MANOR, *June* 3.—A senseless line from the
solitary—you cannot expect much. This place is bright with
bloom; thorns pink and white, and lilac and chestnut; soft
showers in the night and the grass growing all day. Nothing
wrong except they steal the swans' eggs, so that family
does not increase. I had hoped by this time they might have
rivalled the peacocks. . . .

This attack convinced Disraeli that action could no longer be postponed. The Queen herself gave him an opening by a spontaneous offer to call him to the House of Lords.

From Queen Victoria.

BALMORAL, *June* 5, 1876.—The Queen hopes Mr. Disraeli is feeling rested and better.

She was sorry to hear from General Ponsonby that he was feeling the fatigue of his work.

She knows how valuable he is to herself and the country. Should he still feel this, and that the fatigue of the House of Commons is too great, she would be happy to call him up to the other House, where the fatigue would be *far less* and where he would be able to *direct* everything. *No* one, no doubt, can replace him in the House of Commons; still if he felt it too much for his health something must be done, and he has some excellent men—especially Sir S. Northcote—who could no doubt work under him.

The Queen throws this out, as she feels the immense *importance* he is to the Throne and country and how—more than ever now—she wishes and hopes his Govt. may be long maintained.

Everyone agrees that it has gained in strength since the beginning of the Session, as he himself assured her.

Disraeli told the Queen that his physical condition would not permit him to carry on the Government, as Prime Minister in the Commons, after the existing session; but he demurred to Her Majesty's suggestion, and expressed a preference for retirement. He has himself placed on record, in a communication addressed in nearly identical terms to his principal colleagues, the negotiations which followed.

To the Duke of Richmond.

Confidential. 10, DOWNING STREET, *July* 24, 1876.—Some little time ago, when we had extricated ourselves from our difficulties, and the Government was not less popular and strong than at present, I was obliged to inform the Queen, that it would not be possible for me to carry on Her Majesty's affairs after the present Session.

Although, being well acquainted with the Queen's sensitiveness, or perhaps I ought to say Constitutional convictions, on the subject, I did not presume to recommend my successor, I ventured to observe, that, if Her Majesty wished to retain her present Cabinet, I thought there would be no difficulty in keeping them together under an individual, whose fitness would be generally admitted by themselves and the country.

Her Majesty did not seem to believe in this, or to approve of my communication, and wrote to me from Scotland to propose, that I should continue in my present post, and go to the House of Lords, which, she was graciously pleased to say, she had always contemplated since my illness at Balmoral two years ago.

As I have no heir, I was unwilling, in the decline of life, to commence a new career in a House of Parliament of which I had no experience, and where I should be looked upon as an intruder, and I requested Her Majesty's permission to adhere to my original feeling and to make some confidential inquiries on the subject.

I found, to my great surprise, that the Queen had judged the situation more accurately than myself, and that my secession might lead to serious consequences.

Altho' my continuing in the House of Commons for another Session would shorten my remaining life, I was prepared to make such a sacrifice, if, at the end of the year, I could have found the difficulties, occasioned by my withdrawal, removed: but I see no prospect of that.   The identical difficulties would reappear.

Under these circumstances, I have had to reconsider the Queen's proposal, and to bring myself to contemplate, as an act of duty to Her Majesty and my colleagues, the possibility of my going to the Upper House as a Minister, a condition which I had never foreseen.

I invite you as a colleague, whom I greatly value, and with whose Parliamentary position such a step on my part would necessarily, in some degree, interfere, to speak to me frankly on this subject: clearly understanding, that my only motive now is the maintenance of the Ministry and the party, and to secure these, I am ready still to try to serve them, or cheerfully altogether to disappear.

From the Duke of Richmond.

Confidential.   GOODWOOD, CHICHESTER, *July* 26, 1876.—I received your letter late yesterday, and hasten to reply to it. I can conceive nothing more fatal to the party and the Cabinet than your retirement from office.   A party strong and united under you, to whom they have looked up so long as leader, might not be at all willing to follow another, and the result might be jealousies and differences which could not fail to be hurtful.

I regret most sincerely that the state of your health is such as to cause you to wish to retire from the House of Commons. I can well understand how very trying to a person suffering from bronchitis must be the attendance in the House of Commons during the early part of the Session. It seems to me that the course advised by Her Majesty, that you should have a peerage conferred upon you, is by far the best arrangement that can be made.

It is a proper recognition of the long and valuable services you have rendered to the country, and will enable you to continue to lead the party. I speak with all sincerity when I say there is no one who will more cordially welcome you in the House of Lords than I shall. I shall be only too happy to serve under you there as I have now done for so many years in the Cabinet and H. of Commons.

I shall most gladly give you all the assistance in my power upon all occasions. . . .

The replies of Derby and Salisbury to a similar communication from Disraeli illustrate the general feeling among his colleagues that his retirement would be a public misfortune, and their consequent approval of his transference to the Lords.

From Lord Derby.

Confidential. FOREIGN OFFICE, *July 26, '76*.—I was prepared for your communication, and have not the slightest doubt or hesitation in saying that I think you have chosen the right course. You can still lead us in Cabinet: and in the Lords your Parliamentary duties will be almost nominal. Your continuance as you were was a sacrifice which could not be asked of you: your total retirement would have been a misfortune to your friends, and to the public. Only this alternative remained, and it really seems to me open to as few objections as any step you could have taken under the circumstances.

From Lord Salisbury.

Confidential. INDIA OFFICE, *July 27, '76*.—Your letter took me so completely by surprise that I thought I might take 48 hours to think over it. Your health had so manifestly improved that I had banished all apprehensions of any probable change.

The two alternatives you put are—your absolute retirement, or a retreat to the House of Lords.

I have no doubt whatever that your absolute retirement
would be a most serious blow to the Ministry and the party,
especially at this juncture.   Foreign affairs are the absorbing
topic of the day.   It is quite evident, from the quiescence of
Parliament and the country on the subject, that very general
confidence is felt in the present conduct of our foreign policy:
and in the shaping of that policy the largest share is generally,
and justly, attributed to you.   If you were to withdraw, the
most essential element in the public confidence would be taken
away.   Of future possible combinations you do not speak
hopefully: of course I do not know what was suggested; but
no arrangement that seems to me likely would be nearly as
acceptable as that which exists now.

If therefore you feel yourself driven to choose between the
two alternatives—retirement or the House of Lords—I advise,
in the interests of the party and the Ministry, that you should
go to the House of Lords.

But I feel it is a choice of evils.   You would be very heartily
welcomed by the House of Lords: and you would give life
to the dullest assembly in the world.   But the command of
the House of Lords would be a poor exchange for the singular
influence you now exercise in the Commons.   The experience
of those who, having held a first place in the Commons, by
choice or necessity went to the Lords, is not encouraging:
Walpole, Pulteney, the elder Pitt, Castlereagh, Brougham.
In this case it is *facilis ascensus*.   As one of the shades who is
on the wrong side of the stream, I must honestly say that
I think you will regret the irrevocable step when you have
taken it.

However, this is a question of health and feeling, and perhaps
hardly the subject of advice.   We shall be very glad to see
you among us if you do resolve to come.   In the public interest
it would be very desirable that you should so arrange the
charge of business that it should be possible for you to remain
in the House of Commons.   But if this is *not* possible, it is
then infinitely better that you should come to the House of
Lords than that you should retire.

It will be seen that Derby was prepared for the communication, and that Salisbury was not.   Derby, Disraeli's close ally and politically the most important of his
colleagues, and Cairns, whose judgment he had come to
value above that of all others, were early taken into
confidence: and to them was added, shortly afterwards,

EDWARD HENRY, FIFTEENTH EARL OF DERBY.

From a photograph by the London Stereoscopic Co.

Hardy, who had repeatedly acted as his deputy in the Commons and was after himself the protagonist there of the Government. The arrangement which Disraeli had in his mind when he told the Queen that there would be no difficulty in keeping the Cabinet together was that Derby should succeed him as Prime Minister,[1] with Hardy as the leader in the Commons. When, however, he sounded Derby—making use apparently of Lady Derby for the purpose—he found the scheme quite impracticable. Derby 'utterly scouted the idea of his being Premier. That he could never manage H.M., that he did not think he could lead his colleagues on Church questions: in short that nothing on earth would make him take the post. Added to this, he threw out that he would not act with anyone else.'[2] This was decisive. If Derby would neither take command himself, nor serve under any other chief but Disraeli, there was no alternative to a complete break-up except Disraeli's removal to the Lords. To this course, therefore, whether willingly or reluctantly, he was driven. Though to Salisbury his health appeared to be 'manifestly improved,' he had had another warning in this month of July that he could no longer trifle with it.

To Lady Bradford.

2, WHITEHALL GARDENS, *July* 3, 1876.—I could not write yesterday, being so very ill and quite incapable of thought and expression. What irritates me is that Gull, who has now been tinkering me for a week and making a series of conceited mistakes—ordering me, for example, to drink port wine, wh. I have not done for ten years, and wh. has nearly killed me—keeps telling Monty that I am better, who tells of course the same to you and the Queen, altho' I warn him to the reverse; but as he, very plausibly, contends, he is bound to report what Gull says.

Yesterday I drove out for an hour—to try to accustom myself to life again; but the port wine regimen afterwards brought things to a crisis, and I really thought, and not for the first time, that it was all over. . .

---

[1] In the letter to Derby announcing his decision, Disraeli calls him 'My principal colleague, and whom I wished to be my successor.'
[2] Hardy's Diary, July 12: Gathorne Hardy, Vol II., p. 4.

July 4.—. . . I had a very hard night, and did not retire till three o'ck. in the morn[in]g.   Too hard a life for me now —and there is a prospect of a month of it !   It was, however, softened by colossal majorities on a most important measure,[1] and on wh., a fortnight ago, I was told Govt. was to be defeated. . . .

It is difficult to believe that Disraeli did not foresee and desire the issue of the crisis.   With his strong ambition, and his keen interest in India and the East, he can hardly, save in moments of deep physical depression, have seriously contemplated, so long as life and power of work were left to him and he had the confidence of Parliament, the abandonment to others of that forceful Eastern policy which was taking shape under his immediate direction but which was as yet only an outline.   He must have anticipated, and thought it politic to provoke, the urgency of his Sovereign and his colleagues which sent him to the Lords.   On this point there was no division of opinion. The Queen 'absolutely protested' against the idea of his retirement.   The sentiments of Richmond, Derby, and Salisbury on the subject were shared by Ministers generally.   Cairns and Hardy, from the first, were in favour of a retreat to the Lords.   Malmesbury wrote of the 'chaos your retirement from any cause whatever would create in our party.   If I know anything of men there are some excellent heads and hearts in the Cabinet, but only one backbone.'   When Disraeli yielded to the general wish, John Manners wrote emphatically, August 8: 'You have acted in this supreme crisis as you have ever acted in public affairs: rightly, wisely, dutifully. I am confident the Queen, your colleagues, and the country will appreciate and approve the decision at which you have arrived.'

There was that general chorus of approval from press and public which Manners anticipated.   But in one place there was universal regret and sorrow.   If it cost Disraeli,

---

[1] The Prisons Bill, which was eventually withdrawn for this Session, and passed with amendments in 1877.

as he told the Speaker, a 'pang'[1] to separate himself
from the House of Commons, the sense of loss and
bereavement in the House was acute. 'Small groups
are dotted about here and there,' wrote Barrington
picturesquely on the morning of the announcement,
'talking with bated breath, as though there were a
coffin within the precincts of the House.'

From Sir William Hart Dyke.

HOUSE OF COMMONS, *Aug.* 12.—When the news came out
in the early hours here this morning, there was much surprise,
and, amongst our friends, general consternation: Taylor was
frantic, and as to poor Edmonstone, he has done nothing but
cry, and swear, alternately ever since. The deep feeling of
regret is quite universal throughout every corner of the House.
I had no idea, until I heard you make your last speech in the
House, how great the change would prove. All the real
chivalry and delight of party politics, seem to have departed;
nothing remains but routine. . . .
Your constant kindness, assistance, and advice to me here
I shall never forget; always the kind word, when mistakes
have been made: and work which might have been dull and
laborious has been made ever bright and pleasant.

Speaker Brand wrote to Disraeli to say 'on my own
behalf how much I shall miss you, and how much I regret
the cause which has obliged you to leave this House; a
sentiment which is universal throughout the House'—
that 'great assembly' which was 'the scene of your early
struggles and final triumphs.' There is a real sense of
personal loss in the notes written by colleagues in the
Commons. Manners felt especially forlorn. 'It termi-
nates for me all personal interest in House of Commons
life;' 'I cannot bear to think of the future: the change
will be so mournful, the conditions of service in our
House so altered.' Barrington struck the same note.
'My individual interest in the House of Commons is from
this day gone, and nothing will remain but duty—a very
poor substitute indeed.' Northcote's heart was so full

---

[1] On the night of Disraeli's last speech in the Commons, his colleague,
Frederick Stanley, afterwards sixteenth Lord Derby, saw him shedding tears.

that he could not trust himself to express in detail the sadness which he felt. Lord George Hamilton was the exponent of the feelings of those rising young men whom Disraeli had encouraged and cheered when they had difficult work to do. 'I am not the only Under-Secretary who will miss your kindly advice and will feel that he is in a different place now that you are no longer in it.' The feeling of generous opponents in the House was expressed in happy phrase by the eminent Parliamentarian whom Disraeli had answered in his final speech.

From Sir William Harcourt.

NAWORTH CASTLE, BRAMPTON, CUMB, *Aug.* 14, '76.

DEAR MR. DISRAELI,—If I am to call you so for the last time. It is impossible for anyone, and least of all for one who has had so large an experience of your kindness, to hear without emotion that you have sat for the last time in the great scene of your fame. You have made the House of Lords much too rich and you have left the House of Commons by far too poor. Henceforth the game will be like a chessboard when the queen is gone—a petty struggle of pawns.

I little thought when you touched me so deftly with the blunted point of your spear on Friday night that it was to be your last speech in a place where your fame will always live: a fame not only for genius and eloquence but for a kindness to the small quite as uncommon as your force against the great.

I am sure the feeling on our side of the House will be one of universal regret, for the reason which I remember Julian Fane telling me Metternich expressed to him with regard to Napoleon. He said: ' You will perhaps think that when I heard of his death I felt a satisfaction at the removal of the great adversary of my country and my policy. It was just the reverse. I experienced only " un sentiment de regret que je ne devais jamais encore m'entretenir avec cette grande intelligence."' That you should yearn for repose from the weariness of the petty details of the House of Commons I do not wonder. I have felt sad sometimes to see you jaded by them. I hope the *otium cum dignitate* will add long years to a life which is the admiration of Englishmen and is dear to those who have tasted of your friendship. To the imagination of the younger generation your life will always have a special fascination. For them you have enlarged the horizon of the possibilities of the future.

I am sure you will not think this letter an impertinent intrusion. Your constant kindness has given me the right to rejoice in all that concerns you, and yet to regret the great change which will leave an irreparable blank in my House of Commons life. . . .

'Alas! Alas! for the House of Commons and the country. We shall never see your like again. The days of the giants are over. Ichabod! Ichabod!' wrote Sir Philip Rose. Disraeli's career of nearly forty years in the House of Commons exactly coincided with its best days. His entrance followed hard upon the accession of the first Sovereign in English history who accepted its complete ascendancy. Queen Victoria's immediate predecessor had summarily dismissed a Ministry which enjoyed the confidence of Parliament; but King William's failure to secure the endorsement of the country left the supremacy of the House of Commons undisputed. The year after Disraeli quitted it, Parnell, who had been elected in 1875, organised the systematic obstruction of Parliamentary business; and on the Prisons Bill, the Army Estimates, and the South Africa Bill, showed how power-less under its existing rules the House was in face of members determined to discredit and degrade it. To meet the menace, freedom of debate was steadily curtailed, till now the closure and other hampering restrictions are part of the daily machinery of the Mother of Parliaments. But while Disraeli was numbered among its members the House of Commons was at the height of its power and reputation and preserved all its traditional liber-ties. The place which it then held in the mind and esteem of the country may be gauged by the amount of space which the newspapers accorded to the reports of debates. Those who search the files of *The Times* during these years will find that, in the session, the Parliamentary reports not only occupied the most conspicuous pages, but filled, day after day, half or three-quarters of the total news columns, crowding most other matter into short paragraphs and obscure corners. The luminaries of the cricket-field and the river, of the stage and the turf, had not then risen to the rank of popular heroes; and an oration by Macaulay or Bright, a tussle between Disraeli and Peel, or a serious debate in which Palmerston, Russell, Cobden, and Gladstone put forth all their powers, excited the universal interest among newspaper readers which has subsequently, in times of peace, only been secured by the visits of Australian cricketers or the successes of royal horses at Epsom. It was on this wide and universal theatre and among these Parliamentary giants that Disraeli played his striking part, battling with spirit and distinction against succeeding generations of orators and statesmen from O'Connell and the elder Stanley at the beginning to Hartington and Harcourt at the close.

The secret of his astonishing success—the 'singular influence,' to use Salisbury's phrase, which he exercised in the House—may be difficult to probe and to analyse, but undoubtedly one main element was that he was always there. 'The House of Commons,' he wrote in the last year of his life in an unpublished novel, 'is a jealous mistress, and will not grant success without due attention. The greatest compliment you can pay to a woman is to give to her your time, and it is the same with our senate. A man who is always in his place becomes a sort of favourite.' More particularly did he feel it incumbent on him to be always in his place when he became a Parliamentary leader. 'Unless you are always there,' he was wont to say, 'how can you lead the House of Commons? How can you feel their pulse? How can you know the men?' While business was in progress, however dull and irksome it might be, Disraeli would neither leave the bench himself, nor, when in office, permit his colleagues to leave unless they could allege amply sufficient reason. When the House, as was its usual practice in his time, sat through the dinner hour, he remained and took a hasty dinner at the Cabinet table; or sometimes joined his wife in her brougham drawn up

in one of the courts at St. Stephen's, and there in the
carriage ate with her a daintier meal which her solicitude
had brought down for him. In either case, the interval
was short, and he was back in his place almost before he
had been missed.

Being always there, he had a keen perception of all
that was going on; of the tone of the House on this
question and on that; of the nice gradations of feeling
in the course of any important debate. He noted with
constant interest the progress of rising young men,
especially in his own party; and regarded with particular
attention, and a careful scrutiny through his eyeglass,
any new member who rose for the first time to address the
House. To his immediate neighbour on the bench he
would, now and again, drop a caustic reflection on the
newcomer. Thus of the philosopher John Stuart Mill,
whose manner was at once authoritative and ladylike,
he said, 'Ah! I see; the finishing governess!' On
catching sight for the first time of the uncouth figure of
J. G. Biggar, Parnell's precursor, and lieutenant, in
obstruction, he exclaimed, 'What is that?' adding after
a closer examination, 'He seems to be what in Ireland
you call a Leprechaun.' Fawcett, the blind economist,
who deservedly in later years became a favourite of the
House, in his earlier appearances bored and depressed
it by his pedagogic manner and thunderous tones. 'If
this fellow had eyes,' murmured Disraeli during one of
these harangues, 'how we should damn them!' When
a respected leader of the commercial classes was returned
to Parliament by an Irish constituency, Disraeli, after
listening to the new member for awhile, turned to Lord
Rathmore, then sitting, as David Plunket, by his side,
and said impressively: 'My dear David, you usually send
us here from Ireland either gentlemen or blackguards;
but this is neither!'

Observant and alert as both his private asides to
colleagues and his public replies in debate showed Disraeli
to have been, nobody would have guessed it from his

appearance in the House. He was naturally somewhat
restless in manner as, during his days of adolescence, he
was flamboyant in costume; but there was no sign of
extravagance in demeanour or dress as he sat on the front
bench. His clothes were neat and careful, but quiet and
subdued. In place of the gaudy raiment and chains and
rings of earlier days, he wore a dark frockcoat in winter
with a double-breasted plush waistcoat of tabby colour;
and in summer a thin blue frockcoat, tightly buttoned,
with (says Fraser[1]) 'an unquestionable pair of stays' to
be seen through it from the back.[2]   His manner was as
quiet as his dress. He had cultivated early in his
Parliamentary career, and he sedulously matured as
leader, an absolutely impassive bearing which served him
admirably as a mask till it eventually became second
nature. Here is a contemporary description of his
appearance in the year 1847 when he first took his seat
on the front bench.

You never see him gazing around him, or lolling back in
his seat, or seeking to take his ease as other men do in the
intervals of political excitement. He sits with his head
rigid, his body contracted, his arms closely pinned to his
side, as though he were an automaton. He looks like one of
those stone figures of ancient Egypt that embody the idea
of motionless quiescence for ever.[3]

So an observer in 1854 depicts him as sitting 'sunk
into his seat,' his eyes appearing 'to be fixed on the
ground or staring at vacancy,' and 'his whole attitude
that of the most rigid repose.'[4]   Fraser, who watched him,
off and on, in the House from 1852 to 1876, writes of his
'studied behaviour':

[1] P. 149.

[2] Disraeli was extremely reluctant to disturb the neat precision of his
apparel. A Conservative M.P. was once talking to his leader in the House
on a complicated public question, and, fearing to detain and bore him,
tendered him some bulky explanatory papers to be put in his pocket
and read at his leisure. Disraeli firmly waved them aside. 'I never,'
he said 'put papers in my pocket. Give them to Monty Corry; he puts
papers in his pocket.' To realise the full flavour of the reply, it must be
borne in mind that Corry was at least as much point-device in his attire as
his chief.

[3] *Fraser's Magazine*, Feb., 1847.   [4] Ewald's *Beaconsfield*, ch. 11.

He invariably sat with one knee over the other, his arms folded across his breast, leaning against the back of his seat, his hat slightly over his brows. The more vehement the attack of his adversary became, the more he affected somnolence; when it waxed very hot indeed, he, without removing the pendent leg, brought his body round towards the west; placing his eyeglass, with the forefinger of his right hand curved over it, to his right eye, he glanced for about three seconds at the clock over the entrance door; replacing the glass in the breast of his coat, he again relapsed into simulated sleep. [1]

In other passages Fraser adds that he had himself observed Disraeli, when an attack really touched him, shift the pendent leg two or three times, and then curve the foot upwards; and that a colleague had noticed, in similar circumstances, a slight pulling forward of the wrist of his shirt. These were the only signs of feeling that a minute inspection could discover. Disraeli carried this impassiveness and apparent self-absorption into all his actions in the House. 'Observe him anywhere about the House, in the lobbies or in the committee rooms; you never see him in confidential communication with anyone,' wrote the 1847 eyewitness; and he continues: 'See him where you will, he glides past you noiselessly, without being apparently conscious of the existence of externals, and more like the shadow than the substance of a man.' All the accounts of his middle period represent him, when in the purlieus of the House, as quite unapproachable by the ordinary member, whether foe or friend. Towards the close of his career, this unapproachableness in the lobbies was greatly modified, mainly owing to his interest in, and desire to keep in touch with, the promising young men of his party. He liked them, Lord George Hamilton, who entered Parliament in 1868, tells us, 'to come up and talk to him in the lobby during divisions. He nearly always stood with his back to a fireplace, and he was interested in any little piece of gossip or rumour relating to current events, as he wished to know what was going on outside Parliament.' [2]

[1] Fraser, pp. 400, 401.
[2] Lord G. Hamilton's *Parliamentary Reminiscences*, p. 60.

When he rose to speak, though his delivery by no means
lacked animation, he did not discard the same general
reserve, and he eschewed all extravagance of gesture.
He never 'let himself go,' never, like the born orator,
allowed himself to be carried away on an impetuous
torrent of words; but always kept his powers in hand,
prepared to make his points when and how he had
originally designed.   Here is Fraser's careful observation
of his method.

He rose with his coat buttoned across his breast; he usually
moved his open hands downwards above his hips; he then
pulled his coat down in front, and threw his shoulders back.
He began slowly and very deliberately.   Whenever he was
about to produce a good thing, and his good things were
very good, anyone in the habit of watching him knew precisely when they were coming.   Before producing the point,
he would always pause, and give a nervous cough: the action
of his hands was remarkable.   He carried a cambric handkerchief, of spotless whiteness, in his left skirt pocket.   He
would place both hands in both pockets behind him; then
bring out the white handkerchief, and hold it in his left hand
before him for a few seconds; pass it to his right hand: then
with his right hand pass the handkerchief lightly under his
nose, hardly touching it; and then with his left hand replace
the handkerchief in his pocket; still holding his hand, with
the handkerchief in it, in his pocket, until a fresh topic.[1]

The picture which this eyewitness draws, of tricks
and mannerisms, none of them on the grand scale, gives
no suggestion or indication of the mighty power which
his hero wielded for thirty years over the House of
Commons.   Fraser himself despairs of making his readers
understand it.   Very few persons, as he has pointed out,
could ever have had an opportunity of hearing Disraeli
speak.   Gladstone, in his day, owing to his many popular
progresses, must have been heard by hundreds of thousands
of his countrymen; and the same is true of the generation
of politicians who have swayed men's minds in the last
twenty or thirty years.   But Disraeli, in the nineteenth
century, practised the reserve of an eighteenth-century

[1] Fraser, pp. 401, 402.

statesman, and was rarely tempted to speak away from
St. Stephen's. His oratory was therefore familiar only
to Members of Parliament, officials of the House of
Commons, and newspaper reporters, and to the few
hundreds of the public whom the extremely limited space
allotted to visitors in the House could accommodate.
Those favoured individuals, however, who did hear him
are in general agreement with Fraser's verdict that

No one, who has not done so, can form any idea of his
powers. His speeches when read give no adequate idea of
their effect. The impression made on an emotional assembly
like the House of Commons can never be put in print. The
varying sensations, fluctuating like the breast of the ocean;
the minute rhetorical effects, which moved his audience so
powerfully; the alterations of voice; the pauses; the grand
gestures, which he occasionally, but not frequently, used:
all these are utterly lost upon the reader of a debate. Disraeli had a perfectly melodious voice; and, what is rare, a voice
increasing in beauty of tone the more loudly that he spoke:
he had the proud consciousness of having a master-mind;
and a masterly power of influencing men. . . . To the reader
who has read and admired his speeches I say, ' Quid si tonan-
tem ipsum audivisses !' [1]

An imperfect attempt must be made, by the collation
of the evidence of many witnesses, to describe and explain
the indescribable and inexplicable. In the first place, as
Fraser says, Disraeli was endowed with a magnificent
organ—a voice which was singularly pure and attractive
in tone, without any accent such as Gladstone's northern
burr, and which carried easily to the farthest corners of
the House, even, in his last years, proving thoroughly
audible in the most unacoustic of chambers, the House
of Lords. It is well characterised in a Parliamentary
sketch of 1854 as at once clear, powerful, and penetrating;
and completely under its owner's control. ' It is not a
sea of sound, in which the language and articulation of
the speaker are drowned and dissolved; but a pure,
gushing stream, which, at the will of the orator, expands
so as to fill the spacious hall, and contracts so as to

[1] Fraser, pp. 292, 293.

concentrate upon a single individual the full force of his invective, or the scathing sarcasm of his irony.'[1]   Writing of the manner in which this splendid instrument was used, a *Quarterly Reviewer*[2]—an unfriendly witness— testifies in the same year to Disraeli's 'masterly, passion- less, finished delivery.' 'Perhaps the art of compelling a hearer to listen to every word spoken by an orator was never carried to higher perfection.' The tone, though very distinct, would usually at the beginning be low and quiet. 'Towards the end of his speeches Mr. Disraeli gets very loud, but his voice takes a purely artistic tone— passion has nothing to do with it—and he drops from an angry clamour to a smooth colloquialism.' Then would come ' a capitally constructed closing sentence, of which the last syllable rings as distinctly in the ear as the first.' Not a little of his impressiveness was due to the clearness of his enunciation and the care with which he gave their full value to words usually slurred over. When Disraeli spoke, says Fraser, the listener could hear the four syllables in ' Parliament,' and the three in ' business.' John Stuart Mill, a candid opponent, said that it was a real pleasure to him when Disraeli rose ; his voice and manner were so satisfying after an overdose of the voices and manners that prevailed in the House of Commons.

Besides a fine voice and skill in managing it, Disraeli, owing to his long apprenticeship to literature, had a great and varied command of language; knew how to select the suggestive epithet, how to turn the appropriate phrase. It is true that literary qualities, though they may preserve speeches for the delectation of succeeding generations, are often useless, as in the case of Burke, to render them impressive at the moment; and that some of the greatest orators, such as Chatham, have produced their effects without much aid from literary form.   Still, Demosthenes and Cicero among the ancients, Canning

[1] *Reynolds' Newspaper*, Feb. 26, 1854.
[2] *Quarterly Review*, June, 1854.

and Macaulay among the moderns, show what a powerful reinforcement literary graces may bring to argument,
invective, and exhortation. Disraeli's most marked
literary quality was the power of phrase-making and
phrase-adaptation, of illuminating collocations of words,
now in the shape of ironical aphorism, now of convincing
epigram, now of audacious paradox, now of stinging
satire. This quality was pre-eminent in his speeches.
They seldom lacked these

> jewels, five words long,
> Which on the stretched forefinger of all Time
> Sparkle for ever.[1]

The diamonds may sometimes have been paste, and the
setting sometimes rococo, but the brilliance of all was
undoubted; and again and again the phrases were of the
happiest and aptest kind, and have become part and
parcel of Victorian history.

But voice and language are the mere externals of
public speaking ; 'the foundation of eloquence,' as
Disraeli was wont to say and to write, is to be 'completely
master of the subject.' That foundation Disraeli had
well and truly laid. From the time when his return to
Parliament had definitely settled in favour of politics the
contest which had been waged within him for some years
between that engrossing mistress and his other love,
literature, he had given himself wholeheartedly to
master the subject-matter of what was to be his life's
work. He was unremitting in his study of political
history, domestic and foreign, of political and economic
science, and of Parliamentary papers and bluebooks.
Even when he turned for a relief to letters, there was
always—in the famous trilogy, in *Lord Geor e Bentinck*, in
his newspaper activity, and in *Lothair*—either a political
object to be advanced or a political background to his
story. He not only read and wrote on politics; but, in
spite of his enjoyment of country sights and sounds, of

---

[1] Tennyson's *Princess*, Sec. 2.

trees and flowers and birds, he pondered long and deeply over political questions in his Bucks retreat. 'Ah ! now we shall be obliged to talk politics ' was the rather rueful observation of his old chief, Derby, on learning that a shooting party at Heron Court was to be joined by Disraeli. When he was in office, he kept, as Chancellor of the Exchequer and Leader of the House, thoroughly in touch with the main business of the principal departments, and encouraged his colleagues to come to him in any difficulty. He studied political men, as well as political matters. He was, as we have seen, always in his place when the House was sitting; he went much into society in London and in country houses. He was a regular attendant at Quarter Sessions and agricultural meetings in his county; and he made due use behind the scenes of the Rigbys and Tapers and Tadpoles of politics. Few Parliamentary questions or situations could find him unprepared. When, therefore, he rose to speak, he had a full mind; he was master of his subject.

Disraeli was also gifted with a marvellously retentive memory, which often indeed betrayed him into plagiarisms of a sustained character in speech and writing, but which, at any rate, enabled him altogether to dispense, in his ordinary practice, with the use of notes. Not only did his memory register faithfully the points on which he meant to dwell and the choice phrases with which he meant to drive them home, but also the statements and arguments of the opponents whom he set himself to answer or to ridicule, and the very words and tones which they had employed. At the same time he was, in Fraser's words, ' a chivalrously fair ' speaker; though he turned his opponent's words into absurdity, he never altered them, or pretended to mistake what had been said. Once, when speaking in Parliament, he was observed to pull a scrap of paper out of his waistcoat pocket and make great play with it; he held it up in front of his eyes, and, fixing his eyeglass, seemed to read from it, with deliberation and emphasis, some statement of Gladstone's which he was controverting; then he tore it up and threw the pieces on the floor. An eyewitness, who was curious enough, when the House rose, to pick them up, found them without any writing on them whatever. Hardy preserved in his diary, as a unique specimen, a sheet of paper on which Disraeli, then in Opposition, had jotted down during a speech of Gladstone's the three words 'at another time'—the sole text for an effective reply delivered on the instant.[1] He did not escape from the inevitable consequence of depriving himself of all artificial means of reminder, namely, the occasional omission of good things which he had intended to use; as his letters to wife and friends after speeches prove. But he justified his practice to Fraser by saying, 'If I once used notes, I should lean upon them; and that would never do.'[2] Like all orators who really move men, though not to the same extent as his rival Gladstone, he depended in some degree on catching inspiration from his hearers; he told Delane, he was 'much influenced by my audience and the impromptu.'[3] This does not, of course, mean that there was not careful preparation before any great effort, or that, in particular, the biting phrases by which he will always be remembered were not deeply studied in his mind and assiduously polished, before they were launched, apparently at random, upon the world. In preparing the few speeches of importance which he delivered outside Parliament he often made use of a highly original method; he privately rehearsed them, either in whole or in part, to an experienced reporter of *The Times*, J. F. Neilson, in whom he placed especial trust.[4]

Above all, Disraeli was armed, in addressing the House of Commons, with a superb self-confidence. Four years before he became a member, he watched its proceedings as a visitor, hearing, among others, orators so renowned

---

[1] Gathorne Hardy, Vol. I., p. 299.   [2] Fraser, p. 206.
[3] See Vol. IV., p. 360.   [4] See Vol. III., p. 5.

as Bulwer Lytton and Sheil, and 'Macaulay's best speech,' that in which he denounced O'Connell's ingratitude to Lord ,Grey and the Whigs; and then told his sister: 'Between ourselves, I could floor them all. This *entre nous;* I was never more confident of anything than that I could carry everything before me in that House. The time will come.'[1]   That confidence never left him.   It carried him through his initial failure, and enabled him to retrieve that failure almost immediately; it buoyed him up through the years of mediocre success which followed; it nerved him for the titanic struggle against Peel which established his fame.   Neither he nor the House ever forgot that he was the man who had over- thrown 'the greatest Member of Parliament that ever lived.'   He thereby made good his claim to be, as Froude has pointed out, the strongest Member of Parliament in his day; a position which, as early as 1854, was so well recognised that the *Quarterly Reviewer,* whom we have, already quoted, remarks that, though Disraeli was assailed, out of the House, with exceeding ferocity, 'in the House it is rare for anyone but Mr. Gladstone to meddle with him.'   Absolute unanimity of opinion has not yet been reached as to who had the better in the long rivalry of these two famous men in the House of Commons; but the prevailing judgment seems to be that, while, in individual debates, at one time the glowing eloquence of Gladstone, at another the pungent sarcasm of Disraeli, secured the victory, Gladstone never attained the general mastery of the House in all its moods which Disraeli gained, and kept for years, by patience, self-control, force of will, command of phrase, and unvarying attendance in his place.

A notable tribute to Disraeli's powers in debate was published a few years ago by George W. E. Russell.   The Whigs, among whom George Russell was brought up, despised Disraeli and would not take him seriously; but Russell had the opportunity, as the son of the Sergeant-

[1] See Vol. I., p. 223.

at-Arms, of attending as a boy the great Reform debates
and there judging for himself. He heard all the famous
speakers, Gladstone and Bright and Lowe and Cranborne.
'But one figure appeared to me to tower head and shoulders
above the rest, and that was the leader of the Conservative
party, the ridiculed and preposterous "Dizzy." His
mastery of the House, on both sides, seemed absolute.
Compared to him Gladstone played a secondary and an
ambiguous part.' The debates, he adds, 'displayed, in
the contrast between Disraeli and those who surrounded
him, the difference between genius and talent.'[1] Except
Gladstone, nobody in the later days, when Peel and his
generation had passed away, could challenge Disraeli
with success; and that may explain why good judges
have been disposed to consider that his high-water mark
in oratory was reached in the fighting years between the
opening of the attack on Peel and the fall of the Coalition
Government. Certainly a review of the marvellous
series of speeches chronicled and commented on in the
last two chapters of the second volume, and in the third
volume, of this biography, tends to confirm this verdict.

Writing in 1851, during this period, Disraeli told the
world that 'what Lord George Bentinck appreciated
most in a Parliamentary speaker was brilliancy: quickness of perception, promptness of repartee, clear and
concise argument, a fresh and felicitous quotation, wit
and picture, and, if necessary, a passionate appeal that
should never pass the line of high-bred sentiment.'[2] We
know that there was no speaker whom Bentinck more
appreciated than Disraeli himself; and we can hardly
be wrong in assuming that we have in this summary
the qualities which Disraeli believed his own oratory
to possess. He could gauge his own powers pretty
accurately. The description closely fits the speeches of
that time, the late forties and the early fifties, beginning
with the philippics against Peel. As Disraeli became an

[1] *Portraits of the Seventies—Lord Beaconsfield.*
[2] *Lord George Bentinck*, ch. 10.

old Parliamentary hand of undisputed eminence, the brilliancy suffered some diminution; the crisp literary style became, through bad association, diluted with the verbiage and tautologies familiar to every student of Parliamentary eloquence in *Hansard;* but, in compensation, there was a steady increase, especially when he held office, in conscious power and authoritative weight.

So far as print and description can reproduce the effect of speeches, the readers of this biography have had ample opportunity of forming a judgment of Disraeli's oratory. They will have noticed that in one great quality he was deficient. There was no fiery impetuosity, no whirlwind of passion, no rush of torrential words, the speaker seeming, as it were, to be taken out of himself and inspired; to heights of this kind Disraeli never soared. He never assumed in the House of Commons the part of a prophet revealing the eternal verities, but rather that of the man of the world, no better or more intelligent than his hearers, who would state facts and arguments as plainly as possible, confident that the intelligent persons whom he addressed would recognise that there was only one conclusion possible. If he ever attempted to sound the note of passion, he did not, in his own somewhat frigid words, 'pass the line of high-bred sentiment.' But practically all the other resources of oratory were at his command; and the reflection may be hazarded that the missing quality has as often been used to mislead as to enforce reason. He was a master of the lofty, grave, and authoritative rhetoric of the statesman and patriot; he could elaborate a close and consecutive argument; he could expound a complicated Budget or Bill, so as to carry the intelligence, if not the sympathy, of his hearers with him; he could pile up a convincing case by quotation and analysis of public documents; he could make deadly use of that 'ornament of debate,' invective. The perorations of most of his great speeches afford admirable examples

of statesmanlike rhetoric; take some of those on Agricultural Depression in his first year of leadership, 1849,
or the Manchester and Crystal Palace speeches of 1872.
Disraeli's faculty of careful and connected argument
may be well illustrated by his speech on going into
committee on Peel's Corn Law Bill in 1846; his capacity
for exposition was shown in his Budget of 1852 and his
Reform Bills of 1867; for powerful analysis of a blue-
book there is no better example than the impeachment
in 1864 of the Schleswig-Holstein diplomacy of Palmerston and Russell; while the sustained invective of his
denunciations of Peel will never be forgotten.

In all these respects, however, other men have been as
great, or greater than he. Where he was unsurpassed
was in the wit and humour that illuminated his utterances.
He was a complete master of all the arts of irony, sarcasm,
satire, and ridicule; and he employed these, sometimes
in long and elaborate passages, sometimes in concentrated
phrases and epigrams. These passages and phrases are
the 'good things' to which Fraser is so fond of referring;
of which he truly says that Disraeli's good things were
very good. To the reader these need no introduction;
they are scattered all over these volumes. The more
sustained passages are, indeed, too long to quote, and
often too dependent on topics of the moment to be readily
understood. Referring to the 'matchless strain of irony'
in which Disraeli loved to address the Coalition Ministry,
T. E. Kebbel[1] has acutely pointed out that 'the effect
is often not produced by felicitous images or pungent
epigrams, but by one continuous flow of elaborate mockery
which does not admit of being broken up, and which
cannot be appreciated even as it stands without a minute
acquaintance with the political and Parliamentary
circumstances to which it is addressed.' These weapons
are more suited to the attack than to the defence; and it
is partly owing to his mastery of them that Disraeli was
such an incomparable leader of Opposition. To the

[1] *Life of Lord Beaconsfield*, p. 185.

' good things ' which he had prepared he would lead up
in the most artistic fashion, with all the by-play which
Fraser has preserved for us.   The moment arrived, and
the audience duly warned (writes the *Quarterly Review*
of June, 1854), ' not a blow misses ; not a platitude irritates ;
not a sarcasm is impeded by a weakening phrase.   The
arrow, stripped of all plumage except that which aids and
steadies its flight, strikes within a hair's breadth of the
archer's aim.'   Disraeli's strong dramatic sense enabled
him to get the last ounce of value out of situations thus
created.   But he was a generous opponent.   He never
put forth his strength against small men.   Great Ministers
such as Peel, Russell, Palmerston, and Gladstone were
his quarry, or men such as Graham, Charles Wood, and
Lowe, who, though not in the first flight, loomed large in
the eyes of the House.

With regard to quotation, Disraeli has left a note,
written apparently in the sixties, stating what he understood to be the recognised custom of Parliament, and what
had been his own practice.

There used to be well understood rules in the House of
Commons in old days (before the Reform), respecting quotations.
No English poet to be quoted, who had not completed his
century.   Greek and French never under any circumstances.
Latin as you liked : Horace and Virgil by preference ; then
Juvenal. [1]
Now quotation (in the House of Commons) is what we are
most deficient in.   Very few will venture on Latin.   But it
is not that the House has relinquished quotation, but the
new elements find their illustrations and exponents in illegitimate means.   It is not merely, that they quote Byron and
Tennyson before they have completed their quarantine : but
Bright and Cobden, and all those sort of people, are always
quoting Dickens and *Punch,* etc.   Our quotations are either
tawdry or trashy.   The privilege of quotation should not be
too easy.   It should be fenced in.   When I took the lead
of the Opposition, I, temperately and discreetly, somewhat
revived the habit of classic quotation.   (I had done it before

[1] In *Endymion,* ch. 76, Beaconsfield quotes Charles Fox as laying down,
in almost identical terms, the unwritten rules about quotation in Parliament.

to some degree, when I had got the ear of the House.)   Applied with discretion, it was not unsuccessful; and I was rather amused in course of time to find Lord John Russell, who was then Prime Minister and Leader of the House, brushing up his classical reminiscences and coming down frequently with Virgilian passages, so that he might keep up the credit of his party.   If it were worth while to examine Hansard for such trifles, this would be found to be accurate.

Disraeli was not copious in quotation, save of inconvenient expressions of opinion which his opponents had incautiously used and had hoped were forgotten; these he often quoted with telling effect.   But every now and then, as his note intimates, he introduced in a felicitous way a few lines from the Latin poets; instances have been given in previous volumes of this biography.[1]   His most famous collocation of Latin words, which he employed both at the beginning of his leadership[2] and at the height of his power to denote his view of the rightful aim of British policy—*Imperium et Libertas*—was a misquotation, into which he was betrayed by the authority of Bolingbroke and Bacon.   Bolingbroke wrote in the *Patriot King:* 'A King, in the temper of whose Government, like that of Nerva, things so seldom allied as Empire and Liberty are intimately mixed.'   So Bacon in his *Advancement of Learning*, Book I., had written: 'Nerva, the excellent temper of whose Government is by a glance in Cornelius Tacitus touched to the life: "Postquam divus Nerva res olim insociabiles miscuisset, imperium et libertatem." ' But both Bolingbroke and Bacon were quoting from memory; Bolingbroke, indeed, was perhaps quoting from Bacon.   The actual words of Tacitus in the *Agricola*, sec. 3, are: 'Quamquam . . . Nerva Cæsar res olim dissociabiles miscuerit, *principatum ac libertatem*.'   Though there is little difference of meaning, undoubtedly *Imperium et Libertas*, Empire and Liberty, is for the modern world the more impressive phrase.

In his management of the House of Commons, Disraeli kept a light, if firm, hand upon the reins.   Here his

[1] See Vol. II., p. 384; Vol. III., p. 101.   [2] See Vol. III., p. 283.

complete command of temper served him well.   Where
Gladstone would have fulminated and insisted, he was
content to allure and persuade.   A timely jest or a mirth-
provoking epigram would often conjure the storm-cloud
away.   At question-time, though ready if necessary to
administer a crushing snub, he adopted in general the
attitude of polite and welcoming consideration.   But,
both at this stage and in debate, he intervened very
rarely; he allowed no one to draw him; the tactics by
which, in the 1880 Parliament, Randolph Churchill
contrived to make Gladstone himself occupy in explanatory and exculpatory speech the time which should have
been devoted to forwarding Government business, would
have had no success with Disraeli.   He seldom made any
attempt to drive the House, when it was in a recalcitrant
mood.   There was in those days, of course, no closure,
and in order to get business through the choice often lay
solely between threatening and humouring a stubborn
minority.   Gladstone, in the strenuous times of 1869-1873,
had frequently endeavoured to extort the passage of his
measures by insisting that the House should not rise for
the night till some particular stage had been taken,
should not be prorogued for the vacation till certain Bills
had been passed.   Tactics of this sort were distasteful
to Disraeli.   Much as he deprecated and discouraged
obstruction, from whatever quarter it might proceed,
yet, when he found that late at night a determined
minority would not give way, he would often, after one
division, accept the adjournment with a good grace; with
the frequent result that the clause, or the measure, which
was to have been resisted to the death at one in the
morning, was passed after a few minutes' good-humoured
discussion in the early hours of the following afternoon.
Whether methods of this character would have had any
effect upon the organised obstruction started by Parnell
in 1877 may perhaps be doubted.   Happily for Disraeli's
comfort he had then quitted the Commons.

     The dignity of the House was very dear to him.   'Let

us remember we are a senate, not a vestry,' he was wont to say. His attitude towards its traditional rules was almost one of veneration, and it was only with the greatest reluctance that he assented to the slightest modification of them. But he insisted that 'the rules were made for *gentlemen*,' and must be observed in that spirit. For his colleagues he was a strict disciplinarian. He required, as we have seen, steady attendance on the bench and in divisions; and the reproof he administered by word of mouth or by letter to absentees was such that they did not court a second. He strongly disapproved of interruptions during speeches in debate. He would neither interpose himself, save on a very special occasion, nor permit a colleague to interrupt, when an opponent was speaking; and, if interruptions proceeded from any of the benches behind him, he would turn and frown the offender down. To interrupt, he would say, was not merely bad manners, but it did not pay; it only gave the speaker an opportunity for an apt retort. He often profited himself in this way by the unmannerly interruptions of the other side. But he would not allow members of his Government to call an opponent their honourable or right honourable 'friend.' Ostentatious intimacy of that sort would make the struggle a mere game.

No wonder a magnanimous and generous figure of the kind we have tried to depict, a unique and magical personality, exotic in appearance, masterful in quality, was sorely missed when he left the House. After little more than a couple of months' experience of the next Session Sir Henry Lucy bitterly lamented the dulness of the place without Disraeli. 'He was not only brilliant himself, but the cause of brilliancy in others. He wound up the House of Commons to a certain pitch, at which it was constantly kept going. His mere presence supplied a focus towards which the minds of speakers were bent.'[1]

Disraeli's final act as a commoner was to bid farewell

---

[1] *Diary of Two Parliaments*, Vol. I., p. 218.

to the constituency, the fidelity of whose feelings, as he gracefully said, had given him an assured position at Westminster. In his short but dignified address to the electors of Bucks, he summed up in one sentence the two chief objects at which he had aimed throughout his public life.

Not insensible to the principle of progress, I have endeavoured to reconcile change with that respect for tradition which is one of the main elements of our social strength; and in external affairs I have endeavoured to develop and strengthen our Empire, believing that combination of achievement and responsibility elevates the character and condition of a people.

In the titles which Disraeli took—Earl of Beaconsfield and Viscount Hughenden of Hughenden—he was faithful to the memory of his wife and to the country home which they both loved. He based himself on a great historical precedent. 'He would prefer,' he wrote to the Queen, 'following the precedent of Lord Chatham, suggested by your Majesty, and take the same title as his wife, with a step.' Moreover, he was not, we may be sure, insensible to the association of the name of Beaconsfield with so eminent a pillar of the British Constitution as Edmund Burke. Disraeli was somewhat annoyed by a disposition on the part of the public to pronounce the first syllable of his new title with a short vowel sound. When Granville and Bradford used this fashion, basing themselves on the recollections of schooldays spent forty years before in the town of Beaconsfield, he humorously said he was not going to be dictated to by two aristocratic schoolboys.[1] 'It is like the Whigs,' he said, on another occasion, 'to call me out of my name.' He told a lady who asked for information, 'My name is BEACONS-field—not "Becc";' and a foreign inquirer that it meant 'the field of the beacon.' It may be added that the Queen expressed her willingness to settle any part of Disraeli's titles on his nephew and heir, Coningsby Disraeli; but the offer was for family reasons declined.

[1] Fitzmaurice's *Granville*, Vol. I., p. 12.

To Queen Victoria.

CASTLE BROMWICH, *Aug.* 20, 1876.—. . . Lord Beaconsfield asks leave to take this opportunity of again thanking
your Majesty for all the honors your Majesty has graciously
conferred on him. They would not be mean distinctions,
even for the most exalted, but what enhances them to him
beyond all price, is that your Majesty has condescended to
express your Majesty's personal gratification in rewarding a
servant who, whatever his deficiencies, is, he hopes, from his
very heart, devoted to your Majesty.

If there was nothing dramatic about Benjamin Disraeli's
manner of leaving the House of Commons, the first
appearance of the Earl of Beaconsfield in the House of
Lords had a certain piquancy of its own. When, on
February 8, 1877, the Queen opened Parliament in state,
all eyes were turned on 'a familiar face, but a strangely
disguised figure,'[1] at Her Majesty's left hand as she sat on
the Throne. It was the Prime Minister, in scarlet and
ermine, bearing aloft the Sword of State; standing mute
and motionless, with all the dignity of pose, and lack
of facial expression, that distinguished him on great
occasions. He was but lately risen from a bed of sickness,
and the Queen had offered to release him from the ' cumbersome ' burden; but he was resolved, once at least, to
play in due form the Minister's part in the historic
pageant. 'He quite counts,' he wrote on January 28,
' on the honor of carrying the Sword of State and standing
next to your Majesty. He would not like to miss so
great an incident. It is a chapter in life !'
The brilliant throng of peeresses who attended the
function returned a couple of hours later to see the Prime
Minister of Society take his seat as a peer. According to
the practice of the Lords a newcomer has to be introduced
by two members of that order of the peerage to which he
has been raised. The earls whom Beaconsfield chose as
sponsors were Derby and Bradford; the one the son of
his old chief and himself his leading colleague in the

[1] *Diary of Two Parliaments*, Vol. I., p. 172.

Ministry, the other the husband of his intimate friend. Conducted by them, and preceded by Garter and other high officers of state, he and they all duly robed, he went through the bowings and handshakings, the peregrinations to various benches, the liftings of the three-cornered hat, that constitute the quaint old-fashioned ceremony of introduction, with the same stateliness and dignity which had marked his manipulation of the great Sword. The notes that passed with reference to Derby's sponsorship have a pathetic interest in view of subsequent events.

To Lord Derby.

2, WHITEHALL G'DNS, *Jan.* 24, '77.—What do you think of introducing me to H. of L. ? I know it would bore you, and I, always, try to save you from being bored. But one has a feeling, that it would be the proper thing. Perhaps the feeling may have no foundation, and there are 1,000 reasons why you should [not] be trespassed on at this somewhat anxious moment. That chivalric being, the premier earl, is a candidate for the office, but I ventured to observe, that I thought it was the custom to appeal, in such a situation, to one's colleagues.

Bradford would be the second, and if you thought, on the whole, it was more convenient for you not to join him, there is, at least, Beauchamp.

From Lord Derby.

FOREIGN OFFICE, *J[an]*. 24.—I am not disposed to be sensitive on such matters as that to which your note refers; but I should have felt sorry, though not aggrieved, if you had applied to anyone but me on the occasion of your introduction to the H. of Lds. Considering that we have pulled together for nearly 30 years, I think that office of friendship is mine by right; and I accept it with real pleasure.

The old familiar friendship of the two men was still strong; but the coming twelve months, with their searching trial of character, were to sunder the relations of thirty years; and the willing sponsor of the early days of 1877 was to become the deserter of 1878, and, for the remaining few years of Beaconsfield's life, his declared opponent and severe critic.

It was by Derby's side, between him and Richmond, that Beaconsfield took his seat as leader; assuming the leadership here, as in the other House, under unprecedented conditions. He had become Leader of the Commons without ever having been in office, or even sworn in as a Privy Councillor; he now became Leader of the Lords directly he entered their House. That historic assembly, to which so notable a figure had been added, then included, among those regularly taking part in its business, many men eminent in the public life of the country. On the woolsack sat a Chancellor, Cairns, hardly inferior to any of his great predecessors in legal acumen and judicial weight, and superior to most of them in statesmanlike wisdom and oratorical power. As colleagues on Beaconsfield's own bench, besides Derby, the mainstay of the sober middle classes, and Richmond, who had proved an acceptable interim leader, there were Salisbury, who after Beaconsfield's death was to exercise undisputed sway in the House for twenty years, and the scholarly and idealistic Carnarvon. A renowned personality, only occasionally present in his place, was the veteran Whig chief, Russell, who had welcomed Beaconsfield in a short but graceful note, written in a trembling hand: 'Let me congratulate the House of Lords that you are one of its members, and that a man of genius and literary fame has been added to its roll.' The actual Liberal leader was the urbane and adroit Granville, who had efficient lieutenants in men like Kimberley, Cardwell, Aberdare, Selborne, Spencer, and Northbrook. The day of Lord Rosebery, still under thirty, and of Lord Lansdowne, just over that age, was not yet, though both had begun to interest the House. But the great Opposition orator, whose duels with Beaconsfield were the only episodes that gave the debates of the next few years anything of the animation to which the newcomer had been accustomed in the Commons, was the proud and fiery Duke of Argyll. Others in an independent position, who contributed weight or distinction to the proceedings, were Shaftesbury, still at

the height of his philanthropic renown; Grey, who represented the Whig traditions of his father, the Reform Premier;
and, on the episcopal bench, the statesmanlike Tait, of
Canterbury, and the eloquent Magee, of Peterborough.

Distinguished as were the *élite* of the peers, there was
none among them to give pause to one who had successfully encountered in debate Peel and Palmerston, O'Connell and Cobden, Gladstone and Bright.   Beaconsfield
spoke for ten minutes the very first evening on the
Address, and Fraser, who was present, notes that he
seemed at once to be at home in his new surroundings.

I was particularly struck with the perfect ease with which
he leaned forward, glanced at the Chancellor, and moved the
adjournment of the House.   One could have thought that he
had passed his life there: this was always his demeanour in
the House of Lords.

In not one of his speeches in the House of Lords was there
the slightest trace either of too much self-consciousness,
too much familiarity, illness of ease, nor indeed of any quality
that a gentleman would not show under the circumstances.
Having been for many years used to address the Speaker as
' Sir,' he never made the mistake of substituting that word
for ' my Lords ': he adapted himself to the new situation ' as
to the manner born.'[1]

' I am dead; dead, but in the Elysian fields,' was
Beaconsfield's reply to an acquaintance among the peers,
who, when welcoming him to the Lords, expressed a fear
lest he should miss the excitement of the Commons.   The
shortness and comparative rarity of the sittings, the
chilliness of the atmosphere, the abstinence from noisy
demonstration, may have sometimes caused the Parliamentary gladiator to sigh for the strenuous triumphs of
the past.   But one who was a Jewish aristocrat at
heart felt himself naturally at home in an assembly
of aristocrats, where business was conducted with dignity
and manners were urbane; and the leisure of the new
Parliamentary conditions enabled him both to satisfy the
claims of private friendship, and to concentrate his

[1] Fraser, pp. 414, 415.

attention more fully and exclusively on foreign affairs. Far from being dead, in regard to the higher direction of policy he was never more alive and active.

In the *Young Duke* Disraeli had laid it down, with the assurance of youth, that two distinct styles were requisite for speaking in the two Houses of Parliament, and that he meant, if he had time, to give a specimen of both; taking *Don Juan* as his model in the Commons, and *Paradise Lost* in the Lords. In actual fact there was no great difference in his manner in the two Houses; though *Paradise Lost* certainly contains some lines, taken from the great debate—not in the Elysian fields—of Book II., which admirably describe the Minister's appearance, as he was wont to rise to address the Peers.

> With grave
> Aspect he rose, and in his rising seemed
> A pillar of State.   Deep on his front engraven
> Deliberation sat, and public care.[1]

But, though such was Beaconsfield's manner as Leader of the Lords, it was only a continuation of the later and authoritative manner of Disraeli, the Leader of the Commons. Moreover, the good things in his speeches were heralded with just the same play of the handkerchief. Fraser gives an amusing instance;

I was fortunately in the House of Lords, shortly before his departure with Lord Salisbury for the Berlin Conference. Lord Granville had spoken, and had expressed real or affected regret that Lord Beaconsfield and Lord Salisbury should both be absent at the same time from the councils of the Queen. Disraeli replied, ' The noble earl has expressed his regret that my noble friend sitting on my right and myself should be abroad at the same time: he has been pleased to add that he considers that the absence of the noble marquis and of myself from the Cabinet will diminish the personal importance of those that remain. My Lords;' here out came the handkerchief; ' I can conceive no circumstance, ahem ! more calculated to add to it !' [2]

[1] My attention was called to this apt quotation by an article on ' Disraeli's Meridian ' in the *Fortnightly Review* for June, 1916, by Mr. A. A. Baumann.
[2] Fraser, pp. 402, 403.

If there was no serious difference in Disraeli's manner
in addressing the two Houses, there was also no difference
in the ascendancy which he exercised over both.   He
assumed in the Lords, at once, as of right, that dominance
which he had after years of combat established in the
Commons.   Before his elevation to their ranks, the
Lords had not shown any particular complaisance to
his wishes, whether he was Leader of Opposition or
Prime Minister.   Conservative as they might be in
general political complexion, they had acknowledged no
special allegiance to any Conservative leader since the
death of the fourteenth Lord Derby.   They had forced
Disraeli's Government to remodel its judicature scheme,
and had, even in the last Session, come near, under
Shaftesbury's inspiration, to a revolt against Disraeli over
the Royal Titles Bill.   But as soon as they experienced
the personal influence of his genius, they willingly submitted to his claims; and what has been described as the
most independent and unenthusiastic assembly in the
world accorded, again and again, to the ennobled Jew
the loud cheers which few other members of their House
have been able to elicit.

By the transfer of the Prime Minister to the Lords the
balance of the Cabinet between the two Houses of Parliament was disturbed.   It was restored by the retirement
of Malmesbury, who was in indifferent health, from the
post of Privy Seal, which Beaconsfield himself assumed
in addition to the First Lordship of the Treasury, and
by the promotion to Cabinet rank of Hicks Beach, the
Chief Secretary for Ireland—'without question,' wrote
Beaconsfield, 'our most competent man' outside.
This rearrangement presented no difficulty.   It was
otherwise with the vacancy in the commanding position
of Leader of the House of Commons.   In many respects
the natural choice would have been Gathorne Hardy,
and Disraeli's thoughts undoubtedly turned to him in
the first place.   Ever since Cairns had gone to the Lords
ten years before, Disraeli had regarded Hardy as his

'sword-arm' in debate; and he had constituted him his deputy in his absence, always when in opposition, and occasionally since the Tory return to office. Hardy, after his chief, was without a doubt the member of the Cabinet whose intervention exercised most influence in the House. Neither Cross, Manners, nor Ward Hunt carried heavy guns; and even Northcote, though always ready, well-informed and persuasive, had none of the sacred fire which moves an audience. Nevertheless, Disraeli came reluctantly to the conclusion that North-cote would be the more suitable successor. Recognising that Hardy had every right to anticipate that the choice would fall upon himself, he took him into his confidence as to the difficulties of the situation at an early stage; and, while leaving him in no doubt as to his anxiety to meet his wishes, appreciation of his services and deep respect for his character, prepared him gradually for a disappointment of his hopes. Finally, when formally communicating to him on August 2 his own resolve to go to the Lords but to remain Prime Minister, in words similar to those which he had used to Richmond and other colleagues, he added the following significant paragraphs, intimating not obscurely what would be the solution of the problem of leadership.

To Gathorne Hardy.

10, DOWNING ST., *Aug.* 2, 1876.—. . . Of the many anxious points connected with this subject, there is none more grave, than the management of the House of Commons after my departure. The choice can only be between yourself and the Chancellor of the Exchequer. You both entered the Privy Council, and the Cabinet, on the same day, and, almost at the same time, you were both promoted to Secretaryships of State. In commanding eloquence, your superiority is quite acknowledged, while, in transacting the various business of the House, the fact of his having no heavy department to engross him, and the miscellaneous character of his duties, have necessarily placed him during this Ministry in more frequent communication with the members.

In mentioning your name to the Queen, I observed, that

the heavy duties of your office might be incompatible with the management of the House of Commons, and I said that some arrangement might be made to meet, perhaps, this difficulty; but the Queen expressed herself very strongly as to her personal wish, that you should not leave the Army, saying that you possessed her entire confidence, and that there was no person, in that respect, to whom she could extend equal trust.

I feel much the responsibility of life in the step which I am probably about to take, and I regret that my original purpose has not been practicable; but I am going to Osborne in a few days, and I must go there with a definite plan.

I speak to you without the slightest reserve, and an anxiety to meet your wishes in every practicable way. I acknowledge your claim to that consideration on public grounds, but believe me, I also extend it from a deep respect for your character, and from a strong personal regard.

Oblige me, then, by communicating to me in the same spirit, and assist me by your advice in one of the most difficult passages of my life.

Hardy, while confessing to a pang of disappointment, accepted the decision with a loyalty beyond praise, and a generosity which Disraeli fully appreciated. Only he expressed a wish that he might be allowed before long to follow his chief 'into a more tranquil sphere'; and received the immediate promise that 'every wish of yours, so far as I am concerned, will be gratified, and I shall rejoice in their gratification.'[1] Beaconsfield, the most grateful of men, never forgot the fine loyalty and self-sacrifice which Hardy exhibited at this juncture; and at the next vacancy, in August, 1877, in a Cabinet post, he marked his high consideration for him by saying, in Hardy's own words, 'that I must consider it a standing order that an offer was made first to me in case of any change: the choice was always open to me, so great were my services to the party and to him '[2]—an assurance subsequently repeated on similar occasions.

[1] The correspondence is fully set out in Gathorne Hardy, Vol. II., ch. 19
[2] Ibid., Vol. II., p. 28.

From Sir Stafford Northcote.

Confidential.   86, HARLEY ST., *Aug.* 2, 1876.—Hardy will probably have told you that he spoke to me after receiving your letter to-day. Nothing could be kinder or more handsome than his language, and I hope there may be no diminution of cordiality between us. Working together, as I think we shall do, we may be able to serve the party.

I cannot write to you all that is in my mind; but I console myself with the reflection that you have a wonderful power of reading men's thoughts, so I hope you know mine, and that it is unnecessary for me to tell you how much the story of the long years of kindness I have received, and of lessons that I have learnt, is filling my heart, or how much of sadness mingles with it.

> Multa ferunt anni venientes:
> Multa recedentes adimunt;

and how much is receding now !

I trust you may find strength and happiness in the change. and there is much consolation in the thought that it will preserve you to us the longer.

But I must not trust myself to say more.

Though the reasons which Disraeli gave to Hardy undoubtedly counted for much in the decision taken, they were not the whole, probably not even the weightier part, of the motives which actuated him.   It was perfectly true that Northcote's relations to Members of Parliament, and his more frequent communication with them in regard to public business, when contrasted with Hardy's immersion in the work of a great spending department from which both the Queen and the Prime Minister would be loth to spare him, seemed to mark out Northcote as more qualified to succeed. But many other considerations pointed in the same direction. Remonstrances against the selection of Hardy were made in two important quarters. The Whips, whose opinion could not be neglected, were afraid lest Hardy's quick temper should land the party in difficulties. Derby, who in spite of his reluctance might be forced by a sudden failure of Beaconsfield's health into the first place, recognised in Hardy a temperament and standpoint much less congenial than

Northcote's to his own.   Moreover, Hardy did not come
up to Disraeli's strict standard in the matter of constant
attendance at the House; and he incurred more than
once the reproof of his chief for missing a critical
division owing to his otherwise praiseworthy habit of
going home, whenever possible, to dine with his wife.
Lastly, Northcote was Disraeli's man in a sense in which
Hardy never had been.   He had entered Ministerial life
as Disraeli's immediate subordinate at the Treasury, and
was never quite able to sink the lieutenant in the colleague;
always, for example, addressing his chief in writing as
'Mr.' Disraeli or 'Lord' Beaconsfield, a formal mode
used by no other colleague occupying a position at all
comparable to that of Chancellor of the Exchequer.
Considering the many possibilities of friction and misunderstanding between a Prime Minister in the Lords
and his deputy in the prerogative House, we can well
understand the preference which Beaconsfield showed
for a leader who combined an immense capacity for
Parliamentary business with an attitude of peculiar
deference to himself.

The leadership of the Commons has often made, or
marred, British Governments; witness the crisis in 1834
caused by the succession of Lord Althorp to the earldom
of Spencer.   And critics have attributed some of the
troubles which befell the Conservatives between 1877 and
1885 to the selection by Beaconsfield of Northcote as
leader instead of Hardy.   Beaconsfield himself, in later
years, came to think that he had made a mistake, and
had presumed too much on the prospects of a period of
political calm, during which the vagaries of Gladstone's
occasional interventions would be controlled by the
abundant common sense of Hartington as Opposition
leader.   To the demands of such a period he felt sure
that Northcote would be adequate.   Had he anticipated
the new crusade which Gladstone was about to launch,
he might have preferred the more combative leader.   It
is, however, only fair to recognise that, in spite of Glad-

stone's impetuous return, Northcote was not unequal
to the calls which the Parliament of 1874 made upon
him, and was able, by the sweet reasonableness of his
expositions of Ministerial policy, to maintain the majorities
of the Government at a satisfactory figure.   It was not
until the period of opposition after 1880, when dashing
and harassing tactics were demanded, and when his own
health was failing, that Northcote came to be regarded
as too yielding and conciliatory for the chief of a fighting
confederacy.   And, whether in office or in opposition,
his readiness, experience, candour, and courtesy won him
the respect and affection not only of his own followers
but of the House of Commons as a whole.

APPENDIX.

AN UNFINISHED NOVEL,

BY THE EARL OF BEACONSFIELD, K.G.

PUBLISHED, IN THREE INSTALMENTS, IN "THE TIMES" OF JANUARY 20, 21, AND 23, 1905.

CHAPTER I.

Of all the pretty suburbs that still adorn our metropolis, there are few that exceed in charm Clapham Common. An unenclosed park of 200 acres, well turfed and timbered, and, though free to all and without a paling, so well managed that a domain in a distant county could scarcely be more orderly and refined.

Those who live about this agreeable spot have shown, by the solid convenience and rich comfort of their dwellings, that they appreciate the pleasant place where their lot has been cast, and do not contemplate that they or their posterity should quit or desert it. Many of the red-brick structures have the true character of the manor-house, and are varied now and then by buildings of a more ornate and villa style, but still firm and compact, in the manner which the brothers Adam introduced at the beginning of this century. All of them are surrounded by ample and old-fashioned gardens; of late, however, much modernized, and so losing something of their picturesque stateliness, though they now abound with houses of glass of every form and for every purpose.

The dwellers in these homes have, generally speaking, a peculiar character. They have an idiosyncrasy. They are chiefly rich merchants, directors of the Bank of England, men whose fathers were directors of the East India Company, or chairmen of the great docks that were built in the Port of London during the great war. The new class of railway magnates are rarely found here. Their fortunes have been made in modern times, and by means which allow them to live much further from the City and yet find themselves as early every morning at their boards and counting-houses as the old families at Clapham, who, after all, are only four miles from Cornhill. But the very fact that, comparatively speaking, they are old families, and that there is no inglorious tradition among them of philanthropy and piety, of good and great works, and of some names that are even illustrious, binds them to the sacred soil by that local spell which is one of the most powerful influences over mankind.

Mr. Falconet was the head of one of the most considerable of these families. His father, an East Indian director, had been an intimate friend and companion of Mr. Wilberforce, who lived in his immediate neighbourhood and who was the godfather of his son. He had supported Mr. Wilberforce in all his great enterprises with his purse as well as his personal energy. His son, Mr. Wilberforce Falconet, had married, according to the Clapham custom, at an early age, a young lady who lived at Lavender Hill, and whose father was another friend of Mr. Wilberforce. Even in the enthusiastic world in which she was born, the bride was remarkable for the exaltation of her ideas. She was the founder of many institutions and the soul of all. Schools and hymns and Bible classes and tract distributions and industrial homes engrossed her life. But she was pretty, and Wilberforce Falconet lost his heart to her. He himself quite sympathized with all her pursuits and purposes, and had, indeed, been born and bred in a similar religious and moral atmosphere to her own. This, however, did not prevent him from having the reputation of being a first-rate man of business. Indeed, he was sometimes thought to be a little too sharp in his transactions, in which a fuller and larger degree of Christian forbearance, some intimated, might be desirable. As it was, at the head of one of the most considerable East India houses, he succeeded, on the death of his father, to a large realized fortune and was so wealthy that he need not have been appalled by the large family of both sexes which the pretty and enthusiastic partner of his life had presented to him.

It was not the thirty thousand pounds with which he endowed each of his daughters when they married that was the sole or even principal cause of their soon quitting the paternal roof. It was really the custom of the county; and as they were all pretty, like their mother, and full of enthusiasm, they quickly captivated young gentlemen of the neighbourhood, who were generally about the same age and yielded to the blended spell of religious devotion, female charms, and the most comfortable and piously luxurious domestic establishment in the whole neighbourhood.

The sons, though stalwart youths, had not inherited the fair mien of their mother. They resembled, and strongly, their other parent, who, it was the custom to aver, was descended from a Huguenot family. In truth, his father was the son of a Genevese watchmaker, and he had himself been a clerk to an eminent English firm, where his talents and knowledge of foreign tongues were appreciated. The revocation of the Edict of Nantes with the rich middle-class of this country occupies the same position as the conquest of England by the Normans does with our patricians. It throws a halo of imagination over many a humble or obscure origin.

The countenance of Mr. Wilberforce Falconet was austere, and its expression would have been saturnine had it not been in a state of constant mitigation from his thrilling sense of domestic happiness, worldly prosperity, and religious satisfaction. In the management of his family, Mr. Wilberforce Falconet was a despot, but he was an affectionate one. He often required sacrifices, but he occasionally made them, and, in either case, he was satisfied he was acting in a manner becoming the patriarchs.

His two elder sons were in his counting-house, and were soon to be his partners, when they both were engaged to marry young ladies who were the bosom friends of their sisters and were members of the same committees and distributors of the same tracts. Another son was a sailor. Permission to enter the naval profession had been long contested, but with the prospect that his services would be confined to the South African squadron had at length been obtained. Another son, who seemed inclined to be a soldier, was turned by the panic-stricken family into a clergyman without delay, and there only remained the youngest son for whom a career was to be provided.

Joseph Toplady Falconet had been a child of singular precocity. His power of acquisition was remarkable, and, as he advanced in youth, his talents were evidently not merely those which ripen before their time. He was a grave boy, and scarcely ever known to smile; and this not so much from a want of sympathy for those among whom he was born and bred, for he seemed far from being incapable of domestic affection, but rather from a complete deficiency in the sense of humour, of which he seemed quite debarred. His memory was vigorous, ready, and retentive; but his chief peculiarity was his disputatious temper, and the flow of language which, even as a child, was ever at command to express his arguments. In person, with a commanding brow, his countenance was an exaggeration of that of his father; austere even to harshness, and grave even to melancholy.

A learned man, who had guided his early studies, struck by his acuteness and his powers of rapid attainment, had, after much difficulty, persuaded his father to send him to a public school. This decision cost Mrs. Falconet great sorrow, who believed a public school was a place of much wickedness and cruelty. Her fears and anxiety were, however, unnecessary, for her son was at once placed in a position in the school which exempted him from the servitude which she dreaded, while a very short time elapsed before, even with so many competitors, his singular powers began to be remarked and admired.

His success at school secured for him the University. He was always the favourite son of his father, though that feeling on the part of the parent was never acknowledged or evinced. Secretly, however, the elder Falconet began to muse over the future of this gifted child, and indulge in dreams, which he never communicated to his wife. It was agreed, in due course, that Joseph should study for the Bar, having left the University in a blaze of glory as Senior Wrangler, and recognized as the unrivalled orator of its mimic Parliament.

And what were the dreams of the youth himself ? Had he any ? Though of an eager and earnest temperament, his imagination was limited, and quite conscious of his powers, being, indeed, somewhat arrogant and peremptory, aspired only to devote them to accomplishing those objects which, from his cradle, he had been taught were the greatest, and the only ones, which could or should occupy the energies of man.

Firm in his faith in an age of dissolving creeds, he wished

to believe that he was the man ordained to vindicate the sublime cause of religious truth. With these ardent hopes, he had renounced the suggestion which he had once favoured of taking Orders. It was as the lay champion of the Church that he desired to act, and believed that in such a position his influence would be infinitely greater than in that of a clergyman whatever his repute. The career of Mr. Wilberforce, ever before the eyes of the domestic circle in which he moved, doubtless much influenced him. It certainly did his father, for the secret scheme of the elder Falconet over which he mused alone was to obtain a seat in Parliament for his son.

No easy matter in these days, when men think themselves fortunate to reach the House of Commons with a grey or a bald head. And yet men of influence by pondering over an affair generally strike fire at last. If they be not men of influence the luminous particle generally will not appear and they are called visionaries, crotchety, or adventurers.

Chapter II.

The house of Falconet held a mortgage on the West Indian property of a noble lord, who was also a Minister of State. It was not in itself a good security, but the noble lord possessed ample property of a more substantial character, and so the firm was safe. The firm had taken a leading part in that abolition of West Indian slavery which had seriously reduced the value of the property in question. Whether the memory of this fact entailed some remorse, or whether they were influenced by the recollection of happier times, when, for a long series of years, they had been the agents of the noble lord, and had received in consequence a considerable income in the shape of commissions and interest on advances, there is no doubt that the existing relations between the peer and his former factors were always friendly, and, on the part of the commercial firm, frequently obliging.

Now this noble lord was so fortunate as to have an interest in a borough which his opponents always denounced as a nomination borough, though in truth he had no property whatever in it and could not command a single vote. But he and his wife, being wise and good people, were very civil and courteous to the inhabitants of this borough, which reached almost to their park gates; gave them every year a ball or two, went to theirs, asked them to shooting-parties, subscribed to their charities, presided over their meetings, religious and horticultural, supplied all the wants of the great house from the borough instead of from co-operative stores— and so the lord and lady were what is called " adored," and the borough always asked leave to return their sons or nephews to Parliament.

It seems that the son and heir-apparent of the noble lord, who was at present member for this grateful community, had thought fit to change his politics—what are called the family politics—a great sin, and being a gentleman of honour and spirit, nothing would content him but making this known in an address unnecessarily offensive, and then resigning his seat. Mr. Falconet, through the solicitor of the noble lord, had been aware of all this some time before it was publicly known, and had let the noble patron of the borough become aware that if it could be arranged that his son Joseph could succeed to the representation he should not only be singularly grateful, but should be very happy to prove that his gratitude was not shadowy, but of a substantial character, and so it came about that Mr. Falconet and his son were invited to spend the Whitsun week at the great house, and a public meeting in the borough, on the revival of the slave trade in the Red Sea, having been arranged, Mr. Joseph Toplady Falconet had the opportunity of making a speech, which literally electrified the audience. The speech, indeed, became not only famous in the place where it was delivered, it was reported in the London papers, and leading articles were written, attesting its commanding eloquence, and announcing the advent of a new and powerful candidate for the honours of public life. True it was that it subsequently appeared that there had been no revival of the slave trade in the Red Sea, but that the misapprehension had occurred from a mistake in the telegraph, manipulated by a functionary suffering from a *coup de soleil* or *delirium tremens*. But this did not signify and made no difference whatever in the eloquence of Mr. Joseph Toplady Falconet, or the result which that eloquence was to accomplish.

There was a dinner to be given at "the Common" to

celebrate the return of Joseph. There was a good deal of mystery about this coming event; some little hesitation for some time, and then immense preparations. The truth is Mr. Falconet had conceived the idea of asking the noble lord to be his guest on the occasion, and it was a long time before he could induce Mrs. Falconet even to comprehend his purpose, much less to sanction or encourage it. The Falconets gave many dinner-parties, but their guests were always their own family or intimate connexions, or persons who entirely sympathised with their chief thoughts and pursuits. In short, their banquets generally led to some religious ceremony, and were always accompanied by psalmody. Though he regretted the necessity, Mr. Falconet felt that it was possible his noble guest was scarcely accustomed to such pious practices, and as the noble lord would be the only one present who was unused to them, he could not but feel that a due consideration of all the circumstances might justify him in this instance of finding refuge in a compromise by a grace, both before and after the meal, of unusual length.

At length all was settled, the invitation was accepted and the day was fixed. It was a fine summer afternoon, and the noble guest asked permission to arrive an hour before dinner so that he might "enjoy the country a little and see their place." All were a little uneasy, and some were quite frightened, but Mr. Falconet himself felt he must make an effort and his demeanour was outwardly calm. But there was not the slightest necessity for this embarrassment. The noble lord was the personification of tact and polished sympathy. His eyes smiled with gentle kindness when he was presented to Mrs. Falconet, and his general bow was so skilful that everyone appropriated it to him or herself. He was almost enthusiastic about the Common, which, it seems, he had seen for the first time, and said it was worthy of *As You Like It*. He much praised the conifers in the private grounds, and intimated he had never seen any so fine; though the truth was he was himself unfortunately lord of the most rare and extensive arboretum in England. He visited several of the glasshouses and hinted that there could be few in England equal to them, though he had at home acres of these structures which he had unhappily inherited, and which it cost him annually thousands to maintain.

The dinner was quite a family party. Three married daughters and their husbands were present; the two sons in the business and the young ladies to whom they were engaged; two unmarried daughters; the clergyman brother, who had travelled all night to be there, and was to return at dawn so that he might assist at a Bible class, from which he never had been absent. Of course, the new M.P. was there, and the only child away was the sailor, but then, as a compensation, Mrs. Falconet had just received from him a letter on very thin paper and crossed, and which gave a most animated account of the capture by his vessel of one of the most terrific slavers in the Bight of Benin. She wished their noble guest to read this epistle, which he took with much courtesy, and then glancing at its calligraphy with a somewhat humorous expression put the letter in his pocket, saying he should like to show it to the Secretary of State.

The dinner was, of course, too elaborate, and much too long. The dessert itself lasted as long as a dinner ordinarily ought to do, but nothing would satisfy Mr. Falconet, on these occasions, but a procession of all his wondrous fruits—golden pines of vast shape, green melons like gigantic emeralds, rare figs of all sizes and colours, and bananas which in form and flavour beat Egypt. Indeed he had on this occasion some from that sultry land handed round, in order to prove the pre-eminence of Clapham Common.

The evening was short and went off pretty well. The young ladies had sweet voices and were skilful musicans. They did sing some psalms, but his lordship did not find it out. He sat on a sofa in the evening between Mr. and Mrs. Falconet, Joseph Toplady on a chair opposite to them, looking earnest and rather grim. They discussed his new life in the House of Commons, and Joseph took the opportunity of remarking that he had received some new information respecting the s ave trade in the Red Sea and thought of bringing the matter forward. "I think I would leave the Red Sea alone," said the Earl. "It was a miracle that saved us from being drowned in it before."

Mrs. Falconet looked grave, and her husband quickly turned the conversation by remarking that there was great difficulty in settling the habitation of Joseph now that he had become a Parliament man. He wished to live at home, but that seemed incompatible in the long run with the late hours of the House of Commons.

"When I was a young man," said the Earl, "I had to rough it, for I started as a cadet with no great allowance and with little prospect of my inheritance. I found the Albany a very suitable place for a young man, convenient and inexpensive. Why not try the Albany?"

"We had hoped," said Mrs. Falconet, "that Joseph might have found an abode with some serious family."

"Ah!" said the Earl, "I fear that serious families are rarer than they were in Westminster, and he must not be too far from the House. And now I will say Good-night. I have enjoyed myself greatly, and I only wish I had asked permission to bring Lady Bertram with me."

CHAPTER III.

There are few things more striking than arriving in the Port of London on a Sunday and then proceeding to some distant hotel. An enormous and illimitable city stretches out before you, apparently without an inhabitant. The windows are closed, the shops shuttered up, and in mighty thoroughfares, groaning on week-days with the weight of wains and carts and carriages, and streaming with population, perhaps the hansom cab that you have been fortunate enough to secure when you disembarked is the only vehicle visible—and no voice is heard except perhaps your own giving unintelligible directions to some obstinate or silently supercilious driver.

In the present case, however, the individual who had secured the cab had a companion, for when they had landed he had courteously offered a seat in his vehicle to one whose acquaintance he had only made during a short voyage, but whose conversation and manner had interested him.

"There is nothing to me so striking and so unexpected as this appearance of London," said his guest. "I came here with the persuasion that the English were rapidly renouncing, not only their own religion, but the religious principle altogether, and I find a scene which, for the cessation of labour, could only have been equalled in old Jerusalem."

"Manners and customs outlive superstitions," said his

companion, a man who, if he had lost his youth, was in the prime of middle age—of middle stature, still slender, with an inscrutable countenance, for the colour of his eyes seemed to change while he spoke. On the whole, it might be described as a compact face, the features regular but inclined to delicacy; the brow square and the mouth resolute. In these days costume is little guide to a man's station, except to the very practised, and after a voyage the most fashionable and fastidious are somewhat soiled and shattered. Nevertheless, it would be at once felt that the manner of this person was high-bred; natural, easy, and yet dignified.

" I do not disapprove of the Sabbatarian institution," said his companion; " on the contrary, I approve of it. It was a step in the right direction. It secured repose for one day in the week. True religion would secure repose for every day."

" That would be the Kingdom of Heaven," said his companion, " with which you were just saying these English people were not so content as in old days."

" When we were talking together on deck," replied the other, " I told you that I was a missionary, and I saw that you despised me, though you were too polite to express such a sentiment. I am a missionary, and of a faith held by many millions. It will some day, and perhaps sooner than is generally credited, be professed by all, and then there will be an end of all our troubles. I am a subject of Her Majesty and an inhabitant of Ceylon. I have heard much of late of the decay of faith in England, and the evil consequences which may ensue from this. Being independent, and long educated in these high matters, I resolved to visit Europe, and especially England, and see whether steps might not advantageously be taken to advance the great remedy which can alone cure the evils of the human race."

" And establish the Nirvana ?" said his companion with a scrutinising glance.

" I see you are not altogether unacquainted with the truth."

" I am myself in favour of a Sabbath of seven days," said his companion, " of a real Nirvana, but my perpetual Sabbath can only be celebrated in a city of the dead."

" Death is only happiness, if understood," said the Buddhist.

" We are at your hotel. This is Blackfriars. Can I be of service to you ? Have you friends ?"

" I have a private letter to my banker, besides my letter of credit, and I am assured he will take care of me. Falconet and Co.—they are eminent, I understand. Do you know them ?"

" No," replied the other carelessly, " but bankers, if you have a good letter of credit, are generally obliging. What is your name ?"

" My name is Kusinara—and yours ?"

" I have no name," said the unknown.

Chapter IV.

The receptions of Lady Bertram were distinguished; almost amounted to being celebrated. An illustrious foreigner, for example, after the Thames Tunnel and the Crystal Palace, noted among his agenda, during his London visit, the opportunity, if possible, of making his bow to that great lady. Invitations were not a matter of course even to her own political friends, and murmurs were not infrequently heard by expecting, but omitted, guests that their room seemed to be occupied by " the other side." No individuals, however, foreign or domestic, experienced any difficulty in entering her saloons, provided they were famous or even eminent, and provided they properly appreciated the transcendent qualities of their hostess.

Claribel, Countess Bertram, was a very young widow when she consented to become the second wife of her present husband. Herself a member of one of our most ancient and noblest families, beautiful, highly jointured, and with an only child who was a great heiress, if the world did not exactly express their wonder at her union with Lord Bertram, they still, with frequent kindness, would observe that he was the most fortunate of men. But Lord Bertram was one of those who understand women, and he was a favourite with them.

Tall, pale, and somewhat fragile, but of a distinguished mien, her large dark eyes full of inscrutable meaning, while a profusion of rich brown hair, all her own, veiled in a straight line her well-moulded brow, and shaded with rich masses her oval cheeks, Claribel received her guests; her voice low, but musical, and quite distinct, though she scarcely condescended to raise it beyond a whisper. She listened, rather than conversed, but could seem deeply, or what is styled intensely, interested with her companion, and generally herself summed up with an epigram, or what sounded as such. Then the favoured guest might retire, and record the words of wit and wisdom in his journal, if he kept one.

It was amusing, unobserved, to watch the various modes with which she welcomed her guests. Generally speaking, the mass, of either sex, passed by her absolutely in fear and trembling. The beautiful head, grave almost to sadness, with a slight touch of celestial pride in the recognition, just divinely inclined itself; but occasionally her countenance became animated, a phosphoric flame shot forth from those eyes of Olympian repose, and she held forth the most beautiful hand in the world for them to touch, and even to press. These favourites were almost always men: statesmen of both sides, who habitually consulted her, neological professors from foreign Universities, or wild Radical poets, who found occasion, notwithstanding their screaming odes to coming men and coming times, privately to indite impassioned sonnets to the queen of beauty, of fashion, and of genius.

With her own sex she was courteous, but rarely cordial, except with some young ladies who were her worshippers and certainly except with her own family, whom she habitually welcomed with a courtly embrace. It was a divine condescension, and meant to intimate, what she was in the habit of asserting, that there was no family in the peerage which, for blood and historical achievement, could for a moment be classed with her own.

The daughter of Lady Bertram, the Lady Ermyntrude, had just been presented, though young even for such an initiation. Her future was a subject of frequent discussion in what is called "society." Whom she would marry, and when she would marry? Large questions—and then there were some who fancied she would never marry, and why? Because she was eccentric. Eccentric in what? Well, they say, she has ideas of her own. That is certainly serious. To-night, it might have been expected, that she would have been by the side of her mother, as Lady Bertram received her guests; but Lady Ermyntrude had an instinctive feeling that Lady Bertram was not particularly anxious for her

contiguous presence, and she found it more amusing to move
in her own orbit—but not unattended. There was a German
lady, Fräulein von Weimar, who was her official and inseparable companion, and generally one of her guardians; a Bishop
of captivating gifts, sufficiently serious yet of a lusory mind,
a prelate who ever remembered how much the Church owed to
holy women, contrived to hover round her, and was usually
welcomed and encouraged by her smile.

It must not be supposed, however, that Lady Bertram was
not a devoted mother. She was a perfect parent—in theory.
She wished her daughter to have every advantage and enjoy
every delight that was alike proper and practicable, only she
was too much interested about herself to be able to spare any
time to carry her theories into practice. Fortunately she
had become acquainted with Fräulein von Weimar, who had
gained her confidence and her heart by her appreciation of
Lady Bertram's genius and her wondering recognition of Lady
Bertram's resistless influence over men. This last ascendant
power, however, was of so fascinating a character and it
absorbed the life of Claribel to such a degree that, in due
course, she found it was impossible to spare any longer any
portion of her existence even to the sweet tongue and subtle
mind of Fräulein von Weimar. So, after some scenes and
much unnecessary diplomacy on both sides, this lady became
the guide, the preceptress, and inseparable companion of the
Lady Ermyntrude.

Her pupil had not the lustrous beauty of her mother, and
yet her appearance was hardly less striking. She had a
beautiful figure: rare to see anyone more shapely, and she
moved as if she were conscious of her symmetry. Her countenance was delicate, aquiline, with grey eyes, but there was
a want of mobility about her features, and it seemed doubtful
whether their habitual expression were a simper or a sneer.
Fräulein, although very few years older than Lady Ermyntrude, had the mien and carriage of a matured woman. She
was rather under the middle size, and her stature was scarcely
redeemed by grace, but she had a bright complexion, beautiful
teeth, a commanding brow, and a large blue eye of searching
power.

It was rather late in the evening; Lord Bertram, who, at
its commencement, as was his custom, had assisted his wife

in the reception of her guests, and then wandered about the crowded saloons talking with those he wished or cared to meet, had quietly stolen away to his red boxes. The rooms were still full, though thinner. Mr. Chatterley was standing by the side of Lady Bertram. He was one of the favoured, though never welcomed with enthusiasm, and sometimes scarcely treated with consideration. He was Lady Bertram's man of letters and, as he flattered himself, the only one of his class really in society. His chief business was to carry to her gossip, and to take care that she was properly worshipped in the lettered world. Servile to her and adulatory, he vindicated his independence by his arrogance in the inferior circles which he sometimes deigned to re-enter, and where his quotation of great personages made his conversation somewhat resemble the columns of the *Court Circular*.

" Lady Ermyntrude is looking charming to-night," observed Mr. Chatterley.

" Dearest Ermyntrude !" exclaimed her mama.

" She has just had a joust with the Bishop," said Mr. Chatterley, " and I do not think had the worst of it."

" Indeed," murmured Lady Bertram, with a vacant look. " Have you no news to give me to-night ?" She could not for a moment suppose that Mr. Chatterley had ventured to stop by her side merely to praise her daughter.

" All the world is talking of young Mr. Falconet's speech," said Mr. Chatterley.

" Yes; he seems a considerable person. He dined here to-day."

" I am told he is a great admirer of Lady Bertram," said Mr. Chatterley.

" He knows very little of me," said the lady, trying to veil her curiosity.

" He knows what all know, and feels what all feel, who have the honour and delight of Lady Bertram's acquaintance; only what we feel or know goes for nothing; we alas ! who are not orators, or poets and statesmen."

" What did he say ?" said Lady Bertram in a hushed voice.

But before he could answer, he was obliged to retire, for a young man quickly and unceremoniously approached and addressed Lady Bertram.

He was handsome; the highest order of English beauty;

the Norman tempered by the Saxon; his complexion bright, his dark blue eye delicately arched, regular features, the upper lip short, and with hyacinthine locks of auburn hair.

"I thought I was not to see you to-night, Gaston," said the lady of the house.

"Well, I do not know whether I ought to be here. I have not been exactly cut by some of your friends, but they were rather queer. I suppose being in my father's house they could scarcely refrain from noticing me."

"I have made the acquaintance of your successor," murmured Lady Bertram. "He dined here. I have had much conversation with him."

"Ah!" said Lord Gaston. "Then I suppose you are in an orthodox mood."

"The English are essentially a religious people," said Lady Bertram.

"You did not think so the last time we talked about these matters."

"I think I might now sit down," said Lady Bertram, as if his words had not reached her; and she took his arm before even it could be offered, and they were soon seated on a sofa.

"This Mr. Falconet is an extraordinary man," said Lady Bertram. "I never knew anyone so eloquent. He talks, of course, too much, but that will wear off. I am sorry now that you left Parliament."

"I am not. Parliaments are worn out."

"But you say that of everything," said Lady Bertram.

"And it is true of everything; but of the whole affair nothing is so exhausted as the human race itself."

"But what, then, is to happen?" inquired Lady Bertram.

"Many things may happen. I do not suppose that because man is worn out even this little planet which we call ours has not yet some future. The mistake which our self-conceit has always made has been to suppose that this planet was made for man. There never was any foundation for such a belief, and now we know it is mere folly. The fact is that man has really never very much taken to this globe. And no wonder. It clearly was never intended for him. It consists of more water than land, and of that land a great portion is uninhabitable desert. Look at the miserable amount of population that, after millions of years, he has just contrived to procreate! Scarcely equal to the spawn of a shoal of herrings."

"Then you think the world was made for herrings?" sweetly whispered Lady Bertram.

"I cannot tell what it was made for, but I think I can tell what it was not made for."

"Then you can have no interest in life?"

"Yes; I have in you."

"If you begin talking nonsense I will go and fetch my lord."

"I suppose it is only Mr. Falconet who may talk nonsense."

"Mr. Falconet has none but the most exalted ideas. His life is devoted to the vindication and the triumph of religious truth."

"I am also capable of devotion," said Lord Gaston, "and that is to the happiness of my species. For that reason I wish it to become extinct."

Two young ladies with very long trains bowed to Lady Bertram from a distance and kissed their hands. "I must say a word to them," she said, as she returned their salute. "You do not mind?"

"No, I like them both. They have more sense than half the girls I know."

The ladies approached. "I was so sorry, Lady Bertram," said one of them, "not to meet Professor O'Galaxy here to-night. We were at his lecture to-day at the Royal, and I wanted so much to ask him a question. I see my way so far as Protoplasm clearly; but there I stop. I think we ought to be satisfied; but Blanche De Grey says, No; that will not satisfy her; she must go further."

"If Lady Blanche goes further she will not get rid of her difficulties," said Lord Gaston.

CHAPTER V.

Though in the formation of our character the influence of individuals cannot be doubted or denied, nevertheless there are some persons born with a predisposition so strong that it is difficult to believe that, under any circumstances, that native vein would not have asserted itself. Lord Gaston was of this kind and class. Even as a child he was inquisitive, sceptical, and eccentric; doing things which were forbidden, or, if too original to have been contemplated, anticipated by the censure of others, when done, disapproved. He had the awkward habit of asking questions which could not be easily answered, and expressing opinions which perplexed and sometimes shocked. Nevertheless he was a favourite, and at first universally so; and this was owing to two causes—his good looks and his good temper. Nothing could disturb the last, and his first glance fascinated. Still it was a lamentable fact that, in the long run, he could not, as the phrase goes, " get on " with anybody. At a great public school he was soon idolised, but it ended by the authorities privately communicating with his father that they thought, on the whole, it would be advantageous that his son should be withdrawn from their control. Not that he ever did anything disgraceful, mean, or ignominious, or even committed violent or rebellious acts, but he was in the habit of circulating opinions which injuriously affected the discipline of the school; was in the habit of reading and advising others to read books which, while affecting to be philosophical, could not for a moment be tolerated, as tending, in the opinion of the masters, to the destruction of morals and religion. What, however, brought affairs to a crisis was a motion which he made in the boy's debating society condemning the system of public education. Had he not been the son of a great noble, who himself in his day had been one of the bright ornaments of their institution, he would probably have been expelled, but, as it was, he surrendered and marched out with all the honours of war.

Lord Bertram was such a complete man of the world that he resolved never to quarrel with his son, and he endeavoured by indirect means to guide him in the right path and counteract these evil tendencies. He thought Oxford would remove them, and he sent him there at an unusually early age. But the Oxford of Gaston was no longer the Oxford of his father, and Lord Bertram, who had many things to think about, was not sufficiently aware of this. A spirit almost as inquisitive as that which influenced his son had begun to pervade the great University, and it unfortunately happened that the head of the house of which Gaston had become a member was one of those distinguished divines who do not believe in divinity. Of this Socrates he soon became the favourite pupil, and, considering his rank, his fine looks, his fine temper, and the reputation for talents which was soon circulated about and easily and eagerly accepted, Oxford came to believe that it cherished in its bosom one who in due season would become its most brilliant ornament and its shining light.

Nevertheless, when he had exhausted all the nebulous interpretations of his master, which would prove that things, though entirely profane, were yet essentially sacred, Gaston engaged in a controversy on the origin of evil which terminated by his somewhat abruptly quitting his Alma Mater and informing his father that he should not return to Oxford, which he looked upon as a nest of sacerdotal hypocrisy.

This was a great disappointment to Lord Bertram, who, however, was a man never without resource, and Lord Gaston was soon gazetted as an attaché to one of our most important Embassies. This seemed a successful arrangement. Nobody could be more popular than Lord Gaston in his new world. All the great ladies were enchanted with him and invited him to their tea-parties. He was called the handsome Englishman, and then he was so kind and obliging, too. He was as good-natured as he was beautiful. Apparently he was well pleased with his new life. Two years passed away and he never asked for leave of absence, though he wrote charming letters to his father, who read extracts from them sometimes to his colleagues, and sent the most exquisite presents to Claribel, whom he called Mama. Unhappily, one morning he appeared without notice at Bertram House, and ordered breakfast as calmly as if he never had left his home. He had travelled night and day, for he had been ordered by the Government of the country to leave it at an hour's notice, some correspondence having been discovered between the noble British attaché and a revolutionary leader. A secret communication was made to Lord Bertram, but it was the interest of all parties that the affair should be hushed up.

" There is nothing to be done for him now but to push him into Parliament," said his father. " If anything can get the nonsense out of a man, it is the House of Commons."

The reader will have seen that this last expedient had not been quite successful. Lord Bertram forgot his annoyance in the pressure of public business, and Lady Bertram found a substitute for the sceptical confidences and revolutionary principles of her stepson, with which she was beginning to sympathise, in the unflinching orthodoxy and ultra-Conservatism of his Parliamentary successor, urged as they were by him with irresistible dialectics and a torrent of words which no improvisatore could excel, and to which Lady Bertram in veiled ecstasy listened as she would to a cataract in the Alps.

On a certain day in every week it came to be understood that Mr. Joseph Toplady Falconet would probably be drinking a cup of tea at Bertram House and expounding his schemes of regeneration for a society which he was resolved to save, though he admitted its condition was somewhat desperate. He had already achieved success in the House of Commons, where rapid success is difficult. Very shortly after his entrance into that still fastidious and somewhat incredulous assembly he took up the Sabbatarian question, and the notice of his motion was received with contemptuous respect. But the feeling was far otherwise when they had listened to him. The old hands at once recognised that this was a man who would mount and looked forward with interest to the occasions when he might deliver himself on some practical subject and not on such moonshine as that with which he had favoured them. But here the old hands, as they often do, made a mistake. There was a great, though latent, fund of Religionism in the House; much of it sincere, a large portion, no doubt, inspired by the constituencies; but the members who acknowledged these sentiments, were, generally speaking, not of a class calculated to enthral listening Senates. They were respectable men, usually opulent, and their opinions on matters of trade and taxation always commanded deference, but they were quite incapable of grappling with the great questions that touch the convictions and consciences of nations, and they hailed with satisfaction a commanding expounder of opinions which in their hands they felt would have assumed a character of feebleness which they were persuaded was undeserved. These men, sitting on both sides of the House, rallied round Falconet. He gathered other allies. With all his abilities and acquirements, Joseph Toplady Falconet was essentially a prig, and among prigs there is a freemasonry which never fails. All the prigs spoke of him as of the coming man.

Lady Bertram always returned from her daily drive at five o'clock, and she was always at home. There never had been formal invitations, but the initiated came—a small, refined circle. There were always a few ladies of great fashion, sometimes a Royal Duchess, an Ambassador, a dandy or two— for Lady Bertram could even command dandies—and half a dozen other men, native or foreign, but of European celebrity. When it was in his power Falconet was there, but that was uncertain, for the House of Commons is a jealous mistress and will not grant success without due attention. The greatest compliment you can pay to a woman is to give to her your time, and it is the same with our Senate. A man who is always in his place becomes a sort of favourite. But there were other means of communication between Claribel and her new prophet; books were mutually lent to each other, and every day there were letters exchanged: on her part, little emblazoned notes; on his, treatises, pamphlets, where everything was divided under heads and every question exhausted and settled.

CHAPTER VI.

The clubs, which, in their fanciful invention, are only inferior to the Arabian Nights' Entertainments, speculated much on the future of the Lady Ermyntrude. Some thought her so matured in her mind and manner that she would marry immediately; others, on the contrary, held that she would hesitate for a long time before she decided; a third party ventured on an opinion that she would probably never marry at all.

The names of some persons, however, were already intimated as the possible, or even probable, partners of her life and fortune. Gaston, from his connexion with the lady, was always the first mentioned, and yet his name was almost invariably dismissed as that of a man who had no thought of marriage. Then there was Lord Fitz-Alb. He was supposed to have a very good chance, being the great favourite of the Bishop, and quite fit, though youthful, to be a prelate himself. The Bishop was one of Lady Ermyntrude's guardians, who, it was understood, consulted him on all occasions. Some thought that Hugo Bohun would be the lucky man. Heiresses, somehow or other, always seemed to like him, though somehow or other eventually they had hitherto never united their fate with his. Hugo Bohun was an ostentatious pauper, and had a theory that rich women like to marry paupers, particularly if they were personages so *comme il faut* as himself. The knowing ones on the whole backed Lord Warrener against the field. It was circulated that Lady Ermyntrude in one of her morning rides had more than once inquired whether Lord Warrener was in the Park, and seemed disappointed he was not at her side.

Lord Warrener was a good-looking, accomplished cosmopolitan. He ostentatiously announced, though of ample estate, that he cared for nothing but money, but it was generally held that he would prefer obtaining it by a race or a rubber rather than by the aid of an heiress, however wealthy or distinguished.

There was a ball, and the Lady Ermyntrude had danced twice with Hugo Bohun; he had even attended her to the tea-room.

" This is one of the happiest nights of my life," he said to her. " Do you know, I think it wonderfully kind of you to dance with such a miserable wretch as I am."

" One meets with so many happy people," said the Lady Ermyntrude, " I rather like sometimes to meet a miserable wretch."

" What other miserable wretch do you know except myself ?" asked Hugo.

" I know several wretches," replied the lady, " but I am not at all sure they are miserable wretches."

" Well, what is your idea of a wretch ?"

" I think a man who is discontented with his lot in life is a wretch."

" Everybody is discontented with their lot in life."

" I thought just now you said you were most happy."

" So I am when I am with you."

" Then, after all, you are not a real wretch," said the lady

" Do you think Gaston is ?" inquired Hugo.

" His wretchedness is on so great a scale that it amounts to the sublime."

" I should think you were contented with your lot in life," said Hugo.

" I have not yet considered that question so deeply as it deserves," said Lady Ermyntrude. " At present my thoughts are limited to these walls and to the cotillon which I am now going to dance."

" Alas ! not with me ?"

" No," said Lady Ermyntrude, withdrawing her arm, and taking that of Lord Warrener, who at that moment joined her, and bowed.

" Now I feel this is the most miserable night of my life," murmured Hugo.

The lady, departing, looked over her shoulder and smiled.

CHAPTER VII.

One of the most important neighbours of Mr. Falconet died about this time.   He was a German gentleman, and lived at Lavender Hill in a mansion situated in unusually ample grounds for a villa residence, and approached through lodges and by roads ingeniously winding.   Mr. Hartmann was a bachelor; the firm a distinguished one—Hartmann Brothers.   They were bankers to more than one European potentate, and whenever any member of the Royal or Imperial families paid a visit to England they spared one day to be entertained at Lavender Hill with much magnificence; banquets and balls in colossal tents, and all the bowers and groves of Lavender resonant with musicians and illumined with many lamps of many colours.

It was understood that Mr. Hartmann had died very wealthy, and that the bulk of his large fortune had been bequeathed to his brother, who resided in a foreign capital.   It was still more interesting news when it began to be rather authoritatively rumoured that in future England was to be the residence of the heir, and not only England but Lavender Hill.

In due time, architects and builders and workmen arrived at the spot, and it was said that great alterations were making there, with that disregard for expense which became the proprietor of means so ample.   Among other changes, it was said that a library had arrived from Germany, rich and rare, and which was to be housed in a new chamber becoming such treasures.

Mr. Falconet had great respect for the house of Hartmann Brothers, and took the earliest opportunity of personally

paying his respects to the newcomer.   His arrival among
them was rendered not less interesting by the circumstance
of his not being a bachelor.   He was a widower, but with an
only child, a daughter still in her teens, yet already, it was
understood, recognized as the head of his establishment.
The arrival of the Hartmanns, therefore, created no little
excitement in the Falconet family, both among the sons and
the daughters.   Especially was there no lack of speculation
as to the character and appearance of Miss Hartmann.

The first visit was made and returned, and the first impression of their new neighbours on the Falconet family highly
favourable.   Mr. Hartmann was a man singularly calm, with
an intellectual countenance; reserved, a little shy, perhaps,
but not dull.   As for his daughter Angela, all the young
ladies fell immediately in love with her, and, after having
walked twice round their own grounds with her, were quite
prepared to vow eternal friendship.   Their brothers were less
vehement, restrained, perhaps, by their engagements to their
sisters' coadjutors in the Bible class, but their glance betrayed
their appreciation of the charms and manner of their new
acquaintance.

Not that Angela Hartmann was an ideal beauty—a Phryne
to be painted by Apelles or modelled by Praxiteles, or a
Titian's Flora, or even a Madonna of Raffaelle; but there were
a sweetness in her voice and a softness in her demeanour
which at once attracted, while, though the habitual expression
of her mild cheek and pencilled brow was grave, it was, at
the same time, not rigorous but sympathetic.   Nevertheless,
as time flowed on, the enthusiasm of the Falconet family in
her behalf, and especially of its female portion, abated.   They
embraced her when they met, but they did not meet very
often; they still much talked of her when she was not present,
but amid varying comments and criticism there seemed a
general agreement that they could not quite make her out.
She had sweetly declined to assist them in their Bible classes;
and had softly refused to teach at their Sunday schools.   She
was not uninterested in hymnology, but her songs of adoration
were different from those in their orthodox collection.   Miss
Hartmann regularly attended Divine service at their parish
church, but unfortunately she was never accompanied by her
father.   This greatly disquieted Mrs. Falconet, who at first

wished Mr. Falconet to speak to him, and eventually did send him a sheaf of tracts. Mr. Falconet, however, though as devout as his better half, was still, to a certain degree, a man of the world, which truly every merchant must be, and he intimated to his wife that Mr. Hartmann was probably a German philosopher; a difficult kind of animal in these matters to deal with. " He was showing to me his library the other day," said Mr. Falconet, " and there were two portraits in it, very fine pictures; one was of Spinoza, the other of Kant."

" Good gracious !" exclaimed Mrs. Falconet.

" You need not be too much alarmed, my dear, for I said to him—I thought it just as well to say to him—'You have two advanced thinkers there, Mr. Hartmann.'"

" Yes," he replied, " I owe them much; they did their work in their time, and I am grateful to them, but I have long ceased to share their opinions."

" I feel greatly relieved," said Mrs. Falconet.

Chapter VIII.

It was a Bank holiday, and Mr. Hartmann was absorbed in a new work of a friend of Schopenhauer which had just arrived, when a visitor was announced. He looked at the card which his servant brought in to him, and the spleen which, for a moment, was excited at being disturbed vanished instantly as he glanced at the superscription. So the servant was ordered to usher in the guest, and there entered the room the same gentleman who had behaved kindly at the beginning of this history to the Indian who landed on a Sunday at the Port of London.

" My first visit to your new home," said the guest, " a pleasant quarter."

" I might have chosen a more picturesque spot, and one equally convenient," said Mr. Hartmann, " but I passed my childhood here and had a weakness here to close my life."

" The local influences are the strongest," said his companion. " It is almost vain to struggle against them, though they are exceedingly mischievous. I see you have a new book. He has also sent me a copy."

" I do not know that there is anything new in it," replied

Mr. Hartmann, " but what is old to us is new to the world. He is one of the few men who can write on an abstruse subject with clearness."

" They never really answer him," said the visitor.

" So they call him a visionary," said Mr. Hartmann.

" A visionary!" exclaimed his friend. " So are you a visionary; so am I; so was Mahomet; so was Columbus. If anything is to be really done in this world, it must be done by visionaries; men who see the future, and make the future because they see it. What I really feared about him was that he had the weakness of believing in politics, of supposing that the pessimism of the universe could be changed or even modified by human arrangements."

" I heard he was a Communist."

" He might as well be a Liberal or a Conservative—mere jargon; different names for the same thing. You and I know that in attempting to terminate the misery of man, there is only one principle to recognize, and that is the destruction of the species. You and I hold the same tenets, and we desire the same end. We differ only in our estimate as to the time required; but that is of no import. You think that centuries must elapse before the consummation. I would fain believe our release and redemption were nearer; but you are a sedentary man, a man of books. Action and some instinct have taught me what you have derived from pondering on your own observations and the thoughts of others. All that is happening in the world appears to me to indicate a speedier catastrophe. These immense armies, these new-fangled armaments—what do they mean ? In the Thirty Years' War they would have depopulated Europe. What commissariat can support these hosts ? I trust more to the disease and famine of campaigns than to the slaughter of battles."

" Remember what Condé said when he lost his best troops," remarked Mr. Hartmann. " One night at Paris will supply their place."

" Ah ! but a night at Paris is different now from what it was in the days of the Condés. The French are the most civilized nation and the most sterile. But, reverting to what I was saying, there are indications of habitual dearth in this globe which are encouraging."

"Surely these are comparatively slight means to achieve such a result as the total destruction of the human species."

"Not so slight as you may imagine. Besides, we must accept all means. Destruction in every form must be welcomed. If it be only the destruction of a class it is a step in the right direction. Society is formed of classes, and it may be necessary to destroy it in detail."

"What I fear will be the great obstacle to accomplishing our end," said Hartmann, "to which, as you really know, I am not less devoted than yourself, is the religion of Europe, and which has unhappily been colonially introduced into America."

"It has many assailants," said his companion.

"And in its time it has defeated many assailants," replied Hartmann. "I doubt whether my neological countrymen will be more fortunate and effective than the French ency-clopædists."

"Ah, but you do not sufficiently allow for the influence of science at the present day."

"Query, whether science was less influential at the end of the eighteenth century than at the present moment. D'Alembert, and Diderot, and Holbach (? Lamarque) were no mean authorities, and as for mathematics, the French were always supreme. No, the more I ponder over this religious question, the more I am convinced that we shall never succeed in our mighty aim unless we contrive to enlist some religious faith in our resources. If it be true that the confidence of Europe and her colonies in their creeds is falling away, cannot our principle of extermination be clothed in a celestial form ?"

"Secure the future by destroying the present," said his companion musingly.

"You know I have always had some views of this character," said Mr. Hartmann, "but they are fresh in my mind at this moment from some conversations I have recently had with an Indian gentleman, who has been visiting in this neighbourhood, and whom I met at a house certainly not renowned for its philosophy. This Indian gentleman, a man of great culture, is from Ceylon. He is a Buddhist and a self-appointed missionary of that faith, which, if imbibed in its pure and original spirit, would consummate our purpose."

"I fancy I know your friend, and have regretted that the

pressure of affairs has prevented me from cultivating his acquaintance. You are speaking, I am sure, of Kusinara. I came over from Rotterdam with him some little time ago; a remarkable man."

" 'Tis the same person," said Mr. Hartmann.

" He might give lectures. Lectures are grains of mustard seed. Or, what would be better, we might give him a chapel, and let him celebrate, at the same time that he expounded his doctrine, the services of his sect. There must be among the Chinese about the Port of London and other places the elements of a congregation. The English like a congregation. The moment there is a congregation, they think the affair practical."

" There is no doubt," said his friend, " that if we could enlist the religious principle on our side, it might produce great effects. There is nothing to be compared to it in power except the influence of women—and they generally go together. I once thought I had gained one of the greatest ladies in Europe to our creed; I gave, I might say, years to the effort and travelled thousands of miles. I should think nothing of going to the Brazils to-morrow were there a chance of enlisting the sympathies in our cause of any woman of influence. In these matters, they are stronger than armies."

" Here comes my daughter," said Mr. Hartmann. " She wants to give you some luncheon. She is not one of those women who are stronger than armies, but she is a dear girl."

CHAPTER IX.

There was an assembly at Lady Clanmorne's, a popular person, a friend of Lothair. Lady Bertram was present, and moved about with the consciousness of her irresistible fascination. She had received the homage of all the illustrious who were present with a mystical glance from her soft rich eyes, and occasionally had deigned to breathe forth a sentence worthy of a Sibyl. Then, as was rather her wont, she retired from the principal saloons, and seated herself alone on a sofa in a chamber less frequented, meditating on the variety of her charms and her magical influence over mankind. Self-introspection was ever the delightful and inexhaustible pursuit of Claribel, and she never closed these bewitching reveries without increased admiration of her own idiosyncrasy.

A gentleman approached her of distinguished mien. He was young, but of matured youth; his fine countenance serene, but commanding. His costume, though simple, was effective, and, though he wore no ribbon, he was decorated by a star in brilliants.

"Lady Bertram," he said, "I am commanded by Lady Clanmorne to attend you to the tea-room, where you will find Lady Clanmorne, who particularly wishes to see you."

Claribel a little lost her presence of mind. She did not know the envoy of her friend, and yet she ought to know everybody who was anybody. And this, too, a stranger so distinguished! He seemed made to appreciate her. She was already contemplating her irresistible influence over him, though certainly before she commenced her mystic charms she would have liked to have known exactly who he was. But aspiring to control, she felt herself controlled. She rose and with a slight bow took his offered arm.

He gave her some tea, observing Lady Clanmorne had not arrived, and then, without any formal suggestion on his part, she found herself seated, and the stranger by her side.

"I owe Lady Clanmorne much," he said, "but am most grateful to her for giving me this opportunity of speaking to Lady Bertram."

"And why should you be grateful for that?" murmured Claribel, with a glance of voluptuous penetration.

"Because it has been the object of my life that I might have the opportunity of conversing with one of the most gifted of women."

"The most gifted woman, I fear, can do little."

"She can do everything."

"There is much to be done," replied Claribel mysteriously, but as she really had nothing to suggest she only looked like a high priestess bound to betray no secrets of the initiated.

"Certainly there is much to be done," said the stranger. "Society is resolving itself into its original elements. Its superficial order is the result of habit, not of conviction. Everything is changing, and changing rapidly. Creeds disappear in a night. As for political institutions, they are all challenged, and statesmen, con cious of what is at hand, are changing nations into armies."

"What you say is true," said Lady Bertram moodily; and then she added with a subtle, knowing look, and in a cadenced whisper, "but is it the whole truth?"

"Those who know the whole truth are the lords of the world," said the stranger; "and it is because I feel that I am perhaps speaking to one of such Sovereigns that I hail this night, which has given me the advantage of listening to her counsels."

"We must think," said Lady Bertram.

"Pardon me, Madam, but I am mistaken, if you have not exhausted thought. There are thinkers, I know many, not unequal to the times in which we move, but they are all of opinion that what we require now is not so much further thought as a transcendent type of that thought alike to guide and inspire us."

Claribel unfurled her fan and gracefully waved it. There was a gentle tumult in her frame which indicated an increased action of the heart, her cheek slightly glowed. It was delicious to hear, and, as she could not refrain from believing, from high authority, that her mission was to guide and inspire. She had been trying to do this all her life, but, not knowing the way, she had found it difficult to direct what path to follow, and instead of inspiring others she generally imbibed the last ideas which were infused into her. Now it was absolutely necessary to say something, and so she said in a tone of mystical decision, "It is impossible to resist one's destiny."

"Impossible—and yours is a commanding one."

"You were speaking of your friends and some peculiar views of theirs?" remarked Lady Bertram, vanity and curiosity combining in an effort to discover who were these unknown admirers of her consummate self.

"Their views are peculiar only because they are conscious, and have long been conscious, that the pretended principles* upon which society is formed have ceased to exist, and that they are merely conventional phrases which, for the moment, are convenient to employ."

"We must resist conventionalism," observed Lady Bertram with much authority.

"These are good tidings from such lips," said the stranger.

" It will give courage to those who would extricate us from the blunders of ages."

At this moment, smiling, yet with an air of curiosity blended with her smiles, Lady Clanmorne entered the tea-room and approached Claribel. Her attendant, murmuring that he had now fulfilled his mission, rose, and, bowing to both ladies, left the room.

" I am most anxious to know who is your friend. I saw you from a distance on his arm," said Lady Clanmorne. " I thought he must have come with one of the Princes and yet I should have remembered him had he been presented to me."

" He brought to me a message from you," said Lady Bertram, amazed, and a rendezvous in the tea-room.

" From me ! Let us follow him !"

The two great ladies returned to the ball-room, but the stranger was not there. They walked through the other saloons. He was not visible. Lady Clanmorne, describing her unknown guest, made inquiries about him of the attendants. They agreed that he had just quitted the house. He was for a moment in the cloak-room, but there he had only figured as a number. There was a scribe in the hall making a catalogue of the guests. It seemed that the stranger had avoided giving his name, and, as he was decorated with a diamond star, the scribe thought all must be right.

CHAPTER X.

In the meantime, Kusinara, the gentleman from Ceylon, became very intimate with the Falconet family. He had been invited at once to Clapham, for his letter of credit also announced that he was a man of considerable station and distinction. Mrs. Falconet soon discovered that he was also half a Christian, and resolved, that he should become a whole one. The expected neophyte was extremely docile, was interested in all he heard, and if not at once a convert, was always a candid, and often an admiring, listener. . . .

BILLING AND SONS, LTD., PRINTERS, GUILDFORD, ENGLAND